W9-ABV-613

HIGH VICTORIAN CULTURE

High Victorian Culture

David Morse

Lecturer in English and American Studies
University of Sussex

 NEW YORK UNIVERSITY PRESS
Washington Square, New York

First published in the U.S.A. in 1993 by
NEW YORK UNIVERSITY PRESS
Washington Square
New York, N. Y. 10003

Printed in Hong Kong

Library of Congress Cataloging-in-Publication Data
Morse, David.
High Victorian culture / David Morse.
p.   cm.
Includes bibliographical references and index.
ISBN 0–8147–5487–2 (cloth)
1. English literature—19th century—History and criticism.
2. Great Britain—Intellectual life—19th century.   I. Title.
PR461.M64   1993
820.9'008—dc20   92–18942
                                                          CIP

For Carole

Contents

Author's Note

Although, as I point out in the first chapter, the primary focus of this study of Victorian culture is on the first four Victorian decades, I have not hesitated to go beyond these limits where it seemed appropriate to do so – most notably in the case of Thomas Hardy, where, rather than break off the discussion of his fiction after *The Hand of Ethelberta* or *The Return of the Native*, it seemed more appropriate to conclude with *Jude the Obscure*.

I should like to thank my Sussex colleagues Alan Sinfield, Norman Vance, Lindsay Smith and Frank Gloversmith, for reading and commenting on sections of the manuscript.

1

Introduction

High Victorian Culture is a study of the first four decades of Victorian Britain, from Victoria's accession to the throne in 1837 to her proclamation as Empress of India in 1877 – or, to transpose the chronology into a more literary key, it covers an era that runs from Dickens's first novel, *The Pickwick Papers* (1836–7), to George Eliot's last novel, *Daniel Deronda* (1876). There has never really been much argument that from the 1870s onwards the landscape of Victorian England is so significantly altered as to make 'late Victorian' an indispensable modification but this has had the unfortunate effect of developing an binary opposition between early and late Victorian, as a result of which several decades between 1850 and 1890 have a way of dropping out of the picture. This problem has been addressed by the simple and useful expedient of introducing the term 'mid-Victorian' to refer to the 1850s and 1860s, but the danger here, I feel, is of over-periodising, of developing a chronological framework that is at once too specific and too unwieldy. The merit of the designation 'High Victorian' from my point of view is that it permits a more detailed, sustained exploration of mid-nineteenth century Britain, whilst hopefully it averts the danger of generalising about 'the Victorians' as if Bulwer-Lytton and W. B. Yeats, Robert Owen and Beatrice Webb somehow inhabited the same cultural world. If it further implies both that this is a period of great literary and intellectual achievements and also that they originate from within a relatively homogeneous middle-class élite, amongst whose ranks are many who were fearful of the development of mass culture, then those additional resonances will not be inappropriate. In general, Victorian culture is extraordinarily difficult to generalise about, because of the sheer pace of industrial and social change, and because differences between different social classes and between different sections of the British Isles are sharply intensified. An exploration of Victorian 'attitudes' or of a Victorian 'frame of mind' can help to clarify our perceptions of what issues are perceived as being at stake by a middle-class reading public, but there is a great need to ensure that

1

such discussions are more precisely focused. A particular and recurrent danger is the assumption that we can speak of a Victorian 'response' to, say, industrial society, with its connotations of spontaneity, sincerity and immediacy, as if we could somehow see the reality on the one hand, the response on the other. In studying Victorian Britain we need to think more carefully about the ways in which the Victorian world was itself the product of representation and ideological construction. It is, for example, a strange paradox, which I shall touch on at various points in this book, that whilst Victorian society was indeed complex and diverse and whilst innumerable Victorian public figures saw this diversity coupled with freedom of speech and expression as the definitive mark of Britain's national greatness, in practice such diversity of opinion was almost invariably perceived as anarchic and potentially subversive.

Any examination of Victorian society is bound to attach considerable importance to the tremendous improvement in communications. Between 1840 and 1870 more than 15,000 miles of railways had been opened, which was one-half of the total amount of railway construction in the whole of Europe. The speed of rail travel also made possible an improved postal service. Moreover improvements both in the circulation of newspapers and also in their own coverage of the news both at home and abroad meant that those who were in a position to afford them could have immediate access to an extraordinary and unprecedented range of information. However, it was the aristocracy and middle class that benefited most. In 1846 *The Times* and other quality newspapers cost 5*d*., of which 1*d*. was stamp duty – not until the decade following the abolition of stamp duty in 1855 was it possible to buy a daily newspaper, such as the *Morning Star*, the *Evening Standard* or the *Daily News* for a penny. Although the Chartist *Northern Star* paid the stamp duty and sold at 4$^{1}/_{2}d$. it nevertheless claimed a circulation of 42,000, but such prices cannot easily have been within the reach of working men, which suggests that many such papers must have been purchased collectively. *The Times* itself typically sold no more than 7000 copies in the early Victorian period but in the 1860s the market for newspapers expanded so rapidly that by 1870 the *Daily News* was selling 150,000 copies a day. Similar changes began to affect rail travel in the 1870s after the Midland Railway first introduced third-class carriages on all its trains in 1872 and then, in 1875, abolished second-class travel while simultaneously improving the standard of accommodation in third-class coaches. Prior to this there were extraordinary disparities in standards between first- and second-class travel on the one hand and third-class travel on the other. For example, prior do the introduction of railways the journey by stage coach from London to Liverpool took thirty hours, but by 1845 an express train could complete the journey in seven hours. For the unfortunate third-class traveller, however, it was a different story since the journey took two days and even a second-class passenger was required to stay overnight in Birmingham. Third-class carriages always went on separate trains and were often attached to the back of goods trains. Despite the railway, the gulf between different parts of the country could still seem enormous. When Queen Victoria visited Leeds in 1858 it was almost as if she was visiting a foreign country (though she had already built a house at Balmoral in 1853) and *The Times* (9 September) was relieved to find that even in a large manufacturing town, lacking most of the traditional methods of social control, a quarter of a million people could nevertheless gather to greet and pay their respects to their sovereign: 'this democratic and strong-minded race, who spin and weave and forge under their thick canopies of smoke – who know and care little about lords or squires or rectors, are capable, as we see, of the deepest and most heartfelt attachment to the Crown and the illustrious person who now wears it'.

It would be easy to assume from these developments and from the rash of reforming legislation that we associate with early Victorian England that the country was becoming increasingly centralised, but such a conclusion would be highly misleading. Power in England was typically exercised at local level, whether by the aristocracy in the countryside or by the manufacturing millocracy of the towns. They sought to maintain their influence through local political patronage and through the holding of such positions as Lord Lieutenant of the County or as local magistrates. It was taken for granted that the local landowners would work hand in hand with the clergy in dealing with such issues as emerged. The local gentry were undoubtedly paternalist in their attitudes, even though this might imply allowing cottages to fall down just as much as assuming a responsibility for their renovation. What mattered was that they must take the decisions and be seen to take the decisions. They fiercely resisted any idea of interference with their role at national level. As David Roberts has pointed out: 'It would be difficult to exaggerate the importance of locality and local government in paternalist thought: they were central to its most basic assumptions.'[1] Symptomatic of this distrust of any centralising authority was the opposition Edwin Chadwick encountered on the General Board of Health, which was given overall responsibility for sanitation in London. The problems it faced were urgent since in 1849, in a general cholera epidemic, 15,000 people died in London alone. But Chadwick's high-handed attempts to dictate policy, his refusal either to compromise or negotiate, his disregard for local opinion, aroused considerable opposition and by 1854 he had been obliged to submit his resignation. *The Economist* acknowledged his role in public service but commented:

> these services are vast; – but there Mr Chadwick's powers of usefulness end. In spite of his extensive information, in spite of his great sagacity, in spite of his wonderful and unwearied industry, in spite of his sincere benevolence, he has one mental peculiarity which utterly disqualifies him for the executive services of his country. He is essentially a despot and a bureaucrat. He thinks that the people ought to be well governed, but does not believe in the possibility of their governing themselves well. He would coerce them to their own good.[2]

What this really means is not that the people should rule but that the local powers that be should be able to deal with these matters without outside interference. Considering that the population of Great Britain exceeded 25 million in the period covered by this book, the size of the Civil Service was extremely small and comparisons with France make the figures even more striking. Clive Church, discussing the administration under the July Monarchy, writes: 'By 1845 it accounted for 20 per cent of the royal budget, thanks to rising salaries, and its numbers were estimated at anything between 90,000 and 670,000, of whom two to three thousand were in the central administration.'[3] Sir Norman Chester in *The English Administrative System*[4] estimates that the number of government employees rose from 22,367 in 1829 to 39,147 in 1851. Of the 1829 total, nearly 20,000 were employed in Customs, Excise, Stamp Tax and the Post Office, and he estimates that 14,000 of the additional employees were in the Post

Office. More significant are the figures for the Foreign Office, Treasury and Home Office, which rose from 82, 39 and 30 respectively to 105, 85 and 86. Clearly we are not comparing like with like, but even so the numbers in such key departments do seem remarkably small. Moreover, the existence of improved communications actually meant that a devolved system, if system it was, could work better since central government could keep more easily in touch with local areas, and if there was disorder or social unrest troops could be sent by train that much more rapidly. As good a guide as any, both to the topography and the attitudes of early nineteenth-century England, is provided by *Paterson's Roads*, a publication that predates the Victorian era but went through edition after edition until the 1830s. Clearly the development of railways effectively rendered it obsolete but it nevertheless shows that every locality, no matter how remote, was perceived as a centre of personal power and influence, so that to ride around the country was always to pass from one specific force field into another. *Paterson* does not simply tell you, for example, how to get from London to Leeds: it tells you just who are the local dignitaries, who owns what and where. Thus under Ripon the reader is given an elaborate description of Studley Royal 'the very elegant seat of Mrs Lawrence' and afterwards of Fountains Abbey: 'Built in the most elegant style of Gothic architecture, the tower and all the walls are yet standing, the roof alone being gone to ruins – 6 miles distant from Ripon, Hackfall belonging to the same lady.' We are also told: '4m distant from Ripon, Grantley Hall, Lord Grantley; 2m distant from Ripon, in the road to Masham. Brecka Moor, Marmaduke Hodgson, Esq.; 4m distant, Azerley, William Dawson, Esq., and at Kirkby Malzeard, T. Dickens Esq.'[5] England may no longer have had its Doomesday Book but it nevertheless had a multiplicity of fiefdoms, both small and large, and both the grand and the lowly have a very distinct idea as to whose personal fiefdom it is.

This localised influence obviously left its mark on the parliamentary constituencies, which continued to be in the gift of influential local families even after rotten boroughs were abolished. Moreover, although we discuss leading the Victorian politicians as if they were national leaders in a more modern sense, this is often highly misleading as they did not necessarily command a national following in the way that political figures do today. Obviously Cobden and Bright saw themselves as representing Manchester, Lancashire and the northern industrial interest, yet such a prominent figure as the Conservative Prime Minister Sir Robert Peel was very closely identified with the same area through his representation of the Tamworth constituency and throughout his career he showed a quite remarkable involvement in local politics. After Peel's death, apart from London, commemorative statues of him were erected in Tamworth, Manchester, Salford, Preston, Birmingham, Liverpool, Blackburn, Huddersfield, Leeds, Bradford, Glasgow, Montrose and Bury. This indicates quite clearly that the real depth of admiration for his leadership – and especially for his repeal of the Corn Laws – was centred in the industrial north and that those who put up these statues thought of him as a local man. Gladstone was another major figure who was able to draw upon strong regional loyalties – indeed, so many were the areas with which he could claim a personal tie that he was able to use this fact to help put together a national coalition. Gladstone was born and brought up in Liverpool and his tenure as MP for South Lancashire from 1865 to 1868 established a connection with the north of England. Gladstone's home was at Hawarden Castle in North Wales and he also owned much land in this part of the world, which helped him to suggest that he had the interests of Welsh people at heart. Moreover Gladstone's father had been a Scotsman and in addition Gladstone was elected as the first rector of Edinburgh University in 1859. This laid the foundation for his celebrated Midlothian campaign of 1879. With Disraeli, Gladstone was the first politician who could claim to be a truly national figure – indeed, by comparison with Disraeli his own claim was much stronger especially when his involvement in Irish affairs is taken into account – but in his case this involved combining a number of local followings. In Victorian England the sense of locality was both powerful and important.

Nevertheless London still continued to exert its fascination as an unrivalled centre of entertainment and conviviality. The aristocracy and all those with any social pretensions flocked to London for the annual social season. In many ways membership of the House of Commons had a similar appeal, since the sessions were comparatively short and even a comparatively attentive member of the House would be able to find ample time for socialising and other business, owing to the lateness of the sitting. London at this level of society was above all a place for meeting people. Doubtless in most societies prominent people find ways of encountering one another, most often on a comparatively superficial basis, but in examining the various Victorian élites that intermingled, circulated and coalesced it is the depth, complexity, intensity even of these connections that is striking. Dickens was friendly with Wilkie Collins, Tom Taylor the playwright and Macready the actor, but he also knew a surprising number of artists, quite apart from his own illustrators, Browne, Cruickshank and Leech – Maclise, Clarkson Stanfield, Augustus Egg, Charles Collins, even Millais, whose work he had earlier abused. Such figures as Tennyson, Browning, Ruskin and Carlyle would mingle at the Coventry Patmores and Patmore also knew Robert Bridges and Gerard Manley Hopkins. It was Moncton Milnes, Lord Houghton, who really did know everyone, who got Patmore his job as Assistant Librarian at the British Museum. Although there were a multiplicity of informal contacts, the leading journals and magazines brought many eminent Victorians together. It was through the *Westminster Review* that George Eliot was brought in contact with G. H. Lewes, Herbert Spencer and Harriet Martineau. It goes without saying that she knew Lord Houghton, but others with whom she was acquainted included Barbara Bodichon, Mark Pattison, Millais, Burne-Jones, Browning and Tennyson. Through his editorship of the *Cornhill* Leslie Stephen widened his already vast circle of friends, associates and acquaintances, but to say this almost understates the case. Stephen's elder brother was Fitzjames Stephen; A. V. Dicey was his cousin. He married Thackeray's daughter Harriet. Virginia Woolf was his daughter. John Morley, editor of the *Fortnightly Review*, Henry Fawcett, the economist and MP, and George Meredith were his close friends. When he wanted someone to witness his signature on a document renouncing Holy Orders, he called, most appropriately, for Thomas Hardy. Stephen was a member of the Metaphysical Society, whose membership included T. H. Huxley, John Tyndall, Henry Manning, W. G. Ward, R. H. Hutton, Gladstone, Henry Sidgewick and Frederick Harrison. Stephen, Huxley, Sidgewick and Harrison were members of the Athenaeum, along with Spencer, Morley, Matthew Arnold and Mill. Such was the Victorian cultural web.

If the Victorian world was organised topographically by county, town and country estate, it was also divided vertically by social class. Yet class relations acquired an element of mystery that they never possessed where squire and vicar presided over a largely deferential population of rural labourers. The working classes were to be found in the industrial towns of the north of England, yet many had never travelled there and many had never ventured or dreamt of venturing into those parts of London where the poorer people resided. The poor were drab but they were also strangely exotic. In the opening chapter of *Mary Barton* Mrs Gaskell introduces the lively working-class girls who gather at Green Heys Field, near Manchester, and explains how, towards evening, the shawl that they habitually wore 'became a sort of Spanish mantilla or Scotch plaid, and was brought over the head and hung loosely down, or was pinned under the chin in no unpicturesque fashion'. Mrs Gaskell is no romantic observer of the working classes but we cannot avoid recognising how, when alien customs are to be described, they cannot help but be marshalled under the sign of the picturesque. What I want to argue is that Victorian observers, as they attempted to write about the working class, very naturally fell back on already existing categories, and that, sometimes consciously, sometimes unconsciously, they tended to think about them as if they were gypsies. The Victorians were fascinated with gypsies in any event, as is evidenced by such diverse figures as Queen Victoria, Emily Brontë and Mrs Ewing, George Borrow and Matthew Arnold. George Borrow introduces *The Zincali*, an account of the gypsies in Spain, by saying: 'Throughout my life the Gypsy race has always had a peculiar fascination for me. Indeed I can remember no period in my life when the mere mention of the name of Gypsy did not awaken within me feelings hard to be described. I cannot account for this, I merely state a fact.' The gypsies were everything middle-class Victorians were not – while the middle classes prided themselves on their self-discipline, their stability, their integrity, their capacity for hard work, their general sobriety, the gypsies, it seemed, were flamboyant, romantic wanderers who enjoyed a free and easy, not to say uproarious, lifestyle. Where people were enjoying themselves, whether at the racecourse or the country fair, gypsies could be expected to be there. They were almost certainly heathen and were thought to have a very casual attitude to that crucial distinction between mine and thine. In George Borrow's *The Romany Rye* – a gypsy appellation like *Lavengro* that Borrow is happy to assume – the gap between respectable and disreputable society becomes manifest when Borrow accompanied by the Petulengros swaggers into the village church for Sunday service. The gypsies stand up and sit down in all the wrong places, and by awkwardly holding their hymn books at the top instead of at the bottom make it all too apparent that they cannot read. In his sermon the clergyman laments the example of those who have sacrificed their immortal soul solely to obtain fame or worldly goods, but he concludes his sermon by referring to those 'others who lost their souls, and got nothing for them – neither lands, wealth, renown, nor consideration, who were poor outcasts, and despised by everybody. My friends,' he added, 'if the man is a fool who barters his soul for the whole world, what a fool he must be who barters his soul for nothing.'

The eyes of the clergyman, as he uttered those words, wandered around the whole congregation; and when he had concluded them, the eyes of the whole congregation were turned upon my companions and myself.

For Borrow, the archetypal transgressor, this is a moment of both ecstasy and shame. On the one hand he is proud to be the cynosure of all eyes and the object of scandalised rebuke, but on the other, deep down, he knows that the vicar is right. Borrow is attracted towards outcasts for the very reason that they diverge from the norms of respectable society, just as Henry Mayhew is fascinated by the exotic cast of outcast London, yet both are conscious of the perversity of their interest and are anxious not to become *too* closely identified with the unknown territory they have chosen to explore. Inhabiting a no-man's land between diverse cultural worlds and in danger, as in the above incident, of acquiring guilt by association, they attempt occasionally to cleanse themselves by flinching back with exaggerated gestures of disapprobation and distaste.

The parallels between the gypsies and the working class are complex but one of the most important of these is that they live apart from the rest of society. In the introduction to *The Zincali* Borrow says of the English gypsies: 'the Gypsies are no longer the independent people they were of yore – dark, mysterious, and dreaded wanderers, living apart in the deserts and heaths with which England at one time abounded'. Perhaps: but in *Sybil* Disraeli describes a place called Wodgate, which is remote from any area of regular settlement and which for that very reason has always retained a 'heathen character':

Wodgate had advantages of its own, and of a kind which touch the fancy of the lawless. It was land without an owner; no one claimed any manorial rights over it; they could build cottages without paying rent. It was a district recognised by no parish; so there were no tithes, and no meddlesome supervision.

Wodgate is no-man's land, an arena of lawlessness. It is now a large,

anarchic industrial town. There are some interesting parallels between Disraeli's *Sybil* and Scott's *Guy Mannering*, based on an assumption that Scott and Disraeli share, which is that the aristocracy
have a responsibility towards the lower classes. In *Guy Mannering*
the House of Ellangowan is nearly destroyed by the rash decision of
the laird to drive the gypsies from their traditional place of encampment on his estates. In *Sybil* similar retribution is visited on the
Mowbray family as a result of their thoughtless and callous attitude
towards the poor. Those who have been uprooted to live in Wodgate
return in a lawless riot to loot and ransack the ancestral seat of the
family, Mowbray Castle. The sense that both gypsies and the urban
working class are to be associated with a alien and anarchic way of
life is particularly evident in *The Old Curiosity Shop*. In chapter 42 of
that novel Little Nell, as so often, has been left alone at night and she
finds herself drawn towards the fire of a gypsy encampment, where
she overhears a sinister conversation between her grandfather, Isaac
List and Joe Jowl, two professional cardsharps, and a gypsy who
passes around tin cups filled to the brim with brandy. It emerges that
they are trying to persuade the old man to rob Mrs Jarley's cashbox.
Little Nell is terrified by this whole scene and insists to her grandfather that they must flee immediately. But it is a case of out of the
frying-pan into the fire for they arrive in an ugly and terrifying
industrial town that is filled with equally lawless activity:

> night, when the noise of every strange machine was aggravated by
> darkness; when the people near them looked wilder and more
> savage; when bands of unemployed labourers paraded in the
> roads, or clustered by torchlight around their leaders, who told
> them in stern language of their wrongs, and urged them on to
> frightful cries and threats; when maddened men armed with sword
> and firebrand, spurning the tears and prayers of women who
> would restrain them, rushed forth on errands of terror and
> destruction.

There were many obvious resemblances between the working classes
and the gypsies. Like the gypsies, the working classes were uprooted
and dispossessed, with few possessions they could call their own.
They spoke in their own arcane dialects, practised their own strange
customs and rituals, often brought up their children in a state of
godlessness, lived in a state of general indifference to the rule of law,
yet were bound together by a deep sense of tribal solidarity. Al-

though their clothing was often tattered and shabby, they neverthe-less loved to adorn themselves with finery and with touches of brilliant colour. This sense of the working classes as colourful and picturesque is particularly evident in Ford Madox Brown's celebrated painting *Work*. Brown stressed that the British navvy was just as worthy a subject for painting as 'the fisherman of the Adriatic, the peasant of the Campagna, or the Neapolitan Lazzarone', and noted that the costume of his workmen is 'manly and picturesque'.[6] Al-though there are two flashily dressed women on the left of the picture, it nevertheless reverses the conventional clothing code. At the rear of the picture in shadow are the sombre figures of a lady and gentleman on horseback, to the right the intellectuals, Carlyle and F. D. Maurice, both conservatively dressed, while in bright sunlight the centre of the picture is dominated by colourful working-class figures.

That the working classes were colourful was certainly the belief of Henry Mayhew, who in his *London Labour and London Poor* unveiled all the teeming complexity of London street life of the capital before the astonished gaze of a middle-class public. Certainly Mayhew gave the whole idea of work a curious resonance that it never pos-sessed in the pages of Carlyle. All those who had naïvely imagined that work was something carried on with needles or spinning machines, ploughs, spades or scrubbing brushes were introduced to a strange and miraculous new world where people maintained their existence in a much more unorthodox fashion. There were the dog-dung gatherers, the bone-grubbers, the sellers of sham indecent literature, the vendors of damaged fruit, the barkers, the stook-buzzers, noisy-racket men, toshers, lumpers and mudlarks. Mayhew made a crucial distinction – also reflected in Ford Madox Brown's painting – between those who will and will not work, but in all this picturesque enumeration it was often hard to remember which was which. There were certainly many remarkable ways of snapping up unregarded trifles – not all them legal. In Mayhew's relentless, ency-clopaedic enumeration of occupations it was easy to forget that the majority of people worked in familiar, commonplace occupations while by comparison with the élite of snoozers, noisy racket men and pretended destitute Poles, Members of Parliament were com-paratively thick on the ground. But Mayhew claimed to have a scientific purpose. What he offered to his cultivated readers was an account of how the working classes, as a nomadic people, were to be differentiated from 'civilised' man:

The nomad then is distinguished from the civilised man by his repugnance to regular and continuous labour – by his want of the providence in laying up a store for the future – by his inability to perceive consequences ever so slightly removed from immediate apprehension – by his passion for stupefying herbs and roots, and when possible, for intoxicating fermented liquors – by his extraordinary powers of enduring privation – by his comparative insensibility to pain – by an immoderate love of gaming, frequently risking his own personal liberty upon a single cast – by his love of libidinous dances – by the pleasure he experiences in witnessing the suffering of sentient creatures – by his delight in warfare and all perilous sports – by his desire for vengeance – by the looseness of his notions as to property – by the absence of chastity among his women, and his disregard of female honour – and lastly, by his vague sense of religion – his rude idea of a Creator, and utter absence of all appreciation of the mercy of the Divine Spirit.[7]

Gypsies were, of course, the nomadic people *par excellence*, and in his account of the nomad Mayhew reproduces much of the folklore and prejudice that surrounded them. In particular Mayhew stresses that nomadic peoples always prey on civilised ones and therefore 'such wandering hordes have frequently a different language from the more civilised portion of the community, and that adopted with the intent of concealing their designs and exploits from them'.[8] Mayhew thus alerted his readers – if they were not already aware of it – of the manifold dangers that a 'nomadic' working class presented, yet he also offered them much in the way of consolation and reassurance. The working class was the lazy grasshopper that played all summer long with no thought of the future, while the middle class was the bee tirelessly gathering honey for the winter. The 'nomadic' peoples were less intelligent, marked out by high cheekbones and protruding jaws. Moreover, since nomadic peoples were completely unscrupulous and had an extraordinary ability to withstand hardship, there was no particular reason to feel sorry for them. If you gave money to the poor, the sick or the lame you were almost certainly being conned. Mayhew was a deeply contradictory character. He clearly relished the company and the anecdotes of the street people he met, he was genuinely interested in their way of life and did his best to understand their point of view, yet the overall perspective that he brought to their situation was deeply patronising and offensive. In *Bleak House* (1853) Dickens picks up on this way of speaking about the poor as nomadic wanderers and is acutely sensitive to the self-righteous complacency that underlies it. The sanctimonious Mr Chadband introduces Jo, the crossing sweeper, to the assembled faithful by saying:

> We have here among us, my friends . . . a Gentile and a Heathen, a dweller in the tents of Tom-all-alone's, and a mover-on upon the surface of the earth. . . . Devoid of parents, devoid of relations, devoid of flocks and herds, devoid of gold, and silver, and of precious stones. Now, my friends, why is he devoid of these possessions? Why? Why is he? . . . I say this brother, present here among us, is devoid of parents, devoid of relations, devoid of flocks and herds, devoid of gold, of silver, and of precious stones, because he is devoid of the light that shines in upon some of us. What is that light? . . . It is the ray of rays, the sun of suns, the Moon of moons, the star of stars. It is the light of Terewth.

In Chadband's absurd rhetoric we see more clearly than in Mayhew how possessions are equated with righteousness and how the moral superiority and spirituality of the middle class is taken as axiomatic.

In *The Idea of Poverty* Gertrude Himmelfarb has argued that the Victorians, in the spirit of Mayhew and Ford Madox Brown, drew a clear distinction between those who worked and those who did not. It was the very emergence of a clean, hard-working and conscientious class of people who were neither ragged, immoral, criminal or dangerous that made it possible to speak of them as the 'working class'. Of the ragged classes Himmelfarb writes:

> There had always been marginal types among the poor – paupers, beggars, vagrants, street-folk, drunkards, brawlers, thieves and prostitutes. And they had always been distinguished, to some degree, from the labouring poor; they were the lowliest of the poor, the lowest of the lower classes, the most inferior of the 'inferior orders' but they had previously existed in continuity with the poor. . . . The break-up of the continuum, the sharpening of lines of demarcation was partly a result of industrialism and urbanism, partly of ideology and social policy.
>
> So long as all the poor were ragged, there were no 'ragged' classes. . . . Under that distinctive appellation they become a distinctive social problem – a problem to the poor who were not themselves in that condition and fearful of lapsing into it, and a

problem to social reformers who sought to prevent that lapse, to redeem at least the ragged children, and to forestall the degeneration of the ragged classes into the dangerous classes.[9]

Although I agree with Himmelfarb that such terms were used in this way, I would nevertheless disagree with the general thrust of her analysis. For one thing it implies that the Victorians recognised that the ragged and dangerous classes formed a small minority of the working class as a whole; whereas the general drift of middle-class discussion of the working class was if anything to suggest the reverse: to imply that it was the thrifty, hard-working, temperate, God-fearing people who were the saving remnant. Moreover, although they feel inclined to speak favourably of such people in the abstract, whey they encountered them in the real world in the disconcerting form of Methodists and uppity chapel folk their enthusiasm rapidly dwindled, as is all too evident in such works as Mrs Oliphant's *Salem Chapel* and Trollope's *The Vicar of Bullhampton*. Mayhew is at pains to distinguish the working from the non-working classes, yet the overwhelming effect of his book is to criminalise the working classes, to conjure up an immense underworld in which nobody likes work very much and where virtually everyone is on the fiddle. A similar impression is conveyed by John Hollingshead, despite the fact that the overall picture painted by Hollingshead is sombre and grey by comparison with Mayhew's lurid laying on of colour. Thus, of Southwark he writes:

> A vast and melancholy property it is. Within the boundaries before mentioned, and down in the hollow of the water-side basin of London, lighted up at intervals with special markets of industry, or budding into short patches of honest trade, sinking every now and then into dark acres of crime, and covered everywhere with the vilest sores of prostitution, are something like four hundred thousand people, or one seventh part of the whole metropolitan population. . . . It has scores of streets that are rank and steaming with vice; streets where unwashed, drunken, fishy-eyed women hang by dozens out of the windows, beckoning to the passers-by. It has scores of streets filled with nothing but thieves, brown, unwholesome tramps' lodging-houses, and smoky receptacles for stolen goods.[10]

Southwark, admittedly, is worse than parts of the east end to the north of the river – but they are pretty bad too – and Southwark houses, if that is the word, a massive chunk of the population of the capital. In Hollingshead's description the small patches of honest activity are so small as scarcely to command attention. Everything blends together into a vast miasma of evil, as thick and all encompassing as the London fog. In the face of such an unending panorama of crime and misery it seems that there is very little that can be done. With a predictable Victorian emphasis, stark, uncompromising, unforgiving, Hollingshead prefaces his book by saying: 'The evils shadowed forth by this and like books cannot be remedied by Government, nor tinkering philanthropy. . . . Those few of the poor and miserable who wish for improvement – they are not the majority – must shut their ears to such debates, and learn to help themselves.'[11] As sentimentalists fail to grasp, the underworld will always be an underworld because it is inhabited by a tribe of people altogether different from the respectable middle classes. It is a world without moral standards, where criminality rules.

In the field of Victorian painting it is William Powell Frith who most eagerly takes up Mayhew's challenge to depict English society in all its diversity. Frith shared Mayhew's interest in the classification of social types and he was also concerned to interpret the figures he painted in the light of physiognomy, which distinguished between the higher and lower forms of humanity. It is fitting that Frith's most famous paintings, *Derby Day* and *The Railway Station*, should depict the few places and moments in Victorian society where all social classes could mingle or at least temporarily converge. These subjects gave Frith an unrivalled opportunity to construct a representation in which all social classes figured, and he made use of photography to ensure their accuracy. So Frith is generally taken to be *the* master of mid-Victorian realism. But his pictures are not quite what they seem. The point I wish to emphasise here is that – as Mary Cowling's meticulous analysis of both paintings makes clear[12] – despite the very large number of figures, scarcely any of them belong to the working class, and in both paintings there is characteristic emphasis on criminality. In *Derby Day* the most prominent figures in the painting are members of the aristocracy in their carriages, around whom have congregated a number of low-life types, notably gypsies, pickpockets, prostitutes, acrobats, card-sharpers, thimble-riggers and both Jewish and Scottish swindlers. The picture could not illustrate more graphically Mayhew's distinction between the civilised classes and those who live off them. It also points a moral –

anyone who consorts, however briefly, with the lower classes risks being robbed or duped. In *The Railway Station* the middle classes are much more conspicuous. The centre of the painting is dominated by Frith's own family – unmistakably belonging to the affluent middle class – who are shown seeing their two boys off to public school. Also shown is a wedding party, a sailor and his tearful wife, some tradespeople, a naval officer and some humbler military types. But the painting also depicts a dramatic event – the arrest of a criminal for fraud by the famous detectives, Brett and Haydon. Once again the criminal theme intrudes. The message of the two paintings is subtly different, but both articulate a middle-class point of view. In *Derby Day* foolish, dissolute aristocrats put themselves at the mercy of cheats and confidence tricksters; in *The Railway Station* the prosperous middle class calmly goes about its everyday business secure in the knowledge that it is protected from crime by the watchful presence of the police.

Outside such zones of more or less indiscriminate mingling, Victorian cultural spaces were very carefully demarcated and patrolled. In the towns suburbs were for the more affluent and many slum areas became virtually no-go areas. Within upper- and middle-class households, there were separate servants' quarters, themselves hierarchically organised and sexually segregated, and whole areas such as the dining room, billiard room, smoking room, library and study which would be aside as male preserves. In church the well-to-do had their own specially designated pews. Upper-class gentlemen had their clubs. The ladies tended to spend rather more time at home, engaged in needlework, painting and playing the pianoforte. Hotels, as potentially dangerous zones where class divisions might be eroded, had complex regulations designed to discourage prostitutes, whose threat to Victorian society stemmed not so much from their immorality as from their ability to pass themselves off as ladies. Public houses and music-halls were the places of recreation for the working class. In a pub in Wales George Borrow was somewhat taken aback when a man came up to him and asked him if he could understand Welsh. Borrow answered somewhat complacently that he could understand 'a considerable part of a Welsh conversation' since his knowledge of Welsh had often enabled him to get on good terms with the locals to which his interrogator replied: 'Well, sir, that's speaking plain, and I will tell you plainly that we don't like to have strangers among us who understand our discourse, more especially if they be gentlefolks.' While football was a game for the lower classes their social superiors went hunting and shooting, they engaged in cricket, rugby and rowing. While all could depart from the same railway station, until the 1870s third-class passengers travelled on different trains from first- and second-class passengers – they were herded into wagons that were attached to slowly moving goods trains in conditions of extreme discomfort.

In the nineteenth century one of the most crucial aspects of life that differentiated the middle and upper classes from the working class was access to clean water. In the countryside water had never really been a class issue, though doubtless the affluent, since they did not work, were distinctly cleaner, but in the towns and especially in the large cities water became an important issue. The better-off members of society were able to bathe on a regular basis. After 1870 the use of water closets became widespread. They were able to wash with soap. Sales of soap rose – in part, due to Gladstone's repeal of the 3*d*. in the pound duty on soap – from 47,768 tons in 1831 to 150,000 tons in 1871. But what was of far greater significance than cleanliness as such was that their access to comparatively clean supplies of water meant that they were generally untouched by the epidemics of cholera, typhus and typhoid that were such a marked feature of Victorian life. In London 14,000 people died of cholera in 1849, 10,000 in 1854 and 5000 in 1866. Deaths from typhus and typhoid in London were of the order of 100 deaths in every 100,000 until 1890, after which date the proportion dropped significantly to 15 in every 100,000. Nevertheless the great were not exempt and in retrospect it seems quite astonishing that Prince Albert, the highest in the land, should have died such an early death as the result of infection from typhoid fever. Outside Buckingham Palace the risks were still greater. Out of 270,000 homes in the London area, it was estimated that 70,000 had no access of water. Moreover the River Thames itself was deeply polluted – Dickens indicated how closely the idea of the river was associated with dire poverty and extremely insanitary conditions when in *Our Mutual Friend* he referred to the river from the tower of London to the docks and Rotherhithe 'where the accumulated scum of humanity seemed washed from higher grounds, like so much moral sewage'.

Efforts were made to improve urban sanitation through the provision of sewers. In 1865 a new drainage system for London was opened which involved 80 miles of sewers, which drained 100 square miles of built-up area and which were capable of carrying 420 million gallons a day. However, the invocation of statistics such as this in discussions of Victorian society does produce that characteristically Victorian emphasis on *improvement* as the result of which shocking living conditions are made to seem 'temporary' and comparatively unimportant. So we should rather emphasise, as some more socially conscious contemporaries did, that it was positively scandalous that access to clean supplies of water had become a form of social privilege. Charles Kingsley was especially concerned with questions of sanitation and two of his best-known novels, *Yeast* and *The Water Babies*, are effectively allegories of water. In *Yeast* Kingsley seems to have deliberately chosen a rural setting for his exposure of insanitary conditions, for while his readers would have been at least partially prepared for his description of pools of foul and stagnant water in *Alton Locke*, they would not have expected to find similar evils in a village. But as Kingsley points out, appearances can be deceptive, for behind the appearance of rural idyll is something very different: 'There, if anywhere, one would have expected to find Arcadia among fertility, loveliness, industry and wealth. But, alas for the sad reality! the cool breath of those glittering water-meadows too often floats laden with poisonous miasma.' Moreover, as Kingsley points out, what makes the incidence of such diseases as cholera and typhoid particularly unjust is both that they are caused by the carelessness, neglect and miserliness of upper-class landlords, who are themselves exempt from terrible consequences of their own criminal indifference:

> It is most fearful, indeed, to think that these diseases should be confined to the poor – that a man should be exposed to cholera, typhus, and a host of attendant diseases, simply because he is born into the world an artisan; while the rich by the mere fact of money, are exempt from such curses, except when they come in contact with those whom they call on Sunday 'their brethren' and on week days 'the masses'.
>
> Thank Heaven you do see that – in a country calling itself civilised and Christian, pestilence should be the peculiar heritage of the poor! It is past all comment.

In *Yeast* retribution is brought about through the death of Argemone Lavington from cholera after visiting one of the tenants of her family who is suffering from fever. For Kingsley this demonstrates the deep inauthenticity of a class society, in which there is no real recognition of the working classes as fellow human beings. This division is presented from a different point of view in *The Water Babies* where Tom, the boy chimney-sweep is made angry and ashamed of his physical dirtiness through his encounter with Ellie, the clean and beautiful upper-class child. Tom's immersion in the water is intended to symbolise the possibility of moral improvement and re-generation, and it is significant that in this process Ellie serves as his moral instructor. What Kingsley is anxious to show is that the lower classes are not inherently degenerate but can be made capable of reformation. If only they will refrain from doing as they like and submit themselves to discipline they can eventually brought within a middle-class system of values. What is rather disconcerting about all this is that Kingsley's is the relatively progressive view. Yet Kingsley's obsession with water is interesting as it shows that he was conscious, as so few of his contemporaries were, of England as a deeply polluted land, where water itself could no longer be regarded as clean. This very fact seemed to put moral absolutes in question. The very idea of water has become associated with Utopia and fantasy. The same connection is to be found in William Morris's *News from Nowhere*. Morris's socialist world is also a better world because it has been cleaned up, and Morris devotes much of his narrative to descriptions of the River Thames, which is now a pure and beautiful stream and no longer a foul sewer bordered by smok-ing chimneys. Water brings into the sharpest possible focus all that is wrong with Victorian society.

As well as injustice based on class there was injustice grounded in gender. Victorian women were significantly disadvantaged. They were excluded from the universities and from other educational opportunities. They were debarred from pursuing such professional careers as medicine, law and accountancy. They did not have the right to vote. The occupations they pursued, whether governess, seamstress or domestic servant, were extremely badly paid. Yet to focus too exclusively on inequality and on the obstacles that stood in the path of women is to miss the real cutting edge of Victorian ideology: the belief, so widely promulgated, especially by ministers of the church, that a woman's primary duty in life was to aid and support her husband. In this way the whole question of how a woman's role was elaborately circumscribed and restricted could scarcely figure as an issue, since no right-thinking woman could possibly conceive of a role in life that would be as fulfilling as that of comforting and sustaining her husband. The Victorian middle class especially was very preoccupied with the concept of duty, and where a wife was concerned there could be absolutely no question where her duty lay. There is a great preoccupation with the supportive woman in the iconography of Victorian painting, but because our interest in Victorian art is by no means identical with that of the Victorians themselves, this theme can easily go unnoticed. For example, where the Pre-Raphaelite movement is concerned we are prone to think of the ethereal, otherworldly women of Rossetti, Morris and Burne-Jones, yet if we consider the movement more widely it becomes very clear that Pre-Raphaelite painters had a very definite interest in painting women who would, at all costs, stand by their man. A favourite theme was that of the man who, in difficulty or danger, nevertheless is aided and supported by a woman. In Millais's *The Order of Release* a wounded soldier, released from confinement, is comforted by his wife with a baby on her arm; in *The Black Brunswicker* a beautiful young girl clings to her handsome soldier hero; in *The Huguenot* a Huguenot, in danger of religious persecution, is supportively embraced by his lover. Arthur Hughes, who was clearly influenced by Millais, espoused similar themes. His *Home from the Sea* shows a grief-stricken sailor lying by his mother's grave, while his girl-friend, dressed in mourning, sits sympathetically by his side. What is particularly noticeable about this theme is the way in which it privileges the emotions of men over women – it is the men who feel, the women who offer comfort and sympathy. Thus, in Hughes best-known painting *The Long Engagement* it is clear that it is the man who suffers, his tender fiancée who must sustain him. This is even the case in Holman Hunt's *Claudio and Isabella*, where it seems that Isabella seems more concerned with comforting Claudio in his hour of need than with showing indignation at his suggestion that she should sacrifice her virtue to save his life. What links paintings as superficially diverse as James Campbell's *The Poacher's Wife* and Ford Madox Brown's *The Last of England* is their admiration for the woman who dedicates herself totally to her husband's welfare. The title of *The Poacher's Wife* foregrounds the fact that it is the woman who is the heroine of the picture, supporting her husband even when the price for all of them may be very high. In *The Last of England* we are, of course, conscious of the dimensions of a human tragedy that has driven so many Englishmen to seek a new life overseas, but we are also acutely aware of the sustaining role of the woman, who holds her husband's hand with one hand and grasps that of her tiny baby with the other. It is the woman who assumes the full burden of their grief. An intriguing twist to the theme of the nurturing, sustaining woman is provided by William Shakespeare Burton's *The Wounded Cavalier*, in which the wife of a Puritan courageously goes to the rescue of a wounded Cavalier, despite the evident disapproval of her husband. This painting – and we should note that some contemporary observers found it shocking – suggests that a wife's first duty may not necessarily be to her husband, but it confirms woman in her general obligation to concern herself above all with the welfare of men. The depths of a woman's devotion to her man, her willingness to go to any lengths for him, is illustrated by William Lindsay Windus's *Burd Helen*, based on an old Scots ballad, and highly praised by both Rossetti and Ruskin, in which Helen, who has run all day, following the horse of her heartless lover, will even swim the waters of the Clyde rather than risk losing him.

This preoccupation with sacrificial, sustaining women is also reflected in the fiction of Dickens, though the particular inflection that Dickens brings to it is to present such women as always implicitly children and daughters – Dickens's cast of such selfless women includes Little Nell in *The Old Curiosity Shop*, Florence in *Dombey and Son*, Agnes in *David Copperfield* and Little Dorrit, yet through this emphasis on youth Dickens seems to imply that woman's capacity for self-abnegation is somehow imperilled as adulthood looms. The archetypal Victorian sacrificial heroine was not, however, a fictional character, but a real woman, Florence Nightingale, who achieved celebrity in her thirties through her efforts to save the lives of soldiers in the Crimean War. The irony is that Nightingale, a forceful, independent woman, who in her life did so much to challenge conventional notions of what was either proper or seemly in a woman, nevertheless was taken to exemplify woman's infinite capacity for subordination and self-denial. As Nancy Boyd has pointed out:

The legend of Florence Nightingale contained much that people wanted to hear over and over again. It centred on two folk heroes – the British soldier and the woman who serves him. It shows each in a noble light. Furthermore it epitomised what the Victorians believed to be the ideal relationship between man and woman. The man to whom England owed her power and her wealth was long-suffering, brave, patient and kind. The woman was hard-working and gentle; furthermore she reached a final fulfilment and happiness in a life of service, offering herself wholly to caring for the male.[13]

Nevertheless the example of Nightingale and of other nurses who had worked under desperately difficult conditions could be used in a contrary way: to argue that there could be no justification for debarring women from pursuing a medical career when they had already displayed such skill and dedication in caring for patients. In his novel *A Woman-Hater* (1877), written in support of the right of women to pursue a medical career, Charles Reade acknowledges the extent of contemporary prejudice against careers for women, by having Rhoda Gale, an American girl who has studied medicine on the Continent, report a clergyman's arguments against the admission of women to Edinburgh University as follows:

> Women's sphere is the hearth and the home: to impair her delicacy is to take the bloom from the peach: she could not qualify for medicine without mastering anatomy and surgery, branches that must unsex her. Providence, intending her to be man's helpmate, not his rival, had given her a body unfit for war, or hard labour, and a brain four ounces lighter than a man's, and unable to cope with long study and practical science. In short, she was too good, and too stupid, for medicine and science. Lacking the scientific preacher's whole theory in theology and science, woman was high enough in creation to be the mother of God, but not high enough to be a sawbones.

As with questions of poverty and social class, the combination of religious argument with what purported to be the latest scientific wisdom could make a compelling combination. Yet as Rhoda points out there us a vast amount of humbug involved.

> As to the study and practice of medicine degrading women, he asked if it degraded men. No; it elevated them. Nurses are not as a class, unfeminine, yet all that is most appalling, disgusting, horrible, and *unsexing* in the art of healing is monopolised by them. Women see worse things than doctors. Women nurse all the patients of both sexes, often under horrible and sickening conditions, and lay out all the corpses. No doctor objects to this on sentimental grounds; and why? because the nurses get only a guinea a week, and not a guinea a flying visit: to women the

loathesome part of medicine; to man the lucrative! The noble nurses of the Crimea went to attend *males only*; yet were not charged with indelicacy. They worked gratis.

A high-flown and ostensibly reverential attitude towards women in practice could serve as a cover for more self-serving motives. By presenting women with the ideal of the long-suffering, self-sacrificing woman, men were able not only to transform the task of ministering to their own selfish needs into the highest of virtues, but they could also ensure that they were confined to the lowliest of occupations. A work that expounds the characteristic Victorian allocation of sex roles is the Reverend William Landels's *Woman's Sphere and Work*, published, perhaps significantly, in 1859, in the immediate aftermath of the Crimean War. A large part of Landels's book is devoted to reconciling women to the hardships they will encounter in various women's occupations – thus, of governesses Landels characteristically observes: 'And even if her hardships were greater than they are, they might well be borne cheerfully for the influential position which she occupies, and the great and glorious work which she has in her power to perform.'[14] Yet, inevitably, Landels's principal emphasis falls on the role of married women and he is anxious to present the wife in the role of saviour of her husband: 'How many a wife has saved and, as we say, *made* her husband?'[15] and to demarcate it very sharply from any irreverent talk that leads to any notion of the personal autonomy or political enfranchisement of women:

> That enfranchisement would be the veriest thraldom, and that elevation the deepest disgrace, which would lesson or interfere with the influence which woman exerts, or the offices which she performs, within the sacred precincts of home. Beware, my sisters, how you listen to those who would turn you aside from a work which even angels might covet, and rob you of that which, after all that may be said, constitutes your true glory.[16]

What is striking in Landels's discussion is the intransigent, absolutist nature of the argument, the starkness of the alternatives presented. There is no hint that a woman might be able to vote as well as support her husband, no indication even that she might occasionally pursue her own needs and inclinations when not devoting herself to her task as helpmeet – no, this imperious and sacred duty must engross every minute of her waking hours and the woman who listens to any siren voices whispering the contrary is fallen indeed. To be an angel is a full-time occupation! Landels does not merely argue that such behaviour is desirable; he suggests that it is determined by the very nature of woman. Women, he claims, have an inherent 'love of dependence': 'she finds her happiness in her entire devotion to the happiness of others. Her life is a constant sacrifice which never pains her, because to make it accords with the deepest instincts and the most powerful prompting of her nature.'[17] So the woman who feels stifled and frustrated at home and who seeks some other outlet for her energies and ambitions is not simply selfish but actually unnatural as well. Given the choice between being angels and devils, it was hardly surprising that so many Victorian women opted to be angels. Even Harriet Martineau, an independent woman who had made a career for herself as a successful writer, felt this pressure to live up to cultural expectations of a woman's role. Thus, she wrote to Richard Moncton Milnes: 'It is strange that I did not foresee it, for my whole life has been a series of such lessons, – that I was to live for others.'[18]

In saying this, I am not attempting to decry self-sacrifice, when clearly it is a characteristic which in so many circumstances, can only call for our respect and admiration, my purpose is rather to show how Victorians ministers of the gospel and others used this deference to manipulate women purely in support of male comfort and convenience, which is another matter altogether. The demand that women be angels was a sinister one, since in becoming angels they were asked to give up all their rights as an individual person. To be an angel was also to be a slave.

Perhaps the most famous and popular of Victorian works celebrating this domesticated ideal was Coventry Patmore's cycle of poems *The Angel in the House*. In fairness to Patmore, it can be argued that his desire to celebrate married love was in many respects admirable, precisely because it had so often seemed too humdrum and banal to be a worthy subject for verse, as Patmore himself implied in the Prologue to the poem:

> Then she: 'What is it, Dear? The Life
> Of Arthur, or Jerusalem's Fall?'
> 'Neither: your gentle self, my Wife,
> And love, that grows from one to all.'

Yet *The Angel in the House*, like *In Memoriam*, was very much the poem the Victorians wanted. Patmore artfully anchored his rhapsodies celebrating the powers of love within a narrative describing Felix's courtship of his future bride, Honoria, so that lofty sentiments are intermingled with touches of homely realism. There is afternoon tea with the dean in the cathedral close; there is picnicking and the picking of harebells on Salisbury Plain; there is the fortunate delay on going into church, as Honoria pauses to adjust her lilac glove, that enables Felix to offer her his arm; finally, there his realisation, after they are married, that this means that he will have to pay for her sand-shoes! But this willingness to celebrate the humdrum and the ordinary has another side – it implies that men are never so ready to flatter and praise a woman as when she is humble, gentle, mild, compliant, so that praise of a wife also involves a quite complex specification of what a wife should actually be. In the poem, Felix speaks of his ambition 'To live, not for myself, but her', but despite this it is very clear that it is the woman who will be called upon to make the sacrifices. As Patmore perceives it, women can only express their personal volition through their instinctive desire to be subservient to a man:

> Her will's indomitably bent
> On mere submissiveness to him.

She seeks nothing more from life than to make him happy and to devote herself unreservedly to his service. Indeed this is what the whole idea of a wife, an angel in the house, actually means:

> The gentle wife, who decks his board,
> And makes his day to have no night,
> Whose wishes wait upon her lord,
> Who finds her own in his delight.

For Patmore this ideal of womanhood implies not simply dedication to her husband but a total emptying out of self. She can desire nothing more than to become a vacuum that will be filled by *his* presence, *his* will, *his* intelligence:

> A rapture of submission lifts
> Her life into celestial rest;
> There's nothing left of what she was;
> Back to the babe the woman dies,
> And all the wisdom that she has
> Is to love him for being wise.

There is, no doubt, a convenient symmetry in the fact that Patmore, in placing woman on a pedestal, places man on one as well, yet there can be no doubt that woman is the victim of this well-thought-out arrangement. Her's not to reason why – not for her the daunting struggles over truth – her great mission in life is to live up to an ideal of doglike devotion and obedience!

It is within this context that we must set Elizabeth Barrett Browning's *Aurora Leigh*, a narrative poem written with extraordinary brio, which manages to develop its story and its complex arguments as if there were no contradiction between these objectives. Her case against male domination in marriage is the more telling because the man in question, Romney Leigh, is apparently not a domineering, self-centred and self-satisfied male but a thoughtful and genuinely sensitive man, whose primary concern in life is to use his fortune and social position to help others. But Barrett Browning quite subtly shows, in a way that anticipates Henry James and may well have influenced him, how such apparently benevolent motives may involve a well concealed will-to-power. Romney, enlightened as he apparently is, has no sense of equality or partnership in marriage, and his proposals, first to Aurora Leigh, and then to Marian Earle, a girl whom he has rescued from desperate poverty, conceal a drive towards domination and self-aggrandisement. Moreover his refusal to accept Aurora Leigh's vocation as a poet, which is ostensibly bound up with his sense of the irrelevance of art given the urgency of the contemporary social crisis, actually shows how very conventional is his conception of a woman's role:

> Women as you are,
> Mere women, personal and passionate,
> You give us doating mothers, and perfect wives,
> Sublime Madonnas, and enduring saints!
> We get no Christ from you, – and verily
> We shall not get a poet, in my mind.

In reading *Aurora Leigh* we have to recognise that Barrett Browning is trying to find her way out of a complex double bind, which no longer has the power that it once exercised: that a woman in wanting to be an artist cannot necessarily be expected to give up love and a relationship with a man. So that although in a way Aurora Leigh is right to refuse Romney because she perceives his real intentions towards her, in another way this is also wrong because in so doing she denys both her feelings as a woman and a very real principle of spiritual growth:

> Passioned to exalt
> The artist's instinct in me at the cost
> Of putting down the woman's, I forgot
> No perfect artist is developed here
> From any imperfect woman.

But, of course, it was Victorian culture that created the powerful myth that any woman who devoted herself to any object other than her husband's welfare would in some way unsex herself – a myth that Barrett Browning's writing shows traces of even as she challenges it. What the poem also reveals is just how difficult it was for a Victorian woman to take her own sense of identity seriously, though this is obviously a central concern for Charlotte Brontë and George Eliot also. When Aurora Leigh says:

> God has made me, – I've a heart
> That's capable of worship, love, and loss;
> We say the same of Shakespeare's. I'll be meek
> And learn to reverence, even this poor myself.

there is a subtle yet powerful irony in such an apparently innocuous sentiment, since for the Victorians meekness in a woman meant submission to her husband, and most emphatically not any subversive desire to reverence herself!

Courageous and perceptive as *Aurora Leigh* undoubtedly is, an awareness nevertheless obtrudes that Barrett Browning in making her case for equality of the sexes is careful to differentiate and indeed set this whole question quite firmly apart from other forms of injustice and inequality in society. If Romney's desire to enrol first Aurora and then Madeleine as ancillary workers in his own personal mission to reform society is both the expression of male arrogance and the ultimate barrier that stands between them, then it follows that they can only be reconciled when Romney, the deluded philanthropist, blinded when rioting workers set fire to his ancestral home, finally admits the folly of his ways:

> I built up follies like a wall
> To intercept the sunshine and your face.
> . . . I was wrong,
> I've sorely failed, I've slipped the ends of life,
> I yield and you have conquered.

Barrett Browning adopts the strict self-determining Victorian moral code by which individuals must always be regarded as self-sufficient individuals. While such a view necessarily precludes any short-sighted schemes for helping the poor, who will have to help themselves, it nevertheless offers a basis for challenging the husband's dominance in marriage;

> If marriage be a contract, look at it then,
> Contracting parties should be equal, just.

Such a view lead specifically to the Married Women's Property Act of 1870, which secured a married woman's control over her own personal property. Nevertheless we cannot ignore the fact that the small improvements in the position of women in marriage through this and the Divorce Law of 1857 only aided the affluent middle classes, since the legal costs of divorce were very high.

In considering the overall position of women in Victorian society it is difficult to decide what is the more crucial, the actual role of marriage itself or the disabilities and impediments that women faced outside it. As I have already emphasised, the doctrine that a woman must subordinate herself to the needs of her husband effectively made any kind of independent and autonomous action on the part of a woman into a mortal sin and led to feelings of guilt on the part of those few women who did pursue a career. Nevertheless I also feel that it is a mistake to focus too exclusively on the issues connected with marriage and that Victorian reformers who did so were misled by the very ideology that they were trying to combat. In Trollope's *Barchester Towers* Madeline Neroni says:

> you know what freedom a man claims for himself, what slavery he would exact from his wife if he could! And you know also how wives generally obey. Marriage means tyranny on one side and deceit on the other. I say that a man is a fool to sacrifice his interests for such a bargain. A woman too generally, has no other way of living.

It is this final sentence that is the most important. It is precisely because woman's work is so poorly paid that in many cases it is scarcely possible to survive on it that women are driven into early marriage; it is precisely because women's work involves such servitude and humiliation that marriage can seem a relatively attractive option. If only women could pursue worthwhile jobs and careers, this would have the effect of raising the status of women in society in general. Admittedly in an age without adequate means of birth control, women's options were certainly more limited, yet even John Stuart Mill could argue that women should not contribute to the family finances, even though he also admitted that the partner who earned would have more decision-making power. Mill's statement also brings out the middle-class bias of this kind of thinking, since for working-class families the woman's income was often indispensable. What we have to recognise is that any sustained campaign by middle-class reformers to bring about real improvement in the status and remuneration of working women was virtually out of the question, since it was precisely middle-class families that benefited most from the exploitation of such working women. It was they who employed governesses to teach their children on a pittance; it was they who relied upon poorly paid servants to support their middle-class lifestyle; and it was they who wore the elaborate dresses over which undernourished seamstresses endlessly laboured. So, although John Stuart Mill's *The Subjection of Woman* makes a notable case for woman's equality at a time when such claims were invariably either rejected or deflected, it does seem to me that in focusing so obsessively on the whole question of marriage he is often in danger of turning sexual inequality into a single issue. It is all very well for Mill to thunder that 'The law of servitude in marriage is a monstrous contradiction to all the principles of the modern world',[19] and to state that 'Marriage is the only actual bondage known to our law',[20] yet Mill also knew very well that Victorian society had many other forms of servitude and that at this very moment workmen were struggling to form trade unions in order to resist the forms of bondage to which they were subject. Moreover Mill says elsewhere 'I readily admit (and it is the foundation of my hopes) that numbers of married people even under the present law, (in the higher classes of England probably a great majority), live in the spirit of a just law equality',[21] so it seems that he is in effect objecting more to certain legally established principles than to the institution of marriage as it exists in practice. Moreover the actual corollary of his argument must be that if the majority of the women who are abused, ill-treated and tyrannised over by their husbands belong to the working class, then it should be made easier for such women to obtain a divorce. The Divorce Law of 1857 was passed immediately before Mill published *The Subjection of Women* in 1869, yet Mill does not comment on the highly restrictive class nature of this legislation, and indeed, considering that marriage is so much at the centre of his argument, he has surprisingly little to say about divorce and even pointedly remarks: 'The question of divorce, in the sense involving liberty of remarriage, is one into which it is foreign to my purpose to enter'[22] – despite the fact that Mill himself was not able to marry Harriet Taylor until 1851, though they had been emotionally involved for very nearly twenty years. There could be no significant improvement in the position of women until women were prepared to think more broadly about their position on society and to remove the mental blinkers created by middle-class respectability and middle-class family life.

During the nineteenth century the scale and importance of the British Empire steadily increased. There was the acquisition of Hong Kong in 1839 and of New Zealand in 1840. In Africa Natal was annexed in 1843 and Basutoland in 1868, while possessions on the Gold Coast were acquired from Denmark and Holland. Most notable of all was the consolidation of British power in India, despite the Indian mutiny, with the annexation of Sind in 1843, of the Punjab in 1849, and of Oudh in 1856 – a power that was symbolised by the proclamation of Victoria as Empress of India in 1877. However, at this time the typical middle-class Englishman did not particularly pride himself on the extent of Britain's imperial possessions but rather on the superiority of the English as compared with all other nations, including the Scottish, Welsh and Irish. England was *sui generis*, an example to all other nations, by virtue of her political institutions, her legal system, the freedom of the press and her unparalleled technological and economic progress. Indeed it was this very superiority of England as such that began to make the extension of British power of overseas seem both right and natural, since clearly more backward nations could only be glad and grateful if they were set on the right path and permitted to follow, at a respectful distance, in England's footsteps. Macaulay, admittedly, was an early enthusiast for empire but he was dismayed at the ignorance that persisted in England about her great, if sometimes tainted achievements. His essay on Clive begins with a famous lament:

> Every schoolboy knows who imprisoned Montezuma, and who strangled Atahualpa. But we doubt whether one in ten, even among English gentlemen of highly cultivated minds, can tell who won the battle of Buxar, who perpetrated the massacre of Patna, whether Sujah Dowlah ruled in Oude or in Travancore, or whether Holkar was a Hindoo or a Musselman.[23]

Even the élite would have been indignant at being offered such recondite questions as their starter for ten, but Macaulay is dismayed not only at the lack of knowledge but the lack of interest that such bafflement points to:

> It might have been expected, that every Englishman would be curious to know how a handful of his countryman, separated from their home by an immense ocean, subjugated, in the course of a few years, one of the greatest empires in the world. Yet, unless we greatly err, this subject is, to most readers, not only insipid, but positively distasteful.[24]

Macaulay recognised that the task of glorifying the morally dubious Clive and Warren Hastings might even be beyond his own considerable powers, and the climate of his own time made this even harder, since when he wrote, in the 1840s, London seemed to be bursting with lately returned nabobs, whose lifestyles made people all too aware of the extent of their ill-gotten gains. The whole idea of a British Empire signified little, either in general or specific terms. Even readers of *The Times* could scarcely have outlined the skeleton let alone put flesh on the bones. Nevertheless there is an unmistakable development in England's perception of herself as an imperial power, which I propose to explore through an analysis of some of the leading monuments of the Victorian age: Trafalgar Square, the Crystal Palace and the Albert Memorial.

Of these, the memorial to Nelson in Trafalgar Square is the most difficult to decipher. On the face of it the memorial is simply England's tribute to a great man, a reminder of England's darkest hours in the Napoleonic Wars and a celebration of the great naval victory that marked the turning of the tide, just as surely as did the Battle of Britain in 1940. In theory the references made by the whole monument are quite specific. There are reliefs showing some of Nelson's other naval victories, such as the Battle of the Nile. The four memorable lions, sculpted by Landseer from the actual animal, which were only completed in 1867, are intended to symbolise Britain's naval defences. So in theory the message of the memorial is backward-looking and defensive; in practice it communicates a much more vainglorious message. In this the decision to combine the representation of Nelson with an imposing column was crucial. For since Nelson can scarcely be seen, let alone viewed as some actual existing person, it is the imperial message of the column – conveying as it does the grandeur with which great empires honour their warrior heroes – that predominates. The monument celebrates not so much the achievement of Nelson as the past and present greatness of Britain. Through its domination of the whole square in conjunction with such proud and formidable lions, the monument seems to proclaim Trafalgar as the moment when Britain's domination of the seas laid the basis for an imperial destiny. With the erection of the Albert Memorial the homologies between the two displays make such a reading seem virtually inescapable – misreading though it may technically be.

By contrast the gigantic edifice of glass and iron that was the Crystal Palace proclaimed through its very structure – one vast universal greenhouse – that Britain was above all dedicated to the arts of peace. The Great Exhibition of 1851 was always more than an exhibition; it was the moment when England definitively proclaimed and demonstrated her superiority over the rest of the world. At a moment when the whole of continental Europe was still reeling from the shock of the revolutions of 1848, England, with the local difficulty of Chartism behind it, could demonstrate that here at least it was business as usual. If there was ever a moment when that old and probably apocryphal headline 'Storm in Channel – Continent Isolated' might have seemed true, it was in 1851. The exhibition underlined the importance of the new middle classes, both because the middle classes attended in such large numbers and because through the objects on display it defined England as an industrial and trading nation rather than as one that was agricultural and aristocratic. The exhibition was also a moment when sovereign and people were brought together with a new kind of informality, since Queen Victoria visited the Crystal Palace on more than forty sepa-

rate occasions. Indeed there was a general pattern of paying repeated visits to the exhibition, which meant that patriotic Englishmen did not simply attend to be instructed and informed, they
positively wallowed in the image of national greatness that the
exhibition represented. In 1851 London saw itself as the commanding centre of the world – a status that would eventually be confirmed
by the adoption of the Greenwich meridian as the universal meridian in 1884. What the Great Exhibition foregrounded more clearly
than ever before, as machines and machine-made artefacts were
assembled under one roof along with simple craft products from all
over the world, was the enormous gap that had opened up between
the industrialised and non-industrialised nations. Within that industrialised world Britain stood supreme. The Great Exhibition also
inaugurated the categories of the nineteenth-century museum. For
here, on display, was progress and here also were assembled the
past and the primitive, filled with their own distinctive pathos –
artefacts that would need to be preserved as a reminder of a way
of life that would soon be ground to dust under the boots of the
modern. England's ability seemingly to enclose the whole world
within this enormous structure of iron and glass was laden with
intimations for the future.

Prince Albert had been the guiding force behind the Great Exhibition and so it was natural that he should be commemorated after his
death by a monument that would symbolically express the values of
the Great Exhibition. But just as Nelson could scarcely be seen from
the top of his column, so it was perhaps appropriate that the statue
of Albert himself was finally installed in the central podium four
years after the monument was opened to the public in 1872. In this
complex assemblage of sculptures England, represented with a certain irony by a German prince, is at the commanding centre. He is
surrounded by sculptures representing Commerce, Engineering,
Manufacture and Agriculture, while the four corners of the monument are representations of all four corners of the world: America,
Africa, Europe and Asia. In this monument we see England's imperial mission to diffuse her industrial culture throughout the world
unmistakably represented. It asserts not simply England's leading
role in the world but makes world conquest seem the inescapable
consequence of her commercial and cultural supremacy. While the
Roman world order was confined to the Mediterranean, the new
British world order will be universal, bringing with it prosperity,
order, peace. But there is nothing vainglorious about the monument.

It simply seems to depict an already existing state of affairs. Simply the British 'presence' is everywhere.

There never seemed to be any real need to justify British colonialism since it was taken for granted that such a British presence was more or less inescapable. The curious bundle of benefits that such a presence would involve is nicely indicated by Eliot Warburton in *The Crescent and the Cross* when he writes: 'Egypt is become our shortest, and, therefore, our *only* path to India; the Church of England is at last represented at Jerusalem; and the brave, industrious and intelligent tribes of the Lebanon have made overtures for our protection and our missionaries.'[25] Britain is like the sun, a powerful, generous, fructifying force, sending waves of benign energy rippling across the globe.

Progress, as Adam Smith had argued, meant the uniting of nation with nation through trade, and therefore distant nations could only be grateful if they were introduced into the harmonious world system through British shipping and through British explorers, traders and entrepreneurs. Moreover, since Britain was the most progressive, civilised and advanced nation, it followed that a British presence would bring with it the prospect of social advance in a multiplicity of ways. Six years before the annexation of the kingdom of Oudh Sir William Sleeman wrote in a letter: 'A few years of tolerable government would make it the finest country in India.'[26] Similarly, Richard Burton wrote of the province of Sind, which had been annexed in 1843: 'The chief merits which Sindh in its present state possesses, are its capability of improvement, and its value to us as a military and commercial possession.'[27]

Sind was one of the poorest states in India, Oudh one of the most prosperous – what they have in common is their capacity for *improvement*, that most crucial of all Victorian words, at the hands of the British. The British presence brings greater stability, greater prosperity, a superior system of justice and a nobler religion. It is also a dynamic principle. It introduces the prospect of progress and change into societies that have been stagnant for centuries. Although it would be misleading to present David Livingstone, the great African missionary and explorer, as one of the great architects of imperialism, in his *Missionary Travels and Researches in South Africa* (1857) he nevertheless links the development of religion and trade, and suggests that it was essential to bring these backward nations into the commercial and cultural orbit of Europe. Moreover he makes it abundantly clear that missionary activity on its own is not enough:

Sending the Gospel to the heathen must, if this view be correct, include much more than is implied in the usual picture of the missionary, namely, a man going about with a Bible under his arm. The promotion of commerce ought to be specially attended to, as this, more speedily than anything else, demolishes that sense of isolation which heathenism engenders, and makes the tribes feel themselves mutually dependent on, and mutually beneficial to each other. . . . My observations on this subject make me extremely desirous to promote the preparation of the raw materials of European manufacture in Africa, for by that means we may not only put a stop to the slave-trade, but introduce the negro family into the body corporate of nations, no member of which can suffer without the others suffering with it. Success in this, in both Eastern and Western Africa, would lead, in the course of time, to a much larger diffusion of the blessings of civilization than efforts exclusively spiritual and educational confined to any one small tribe.[28]

Livingstone could see that missionary work can only be carried on effectively within a much larger process of Westernisation, which will insert the tribes into much larger economic and political structures and so break down their self-sufficiency and general distrust of outsiders. Although he does not actually say so, it is clear from his analysis that Christianity can only begin to make serious inroads into African societies when the existing social structures are put under considerable pressure. Published in the same year, 1857, R. M. Ballantyne's *Coral Island* is equally enthusiastic about the role of missionaries but considerably cruder in its perception of the issues at stake. Ralph, Jack and Peterkin are three boys who are cast away on an island in the South Seas, but far from finding an island paradise they are progressively drawn into scenes of extraordinary brutality and violence. It is here that the missionaries come in. From Bloody Bill, a trader not averse to violence himself, Ralph learns that the locals are wont to murder their babies by strangling them or burying them alive, but, he continues: 'it's a curious fact, that when the missionaries get a footin' all these things come to an end at once, an' the savages take to doin' each other good and singin' psalms like Methodists', which evokes from Ralph this emotional response: ' "God bless the missionaries!" said I, while a feeling of enthusiasm filled my heart, so that I could speak with difficulty, "God bless and prosper the missionaries till they get a footing in every island of the sea!" '

Subsequently Ralph, Jack and Peterkin are themselves delivered from imprisonment and probable death by the providential arrival of a missionary who converts the Tararo to Christianity and persuades them to burn their wooden idols. Now all is transformed and the natives immediately commence the erection of a large and commodious church. The boys must now return home but they are seen off by the missionaries and thousands of the natives, who are there to wish them godspeed. A tropical paradise can actually only become a paradise through the presence of the white man.

In William Hughes's *The Treasury of Geography* (1869) we find the authentic note of pride in the British Empire and the English race that has built it: 'The British Empire includes a vast number of foreign and colonial possessions, embracing territory situated in every quarter of the globe.'[29] There are 8,212,596 square miles of it and a total population of 237,100,000. We may note – though Hughes does not make this specific point – that of this total population, 180 million are inhabitants of India. For Hughes the British presence in Asia is an unmitigated blessing. It is Britain that is breathing life into a moribund continent:

> But the social and political development of Asiatic nations belongs to the *past* – that of Europe constitutes the active and vigorous life of the *present*. We shall have occasion as we pursue our descriptive progress through the countries of the world, to point the reader's attention to the striking evidences of Asiatic wealth, Asiatic refinement, Asiatic magnificence; and shall dwell with interest upon the countless monuments of human skill (many of them belonging to periods of hoar antiquity) which the gorgeous East presents to the observant eye. But these monuments, and the empires whose greatness they commemorate, belong to a condition of society that has long since passed, and that can return no more. Whatever of progress and improvement belongs to the countries of Asia and Africa in the present day is due to the infusion of European skill, intelligence, and wealth. Asia, though containing more than half the population of the globe, is in great measure subordinate to the influences of European energy, and many of the most fertile regions are under the direct dominion of our own countrymen.[30]

There is certainly something very artless about these lines. Are we to take it, for example, that the most fertile areas are fertile because of the presence of Englishmen, or that Englishmen have wisely concentrated their dominion on the most fertile areas. But clearly such pedantic interrogation is beside the point. Asia and everywhere else must succumb to progress and improvement since such is the way of the world. Happily for them, and happily for us, it is Englishmen who are the bearers of such progress, of such undoubted blessings.

In looking back at Victorian Britain we may well concede that it was in certain respects at least an age of progress and we may also be inclined to assume that freedom of discussion, an acceptance of conflict and controversy as a necessary part of the liberal and progressive society, could be taken for granted. Our photographic album of the Victorian world consists very largely of snapshots of such controversy – the battles over the Reform Bill of 1832; Carlyle's fierce denunciations of the condition of England when Chartism was in the ascendant; Huxley versus Wilberforce over evolution; Gladstone and Disraeli engaged in regular and ritualised confrontations on the floor of the House of Commons. Nevertheless Victorian society found debate, conflict and controversy very difficult to come to terms with. To begin with, Britain, at war with France under Pitt and Castlereagh, had for a very long period of time been inured to the suppression of dissenting voices. Censorship had been taken for granted. In the late 1820s critical voices once again began to be heard, but for many the passing of the 1832 Reform Bill was seen as a way of putting an end to rough grievances and of restoring tranquillity and order. If there were any sound conclusions to be drawn from the French Revolution, they were that stability, order and continuity in government were all important; that criticism and controversy were always potentially dangerous, especially if they were allied with popular discontent; but that governments must be prepared to make specific, carefully delimited concessions in order to maintain their credibility and ward off more serious trouble. Again, the political and social life of Victorian England was dominated by the aristocracy. Like most aristocracies it tended to be very set in its views; to perceive discussion as at best unnecessary, at worst socially subversive; and to believe that anyone who persisted in it was deliberately rocking the boat. Carlyle himself, who tried as hard as anyone to rock the boat, nevertheless distrusted debate and discussion himself and regarded Parliament as nothing more than a futile talkshop. The middle classes were also ill at ease with controversy.

Clearly they had their own specific interests to press, which did not always coincide with those of the aristocracy, as was the case with parliamentary reform and the campaign to remove the Corn Laws. But because they perceived themselves as realists and pragmatists, who always had specific solutions to offer, they preferred to home in as rapidly as possible on actual policy recommendations. Indeed the campaign to repeal the Corn Laws was a classic instance of this. Repeal benefited northern manufacturers since it meant that they could pay their workers less. The workers themselves could be mobilised in support of it.

The aristocracy could be shown to be blinkered, selfish and obstructive in defence of it. The issues could not be clearer. For Cobden and Bright the beauty of it all was that there could be absolutely no doubt where right lay. Theirs was always a monologic discourse. Yet it was not enough simply to assert this point of view in the House of Commons since the aristocracy would not listen. Indeed at one point, in 1843, Cobden suffered a serious loss of face in the House when Peel alleged that Cobden had claimed that he was *personally* responsible for the distress and misery in the country. But the strategy of the Anti-Corn Law League involved 'going on two legs', that is combining attacks in the House of Commons with agitation in the country at large, so it was possible for Cobden to regain outside the Commons the credibility that he had lost within it. Later in the same year *The Times*, in a editorial in the issue of 18 November, announced in capital letters: 'THE LEAGUE IS A GREAT FACT . . . A NEW POWER HAS ARISEN IN THE STATE.' What was significant about this was the fact that *The Times* was another dogmatic and monologic voice, which prior to 1850 was able to dictate the general parameters of public discussion, so that this announcement gave the Anti-Corn law League further credibility. From now on the League was itself able to dominate the debate, and when a serious potato famine arose in Ireland there was no real alternative to repeal. Yet for Cobden this was a Pyrrhic victory, for with repeal went the one single issue that he could rely on to generate broad popular support for middle-class politicians like himself.

Ironically the turn towards a more democratic style of politics by Gladstone and Disraeli in the late 1860s and 1870s, in which both attempted to organise their respective political parties around a more clearly defined programme, was not so much a response to new circumstances as a way of strengthening their own always imperilled authority. It was also an attempt to break away from the ineffectuality of the old élitist politics, whose shortcomings were most cruelly exposed during the Crimean War, when the whole system of government virtually broke down under the stress of personalised confrontations between Aberdeen, Palmerston and Russell. At this time it was men not measures that really counted. Even when considered dispassionately it still seems hard to believe that for more than three decades one of the major problems for the English political system was that of finding a suitable position for Lord John Russell. As Dickens wrote sardonically in *Bleak House*, in an account that could equally well refer to Palmerston:

The giving the Home Department and the Leadership of the House of commons to Joodle, the exchequer to Koodle, the Colonies to Loodle, and the foreign office to Moodle, what are you to do with Noodle? You can't offer him the Presidency of the Council; that is reserved for Poodle. You can't put him in the Woods and Forests; that is hardly good enough for Quoodle. What follows? That the country is shipwrecked, lost and gone to pieces . . . because you can't provide for Noodle!

It was the comparative failure of this personalised system of government that led to the re-emergence of an ideological politics.

The middle-class approach to political controversy is perfectly exemplified by the long serious articles that appeared in the quarterlies and especially in the *Edinburgh Review* and *The Quarterly*. They were written by gentlemanly amateurs, but by amateurs anxious to prove that they were experts. The articles appear to be exhaustive and to survey their chosen topic from every conceivable point of view. But their purpose was not to inaugurate discussion and debate so much as to close it. They were, or aspired to be, the unofficial White Papers of their day. By their authoritative tone they sought to convince the reader that the opinions they promoted were not the product of bias or sectional interest but that they embodied the claims of a higher disinterested and critical reason, which since it seeks to transcend conflict cannot itself be easily controverted. Matthew Arnold also approved of this style of writing. In 'On the Literary Influence of Academies' he calls for a criticism that will, effectively, lay down the law and impose a strict standard. In this way the dangers of dilettantism, mere narrow partisanship and parochialism can be averted. What is needed are 'influential centres of correct information',[31] such as exist, Arnold claims, in France.

The general dislike of controversy in the England of the 1830s is particularly evident in responses to the Oxford Movement.

The Anglican Church was widely perceived as a stabilising force in British society, and it was accorded such a role precisely because its status as a national church seemed to place it beyond any possibility of intellectual interrogation or challenge. No matter how forcefully dissenters or Catholics might object to its pre-eminence, this pre-eminence was not a matter of opinion but an indisputable political fact. Membership of the Church of England involved assenting to the Thirty-Nine Articles, but since these Articles were very broadly framed and since it was generally accepted that assenting to them was a mere formality, it did not really matter whether you believed them or not. Newman, by subjecting the Articles to a very searching interrogation and by drawing attention to the specific circumstances under which they were framed, made it much more difficult for people to think that these Articles were unimportant. Worse still, the Articles became a matter of contention when the whole point of them was that they served very effectively to silence controversy. For many people Newman, by raising the matter at all, was deliberately rocking the boat. His decision to go over to Rome was effectively treason. But what Newman's critics did not fully recognise was that they were just as anxious to silence controversy as the Catholic enemy. Newman's crime occurred long before his defection and consisted, as much as anything, in his alarming readiness to regard the Thirty-Nine Articles as open to discussion.

Historians are always prone to look for turning points or pivotal moments in history, and there is always a strong element of the arbitrary and *ex post facto* in this, but even so I feel there are strong grounds for regarding the year 1860 as the historical moment when Victorian culture began to come to terms with the idea of controversy. 1860 was the year in which *The Cornhill* magazine first appeared under the editorship of Thackeray. From the outset it was a tremendous success. It rapidly achieved a circulation of a 100,000 copies – which was positively astronomical by comparison with the quarterlies of the old school. 1860 was also the year in which the historian J. A. Froude took over the editorship of *Fraser's* magazine. *The Cornhill* (edited by Leslie Stephen from 1871), *Fraser's* and the *Fortnightly Review* (edited by John Morley from 1967) together created a new kind of middle-class reading public and also a new kind of periodical, which was more catholic, more diverse and more readable than its predecessors. This is not to say that they were necessarily very tolerant – in sexual matters they were prurient in the extreme. But the editors were certainly not spokesmen for orthodoxy and the religious establishment. Both Stephen and Morley thought of themselves as agnostics, while Froude had publicly given up his faith many years before. So a more flexible and more tolerant style of editing began to develop. There was a greater willingness to give space to dissident or faintly unorthodox views. However, what makes this year a particularly significant date is that it was in 1860 that T. H. Huxley had his famous confrontation with Bishop Wilberforce over Darwin's *Origin of Species* and it was in 1860 that *The Cornhill* published Ruskin's attack on classical economics that was to be *Unto This Last*. Nevertheless there was still a strong sense of decorum at this time, which both Huxley and Ruskin were deemed to have violated. Huxley may well have got the better of the Bishop – but should not he have shown more respect for his high office? Ruskin was certainly felt to have gone too far. His articles drew a storm of protest both from critics and the general public. In Victorian society classical economics was second only to holy writ – indeed, post-Darwin it may even have seemed more certain than holy writ – so Ruskin's attack on it was certainly shocking. The very idea of attacking it was unthinkable. Nevertheless Ruskin had attacked it and little by little the Victorian middle class became accustomed to the idea that there could be a diversity of opinion on quite a number of issues. Trade unionism is an interesting case in point. The habitual response to trade unions and to strikes was to deplore them. Strikes set man against man and employer against workman. They prevented the honest and independent workman from freely seeking employment at a rate that he found suitable. They caused hardship and dislocation of production. They necessarily involved illegitimate coercion, intimidation and violence. Yet wage fund theory proclaimed that the amount of money that could be paid out to workers was strictly limited, so the idea that workers could hope to obtain more money through striking was actually a fantasy. The 'experts' shook their heads, in mingled disbelief, disgust and despair. Yet the workers went on striking. What could be more irrational. Little by little the middle-class readership began to see that the workers might have a case. When G. H. Lewes inaugurated the *Fortnightly Review* one of the first things that he did was to publish two articles by Frederick Harrison, which questioned the conventional orthodoxy. In 'The Limits of Political Economy' Harrison argued that the principles of political economy were based on the assumption that society was not susceptible to improvement, and he denied that the relationship between wages and profits was governed by immutable laws. In 'Trades-Unionism' he argued strongly in their defence, writing: 'in the midst of the increasing power and recklessness of capital, one can see no immediate safeguard but this against the ruin of the workman's life, his annihilation as a member of society – against the deterioration of the community, and ultimate social revolution'.[32]

To write this and to publish this at a time when trade unions were still the subject of hysterical abuse and widespread middle-class alarm took a good deal of courage. What was at stake here was not simply recognition of strikes as a legitimate form of activity, but the recognition of magazines as places where a diversity of opinions could be given expression. Almost imperceptibly the reading public had come to accept such an openness to controversy not as a cause for alarm – as had been the case with Ruskin's articles of 1860 – but as a natural state of affairs. Clearly much was still taboo and off-limits, but the principle itself was more widely accepted. In his *Physics and Politics* (1872) – itself based on articles that had earlier appeared in the *Fortnightly Review* – Walter Bagehot, in 'The Use of Conflict' stressed the importance of conflict for progress. In 'An Age of Discussion' he stressed the value of discussion for promoting both progress and tolerance: 'I believe that the reason of the English originality to be that government by discussion quickens and enlivens thought all through society.'[33] A society that had feared and distrusted debate and controversy was beginning to claim this as one of its most prized and treasured virtues!

W. H. Mallock's *The New Republic* (1877) typifies this new interest in the diversity of opinion. It consists of a dialogue conducted over a country-house weekend between characters who represent a number of influential figures of the day. They are, in the idiom of *The New Republic* itself, either deniers or doubters. The deniers are the self-proclaimed atheist William Kingdon Clifford, supported by the leading scientists Huxley and Tyndall. The doubters who espouse various forms of aestheticised belief are Pater, Jowett, Arnold and Ruskin. Although Mallock may occasionally attribute to his fictionalised figures opinions that their real-life prototypes would not share, he is in general careful to discriminate shades of opinion and varieties of emphasis that exist among the participants and to bring out something of their personal character and style. Mallock undoubtedly relishes this extended style trial and he has his host, Otho

Laurence say: 'We certainly are a curious medley here, all of us. I suppose no age but ours could have produced one like it – at least, let us hope so, for the credit of the ages in general.'

So here again we have the assumption that Victorian society has come both to accept such intellectual diversity and to regard it is characteristic of the age. Yet in another way Mallock is made uneasy since he feels that his protagonists have come to terms with the death of God all too easily, and he concludes their suave discussions with an astonishing outburst from Mr Herbert (Ruskin):

'You have taken my God away from me, and I know not where you have laid Him. My only consolation in my misery is that at least I am inconsolable for his loss. Yes,' cried Mr Herbert, his voice rising into a kind of threatening wail, 'though you have made me miserable, I am not yet content with my misery. And though I have said in my heart that there is no God, and that there is no more profit in wisdom than in folly, yet there is one folly that I will give tongue to. I will not say Peace, peace, when there is no peace.'

Mallock implies that the conflict of opinion that he depicts is the product of unsettled and disordered times. As Dr Jenkinson (Jowett) remarks: 'In every state of transition there must always be much uneasiness.' But, like most Victorians, Mallock did not like to be left in a state of uneasiness, which is why he feels obliged to terminate his many-sided discussions with a stern moral rebuke.

In the course of *The New Republic* Otho Laurence regretfully observes to Miss Merton, a staunch Catholic:

You, happy in some sustaining faith, can see a meaning in all life, and all life's affections. You can endure – you can even welcome its sorrows. The clouds of ennui themselves for you have silver linings. For your religion is a kind of philosopher' stone, turning whatsoever it touches into something precious. But we – we can only remember that for us, too, things had a meaning once; but they have it no longer. Life stares at us now, all blank and expressionless, like the eyes of a lost friend, who is not dead, but who has turned an idiot. Perhaps you have never read Clough's Poems, did you? Scarcely a day passes in which I do not echo to myself his words:-

Ah well-a-day, for we are souls bereaved!
Of all the creatures under heaven's wide cope,
We are most hopeless who had once most hope,
And most beliefless who had once believed.

It is Clough's sardonic and unquiet spirit who, above all hovers over the deliberations of the long weekend, and it is his sense of inconsolability that the suave lucubrations of the distinguished company somehow fail to address. Clough, the largely unread, somehow continues to make his presence felt as a man, like Nietzsche, who will persist in uttering thoughts that seem out of season even when their time has come. Moreover Clough's example brings out very clearly just how much is left out and distorted in that familiar Victorian melodrama of Faith slain by Darwinism. The oddity of Clough is that in one way he seems at the centre of the Victorian world – educated at Rugby and Oxford, Fellow of Oriel, a friend of such luminaries as Arnold and Thackeray, Emerson and Charles Eliot Norton – and yet is at the same time a very peripheral figure. In some sense Clough was always a dissident and rebel against the values that Thomas Arnold had propagated both at Rugby and beyond. Clough rejected moral earnestness, the sense of duty, the desire for a life of purpose and constructive activity not so much because he was an iconoclast but because he found the prospect too tempting. As *The Bothie of Tober-Na-Vuolich* makes evident, there was much in Christian manliness that Clough found appealing, but he was a passionate sceptic who would always refuse to take any intellectual baggage on board until he had subjected its contents to a very thorough examination. Already, before Nietzsche, Clough had an inkling that it might be better to be void of purpose than to have a void for a purpose. Clough was not a popular poet in his own day – indeed he was not generally well known – he is certainly quite untypical, yet he does have a certain strange representativeness as the man who deliberately said out loud the sort of thing that many others also thought, but consciously pushed to the backs of their minds. A marginal and unregarded figure, Clough seems like a tic-tac man on the edge of a racecourse crowd who gradually becomes a centre of attention through the strangeness and concentrated vehemence of his gestures. As a poet Clough has a fine ear for rhythm and vernacular speech, writing with great intelligence and sensitivity; if he cannot quite muster the most complex resources of poetic language, he almost makes up for it through the clarity and directness of what he has to say. 'How beautiful a thing is candour' says Emerson in 'Self-Reliance', and since Clough is quintessentially the poet who defines himself through his candour and his strong sense of his own personal integrity, it was perhaps fitting that his greatest poem *Amours de Voyage* should first appear in an American setting, in the pages of the newly founded *Atlantic Monthly* in 1858. It is characteristic of Clough's hero Claude in this poem that all he can really do is consistently fail to rise to the occasion. In Rome to admire the antiquities, he can only admit to his feelings of disappointment. Confronted with the spectacle of the Italian people fighting for their independence under Garibaldi, he can only express his own distinct unwillingness to become involved:

> *Dulce* it is, and *decorum*, no doubt, for the country to fall – to
> Offer one's blood an oblation to Freedom, and to die for the
> 　　Cause; yet
> Still, individual culture is always something, and no man
> Finds quite distinct the assurance that he of all others is
> 　　called on,
> Or would be justified, even, in taking away from the world
> 　　that
> Precious creature himself. Nature sent him here to abide here,
> Else why send him at all?

Here we see Clough's characteristic delight in marshalling compelling, casuistical arguments that simultaneously invite the reader to conclude that he does not mean to be taken seriously and at the same time alarm him with the prospect that he does. For Clough *life* was very important, which meant that you did have to scrutinise every commitment very seriously. In *Amours de Voyage* Clough sees religion as one of the grand delusions of Western culture, but this very grandeur is not therefore a reason for succumbing to it. Claude will not succumb to love either, even though he does fall in love with Mary Trevellyn and pursues her inconsequentially and inconclusively around Italy. What Claude resists is not so much Mary herself but the ideological investment that everyone is expected to make in the very idea of love, the illusion of permanence and transparency, the commitment to idealisation. Instead Claude decides to give Mary up and submit himself to the arbitrary and contingent:

> Let me, then, bear to forget her. I will not cling to her falsely
> Nothing factitious or forced shall impair the old happy relation.

I will let myself go, forget, not try to remember;
I will walk on my way, accept the chances that meet me,
Freely encounter the world, imbibe these alien airs, and
Never ask if new feelings and thoughts are of her or of
    others.
Is she not changing herself? – the old image would only
    delude me.

Of course, from the conventional standpoint of Victorian morality, Claude's behaviour is consistently selfish, frivolous, unmanly. At best the hero is a latter-day Hamlet, at worst a downright coward and a rotter. Characteristically, an old friend of Clough's, W. Y. Sellar, wrote of *Amours de Voyage*:

> A very modern Hamlet is seen playing a weak and common-place part in the very commonplace drama of modern English society. Mr Clough may have passed through some transient phases of feeling and inward experience, which gave him insight into such a character; but the evidence of his other writings, and the respect of his friends, prove that his own manly nature was in no way identified with the subtle but unfortunate creation of his mind.[34]

Even his close friends could not see that what they perceived as weakness – his refusal to accept their own unexamined complacencies – was not weakness but on the contrary showed great independence of character and great strength of mind. What made Clough unusual in Victorian times was his determination to refuse 'consolations' if he could not honestly believe in them. But within the proud towers and behind the well-fortified battlements of High Victorian Culture even such a man a Clough could seem like the traitor within the gates.

2

England

In nineteenth-century history 'England' is a name to conjure with, apparently transparent yet often perplexing, at once the site of struggle and contention but always – and no matter in what hands – endowed with a certain irresistible glamour. It might seem that those who invoke 'England' in this way are always acting manipulatively and in bad faith, that whether they would mobilise chauvinism and self-interest or nostalgia and anxiety, they will always be wading in shallow waters. Nevertheless I would want to argue that these shallow waters are also deep; that the issues raised by a debate over the nature of English culture or the state of English society were both complex and important. Of course the naming of England in this way is always a cloak for powerful ideological purposes since 'England' is at once an all-inclusive term that generously and openly refers to everyone and an elaborately coded discourse: it means to be English, as against Irish, Scottish or Welsh, to be Saxon rather than Celt; it designates the interests of the aristocracy and the middle class, which have to be defended against the workers; it means having property and 'a stake in society'; it is to be Anglican rather than a Catholic or a Dissenter; to be male rather that female; to be law-abiding and opposed to violence; it is to be respectable and contented rather than disreputable and discontented. Englishness, in this sense, is both something you have and aspire to. But in recognising this, we should not therefore skimp the debates in which conceptions of 'England' were articulated, nor should we overlook the curious fact that those most active in the construction of this model were very largely Scottish. It was Hume and Mackintosh who laid the foundations for a modern history of *England*. It was Adam Smith who elaborated an economic theory that could serve as a framework for England's destiny as a trading nation. It was James Mill who in his classic *History of British India* (1818) mapped out Britain's future as an imperial power and legislator for mankind. It was Sir Walter Scott who in *Ivanhoe* produced the definitive myth of a proud Saxon race indomitably struggling against the Norman yoke. It was Thomas

Carlyle who extended and developed this into a philosophy of the English character and a critique of industrialisation, and while Macaulay, who was perhaps the one single writer to produce a view of England that was more influential than Carlyle's, was not himself Scottish, he was deeply influenced by the ideals of the Scottish Enlightenment, the foremost protégé of Francis Jeffrey at the *Edinburgh Review* from 1839 to 1847, and from 1852 to 1856 MP for Edinburgh itself. In this context Cobbett, as the one unquestionable and incontrovertible Englishman, looks strangely isolated – an irony that one suspects he would have relished. But to invoke Cobbett is also to bring out more clearly how this Scottish perception differs. For although Cobbett's sense of the English past was often rose-coloured and profoundly mythic, he nevertheless believed when he spoke of England that he was referring to real and actual states of affairs, whether in times past or present, whereas for the Scottish thinkers 'England' is always a construction, a model and an ideal type – an example to be held up to the rest of the world, and perhaps even to the English as well.

To the intellectuals of the Scottish Enlightenment, England represented the possibility of progress out of the conflicts and confusions of a feudal past into a freer, more prosperous and more harmonious world, where economic change takes place against a background of order and stability, where social life is governed by law and where debate is always calm and rational. In *That Noble Science of Politics*, Stefan Collini, Donald Winch and John Burrow have perceptively demonstrated that the conceptual field covered by the idea of 'politics' was very different from any present understanding of the term precisely because of its territorial ambitions; as 'political economy' it included economics almost as a matter of course but went beyond this to address the whole field of policy-making in society. Indeed this very idea of policy-making may be its most significant legacy. What particularly needs to be stressed is that the whole coupling of politics and political economy predicates England as the exemplary model, since it is the English mixed style of government with its space for representation of the commercial classes that creates a framework in which economic progress is possible. England is not simply the middle way between autocracy and tyranny on the one hand, anarchy and license on the other, it is also the only type of society in which economic progress is possible since autocratic governments stultify commerce through bureaucracy, imposts and taxes, while a society that embodies the popular will be too erratic and unstable to provide the framework businessmen need to make rational decisions. What is also significant here is that while a more democratic society is broadly postulated as desirable, it is seen in largely instrumental terms, that is as a context for economic growth. The reason why a science of politics began to look old-hat was not simply that it was being supplanted by sociology but rather that the dazzling clarity of England as an exemplary model became progressively occluded. This was partly because industrialisation could be seen to have occurred in other social circumstances (i.e. Germany) but also because the price of industrialisation in terms of suffering and social and political unrest made it increasingly difficult for people to imagine that England had taken a trouble-free middle way between unpalatable extremes, as had seemed plausible in the immediate aftermath of the Napoleonic Wars. Yet the power of the model persisted nevertheless, most notably in Russia, where the attempt to synchronise a limited constitutional government with economic growth turned out in a way that the Scottish pundits could scarcely have envisaged.

Political economy is more important for the construction of a discourse that focuses specifically on *England* rather than on Great Britain because the kind of theorising that it is concerned with is specifically addressed to the situation of England, which is successful manufacturing, commercial nation in a way that Scotland and Ireland are not. Such Scottish economists are Adam Smith, McCulloch, Buchanan and James Mill approached the problem via the four-stage theory of human development, whereby human society passed successively through hunting, pastoral, agricultural and commercial stages: thus, England was ahead of the rest, while Scotland and Ireland, along with Germany and Russia, lagged behind. Since, after the Napoleonic Wars, England had emerged as the indisputable great power of Europe, the task of political economy was to explain both how this pre-eminence had been achieved, and to lay down the conditions – primarily through free trade – whereby that superiority might be maintained. So the new science of political economy, for all its universal pretensions, both addressed itself to Englishmen and always had England in its theoretical sights. Thus, David Ricardo in *The Principles of Political Economy and Taxation* (1817), which rapidly established itself as the economist's bible to which all problems could be referred, while never abandoning the ground of high theory, could scarcely avoid noting the general superiority of English life. He observed that 'Many of the conveniences now enjoyed in an

English cottage would have been thought luxuries at an earlier period in our history',[1] and he drew attention to the relative superiority
of English agriculture compared with a backward nation such as
Poland; England was able to produce vastly more corn, both because
of the greater fertility of the land and the superior skills and imple-
ments of the English labourers.

But of course Ricardo's real interest was in England as a commercial nation and England's problems, though not referred to as such,
were very much on his mind. So on the subject of the terms of trade
he points out that 'A great manufacturing country is peculiarly
exposed to temporary reverses and contingencies, produced by the
removal of capital from one employment to another',[2] and with the
falling rate of profit in mind he observes:

> Man from youth grows to manhood, then decays, and dies; but
> this is not the progress of nations. When arrived to a state of the
> greatest vigour, their further tendency may indeed be arrested,
> but their natural tendency is to continue for ages to sustain undi-
> minished their wealth and population.[3]

This discussion makes it quite explicit that Ricardo believed England to be at the apogee of her fame, reputation and influence, which
had been produced by the growth of manufacturing industry; the
problem now is to ensure that that power is maintained by appropriate measures, the most important of which, from the Ricardian point
of view, was a repeal of the Corn Laws, which was belatedly achieved,
from the point of view of classical economics, only in 1845. Ricardo's
definition of England as the manufacturing nation *par excellence* means
that agriculture and the landed interest are seen increasingly as
marginal in British society, even though Ricardo denied this implication and had joined the landed interest himself, after a successful
career on the Stock Exchange! Yet Ricardo was no tub-thumping
patriot; it was rather that the whole science of political economy took
its starting point from English developments and tried to develop
general laws from that experience. Thus there is something quite
inexorable about the turn taken by Edward Baines in his pamphlet
On the Moral Influence of Free Trade (1838) where he writes:

> Let me take a single country, by way of giving reality and force to
> the illustration, and show how an extensive commerce binds it in
> the times of profitable connexion to all the principal countries of

the earth, – how the wants and comforts of its inhabitants are supplied by that commerce, – and how the country is thereby interested in the peace and prosperity of the whole world. No other country will answer this purpose as well as England.[4]

And how could it be otherwise? After all England is the vanguard nation; England is the bearer of peace and tranquillity; it is English commerce that makes the world go round; and, if any nation, it is England who will usher in the Golden Age of universal prosperity. The explanation and prophecy of how all this will come to pass is provided by the science of political economy.

Yet for many the vision was far from irresistible. The claims of political economists and Whigs – for the conjunction was significant in the period – to be sturdy patriots was one that could not fail to be challenged since the Tories, with the Duke of Wellington in their midst, felt that they epitomised the traditional greatness of the English nation, a nation that they identified with pre-eminence of the landed interest. From this point of view the attempts of the Whigs to secure power by influencing a wider constituency than those who actually had the vote was necessarily destabilising, while the prevalence of machine-breaking and Luddite riots suggested that England's traditional peace and stability was being shattered by a mercenary spirit of commercial innovation. It is therefore significant that McCulloch felt obliged to address the argument that commercial pursuits were always potentially unpatriotic in his *The Principles of Political Economy* (5th edn 1864). There he argued that despite the anti-commercial thrust of much ancient philosophy, there was evidence of a patriotic spirit in such trading nations as Athens, Corinth, Carthage and Tyre, while such modern nations as the English and the Dutch have combined prosperity with 'extraordinary sacrifices and exertions' in the cause of freedom and national independence.[5] Moreover, McCulloch argued, while in many countries the patriotic spirit is ignorant and ill-informed, English patriotism is grounded in a dispassionate assessment of the truth:

A Turk, or a Spaniard, may be as patriotic as an Englishman; but the patriotism of the former is a blind undiscriminating passion, which prompts him to admire and support the very abuses that depress and degrade himself and his country; whereas the patriotism of the latter is comparatively sober and rational. He prefers his country, not merely because of its being the place of his birth, and of the many ennobling recollections connected with its history, but because, in addition to these circumstances, he finds, upon contrasting it with others, that though not faultless, its institutions are comparatively excellent.[6]

If for Hegel the rational was the real and possibly identifiable with the Prussian state, for the classical economists the rational was commercial and *English*.

That there was such an inescapable connection between English and the English science of political economy was argued by Nassau Senior, co-architect with Edwin Chadwick of the Poor Law Amendment Act of 1834 and for long one of the principal economic pundits of the *Edinburgh Review*, in his 'Introductory Lecture on Political Economy' (1826):

> To us, as Englishmen, it is of still deeper interest to inquire whether the causes of our superiority are still in operation, and whether their force is capable of being increased or diminished; whether England has run her full career of wealth and improvement, but stands safe where she is; or, whether to remain stationary is impossible, and it depends on her institutions and her habits, on her government, and on her people, whether she shall recede or continue to advance.
>
> The answer to all these questions must be sought in the science which teaches in what wealth consists, – by what agents it is produced, – and according to what laws it is distributed, – and what are the institutions and customs by which production may be facilitated and distribution regulated, so as to give the largest possible amount of wealth to each individual. And this science is Political Economy.[7]

Thus, political economy addresses itself to all the most urgent questions that any patriotic Englishman can formulate about the future of his country and promises to answer them with a certainty infinitely greater than the Delphic oracle. For Senior one of the greatest threats to England's prosperity was the giving of relief through the Poor Laws, and though the Amendment Act stipulated that relief could only be given within the strict disciplinary context of the workhouse, even this did not satisfy Senior who felt that any infringement of the subject's liberty, defined in terms of a moral obligation to feed himself and his family, was positively dangerous. For Senior all such provisions savoured of idleness and laxity, whether on the part of the labourers themselves or on the part of the indolent rich who would rather pay higher rates than address themselves to the stern obligations of moral rectitude. Senior had an exalted conception of the worth of an Englishman's work. He claimed that the well-directed labour of an Englishman was worth twice as much as that of any European and between twelve and fifteen times as much as that of any Asian. Yet far from being complacent about this he was concerned that England's competitive advantage might be lost and that the workforce should be kept on their toes. The whole point of a rigorous Poor Law (or better still nothing at all) was not so much to punish the unemployed – though, after Malthus, Senior was probably as responsible as anyone for the image of political economy as a 'dismal science' – as to ensure that those who were actually in work were kept up to the mark. Senior recognised more clearly than most that industrial work required new levels of discipline that could not be maintained if the option of outdoor relief was available. Yet Senior purported to trace this spirit of 'freedom' back to our Saxon forefathers and claimed that, unlike other nations, the English pauper was characteristically healthy and able-bodied. The convenient result of this manly spirit of independence, when not undermined by strong drink, was that the factory owner would always have an abundant and compliant workforce at his disposal.

The world that Senior viewed with so much satisfaction was described by Alexis de Tocqueville on a visit to Manchester in 1835:

The footsteps of a *busy* crowd, the crunching wheels of machinery, the shriek of steam from boilers, the regular beat of the looms, the heavy rumble of carts, those are the noises from which you cannot escape in the sombre half-light of these streets. You will never hear the clatter of hoofs as the rich man drives back home or out on expeditions of pleasure. Never the gay shouts of the people amusing themselves, or music heralding a holiday. You will never see smart folk strolling at leisure in the streets, or going out on innocent pleasure parties in the surrounding country. Crowds are ever hurrying this way and that in the Manchester streets, but their footsteps are brisk, their looks preoccupied, and their appearance sombre and harsh.[8]

If they are busy, so much the better, for vice is the flower of idleness and their stressful existence and desperate attempts to make ends meet are nothing less than the Englishman's priceless birthright of freedom.

The political economists of the age, such as McCulloch and Senior, were never happier than when giving the impression that theirs was an exact and rigorous science, founded securely on principles laid down by Adam Smith, Malthus and Ricardo, yet in practice they found it possible to diverge quite markedly from what the theory ostensibly prescribed. Thus, while Malthus was a useful scarecrow with which to dismay the multitude, neither Senior nor McCulloch really accepted Malthus's claim that population must always tend to outstrip the food supply since it increased in a geometric as opposed to an arithmetic ratio. For Senior man's desire to better himself when combined with technological improvements in the field of agriculture meant that the Malthusian nightmare would not in practice occur. McCulloch was persuaded of the force of the argument that, when population trends and agricultural production were examined on a historical basis, they demonstrated that the reverse had been the case: the food supply had historically increased faster than the population. Both men modified their views on the Poor Law. Senior, in principle opposed to the granting of any relief whatsoever, was nevertheless a principle architect of the new Poor Law, while McCulloch actually came to favour the Poor Law in its earlier, more generous form and even advocated its extension to Ireland. An article by McCulloch in the *Edinburgh Review* was a prime factor in the abolition in 1826 of the Combinations Laws, which had made trade union activity illegal. With the typical pedantry of the classical economist, McCulloch argued the combinations among working men could do nothing to raise real wages above existing levels because of market forces but the existence of combination laws was an irritant that actually caused trouble. McCulloch even hung onto this view into the 1860s when trade unions were becoming much more powerful and their power to influence the situation could not so easily be shrugged aside. But at bottom what Senior and McCulloch offered was an ingenious mixture of grand theory and pragmatism. The grand theory was designed to impress – but recognising that too much insistence on the theory would only create hostility, Senior and McCulloch knew just how to temper the wind to the shorn lamb. Their primary goal was to increase the profitability of manufacturing industry by holding down wages. Crucial to this purpose was repeal of the Corn Laws and, for Senior at least, the use of the Poor Laws to hold down wages and ensure that the poor were always industrious. But the other side of the much-abused Poor Laws was that they *were* needed when manufacturing industry went into a period of recession. But this also meant that the classical economists and the businessmen with whom they were allied had to play a complicated game: promoting a certain amount of agitation among the working class in order to pressurise the landed aristocracy over the Corn Laws, yet standing shoulder to shoulder with landed society over social disturbance and unrest. This also meant that classical economics was also a *moral* science, whose task was to lecture all sections of English society as to what was demanded of them. What England expected was that every man should do his duty according to the infallible prescriptions of the classical economists.

An egregrious yet characteristic instance of the new commercial rhetoric is an article that appeared in the *Edinburgh Review* of February 1843 in the wake of popular agitation over the Charter and at a time when strikes and disorder provoked by low wages and long working hours were at their height. It was written by Thomas Spring-Rice – later Baron Mounteagle – an long-time Irish Whig from Limerick whose complacency about 'England' seems particularly misplaced in view of Ireland's own desperate situation. Ostensibly this article addressed the topic 'Distress of the Manufacturing Districts – Causes and Remedies', yet in practice it skirts away from that subject as much as possible and in so far as remedies are involved all that is offered is the familiar nostrum of setting commerce free – that is repeal of the Corn Laws. The actual boredom, stress and hardship of factory work is scarcely acknowledged at all – indeed our sanctimonious author responds to de Tocqueville's alarm at its possible effects on the mind as follows: 'We have known instances in which workmen were able to read whilst discharging a function purely mechanical. We recollect to have seen one of the Parts, periodically published, even of such a work as the "Encyclopaedia Britannica", lying open on the working place of an artizan.'[9] Yet even this preposterous line of argument demonstrates that the author is not so much interested in the question of suffering as of justifying the place of commerce and industry in English life. The distress is only of any importance because it seems to offer ammunition to those who speak for the landed interest, like Disraeli and Young England, and to those, like Carlyle, who have seen Chartism as symptomatic of the evils of an uncaring society.

The author sees it as his principal task to restore the image of commerce and to insist on its centrality to the identity of the English nation. Thus the article begins not with the smoky cities of the north of England but rather with England's finest hour, the battle of Waterloo. When the author rhetorically asks how it was that such a mighty victory came about, the answer is unhesitating:

> The triumph of England is attributable to fortitude, founded on religious and moral principle; to energy, the fruit of free institutions; to unbounded credit, the consequence of a strict maintenance of public faith; and to wealth, the effect of industry and commercial enterprize. Had any one of these elements been wanting, our struggle might have been as heroic, but it could scarcely have been as successful; and even if we have been enabled for a time to preserve our national independence, we could never have hoped to become the liberators of Europe. We owe as much to our traders as to our warriors. The general war had made us monopolists in commerce, and we became all but monopolists in glory and success. The industry of Peel and the inventive genius of Arkwright, contributed to the result as well as the heroic genius of Nelson, and the surpassing capacity, energy, prudence and fortitude of Wellington.[10]

Figuratively and syntactically it seems that the military victories of Wellington and Nelson are parasitic upon the achievements of commerce, that courage and valour upon the battlefield would all have been as nought without the massive weight of England's commercial and financial power behind them. While the landed gentry habitually regards themselves as constituting the backbone of English society, Englishmen need to acknowledge that England's present greatness is the creation of merchants and entrepreneurs. England's mighty cities, canals, railways and factories are wonders of the world and since 'commercial and manufacturing industry are inseparably connected with civilization',[11] it follows that 'it is the duty of the state to promote, by all means, their further and unlimited development'.[12]

Indeed it would be impious to do otherwise since England's commercial prosperity, resting as it does on many favourable natural circumstances, that is 'a supply almost inexhaustible of coal; abundant mines of valuable metals; raw materials for various manufactures; timbers for naval and domestic architecture; rivers adapted for transit and for use as moving power',[13] must have been directly willed by divine providence:

Are they not the very gifts which Almighty benevolence would delight in pouring forth for the good of its most favoured creatures? Can we conceive it possible that these blessings are conferred on any nation without leading to useful discoveries, to successful industry, to manufactures and commercial enterprize?[14]

With this theodicy firmly in place, dark satanic mills fade into the background and the question as to whether the commercial and manufacturing system is productive of good or evil virtually answers itself. Admittedly the beauties of a rustic world may be replaced by 'the ungraceful lines of a dark factory, with its gigantic chimneys alternately breathing flame and smoke', the air may be polluted with 'murky clouds', the waters of the river may be stained with 'the dyestuffs and refuse of a thousands mills',[15] and the life of the collier may seem less pleasant than that of the shepherd, but we should consider that the rise of commerce has led to 'The cessation of civil wars, the suppression of feudal enormities, the mitigation of our criminal code, the refinement of manners',[16] and that 'it is the annals of great cities, and their commercial inhabitants, that we trace the growth of civilization'.[17]

Moreover the industrial system itself produces no miseries – these are all produced by artificial restraints on trade – and so our genial author concludes his survey of 'distress' with a sublime amalgam of Malthusian and Adam Smithian wisdom:

> But we should not presumptiously attempt to counteract the dispensations of Providence in its varied distribution of gifts; we must not daringly fragment the system of the universe which by contrasts of soils and climates, by the infinitely diversified habits, energies, and inclinations of men, makes the ingenuity of each subordinate to the happiness of all; and renders commerce not only the source of civilisation and wealth, but likewise the best check upon the ambition of princes, and the most effectual security for the repose of the world.[18]

We should not question the divine dispensation that requires that millions should live in poverty, just as we should not question the providential design that would ensure that the whole world could be exploited for the benefit and greater prosperity of the English middle classes. From the perspective of political economy there is a fallen world ordained for the many and an economic paradise of plenty reserved for the fortunate and deserving few. This is what England's 'greatness' really means.

Nevertheless, although England undoubtedly was a powerful trading nation, there was something rather unsatisfying about defining the nation's greatness purely in terms of a commercial and industrial success that was of comparatively recent origin. The story of England's rise to pre-eminence must itself involve the unfolding of an epic narrative in which the English people themselves must play a remarkable part: national greatness must necessarily involve qualities of greatness in the national character. Yet to construct a history of England was by no means straightforward. The easiest part was to describe England's part in the history of the Reformation from Henry VIII to Cromwell and to trace the development of constitutional liberty in England from Elizabeth to William of Orange where the evidence was more abundant and the issues, even though they offered plenty of scope for controversy and partisanship, seemed to be quite clearly defined. But this was very far from being the case where England's earlier history was concerned. Hume, who had made the most comprehensive attempt to write a complete history, nevertheless devoted comparatively little space either to pre- or post-Conquest Britain, and he made it clear that he regarded many stories concerning the ancient Britons as essentially mythic. Moreover the rationalist Hume found little to admire in the blood-thirsty and superstitious aboriginals. He deplored the fact that 'No idolatrous worship ever attained such an ascendancy over mankind as that of the ancient Gauls and Romans',[19] and he could scarcely admire a nation in which 'wars were the chief occupation, and formed the chief object of ambition among the people'.[20]

Yet he was scarcely more enthusiastic about what the Victorians liked to call 'our Saxon forefathers'. For Hume the Saxons were an idolatrous and brutal people, and with a frankness that must have disconcerted latter-day antiquarians he announced: 'there have been found in history few conquests more ruinous than that of the Saxons'.[21] For Hume the fact that the Saxons were Christians, which for his successors was one of their most outstanding characteristics, gave no cause for rejoicing; on the contrary it was responsible for the most extensive moral depravity – though Hume was careful to lay responsibility for this at the door of Rome:

The Saxons, though they had been so long settled in the island, seem not as yet to have been much improved beyond their German ancestors, either in arts, civility, knowledge, humanity, justice, or obedience to the laws. Even Christianity, though it opened the way to connexions between them and the more polished states of Europe, had not hitherto been very effectual in banishing their ignorance, or softening their barbarous manners. As they received that doctrine through the corrupted channels of Rome, it carried along with it a great mixture of credulity and superstition, equally destructive to the understanding and to morals: the reverence towards saints and reliques seems to have almost supplanted the adoration of the Supreme Being: monastic observances were esteemed more meritorious than the active virtues: the knowledge of natural causes was neglected, from the universal belief of miraculous interpositions and judgments: bounty to the church atoned for every violence against society: and the remorses for cruelty, murder, treachery, assassination, and the more robust vices, were appeased, not by amendment of life, but by penances, servility to the monks, and in abject and illiberal devotions.[22]

Although Hume did pay tribute to at least one of the poetic myths of English history – namely that Alfred was a great guardian of the liberties of the people – in general he seemed quite prepared to dump the Saxons, along with the Britons, on the scrapheap of history. The problem for the Victorians was precisely the reverse: how to rescue the Saxons from an undeserved oblivion and reconnect them to the mainstream of English history. The way to go about this obviously was not to follow Hume and begin at the beginning, but rather to start with the undoubted fact of England's present greatness and then decide how much of this might reasonably be traced back to our Saxon forebears. In Saxon England and the common law might be discerned the origins of England's birthright of freedom; it was from a Saxon acorn that the stalwart oak of the English national character had grown. As Christopher Hill has persuasively argued in his seminal essay in *Puritanism and Revolution*, 'The Norman Yoke', the work that more than any other revived the theory of the Norman yoke and stimulated a rewriting of English history was the anonymous *Historical Essay on the English Constitution* published in 1771. The *Historical Essay* initiated the obligatory pious and unproblematic references to 'our Saxon forefathers' and proposed an interpretation of English history in terms of a struggle between a Norman spirit of domination and a Saxon impulse towards freedom that was given wider currency by Scotts' *Ivanhoe* and by the *History of England*, written by the influential French historian Thierry. The whole point about the Saxon 'origin' of contemporary England was it was something that scarcely needed to be argued for. Englishmen needed forefathers and, for obvious reasons, these could not be the Normans, who were, after all, French. But equally the candidature of the ancient Britons was weak. Once their claim to have been founded by Brutus was demolished they seemed to have little going for them. They were undoubtedly primitive and pagan, worse still they had ended up on the losing side with a demoralising predictability. It was simpler to imagine that the Britons had effectively disappeared from the scene – possibly fleeing to mountain fastnesses in Wales and Scotland – and to trace one's origins back to the Saxons, who even if they had originally been defeated by the Normans, were a more promising case, since it could be argued that in the complex dialectic of history they had nevertheless won through in the end – finally conquering and assimilating the alien invader like a giant boa constrictor. If the English were anything they were Saxons; and if the Saxons were anything they were the stuff of which modern England was made. In his *Old England* (1845) Charles Knight remarked:

> In our own times we are accustomed to use the term Anglo-Saxons, when we speak of the wars, the institutions, the literature, and the arts of the people, who for five centuries were the possessors of this our England, and have left the impress of their national character, their language, their laws and their religion upon the race that still treads the soil which they trod.[23]

The connection is not something to be historically demonstrated but rather something you just feel in your bones.

Yet even historians who did not consciously dedicate themselves to the rediscovery of England's Saxon past were nevertheless obliged to invoke this as part of their interpretation of more recent history. Thus, Henry Hallam's classic work *The Constitutional History of England*, which was ostensibly devoted to the development of modern constitutional democracy based on a careful study of the documentary evidence – and thus on techniques equally modern – could not avoid an extensive referral back beyond the self-imposed starting point of the accession of Henry VII. For the whole project of constitutional history was based on the assumption that Englishmen enjoyed certain traditional political rights, which the Stuart kings had sought to invade and which parliament had sought to defend. Thus Hallam found himself arguing:

> The government of England, in all times recorded by history, has been one of those mixed or limited monarchies which the Celtic and Gothic tribes appear universally to have stablished in preference to the coarse despotism of eastern nations, to the more artificial tyranny of Rome and Constantinople, or to the various models of republican polity which were tried upon the coasts of the Mediterranean Sea.[24]

From this point of view James I and Charles I, in claiming the right to rule without necessarily consulting Parliament, were in fact questioning a tradition that had existed from time immemorial. A further implication of this, which Hallam did not pursue, was that one might think of struggles over the constitution as far back as the time of Ethelred the Unready. Moreover it was integral to Hallam's perspective on history to see all historical developments as representing a process of long maturation. If England in the fifteenth century was noted for 'the goodness of her laws and the security of her citizens from oppression',[25] then this state of affairs has not come from nowhere: 'This liberty had been the slow fruit of ages, still waiting a happier season for its perfect ripeness but already giving proof of the vigour and industry which had been employed in its culture.'[26]

We may therefore take it that Hallam in 1827 – the agitation for a Reform Bill notwithstanding – believes that the period of perfect ripeness has now come and that – reading between the lines – what has made that liberty the 'slow fruit of ages' has been the long struggle on the part of Saxon Englishmen to preserve their customary rights in the face of Norman oppression. So a Saxon origin is still required. But what Hallam clearly lacks, as his uncritical lumping together of Celtic and Gothic clearly indicates, is any sense of the English as a distinctively Germanic race with an innate affinity with democratic government that was born, as Tacitus had suggested, in the German forests; that, as Kingsley was to put it: 'We at least brought the British constitution with us out of the bogs and moors of Jutland, along with our smock-frocks and leather gaiters, brown bills and stone axes; and it has done us good service, and will do till we have carried it right round the world.'[27]

If you put it this way, then Hallam's whole way of arguing about the development of the constitution begins to seem slightly pedantic: since freedom is a birthright that Englishmen (Saxons) possess from the very first, it would seem that for the freedoms to have been there later then they must have already been there at the very beginning. Here too we see a characteristic coupling of English democracy with England's imperialist mission that is also found in Thomas Arnold's *Introductory Lectures on Modern History* delivered in 1841, one of the earliest and most influential historical works to insist on England's peculiar racial destiny:

> our history clearly begins with the coming over of the Saxons; the Britons and Romans had lived in our country, but they are not our fathers; we are connected with them as men, indeed, but, nationally speaking, the history of Caesar's invasion has no more to do with us, than the natural history of the animals which then inhabited our forests. We, this great English nation, whose race and language are now overrunning the earth from one end of it to the other, – we were born when the white horse of the Saxons had established his dominion from the Tweed to the Tamar. So far we can trace our blood, our language, the name and actual divisions of our country, the beginnings of some of our institutions. So far our national identity extends, so far history is modern, for it treats of a life which was then and is not yet extinguished.[28]

In this myth of origins the Saxons are alive just so far as they are alive in England's imperial mission, and therefore Arnold significantly is not content to refer back only to place names and institutions: he must also invoke an imperial domination from Tweed to Tamar that is the precursor of greater things to come. In the Victorian period a more upbeat kind of historical writing is required that is neither sceptically dismissive like Hume, or neutral and more or less dispassionate like Lingard, but rather one that will unfold a tale of great expectations, of a destiny always implicit yet in the present finally fulfilled. Thus William Cooke Stafford in expanding Hume's *History of England* for a later age is not content merely to bring the work up to date, or in his introduction to supply vital information about the Britons whom Hume had slighted by disposing of them in five paragraphs. He is determined to out-Macaulay Macaulay in a triumphant vision of progress unalloyed:

> Lord Macaulay remarks that 'the history of our country, for the last 160 years, is eminently the history of physical, of moral and

intellectual improvement.' We may go much further back, and say, that it has been so, more or less, for the last 1800 years. The Britons whom the Romans found here, had no doubt 'improved' the country they inhabited to a certain extent, and were themselves somewhat in advance of the time, when 'wild in the woods the noble savage ran.' The Romans still further civilised that certainly rude race; and, from their time, the successive inhabitants of the island – Saxons, Danes, and Normans – have, with some exceptions, but as a rule, been advancing on the high road of civilisation, till the present foremost position has been attained. One of the pleasantest tasks of the historian is to trace this progress, and to show how, as generation succeeded generation, so have the blessings of true religion, and the benefits resulting from literature, science, and art, been more generally diffused.[29]

Yet despite a more positive assessment of the ancient Britons as one step beyond the noble savage, in the end the island story always goes back to the Saxons who above all *remained* and who 'had much of the energy, the perseverance, and the natural ability, which have since distinguished their race; and their love of freedom stimulated to improvement'.[30] To an earlier generation of historians Buckle's reference in his *History of Civilization* to circumstances that 'as early as the eleventh century, begun to affect our national character, and had assisted in imparting to it that sturdy boldness, and, at the same time, those habits of foresight, and of cautious reserve, to which the English mind owes it leading peculiarities'[31] might have seemed wilfully speculative in its determination to look for recondite historical origins. Now to many it was self-evident that our island story had to begin a good six hundred years earlier.

Yet the construction of a historical narrative that could trace the English character and its progressive spirit over such a protracted historical period was by no means an easy task. It did not simply involve covering a lot of ground or even making the necessary and appropriate connections, but also called for extensive historical research and analysis of periods that had been very little studied. The difficulty can be brought out with particular clarity in the case of Sharon Turner, whose three-volume *History of the Anglo-Saxons* (1799–1803) laid the foundations for the serious study of Saxon history. Subsequently Turner wrote a more conventional history of England covering the period from Henry VIII to Elizabeth (1823–9) but the hiatus between the two was as marked as the interval that elapsed between the writing of them. Turner clearly felt that there was a continuous history to be written but was himself unable to close the gap between ancient and modern. Nevertheless Turner did have a very clear idea of the distinctive genius of the Saxon people, which was at once political, mental and moral. The Saxons should not be seen as yet one more wave of barbarian invaders; they were part of a providential design through which Roman decadence would be supplanted by Germanic vigour, exemplified in 'more just governments, more improving institutions, and more virtuous, though fierce manners'.[32]

\According to Turner, following Tacitus and the German historians, the Germanic tribes were distinguished by democratic values, respect for women and intellectual energy, and it was these qualities that prepared the way for England's future greatness: 'they laid the foundations of that internal polity, of those peculiar customs, of that female modesty, and of that vigour and direction of mind, to which Great Britain owes the social progress which it has so eminently acquired'.[33] For Turner the most significant of all the Saxon innovations – if innovations they were – was their commitment to the principle of limited monarchy whereby the king was obliged to secure the assent of the people to his laws through the calling of a witenagemot:

> Our Saxon ancestors appear to us at first in that state in which a great nation is preparing to be formed on new principles, unattained by human experience before. The process was that of leading their population to such a practical system as would combine the liberty of the people with the independence and elevated qualities of a high-spirited nobility, and with the effective authority of a presiding king, and of such wise and improving laws as the collected wisdom of the nation should establish from the deliberations of its witena-gemot, not legislating only for the powerful.[34]

The problem with Turner's approach to the Saxons, however, was that he could do little more than assert their role as ancestors without giving any satisfactory explanation as to why such an importance should be attributed to them. Doubtless Turner subscribed to the general theory of the Norman yoke and doubtless he saw in the Magna Charta the rearticulation of rights that had been temporarily repressed after the Norman invasion, but despite his assertions, in his account the question of Saxon ancestry still seems problematic and Saxon culture historically remote.

Consequently, the overall interpretation of the Saxons offered by Sir Francis Palgrave in his brief *History of the Anglo-Saxons* (1831) and in his more substantial *The Rise and Progress of the English Commonwealth* (1832) was more suggestive, just because he was more determined to offer an continuous narrative of English history and more concerned to explain, by a consideration of the medieval period – the crucial *tertium quid* in the whole affair – just how it was that the Saxon precedents had proved significant. Palgrave's solution was to minimise the impact of the Norman conquest and to suggest that in legislative matters persistence rather than change is the most common state of affairs:

> We attribute over-much to the Norman Conquest. The subjugation of the English race affords an easy and plausible mode of accounting for the vast difference between the state and the government of England under the Plantagenets, and the institutions of an earlier age. But the simplest theory is not always the truest: and notwithstanding the ascendency of the Normans, the usages and customs of Anglo-Saxon England were retained with much greater pertinacity than in those countries where no foreign ruler attained the throne.[35]

The very fact of alien rule may well have made Englishmen that much more tenacious of their rights. For Palgrave Edward the Confessor was a model ruler, and he believed that the democratic and responsive mode of government established by Edward became a pattern that was never lost sight of even long after the Norman invasion. While William Rufus admittedly had ruled in an alien, arbitrary and tyrannical way, the Charter of Henry I ' "restored the law of Edward", or, in other words, re-established, or intended to re-establish, the Anglo-Saxon jurisprudence as it existed before the invasion'.[36]

Over the whole lengthy and confusing span of English history from the fifth century to the nineteenth, Palgrave purported to discern a persistent but gradual tendency towards political improvement, and in this way, despite apparent discontinuities and reverses, it could be argued that it was precisely this genius for moderation and liberty that characterised the English people:

> Though the modern policy of England may, at first sight, appear to differ most widely from the ancient laws, still the alterations

have been chiefly effected by custom and transmission. Legislation has advanced in a continued path, treading in short and measured steps, and usage has effected more than legislation. By far the greatest portions of the written or statute laws of England, consist of the declaration, the re-assertion, the repetition, or the re-enactment of some older laws, either customary or written, with additions or modifications. The new building has been raised on old groundwork: the institutions of one age have always been modelled and formed from those of the preceding, and their lineal descent has never been interrupted or disturbed.

By these means, the country, notwithstanding its various revolutions has been exempted from any violent shocks or changes, and from their consequent afflictions. . . . Chequered with many dark and dreary scenes of sin and sorrow, the political history of England is, on the whole, less depressing than that of any other state of dominion which has hitherto existed. In no other community can we discern, at the end of each successive cycle, so incontrovertible an advance in the science of political government.[37]

Palgrave's argument is ingenious in the way each proposition reinforces another. Conquest and invasion cannot affect the deeper reality of the persistence of institutions, and these institutions have in turn persisted because they are moderate, democratic and grounded in customary rights; their very persistence is our guarantee that they can be traced back as far as the Saxons. Moreover since each advance is only made possible because it builds upon an earlier foundation, then there could have been no progress towards free institutions in England if the groundwork had not already been laid. So freedom is always already there.

A third contributor to this upsurge in Saxon historiography was the German historian J. M. Lappenberg whose *England under the Saxon Kings* was published in Hamburg in 1834 and translated into English in 1845. As an outsider Lappenberg brought a more complex set of motives to the task of reviving Saxon history. While clearly there could be no question of English patriotism in his assessment of the evidence, patriotism itself was definitely involved. Lappenberg came from a cultural tradition more disposed to a critical weighing of evidence and assessment of sources but he did have several bees in his bonnet that indisputably found their way out of his bonnet and into the narrative. Like many Germans of his day, Lappenberg was deeply resentful of French cultural influence and of the prestige of French culture. He admired the English and was anxious to interpret their success in the light of common German origins. Like Ranke he distrusted the power of the papacy and was anxious to demonstrate that there had been a long-standing northern resistance to papal perversions and corruptions of Christian doctrine. Thus, as far as Lappenberg was concerned, the Saxons were nothing less than Germans on foreign shores and their defeat at the hands of the Normans in 1066 could not be regarded, as with Palgrave, as a mere blip on the oscilloscope – it was an unmitigated disaster. But the writing was on the wall even earlier since Edward the Confessor – no hero here we note – by his undue receptiveness to alien ways and customs was already paving the way for subsequent defeat:

The piety of Eadward the Confessor was hardly less dangerous to his country than Caesar's military and Gregory's spiritual conquest had been, and which in some degree it may be said to have continued. As temporal interests had gained a preponderance at Rome, the least evil which the Anglo-Saxons had to fear was, that England might become a spiritual prey to the Roman system, as well a secular conquest for the rapacious papal court. The greater evil, subjection to the dukes of Normandy, must be accompanied by the other. The civil war with Godwine, therefore, though unattended with much bloodshed, may be considered as highly important on account of views developed in it. Ad Eadward gave the first example of a morbid predilection for Frankish manners and language, so pernicious to modern Europe, in like manner we behold in the resistance of the Anglo-Saxons and their adherence to Godwine a nationality powerfully bursting forth (for the first time in such a manner during the middle age), not yet, indeed, against foreign armies, but against an opposite mental direction. Would that they could always have preserved the British Channel as their boundary; much domestic calamity might have then been spared, the most important national literature of the time not suppressed, and an uninterrupted affinity would have connected the soul, the language and the knowledge of the ancient world with the present, to our incalculable profit and gratification.[38]

So Lappenberg pushes the theory of the Norman yoke back into the reign of Edward the Confessor and links this with papal tyranny and internal collusion which only Godwine is principled enough to resist. For Lappenberg the Channel exists as a kind of *cordon sanitaire* that can protect the true Germanic spirit from Romish and Frankish decadence, but while it may have succeeded at the time of the Spanish Armada it failed in 1066 – with catastrophic consequences for the course of world history. As a result the Saxons have been thrown into the dustbin of history and it is now an act of necessary piety to restore them to their rightful place within it.

In this reconstruction Lappenberg develops a number of fanciful arguments. It goes without saying that Saxon England laid the foundation for 'the most formidable power that the world has witnessed, and a constitution the most perfect, the fundamental principles of which have exercised their influence over the countries of both hemispheres, and will maintain it for many ages to come',[39] but in addition Lappenberg claims that the English church in the purity of its spirituality, its resistance to canon law and celibacy, its persistent use of the vernacular rather than Latin in church services represented a real possibility of purity of faith, which could have resisted the power of Rome:

> The British church, established probably on the oldest direct traditions from Judaea, in closest connexion with conversions of the highest importance in the history of mankind, appeared no less by its geographical position, than by its exalted spiritual endowments, fitted to become the foundation of a Northern patriarchate, which by its counterpoise to Rome and the rest of the South, its guardianship over a Celtic and Germanic population, sanctified by the doctrine of Christ, might have been the instrument to impart to those within its pale that which both meditative and ambitious men, in the middle age, sometimes ventured to think on, but which, in comparatively modern times, Martin Luther first strove to extort for Romanized Europe.[40]

Thus while Palgrave can only look back over the passing centuries in complacency and satisfaction, Lappenberg can only weep at the thought of the immense tract of historical time that has been completely wasted. But it is in the figure of the Saxon's celebrated ruler and law-giver, King Alfred, that Lappenberg's nostalgia is most intensely focused. As a modern, scientific historian Lappenberg was well aware of the dangers of attributing to a single individual changes that may have been the work of many people over a long period of time, but despite this he cannot refrain from eulogy or from suggesting that Alfred is one of the most significant figures in the whole of world history:

Greater and better earned glory has never been attached to the memory of any chieftain than that which encircles the name of Aelfred. What a phenomenon, when compared with the bigoted, dastardly and lawless kings, under whom the independence, prosperity and civilization of the Anglo-Saxons was destroyed! Even when we compare him with all those great princes, who in external circumstances and by the magnitude of their deeds may be likened to him – with the energetic and sagacious Ecgberht, with the lord of half and the wonder of the whole contemporary and after-world – the Frankish Charles, – with the Czar Peter, or the Great Frederick, yet to none of these wonderful men can we yield precedence over the great West Saxon king, whose life-course at once reminds us of all those great rulers, without being sullied by pernicious ambition and lust of conquest. . . .

Even the Norman tyrants have regarded Aelfred with friendly feelings, and gladly claimed the glory of numbering him among their ancestors. But how must such a remembrance, such a bright comfort have operated on the Anglo-Saxon race! No splendour is equal to that which beams forth from the manger and the beggar's garment, and no memorial so well preserved as among the oppressed. But the present time will rather revere the sage, the legislator, and the instructor of his people, and they will revere him the more, because their remembrance of him is unconnected with any of the later excrescences and abuses in the state and of civilization which still perceives the battle-axe only in the hatchet of the executioner, the law in taxes, the church in tithes. But if men like Aelfred belong to every people and to every age in the circuit of the human mind, yet, next to the posterity of his countrymen, the German, – whose speech and culture will by continued re-search gather many golden fruits sown by Aelfred, with joyful pride may say, 'The man is near of kin unto us.'[41]

In this rapturous effusion, in which Alfred appears as positively Christ-like, we are invited to see the Saxon moment as representing the possibility of a paradise, which has indeed been lost, but which by careful scholarship can nevertheless be regained. The true linea-ments of an authentically Germanic civilisation can be discerned even though they have been buried by centuries of Frankish igno-rance and prejudice. So Lappenberg is a significant contributor to the Victorian cult of Alfred, whose achievement is the earliest and most unshakeable warranty that the English people have been marked out by destiny for greatness.

In 1849, four years after the translation of Lappenberg into English, John Mitchell Kemble's *The Saxons in England* appeared. Like
Lappenberg, Kemble's study was an act of piety and respect for the
historic and still underestimated achievements of our Saxon forefathers in which antiquarianism was combined with a strong sense
of their contemporary relevance, but unlike him this was cast not in
the form of a narrative history but in the form of an analysis of their
legal, political and religious institutions. But Kemble was more antiquarian than most. Thus, in explaining that the ceorlas or dependent
freemen of Hurstbourn were expected, in addition to paying six
church-mittan of ale and three sesters or horseloads of wheat, 'to pay
three pounds of gafolbarley, to mow half an acre of gafolmead and
stack the hay, to split four foder or load of gafolwood and stack it, to
make sixteen rods of gafolhedging', Kemble offers in elucidation the
following footnote: 'Gafolbaere, gafolmead, gafolwidu, gafoltuning.
The Saxons knew well enough that all these things were *rent*; and
that all land put out upon rent of any kind was gafolland, gafolcund
or *gavelkind* land.'[42] Kemble evidently imagines that the reader will
admire his respect for the intricacies of the Saxon tradition, wonder
at the depth and profundity of his learning and yet breathe a sigh of
relief that such untutored Saxons, without benefit of Ricardo, should
have such a thorough grasp of such an apparently incomprehensible
system. Undoubtedly our Saxon forefathers knew a thing or two.

Kemble, like Turner and Palgrave, rejoiced in the longevity of
English democratic traditions. The Saxon witenagemot does foreshadow the Magna Charta, and though there may be significant
differences they embody a common tradition that the power of the
monarchy shall not be absolute and that it exists only by consent of
the people:

> We need not lament that the present forms and powers of our
> parliament are not those that existed a thousand years ago, as long
> as we recognise in them only the matured development of an old
> and useful principle. We shall not appeal to Anglosaxon custom to
> justify the various points of the Charter; but we may still be proud
> to find in their practice the germ of institutions which we have,
> through all vicissitudes, been taught to cherish as the most valu-
> able safeguards of our peace as well as our freedom. Truly there
> are few nations whose parliamentary history has so ample a foun-
> dation as our own.[43]

Here Kemble comes close to admitting that it is pleasant to trace the ancestry of our democratic institutions as far back as the Saxons, even if the intellectual justification for doing so is by no means clear cut, and that if we are to respect our traditions, then it makes sense to make them as venerable as possible.

Kemble was writing in the aftermath of Chartism and the revolutions on the continent of 1848, so in Saxon culture and English society he was anxious to identify elements of stability and of an enduring social order. The picture he conjures up of Saxon society after the invasion is as idyllic as anything ever offered by the Pre-Raphaelite painters:

> On the natural clearings of the forest, or on spots prepared by man for his own uses; in valleys, bounded by gentle acclivities which poured down fertilising streams; or on plains which here and there rose, clothed with verdure, above surrounding marshes; slowly step by step, the warlike colonists adopted the habits and developed the character of peaceful agriculturalists. The towns which had been spared in the first rush of war, gradually became deserted, and slowly crumbled to the soil, beneath which their ruins are yet found from time to time, to mark the sites of a civilization, whose bases were not laid deep enough for eternity. All over England there soon existed a network of communities, the principle of whose being was separation, as regards each other: the most intimate union, as respected the individual members of each. Agricultural, not commercial, dispersed, not centralised, content with their own limits and little given to wandering, they relinquished in a great degree the habits and feelings which had united them as military adventurers; and the spirit which had achieved the conquest of an empire, was now satisfied with the care of maintaining inviolate a little peaceful plot, sufficient for the cultivation of a few simple households.[44]

Clearly Kemble's reaction to all this is deeply ambivalent. On the one hand, faced with an England increasingly defined by huge industrial cities with their furiously smoking factory chimneys and disgruntled, exploited and deeply disaffected workers, it is pleasant to conjure up the vision of an England whose inhabitants seek only peace and tranquillity, and where the towns are actually falling down. William Morris would have enjoyed this also. On the other hand

Kemble wants to believe that it is this Saxon, agricultural and law-abiding spirit that still persists. For the Saxon peasants, despite the hardship and the hassle of having to come up with the requisite ale, wheat, gafolbarley and gafolhedging, always knew their place: 'But the Saxon peasant knew his position: it was a hard one, but he bore it: he worked early and late, but he worked cheerfully, and amidst all his toils there is no evidence of his ever having shot at his landlord from behind a stone wall or hedge.'[45]

In this, of course, he was very different from the contemporary Irish or Celtic peasant, who was causing the British government so much trouble. But on balance Kemble was prompted in the aftermath of 1848 to thank God and the Saxons for the stability that England had been vouchsafed:

> On every side of us thrones totter, and the deep foundations of society are convulsed. Shot and shell sweep the streets of capitals which have long been pointed out as the chosen abodes of order: cavalry and bayonets cannot control populations whose loyalty has become a proverb here, whose peace has been made a reproach to our own miscalled disquiet. Yet the exalted Lady, who wields the sceptre of these realms, sits safe upon her throne, and fearless in the holy circle of her domestic happiness, secure in the affections of a people whose institutions have given to them all the blessings of an equal law.
>
> Those institutions they have inherited from a period so distant as to excite our admiration, and have preserved amidst all vicissitudes with an enlightened will that must command our gratitude.
>
> ... It cannot be without advantage for us to learn how a State so favoured as our own has set about the great work of constitution and solved the problem, of uniting the completest obedience to the law with the greatest amount of individual freedom.[46]

So the task of political science, as of political economy, is that of determining all the reasons that have served to make England uniquely favoured among nations. Saxon history necessarily has a bearing on this enquiry. It is with the Saxons that England's unique mission to civilise the world really begins.

In 1849 there also appeared the first two volumes of what was to prove perhaps one of the most influential accounts of England's distinctive identity: Macaulay's *History of England*. For Macaulay, as for Palgrave, the events of 1848 were a catastrophe from which

England had providentially been spared, and he too attributed this escape to the wisdom of England's constitutional arrangements. England had been spared the full force of Jacobinism and radical innovation by successfully pre-empting the moment of absolute monarchy – based on the existence of a large, well-trained standing army and taxation directly levied by the king himself – because she had resisted its emergence with Charles I and had resisted it again in the Restoration period. England had escaped the extremes of anarchy and despotism by following a middle course that had itself always been based on tradition and attention to precedent. The Glorious Revolution of 1688 was unique in that it was not radical and violent but peaceful and conservative:

> As our Revolution was a vindication of ancient rights, so it was conducted with a strict attention to ancient formalities. In almost every word and act may be discerned a profound reverence for the past. . . . To us who have lived in the year 1848, it may seem almost an abuse of terms to call a proceeding, conducted with so much deliberation, with so much sobriety, and with such minute attention to prescriptive etiquette, by the terrible name of Revolution.
>
> And yet this revolution, of all revolutions the least violent, has been of all revolutions the most beneficial.[47]

For a Whig like Macaulay 1688 was in all respects both a crucial benchmark and landmark; it inaugurated a modern world that was sensible, rational, progressive and middle class. It thus made it possible to define the genius of England in middle-class terms. For if 1688 is the definitive event in English culture, and if this event is itself the culmination and the quintessence of hundreds of years of English history, then we may rest assured that the English are essentially practical, law abiding and conservative; yet they are jealous of their traditional rights, patient and thoughtful in the defence of them, stubborn and tenacious when they have to be. Against those Tories who romanticise the House of Stuart and their servants, Macaulay insists on the pre-eminent value of those less-romantic figures who in their struggle to resist the power of the king 160 years before not only saved England then but saved it for their middle-class successors:

> Now, if ever, we ought to be able to appreciate the whole importance of the stand which was made by our forefathers against the

House of Stuart. All around us the world is convulsed by the agony of great nations. Governments which lately seemed likely to stand during ages have been on a sudden shaken and overthrown. The proudest capitals of Western Europe have streamed with civil blood. All evil passions, the thirst of gain and the thirst of vengeance, the antipathy of class to class, the antipathy of race to race, have broken loose from the control of divine and human laws. Fear and anxiety have clouded the faces and depressed the hearts of millions, Trade has been suspended, and industry paralysed. The rich have become poor; and the poor have become poorer. . . . Meanwhile in our island the regular course of government has never been for a day interrupted.[48]

The anxiety is as genuine as the complacency. Macaulay is, in his heart of hearts, terrified of lawlessness and civil disorder, and through the Chartist years he could not be certain that 1832 was the final settlement of accounts, the last piece of fine tuning that would bring the constitution in harmony with the needs of the contemporary world that he and his fellow Whigs believed and wanted it to be. Now with the Chartist threat decisively fading just as European governments were being shaken to their very foundations, Macaulay is able to breathe a deep sigh of relief in the very same instant as he utters a firm and predictable, 'I told you so.' 1832 confirms 1688, and 1848, in England, confirms them both.

Macaulay studied the past for its anticipations of the present, but he also took a perverse delight in viewing the present from what he imagined would be the standpoint of the past. In his own version of Whig history you first look through the wrong end of the telescope in order to behold the diminished landscape of the past and then, from that imaginative standpoint, you turn it round the right way in order to view the remarkable wonders of the present. If Macaulay often stood astonished at the follies and miseries of the past, he could not doubt that our forefathers would by inverse logic stand even more bemused if they could see the amazing beanstalk that had shot up from such a humble shoot. So this is the main reason why he seeks to put himself in their shoes, like the millionaire who surrounds himself with impecunious cronies in order to maintain a more vivid appreciation of the advantages that wealth brings, which otherwise might so easily become dulled. Although Macaulay's celebrated extended chapter on the State of England in 1685 has been deservedly praised for the virtuosity of its imaginative reconstruction, it is doubtful if Macaulay would have written it had he not been so anxious to demonstrate how much things had improved since then. We learn that the position of the armed forces, the government service, the clergy, of women in all social classes, of the middle classes and the common people, all have been immensely improved. With the coming of railways travel is immensely faster and more comfortable. There is an efficient postal service. In the space of 150 years England has been utterly transformed and unquestionably for the better:

> Many thousands of square miles which are now rich corn land and meadow, intersected by green hedge rows, and dotted with villages and pleasant country seats, would appear as moors overgrown with furze, or fens abandoned to wild ducks. We should see straggling huts built of wood and covered with thatch, where we now see manufacturing towns and seaports renowned to the farthest ends of the world.[49]

The advantage of this kind of imaginative time-travelling is that it can dwell on the noticeable differences, in the guise of 'improvements', but there is no particular pressure to look at the downside, which is, after all, not what progress – and Macaulay did insist and insist most emphatically that 'the history of England is the history of progress' – is all about.[50] Macaulay sees only huge commercial enterprises that are exporting their products around the globe and he is not disposed even to examine the human or environmental cost of industrialisation, let alone count the cost. It seems symptomatic of the deliberate blindness of Macaulay's whole approach that in this chapter he should dwell on the evils of Whitefriars as a no-go area, beyond the law, frequented by prostitutes, cheats, forgers and highwaymen, which he regarded as a relic of the barbarism of the darkest ages, when in the very same year that these volumes appeared, the extraordinary depths of poverty, misery and lawlessness that prevailed in the very heart of London should been exposed to the readers of the *Morning Chronicle* by Henry Mayhew. By comparison with this colossal underworld, Whitefriars seems small beer, yet Macaulay is shocked to record that all this went on within a stone's throw of Will's coffeehouse, the great centre of literary culture, where John Dryden held court. Macaulay's past is always designed to strengthen the assurance of the present, not to undermine it. His history never leads to questioning or doubt. What it characteristically produces is such a reflection as: 'The little army thus formed by Charles II was the germ of that great and renowned army which has, in the present century, marched triumphant into Madrid and Paris, into Canton and Candahar.'[51]

But if England is always the epitome of progressive civilisation, this grand narrative always has its darker side in the relative backwardness of Scotland and above all Ireland, which is why it is neither possible nor desirable to conflate England with Britain. But the exemplary history of Saxon England requires the foil of recalcitrant Celtic Ireland if its virtues are to be truly appreciated. The development of a binary antithesis between England and Ireland was already important for the arguments of the classical economists: if England was the example to follow, Ireland was above all a terrible instance of what to avoid. Whereas England was a stable, commercial and progressive nation, where the workforce was both industrious and comparatively well educated and well fed – such at any rate was the classical economists' claim – Ireland was primitive and backward, held back from progress by a lack of capital and popish superstition, its peasantry, idle, ignorant and always on the point of starvation. As Nassau Senior wrote in 1844: 'The Material evils are the want of Capital and the want of small Proprietors, the Moral evils are insecurity, ignorance, and indolence.'[52]

The root of the problem was the Irish system of land-tenure, which encouraged a process by which land was let and sub-let until it had to support a population that was greater than it could bear. Sir Francis Palgrave traced the evil back to the original system of gavelkind, whereby land was held in common: 'which annihilated all inducements to industry, destroyed the sources of individual opulence, and exposed the nation at large to all the evils of sloth and disunion'.[53] However, for the classical economists the evil was of more recent origin and Ireland was a classic instance of population outrunning the food supply: between 1740 and 1840 it was computed that the population of Ireland had increased by 400 per cent. The Irish peasantry were lacking in both industry and prudence, and, it was suggested, were largely responsible for their fate, though it had admittedly been made worse by the high rents charged by the absentee English landlords and by the financial demands of the Anglican and Catholic churches in Ireland. In Macaulay's historical analysis the terms of the opposition are substantially the same but are reworked in terms of a racial antithesis between Saxon and Celt, where Saxons are industrious, commercial and civilised, and the Celts, whether Irish or Scottish, are indolent and barbarous. Indeed Macaulay is just as severe on the Scottish of an earlier era as he is on the Irish – the tacit distinction being that they are now advancing towards civilisation and unification with the English, where the Irish are not. Of the highlanders in the seventeenth century he writes:

> It is not strange that the Wild Scotch, as they were sometimes called, should in the seventeenth century, have been considered by the Saxons as mere Savages. But it is surely strange that, considered as savages, they should not have been objects of interest and curiosity. The English were then abundantly inquisitive about the manners of rude nations separated from our island by great continents and oceans. Numerous books were printed describing the laws, the superstitions, the cabins, the repasts, the dresses, the marriages, the funerals of Laplanders of Hottentots, Mohawks and Malays. The plays and poems of that age are full of allusions to the usages of the black men of Africa and of the red men of America. The only barbarian about whom there was no wish to have any information was the Highlander.[54]

Macaulay is doubtless justified in drawing attention to the regrettable fact that Englishmen knew so little about fellow inhabitants of these islands, and his suggestion that the highlanders belong to an earlier and more primitive state of society is after all one that he derives from the Scottish enlightenment itself. But in the constant reiteration of this terminology of Saxon and Celt in his history Macaulay does more than distinguish between more economically advanced and more backward nations; he suggests that this is itself grounded in ethnic superiority, as when he says of Inverness: 'Inverness was a Saxon colony among the Celts, a hive of traders and artisans in the midst of population of loungers and plunderers, a solitary outpost of civilisation in a region of barbarism.'[55]

What makes it all slightly the less damaging is the knowledge that Scotland is coming closer to England, that the Scottish reviews are respectfully read in London, that the old antagonisms are fading away. So Carlyle, in *Heroes and Hero-Worship*, could frankly describe the Scotland of John Knox as 'A poor country, full of continual broils, dissentions, massacrings; a people in the last state of rudeness and destitution, little better perhaps than Ireland today' (III, 119), secure in the knowledge that if Ireland still is this, Scotland at least is not. Scotland can be and is becoming what England already is; the question is: can Ireland follow her example?

This was also the question for Macaulay. On the face of it the contrast between the Saxon Protestants of Ulster and the debased Catholic Celtic majority is so absolute as to be virtually unbridgeable:

> They sprang from different stocks. They spoke different languages. They had different national characters as strongly opposed as any two national characters in Europe. They were in widely differing stages of civilisation. . . . The English settlers seem to have been, in knowledge, energy and perseverance, rather above than below the average level of the population of the mother country. The aboriginal peasantry, on the contrary, were in an almost savage state. They never worked till they felt the sting of hunger. They were content with accommodation inferior to that which, in happier countries, was provided for domestic cattle. Already the potato, a root which can be cultivated with scarcely any art, industry or capital, and which cannot be long stored, had become the food of the common people. From a people so fed diligence and forethought was not to be expected. Even within a few miles of Dublin, the traveller, on a soil the richest and most verdant in the world, saw with disgust the miserable burrows out of which squalid and half naked barbarians stared wildly at him as he passed.[56]

According to Macaulay, at the time of James I there was still a change of reconciliation between the two races. Just as the old animosities between Norman and Saxon had been overcome, there was still hope for the Celt to move upward on the ladder of civilisation: 'The native race would still have had to learn from the colonists industry and forethought, the arts of life and language of England.'[57] Macaulay thought of the Irish as helots and referred to them as such – which made James II's decision to put Saxon Protestants 'under the feet of Popish Celts' all the more unforgivable and made reconciliation virtually impossible.[58] Needless to say Macaulay still hoped that Ireland would finally blend in with the dominant progressive English, but his terminology of Saxon and Celt nevertheless served to mark absolutely the difference between them and relegated to the very fringes of consciousness the notion that progressive England might actually have a responsibility and a duty to address Ireland's dauntingly serious problems. It was all too easy to feel that the Irish should be left to go on stewing in their own juice, as an example to the world of how not to do it.

The consequence of this kind of progressive discourse is effectively to exclude Ireland from the United Kingdom – even as the Irish petition for Repeal of the Act of Union – and to see the Irish as yet another troublesome outpost of the Empire. It seems symptomatic that Macaulay should perceive Ireland simply as the Achilles heel of British imperial power, as 'the one vulnerable spot near to the heart',[59] or that Palmerston at the time of the Indian mutiny should write to the Viceroy emphasising the importance of displaying in Ireland 'a sufficient Saxon force to make any movement on the part of the Celts perfectly hopeless, and sure to bring immediate destruction on those who take part in it'.[60]

The lesser breeds within the law, whether Irish or Indian, are to be terrorised into submission. It was very difficult to challenge the power of this kind of thinking. Particularly after the passing of the Reform Bill, it made sense for radicals and Irishmen to make common cause against the establishment of a new, complacent consensus between aristocracy and the middle classes. Yet there were always tensions between them, partly because of a long-standing personal rivalry between Daniel O'Connell and Feargus O'Connor, the Chartist leader, and partly because many English working men distrusted the Irish because of their religion and general reputation. In the 1840s this was intensified by the renewed fear of popery after the appointment of Cardinal Wiseman and the increased emigration of Irishmen to England looking for work. Thus the *Manifesto* of the Chartist convention could point to Ireland in the spirit of the classical economists as a dreadful example and warn: 'If you long continue passive slaves, the *fate of unhappy Ireland will soon be yours.'*[61] While the *Northern Star* did make strenuous efforts to combat this kind of distrust and suspicion, it was difficult to develop a coordinated campaign between the radical forces in England and Ireland because their priorities were significantly different. Thus in the issue of 13 May 1843 the *Northern Star* proclaimed: 'let us array ourselves – English, and Scotch, and Irishmen – under one common banner with the flag of freedom and the Charter waving over us, with the Charter, and never before it will Repeal come; and the sacred tree of Liberty shall take root at once in England and Ireland.' Yet the context of this pronouncement, of course, was the Irish demand for Repeal of the Act of Union, which they insisted must take priority over all else, whereas the Chartists believed that the Charter itself was the precondition for all progressive legislation – whether that involved repealing the Act of Union or the Corn Laws. So although the Chartists and the Irish were natural allies, they were never able to cement an effective alliance.

The Chartists differed from the Whigs not just in the fact that they were not satisfied with the limited reform granted in 1832, demanding universal manhood suffrage, annual elections and the secret ballot, but also because they rejected the progressive historical scenario. The Chartists were nothing if not patriotic, but they could not accept the Whig interpretation of English history, which saw 1688 as the landmark event in English history, the moment that had inaugurated England's political and economic greatness and made her a force to be reckoned with in the world. They saw England's recent history as one of decline, in which traditional freedom and been eroded to the point of extinction during the repression of the Napoleonic Wars and where the living standards of the labouring classes had been progressively driven down. Especially during the period of depression and severe economic hardship that followed the ending of the war in 1815 it was natural to look back to earlier days and better times when the common people, as it was believed, had enjoyed both security and relative prosperity. In English radical thought this nostalgia became a complex and pervasive philosophy since it was coupled with two other scenarios of decline: the belief that the lot of ordinary people had actually been better during the Middle Ages – the gospel of 'Merrie England' as it came to be called – and the conviction that the English people under the Saxon kings and especially under Alfred, the all-wise lawgiver, had enjoyed rights and freedoms that were subsequently lost. The first of these propositions found its definitive articulation in Cobbett's *A History of the Protestant Reformation in England and Ireland* – a violently partisan work that was very loosely based on the careful and relatively unbiased work of Lingard, an Irish priest, whose *History of England* was written to correct the anti-Catholic bias in the writing of much English history and in particular to rehabilitate the reign of 'Bloody' Mary. Cobbert saw the Reformation and especially the dissolution and confiscation of the monasteries as a disaster for the common people since it destroyed the traditional basis of Christian charity and produced new, oppressive concentrations of power:

The Reformation despoiled the working classes of their patrimony; it tore from them which nature and reason had assigned to them; it robbed them of that relief for the necessitous which was theirs by right imperscriptable, and which had been confirmed to them by the law of God and the law of the land. It brought a compulsory, a grudging, an unnatural mode of relief, calculated to make the poor and the rich hate each other instead of binding them together as the Catholic mode did, by bonds of Christian charity.[62]

For Cobbett the whole history of modern England had been one of *de*formation – it was a story of financial speculation and manipulation, of coercion directed against the poor, of the great 'Wen' poisoning and corrupting the healthy body of England, of the ruin of a hitherto prosperous and harmonious land.

But this nostalgia could be taken back one stage further to the pristine democracy of our Saxon forefathers. It might not be thought surprising that radicals and Chartists should participate in the great Victorian cult of the Saxons and of Alfred the Great, but this is really to misrepresent the matter, since radicals had done as much as any to promote it. A significant instigator of much of this was Major John Cartwright, who, following Obadiah Hulme's *Historical Essay on the English Constitution* (1771), stressed the Saxon origins of England's constitutional system – a system that had in the past been vastly more democratic that it was at present. Although Cartwright, like Paine, argued that democracy was simply a matter of common sense, he did not simply argue on the basis of universal principles but was also concerned to invoke historical precedent. This apparently conservative method of arguing became integral to the tradition of English radical politics. As distinct from the French libertarian politics, which called for the replacement of a corrupt old regime by democratic government founded on reason, English agitators for reform tended to deny that any innovation was involved and rather insisted that they sought for nothing more than the restoration of traditional rights. Thus in *Take Your Choice* Cartwright invoked from some unknown source praise of 'the godlike sentiment' of the 'all-excellent Alfred'.[63] Cobbett claimed that 'we want *great alteration*, but we want *nothing new*'.[64] Alfred was also revered in the pages of the *Poor Man's Guardian* and the *Northern Star*. As some erstwhile English golden age, Alfred's reign was a popular subject for lyric poetry. In the *Poor Man's Guardian* an anonymous poet compared Alfred with William to the disadvantage of the latter:

> In great King Alfred's glorious reign,
> The pride and boast of Englishmen,
> Albion's brave sons (or history lies)
> Were much more happy, quite as wise
> As we, their 'intellectual' race,
> Under 'the *Brunswick* reign of grace,'[65]

while Thomas Cooper in his *The Purgatory of Suicides* (1845) invoked Arthur as the exemplary king:

> A monarch scorning blood-stained gawds and gold,
> To build the throne in a blest people's love.

Increasingly the radical line tended to be that the Englishman's rights and freedoms dated from time immemorial. Thus an article on 'The Poor Law' in the *Northern Star* of 14 May 1842 suggested that provision for poor relief in England went back very much further than the reign of Queen Elizabeth:

> As far back as the historical records of our country reach, they show that there has existed amongst the inhabitants of this island some sort of provision or other for the relief of the destitute. . . . There is evidence to prove that a provision of this nature existed amongst our ancestors even before the introduction of Christianity; aye, even before the Roman invasion. There is evidence to show that even the DRUIDS, the 'rude,' 'uncouth,' 'ignorant,' 'savage,' 'uncivilised,' DRUIDS had laws which provided *that the people should not be starved to death.*

Of course the radical determination to argue rather on the basis of tradition than of reason, justice and democratic right was in part dictated by the existence of political repression in England over half a century since radicals could claim that they were avoiding all foreign tendencies to subversion, anarchy and innovation, and that in asking for reform and the restoration of traditional liberties they were arguing in the spirit of middle-class Whigs. The appeal to precedent was often designed to disarm. The judge and jury who heard Isaac Johnson defend himself against charges of uttering riotous and inflammatory language at Stockport (reported in the *Northern Star* of 18 April 1840) must have been rather surprised to hear him launch into an lengthy and erudite exposition of England's early constitutional history:

> It was upon the laws of the ancients that the institutions of this country, of which we are liable to boast, were securely fixed, and upon these rests all the present glory and the present renown of England. If there is anything added, we are compelled to admit it is but imitating the track of our forefathers. If there is anything left worthy of admiration or deserving of respect, let us point to the primitive source, and admit our own degeneration. But it may be doubted whether the people, when assembled, possessed the right to deliberate. From Dr Wilkins's Saxon Laws we learn that 'Withred, the King of Canterbury, gathered the people in council.' It is stated that 'there were all the clergy and the herds folk, where the chiefs and the congregation established their laws.' It appears, then, Gentlemen, and we have it there established, that the people were called to council, and did create laws, and to make us certain with regard to the extension of right, we are informed that the 'herdsfolk' were also there, and further that 'the chiefs' and the assembled people all united, forming a 'congregation,' and did establish there. My Lord and gentlemen of the Jury, according to the ancient laws of England, we find that the House of Commons should be chosen by a full, free and uncontrolled voice of the people of this united realm, so that the will of the body of the people be, in a free and equal Parliament, fully and freely expressed and executed.

While it is impossible not to admire the courage and determination of a man arguing this brief under such very adverse circumstances, it is at the same time very clear that such an exposition of the democratic case becomes highly problematic. It is founded on a largely conjectural history and on impossibly remote events. With the best will in the world all that can be extracted from Saxon precedent is a deferential politics, not the arguments for popular sovereignty, which was what the Chartists actually wanted. The Chartists were always tempted to speak in two different languages – amongst themselves excoriating a corrupt and unrepresentative system and effectively calling for its overthrow, yet on the wider stage, when addressing a constituency of the established and enfranchised middle class, they stressed their desire to extend the franchise and participate in the system, claiming that they asked for nothing more than the traditional rights of freeborn Englishmen. In so far as they sought to align themselves with the middle class and allay any anxiety about revolutionary change – even though this seemed the only really viable policy if parliamentary reform was to take place – the actual consequence was that they tended to be taken less seriously, while at the same time they became the more confused and divided about their objectives and aims. The problem about the distinction proposed between physical and moral force Chartism was that it seemed to imply that there could be nothing between open warfare and the pious and utterly unrealistic hope that the middle class and landed aristocracy would be compelled to submit before the overwhelming force of reason. The Chartists simply underestimated the strength of their determination to defend the 1832 bill as a final settlement, and somehow imagined that they were pushing at an already open door. Middle-class public opinion was convinced that the Chartists were dangerous anarchists and no recondite allusion to Saxon law was likely to persuade them to the contrary. Nevertheless when both the aristocracy and the middle classes were presenting their claim to represent England it was not unreasonable that the working classes and their radical spokesmen should insist on their own claim to England's cultural heritage, or that they should want to argue that her democratic tradition was not to be construed solely in terms of representation for ten-pound householders. They had reason to object to the way in which a relatively open debate over questions of representation had been suddenly closed down once the Reform Bill was passed. England's Saxon heritage was a reality to many radicals and Chartists and its relevance was epitomised by the occasion when, in April 1839, the veteran Tory radical Richard Oastler was presented with a trusty wooden spear at the meeting of the Democratic association at the Fox and Hounds in Nottingham. Responding to this gift Oastler said:

> This meeting reminds me of the times long gone by, when an English working man was not afraid to handle his trusty spear, and when his employer did not tremble because his workman was well armed. Our ancestors were wont to meet thus armed, under the shadow of their native oaks, to discuss their national affairs, and, as a pledge of confidence, they would exchange their spears; this was called a weapon take. . . . May the patriotic ardour of our ancestors return with the sight of their well-made trusty spears.[66]

Thus the Saxon spear is an amazingly multiform symbol that suggests at once the roots of Chartist traditions in England's far distant past, a tradition of democratic government in which the people gathered in peace to discuss the nation's affairs, and yet, at a time when many Chartists were arming themselves with simple weapons of this kind, it may also point to a preparedness on the part of Chartists to use physical force if necessary to achieve their democratic ends. But in any event the spear is a deeply patriotic symbol that grounds Chartism in antique national precedents and thereby disassociates itself from any abstract invocation of the Rights of Man. It is doubtful, however, whether such rhetoric disarmed the middle classes – certainly in Oastler's case it could only have alarmed them – and its most significant effect may have been to lull the Chartists into the belief that the struggle for democratic rights would not be resisted as firmly as it actually was.

Much of Thomas Carlyle's most eloquent and impassioned writing was a direct response to Chartism and the industrial unrest that developed with extraordinary rapidity in the late 1830s as a response both to a serious recession in England's manufacturing industry and also to the refusal of Parliament to respond to further pressure to extend the franchise. Yet Carlyle's critique of English society begins with the work in which he announced the inauguration of his own career as a seer and prophet, *Sartor Resartus*, first published in *Fraser's Magazine* in 1833. In the critical discussion of Carlyle a distinction is often made between the subjective, existential Carlyle of *Sartor* and the later Carlyle who is seen primarily as a social critic. Thus, John D. Rosenberg writes: 'In *Sartor Resartus* his subject had been himself and the Universe. In *The French Revolution* he turned from himself to society.'[67]

Yet with such a writer as Carlyle, for whom self and society were always intimately related, such a distinction cannot be but artificial. As a Scotsman seeking to make his way in London Carlyle could only experience England as an alien and alienating culture, a massive portent of the modern certainly, but one that stirred up a teeming multitude of doubts, reservations and misgivings in his mind as he endeavoured to grapple with such a solid, intransigent object. Whereas the Scottish political economists saw England as setting a pattern of economic and moral development that the rest of the world would be compelled to follow, Carlyle responded to England on a existential level, in which culture-shock, future-shock and religious uncertainty were explosively combined. In *Sartor Resartus* Carlyle both dissimulated the real sources of his *angst* and at the same time played ironic games at the expense of his plodding English readers by pretending that his sense of the world as 'one huge, dead, immeasurable Steam-engine' (III, 114) had been produced not by his exposure to Utilitarianism, Malthusianism and the general heartlessness of bourgeois England in its relentless determination to widen still further the disparity between wealth and poverty but, in the case of Teufelsdrockh, by the loss of Blumine's love and a consequent nameless unrest. Carlyle came nearest to telling the truth when he spoke of the terrible sense of isolation and emptiness that Teufelsdrockh experienced not as he wandered by the gurgling River Kuhbach in Weissnichtwo but in the desolate, foggy streets of London. It was here that he experienced that sense of hollowness in the universe that is the crucial perception of *Sartor* and one closely bound to the clothing metaphor:

> Often, while I sojourned in that monstrous tuberosity of Civilised Life, the Capital of England; and meditated and questioned Destiny, under that ink-sea of vapour, black, thick and multifarious as Spartan broth; and was one lone soul amid those grinding millions; often have I turned into their Old-Clothes Market to worship. With awe-struck heart I walk through that Monmouth Street with its empty suits, as through a Sanhedrim of stainless ghosts. (III, 163–4)

It was here, Carlyle insists 'at the bottom of our own English "ink-sea", that this remarkable Volume first took being' (III, 165). This originary context significantly colours Carlyle's complex usage of the clothes figure, since it suggests not simply that all societies will necessarily require 'clothing' in the form of customs, traditions and, most importantly, religious beliefs, but also that such clothing is always becoming at once worn-out and outworn, so that society will sooner or later be brought to the point where it needs to pitch all its old garments into the flames in an orgy of destruction, which will at one and the same time be what Carlyle calls a 'Phoenix Death-birth', a 'Fire-Whirlwind' in which 'Creation and Destruction proceed together' (III, 166).

This demand that renewal take place when faith and custom have become nothing more than hollow shams and empty clothes makes Carlyle's whole parallel insistence on the value of tradition deeply equivocal since traditions can never be celebrated just because they *are* or because they can be regarded as embodying the cumulative wisdom of generations. Although Carlyle follows Burke in proclaiming this and in insisting that 'Custom is the greatest of Weavers' (III, 175), Carlyle's perception of tradition is made the more complex because what he demands above all is the existence of tradition as a living, animating principle to which men genuinely and spontaneously give their allegiance. Once it becomes simply an outworn husk or an antiquated suit of clothes, it then becomes an actual denial of the spiritual imperative in man, a fetishised externality that instead of serving as a supportive and fulfilling environment serves to alienate him from the deepest sources of his being. Carlyle saw the England of his day as characterised by just such a lack. The Church of England had, in his eyes, become a virtually moribund institution and its failure to exercise any socially integrative role meant that society itself was falling apart:

> For the last three centuries, above all for the last three quarters of a century, that same Pericardial Nervous Tissue (as we name it) of Religion, where lies the Life-Essence of Society, has been smote-at and perforated, needfully and needlessly; till now it is quite rent into shreds; and Society, long pining, diabetic, consumptive, can be regarded as defunct. (III, 157)

Coming to England from a simpler, face-to-face culture, where religion in its Calvinist embodiment was still a powerful force, Carlyle experienced the 'modern' that England represented not as progress but as fragmentation, hollowness and sham. He saw the polarisation of England into two sharply divided classes – a 'Dandiacal body' that did not work and an exploited proletariat that did – as its most ominous characteristic. It followed that Carlyle could not be sanguine about England's prospects and he found it impossible to involve himself in a discourse predicated on the assumption that England was an exemplary model. The German alias that he assumed involved a willingness on his own part to admit that any point of view that he was likely to express must necessarily seem naïve, alien and uncouth if it involved a refusal of such a discursive framework. It was dictated by the universal reluctance of Englishmen to think about their country (yet, though it scarcely crossed their minds, the country of Scots, Irish and Welsh men and women as well) in any but the most complacent and self-satisfied terms:

> Perhaps it is proof of the stunted condition in which pure Science, especially pure moral Science, languishes among us English; and how our mercantile greatness, and invaluable Constitution, impressing a political or other immediate practical tendency on all English culture and endeavour cramps the free flight of Thought, – that this, not Philosophy of Clothes, but recognition even that we have no such Philosophy, stands here for the first time published in our language. (III, 5)

There was a great irony in Carlyle thus offering the English reader a philosophy of clothes since he believed they already had one enunciated in Bulwer-Lytton's *Pelham* – the philosophy of a shallow and empty dandyism in which the highest possible value is placed on externals and on making one's mark in the fashionable world through an ostentatious style of dress. For Pelham the introduction of the starched neckcloth was a gesture of unimpeachable genius. To Carlyle's earnest non-conformist conscience the affectations of a Pelham were no trivial matter because they only served to demonstrate how utterly ill-equipped the ruling class was for its task of governing England at such a critical time. From his earliest years Carlyle had been part of a Scottish religious culture in which prophesies of doom and intimations of damnation were uttered almost as a matter of course, and though as a young man his belief was shaken, he continued to share in its deep distrust of worldliness. When he visited London for the very first time in June 1824 he at last encountered a object that was fitted to bear the full weight of moral execration invoked by Calvinist tradition. Carlyle was completely traumatised by this first encounter, perhaps not surprisingly, since the gulf between the capital and his native Ecclefechan was as great if not greater than that between the interior of Brazil and the streets of São Paulo. He found it a Babylon and after only a few months fled back to Scotland and did not return again until 1831. The most significant product of the years in seclusion at Craigenputtock was *Sartor Resartus*, a work that was for Carlyle an eyeball-to-eyeball confrontation with the modern. What was particularly significant was the way in which, though he had never been there, Carlyle made the state of Ireland fundamental to any perceptions about the state of British society. The cultural divide between the 'Dandy' and what he called the 'Irish Poor-Slave' or 'Drudge' was both enormous and morally indefensible. He therefore could not follow the Scottish economists in their belief that the state of English society was both healthy and sound, nor could he acquiesce in the terms of analysis that carefully excluded backward Ireland from any discussion of England. On the contrary Carlyle saw the state of England as essentially abnormal and perverse. England 'as the wealthiest and worst-instructed of European nations offers precisely the elements (of Heat, namely, and of Darkness), in which such moon-calves and monstrosities are generated' (III, 186).

In Carlyle's view this intensifying division between classes is a certain recipe for a social explosion:

> Hitherto you see only partial transient sparkles and sputters: but wait a little, till the entire nation is in an electric state; till your whole vital Electricity, no longer healthfully Neutral, is cut into two isolated portions of Positive and Negative (of Money and of Hunger); and stands there bottled-up in two World-Batteries! The stirring of a child's finger brings the two together; and then – What then?   (III, 194)

So *Sartor Resartus* does not only sketch a personal crisis but links it with a wider crisis in society, and though Carlyle offers work as the resolution of his personal dilemma it is far from certain that he has any answer to the second.

The French Revolution (1837) was Carlyle's attempt to explore more deeply what he saw as the central episode in modern history – indeed as the originary moment of modern history. Moreover Carlyle wrote about these complex and confused events not so much with a view to endowing them with a retrospective and possibly illusory lucidity as to endow them with both the urgency and deceptiveness of a remorselessly dissolving present. Carlyle's complex shifts from narrative involvement to a prophetic gesturing in the direction of the actual outcome manage at once to suggest a world in which a diversity of possibilities remains open as far as the active agents on the scene are concerned, and yet still convey a powerful sense of an implacable, irrevocable principle of destiny at work in the universe. What is still more puzzling is the evident relish and enjoyment with which Carlyle presents the French Revolution as one vast theatrical spectacle that is acted out on the boards of Paris and the great stage of universal history. For on the one hand Carlyle insists on the profound *reality* of these events, however distasteful they may seem to any rational, law-abiding, middle-class person, while on the other he delights in representing them as the sham and surface of the world, whose grandiose pretensions are to be distrusted. Indeed it could well be argued that precisely what lies behind this apparent contradiction is Carlyle's conviction that the 'demonic' (a concept he took from Goethe) is necessarily an irrational force, and the actors in the French Revolution are therefore bound to misrecognise its significance so long as they imagine that it can be explained purely in terms of their conscious motives and intentions. Certainly Carlyle believes that his own interpretation is necessary because the deeper import of the French Revolution can never be grasped so long as it is seen purely and simply in terms of right or wrong, since such language is meaningful only when it refers to actions that are freely chosen. Carlyle believes that the Revolution is the inexorable consequence of the action of a 'Shoreless Fountain-Ocean of Force' (I, 334) which is beyond good and evil and therefore should be rather the occasion for astonishment than for the uttering of moral platitudes. It is at such moments that man is compelled to recognise that history is not what he or his rulers consciously make it, for those new forms of consciousness that have been silently developing within the hollowed-out customary forms suddenly burst out of their shell and demand an accounting. Carlyle draws a strangely religious conclusion from this, which is that the age of miracles is therefore not past and never will be. For Carlyle the French Revolution was in some sense God's judgement on eighteenth-century rationalism, and not the least significance of it is that it reawakens man to a sense of his own insignificance in the scheme of things and restores his capacity for wonder:

When the age of Miracles lay faded into the distance as an incredible tradition, and even the age of Conventionalities was now old; and Man's Existence had for long generations rested on mere formulas which were grown hollow by course of time; and it seemed as if no Reality any longer existed, but only Phantasms of realities, and God's Universe were the work of the Tailors and Upholsterers mainly, and men were buckram masks that went about beckoning and grimacing there, – on a sudden, the Earth yawns asunder, and amid Tartarean smoke, and glare of fierce brightness, rises *SANSCULOTTISM*, many-headed, fire-breathing, and asks: What think ye of *me*. Well may the buckram masks start together terror-struck 'into expressive, well-conceited groups'. It is indeed, Friends, a most singular, most fatal thing. (I, 181)

Carlyle refers elsewhere to the mob as 'a genuine outburst of Nature; issuing from, or communicating with the deepest deep of nature' (I, 213), so although the unpredictable motions of the crowd arouse in Carlyle equally deep feelings of apprehension and disquiet, he never doubts for one moment that the crowd is the supreme instance of *vox populi, vox dei* or that the circumstances that have provoked it into action demand the statesman's urgent attention.

Despite this there is a distinctly Burkean strain running through much of Carlyle and it is this that Carlyle's readers then and now have tended to latch onto, if only because it seems to represent a kind of log of sanity onto which they can cling to as Carlyle hurls them through the maelstroms of popular disruption. But what makes the Carlylean squeeze-box disconcerting is that it has more than one keyboard. Carlyle's romantic doctrine of growth had a violent bipolarity in that it is as capable of gesturing as firmly in the direction of sloughing off the old skin as towards the need for roots and cultural stability. So that when Carlyle speaks, or appears to speak, Burke's language, as he often does, it comes out with distinct elisions and syntactical kinks that produce a somewhat different effect. Carlyle could concur both with Burke's assertion that 'When ancient opinions and rules of life are taken away, the loss cannot possibly be estimated. From that moment we have no compass to govern us; nor can we know distinctly to what port we steer',[68] and also with his suggestion that 'A state without the means of some change is without the means of its conservation.'[69]

The difference is that Burke speaks securely from within cultural traditions and from under the shade of the spreading oak of British custom, whereas Carlyle will never make the indispensable first move of the political conservative, which is to assume that tradition is always self-justifying and beyond any possibility of rational interrogation. Indeed at a significant moment in *The French Revolution* Carlyle aligns himself with the emphasis of Paine rather than with Burke over the plight of the Royal family: 'Unhappy Family! Who would not weep for it, were there not a whole world to be wept for?' (I, 470–1). Carlyle agreed with Burke in rejecting the reckless superficiality of Jacobinism in its arrogant assumption that time-honoured practises should be consigned to the flames and replaced by hastily drawn-up schemes that allegedly conformed to the demands of universal reason. But Carlyle combined this with an unpredictable insistence, given the way the arguments were traditionally polarised, that although men, for their very existence and sanity, require the security of traditional forms, there nevertheless must be times when these must be put in question – not at the bar of reason but at the bar of human feeling and emotion. The question that must be asked of them is not are they universally just or true, but do they correspond to the needs of the people? For Carlyle tradition is a kind of house or dwelling place, which should not be recklessly demolished; but he believes, unlike Burke, that there may be times when it is imperative to ask whether it is still actually serviceable or whether it is time to move on. The effect of Carlyle's Everlasting No is that it leads to a foregrounding in those quotations from Burke of such phrases as 'no compass' and 'void', so that what Burke is simply not prepared to contemplate is in Carlyle already thought. Carlyle does not necessarily wish to sweep away traditions, and he despises those who do, but he does reserve the right to suspend them for the moment and to place them in interrogative brackets. Characteristic of the way in which Carlyle is capable of recasting the whole debate between radical and conservative is his discussion of constitutions in Book 6 of *The French Revolution* where he begins by mocking the attempt by the Abbé Sieyès to draw up a constitution in a way that Burke would certainly have approved of, but he then goes on, more disturbingly either for right or left, to question the value of constitutions themselves and to suggest that there is finally *nothing* that can serve as an ultimate guarantee of stability:

A Constitution can be built, Constitutions enough *a la Sieyès*: but the frightful difficulty is, that of getting men to come and live in them! Could Sieyès have drawn thunder and lightning out of Heaven to sanction his Constitution, it had been well: but without any thunder? Nay, strictly considered, is it not still true that without some such celestial sanction, given visibly in thunder or invisibly otherwise, no Constitution can in the long run be worth much more than the waste-paper it is written on? The Constitution, the set of Laws, or prescribed Habits of Acting, that men will live under, is the one which images their Convictions, – their Faith as to this wondrous Universe, and what rights, duties, capabilities they have there: which stands sanctioned, therefore, by Necessity itself; if not by a seen Deity, then by an unseen one. Other Laws, whereof there are always enough *ready*-made, are usurpations; which men do not obey, but rebel against, and abolish at their earliest convenience. (I, 183–4)

Carlyle set little store by constitutions and he regarded parliaments as little better than talk shops. As far as he was concerned constitutions would simply reflect a society already structured and ordered; they could not hope to support or shore up a culture on the point of collapse. The hero is thus central to Carlyle's whole doctrine of culture since only he can restore its fabric of belief and bring people and institutions into harmony. The problem with the French Revolution was not so much that it happened – for that was inevitable – but rather that its heroes, such men as Mirabeau and Danton, were just not heroic enough.

But the greater problem in reading, or deciphering Carlyle is not trying to establish what he is trying to say about the revolution in France but in divining just what inferences he wants to make about the condition of England. And once again Carlyle is trying to have it both ways. On the one hand he wants to suggest that the English character and the English experience is utterly dissimilar from that of France, and that therefore she is destined to take a completely different path, yet on the other he asks his English audience to take note of the terrible warning that France offers, as if it were the contemporary equivalent of a painting of the Last Judgement. There is much in Carlyle's description of the revolution that stresses the distinctiveness of the French national character: the French are addicted to rumour, they have a 'Gallic-Ethnic excitability and effervescence', the French mob is 'among the liveliest phenomena of our world: so rapid, audacious; so clear-sighted, inventive, prompt to seize the moment; instinct with life to its finger ends' (I, 213).

Yet Carlyle makes the moral judgement that the Gallic temperament, unlike the Teutonic, lacks staying power, which can be taken to imply that while a revolutionary situation would be much more difficult to ignite in either England or Germany it could then never be the short-lived phenomenon that the French Revolution had apparently been:

Rash Coalised Kings, such a fire have ye kindled; yourselves fireless, *your* fighters animated only by drill-sergeants, mess-room moralities and the drummer's cat! However, it is begun, and will not end: not for a matter of twenty years. So long, this Gaelic fire, through its successive changes of colour and character, will blaze over the face of Europe, and afflict and scorch all men: – till it provoke all men; till it kindle another kind of fire, the Teutonic kind namely; and be swallowed up, so to speak, in a day! For there is a fire comparable to the burning of dry-jungle and grass; most sudden, high-blazing: and another fire which we liken to the burning of coal, or even of anthracite coal; difficult to kindle, but then which no known thing will put out.   (II, 226)

Still more disparagingly Carlyle contrasted the quiet determination of the Scottish covenanters, who signed their agreements in a dingy close off Edinburgh High Street, with the flashy French who must make a huge scenic exhibition of themselves on the Champ de Mars. Carlyle symbolically opposes theatricality and truth and implicitly suggests that it is the unpretentious covenanters who are closer in spirit to the private moment of the Last Supper. It is their movement that will therefore prove the more durable; it is a case of Teutonic inwardness versus Gallic outward show – though, of course, Carlyle's ethnic categories were curiously flexible and he was capable also of contrasting Norman discipline with Saxon disorganisation where the occasion suited. But certainly for all the emphasis on national differences it is far from clear that Carlyle does not envisage a similar explosion in England especially when the figure of electrical discharge, used at the end of *Sartor*, pervades the whole of *The French Revolution* whether in allusions to Leyden jars or menacing thunder-clouds: 'the chaotic thunder-cloud, with its pitchy-black, and its tumult of dazzling jagged fire, in a world all electric' (II, 186).

After *The French Revolution* it was inevitable that Carlyle would have to return to the subject of England in order to make clear just how the terms of analysis he had made use of there applied to the English situation. *Chartism* (1839) was that work – Carlyle's searing indictment of the condition of England in the year of the presentation of the Chartist petition and his still more withering criticism of the failure of Parliament to do anything about it. Yet for all the brilliance of its writing, which has made it one of the most memorable and influential commentaries on English politics, it is a curiously botched and aborted work, which follows nine masterful chapters in which Carlyle sets forth his own idiosyncratic but nevertheless compelling and credible perception of the situation with a tenth that is so limp and inconclusive in the 'solutions' it offers that one can scarcely believe it was written by the same man. However, such a hurried and inconsequential bringing down of the curtain only serves to demonstrate that policy recommendations were hardly Carlyle's forte. The *Edinburgh Review* was awash with plenty of those already and the real danger of the *Edinburgh Review* manner was that the house style, of apparently exploring every ramification of the subject in an article over many pages so as to make its magisterial summing up all the more inexorable, succeeded in making many social problems seem a good deal more manageable than they actually were. Thus it was only necessary for some knowing person to suggest that the Irish peasant should work harder and in the London clubs many heads would nod sagely in agreement. The ludicrous inadequacy of such an analysis was scarcely evident from its imposing appearance and context. Carlyle, by contrast, emotional and melodramatic, as he often was, never underestimated the gravity of the situation or tried to brush it aside with some well-chosen disparaging epithets, as he himself pointed out: 'To say that it is mad, incendiary, nefarious is no answer' (xvii, 256).

Carlyle's essay on *Chartism* rather resembles a huge red fire-engine that rushes round and round the city streets at night, violently and continually ringing its alarm bells, in a desperate effort to locate the source of the fire, when the whole city lies under a vast pall of impenetrable black smoke. Carlyle was one of the very few who had grasped just how extensive were the changes that had occurred in England in its transformation into a great industrial nation and he lacked the convenient faith of the political economists that some kind of invisible hand, the presiding deity of capitalism, would ensure that everything would turn out for the best. On the contrary he stressed how radical and how incalculable the whole process was:

English Commerce stretches its fibres over the whole earth; sensitive literally, nay quivering in convulsion, to the farthest influences of the earth. The huge demon of Mechanism smokes and thunders, panting at his great task, in all sections of the English land; changing his *shape* like a very Proteus; and infallibly, at every change of shape, oversetting whole multitudes of workmen, and as if with the waving of his shadow from afar, hurling them asunder, this way and that, in their crowded march and course of work or traffic; so that the wisest no longer knows his whereabouts. With an Ireland pouring down daily in on us, in these circumstances; deluging us down to its own waste confusion, outward and inward, it seems a cruel mockery to tell poor drudges that *their* condition is improving.   (xvii, 274)

In England there was a radically new social and economic landscape in which people were still frantically trying to get their bearings, and refinements to the Poor Law represented a woefully inadequate response to the massive scale of Irish immigration and to the endemic booms and busts in manufacturing industry. As Carlyle rightly stressed, what made the situation so intolerable was that life for the working class was not simply hard, it was also desperately unpredictable as well: 'English Commerce with its world-wide convulsive fluctuations, with its immeasurable Proteus Steam-Demon, makes all paths uncertain for them, all life a bewilderment; sobriety, steadfastness, peaceable continuance, the first blessings of man, are not theirs' (xvii, 275–6). What Carlyle perceived very clearly was that there was no disposition in the upper echelons of English society to recognise the magnitude of the problem: the landed aristocracy knew very little about it, while the commercial middle classes were mainly interested in maximising their financial returns when the going was good, and in resisting any implication that they bore a moral responsibility for those they threw out of work when times were bad. The world of *The Times*, the quarterly reviews and of informed public opinion in general was one that instinctively and automatically identified England with the interests of the middle and upper classes. Within such circles it was natural to feel that the 'poor' generally got what they deserved and that any demand that something should be done about their situation was simply to make improper and importunate demands on the attention of very busy men. As Carlyle suggested, with more than an echo of Swift, 'To believe practically that the poor and luckless are only here as a nuisance to be abraded and abated, and in some permissable manner made away with, and swept out of sight, is not an amiable faith' (xvii, 265). Just as Ireland was being defined out of any definition of England, so too were Scotland, the industrial north and the unemployed, wherever they were to be found. England's 'success' had nothing to do with these, and conversely if such aliens were actually taken into an account, then England's success story would necessarily be undermined.

Chartism as a movement was a response not just to economic hardship; it also represented widespread dissatisfaction among the

working class with the fact that the Reform Bill was not being presented as a final settlement and with the fact that the great Whig
reforming ministry had in practice achieved so very little. Carlyle's
response to what was happening or not happening in Parliament
was equally critical. He recognised that despite all the rhetoric that
had surrounded the extension of the suffrage, parliamentary business still went on pretty much as before and that many of those who
had secured their election in 1832 were more interested in manipu-
lating public opinion for their own ends than in genuinely responding to the needs of the broad mass of the British people. Yet Carlyle
was unusual in imagining that it was their duty to do so, and he was
therefore acutely sensitive to Parliament's persistent failure even to
address the question, let alone do anything about it. Parliament was
in theory the great national assembly where such matters ought to be
urgently debated, yet it remained obstinately and inexplicably silent:

The condition of the great body in a country is the condition of the
country itself: this you would say is a truism in all times; a truism
rather pressing to get recognised as a truth now, and be acted
upon, in these times. Yet read Hansard's Debates, or the Morning
Papers, if you have nothing to do! The old grand question whether
A is to be in office or B, with the innumerable subsidiary questions
growing out of that, courting paragraphs and suffrages for a blessed
solution of that: Canada question, Irish Appropriation question,
West-India question, Queen's Bedchamber question; Game Laws,
Usury Laws; African blacks, Hill Coolies, Smithfield cattle, and
dog-carts, – all manners of questions and subjects, except simply
this alpha and omega of all! Surely Honourable Members ought to
speak of the Condition-of-England question too. Radical Members, above all, friends of the people; chosen with effort, by the
people, to interpret and articulate the dumb deep want of the
people! To a remote observer they seem oblivious of their duty.
(xvii, 257)

Carlyle is often thought of as a rather grim, earnest and unbending
figure, but at least he had enough of the spirit of irreverence to call
in question the whole agenda of parliamentary business, which Parliament itself took so seriously and which was elaborately reported
and commented on in the daily press. Like the child in Hans Christian Andersen's story who drew attention to the Emperor's naked-

ness, so Carlyle with equal perspicacity and apparent naïvety, pointed emphatically at the void that lay at the heart of the great parliamentary public show. Not unreasonably, given the context of the time and in view of the Whig insistence on limiting the role of the state, Carlyle saw the new democratic processes as essentially bankrupt and symptomatic of a deep failure of nerve. The Whigs had ushered in a new political order, and given the controversy and enthusiasm that had surrounded it, it was to be expected that significant initiatives in the field of public policy would follow. Yet these expectations had not been fulfilled and Carlyle therefore had some justification for concluding, of such democracy, 'it abrogates the old arrangement of things; and leaves, as we say, *zero* and vacuity for the institution of a new arrangement. It is the consummation of No-Government and *Laissez-faire*' (xvii, 289).

Few of Carlyle's contemporary readers could follow him in his criticisms of the representative government and they must have found the twists and turns of his rhetoric, the shifts from one register to another, extremely difficult to follow. On the one hand Carlyle at times seemed to speak the language of Chartism and popular radicalism, as when he referred to 'the mistake of those who believe that fraud, force and injustice, whatsoever untrue thing, howsoever cloaked and decorated, was ever or can ever be the principle of man's relation to man, is great and the greatest' (xvii, 310–11), but on the other his insistence that the masses did not really know what they wanted and only sought to be led, that what the moment required was strong government and leadership by the aristocracy, suggested a Tory politics. Matters are made still more confusing by the fact that many other strategic emphases in Carlyle's text suggest an identification with the commercial middle class. Certainly no northern mill owner who read *Chartism* could feel that Carlyle's heart was in the wrong place: he celebrates Arkwright and Watt as culture-heroes of the age; he finds the sound of Manchester cotton-mills as sublime as Niagara and he sees English's cultural identity above all articulated through the spirit of commerce:

> the Saxon kindred burst forth into cotton-spinning, cloth-cropping, iron-forged, steam-engining, railwaying, commercing and careering towards all the winds of Heaven, – in the inexplicable noisy manner; the noise of which, in Power-mills, in progress-of-the-species Magazines, still deafens somewhat. . . . God said, Let the iron missionaries be; and they were.

Thus Carlyle on one level strikes a complacent and patriotic note about what, on another level, he fears and deplores. Moreover Carlyle's own proposals for dealing with the Condition of England question – Education and Emigration, far from being more radical and far-reaching than the consensus, simply repeat nostrums that had long since been peddled by business men and conservative economists. As Herman Merivale commented in the *Edinburgh Review*: 'When asked, what are the remedies which he proposes – he answers, very much in the tone of a man forced to say something – emigration – and education.'[70]

In his own more clear-sighted and more forceful moods Carlyle would certainly have swept both aside as failing even remotely to meet the case. How could emigration help the situation of twenty-four million people? And while the ability to read and write – the aspect of education that Carlyle particularly stressed – might be desirable what relevance did it have to the problem of widespread poverty and immiseration that Carlyle himself had so eloquently described or to the political demands of the Chartists? In this limp and clichéd conclusion with its desperate invocation of an imperialist England that would somehow resolve abroad all the most urgent problems at home, Carlyle did indeed foretell the England of Palmerston and Disraeli but he lamentably failed to rise to his own intimidating challenge.

Although *Past and Present* (1843) superficially resembles *Chartism* in that both offer a comprehensive indictment of the state of British society, it is in reality a very different work. In *Chartism* Carlyle presented his argument both as a criticism of the failure of Parliament to respond to the new situation that the Chartist phenomenon represented while at the same time offering his own solution to the problem. However, in the interval between the books Carlyle clearly came to recognise that it had been a mistake on his part to offer concrete suggestions in response to some presumption on the part of some hypothetical *Edinburgh Review* reader that no analysis of the contemporary situation could be taken seriously unless it was coupled with specific policy recommendations. But Carlyle now saw that if he was to comply with such a demand it could only result in trivialisation of the issues as he perceived them. The inevitable corollary of this would be an abandonment of his far-reaching speculation on the moral integrity of past and present societies, which for him went to the very heart of the matter. What made Carlyle's position complex was that he was not simply filled with a nostalgia

for the medieval past – though this is how he has often been represented – but recognised that there were qualitative changes in human history from which there could be no going back. The problem
was rather: how was it possible to re-create in the present many of
the most desirable features of the past, given the fact that such
radical discontinuity had already taken place? In *On Heroes and Hero-
Worship* (1841) Carlyle claimed that the modern world, which he saw
as an essentially sceptical world that had had its beginnings in the
eighteenth century, was on the verge of coming to an end:

> It seems to me, you lay your finger here on the heart of the world's
> maladies, when you call it a Sceptical World. An insincere world;
> a godless untruth of a world! It is out of this, as I consider, that the
> whole tribe of social pestilences, French Revolutions, Chartism,
> and what not, have derived their being, their chief necessity to be.
> This must alter. Till this alters, nothing can beneficially alter. My
> one hope of the world, my inexpugnable consolation in looking at
> the miseries of the world, is that this is altering. . . . I prophesy that
> the world will once more become *sincere*; a believing world: with
> *many* Heroes in it, a heroic world! It will then be a victorious
> world; never till then!   (III, 144)

In effect the whole of *Past and Present* is an extended meditation on
the puzzling and paradoxical implications of this diagnosis. It would
seem that the upsurge of popular radicalism in France and in the
phenomenon of Chartism in England is nothing more than an aberration in the course of world history that must *necessarily* be corrected if only because the alternative is so intolerable. Yet no one
insisted more than Carlyle on the fact that the French Revolution and
Chartism were *realities* that could not simply be brushed aside, and
in *Past and Present* he translated this into the claim that Englishmen
were living through a wholly new cultural epoch whose demands
were such as to make action absolutely imperative and to make the
arguments of a cultural conservatism of the type that Carlyle in
general approves of finally irrelevant:

> It is true the English Legislature, like the English People, is of
> slow temper; essentially conservative. In our wildest periods of
> reform, in the Long Parliament itself, you notice always the invin-
> cible instinct to hold fast by the Old; to admit the *minimum* of New;
> to expand, if it be possible, some old habit or method, already

found fruitful, into new growth for the new need. It is an instinct worthy of all honour; asking to all strength and all wisdom. The Future hereby is not dissevered from the Past, but based continuously on it; grows with all the vitalities of the Past, and is rooted down deep into the beginnings of us. The English Legislature is entirely repugnant to believe in 'new epochs.' The English legislature does not occupy itself with epochs; has, indeed, other business to do than looking at the Time-Horologue and hear it tick! Nevertheless new epochs do actually come; and with them new imperious peremptory necessities; so that even an English Legislature has to look up, and admit, though with reluctance, that the hour has struck.   (II, 225–6)

Precisely what gives this utterance its prophetic urgency is its insistence that while tradition may well have served its purpose, its moment is now past; Burkean conservatism is thus no longer an available option. Moreover Carlyle denies the whole gradualist scenario put forward by the proponents of England's Saxon traditions. He is nothing if not the prophet of discontinuity even as he laments the circumstances that force him to propound it. The old ways are gone – and even if they were not, they still would not meet the situation. So that what Carlyle is calling for with one voice, is what with another voice he proclaims to be impossible. Moreover since the processes of history are finally inscrutable and beyond the powers of reason to control, it follows that the task of changing things again once they have changed becomes at once a necessity and an insoluble conundrum. Thus, in the comments from *On Heroes and Hero-Worship* quoted above, he insists again and again that the world as it is must alter and he claims to see signs that it is altering, yet finally the belief that this is so is only the desperate conviction on Carlyle's part that it must be so if only because the alternative is so unthinkable. Nevertheless the relentless circularity of the whole argumentative procedure becomes inescapable when Carlyle proclaims that a believing world and a sincere world will be a victorious world and never before; when he himself knows better than anyone that you cannot just go back to an unselfconscious, unquestioning, unproblematic faith when that is exactly what you do not possess. Carlyle seeks to reimpose a cyclical pattern of faith–scepticism–faith on an unstable, unpredictable diachronic development whose very uncertainty is the ground of the apocalyptic utterance.

The abrupt and perpetual shifts of focus that are such a characteristic feature of Carlyle's style in *Past and Present* become expressive of his insatiable desire to explore the contemporary situation from every conceivable angle and to refuse to remain trapped within a single perspective. Carlyle worries away at the problem like a dog with a bone, but the more he worries the more intractable it seems. Like Shakespeare's Owen Glendower he would like to summon spirits from the vasty deep that would have the power to set the world to rights, but he doubts both his power to summon them and their power, when so summoned, to make the crooked straight. In Carlyle's theory of history the hero is crucial, since only the hero, a charismatic religious leader such as Mahomet, has the ability to restore what is absent and give the people the living faith that they lack. The lesson of the French Revolution would seem to be that in the modern age such a task has become impossibly Sisyphean. Again, it behoves the aristocracy to justify their privileges by assuming the constructive leadership of society as they once did in the past: 'Soldiering, Police and Judging, Church-Extension, nay real Government and Guidance, all this was actually *done* by the Holders of the Land in return for their Land. How much of it is now done by them; done by anybody?' (II, 206), but Carlyle well knows that they are not likely to abandon their fox-hunting or the preserving of their game just because he insists that for them the writing is already on the wall. His peremptorary injunction 'Descend, O Donothing Pomp; quit they down-cushions; expose thyself to learn what wretches think and feel' (II, 152) will certainly fall on deaf ears. It would be easier for Carlyle to bring back Abbot Samson than bring back King Lear. Carlyle therefore recognises that he has no recourse but to fall back on the 'working aristocracy' of factory owners and industrialists if his dream of a society of heroes is to be realised. Yet Carlyle knows that there are problems here too since the commercial classes are devoted to the gospel of Mammon and the heartless creed of *laissez-faire*; their sights are set on joining the leisure class as rapidly as possible. The moral distinction that he makes between them and the idle aristocracy is thus likely to be very short-lived. So his appeal to them to restore the fallen world must be something of a desperate, last-resort appeal, based only on his own unshakeable conviction that the hour is late and that therefore something simply *must* be done:

> Captains of Industry are the true Fighters, henceforth recognisable as the only true ones: Fighters against Chaos, Necessity and the

Devils and Jotuns; and lead Mankind in that great, and alone true, and universal warfare; the stars in their courses fighting for them, and all Heaven and all Earth saying audibly, Well done! Let the Captains of Industry retire into their own hearts and ask solemnly, If there is nothing but vulturous hunger, for fine wines, valet reputation and gilt carriages, discoverable there? Of hearts made by the Almighty God I will not believe such a thing. Deep-hidden under wretchedest god-forgetting Cants, Epicurisms, Dead-Sea Apisms; forgotten as under foulest Lethe mud and weeds, there is yet, in all hearts born into this God's World, a spark of the Godlike slumbering. Awake, O nightmare sleepers; awake, arise, or be forever fallen! This is not playhouse poetry; it is sober fact. Our England, our world cannot live as it is. (II, 228–9)

From this it is apparent that there has been a significant switch in Carlyle's general sympathies even since the writing of *Chartism*. In that work and in *Sartor* Carlyle had associated most of the evils of contemporary society with the rise of industrialism – it was this that had turned the world into one vast, godless, soulless steam-engine. But now, although in no way going back on this general indictment, Carlyle began to see matters rather differently. *Past and Present*, like its predecessors, was very much a response to contemporary events and the early 1840s were dominated by two issues in particular: the demand for the repeal of the Corn Laws and the apparent threat posed by Roman Catholicism in the wake of the appointment of Wiseman as Cardinal for England and the defection of Newman to Rome. Although retrospectively it might seem that Newman's desire to restore to the English church a clear and unquestioning faith was very similar to that of Carlyle, Carlyle's low-church hostility to ritual and images meant that he was not prepared to acknowledge the existence of any common ground. On the contrary, he regarded Puseyism as part of the problem. Just as England was afflicted with a sham aristocracy that buried its head in the sand instead of exercising positive leadership and was setting its face against any repeal of the Corn Laws despite the urgent necessity of so doing, so Carlyle was convinced that the doctrines of Newman and his followers were utterly irrelevant to the situation that England was in. The Tractarians were fiddling while England was burning:

but of our Dilettantisms, and galvanised Dilettantisms; of Puseyism, in comparison to Twelfth-Century Catholicism? Little or nothing;

for indeed it is a matter to strike one dumb. . . . That certain human souls, living on the practical Earth, should think to save themselves and a ruined world by noisy theoretic demonstrations and laudations of *the* church, instead of some unnoisy, unconscious, but *practical*, total heart-and-soul demonstration of *a* Church: this, in the circle of revolving ages, this also was a thing we were to see. (II, 99)

For Carlyle Tractarianism represented arid, unprofitable speculation when what was required was strong and effective action – had the Tractarians been monks at St Edmundbury they would have been just the sort of people that Abbot Samson would have had to sort out.

So by comparison with a deaf and self-deluding aristocracy and posturing Puseyism, Carlyle saw positive virtues both in an energetic millocracy, even if dedicated to Mammon, and even in their Benthamite creed. It was in its own way heroic – even if it was 'a Heroism with its *eyes* put out' (III, 142). As Carlyle perceived it, Benthamite Utilitarianism was almost the necessary precondition for a renewal of faith, since if nothing else it was a relentless destroyer of shams and illusions – the problem with it was that it had nothing constructive to put in their place. Nevertheless industrialism and Utilitarianism, by the very bleakness and inhospitability of their vision of human situation, at least compel the world in the direction of something better; they offer the prospect of progress through dialectic and of hope through the very negation of hope, whereas those who live by illusions can remain in thrall of them indefinitely. What Carlyle admired about the twelfth century world of Abbot Samson was its clarity and simplicity – you really knew where you were: 'Monachism, Feudalism, with a real King Plantagenet, with real Abbots Samson, and their other living realities, how blessed!' (II, 109). By contrast for Carlyle the modern world was most aptly represented by the seven-foot-high lath and plaster hat that could be seen being wheeled through the streets of London but which served to supplant honest craftmanship and the making of real hats with grotesque simulacra. The problem was how to restore the world to the fullness, integrity and plenitude that it had once possessed – what was required was something very like the fairy-tale magic that had transformed Cinderella's pumpkin into a golden coach. Carlyle frankly conceded that he had no simple remedy, no 'Morrison's Pill', but in so saying he meant more than that he would not be drawn into peddling such solutions as emigration or instruction in the alphabet, he was also conceding that he was extremely pessimistic about his own chances of affecting the situation through the written word. In the same breath as he is proclaiming 'Awake ye noble workers' (II, 231) he is confessing: 'Certainly it were a fond imagination to expect any preaching of mine could abate Mammonism' (II, 247). Of course, Carlyle claims that divine providence will bring this about anyway but it is still a curious admission in view of the fact that *Past and Present* is a work of continuous and strenuous exhortation, if ever there was one, and it is also unexpected in view of Carlyle's pronouncement in *On Heroes and Hero-worship* of the previous year, that 'of all Priesthoods, Aristocracies, governing classes at present extant in the world there is no class comparable for importance to that Priesthood of the Writers of Books' (III, 138). But now as Carlyle meditated on the image of Abbot Samson and praised deeds at the expense of words, the gap between the real and ideal seemed wider than ever and his own powers of language had the perverse effect of seeming to make it more impassible, rather than bridging it as he desired.

In *Past and Present* Carlyle now looked to the millocracy rather than the landed gentry to provide the leadership that he believed England required, yet it was in the ranks of the Conservative Party that he came closest to exercising a direct political influence, and it was Benjamin Disraeli, who was neither an industrialist nor a member of the established aristocracy, who took on board Carlyle's notion that government must address itself to the needs and welfare of the common people. In *Coningsby* (1844) and *Sybil* (1846) Disraeli simultaneously addressed the Condition of England question as adumbrated by Carlyle and, at the same time, combined this with a Tory alternative to Macaulay's Whig interpretation of history, which presented the history of England since 1688 not as the history of progress but as a narrative of social disintegration and moral collapse. Yet the story also had to be traced back, beyond 1688, for, in the footsteps of Cobbett, Disraeli saw in the Reformation and the Dissolution of the monasteries the originary moment from which stemmed all the distresses of the modern world.

The monasteries had been centres of goodness and piety in English culture, for the monks as well as being noble builders of churches and undemanding landlords had also been genuinely concerned with the spiritual welfare of the people. They were replaced by a rapacious and self-centred breed of upstart nobles who neglected the people, challenged the power of the king and thought of Parliament simply as an instrument for their own power and enrichment. The rebellion of 1640 and the execution of Charles I, the legitimate monarch, had led to a Venetian form of government after 1688 under which English was actually ruled by a tightly knit cabal of Whig magnificoes, while the sovereign was rendered as impotent as a Venetian doge. A further twist is that the Tory Party itself, which should defend the rights both of king and people, had done all too little to rectify the situation. The administration of Lord Liverpool, 'The Arch-Mediocrity', which lasted from 1812 to 1827, did nothing, when by introducing effective measures in respect of Ireland, the franchise and trade it could have forestalled the current wave of agitation. The administration of Duke of Wellington fared no better since the Duke had no real understanding of the situation that he was faced with or any consistent policy with which to tackle it. By his high-handed and opportunist conduct he had only succeeded in wrecking his party. Now Sir Robert Peel in seeking to rebuild it offers only, in his Tamworth Manifesto 'an attempt to create a party without principles'. Moreover, because of the adroitness of the Whigs in passing the Reform Bill of 1832 there is a likelihood that the Tory Party will again face a long period of exclusion from effective power. Symptomatic of its decline is the fact that in *Coningsby* Buckhurst, one of Coningsby's Etonian friends, wins the parliamentary election in Cambridge for the Conservatives yet immediately after his election confesses that he does not know what the Conservatives cause is – to which his friends ironically reply:

'Why, it is the cause of our glorious institutions,' said Coningsby. 'A Crown robbed of its prerogatives; a church controlled by a commission; and an Aristocracy that does not lead.'

'Under whose genial influence the order of the Peasantry, "a country's pride," has vanished from the face of the land,' said Henry Sydney, 'and it is succeeded by a race of serfs, who are called labourers, and who burn ricks.'

'Under which,' continued Coningsby, 'the Crown has become a cipher; the Church a sect; the nobility drones; and the People drudges.'

The moral collapse of the Conservative Party is an especially serious matter since if they do not represent the idea of 'a free Monarchy and a privileged and prosperous People', there is no one else who will.

In this emergency Disraeli believes that what is required is a rebuilding of the Conservative Party on firm and explicit principles by a young and idealistic 'new generation', which will also necessitate an equally explicit repudiation of the opportunism of the Tory old-guard. In place of sects and factionalism there must be national unity and a concern for the general welfare, which also implies reform in the Church of England, for 'the Church is the medium by which the despised and degraded classes assert the native equality of man, and vindicate the rights and power of intellect'. In place of short-sightedness and selfishness England must be regenerated by a saving aristocratic remnant who will have both the courage and the vision to realise for their country a nobler destiny. But Disraeli concludes *Coningsby* with the marriage of the eponymous hero to the beautiful and gifted Sybil on a note of perplexity and interrogation that owes more than a little to Carlyle:

> Will they maintain in august assemblies and high places the great truths which, in study and in solitude, they have embraced? Or will their courage exhaust itself in the struggle, their enthusiasm evaporate before hollow-hearted ridicule, their generous impulses yield with a vulgar catastrophe to the tawdry temptations of low ambitions?. . . Or will they remain brave, single, and true; refuse to bow before shadows and worship phrases; sensible of the greatness of their position, recognise the greatness of their duties; denounce to a perplexed and disheartened world the frigid theories of a generalising age that have destroyed the individuality of man, and restore the happiness of their country by believing in their own energies, and daring to be great?

The idealistic and somewhat rarefied political speculation of *Coningsby* is replaced in *Sybil* by a much closer look at the conditions of the working class and of the sufferings and injustices that have led to the development of Chartism. For Disraeli Chartism is more the symptom of a general *malaise* in English society than a fundamental set of political demands, and more than part of the reason why he focuses so sharply on the injustices of the 'tommy' system – by which the workers are forced to buy food from their employer at inflated prices – is that this suggests that their real grievances are economic. In the Rising Sun tavern Juggins complains:

> 'We had a Chartist here the other day, but he did not understand our case at all.'
> 'I heard him,' said Master Nixon, 'but what's his Five Points to us? Why he ayn't got tommy among them.'
> 'Nor long stints,' said Waghorn.
> 'Nor butties,' said Juggins.

In order to dramatise his own political philosophy Disraeli filters the whole issue of class conflict and of the division of England into two nations, rich and poor, through a romantic historiography based on Scott's *Ivanhoe* in which the poor are perceived as Saxons groaning under an oppressive 'Norman' yoke.

Sybil, as the radiant symbol of a noble but downtrodden race that will ultimately be restored to its rightful inheritance, is linked with the figure of Queen Victoria, who has 'the blood and the beauty of the Saxon' and whose destiny is to 'bring relief to suffering millions' and to break 'the last links in the chain of Saxon thraldom'. *Sybil* is thus a myth of usurpation and of the eventual restoration of legitimacy, and its somewhat contorted plot needs to be seen in this light. What was once the beautiful picturesque structure of Marney Abbey is now the stately home of Lord Marney, the elder brother of the hero Charles Egremont, a man who is 'cynical, devoid of sentiment, arrogant, literal, hard'. Lord Marney pretends that his workers can manage on eight shillings a week and even objects to their being given beer money or allotments. He keeps down the population by refusing to build cottages and by destroying others. When pressed he invokes emigration as the only possible solution. The unreality of this section of the aristocracy is dramatised by the fact that on the very occasion when the clergyman Mr St Lys is arguing the hardships of the poor, Lord Mowbray can say to Lady Marney: 'Oh! how I envy you at Marney. No manufactures, no smoke, living in the midst of a beautiful park and surrounded by a contented peasantry.'

A similar usurpation of right and tradition has also occurred at Mowbray Castle, which is now ruled by the descendants of a valet called Warren, who became an Indian nabob, and who are now known as the Fitz-Warenes. The title rightfully belongs to Walter Gerard, Sybil's father, who comes from an old Saxon family and who has become a supporter of the rights of the common people. Egremont, who is similarly wedded to their cause, nevertheless believes that it can only be advanced by the aristocracy, since popular democracy can only lead to factions and the chaos of mob rule. This view is vindicated in the novel's melodramatic denouement. A huge crowd led by the violent and uncouth 'Bishop' Hatton, bearing a large hammer, assembles to attack the factory of Trafford, a progressive and enlightened mill-owner, but when Gerard persuades them that he is their friend, they march on Mowbray Castle instead. In this assault Gerard is killed, Sybil is rescued by Egremont and documents are discovered that vindicate Gerard's claim to the castle itself. In the marriage of Egremont and Sybil, rich and poor, Saxon and Norman are united, while both Marney Abbey and Mowbray Castle are restored to a legitimate and caring rule, in which the spirit of the monastic past will be revived. This preposterous apotheosis makes the unreality of Disraeli's whole programme embarrassingly obvious – although his belief that the Conservative Party would have ultimately to be something more than the party of privilege, that it would have to learn to speak for the whole nation, was to be triumphantly vindicated. If Disraeli's often impressive political vision is driven by an idiosyncratic view of English history it would be difficult to claim that it was necessarily more whimsical than anybody else's!

Nevertheless, by comparison with Disraeli, Elizabeth Gaskell's sense of the English past and the English present strikes one both as more localised in space and time, and as much more securely grounded. For Gaskell the new industrial society in whose name the classical economists sought to redefine England was undoubtedly an ominous portent and she had great difficulty in accommodating it within the parameters of the old. For while she recognises that the great factories of the north of England and the collective ways of living with which they are associated are a great fact – as Carlyle would say – with which it is impossible to argue, she is nevertheless disturbed at the evident discontinuity with the old. It seems symptomatic that, after having first published *Mary Barton* (1848), which frankly records the ferocity of class conflict and class antagonism in industrial Manchester, she should have turned in her second book, *Cranford* (1853), to a small English country town where nothing very much ever happens and, which, as it is ruled by women, is characterised by the avoidance of extremes. Gaskell knew that England was undergoing dramatic changes but in *Cranford* – and this undoubtedly explains the work's enduring popularity – she painted a delightful picture of a provincial world in which the old ways were lovingly and almost unconsciously perpetuated and which, though undoubtedly affected by the modern, nevertheless displayed an extraordinary power to survive it. Although allusions in *Cranford* to *The Pickwick Papers*, the passing of Catholic Emancipation and Tennyson's 'Locksley Hall' locate the action of the novel in the 1830s and 1840s, the chronological focus dissolves and references back, together with the general archaism of Cranford conduct, suggest a world in which the eighteenth century is effortlessly extended into the nineteenth. The *St James' Chronicle* is required reading. Johnson's essays in *The Rambler* provide a model for literary style, and Lord Chesterfield's letters for social behaviour. The ladies are addicted to old-fashioned brooches and to a variety of anachronistic headgear from jockey caps and turbans to calashes, while Captain Brown, whose espousal of *Pickwick* seems to mark him as a modern, nevertheless wears a curly Brutus wig of a sort that has long since become out of date. At the august Mrs Jameson's, where Preference, Ombre and Quadrille are played against a backdrop of Louis Seize furniture, the sense of having become stuck in a timewarp is particularly overpowering, yet even this pales before the antique stateliness of the sedan-chair that is still in use, borne by some elderly chairmen, who abandon their regular trade of shoemaker to dress up in 'a strange old livery – long great-coats, with small capes, coeval with the sedan and similar to the dress of the class in Hogarth's pictures'.

It is therefore only to be expected that the modern commercial world, in so far as it reaches *Cranford*, should have the most serious consequences: tragedy strikes when Captain Brown, the ladies' favourite, is killed by a train, and again when old Miss Matty, who has never done anyone any harm, loses all her savings in the failure of the Town and Country Bank. Yet what the novel stresses is the way in which these rents in the fabric of domestic life are nevertheless repaired. For the other disaster in the book concerns Peter, Miss Matty's brother, who is so incensed at the beating he receives from his father for dressing up as a woman that he leaves for India, eventually becoming a lieutenant in the army. By returning quite unexpectedly, like the prodigal son, Peter fills up all the gaps that have been created, for he also becomes the ladies' favourite in place of Captain Brown and at the same time restores the fortunes of his sister. At the end of *Cranford* all the 'old friendly sociability' has been restored and it is almost as if the nineteenth century had never happened.

Of course, *Cranford* is a consciously retrospective work just as the concern of *Mary Barton* with strikes and industrial unrest is aggressively modern, yet throughout *Mary Barton* the traces of an earlier way of life persist as a silent reproach to the brutal and unyielding present. It is significant that the novel is framed by images of the peace and contentment of rural life: it opens not in the city of Manchester itself but in Green Heys Fields outside the city where an old black and white farmhouse 'speaks of other times and occupations than those which now absorb the population of the neighbourhood', and it closes with Mary Barton and her husband Jem starting their new life in Canada in a cottage that possesses both a garden and an orchard, surrounded by the beautiful foliage of autumn. In *Mary Barton* the city is a kind of nightmare from which it seems impossible to awake, so remorseless is the pressure it imposes, so that although the decision of Mary and Jem to emigrate might seem a terrible indictment of the system under which they have struggled to live, it also figures as a blessed release. For old Alice Wilson the city is explicitly a place of exile. She still carries on cooking her north-country recipes of clapbread and oatbread, she gathers from the fields medicinal herbs as she had formerly done at home but she never ceases to think of her birthplace, which she remembers as 'the golden hills of heaven':

> Eh, lasses! ye don't know what rocks are in Manchester! Gray pieces o'stone as large as a house, all covered over wi' moss of different colours, some yellow, some brown; and the ground beneath them knee-high in purple heather, smelling sae sweet and fragrant, and the low music of the humming bee for ever sounding among it. Mother used to send Sally and me out to gather ling and heather for besoms, and it was such pleasant work! We used to come home of an evening loaded so as you could not see us, for all that it was light to carry. And then mother would make us sit down under the old hawthorn tree (where we used to make our house among the great roots that stood above the ground), to pick and tie the heather. It all seems like yesterday, and yet its a long long time agone. . . . I sicken at heart to see the old spot once again.

Alice lives in the city and dies without ever returning to her rural birthplace, yet she is so wrapped up in her memories it is as if to her Manchester itself is unreal. So it is Mary and Jem, the survivors, who are finally able to realise a dream of freedom and space that has been denied to all the others. The city is a place of pollution, confinement and repetition where the spirit, little by little, is broken and reduced to silence:

> the next evening it was a warm, pattering, incessant rain, just the rain to waken up the flowers. But in Manchester, where, alas! there are no flowers, the rain had only a disheartening and gloomy effect; the streets were wet and dirty, the drippings from the houses were wet and dirty, and the people were wet and dirty. Indeed, most kept within-doors; and there was an unusual silence of footsteps in the little paved courts.

In the city hope itself becomes a mockery. Old Job Legh, from an earlier generation, tells Mary Barton how, after his daughter and her husband died in London, with his friend Jennings he struggled all the way back to Birmingham and Manchester with their tiny baby. When they are utterly exhausted and the baby has grown extremely weak they are thankful when a kindly woman takes them into her cottage and nurses and cares for the baby despite her husband's disapproval. Job quotes an old proverb: 'Th' longest lane will have a turning.' Yet now times are changed for only a few pages later Mrs Gaskell insists that such wisdom no longer possesses the power to console or even convince:

> In times of sorrowful or fierce endurance, we are often soothed by the mere repetition of old proverbs which tell the experience of our forefathers; but now 'it's a long lane that has no turning,' 'the weariest day draws to an end,' &c., seemed false and vain sayings, so long and weary was the pressure of the terrible times.

The experiences of the 1830s and 1840s are unprecedented and life as it is lived in Manchester in these decades is certainly very different from Cranford. Moreover, although Mrs Gaskell could be sentimental, we should not underrate her achievement in writing so directly about the sufferings of the industrial working class or in presenting them as fellow human beings. Even Charlotte Brontë in *Shirley* (1849), despite the possibility of greater detachment that the context of the Luddite riots of 1811–12 afforded, could only present the underclass as a faceless mob manipulated by unscrupulous outside agitators. The effort of imagination required to see things from the other side of the class conflict was considerable.

Thus when Mrs Gaskell subtitles *Mary Barton* 'A Tale of Manchester Life' we must recognise that what she has in mind is a depiction of conditions in Manchester that will bring home to the reader just how warped and unnatural those conditions are. The event that she chooses to dramatise the nature of the new order is the fire at Carsons' mill. By any standards the fire at the mill is a traumatic event for the mill is a large, imposing structure that dominates the surrounding neighbourhood and the 'magnificent terrible flames' are being fanned by powerful winds. Two men are trapped inside and face almost certain death but they are rescued and carried across a ladder into a window on the other side of the street. Yet far from the fire being a disaster it is, as far the owners are concerned, actually a blessing:

> They were well insured; the machinery lacked the improvements of late years, and worked but poorly in comparison with that which might now be procured. Above all, trade was very slack; cotton could find no market, and goods lay packed and piled in many a warehouse. The mills were merely worked to keep the machinery, human and metal, in some kind of order and readiness for better times. So this was an excellent time, Messrs Carson thought, for refitting their factory with first-rate improvements, for which the insurance money would amply pay. They were in no hurry about the business, however. The weekly drain of wages given for labour, useless in the present state of the market, was stopped. The partners had more leisure than they had known for years.

This description introduces many paradoxes about the capitalist system which the book addresses. The men are simply regarded as a resource that is necessary for industrial production, and if they are out of work then the question as to how they are to survive until trade picks up again is scarcely one that concerns the mill-owners, who, for their part, are quite happy to cut costs and mark time. In another cultural situation an event such as the fire would have united the community, yet here it intensifies still further the divide between the workers and the employers. The fire in its implacable destructiveness seems to inaugurate a new era in which compassion and human solidarity can have no place. In the calculations of the Carsons the fact that their workers are actually starving scarcely signifies. It is in the light of this that we must therefore view their subsequent arguments and behaviour.

As Mrs Gaskell sees it, England has entered a new age in which the old Christian values have broken down and in which the lack of humanity that the employers and the ruling class display is echoed in the bitterness, violence and frustration of the men who face a world that offers them no prospect of amelioration or hope. The workers start out by believing that their cause is so just, their case so clear that it is unthinkable that no one will listen to them. John Barton starts out believing that the Chartists' march on London will evoke a positive response: 'yo see now, if better times don't come after Parliament knows all', but he is soon to be disillusioned. For in London they have no conception of the depths of distress and poverty that people are facing in the industrial cities, and the marchers are reprimanded for distressing the carriage horses that 'were too fat to move quick; they'n never known want o' food, one might tell by their sleek coats'.

The Chartists are ignored, derided and laughed at. The strikers face a similar inhumanity in Manchester when young Harry Carson, who leads those among the masters who are determined to take a tough line, not only refuses to pay the men a living wage but mocks their poverty by drawing a caricature of them as 'lank, ragged, dispirited and famine-stricken' with his silver pencil. In this way he demonstrates that, fortified by the self-righteous 'wisdom' of classical economics, he has lost even the last vestige of human feeling and compassion. It is in this light that we must view Mrs Gaskell's apparently condescending depiction of the common people as Frankenstein:

> The people rise up to life; they irritate us, they terrify us, and we become their enemies. Then, in the sorrowful moment of our triumphant power, their eyes gaze on us with a mute reproach. Why have we made them what they are; a powerful monster, yet without the inner means for peace and happiness.

By this she means the masters have made the workers into a threatening, ominous presence by refusing to acknowledge their legitimate interests and needs; it is they who have created a situation that must necessarily lead to the 'monster's' revenge.

Mrs Gaskell shows that John Barton is a good, noble and idealistic person who places the interests of others before himself but who in the depths of his despair and bitterness is led to reject his wife's sister Esther, to strike his own daughter Mary and finally to kill Harry Carson on a mandate from the union. Mrs Gaskell is certain

that John Barton's act is morally wrong but she also strongly suggests that Harry Carson's behaviour is so criminally irresponsible
that it is as if he has brought this retribution on his own head; like
Frankenstein he has been utterly indifferent to the consequences of
his own actions but he had met with retribution just the same. In the
final scenes of the book it is ostensibly John Barton who is the great
sinner and old Mr Carson, Harry's father, the one who forgives, but
precisely because Mr Carson has been implacably opposed to any
idea of forgiveness his gesture of holding the dying Barton in his
arms seems more a gesture of *submission* – a recognition that it is
actually he and his family who have been in the wrong. It has been
their denial of the Christian spirit of charity that has provoked the
violence and it is only through a return to Christian values and a
recognition of the rights and dignity of others that peace can finally
come. The deepest dislocation of the city is spiritual.

The appeal to Christian values is also prominent in Charles
Kingsley's novel of the Chartist moment, *Alton Locke* (1850), but the
argument of the novel is more tortured and fraught with perplexity
precisely because Kingsley, a clergyman of twenty-nine when he
wrote it, is very far from being sure what Christian values are. The
only thing he is clear about is that in mid-Victorian England they
only exist as hypocrisy and sham. Kingsley was prompted to write
Alton Locke by Henry Mayhew's articles describing the terrible
poverty and exploitation that existed in the London clothing trades,
and through the book's vivid depiction of outcast London alone it
easily eclipses Kingsley's earlier and rather faltering essay in the
Disraelian manner, *Yeast*. On the face of it *Alton Locke* is a wayward
and eccentric work in which we are jerked from the slums of the
city to the pleasures of undergraduate Cambridge; from rural rick-
burning to elaborate descriptions of the working-class poet's dreams,
in which he figures as crab, ape and mylodon; from disquisitions on
Tractarianism to lectures on art. And yet the book nevertheless
carries a strange and impressive conviction. In writing *Alton Locke*
and in thus identifying himself with Chartism and working-class
protest, Kingsley showed considerable intellectual and moral courage, for to a person like himself these subjects were effectively taboo.
Alton Locke is genuinely disconcerting precisely because Kingsley
cannot help revealing that he does not have any answers, because he
is unable to resolve the issues that the novel poses in the way that
Disraeli and Mrs Gaskell more or less manage to do. Disraeli's more
masterful and leisurely style in *Sybil* means that although we are

made conscious of the existence of two nations we move from one to another down magnificent spiralling staircases that give the existence of these levels a certain inevitability. With Mrs Gaskell the vivid depiction of provincial Manchester makes it possible for us to think of the problem as a local one and one that can be resolved with goodwill on both sides, whereas the shifts and juxtapositions of *Alton Locke* are positively surreal and show the undoubted influence of De Quincey, who was not just an opium eater but one of the first recorders of outcast London. Nothing is more brilliant than the moment in the novel when Mr Mackaye, the old bookseller who has become Alton's patron and mentor, insists that he must write not of tropical islands but of the world immediately around him:

'. . . why, if God had meant you to write anant Pacifics, he'd ha put you there – and because He means ye to write about London town. He's put you there – and gien ye an unco sharp taste o'the ways o't; and I'll gie ye anither. Come along wi' me.'
  And he seized me by the arm, and hardly giving me time to put on my hat, marched me out into the streets, and away through Clare Market to St Giles.
  It was a foul, chilly, foggy Saturday night. From the butchers' and greengrocers' shops the gas-lights flared and flickered, wild and ghastly, over haggard groups of slip-shod dirty women, bargaining for scraps of stale meat and frostbitten vegetables, wrangling about short weight and bad quality. Fish-stalls and fruit-stalls lined the edge of the greasy pavement, sending up odours as foul as the language of sellers and buyers. Blood and sewer-water crawled from under doors and out of spouts, and reeked down the gutters among offal, animal and vegetable, in every stage of putrefaction. Foul vapours rose from cowsheds and slaughter-houses, and the doorways of undrained alleys, where the inhabitants carried the filth out in their shoes from the back-yard into the court, and from the court up into the main street; while above, hanging like cliffs over the streets – those narrow, brawling torrents of filth, and poverty, and sin – the houses with their teeming load of life were piled up into the dingy choking night. A ghastly, deafening, sickening sight it was. Go, scented Belgravian! and see what London is!

The description is doubly shocking since in describing the conditions in which Alton Locke lives and works Kingsley might be thought to have descended far enough into the London underworld so that to open up abysses far below this is positively disturbing. But Kingsley is not content with this and heightens the reader's sense of unease still further by actually suggesting that this is appropriate subject matter for poetry. Kingsley subsequently suggests that it is characteristic of the age to find 'poetry in common things' but the imperative that drives him to confront his audience with those aspects of their society that they conveniently overlook clearly suggests a dissatisfaction with the traditional aesthetic categories, for certainly the feeling of nausea played no part in the aesthetics of Aristotle or Kant. Kingsley realised much more clearly than most of his contemporaries that the world of the modern city was such as to render all traditional and moral categories problematic. For the city, terrible as it is with its 'endless prison-walls of brick, beneath a lurid crushing sky of smoke and mist', nevertheless seems the only site of hope and renewal 'where man meets man, and spirit quickens spirit, and intercourse breeds knowledge, and knowledge sympathy, and sympathy enthusiasm, combination, power irresistible'. On this latter characterisation Kingsley immediately comments 'Such was our Babel-tower, whose top should reach heaven', but Kingsley himself could see that England could not possibly remain as such an intolerably Dantesque world and in the face of it the only consolation must be that eventually some good may come out of it. The city necessarily sharpens spiritual values because it is there that the contrast between matter and spirit is most dramatically realised.

Alton Locke significantly differs from both *Sybil* and *Mary Barton* in the fact that it seriously questions the whole paternalist framework, the general assumption that what is needed above all is a better relationship between aristocracy and people, between masters and men. Kingsley's radicalism is the more striking because *Alton Locke*, like *Yeast*, was heavily influenced by Carlyle and by *Chartism* in particular, which would have made it so much more probable that Kingsley would insist that the onus was on the upper classes to adopt a more humane and morally responsible attitude. Yet, as a Christian – though the parenthesis is by no means inevitable – Kingsley recognised that any attempt on the part of the privileged classes to legislate for and control the working classes would be morally suspect: as free individuals they must be allowed to work out their own destiny. So Kingsley's decision to write *Alton Locke* from the point of view of a working man *was* radical because it meant that it had to consider his hero as a self-determining and

developing human being, who would be brought to question his
social superiors and even to rebel against their well-meaning but
ultimately self-interested altruistic gestures. When the Dean decides
to take Alton Locke up as representing all that is worthiest among
the humbler classes of society, Kingsley is acutely aware that such
patronage carries with it severe penalties and that the first casualty
will be the loss of Locke's integrity and independence. Alton Locke
will have to accept that from henceforth his destiny will be determined by someone else – it was taken for granted 'that I felt myself
exceedingly honoured, and must consider it, as a matter of course,
the greatest possible stretch of kindness thus to talk me over, and
settle everything for me, as if I were not a living soul, but a plant in
a pot'.

The nature of the contract between them is such that Alton Locke
is asked to renounce his hostility to the upper classes and his political radicalism in return for the assurance that he will, in consequence, achieve a position commensurate with his abilities. The
Dean insists that political quietism is the precondition for his acceptance in society:

> Now, recollect; if it should be hereafter in our power to assist your
> prospects in life, you must give up, once and for all the bitter tone
> against the higher classes, which I am sorry to see in your MSS.
> . . . Avoid politics; the workman has no more to do with them than
> the clergyman.

Alton Locke defends the validity of political poetry but he succumbs
to the pressure that is put upon him and agrees to publish his poetry
in a heavily censored form in which all political references are removed. In his portrayal of Alton Locke's development Kingsley
shows that self-realisation is a much more complex project than
either Goethe or Carlyle would be prepared to recognise, because
although on the one hand there is a conception of *Bildung* in which
Alton Locke aspires to 'higher things' through his love of such
pictures as Guido Reni's *St Sebastian* and Raphael's *Miraculous Draught
of the Fishes* and his delight in the poetry of Tennyson, Kingsley
clearly grasps that such an aesthetic education carries with it a wilful
blindness towards the real oppressions of a class society. As Alton
rises in the world he also becomes less because he has compromised
his own integrity and lost sight of the social injustices that it is his
God-given mission to address.

The problem Kingsley faces is that the more truthfully, the more powerfully and the more honestly he addresses the condition of the people and the failure of the ruling class even to acknowledge the existence of such widespread misery, the more problematic does his insistence on Christian values as the solution to the problem become. For the radical, egalitarian gospel he advocates is very far removed from the actual practice of the Church of England, as Kingsley himself is well aware. Thus to speak of Christianity as some kind of unified unproblematic creed – at a time when Anglicanism is being simultaneously challenged by Catholicism and Dissent – involves a kind of blinkered nostalgia, which in his more acute and lucid moments Kingsley would be the first to question. Indeed Kingsley himself provides a forceful statement of the continuing failure of the Anglican church seriously to address the most urgent issues and social problems of the day:

> Everywhere we see the clergy, with a few persecuted exceptions (like Dr Arnold), proclaiming themselves the advocates of Toryism, the dogged opponents of our political liberty, living either by the accursed system of pew-rents, or else by one which depends on the high price of corn; chosen exclusively from the classes who crush us down; prohibiting all free discussion on religious points; commanding us to swallow down, with faith as passive and implicit as that of the Papist, the very creeds from which their own bad example, and their scandalous neglect, have, in the last three generations, alienated us; never mixing with the thoughtful working men, except in the prison, the hospital, or in extreme old age betraying, in every tract, in every sermon, an ignorance of the doubts, the feelings, the very language of the masses, which would be ludicrous, were it not accursed before God and man.

But having displayed the depths of suspicion and incomprehension that divides the classes from one another, and having shown that Chartism represents a justified assertion by working people of their right to representation and autonomy, Kingsley, in the final pages, draws back from the conclusion that the class struggle is inevitable by transforming Alton Locke and his fellow Chartist Crossthwaite into the obedient disciples of the Christian doctrine of Lady Ellerton. This of course represents an appeal to the familiar argument that Christianity has not worked because it has never been tried. Given Kingsley's position in society such a conclusion was inevitable, but it seriously compromises what is a brave and often brilliant novel.

What characterises these novels of the 1840s is not just the fact that they deal with social unrest but that class divisions figure as part of a breakdown of any collective consensus as to what England is and represents, even leaving aside the fact that this 'England' necessarily suppresses any recognition of regional divisions. Just because England becomes such a thoroughly problematic, contested subject, claimed by landed aristocracy, industrialists and workers alike, and often defined in quite divergent ways, it has become that much more difficult to appeal to a sense of a common tradition or predicate some instinctive loyalty. Indeed it could well be argued that both the Great Exhibition of 1851 and the Crimean War were events around which a new sense of cultural identity could coalesce. Not the least significant aspect of the Exhibition was that in its mighty halls manufacturing industry symbolically won out; in the face of such a majestic display of technological power, paraded before all the world, it was simply no longer credible to think of England as an essentially rural nation, grounded in the power of the landed interest, even though the landed interest did in fact continue to exercise power. Symptomatic of this attempt to rethink England and to reconstruct it in terms that can give due weight to the traditional and the modern is Mrs Gaskell's *North and South* (1855). Crucially the novel begins with a moment of trauma and dislocation: Margaret Hale is forced to leave the idyllic rural village of Helstone for the smoky industrial town of Milton, because her father can no longer accept the Thirty-Nine Articles, and has to take up a post as private tutor to John Thornton, a prosperous mill-owner. The enforced and unexpected departure from Helstone is like an expulsion from paradise and it casts a long shadow over the development of the novel. Although Margaret's mother always complained about the unhealthy air of Helstone when she was there, her health takes a decided turn for the worst in Milton and the family believe that the move is the real reason for her illness and early death. Mr Hale himself soon follows. Margaret's early boast to Mr Lennox, 'I think Helstone is about as perfect a place in the world', is one that in exile she can derive no comfort from, and in Milton – in her bleak bedroom, looking out through the foggy, smoke-polluted air onto a blank wall immediately opposite – she becomes intensely homesick for her 'beautiful, beloved Helstone'. It seems that she has had to leave tranquil, unchanging Helstone for a world that is not only physically unattractive but one that is characterised by bitter and always potentially violent disputes between masters and men.

Nevertheless *North and South* insinuates that it is in the north that the future of England lies, and though the novel is concerned to work out the reconciliation of north and south it is as if in the process Helstone is subtly marginalised so that it is Milton that now seems to epitomise all that is best in England, in the strength, stubbornness and determination of its people. Although there is industrial conflict in *North and South* that comes to a climax in a scene where Margaret Hale is injured by a stone aimed for John Thornton, it becomes equally the moment from which all the participants in the scene must learn. Unlike John Barton, Nicholas Higgins the trade unionist never becomes totally embittered despite the fact that for a long while none of the mill-owners will give him work. Higgins has been opposed to violence in the strike and can scarcely forgive Boucher, another worker, for instigating it, yet when Boucher commits suicide Higgins insists on taking care of his children. Thornton, though initially an intransigent and somewhat self-righteous figure, nevertheless comes to see that the worker's have a point of view and tries to run his factory on more enlightened principles. The whole novel is consciously an Austenian study in the overcoming of pride and prejudice in which the characters are finally able to bring down the social and ideological barriers that separate them. At the end, the fact that Thornton and Margaret will marry and that her capital will enable him to restart his business, after financial failure, symbolises an England that will characterised by the union of opposites: energy and charity, compassion as well as strength. Yet for this ending to carry conviction it is essential that the spell of Helstone shall be exorcised. Towards the end of the book Margaret returns to her former home but finds that everything is changed and that it is now no longer as she remembered it. For a while she is confused and perplexed by the sense of living in a universe without stability or point of anchorage: 'A sense of change, of individual nothingness, of perplexity and disappointment overpowered Margaret. Nothing has been the same; and this slight, all-pervading instability, had given her greater pain than if all had been too entirely changed for her to recognise it.' But on reflection she concludes that such change, though disorientating, must nevertheless be faced and come to terms with: 'Looking out of myself and my own painful sense of change, the progress all around me is right and necessary.' Looking back has ultimately been illusion. There is no alternative but to face the future courageously.

3

The Menacing World: Dickens, Emily and Charlotte Brontë, and Thackeray

The beginnings of the Victorian novel are uneasy. The incipient turn from the esoteric world of the Gothic towards the depiction of a recognisable contemporary world is troubled and confused by the persistence of Gothic figures and by the perplexed recognition that the tradition of the eighteenth-century novel offers no real guidance on how to proceed. For the Augustan foundling was never far from the prospect of support, tutelage or relief. England then, it seemed, was a tranquil, essentially rural place, a land of small, pretty villages, smiling cornfields, winding country roads and cosy rustic inns, where the local squire, if sometimes given to the swearing of violent oaths, was essentially good natured and the vicar was beaming and bland.

Looking backward England seemed like a pretty safe place – but in the meantime England had changed. The obvious signs of this were glowing furnaces and factory chimneys belching smoke, and intense overcrowding in run-down urban areas – yet these were so clear and blatant as to be almost unproblematic. What produced a deeper sense of disquiet was precisely the feeling that somewhere along the way continuity had been lost and that, in consequence, in multifarious, unspecifiable ways, life had been altered for the worse. There were more obvious signs of poverty. Certainly there were more political disturbances and social unrest. London now seemed to be full of Irish labourers and political refugees. And wasn't it the case that many working people in towns and cities never went to church? Going by the newspapers there seemed to be much more crime – some of which seemed to represent not simply law-breaking but deliberate defiance of the law. Moreover outbreaks of typhoid and cholera showed that the conditions in which many people lived were not simply unhealthy but positively dangerous. So in some sense the reform movement and the novel have a common purpose: they share the belief that if this menacing world would come more clearly into focus so that problems could be identified and solved; moreover if this world were known and understood and its contours became familiar, it would also seem less threatening.

At the beginning of Bulwer Lytton's novel *Paul Clifford* (1830) a characteristic note of menace is struck, which simultaneously reflects the Gothic and the sinister potentiality of the modern city. It was, notoriously, a dark and stormy night, the rain fell heavily and the wind could be heard 'rattling along the housetops, and fiercely agitating the scanty flame of the lamps that struggled against the darkness'. The scene is set in 'one of the obscurest quarters of London, and among haunts little loved by the gentlemen of the police', and Dummie, a small, thin, working-class man, wearing a tattered jerkin and subsequently described as 'grotesquely hideous in feature but not positively villainous in expression' is making the way to a 'nest of low and dingy buildings' where he is to see a dying woman. The room is described in the following terms:

> The walls were whitewashed, and at sundry places strange figures and grotesque characters had been traced by some mirthful inmate, in such sable outline as the end of a smoked stick or the edge of a piece of charcoal is wont to produce. The wan and flickering light afforded by a farthing candle gave a sort of grimness and menace to these achievements of pictorial art, especially as they more than once received embellishments from portraits of Satan, such as he is accustomed to be drawn. A low fire burned gloomily in the sooty grate; and on the hob hissed 'the still small voice' of an iron kettle. On a round deal table were two vials, a cracked, broken spoon of some dull metal, and upon two or three mutilated chairs were scattered various articles of female attire.

To cap it all an apron instead of a curtain hangs over the broken window. The one incongruous note in this pitiful and degrading scene is the presence of a three-year-old boy, 'dressed as if belonging to the better classes', who is to become Paul Clifford, the gentleman highwayman. What this scene explains is how a gentleman can become a highwayman and how a highwayman can be a gentleman. Clifford is subsequently condemned to death for his activities by Sir William Brandon, a judge who turns out to be his own father. Symbolically the scene is not simply sordid but positively hellish and if the reader's apprehension and concern are aroused it is only because the boy so obviously does not belong there. The fascination of the scene is that it represents an imaginative entry into a cultural no-go area; exotic as it is, however, it is not one where either reader or novelist would wish to linger. Bulwer-Lytton rapidly abandons this haunt of vice for more respectable surroundings and more standard English – since Dummie speaks in broad Scots – noting in passing that 'broad Scotch is not yet the universal language of Europe'. Bulwer-Lytton has no idea how the inhabitants of London's rookeries live or how they speak so almost anything that sounds fairly impenetrable will do. The novel exploits the squalor of the city for dramatic effect, yet almost instantaneously seeks to suppress any recognition of what that might actually represent. The menace is both real and unreal.

Nevertheless what gave Victorian society a menacing aspect for so many people was not so much a matter of environment as of the general economic insecurity that they experienced. There were few so fortunate as to be confident that their way of life was secure. For those who worked in factories there was always the prospect of being laid off or of being more permanently unemployed. At the very bottom of the social ladder Mayhew has described the scarcely credible shifts and strategems by which the very poor attempted to survive. Yet even the prosperous and apparently unshakeable middle classes, who were, after all, the main readers of novels, were always anxious about their financial circumstances and concerned about the possible or actual loss of social status. Middle-class society seemed to be in a process of constant flux and perpetual motion as the fortunate few advanced irresistibly towards the aristocracy, while some desperately struggled to maintain their existing place, and others actually fell back. In earlier times it seemed that everyone possessed a secure place in the world, whatever that might be, whereas in the nineteenth century only the first-born of the landed aristocracy could feel so confident. For the majority there was a struggle to find and keep such a place in the face of many uncertainties. At the back of the mind of every working-class person was fear of the workhouse. For the middle classes the danger was bankruptcy or the serious loss of status that might be connected with the loss of suitable employment or with the disgrace attending a socially scandalous alliance. One of the many reasons why nineteenth-century readers so loved a villain was that the villain, whether capitalist, money-lender, lawyer, criminal – or even just an adventuress like Thackeray's Becky Sharp, was a person who seemed to be completely in his (or her) element in this murky and threatening world. While respectable people were often perplexed and confused by the difficulties that they faced, the villain was never at a loss. He always seemed to know just what action to take and precisely what disreputable courses were available to him in even the most apparently desperate contingency. The villain, even if he was ultimately doomed to fail in his deepest and craftiest machinations, was always something of an escape artist. Victorian readers were both fascinated by and envious of the villain's gift for getting out of trouble and what his final come-uppance seemed to show was that no one, no matter how ingenious could escape society's inexorable laws.

The principle subject of the Victorian novel is misfortune. Over and over again the novelist circles around this possibility and much of his or her art is devoted to the task of drawing more tightly the threads of disaster around the protagonist, intensifying the pathos and the peril until it becomes well-nigh unbearable. No doubt Victorian readers enjoyed the suspense and excitement of this narrative art, but they also found it edifying. For in such tales it was possible to confront, if only in the realm of the imagination, the possibility of disaster that haunted their minds, for to embrace such an eventuality, if only hypothetically and vicariously, was to have shown a kind of fortitude already. The novel with which Victorian fiction really begins and which acquires an exemplary significance for the whole developing genre is Oliver Goldsmith's *The Vicar of Wakefield* (1766). For although Goldsmith ostensibly belongs to that serene and untroubled Augustan world, it is in his writings that its passing seems most clearly marked, whether in 'The Deserted Village' with its lament for the lost innocence of a rural past, or in *The Vicar of Wakefield* in its depiction of a shattered idyll. Although *The Vicar of Wakefield* ends happily it disturbs the reader by the series of terrible and relentless blows that descend on the worthy cleric. He loses the whole of his personal income when a merchant goes bankrupt. His daughter, Olivia, is seduced by Squire Thornhill after a mock ceremony of marriage. His home is destroyed by fire. His second daughter, Sophia, is abducted by an unknown villain. He is told that Olivia is dead. It would be hard to imagine a greater catalogue of misfortunes, but the Vicar faces them with extraordinary fortitude and equanamity. As his house is burning he stands 'a calm spectator of the flames', almost oblivious of the fact that his arm has been badly burned, and when he is visited by his tearful family after being thrown into prison 'I gently rebuked their sorrow, assuring them I had never slept with greater tranquillity.' The Vicar insists that their troubles, no matter how numerous, can nevertheless be borne if only they can support one another and stick together – so already here we encounter that familiar Victorian theme: the possibility of creating a cosy domestic environment even in the face of such a hostile and menacing world:

> The real hardships of life are now coming fast upon us, let us not therefore encrease them by dissention among each other. If we live harmoniously together, we may yet be contented, as there are enough of us to shut out the censuring world, and keep each other in countenance. The kindness of heaven is promised to the penitent, and let ours be directed by the example. Heaven, we are assured, is much more pleased to view a repentent sinner, than ninety nine persons who have supported a course of undeviating rectitude. And this is right; for that single effort by which we stop short in the downhill path to perdition, is itself a greater exertion of virtue, than a hundred acts of justice.

What this passage also serves to do is to question contemporary assumptions about the worthiness of those philanthropic and benevolent individuals who go about the world dispensing acts of charity. The vicar himself is potentially such a character but Goldsmith places him in a position where his very existence is in jeopardy and where the very idea of virtue is put under supreme pressure. It is worth noting that Goldsmith himself led a financially precarious existence, marked by his failure for a very long time to establish himself either as a physician or as a writer. In fact it was only the sale of the manuscript of *The Vicar of Wakefield* that saved him from imprisonment for debt. So Goldsmith knew what he was talking about. Many of the leading Victorian novelists had a background of financial and emotional insecurity. Mrs Oliphant turned to writing after her husband, an artist, died and she was left alone to bring up a large family. Dickens's father was imprisoned for debt in the Marshalsea and Dickens himself was sent to work in a blacking factory. Trollope's father contracted extensive debts which often obliged the family to leave England to escape his creditors. Thackeray also experienced financial hardship and in later life was shattered by the discovery that his wife was becoming insane. The Brontë sisters were sent away to a boarding school after the early death of their mother which may have contributed to the death of Charlotte's two elder sisters. Goldsmith's precarious world was therefore one with which the Victorian novelist could readily identify.

Nevertheless if we compare *The Vicar of Wakefield* with its progeny what must strike us is that the Victorian novelists always orientate their narrative towards the future. Their heroes and heroines fully expect the world to be menacing and they are always filled with anxious expectations as they contemplate what lies ahead. By contrast what Goldsmith emphasises is that the vicar is totally unprepared for the misfortunes he is to experience. His family lives a happy, affectionate and untroubled life: 'We had no revolutions to fear, nor fatigues to undergo; all our adventures were by the fireside, and all our migrations from the blue bed to the brown.' It is a major vexation for them if apples are stolen from the orchard or if custards made by the vicar's wife are plundered.

The future is scarcely a concept to them since to be sensitised to the future they would have to imagine that what it held in store would be radically different from the present. Admittedly when the catalogue of disasters had begun the vicar begins to view matters in a rather more pessimistic light, yet even here he can find grounds for consolation:

My health and tranquillity were almost restored, and I now condemned the pride which had made me refractory to the hand of correction. Man little knows what calamities are beyond his patience to bear till he tries them; as in ascending the heights of ambition which look bright from below, every step we rise shows us some new and gloomy prospect of hidden disappointment. . . . Still as we approach, the darkest objects begin to brighten. And the mental eye becomes adapted to its gloomy situation.

When his fortunes are finally restored the vicar concludes his narrative by saying: 'It now only remained that my gratitude in good fortune should exceed my former submission in adversity.'

In contrast the Victorian novelist is convinced that it is morally incumbent on his characters to struggle against such adversity, even though the path may be long and difficult with no prospect of any turning in sight. While it is necessary for them to show as much inner strength as the vicar, they must always remain active and concerned; they are dignified by the unceasing care and effort that they devote to improving their situation and we are asked to share the mixture of courage and anxiety with which they confront the obstacles that lie ahead of them. In *Nicholas Nickleby*, for example, Dickens always makes dramatic use of anticipation. From the outset the situation of Nicholas, his sister and mother is desperately uncertain and Dickens always capitalises on the way in which their forebodings prefigure and intensify a specific outcome. When Nicholas arrives at Dotheboys Hall his mind is filled with 'a host of unpleasant misgivings', and as he looks at the dreary house and bleak Yorkshire countryside he feels 'a depression of heart and spirit which he had never experienced before'.

Subsequently after his departure from the place and his defiance of Ralph Nickleby 'many doubts and hesitations arose in his mind' and 'he gives way to the melancholy reflections that pressed heavily upon him'. When Nicholas rushes back to London in response to a message from Newman Noggs warning him that his sister is at risk, he paces the streets 'agitated by a thousand misgivings and apprehensions which he could not overcome'. Yet Nicholas's worries about his sister are resolved, only to be replaced by a similar concern about the fate of Madeleine Bray, with whom he has fallen in love. After a sleepless night he finds himself still more worried and dispirited in the morning, and Dickens comments:

> As the traveller sees farthest by day, and becomes aware of rugged mountains and trackless plains which the friendly darkness had shrouded from his sight and mind altogether, so the wayfarer in the toilsome path of human life sees with each returning sun some new obstacle to surmount, some new height to be attained; distances stretch out far before him which last night were scarcely taken into account, and the light which gilds all nature with its cheerful beams, seems but to shine upon the weary obstacles which lie yet strewn between him and the grave.

Here, of course, there is a conscious reminiscence of Bunyan, since in *The Pilgrim's Progress* the sun rises just as Christian has passed through the first part of the Valley of the Shadow of Death:

> Now was Christian much affected with his deliverance from all the dangers of his solitary way, which dangers, though he feared them more before, yet he saw them more clearly now, because the light of day made them conspicuous to him . . . the way was all

along set so full of snares, traps, gins, and nets here, and so full of pits, pitfalls, deep holes and shelvings down there, that had it been dark, as it was when he cames the first part of the way, had he a thousand souls, they had in reason been cast away; but, as I said, just now the sun was rising.

Yet we cannot help noting that the Victorian world lacks the consolations of Bunyan's pilgrim. Christian is helped by the clarity with which he sees the obstacles and he believes that God is with him, whereas the Victorian traveller has no such assurance and has no conviction that there is any sort of safe passage to be had through the minefields of contemporary capitalism. *Nicholas Nickleby* is one of the gayest, most light-hearted and humorous of Dickens's books, yet behind the boisterousness and fun the authentic Victorian menace is there.

Before coming on to Dickens, however, I first want to look at *Wuthering Heights*, a novel that reveals with particular clarity how the Gothic was modified to reflect Victorian attitudes. On the face of it *Wuthering Heights* is a novel that is disconnected from historical circumstances and one that bears little relation to the year of its publication, 1848. The narrative of *Wuthering Heights* begins in the year of 1801 and then subsequently reverts in Nellie Deans's account of prior events to 1778, so that the novel is in some sense a historical novel. Moreover, as has often been pointed out, Heathcliff in his misanthropy, morose disposition and in his obsession with his memories of Catherine, long after her death, has many of the hallmarks of the Byronic hero. It is therefore easy to regard *Wuthering Heights* as a belated Romantic work – indeed it would be rather ridiculous to deny it. Yet there is much about *Wuthering Heights* that is distinctively Victorian and what, above all, marks it as such is its anxiety about status and social class. In the 1830s and 1840s the middle classes – to which the Brontë sisters, as daughters of a clergyman, belonged – were becoming ever more anxious about their position in society. On the one hand the working classes were becoming increasingly discontented and more insistent on their rights – they represented an obvious principle of discord in society. Yet, on the other, the development of industry and capitalism was giving rise to a new merchant class, composed of individuals who had become almost inexplicably and incalculably wealthy in a very short space of time. Both groups were prominent in the political agitation over Chartism and the repeal of the Corn Laws; both looked for significant changes in the general order of things. In *Wuthering Heights* the menace to the established order is complexly synthesised in the figure of Heathcliff. Although Heathcliff does become associated with the world of the Yorkshire moors in which the novel is set, he is originally an outsider – unaccountably picked up as an orphan castaway by old Mr Earnshaw on the streets of Liverpool and treated by him with a peculiar irrational favouritism. Heathcliff is dark-skinned and generally thought to be of gypsy blood – his appearance is certainly foreign: 'a little Lascar, or an American or Spanish casta-way'. At the time the novel was written the working classes were thought of as 'dangerous classes' and the character of Heathcliff manifests many of their alleged stereotypical characteristics – Heathcliff as a boy is dirty and proud of it, he is hostile to education, he is taciturn, unpredictable and violent. He is resentful of his own inferior situation and determined to overturn it. He is filled with the resentment of the underdog. Yet he is only able to turn the tables through a mysterious absence of three years, at the end of which he returns quite inexplicably wealthy. In this he is reminiscent of the many nabob figures who throng the early Victorian novel, but his mentality is also very much that of the capitalist, since he is both mean and shrewd with his money, and it is through this expertise that he is able to gain the upper hand over the Earnshaws. The contrast between the traditional landowner and new money could not be more clear, despite the fact that *Wuthering Heights* is not a novel written by Mrs Gaskell but a powerful imaginative fantasy.

Heathcliff embodies in the most vivid form a general disturbance in class relations; however, this is by no means confined to him but is reflected in many of the other characters in *Wuthering Heights*. At an early point in the novel Lockwood praises Nelly Deans for her education and refinement: 'Excepting a few provincialisms of slight consequence, you have no marks of the manners which I am habitu-ated to consider as peculiar to your class.' Nelly Deans by these outward tokens, and by much more besides, is always more than housekeeper. She is not simply a major narrative voice, she also acts as the conscience of many of the characters and attempts, admittedly not always successfully, to assert her authority over them, in a way we simply would not expect in a housekeeper. Even more surprising perhaps, is the authority that Joseph, the puritanical old servant, is able to wield at Wuthering Heights. He defers to no one and is characteristically at once downright rude and morally self-right-eous. He initially obtains a powerful hold over old Earnshaw.

He was, and is yet, most likely, the wearisomest, self-righteous pharisee that every ransacked the Bible to rake the promises to himself, and fling the curses on his neighbours. By his knack of sermonising and pious discoursing, he contrived to make a great impression on Mr Earnshaw, and the more feeble the master became, the more influence he gained.

Joseph's charismatic influence persists after Hearnshaw's death and he gains Hindley's ear and constantly asserts Heathcliff's damnation. It is Joseph above all who provides the moral sanction for the brutality and violence that prevails at the Heights, since if all human beings are backsliders and morally reprobate, a little chastisement can never come amiss. Yet as the humble are raised the great are diminished. Edgar Linton is humiliated by Heathcliff's threats of physical violence. Hareton, though the legal inheritor of the Earnshaw estate, becomes Heathcliff's slave: 'Hareton, who should now be first gentleman in the neighbourhood, was reduced to a state of complete dependence on his father's inveterate enemy; and lives in his own houses as a servant deprived of the advantage of wages'. It is characteristic of this strife-ridden and psychologically unsettled world – a world, we must note, that has been thrown into disorder through the arrival of Heathcliff – that Heathcliff, with no established class-position himself, should be proud that Linton, as his son and heir, can serve both as a principle of legitimacy and revenge, and yet despise and resent Linton himself:

> Besides, he's mine, and I want the triumph of seeing *my* descendent fairly lord their estates; my child hiring their children, to till their fathers' land for wages – that is the sole consideration which can make me endure the whelp – I despise him for himself, and hate him for the memories he revives!

This topsy-turvy world, as Emily Brontë was well aware, is strongly reminiscent of *King Lear*, yet its turbulent atmosphere undoubtedly articulates early Victorian anxieties about tradition, authority and social control.

Through his paradoxical construction as both child of the gutter and wealthy parvenu, Heathcliff becomes an enigma to those around him. The puzzle he presents is suggested at the very outset:

> He is a dark-skinned gypsy, in aspect, in dress, and manners of a gentleman, that is, as much a gentleman as many a country squire:

rather slovenly, perhaps, yet not looking amiss with his negli-
gence, because he has an erect and handsome figure, and rather
morose; possibly, some people might suspect him of a degree of
underbred pride – I have a sympathetic chord within that tells me
it is nothing of the sort; I know, by instinct, his reserve springs
from an aversion to showy displays of feeling – to manifestations
of mutual kindness. He'll love and hate, equally under cover, and
esteem it a species of impertinence, to be loved or hated again.

Already, in this relatively brief description, the difficulty of deciphering Heathcliff is manifest. He is physically a gypsy, sartorially a
gentleman. Does his reserve spring from an aristocratic distrust of
emotional display, or is it rather a sulky show of indifference put on
by a man with a grievance? It is clear that Heathcliff is a man of
powerful emotions, but because these emotions are veiled they constitute an intimidating enigma for others. Isabella, who marries him
pleads to Mrs Deans in a letter: 'Is Mr Heathcliff a man? If so, is he
mad? And if not, is he a devil? I shan't tell my reasons for making
this enquiry; but I beseech you to explain, if you can, what I have
married.'

Here there are distinct intimations of the monstrous – Heathcliff
may be like Frankenstein, some dark dream of deformed humanity
in which man and animality combine – as Catherine warns Isabella:
'Pray, don't imagine that he conceals depths of benevolence and
affection beneath a stern exterior! He's not a rough diamond – a
pearl-containing oyster of a rustic; he's a fierce pitiless, wolfish man.'
Here we should note that the danger stems directly from the fact that
he is a child of the city not the countryside. If he were a countryman
it might be reasonable to assume a heart of gold beneath, but as one
early inured to life as a brutal struggle for survival no pity or mercy
are to be expected. A similar debate as to what kind of man Heathcliff
is takes places later in the novel between Linton and the younger
Catherine. Linton warns her that Heathcliff is 'a most diabolical
man, delighting to wrong and ruin those he hates', but Catherine is
completely baffled by this characterisation: 'But Mr Heathcliff was
quite cordial, papa . . . and *he* didn't object to our seeing each other'.
Heathcliff is inscrutable and unpredictable, a dark enigma onto whom
each character projects his or her deepest wishes and fears.

Heathcliff is driven by a deep sense of insecurity that pursues him
even after he is rescued from the slums of the city. He is never
accepted, never permitted to belong, never regarded as anything but

an outsider. Heathcliff belongs with Dostoevsky's insulted and injured; he harbours a deep sense of injustice at all the blows and indignities that he is compelled to suffer, yet he seems to pride himself on the appearance of indifference that he maintains. Heathcliff is not philosophical. He does not accept that this is how life is. Rather he turns everything into a promise of future revenge. It is only the hope that he will one day be able to repay all that he had endured that sustains him. Above all, Heathcliff detests the comfort and security of Thrushcroft Grange, and Catherine's decision to marry Linton and make her home there represents the deepest and darkest of all betrayals; it opens up a rent in the world that can never be repaired. For when Catherine says that she is Heathcliff, what she really means is that part of her is Heathcliff – part is drawn to the wild and exotic spirit of independence he represents, but part is also drawn to the security of Linton and Thrushcroft Grange. Heathcliff, like Byron's Manfred, confronts a self-generated wasteland, in which he is perpetually reminded of his own loss and where even the blessing of forgetfulness is denied him: 'The entire world is a dreadful collection of memoranda that she did exist, and that I have lost her.'

Heathcliff epitomises the bleakness of the new Victorian moral landscape, a sense of life as a brutal and pointless struggle, in which the existence of each person seems to present an insidious threat to the happiness of someone else, where all the old social contracts have been torn up. Heathcliff's restless and unhappy spirit is the spirit of the new age.

What is obliquely suggested in *Wuthering Heights* becomes overt in Dickens and Thackeray; it is above all the city that is the locus of menace; it is in the city that lurk all the dark forces of the modern age that have the power to oppress the human spirit. The world of the city is baffling, overpowering, indecipherable and enigmatic. As Raymond Williams has pointed out: 'what London had to show . . . was a contradiction, a paradox: the coexistence of variation and apparent randomness with what had in the end to be seen as a determining system: the visible individual facts but beyond them, often hidden, the common condition and destiny.'[1]

The power of the Victorian novel as practised by Dickens and Thackeray is very closely bound up with this dialectic of pattern and contingency – the reader, often baulked, baffled and swamped in a plethora of urban detail nevertheless trusts his fictional guide, who will lead him through all the mazes of the city and finally unfold the significance of all that has been represented. Pattern is denied only to be restored. Moreover the city is daunting because there the individual encounters a massive wall of indifference. No matter how loudly he cries out, his appeals elicit neither response nor echo. He begins to feel his whole existence disappearing down a black hole. He becomes painfully conscious of his own insignificance. It was in the streets of the city that Teufelsdrockh discovered the 'dead indifference' of the world:

> Now when I looked back, it was a strange isolation I then lived in. Then men and women around me, even speaking with me, were but Figures; I had, practically, forgotten that they were alive, that they were not merely automatic. In the midst of their crowded streets and assemblages, I walked solitary; and (except as it was my own heart, not another's, that I kept devouring) savage also, as the tiger in the jungle. (III, 114)

The city is a place where you begin to doubt everything, where meaning progressively leaks away.

Dickens's own exploration of this disconcerting, alienating landscape was to be immensely convoluted and protracted. In *The Pickwick Papers* (1836–7), his first real venture into fiction, it seems clear that his original intention was to present his readers with an anachronistic hero whose general air of cheery and affable benevolence would enable him to surmount all manner of difficulties, which would in turn be created by the very fact that the genial Pickwick was so much at odds with the spirit of the contemporary age. In theory at least, Pickwick with his faithful servant Sam Weller are a modern re-creation of Don Quixote and Sancho Panza, yet in practice they are never quite this – very largely because Dickens for a long while was reluctant to expose his hero to the full rigours and harshness of Victorian society, choosing rather to protect him and enfold him in the nostalgic idyll of Dingley Dell. Nevertheless Dickens does see Pickwick as a tougher character than he looks, not so much because he is a brave man – though Dickens will have it that he is prudent rather than actually cowardly – as because he is strangely impervious to the feelings to which ordinary men are subject. As Mr Tracy Tupman writes: 'You, my dear friend, are placed far beyond the reach of many mortal frailties and weaknesses which ordinary mortals cannot overcome.' Tupman means that Pickwick never experiences the often distressing and perplexing emotion of being in love but his comment has a wider application, since Pickwick does seem psychologically invulnerable, as if a cloak of invincibility shrouds his heart. Pickwick's rubber ball-like resilience is demonstrated at many points in the narrative. Although he is subject to almost perpetual discomforture – his spectacles are knocked off by a belligerent cabman, the coach overturns in his pursuit of Jingle, he is placed in the stocks, he finds himself an intruder both in a convent and in a ladies' bedroom, he makes a spectacle of himself at the Eatanswill election – he is never really discomforted; though battered he remains unbowed. After a few drinks Pickwick is described as 'producing a constant succession of the blandest and most benevolent smiles without being moved thereunto by any discernible cause or pretence whatsoever', and despite his frequent falls on the ice while skating 'his eyes beamed cheerfulness and gladness through his spectacles', he resumes his station 'with an ardour and enthusiasm which nothing could abate'. After a temporary row with Mr Tupman as to whether he is too old to wear a green velvet jacket: 'The unwonted lines which momentary passion had ruled in Mr Pickwick's clear and open brow, gradually melted away . . . like the marks of a black-lead pencil beneath the softening influence of India rubber. His countenance resumed his usual benign expression ere he concluded.'

For if a righteous indignation often stirs in his breast, it seldom disturbs his equanimity for long. If Mr Pickwick is indeed godlike, it is in this transcendental affableness with which he perpetually greets the world. As Edmund Wilson has justifiably stressed,[2] we already encounter the dark side of Dickens in *Pickwick* in the harrowing stories of personal suffering that are inserted for dramatic relief, but it would be unwise to place overmuch emphasis on this without also recognising that part of the irony of these stories is that they leave Pickwick himself totally unmoved. After 'The Stroller's Story' Dickens deliberately frustrates the reader's curiosity as to how Pickwick will respond to this relentless recital of distress by switching his attention to the dramatic entry of Dr Slammer. 'The Convict's Tale', far from disturbing him, has such a 'somniferous influence on him' that he immediately falls asleep. Although he is made somewhat fearful by 'The Madman's Story' he awakens in a very cheerful and light-hearted mood. Pickwick is as indestructible as the animated cartoon characters of Tom or Jerry.

So it was a brilliant reversal on Dickens's part to make Pickwick the defendant in a breach of promise case and to make him experience the full rigours of the judicial system, not only because this makes Pickwick vulnerable as he had never been before, but because it exposes the tacit assumption of the early part of the book that the character of Pickwick, though sorely tested by the likes of Jingle, could only exist in a universe that was thoroughly imbued with a spirit of fair play. And the joke, if joke it is, is that if there is one social institution where such a judicious and even-handed spirit has absolutely no part to play, it is the law. Ironies abound when Pickwick first enters the 'dark, mouldy and earthy-smelling' offices of Dodson and Fogg in the sanguine expectation that all this can rapidly be cleared up and that his mere expression of astonishment will be sufficient to call their bluff. As usual Pickwick is unruffled: '"I came, gentlemen," said Mr Pickwick, gazing placidly on the two partners, "I came here gentlemen, to express the surprise with which I received your letter of the other day, and to inquire what grounds of action you can have against me."'

But Dodson and Fogg not only believe that they have grounds but they are 'strong and not to be shaken.' Far from explaining or justifying themselves, they take Pickwick's guilt as read and treat him in a condescending and censorious manner. For them the truth of the charge against Pickwick is already certified by the fact that it is entered in the *praecipe* book for 28 August 1830 – 'all regular, sir, perfectly'. Pickwick's unfailing presumption of innocence has run into the immovable object of Dodson and Fogg's unfailing presumption of guilt: 'If you are really innocent of what is laid to your charge, you are more unfortunate than I had believed any man could possibly be.' Implicit in the stereotype of the benevolent philanthropist are the assumptions that he at least is secure from adversity or distress – otherwise he could not help others – that the world can never fail to see him for the noble and disinterested individual that he is, and that his own honesty and integrity will meet with a comparable response from others. But with the setting in motion of proceedings in the case of Bardell *v.* Pickwick all these expectations are overthrown and Dickens asks us to see that in many ways the case against Pickwick, preposterous though it is, is nevertheless quite plausible in legal terms. Pickwick's combination of moral spontaneity and bonhomie actually tells against him. Thus when Pickwick gives a violent start at Serjeant Buzfuz's reference to his 'systematic villainy', Buzfuz uses this moment to pillory him, treating this reac-

tion as some futile and improper attempt to deny the obvious that is
tantamount to contempt of court:

> 'I say systematic villainy, gentlemen,' said Serjeant Buzfuz, look-
> ing through Mr Pickwick, and talking *at* him; 'and when I say
> systematic villainy, let me tell the defendant Pickwick, if he be in
> court, as I am informed he is, that it would have been more decent
> in him, more becoming, in better judgement, and in better taste, if
> he had stopped away. Let me tell him, gentlemen, that any ges-
> tures of dissent or disapprobation in which he may indulge in this
> court will not go down with you; that you will know how to value
> and how to appreciate them.'

The courtroom is hardly a *just milieu* for the man of feeling.
　　Similarly Pickwick's unflagging cheerfulness makes Buzfuz's depiction of him as a 'damned smiling villain' quite plausible:

> But Pickwick, gentlemen, Pickwick, the ruthless destroyer of this
> domestic oasis in the desert of Goswell Street – Pickwick, who has
> choked up the well, and thrown ashes on the sward　Pickwick,
> who comes before you to-day with his heartless Tomata sauce and
> warming-pans – Pickwick still rears his head with unblushing
> effrontery, and gazes without a sigh on the ruin he has made.
> Damages, gentlemen – heavy damages – is the only punishment
> with which you can visit him; the only recompense you can award
> my client.

At this point all the old securities are gone. In the eyes of the world
at least, Pickwick is become Jingle.
　　In the Fleet Prison the indefatigable Pickwick maintains his pos-
ture of tourist, man of letters and social investigator as if he were not
actually a prisoner himself:

> 'This' said the gentleman, thrusting his hands into his pockets,
> and looking carelessly over his shoulder to Mr Pickwick,' This
> here is the hall flight.'
> 　　'Oh,' replied Mr Pickwick, looking down a dark and filthy
> staircase, which appeared to lead to a range of damp and gloomy
> stone vaults, beneath the ground, . . . 'My friend,' said Mr Pickwick,
> 'you don't really mean to say that human beings live down in
> those wretched dungeons.'

Pickwick is so confident of his own moral righteousness and so unflagging in his determination not to acknowledge the courts in any way that it never even crosses his mind to obtain his release by the simple device of paying. The more pragmatic Sam Weller points up the dangers of such obduracy by his tale of the man who has eaten four crumpets every night for fifteen years and who responds to his doctor's suggestion that crumpets are unwholesome and that he should give them up by blowing his brains out. But for Pickwick it *is* a matter of principle and he will not bend to the law. Yet even he is finally ground down by the process of incarceration – his optimism and curiosity are finally gone:

> From this spot, Mr Pickwick wandered along all the galleries, up and down all the staircases, and once again round the whole body of the yard. The great body of the prison population appeared to be Mivins, and Smangle, and the parson, and the butcher, and the leg, over and over, and over again. There were the same squalor, the same turmoil and noise, the same general characteristics, in every corner; in the best and the worst alike. The whole place seemed restless and troubled; and the people were crowding and flitting to and fro, like the shadows in an uneasy dream.
>
> 'I have seen enough,' said Mr Pickwick, as he threw himself into a chair in his little apartment. 'My head aches with these scenes, and my heart too. Henceforth I will be a prisoner in my own room.'
>
> And Mr Pickwick steadfastly adhered to this determination. For three long months he remained shut up, all day; only stealing out at night, to breathe the air, when the greater part of his fellows prisoners were in bed or carousing in their rooms.

This is surely a pivotal moment both in the narrative itself and in the development of Dickens's fiction. Even Pickwick can take no more. The philanthropist is transformed into something very like a misanthrope. Yet we should also note that this self-confinement involves a proud assertion of independence, since Pickwick refuses to admit that society has any right to punish him and therefore responds with a gesture of exclusion and denial. But with Pickwick *in extremis* the world seems menacing indeed.

But for all that, we know in our hearts that the world of Pickwick is so elaborately padded, bolstered and feather-bedded that there can never be any real possibility of serious harm, whereas in *Oliver*

Twist (1837–8) the hero, a young boy, is extremely vulnerable and exposed to such possibilities from the very start. The motif of the foundling was one familiar to Dickens from his reading of eighteenth-century fiction, but he gave it a new authority and a new integrity simply by not assuming that such a waif must necessarily take life as he finds it, if only because he knows no better. But Oliver is difficult and obstreperous. He is not prepared to acknowledge misery as his natural station and portion in life. He continually rebels against the terms that he is presented with – notoriously asking for more, but also protesting against being handed over to the chimney sweep, running away from Mr Sowerberry, the undertaker, and stubbornly resenting the plans made for him by Fagin and Sykes. Oliver shows an extraordinary spirit of independence – so much so that we might be inclined to find it implausible – but Dickens wants us to see through the eyes of a child how much of what adults may be inclined to take for granted is actually quite intolerable. Dickens asks us to believe that the rebelliousness that Bumble finds ungrateful and perverse is in reality entirely natural. Through the theoretically very different but actually quite symmetrical characters of Bumble and Fagin, Dickens suggests that in the wake of the new Poor Law a heartless spirit has arisen in society, where there is no longer even any residual sense of care or concern for people as people: they are simply regarded as exploitable commodities. Mrs Mann views the orphans simply as a useful source of income. The chimney sweep values Oliver at three pounds, Mr Limbkins at three pounds ten, yet Fagin, the more adroit exploiter of human labour, says that Oliver is worth hundreds of pounds to him. For Bill Sykes Oliver is simply something of a particular size that can get through a particular window, whose feelings can be disregarded and who does not need to be consulted in any way. Oliver's lack of any real name other than that arbitrarily assigned to him by the beadle suggests both a deeper lack of identity and the possibility that he is correspondingly the more open to being shaped and manipulated by others to criminal ends. The collusion between Monks and Bumble to efface all traces of Oliver's past suggests the heartlessness of the new social order that will erase the last vestiges of a former humanity with the bland efficacity of a wet sponge.

For Dickens it was deeply disturbing that such an innocent boy as Oliver could be so effortlessly sucked into the criminal underworld of London and effectively disappear. Yet it was even more shocking that such a thing could happen without anyone either knowing or caring that this was going on. Dickens's view of this emergent anarchic subculture was by no means that of simple moralistic condemnation. On the contrary he felt that the exploitative nature of the relationships within it, the mutual indifference, the atmosphere of suspicion, distrust and betrayal simply represented the distorted values of Victorian society in an intensified form. Dickens could not altogether accept the view urged by Bulwer-Lytton that the slums were inevitably the breeding grounds for crime and that people were predetermined to become law-breakers by their circumstances and upbringing. The importance of Nancy from this point of view is to show that even a woman of the streets may be animated by noble feelings and generous impulses. At the same time it was crucial to the whole concept of the novel that there would be a real possibility that Oliver could be corrupted by his exposure to evil; thus Dickens writes of Fagin:

> in short, the wily old Jew had the boy in his toils. Having prepared his mind, by solitude and gloom, to prefer any society to the companionship of his own sad thoughts in such a dreary place, he was now slowly instilling into his soul the poison which he hoped would blacken it, and change its hue for ever.

The dark and dismal room, with its mouldering, tightly closed shutters, in which Oliver is incarcerated is the contemporary equivalent of the gloomy turret, high in the Apennines, where the Gothic heroine was wont to be confined. Of course the reader does not expect Oliver to give in and would be horrified even to contemplate such a possibility. Dickens, by specifying so closely the pressures exerted on his hero, tests his own faith in free will to the very limit. These were very real issues for Dickens as his lengthy involvement in schemes for the regeneration of fallen women makes evident. Dickens does not invoke the possible escape clause that a child of such tender years as Oliver cannot really be expected to act as a wholly autonomous moral agent. Yet this problem hovers over the whole novel just the same, for it is precisely Dickens's indictment of the new Utilitarianism that since it does not have any conception of the value of individuality and free will, it does not create a climate in which they can be expected to flourish. Moral behaviour, though in some sense natural, is by no means automatic. It needs to be stimulated and encouraged. Since moral behaviour rests on free choice it is absolutely crucial that the individual should recognise that he or she actually does have the power to choose; yet, as Dickens saw it, the contemporary world increasingly denied this. A figure such as Bumble wants to reduce all his charges to a state of helpless dependency, so that they totally lose the power either to express or assert themselves. For Dickens this unfreedom, this drive to transform people into impotent ciphers that the example of Oliver Twist so clearly illustrates, was a great evil in Victorian society, and it was not the least reason why he perceived the new urban world as menacing. Indeed Dickens's most astonishing effect in the novel is, in the final pages, to force us to see the world through the eyes of his villains, Fagin and Sykes. It is, of course, easy to argue that Dickens does this purely for dramatic effect, to make us the more thoroughly convinced that they are guilty, wicked, utterly damned. Yet the significant consequence of such a perspective shift is that we can no longer clearly perceive Fagin and Sykes as the *source* of all that renders the world menacing. Rather we perceive just how menacing it is to *them*. It is through Sykes's ears that we hear the terrifying shouts of the crowd, and it is through Fagin's eyes that we see people eating and fanning themselves in the court-room, with one man sketching his picture. It is just this lack of care in the world that is a recipe for social disaster.

By contrast with the lurid canvas of *Oliver Twist*, *Nicholas Nickleby* (1838–9) is a return to the manner of *Pickwick*, but it is often a book that contrives to be very much funnier, because, for all the exaggeration and pastiche, it rests on a bedrock of precise observation and the careful delineation of shabby genteel circumstance. *Nicholas Nickleby* is the final demolition of the Silver Fork School since social pretension has never been so painful or so inappropriate as in the depths of this lower middle-class world that daily experiences the whole gamut of emotions of A to B, and where tragedy looms every time the landlord knocks at the door. Yet although Dickens mocks the fantastic delusions of his characters and exposes their strange inhumanity, he also identifies with them, since he knows that having to swallow your pride is a far greater torment than having to go to bed hungry. Although melodramatic dangers continually loom up on the horizon, they really only serve to vindicate a general sense of the precariousness of existence that all the characters, barring Mrs Nickleby, feel. On every side we encounter characters who are hanging onto life by their very fingertips. There are the Nicklebys themselves, thrown on the doubtful mercies of Ralph Nickleby and Wackforth Squeers; there is Madame Mantalini trying to keep her head above water despite the extravagances of her husband; there are the actors in Vincent Crummles's theatrical troupe, who never quite know where they will lay their head; there is Madeleine Bray and her improvident father; perhaps, above all, there is Newman Noggs, who as a gentleman now reduced to the status of a humble clerk, seems an almost totemic representation of the unpredictability and insecurity of modern society. The degree to which they are all desperately trying to keep up appearances on insufficient funds is apparent when Nicholas joins up with Vincent Crummles. After an extensive search through the most insalubrious areas of Dickens's native Portsmouth, Nicholas finally lights upon some very shabby lodgings that are just within his means. He is both surprised and alarmed the next morning to discover that Mr Folair and Mr Lenville are already at the door, ostensibly to enquire about their parts in the play, but in reality to obtain a free breakfast. Mr Folair is to play a faithful servant who is turned out of doors with his wife and child and who is then forced to put up in some very poor lodgings – a situation that would obviously require him to summon up all his histrionic powers in feigning the appropriate moral indignation. Mr Folair insists on the inclusion of a 'dance' to raise their spirits, and in return for such a gem of dramatic invention is rewarded with the breakfast he had sought all along. By such means, whether on stage or off, all sense of financial hardship is agreeably, if momentarily, cancelled.

Nicholas Nickleby is an essentially unstable book since although it seeks to articulate the sense of a world that is genuinely threatening, it nevertheless always seems, on closer inspection, that the anxieties of the characters are disproportionate. They worry so much about small things that anything that is even remotely beyond their ken can only seem positively monstrous. Here, Dickens's worthy characters are as incapable of tragedy as his would-be villains are incapable of villainy. The lack, the perpetual gap between aspiration and accomplishment seems typified by the arrival of Nicholas and Smike on the stage of the Portsmouth Theatre:

> Among bare walls, dusty scenes, mildewed clouds, heavily daubed draperies, and dirty floors. He looked about him: ceiling, pit, boxes, gallery, orchestra, fittings, and decorations of every kind, – all looked coarse, cold, gloomy and wretched.
>
> 'Is this the theatre?', whispered Smike in amazement; 'I thought it was a blaze of light and finery.'

'Why, so it is,' replied Nicholas, hardly less surprised, 'But not by day, Smike – not by day.'

This is precisely the irreducibly drab and humdrum world of the novel itself, where the melodramatic can scarcely obtain a point of entry, no matter how desperately Dickens tries. Even the Demon King himself could only figure as some other importunate sponger. All the characters in *Nicholas Nickleby* from Mr Lenville and the Kenwigs to Ralph and Gride continually strive to create an effect, but their efforts are undermined by the pathetic recognition that they can never hope to maintain the illusion.

To transpose Marx, Dickens created Ralph Nickleby to epitomise and personify the heartlessness of a heartless world, to represent everything that the lower middle classes feared. It is immediately after the introduction of Ralph that Dickens launches into his description of Snow Hill, where the pitiless indifference of modern society seems most unselfconsciously laid bare:

> There, at the very core of London, in the heart of its business and animation, in the midst of a whirl of noise and motion: stemming as it were the giant currents of life that flow ceaselessly on from different quarters, and meet beneath its walls, stands Newgate . . . when curious eyes have glared from casement, and house-top, and wall and pillar, and when, in the mass of white and upturned faces, the dying wretch, in his all-comprehensive look of agony, has met not one – not one – that bore the impress of pity or compassion.

Yet this pity and compassion, excluded from the scene, is also excluded from the novel since it seems that only someone actually out of the world would be capable of feeling it – those who try to struggle on within it are necessarily desensitised. For Dickens London is a world of speed, of energy, of transitory impressions, where the only response that suffering is likely to evoke is a kind of bemused curiosity. Ralph Nickleby, with his henchman Wackforth Squeers, possess a hard, unflinching indifference that could never reach the point of softening, unlike say Scrooge in *A Christmas Carol*, yet they nevertheless fail to convey the full menace that Dickens undoubtedly intends. Ralph Nickleby is simply *not indifferent enough* – he seems to put such an inordinate amount of effort into making the lives of his relatives uncomfortable that it is hard for us to grasp why he should take such pains, or, having taken them, have never-theless been so utterly ineffective. Such conviction as Ralph Nickleby possesses stems from the fact that he is the ideologue and oracular spokesman for that cheesepairing environment which all the other characters must reluctantly come to terms with. In a way he is the voice of unpalatable common sense. When he tells Mantalini that money is scarce, for example, he only states what Miss Snevellicci knows to her cost when Mr Curdle gives her sixpence less than he rightfully should, but it is as if Ralph is prepared to look this axiom firmly in the eye, when everybody else flinches from the recognition. The villains in *Nicholas Nickleby* make no bones about what they are up to, whereas the would-be respectable characters are so anxious to preserve appearances that their world must be swathed in Roman drapery. Lillyvick is raised to such heights of indignation at the winks and kisses blown in the direction of his new wife by Mr Snevellicci that he leaps on him in a state of uncontrollable fury. Squeers, of course, is a great comic creation and this in itself is striking evidence of a strange characteristic of Dickens's writing: that when he deplores evils in society he seems simultaneously to find them funny. It is never Dickens's view that there are some matters that are too serious for humour; he seems compelled to ridicule everything that arouses his anger, as if he resents the very admission that they really should be taken seriously. We cannot help finding Squeers's cruel mistreatment of the boys at Dotheboys Hall laughable, and the effect is to diminish the sense of evil that Squeers is supposed to represent. Perhaps, for Dickens, evil is always marked by a certain ludicrous banality, a kind of blindness to the futility of it all, but when Nicholas thrashes Squeers, as when he thrashes Sir Mulberry Hawke, the victory is somehow less satisfying than it ought to be. Indeed the Squeers's preposterous efforts at economy only serve to link them the more firmly with the more sympathetic characters in what is clearly a universal struggle to make ends meet. Dickens desperately tries to polarise his narrative by opposing Ralph Nickleby with the Cheerybles, and by augmenting a villain who never seems quite able to deliver what he promises with his double, the miser, Gride. Yet we sense that the real ground for Dickens's concern lies elsewhere. What *Nicholas Nickleby* presents is a world where children are compelled to act beyond their years with a sense of maturity, courage, responsibility and concern for others, while the adults, who should be concerned for their welfare, act with a mix-ture of selfishness, carelessness and stupidity. Here Dickens clearly

wrote from the heart, from a deep sense of indignation at the irresponsibility of his own father. Ralph, as it turns out, has abandoned
his own son to the tender mercies of Squeers; Bray for his own
convenience is determined to marry his daughter to a heartless
miser; while Mrs Nickleby is so lacking in judgement and any awareness of what is going on that she is prepared to entertain a proposal
of marriage from a madman and abandon her daughter to Sir Mulberry Hawke. It is a significant irony in the novel that when Nicholas
complains about the wrongdoing of his uncle, Smike is determined
to memorise the name: 'Ralph, I'll get his name by heart', for it as if
his own determination to remember doubles his father's determination to forget. If there is such an indifference even in the family itself,
how can the world seem other than profoundly hostile. In a poignant
passage Nicholas tries to explain to Smike what a home is: 'When I
speak of a home, I speak of a place where – in default of a better –
those I love are gathered together; and if that place were a gypsy's
tent or a barn, I should call it by the same good name notwithstanding.' Yet Dickens's real fear is that in the new hostile environment
such good names may no longer be enough – the capacity for care
that the name 'home' implies may not actually be present.

Perhaps Dickens felt that the humour of *Nicholas Nickleby* had
undermined his project of representing the indifference of Victorian
society, for his next work, *The Old Curiosity Shop* (1841), was a return
to the manner of *Oliver Twist*, in which childish innocence is threatened by the menace of the modern city as embodied in that spectacu-
larly grotesque figure, Quilp, the malignant, grimacing, red-headed
dwarf. Quilp is such a preposterous figure that it is hard to take him
very seriously, even as or especially as a figure of evil, but again we
have a totemic figure who Dickens offers to the reader as the very
incarnation of the alienated humanity, the monstrosity that the modern city could engender. Quilp is a nightmare or he is nothing, but
nightmares are rarely handed on from generation to generation.
What is rather more of a problem is why such a shrewd and preter-
naturally cunning figure should continue to believe that Nell's grandfather has vast stores of money at his disposal when he is the one
person who is in a good position to know that he hasn't. So *The Old
Curiosity Shop* is always on the point of sliding into self-parody,
always struggling to extract powerful emotional effects from essentially exiguous plot materials. Nevertheless the enthusiasm with
which Dickens wrote it, and the powerful response that it evoked,
shows how deeply committed Dickens was to the representation of

a menacing world and how readily a modernised Gothic could resonate in the minds of his readers. Quilp is a prophetic anticipation of the many curious, not to say perverse, occupations that fill the pages of Henry Mayhew. Quilp is a kind of master of rubbish, debris and bric-à-brac, whose undoubted power seems to consort oddly with the world of dereliction he actually inhabits – though Milton's Satan might be a significant precursor:

> On the Surrey side of the river was a small rat-infested dreary yard called 'Quilp's Wharf', in which was a little wooden counting-house burrowing all awry in the dust as if it had fallen from the clouds and ploughed into the ground; a few fragments of rusty anchors; several large iron rings; some piles of rotten wood; and two or three heaps of old sheet copper, crumpled, cracked and battered. On Quilp's Wharf, Daniel Quilp was a ship-breaker, yet to judge from these appearances he must either have been a ship-breaker on a very small scale, or have broken up his ships very small indeed.

The strange materialisation of a counting-house seems to epitomise the magic of capitalist society, whereby profit can seemingly be extracted from the most unfavourable and unpropitious circumstances. Old-fashioned notions that you should carry on a definite occupation and get a fair day's work for a fair day's pay, or that successful undertakings should identify themselves by a general sense of the well kept, by a general air of prosperity are totally contradicted by the example of Quilp. Quilp epitomises the strangeness and complexity of the modern city, which seems to offer so many unorthodox and probably illegal ways of gaining a livelihood. Quilp seems to occupy an imaginative space of his own, beyond the margins of society in his self-generated, dematerialised yet curiously tangible wharf. There is really no way of deciphering Quilp – his associates, his occupations, his motives are all shrouded in the deepest mystery. The only thing that seems certain is that he preys on others, that he is the kind of human louse, the unshakeoffable parasite that the urban world engenders. Whatever Quilp means – it can only mean harm. Yet Quilp is not the only figure in the novel who is identified with this *malaise*. The *donnée* of the book is given at the very outset, when the elderly narrator, wandering the streets of the city at night, is disturbed to come across a little girl who is on her own and who seems to have lost her way. He accompanies her home and is yet more disquieted to learn subsequently that the old man, her guardian, regularly goes out at night, leaving the child alone. What Dickens's readers subsequently discover is yet worse: the old man regularly goes out late at night to indulge in reckless gambling, in the perverse belief that by this means he will eventually be able to provide for the security of Little Nell after he has passed away. Dickens suggests that the old man, left to himself, is a kind, well-meaning and essentially harmless fellow, but that, in the city, he becomes possessed by a sinister double, an alien within, who (at night) assumes control and by his excesses threatens the very fabric of their existence together. When Nell is awakened one night by her grandfather, who is secretly leaving to gamble, she is frightened by the sight of a 'dreadful shadow', which she believes intends the old man some harm. She can scarcely believe that this person actually *is* her grandfather:

> The feeling which beset the child was one of dim uncertain horror. She had no fear of the dear old grandfather, in whose love for her this disease of the brain had been engendered; but the man she had seen that night, wrap in a game of chance, lurking in her room, and counting the money by the glimmering light, seemed like another creature in his shape, a monstrous distortion of his image, a something to recoil from, and be the more afraid of, because it bore a likeness to him, and kept close about her, as he did.

This other – who cannot actually be named as the 'grandfather' – represents the perversion and destruction of all normal family feeling, the sinister confirmation of the anxiety of the narrator at the beginning that such unthinkable things are actually going on. What Dickens fears – a fear that he was to articulate more powerfully and more profoundly in his later work – is this possibility of dehumanisation: that in the strange and oppressive circumstances of modern life people will actually lose touch with that aspect of themselves that is bound up with a compassionate, tender concern for others. Quilp with his 'ugly face' and 'stunted figure', with his menacing, mindless self-centredness, is an almost allegorical representation of the narrator's original speculation, when he imagines Nell 'holding her solitary way among a crowd of wild, grotesque companions; the only pure, fresh, youthful object in the throng'. It is significant that as the embodiment of such dehumanisation, Quilp becomes strangely intermingled in Nell's mind with the stern, impassive faces of Mrs Jarley's waxworks: 'she tortured herself – she could not help it – with imagining a resemblance, in some one or other of their death-like faces, to the dwarf, and this fancy would sometimes so gain on her that she would almost believe he had removed the figures and stood within the clothes'. This unnerving tableau encapsulates the ill-articulated nightmare of *The Old Curiosity Shop*, on the face of it a crude melodrama of innocence threatened by a motiveless malignity, but more fundamentally and earnestly an emotional *cri de coeur* that we should not – as many Victorians did – take assumptions about an unchanging human nature too much for granted. Oliver Twist always remains virtuous – so too does Little Nell. But Nell dies – and her death is not purely sentimental, for in that emotionally super-charged moment there also dies much of Dickens's earlier Pickwickian optimism.

In Dickens's earlier fiction there always looms up, like a mirage in the desert some appealing vision of an earlier, simpler, untroubled England that seems to offer some kind of refuge from the looming menace of the present, yet such oases of tranquillity were themselves imperilled even at the very moment when they were invoked. After his brutal initiation into the life of the city at the hands of the Artful Dodger, Fagin and Sykes, Oliver Twist is taken into the country by Mrs Maylie and Rose, and Dickens is at pains to suggest that the countryside possesses a restorative power that can bring back to normality even those, such as Oliver, who have been exposed to the corruption of the city:

> Who can described the pleasure and delight, the peace of mind and soft tranquillity, the sickly boy felt in the balmy air, and among the green hills and rich woods of an inland village! . . . Oliver, whose days had been spent among squalid crowds, and in the midst of noise and brawling, seemed to enter on a new existence there. The rose and honeysuckle clung to the cottage walls; the ivy crept round the trunks of the trees; and the garden-flowers perfumed the air with delicious odours.

Yet this happiness cannot remain untroubled. One day when Oliver is sitting at the cottage window, surrounded by the perfume of jasmine and honeysuckle, he is shocked to see the figures of Fagin and Monks standing before him. Their power can reach even here. Nell and her grandfather flee the city for rural tranquillity, yet Quilp nevertheless catches up with them. Towards the end of *Nicholas Nickleby* Nicholas takes Smike into the countryside to the scene of his own happy childhood memories, yet Smike can find no peace since he is haunted by visions of the man who first took him off to his bitter existence at Dotheboys Hall, and though he also had pleasant dreams it is at this moment that he dies. In every case the rural idyll is disrupted, yet the appeal of the pastoral ideal remains a powerful one. In early Victorian England in particular it was always easy to hypothesise some other England untouched by modernity, which could be seen as a repository of enduring values. Dickens himself was certainly attracted to the idea that the English past was in some sense more substantial than the English present, even though it might often seem as if the reverse were the case. For Dickens the most potent symbols of the English past were the old coaching inns, which were entering into a period of decline. In *The Pickwick Papers* we first encounter Sam Weller at one of these establishments, 'The White Hart', but Dickens points out that now you will have to search for them – the reader 'must direct his steps to the obscurer quarters of the town; and there in some secluded nooks he will find several, still standing with a kind of gloomy sturdiness, amidst the modern innovations that surround them'.

Though banished to the fringes, these old inns are a kind of living reproach to the flashiness and insubstantiality of the modern. So Dickens's first historical novel, *Barnaby Rudge*, takes as its subject the Gordon Riots of 1780, a violent explosion of anti-Catholic sentiment, but it is equally crucially focused on the Maypole Inn, which, as its name suggests, is taken to be symbolic of 'Merrie England'. The Maypole Inn seems to represent all that is best in English life, a sense of stability and permanence, a genial and unquenchable fountain of refreshment. Cobbett's claim that the English were better fed and more prosperous before the tax-eaters came seems sublimely vindicated at that moment when the Vardons arrive in the bar of the Maypole, 'the very snuggest, cosiest, and completest bar, that ever the wit of man devised', to hear their host, John Willett order their dinner: '"A bit of fish", said John to the cook, "and some lamb chops (breaded, with plenty of ketchup), and a good salad, and a roast spring chicken, with a dish of sausages and mashed potatoes, or something of that sort"', and Dickens comments wonderingly, 'Something of that sort! the resources of those inns. To talk carelessly about dishes, which in themselves were a first-rate holiday kind of dinner, suitable to one's wedding-day, as something of that sort.' To the visitor the Maypole offers such a cheery invitation to the traveller that it prompts Dickens to create a Victorian Christmas card in prose:

> Blessings on the red – deep, ruby glowing red – old curtain of the window; blending into one rich stream of brightness, fire and candle, meat and drink, and company, and gleaming like a jovial eye upon the bleak waste out of doors! Within, what carpet like its crunching sand, what music merry as its crackling logs, what perfume like its kitchen's dainty breath, what weather genial as its hearty warmth! Blessings on the old house, how sturdily it stood.

Yet this description is deeply ironic. For we already know that John Willett, though subservient to those whose social station is superior, is brutally authoritarian to those whom he deems beneath him and especially his son Joe, who is not even allowed to speak or utter an opinion within the walls of the Maypole Inn. It is immediately after Joe has left the Maypole to enlist in the army – a decision that will lead to the loss of an arm in the American Wars – that Dickens launches into this deceptive encomium. Moreover there can be no doubt that the real climax of the book occurs when, in a veritable orgy of destruction, the serenity of the Maypole is finally and irrevocably shattered by the Gordon rioters. What exactly does Dickens intend by his presentation of this scene as it is clear that he is in sympathy with the rioters and that he exults quite as much as they in the desecration of this ritualised space, and in John Willett's bewilderment and bemusement as he witnesses the unthinkable taking place before his very eyes?

> Yes. Here was the bar – the bar the boldest never entered without special invitation – the sanctuary, the mystery, the hallowed grounds: here it was, crammed with men, clubs, sticks, torches, pistols; filled with a deafening noise, oaths, shouts, screams, hootings; changed all at once into a bear-garden, a mad-house, an infernal temple: men darting in and out, by door and window, smashing the glass, turning the taps, drinking liquor out of China punchbowls, sitting astride of casks, smoking private and personal pipes, cutting down the sacred grove of lemons, hacking and hewing at the celebrated cheese, breaking open inviolable drawers, putting things in their pockets which didn't belong to them, dividing his own money before his own eyes, wantonly wasting,

breaking, pulling down and tearing up: nothing quiet, nothing private: men everywhere . . . more men still – more, more, more – swarming on like insects: noise, smoke, light, darkness, frolic, anger, laughter, groans, plunder, fear and ruin!

Dickens focuses the scene through the eyes of John Willett and he positively gloats over the fact that, while so many are thoroughly enjoying themselves, only one in the midst of it is disconsolate, only one in the midst of so much movement and energy sits motionless. Of course, like revenge, this scene represents a kind of wild justice and the reader may feel that the suppression of one rebellion has led inexorably to another that cannot be so easily repressed. So harsh a patriarchal order both cannot stand and cannot be overthrown except by violence. The arguably morally ambiguous task of struggling against unjust fathers is thus displaced from such innocent victims as Joe Willett and Edward Chester onto a mob that knows not what it does and which is itself headed by two confused victims of irresponsible patriarchy: Hugh, the illegitimate son of Sir John Chester, and Barnaby, son of the murderer, Rudge. Since *Barnaby Rudge* was written at the height of Chartist agitation it has often been taken as some kind of comment on contemporary social unrest, yet the provenance of such scenes of riot in such obvious sources as Scott's *The Heart of Midlothian* and Carlyle's *The French Revolution* would have made it difficult simply read out of the novel some generalised condemnation of violence, even if Dickens had not made his sympathy with the spirit of misrule so evident in many of the scenes. More likely than this is that Dickens might have conceived *Barnaby Rudge* in a Carlylean spirit, as involving a perpetual struggle between the old and the new. Certainly Dickens was always acutely conscious of the oppressive weight of the past and from *Bleak House* onward he was disposed to see the living as sacrificial victims on the altars of tradition. This is particularly evident in his later novel of the French Revolution, *A Tale of Two Cities* (1859), where the substitution by which Charles Darnay must pay the price for the evils committed by his uncle, the Marquis de St Evrémonde, can only be rectified by a second substitution in which Sidney Carton takes Darnay's place at the guillotine. In both *Barnaby Rudge* and *A Tale of Two Cities* the blame is laid at the door of an egocentric older generation that seems quite unconcerned about the dragon's teeth it has sown.

But whatever Dickens's intentions may have been, the real significance of *Barnaby Rudge* for him was that he finally acknowledged the futility both of the pastoral ideal and of any kind of appeal to the example of the past. For the past as represented by the Maypole Inn may have been just as much a sham and a phantasm as the present. Then as now, life may have placed daunting obstacles in the path of a younger generation. Thus in his later novels Dickens abandoned the delights of antithesis to concentrate unremittingly on the present.

Before the quantum leap to *Dombey and Son*, however, Dickens was to write his first and only poor novel, *Martin Chuzzlewit* (1844). The comparative failure of *Chuzzlewit*, despite many incidental brilliances, has an honourable source in Dickens's desire to replace such an obviously menacing villain as Quilp with a more insidiously threatening figure such as Pecksniff, whose serene and imperturbable blandness most effectively dissimulates his selfishness and indifference to others. However, the problem with Pecksniff was that Dickens could never really think of anything very satisfactory to do with him, and in consequence the novel loses focus, thrust and momentum. More seriously, and here *Martin Chuzzlewit* is unlike any other Dickens novel, it fails to present any kind of recognisable world and this is not through the introduction of the American scenes, rather those scenes are a symptom of that failure. As John Lucas rightly points out:

> Yet for all Dickens's ingenuity, the Chuzzlewit family cannot compose a vision of any genuine typicality; hence the desperate plotting to keep members in touch with each other and with the various other characters of the novel . . . in the end things fly apart, the centre will not hold. You cannot have a novel that is as socially unfocussed as *Martin Chuzzlewit* is, and also pretend that it is somehow a central statement about capitalism.[3]

Martin Chuzzlewit represents a parting of the ways for critics of Dickens: over those who see Dickens as a comic novelist or a creator of characters first and foremost it will continue to exert an appeal; for others, including myself, overcoming that obsession with the creation of character as such was the precondition for his achieving real greatness as a novelist.

Dombey and Son (1847–8) was Dickens's most mature, most complex and most comprehensive indictment of Victorian commercial society, but though it was written in the culminating moment of the Chartist campaign, Dickens, in the footsteps of Carlyle, chose to see working-class discontent not as the fundamental issue but rather as a symptom of a more deep-seated spiritual *malaise*. For Carlyle what was at stake was a crisis of values: there was a hollowness at the core of Victorian society that stemmed both from a lack of belief and a lack of personal conviction. It was a world of shams epitomised by the seven-foot lath and plaster hat. Yet it was also a world given over to what he called the Gospel of Mammonism:

> We have profoundly forgotten everywhere that Cash-payment is not the sole relation of human beings; we think, nothing doubting, that *it* absolves and liquidates all engagements of man.
>   'My starving workers?' answers the rich mill-owner: 'Did I not hire them fairly in the market? Did I not pay them, to the last sixpence, the sum covenanted for what have I to do with them more?' (II, 124)

For Carlyle those who affected to live by the *laissez-faire* code had not only lost touch with their own humanity and with their fellow human beings, they had also become disconnected from any sense of reality – they were insisting on a programmatic and ideological representation of the world that effectively excluded both their own awareness of suffering and their own moral responsibility. Dickens was deeply affected by Carlyle's perception of the contemporary crisis, but Dickens was also much more deeply concerned with relations within the family and with the universal need for love. Carlyle too recognised this exclusion of love in *Past and Present*: 'Love of men cannot be bought by cash-payment; and without love men cannot endure to be together' (II, 229), but for him this was primarily a social issue, the need for strong processes of bonding between individuals, for deep and sustaining collective loyalties. But where Dickens took this one powerful step further was to show how personal relations within the family – between father and son, father and daughter, man and wife – could be damaged by this ideology: Dombey, by treating his own family as his satellites, minions and subordinates, not only makes his children and his wife deeply unhappy but brings an even greater emptiness and unhappiness into his own life. Paul Dombey, Florence and Edith at least have their own sense of personal integrity to sustain them, but Dombey has no positive qualities. He has proved unable either to give love or to accept it precisely because such reciprocity threatens his weak identity, which is founded solely on the exercise of personal power. By denying, or attempting to deny, any personal freedom to those who are ostensibly closest to him, he demands that they live a life that will be as hollow as his own. Dickens's subtitle 'Dealings with the firm of Dombey and Son' clearly focuses these issues, not just because Paul is thereby simply a kind of corroboration of the whole commercial undertaking, but because Dombey's life is made of nothing else but dealings – he comes to the same sort of understandings with his wife as he does with Carker, his manager, and even uses Carker to pursue those dealings. The terrible failure in Dombey's life is not so much that he is insensitive or hard-hearted, but that he seems incapable of being a human being, he lacks any real core to his personality. Throughout the novel Dickens emphasises that Dombey was a person who defined himself through externals, but never more powerfully than when, in the very first chapter, he describes Florence looking up at him: 'the child glanced keenly at the blue coat and stiff white cravat, which with a pair of creaking boots and a very loud ticking watch, embodied her idea of a father'.

For Dombey such indicators of the successful commercial life are signifiers of plenitude: they mark him off from others as at once prosperous, punctilious and correct; they show him forth in just the manner that he wishes to be displayed. Yet to Florence they indicate only a terrible lack and absence. There is no way in which these things can really mean 'Father' to her, especially when Dombey seems incapable of love, which could only indicate, as far as he is concerned, some kind of flaw in his authority. He must be respected and reverenced for what he is, not merely loved and loving in return. For Dombey money is, above all, an instrument of power. He answers Paul's innocent but deadly question 'what is money, after all?' by saying 'Money, Paul, can do everything', and subsequently he insists on the power of money to Mrs Skewton and his wife. Dombey cannot allow freedom because he believes that money gives him the power to own, possess and control. He is even proprietorial where Major Bagstock and his interminable anecdotes is concerned. Yet the irony is that the more he seeks to extend his power, the weaker he becomes – utterly despised and repudiated by his wife, Edith, and altogether at the mercy of Carker and his financial manipulations. After the financial collapse the hollow shell of Dombey's house symbolises the real emptiness he has brought about. It has never been a home in any sense – simply the apogee of Dombey's programme of self-promotion and self-glorification. In *Dombey and Son* clothing and identity are always bound up together. As a dedicated follower of Fielding and Smollett, Dickens well knew how clothing could serve to articulate an idea of character, yet he was equally aware of its problematic relationship to the individual. It is significant that Rob the Grinder, who incurs hostility through his possession of an expensive school blazer, should be the most chameleon-like character in the book, working for Mrs Brown, Carker and Solomon Gills. It is also noteworthy that Florence, whose own identity is never acknowledged by her father, should suffer the trauma of having all her clothing stripped off and of having to search for her father's office in rags, well knowing that she has probably not even been missed. Here, the clothing figure actualises Florence's plight as a kind of Cinderella figure, who all through the novel is despised, rejected and ignored. This fairy-tale character is subsequently intensified, when Dickens describes how

> Florence lived alone in the great dreary house, and day succeeded day, and still she lived alone; and the blank walls looked down on her with a vacant stare, as if they had a Gorgon-like mind to stare her youth and beauty into stone.
>
> No magic dwelling place in magic story, shut up in the heart of a thick wood, was ever more solitary and deserted to the fancy than was her father's mansion in its grim reality, as it stood lowering on the street.

Florence is a Gothic heroine who is forced to suffer deprivation and imprisonment, the helpless spectator of puzzling events in which she is too insignificant ever to play a conspicuous part. Yet Edith too is a parody Cinderella who instead of being miraculously transformed by her costly garments into a more esteemed and valued person, finds on the contrary that they are only a form of display for Dombey, not for her, and that their magnificence is a badge of servitude. He asks that she be extravagant on his behalf and then has the gall to accuse her of being 'too expensive'. When he finally tears off her tiara and jewels and hurls them on the floor we finally begin to grasp the power that money truly has: to construct a world of appearance where nothing genuine can hope to survive. This notion of appearance is, of course, most strongly registered in the case of Edith's mother, Mrs Skewton, who has devoted her life to creating illusions about herself – most notably with the rose-coloured curtain, which, she believes, adds lustre to her complexion – and whose insincerity Dickens heavily underlines, by having her say on her very first appearance in the novel: 'What I want is frankness, confidence, less conventionality, and freer play of soul. We are so dreadfully artificial. . . . I want Nature everywhere.' Yet while this lack in her case is merely comic and absurd, for Dombey, and for everyone with whom he comes into contact, the consequences are much more far-reaching.

It was in *Dombey and Son* that Dickens first brought into question his deeply cherished belief that the inherent virtues of human nature were always capable of resisting the force of circumstance. Dickens could never accept with a clear conscience the view that urban squalor and poverty created crime. Yet at the same time he did believe that the warped priorities of Dombey were unnatural, and if this was so then there must be a strong presumption that those who lived among circumstances vastly less favourable than he must necessarily be led to perverted forms of conduct:

> Alas! are there so few things in the world, about us, most unnatural, and yet most natural in being so? Hear the magistrate or judge admonish the unnatural outcasts of society; unnatural in brutal habits, unnatural in want of decency, unnatural in losing and confounding all distinctions between good and evil; unnatural in ignorance, in vice, in recklessness, in contumacy, in mind, in looks, in everything. But follow the good clergyman or doctor, who, with his life imperilled at every breath he draws, goes down into their dens, lying within the echoes of our carriage wheels and daily tread upon the pavement stones. . . . Breathe the polluted air, foul with every impurity that is poisonous to health and to life; and have every sense, conferred upon our race for delight and happiness, offended, sickened and disgusted, and made a channel by which misery and death alone can enter. Vainly attempt to think of any simply plant, or flower, or wholesome weeds, that, set in this foetid bed, could have its natural growth, or put its little leaves off to the sun as GOD designed it.

Like many of his contemporaries Dickens thought of the slum areas of London as a centre of contagion and moral corruption, since not only were they the source of cholera outbreaks and centres of venereal disease, but they contained 'a Moral pestilence' leading to 'depravity, impiety drunkenness, theft and murder'.

The development of slums and rookeries and centres of crime was associated with the destruction of traditional centres of working-class life such as Stagg's Gardens, which had been destroyed by the railway, where the old friendly communities had been replaced by streets that suddenly stopped and bridges that led nowhere, by a labyrinth of railway hotels and lodging houses. Nevertheless in *Dombey and Son* Dickens chose to offset and alleviate the overall pessimism of this picture with the nautical instrument shop at the sign of the wooden midshipman, the home of Solomon Gills and subsequently of his old friend Captain Cuttle. The instrument shop is something of anachronism and scarcely anyone ever comes to buy, but it is also the sign of unchanging rectitude in a world where such virtues are hard to come by. Significantly in the case of both Gills and Cuttle the clothes express the man. Sol Gills in 'his old welsh wig and old coffee-coloured coat and basket buttons, with his old infallible chronometer ticking away in his pocket' is the very picture of old-fashioned honesty and the watch itself underlines his own moral constancy. Similarly there is an engaging if ridiculous integrity about Captain Cuttle, who is so utterly unworldly as be positively saint-like and even his attachment to his sugar-tongs and two twisted silver teaspoons in reality shows how very unmaterialistic he is. Dickens observes: 'No child could have surpassed Captain Cuttle in inexperience of everything but wind and weather; in simplicity, credulity, and generous trustfulness. Faith, hope and charity, shared his whole nature among them.'

Cuttle is so invariably attired in a 'wide suit of blue' with a 'hard glazed hat' that Dickens comments: 'The Captain was one of those timber-looking men, suits of oak as well as hearts, who it is almost impossible for the liveliest imagination to separate from any part of their dress, however insignificant.' The Captain and Solomon Gills can never be other than what they are. In a world of change they represent all that is most permanent and abiding, just as the solid, imperturbable wooden midshipman is symbolically contrasted with Carker's gaudy parrot, which embodies all the qualities of his owner – imitative, flashy, unstable and unpredictable: the very sign of the modern. Gills and Cuttle are loyal, devoted and steadfast. Solomon Gills goes away secretly to search for Walter, who is presumed to be drowned. Cuttle gives aid and comfort to Florence when she is most bereft and deserted. In their world there is a place neither for pretension nor pretence. The wooden midshipman represents the heart of a heartless and restless world.

In *Dombey and Son* the motif of substitution plays a very significant part. In particular Dombey is obsessed with the idea that various people are attempting to usurp a position that is rightfully his.

Ironically he never even suspects Carker, who is the individual plotting most deeply to succeed him, but in various ways he fears that Mrs Toodles/Richards, Florence and Edith may have access to a power (or love) that is denied him. Substitution is also important where Florence is concerned since she loses a mother, a brother and a father who must in some way be replaced. Moreover although Paul Dombey is actually irreplaceable, the vacuum that he leaves behind him serves to generate so many of the events of the plot. For Florence, Walter Gay becomes a replacement for her brother, Solomon Gills for her father and Toodles/Richards for her mother. But all three disappear from the scene and must in turn be replaced. Edith Dombey becomes her new mother, Captain Cuttle becomes a substitute father and actually fulfills the role of escorting her down the aisle at her wedding. In some sense the faithful dog, Diogenes, who has belonged to Paul, also functions as a kind of substitute for his former master. Hence the most pathetic substitute is Toots, who in his role as suitor for Florence's hand, confesses his inadequacy by saying: 'If, at the sacrifice of all my property, I could get transmigrated into Miss Dombey's dog I really think I should never leave off wagging my tail.' The chain of substitutions serves as a delaying mechanism whereby both Walter and Florence can eventually takes Paul's place, substituting husband and daughter for brother and son. There is also a significant substitution/transposition in the relationship of Dombey to Paul, since Dombey only sees Paul as his successor, whereas Dombey actually becomes a kind of successor to his son, in learning the unimportance of money. At the beginning Dombey seeks only to abolish childhood, but at the end he learns to become a child again. Thus the idea of progress is rejected not only on a material level but on a psychological level as well.

If for Dickens the world so often assumed a menacing shape, this was in part because of his childhood experiences, not least the notorious if brief spell in the blacking factory. In retrospect it would seem that what Dickens particularly resented was the fact that his father steadfastly refused to acknowledge either his own responsibility for the misfortunes that beset his family or, indeed, the very existence of the misfortunes themselves. His response to the congenital evasiveness of John Dickens was the portrait of Mr Micawber in *David Copperfield* (1849–50). What we should especially note is that in the novel the *malaise* is not confined to Micawber himself – David is anxious to avoid the weakness and passivity that afflicts so many others in the novel, whether Mr Dick, Mr Wicksteed or Traddles, yet even he is not unaffected. His aunt, Betsy Trotwood, recognises that part of the fascination that Dora holds for him stems from her determination to refuse adulthood and to go on living as a child, who can know nothing of money or domestic duties and who feels entitled, because of her privileged background, to close her eyes to the harshness of the world in which David must make his way. Throughout we perceive that David is weak and easily imposed upon: the humorous incident in which the waiter polishes off the meal he has ordered figures as an early allegory of his character. Yet even David does not share Micawber's delusion that the world somehow owes him a living and that therefore as he is unfortunate enough to possess no steady source of income, it is incumbent on the world to rectify that omission as soon as possible. As Mrs Micawber observes:

> 'And here is Mr Micawber without any suitable position or employment. Where does the responsibility rest? Clearly on society. Then I would make a fact so disgraceful known, and boldly challenge society to set it right. It appears to me, my dear Copperfield,' said Mrs Micawber forcefully, 'that what Mr Micawber has to do, is to throw down the gauntlet to society, and say, in effect, "show me who will take that up. Let the party immediately step forward."'

The absurdity of a demand such as this and John Dickens's readiness to exculpate himself from any part in his own downfall goes a long way to explain why Dickens was so resistant to any sociological explanation of crime, even when the evidence of his own experience pointed strongly in that direction.

Even in early childhood David Copperfield's existence is threatened by the arrival of Mr Murdstone – an implacable and powerful rival for his mother's love. From then on his whole life is to be a quest to find some kind of replacement for the love and security he has lost. The importance of this surfaces when David remembers 'with a grateful heart how blest I was in having such a friend as Steerforth, such a friend as Peggotty, and such a substitute for what I had lost as my excellent and generous aunt'. Yet all the happy, stable places, whose twinkling lights beckon so invitingly to David through the surrounding darkness, prove to be fragile and transitory themselves. Even Betsy Trotwood, whose place in the world seems so unassailable, is not only plagued by visits from her former husband but subjected to severe financial losses, which are eventually attributed to the machinations of Uriah Heep, who also brings misfortune on Mr Wickfield and his daughter. A shadow is cast over the genial existence of the schoolmaster Dr Strong, through the involvement of his young wife with her cousin, Jack Maldon, and even the simple working-class conviviality of the Peggottys is suddenly shattered when Little Emily is calculatedly seduced by David's friend Steerforth. This devastation of such a place of refuge from all the evils of the world is made the worse because it is David who has brought the serpent with him. His lack of confidence, his general indecisiveness affects those whom he cares for just as much as himself. It is actually hard to believe that he possesses the qualities to become, like Dickens, a House of Commons stenographer and a successful writer, and we can only share Traddles's surprise when he says to David 'Dear me. I had no idea that you were such a determined character, Copperfield.'

Most of David's energies go into the search for a variety of mentor figures, ranging from Steerforth and Traddles to his aunt and Agnes. At bottom, though Dickens might strongly resist the implication, Mr Micawber is David's double – both attempt to solve the difficulties they encounter in life by seeking to place themselves trustingly in the hands of others. This is so quite as much at the end of the novel as it was in its beginnings. After the death of Dora and the tragedy of the Peggottys, David goes abroad an utterly devastated and broken man:

> The desolate feeling with which I went abroad, deepened and widened hourly. At first it was a heavy sense of loss and sorrow, wherein I could distinguish little else. By imperceptible degrees it became a hopeless consciousness of all that I had lost – love, friendship, interest; of all that had been shattered – my first trust, my first affection, the whole airy castle of my life; of all that remained as a ruined blank and waste, unbroken to the dark horizon.

At this moment David's constant fear that the world is not to be relied upon seems all too brutally corroborated. Yet his loss, so overwhelming, can nevertheless be made up for by the one final substitution that can make life whole again – of Agnes for Dora, who does possess that greatest of Victorian virtues, a 'deep downright faithful earnestness'. David can find in Agnes what the world itself lacks. Moreover this final stability is peculiarly satisfying because the promise has been so long withheld. Although David's love for Agnes is presented as something salvaged from a more general wreckage, taken in conjunction with the salvation of Mr Micawber, it does offer a sense of completion and closure that Dickens would never permit himself again.

One of the strangest disclosures in *David Copperfield* is when Uriah Heep accuses David of being an 'upstart'. We do not expect to hear the hero spoken of in such a way even if he is a man who has risen in the world, and, unlike Heep, by perfectly legitimate methods. Yet once the connection is made the parallels become irresistible. David's relationship with the Spenlows is very like Uriah's situation at the Wickfields, and at least part of the reason why David prefers to think of Agnes as a friend rather than as a lover is that he is reluctant even to contemplate the idea of Uriah as a rival. David always conceals, muffles and dissimulates his desire to a point where he scarcely knows any longer what he wants himself, whereas both the revered Steerforth and the despised Heep are perfectly open about what they want and absolutely determined to get it. What they want is also what David wants, but they are not inhibited by social taboos and prohibitions in the way that David is, which gives them an 'unfair' advantage. When David says of Steerforth's seduction of Emily: 'Deeply as I felt my own unconscious part in his pollution of our honest home, I believe that if I had been brought face to face with him, I could not have uttered one reproach', he speaks sincerely not just because of his love for Steerforth but because of his complicity in Steerforth's desires, and his admiration for the man who has the bravado and confidence to achieve them. On the one hand David reverences the innocence and security of the Peggotty household; on the other, on some more primitive level he resents it because he himself has been denied it. Moreover the whole question of the Peggottys is complexly bound up with the taboo against female sexuality in the novel. So many of the women in *David Copperfield* are child-like: little Emily, Annie, Dora, David's mother, even, though to a lesser degree, Agnes herself. The illicit and sinister hold that Mr Murdstone obtained over David's mother with his luxuriant black moustaches is repeated in little Emily's fascination with Steerforth and Annie's compromising involvement with her cousin. It is this very possibility that menaces the idea of the home as a place of security. Yet equally the dilemma of the novel is that a relationship with a child bride like Dora, while unthreatening, is also deeply unsatisfying since she has no strength of character or spirit of independence. She cannot offer David the security he craves because she in turn wishes to place the whole burden of existence on him. Although Agnes has never been for David this object of desire, this also means that his love for her has never become entangled in a net of misrecognitions. He need no longer be haunted by the spectre of rivalry.

In his earlier fiction Dickens had been comparatively sanguine about the state of English society and had tended to see social problems as being called into existence by such innovations as the new Poor Law. With *Bleak House* (1852–3), however, under the influence of Carlyle and utilising his own experience of the legal system 'at work' in Chancery, he painted a gloomy picture of England as a torpid, moribund society in which the living generations are shown as being slowly suffocated out of existence by the protocols, precedents, laws and traditions of the past, by a legal system that has intentionally lost sight of its ostensible *raison d'être* – to deliver justice. This image is all the more remarkable, occurring as it does in the immediate aftermath of the Great Exhibition, which had demonstrated beyond any possible hint of doubt that England was in the forefront of nations. It is now that we see all the more clearly Dickens's stubborn integrity as a writer – his refusal to be seduced by commonplaces when they were in sharp contradiction with his own experience. Now Dickens recognised more clearly than ever before that the forces which made for change, though significant, nevertheless seemed comparatively lightweight when weighed against the massive inertia of English society in general. Through Carlyle he became conscious of the ways in which societies can be transformed into hollow shells as life and vitality progressively ebbs out of institutions that once possessed an authentic collective significance. In consequence people become enchained and enchanted by a set of illusory appearances that no longer correspond to the real forces actually at work in the world, and they can find no meaningful outlet into which to direct their energies. Carlyle insists: 'Nature and Fact, not Redtape and Semblance are the basis of man's life' (II, 21). Needless to say, Carlyle's analysis of the continuing role of an outworn past in human affairs has a special pertinence to the law. As Carlyle characteristically insists it is *not* the legal forms in themselves that matter but their connection with the preservation of justice:

> For the gowns of learned-serjeants are good; parchment records, fixed forms, and poor terrestrial Justice, with or without horse-

hair, what sane man will not reverence thcse? and yet, behold, the man is not sane but insane, who considers these alone venerable. Oceans of horse-hair, continents of parchment, and learned-serjeant eloquence, were it continued till the learned tongue wore itself small in the indefatiguable learned mouth, cannot make unjust just. (II, 9)

Carlyle's perception of the law is all of a piece with his view of a hereditary aristocracy: 'Aristocracies, actual and imaginary, reach a time when parchment pleading shall not avail them' (II, 153). Carlyle believes that no section of society has the right to rest on its laurels, the aristocracy in particular must continually justify its existence by renewed efforts and fresh achievements. There has been a revolution in France precisely because of the terrible fixity and inertia of the system. Dickens was certainly influenced by this overall assessment but his own view of the state of England was, if anything, even more pessimistic. For Carlyle there is a certain dynamism in history which ensures that even if suppressed energies are blocked in one place, they will inevitably surface in another, like an earthquake or volcanic eruption. Sooner or later, something somewhere will have to give and the explosion, when it comes, will be the more terrifying the longer it is delayed. So the ruling class can never be tranquil.

Dickens, on the contrary, was impressed by England's massive imperviousness to change. More than any of his contemporaries he saw just how superficial the few changes cranking laboriously through the system actually were. He saw how tenaciously and jealously the vested interests in society, from the landed aristocracy to the legal profession, guarded their powers and he recognised that there was no contrary force that could winkle them out of their entrenched positions. Certainly Parliament would not do it for Parliament was their first and last line of defence. So Dicken's famous description of Tom-All-Alone's is very much more than an expressive use of local colour. The very existence of such a place, such an ambience, stands as a massive indictment of a system that not only will do nothing about it but has never even remotely considered doing anything about it:

Jo lives – that is to say, Jo has not yet died – in a ruinous place, known to the likes of him by the name of Tom-All-Alone's. It is a black, dilapidated street, avoided by all decent people; where the crazy houses were seized upon, when their decay was far advanced, by some bold vagrants, who, after establishing their own possession, took to letting them out in lodgings. Now, these tumbling tenements contain, by night a swarm of misery. As, on the ruinous human wretch, vermin parasites appear, so these ruined shelters have bred a crowd of foul existence that crawls in and out of gaps in walls and boards; and coils itself to sleep, in maggot numbers, where the rain drips in; and comes and goes, fetching and carrying fever, and sowing more evil in its every footprint than Lord Coodle, and Sir Thomas Doodle, and the Duke of Foodle, and all the fine gentlemen in office, down to Zoodle, shall set right in five hundred years – though born expressly to do it.

Just a few years earlier Dickens might have been tempted, like so many of his contemporaries, to present the squalor of urban London as some kind of adventitious scar on the smiling face of England's green and pleasant land; now he was determined to insist on the urgency and intractability of the problem. Tom-All-Alone's can no longer be seem as some little local difficulty, some freak or aberration, but as representative of the desperate pass that England has been brought to. Tom-All-Alone's is Carlyle's imperious fact that by its very nature puts in question the political and juridical institutions that would seek to ignore it. In this way *Bleak House* subtly parodies the style of writing practised by Bulwer-Lytton, where the seedy picturesque is but prelude and dramatic relief for a drama whose setting will be predominantly within stately walls and behind lofty porticoes. Dickens, of course, freely acknowledges that the only thing that can make outcast London interesting is that it possesses some obscure connection with the august affair of Sir Leicester and Lady Dedlock in Chesney Wold. Ordinarily the life and death of some obscure opium addict in a seedy garret, the circumstances of a crossing sweeper like Jo would be of interest to no one. These are everyday tragedies, so commonplace as to be hardly worth commentating on. It is only when they touch the lives of the high and the mighty that they become of interest to such voyeuristic manipulators as Tulkinghorn or Guppy. Dickens forces us to recognise our own complicity in such a perspective. The famous scene in which Jo is moved on has a complex representational significance, for as Dickens notes 'the great lights of the parliamentary sky have failed for some years in this business, to set you the example of moving on'.

This is just one of the many manoeuvres that society adopts to mask, conceal and dissimulate all the disasters in its midst. As Dickens knows, the problems themselves will not go away. So the novel itself in endlessly moving on, in pursuing dynamically its narrative threads through an atrophying, stagnating world always risks deflecting attention from the social questions that it so persistently tries to address. Dickens the concerned individual risks becoming like Mrs Flite or Mr Gridley, an ineffectual interrupter of his own more imperious novelistic proceedings. In *Bleak House* Dickens, in the terminology of the Russian formalists, lays bare the device, exposing the law of narrative as complicit with the laws of a class society.

In relation to the melodramatic tale of Lady Dedlock, the fallen woman enshrined within the citadel of the English aristocracy, the tale of Esther Summerson is deliberately hum-drum and low-key, despite her ostensibly pivotal role in the narrative as the conclusive evidence in the case, as Lady Dedlock's illegitimate daughter. For Dickens this connection cannot be the *raison d'être* of Esther's life – it is on the contrary the menacing fact of her existence which she must endlessly strive and struggle to overcome. Here we cannot fail to recognise the desire on the part of Dickens himself to be able to live a stable and ordered existence, where he himself would always be personally in control, despite the misfortune of having been brought up as the son of a spendthrift and perennial debtor, whose existence could well have cast even longer shadows over the life of the son that it actually did. Dickens's determination to hack himself free, first from his father's all-enveloping webs and then from the family life that he had established with his first wife, led to a definite ruthlessness on his part that is not reflected in the character of Esther Summerson. Dickens nevertheless asks us to recognise that in life a moment may come when, through the sheer desire for survival, the individual may be compelled to limit his or her involvement in the predicament of others. Esther is concerned about Lady Dedlock's fate, yet she is equally determined to avoid the temptation of being dragged under the wheels of her mother's funeral car, just as she refuses to become emotionally involved in the long drawn-out proceedings of Jarndyce *v.* Jarndyce. Despite appearances Esther can be hard as well as soft. Dickens sees Esther's whole mode of being as having much wider application. We should orientate our lives around that which is closest and most immediate to us (unlike, say, Mrs Jellaby) and not allow ourselves to be distracted by more fascinating and glamorous events that seem to reduce and even trivialise the possibility of domestic happiness. In a sense such a moral axiom can be seen as expressing a curiously Victorian complacency about the integrity and priority of the private life that makes it possible and even easy to let the rest of the world go hang. What to Dickens and the Victorians seemed sheer sanity, can to us, in the aftermath of Stalin, Auschwitz and Ceaucescu, look much more like insanity and criminal irresponsibility. Yet if the need for self-preservation is not always a such unproblematic imperative as it might seem, it is never theless a powerful one, and in Esther's case the need for a radical simplification very real. If there is a desire at Chesney Wold to suppress any recognition of Tom-All-Alone's and what it represents, we must recognise that there is a certain smugness at Bleak House too.

In Scott's *Redgauntlet* the young hero is haunted by his fateful resemblance to Redgauntlet, the veteran supporter of the doomed Jacobite cause, and in consequence becomes almost involuntarily entangled in political plots whose momentum persists even when the passions that once generated them seem to belong to a bygone age – the past has a python-like power to envelop and engorge the present. Yet Darcy must find his own destiny as Esther finds hers. In *Bleak House* the resemblance between Esther and Lady Dedlock's portrait is constantly alluded to, with the implication both that they share a similar beauty and that their destinies are inescapably coupled together. In a crucial scene, after her illness, Esther looks at herself in the mirror and sees herself as some *other* person. The smallpox she has caught from Jo is in one sense the curse of her mother that also risks disfiguring her own life; yet from another point of view it marks the crucial *difference* that will make another life possible for her. Esther denies that she was ever a beauty, but the reader interprets this as both modesty and *post-facto* rationalisation. The real significance of her *alteration* is that it makes possible a new, more ordinary life that can actually be her own. The power of grand narrative *can* be resisted as the separate articulation of Esther's *own* story attests.

Vanity Fair is a novel without a hero, for a long time the problem of Dickens had been reverse, that of writing a novel without a villain. Even in *Dombey and Son*, with its powerful depiction of the hollowness of Victorian values, he had nevertheless to introduce a villain as a means by which to engineer the downfall of the haughty Dombey. The villain was the way in which the menacing world was made manifest. But in *Bleak House* Dickens brilliantly and powerfully expressed his dispiriting yet recalcitrant sense of the world. *Bleak House* takes the law as its focus, yet the law is just a compelling symbol of a human world that has grown impervious to human desire. In the world of *Bleak House* you have to surrender hope just as surely as in Dante's Hell. The law, like the mythical Minotaur, is only encountered at the end of myriad winding passages, and when the moment of truth comes it offers not justice but destruction. In a way the financial cost is the least of it all. It is, of course, well nigh incomprehensible that such a vast estate as that at stake in Jarndyce *v.* Jarndyce should be wholly consumed in legal costs, but Dickens shows that the real cost is in human suffering, in hope endlessly postponed, delayed, betrayed. We first encounter Miss Flite and the man from Shropshire as ludicrous and maladroit disruptors, whose obsessiveness verges on madness. They are comic we think. Only gradually does Dickens bring home to us that these figures of farce become ridiculous through their own blighted hopes. We have to adopt a different perspective. Living with 'justice' becomes a complex figure for the whole problem of existence in general – how it is possible to live from day to day without ever expecting anything; or how contrariwise is it possible to live from day to day in a constant state of expectation? If there were no future, life would be difficult but it would not be threatening. In effect Harold Skimpole, though mercilessly satirised, nevertheless does offer a hypothetical solution to this dilemma. Harold follows the biblical injunction to take no thought for the morrow. His existence is radically simplified through his childlike immersion in the present and through his refusal to think of the consequences; Skimpole has found his own idiosyncratic way of evading the difficulties of existence, yet no one could seriously consider following him. In the figure of Richard Carstone Dickens crystallises the psychological impossibility of living in a state of dependence on the outcome of events that must necessarily be imponderable and unspecifiable. It would be easy to be censorious of his constant switches of mood but Dickens understands very well the psychology of his character and shows just how easy it is for a person to lose his way under the pressure of contingency. Richard loses sight of the fact that he is responsible for his own life. He cannot decide on a career.

He signs contracts without the ability to pay for them. He tries to stabilise his existence by marrying Ada. He dares to hope. With a young man's natural enthusiasm he tries to channel his energies into pursuing the case. He tries to be self-reliant. Later he falls back to a state of dependency on Vholes, taking Vholes's pertinacity to be a kind of worthy, self-validating activity and never quite recognising

that Vholes, like everyone else, is finally only after his own percent-
age of the costs. Yet, at bottom, no one can be blamed, just as Coavins
cannot be blamed for asking Harold Skimpole for twenty-four pounds
sixteen and sevenpence ha'penny: they are all doing their job. Even
Tulkinghorn is only doing his job according to his own lights –
safeguarding the interests of his employer even if his employer dies
in the attempt. As David Trotter points out: 'Tulkinghorn's vocation,
his very being, is secrecy. He neither explains anything, nor is explained. He represents a *NO THOROUGHFARE* sign, a block to the
hermeneutic activity on which the moving world depends for its
movement.'[4] Tulkinghorn is not himself the villain, he is only the
supreme embodiment of the relentless, pitiless workings for the
whole infernal and incomprehensible system. When Lady Dedlock
tells Esther that she is unable to shake Tulkinghorn off, Esther asks
'Has he so little pity or compunction?', to which her newly discovered mother replies: 'He has none, and no anger. He is indifferent to
everything but his calling. His calling is the acquisition of secrets,
and the holding possession of such power as they give him, with no
sharer or opponent in it.'

The nightmare of *Bleak House* is at once genuine parodic, since it is
based on the strange inversion by which a world on paper becomes
more important than the real and actual world in which that paper
figures also as so much garbage and detritus. The power of the law
rests on its multitudinous documents, its wills, affidavits, pleas,
warrants and petitions, and of course the more this paper prolifer-
ates, the more powerful and more impenetrable the law becomes.
The monstrosity of the law consists in the fact that the more labori-
ous its workings, the more imposing its proceedings must seem; the
more incompetent it is, the more profitable for its practitioners it
becomes. As Dickens wryly notes at the opening of the novel, as a
massive panoply of blue bags are laboriously carried away: 'If all the
injustice it has committed, and all the misery it has caused, could
only be locked up with it, and the whole burnt in a great funeral pyre
– why so much the better for other parties than the parties in Jarndyce
and Jarndyce.' Yet Dickens's attitude to this world of writing is more
ambivalent than it might seem. We must remember that Dickens's
own successful attempt to raise himself from reduced circumstances
to a position of social eminence itself derived from the power of
writing, first as a stenographer, then as a successful novelist. Dickens
therefore had every reason to believe, in a world in which the major-

ity could not read and write, that writing was a phenomenon charged with immense cultural significance. What his work as a stenographer in particular revealed to him was that those things that were written down were those to which society assigned a particular value. What was written was preserved and when weighed against its massive and copious documentary reality the ordinary world must appear by contrast as ephemeral and insubstantial. Although Dickens is acutely conscious of the injustice, perversity and confusion generated by this fetishisation of the written word, he nevertheless accepts that the reality that it serves to define cannot be ignored even if it can be deplored. Only the Harold Skimpoles of this world can affect to ignore the significances of writs, summonses and written loans, and perhaps not even he. The power of the world on paper is testified to by Jo, the crossing sweeper, who, on his deathbed, seeks to give some title and status to his sorrow that he has given Esther her disfiguring illness by having it written 'Uncommon precious large'.

Whenever there are matters of importance and deep significance in *Bleak House* they are necessarily written down, even though this very act of writing may lead to confusion, unhappiness, further litigation, perhaps even to death. Seemingly to enter the world of writing is to be powerful, and yet the world of inscription itself cannot be mastered but becomes an alien power, a monstrous web of writing that entangles and captures all who enter its domain. Hence Inspector Bucket's distrust of letters:

> He is no great scribe; rather handling his pen like the pocket-staff he carries about with him convenient to his grasp; and discourages correspondence with himself in others, as being too artless and direct a way of doing delicate business. Further, he often sees damaging letters produced in evidence, and has occasion to reflect that it was a green thing to write them. For these reasons he has very little to do with letters either as sender or receiver.

In effect Bucket, acutely conscious of the dangers of writing, and Tulkinghorn, the apparent master of everything connected with the written text, represent the opposite polarities of the novel. Yet virtually all the other characters either maintain their livelihood through the written word or find their existence controlled by it. There is Mr Snagsby, the law stationer, who deals in all sorts of blank forms of legal process; in skin and rolls of parchment; in paper – foolscap, brief, draft, brown, white, whitey-brown and blotting; in stamps, in office-quills, pens, ink, India-rubber, pounce, pins, pencils, sealing-wax, and wafers; in red tape and green ferret, in pocket-books, almanacks, diaries, and law lists; in string boxes, rulers, inkstands – glass and leaden, penknives, scissors, bodkins, and other small office cutlery; in short in articles too numerous to mention.

Part of Dickens's peculiar genius as a novelist is not just his very Victorian fascination with bric-à-brac – since it was the Victorian age itself which brought into being so many of these multitudinous objects – but that he recognises that even an activity so apparently abstract as the law nevertheless has a material base, in terms both of the practical requirements that it specifies and the opportunity for employment that it provides. The power of documents extends far and wide. There is Hawdon, who, though a protagonist in the Deadlock affair, is nevertheless reduced to the role of humble copyist for Jarndyce and Jarndyce and betrayed by his own distinctive hand. Although he is so enigmatic and so elusive and individual, his existence is nevertheless memorialised in paper – in 'crumpled paper, smelling of opium, on which are scrawled rough memoranda – as took, such a day, so many grains'. There is Grandfather Smallwood with his documents secured in two black leather cases, which in turn are further secured within a locked bureau. There is Tulkinghorn who lives surrounded by the files and documents of those who believe they employ him as their confidential servant even when he, armed with all this information, is actually the master. There is Guppy who in his humbler way nevertheless recognises the possibilities within the law for blackmail and extortion. There is the honest, dependable, reliable Mr Vholes who nevertheless succeeds in depriving Richard of whatever resources he possesses. *Bleak House* shows that such parasites are always more powerful than those who lack this control over the written word. Worse still, the hegemony of writing is such as to have the effect of devaluing everything that has not been accorded inscription. Mrs Jellaby is one of a vast retinue of heartless parents in *Bleak House*, but her massive indifference is significantly associated with the power of writing. The first impression of the Jellaby household is one of paper that has got out of control: 'The room, which was strewn with papers and nearly filled by a great writing table covered with similar litter, was I must say, not only untidy, but very dirty.'

Of course, through Mrs Jellaby Dickens castigates those for whom causes far from home will always be more pressing than those that are near and immediate, but he also shows how deeply this is connected with the idea of correspondence and documents. Mrs Jellaby's general air of abstraction in the real world is deeply bound up with her privileging of the signifier. Those who are alienated and disconnected from the written word are victims. There is Jo, there is the bridegroom whom the bride will not shame by writing her own name, there is Mr George, the honest trooper, who freely confesses to Tulkinghorn: 'I have no head for papers, sir.'

In the world of *Bleak House* there could be no more damaging admission of frailty – and no more damaging person to confess it to. The most pathetic instance of the fetishisation of written texts and documents is Mr Krook, who though he owns a rag and bottle warehouse and is a dealer in marine stores is nevertheless obsessed with the power of written documents precisely because he cannot read or understand them. Krook can make out the letters but the actual meaning or sense escapes him. As such he is a fitting analogue for the Chancery after which he is named. Krook is tortured by his inability to read. He is haunted by the intransigent word that will forever elude him. Krook is not merely emblematic of the obscurity of legal processes, he epitomises the nightmare of *Bleak House* – a world in which the quest for meaning can only appear as a vain endeavour.

At the centre of *Bleak House* are two characters whose lives are dominated by the act of writing: Esther Summerson and her mother, Lady Dedlock. Esther is the author of her own narrative, her attempt to describe her life from her own point of view. Yet this writing is itself crucially dependent for its construction on other written documents. There is the letter she receives from Kenge and Carbury, which changes her whole life and delivers her into the guardianship of Mr Jarndyce. There is the written proposal of marriage, which she receives from Mr Jarndyce himself – as if the infringement of a taboo is only possible through the written word. There is the letter she receives from Lady Dedlock, in which she acknowledges, and which she also asks her to burn. There are the letters that Lady Dedlock wrote to Hawdon, which now offer the possibility of blackmail. There are the messages that Lady Dedlock sends to Esther before her death. It is as if everything that is really crucial to Esther's life is set down on paper. Yet there is a strange discrepancy between the abstract and formal tone of the letter she receives from Kenge and Carbury and the effect that it has: 'O never, never, never shall I

forget the emotion this letter caused in the house.' For all its apparent abstraction, writing can nevertheless be the occasion and the
signifier of powerful emotions. Everything connected with Lady
Dedlock is inscribed on paper, which signifies both its illicit power
and truth, and yet, at the same time, its potential for social disruption. Again, Dickens seems ambivalent here. On the one hand there
is a certain justice in the revelation of the truth, in the unforeseen
connections between the world of Tom-All-Alone's and Chesney
Wold, and yet it cannot be denied that that power is destructive. All
the characters of *Bleak House* are at the disposal of this merciless
power of inscription – hence the strange pathos of the moment
whereby Sir Leicester Dedlock, himself psychologically devastated
by the written evidence that Inspector Bucket has uncovered, nevertheless tries to cling on to his sense of things by *writing* 'Chesney
Wold'. Writing is the power to control.

As we have seen, Dickens believed very strongly in individual
free will, yet at the same time he could not deny that Victorian
society, both through its material circumstances and its ideology,
was able to shape and modify the lives of individuals to the extent
that they became either the prisoners of circumstances or of a particular kind of education – though mental conditioning might actually be a more appropriate term. Typically Dickens in his fiction
showed his characters enmeshed in complex webs and their desperate struggles to break free, yet he was usually content to do this
without necessarily drawing any explicit conclusion. *Hard Times*
(1854) is different. In this novel Dickens frankly showed how the
human personality could be warped and distorted both by a utilitarian system of values but also by the conditions of industrial society.
Hard Times is often seen as Dickens's belated attempt to write a social
novel in the manner of Mrs Gaskell. Dickens has been criticised for
his failure fully to acknowledge the right of the working class to
freedom and self-determination, and on this level the criticism is
entirely just. Dickens was not sympathetic to social disorder or to
striking workers – indeed these were thing he deeply feared and his
silence during the heyday of Chartism was certainly significant.
Dickens could only address the issue once the Chartist threat to
middle-class society had collapsed, and he could only approach it in
middle-class terms. Nevertheless, deliberately depoliticised as the
novel is, it remains a powerful critique of the sources of contemporary alienation. What Dickens recognises is that the breakdown of
family life, whether it is that of Sissy Jupe, the Gradgrinds or Stephen

Blackpool, is directly created by a society that places the majority of people under intolerable economic and psychological pressure and denies them any sense of their own worth and significance. Mutual respect is a very rare quality in *Hard Times*. Bounderby values no one but himself and even denies his own mother's life to increase his own self-importance. Gradgrind asks his children to meet targets and jump through hoops. He cannot accept them for what they are. Louisa finds some comfort and consolation in the company of James Harthouse, yet she cannot recognise him as the shallow and self-centred person that he is simply because she has never known anything any better. Stephen Blackpool alone is sustained by the love and respect of Ruth, despite his unhappy marriage and isolation from his fellow workers, but the pressures that he experiences are so great that even this is not enough. Stephen seems to be a reactionary figure, precisely because Dickens does not wish to be interpreted as supporting industrial unrest, yet he is nevertheless used to mount a powerful critique of contemporary society. For what Stephen's apparently vague words focus on is the psychological oppression that denies people rights to express themselves freely and to possess any individual identity: 'to piece out a livin', aw the same one way, somehows, twixt their cradles and their graves. Look how we live, and wheer we live, in what numbers, an by what chances, and wi' what sameness.'

Dickens knew from the frustration of his own marriage and the need to keep up respectable appearances how the ethic of Victorian society worked to impose a rigid set of appearances on all members of society, and despite the plethora of 'characters' for which his novels are justly celebrated, he also knew just how fragile such individuality was. Here, symbolically, we see the connection with *Dombey and Son* where Dombey's stiff cravat seems to exemplify a whole mode of being. Dombey denies individuality in himself, in his family, in others. He seeks to impose his will on others even though he is the hollowest man of all, a man who at bottom has no idea of what he really wants. And what goes for Dombey goes for Gradgrind and Bounderby too. They are both self-righteous and emotionally crippled. Consciously they try to make others follow their pattern, in the belief that they are superior human beings; subconsciously, like Dombey, they feel threatened by those who love, care and are able to express their feelings. Dickens shows us that Utilitarianism is not simply a 'philosophy' but a pathology as well.

Little Dorrit (1855–7) is Dickens's finest novel, not just one of the classic works of Victorian fiction but one of the great masterpieces of world literature, a work that not only offers an extraordinarily complex vision of Victorian society, but also displays the most profound insight into questions of human identity and behaviour. It would not be wrong to describe *Little Dorrit* as fatalistic: all of Dickens's characters struggle desperately against the forces that seems to have determined their lives, for we see that they are doubly constrained – as much in terms of their own identity and behaviour as in the objective circumstances with which they must contend. Whereas in his earlier fiction Dickens had pitted his protagonists against a menacing and unstable world, his heroes themselves were sound in wind, limb and mind, ready to encounter any hard knocks they might receive without either complaining or flinching. But in the later novels, and especially in *Little Dorrit*, it is a different story. From the outset virtually all the characters that Dickens presents us with are the walking wounded. They have already been damaged by life and though they may somehow struggle on, make their way, survive, he never allows us to lose sight of the price they have already paid as well as the price they continue to pay. Perhaps the influence of Carlyle, always great, is greatest here. For the world of *Little Dorrit* is a world that has lost all theological meaning and all secular meaning as well. It is a monstrous engine, as infernal machine that continues to puff out stream, make a terrible noise and rotate its massive wheels, yet without any presumption or expectation that this all amounts to anything whatsoever or that it is actually going anywhere. There is the grand capitalist exploitation of Merdle, and on a lower level there is the petty but relentless exploitation of Casby, there are interminable manoeuvres and delays of the Circumlocution Office – but all this only serves to proclaim a society that functions without even understanding how or why it is functioning, a society that lacks not only justice but any conceivable *raison d'être*. But Dickens cannot disconnect this lack of purpose in society from its effect on the lives of individuals, and he shows just how demoralising and how stultifying it is to try to survive in such a world. For Dickens society is now an inherently repressive force. Its effect is to choke and suffocate the life of every individual. If there is no purpose there is no hope. Hope, of course, can never be totally destroyed, but Dickens well understands the inner anguish of those whose lives are haunted by repetition, in which hope is so often delayed and deferred that it has become a terrible parody of the thing that it still, faintly, aspires to be. Carlyle saw the French

Revolution as the volcanic bursting forth of forces that had been long stifled and repressed and Dickens picked up this analogy in *Hard Times* when, referring to the rebellion of Louisa Gradgrind, he wrote 'All closely imprisoned forces rend and destroy.'

But in *Little Dorrit*, while the suffocating, choking force of culture is powerfully represented, there is very little sense indeed of a humanity bursting free. What is particularly striking about *Little Dorrit* is the way the psychology of the central characters is linked with those who fill out the canvas – so many of them live in a state of suspended animation, a state of 'living on' after they have seemingly lost the sources of energy that once made life meaningful to them. A classic instance of this is the old musician whom Little Dorrit sees on a visit to the theatre:

> He had been in that place six nights a week for many years, but had never been observed to raise his eyes above his music-book, and was confidently believed to have never seen a play. There were legends in the place that he did not so much as know the popular heroes and heroines by sight, and that the low comedian had 'mugged' at him in his richest manner fifty nights for a wager, and he had shown no trace of consciousness. The carpenters had a joke to the effect that he was dead without being aware of it; and the frequenters of the pit supposed him to pass his whole life, night and day, and Sunday and all, in the orchestra. They had tried him a few times with pinches of snuff offered over the rails, and he had always responded to this attention with a momentary waking up of a manner that had the pale phantom of a gentleman in it: beyond this he never, on any occasion, had any other part in what was going on than the part written out for the clarionet; in private life, where there was no part for the clarionet, he had no part at all. Some said he was poor, some said he was a wealthy miser; but he said nothing, never lifted up his bowed head, never varied his shuffling gait by getting his springless foot from the ground.

What is particularly tragic about this old man is not just that his own existence seems to have no meaning and he had become nothing more than a Hoffmann-like automation, playing the same notes over and over again, but that in the process he seems to have lost any connection whatsoever with human society. An equally abject figure is old Nandy, who also possesses a musical talent:

The poor little man knew some pale and vapid little songs, long out of date, about Chloe, and Phyllis, and Strephon being wounded by the son of Venus; and for Mrs Plornish there was no such music at the Opera as the small flutterings and chirpings wherein he would discharge himself of these ditties, like a weak, little, broken barrel-organ, ground by a baby.

Once again there is the analogy with a machine, the sense of a life that has become meaningless – an emptiness that for others becomes a form of amusement. Nandy is such a nondescript individual that even his clothing expresses no sense of identity: 'his coarse shirt and his coarse neckcloth have no more individuality than his coat and hat: they have the same character of not being his – of not being anybody's'. Old Nandy has sunk so low that even William Dorrit – hardly the most psychological robust of individuals – says of him: 'The poor old fellow is a dismal wreck. Spirit broken and gone – pulverised – crushed out of him sir, completely.' Dorrit's jerky delivery cannot but remind us of Jingle in *The Pickwick Papers* and of a world that was utterly different, where it seemed that almost everyone was possessed of preternatural quantities of energy, the energy of Dickens himself. Yet although the old musician and Nandy are two of the most pathetic characters in the novel there are many others who seem to have lost all purpose in life and who seem to persist in a state of suspended animation like a clock that has finally run down – there is Flora Finching and Mr F's aunt; there is Mrs Clennam, and the Flintwichs; there is William Dorrit and his brother Frederick; there is Arthur Clennam. In *Little Dorrit* the ability to go on living, the reasons for doing so, have become the greatest of mysteries.

If the world of *Little Dorrit* seems menacing, it is not just because there is a pervasive sense of financial insecurity that affects everyone in society from Dorrit to Clennam, from Merdle to Pancks, or even that so many of the characters seem crippled and maimed. On a more fundamental level it is because life itself seems to have no meaning. The world is hostile because it is ultimately incomprehensible. Indeed one reason why the Marshalsea, tragic pit of human desolation that it is, seems actually less menacing is because the characters, having reached the lower depths, are consoled by the thought that there is nowhere further for them to fall. As the doctor points out:

We are quiet here; we don't get badgered here; there's no knocker here, sir, to be hammered at by creditors and to bring a man's heart to his mouth. Nobody comes here to ask if a man's at home, and to say he'll stand on the door mat till he is. Nobody writes threatening letters about money to this place. It's freedom, sir, it's freedom! . . . Elsewhere, people are restless, worried, hurried about, anxious respecting one thing, anxious respecting another. Nothing of the kind here, sir. We have done all that – we know the worst of it; we have got to the bottom, we can't fall, and what have we found? Peace. That's the word for it. Peace.

Of course it is scarcely possible to accept the doctor's words at face value. The imprisoned debtors are indeed free from the manifold threats, anxieties and insecurities of the outside world but they are scarcely free in any customary sense of that word. Indeed we might rather say that they have given up all thought of freedom because it is a prospect that they find it impossible to cope with. If they find peace it is not so much a tranquillity of the heart as an exhaustion and apathy of the spirit.

Initially in the Marshalsea Clennam felt 'a burning restlessness' and an 'agonised impatience' – 'his dread and hatred of the place became so intense that he felt it a labour to draw breath in it. The sensation of being stifled sometimes so overpowered him, that he would stand at the window holding his throat and gasping.' Yet this violence of the spirit is soon spent. Soon 'a desolate calm succeeded' and Clennam has resigned himself to his monotonous existence just as surely as the old clarinet player. It is one of the great paradoxes of *Little Dorrit* that although Dickens implies that Clennam's whole life has been blighted by Mrs Clennam's morbid religiosity and fanatical obsession with sin, the novel nevertheless seems to share her sense of the world as a dark and depressing place of suffering and punishment: 'this scene, the Earth, is expressly meant to be a scene of gloom, and hardship, and dark trial, for the creatures who are made out of its dust'.

The important difference, however, is that Mrs Clennam presumably believes that there is some sort of point to all this despondency and pain, whereas Dickens can see no redeeming meaning in it whatsoever. And it is here that we have to consider the strange, perverse, preposterous heroism of William Dorrit. For, when all is said and done, Dorrit is a great survivor and he manages to accomplish the extraordinary feat not merely of becoming, through his role of 'Father of the Marshalsea', a person of dignity, of substance and respect even in a debtor's prison, but to become the very core of that odd community. There is scarcely a person in the Marshalsea whose life does not revolve around William Dorrit, scarcely a person there who does not attend to his wants, scarcely a person who does not pay him fealty, homage and respect. On the one hand we must wonder at such a monstrous ego, that insists that every single person there shall minister to its insistent and overwhelming need for massage; yet on the other we are compelled to respect the courage and determination with which he builds up this fantasy world, in the process making the prison more psychologically acceptable, not only for himself but for others as well. If the prison is not only a community but a caring community at that, Dorrit in his own heedless, narcissistic way is responsible. By keeping his dignity, through a whole series of absurd machinations and exaction of financial tribute, he makes its easier for others to keep up at least a shred of their own self-respect as well. Of course it may well be argued that all this is nothing more than a sham and a pretence that ultimately deceives no one, and as Dickens sardonically comments on characterisation of his twenty-three years in the Marshalsea, 'It is all I could do for my children – I have done it' –

> Enough, for the present place, that he lay down with wet eyelashes, serene, in a manner majestic, after bestowing his life of degradation as a sort of portion on the devoted child upon whom its miseries had fallen so heavily, and whose love alone had saved him to be even what he was.

Such a high level of self-deception and complacency is undoubtedly shocking. Dorrit's airs, graces and pretensions, if taken at their face value, are well-nigh intolerable, but we well know also that no one is really deceived – these are all just spells, charms and incantations that keep the oppressiveness of the void at bay.

In *Little Dorrit* Dickens turned the whole question of human identity into a fantastic and intractable puzzle. That every person has a vital need for independence, autonomy and self-respect is powerfully demonstrated by Tattycoram, the foundling child, who like Oliver Twist has no real name but only a complex designation that can never really serve as the signifier of a person. The single word goes against the traditional modes of classification and makes her name more like that of a dog than of a human being. Dickens makes us understand very well how suffocating and claustrophobic her existence is with the Meagles, who kill her with a combination of patronising condescension and kindness so that her every impulse to rebellion is countered by Meagles's ingratiating plea 'Count to twenty five Tattycoram.' It is hardly surprising that Tattycoram should finally protest against all this or that she should seek refuge with Miss Wade. The modern reader is strongly disposed to identify with Tattycoram's revolt and with Miss Wade who stands out against so much of the Victorian humbug about the family. Dickens, however, in a way with which we are distinctly uncomfortable, does not see this emphasis on independence and self-realisation as wholly desirable. For Dickens the desire to reject others and strike out on a path of one's own always carries with it the implication of emptiness and despair. He believes that we can never be fully human if we cannot accept the humanity of others, if we reject the love and concern of others, however suffocating and misguided. Tattycoram is a kind of obbligato to the principle theme of the novel – the way in which the relationships between William Dorrit, his daughter Amy and Arthur Clennam are radically changed by the news that William Dorrit, far from being a lifelong debtor, is actually a person of substance. For Dickens does not flinch from the conclusion that the emancipation of the Dorrits from their interminable incarceration in the Marshalsea, far from being a liberation from misery and hopelessness, is actually a form of privation. In the Marshalsea the open display of love, care and tenderness is taken as a matter of course. It is the presence, the persistence of these honest and powerful feelings that gives dignity to a life that in all other respects has little to recommend it. Once William Dorrit is a wealthy man he again has no need for the well-intentioned ministrations of a Clennam, which are, on the contrary, now the source of a distinct unease and embarrassment, an uncomfortable reminder of a moment when help was not merely welcome but positively indispensable. Now that Dorrit is a man of power and position he has waiters, innkeepers, ostlers, major-domos leaping to his call; the unselfish dedication of Little Dorrit to her father's welfare is no longer called for. Indeed everything that Little Dorrit once represented to him is, on one level, precisely everything that he would prefer to forget. So William Dorrit becomes a split personality – one half seeking to be the aristocrat he always believed himself to be, and to free himself absolutely from all memories of a degraded past; the other still chained to the Marshalsea and the identity he lived out there, both trapped and cossetted in a world of memory. Yet what to her father and her sister Fanny is a release and liberation is, paradoxically, to Little Dorrit a denial of her whole identity. She has defined herself as a loving and caring person and she has made it her mission in life to preserve her father's dignity and self-respect. But now, on the Grand Tour, her self-sacrifice is suddenly rendered valueless. Everything her existence has been predicated on has vanished in an instant. The opening of book II symbolises her predicament. The darkness recedes, to be replaced by brilliant clarity and light, yet the landscape they enter is hostile, bleak and inhuman. It is as if the ordinary world of human care has been left behind. In Venice, the icy and ethereal city, Little Dorrit becomes conscious of the fact that 'she had no one to think for, nothing to plan or contrive, no care of others to load herself with', and she looks wistfully after some diminutive Italian girl leading her grey father. In the upper-class world into which she has been translated, decorum, defined by Mrs General, is a form of sophisticated indifference: 'A truly refined mind will seem to be ignorant of the existence of anything that is not perfectly proper, placid and pleasant.'

There is no place for the open and honest expression of emotion. So although Little Dorrit longs to show her father how much she loves him – and in reality he needs this declaration now as much if not more than he ever did in the debtor's prison – she knows that to do so would be to violate all the taboos of his newfound, or rediscovered, social status: 'I want to put my arms around his neck, tell him how I love him, and cry a little on his breast. I should be glad after that, and proud and happy. But I know I must not do this; that he would not like it.'

Little Dorrit has become an embarrassment to the social pretensions of the Dorrits because her identity had become so bound up with their incarceration in prison that she will neither give it up nor repudiate all that it signified. To others, to Fanny especially, but to her father also, she appears as a regressive figure, who will make no effort to free herself from the shadows of the past. Paradoxically the father puts himself forward to the daughter as an example of the ability of the human spirit to free itself from the determining power of circumstance:

I have suffered. Probably I know how much I have suffered better than any one! If *I* can put that aside; if *I* can eradicate the marks of what I have endured, and can emerge before the world – a – ha – gentleman unspoiled and unspotted – is it a great deal to expect – I say again – is it a great deal to expect – that my children should – hum – do the same and sweep the accursed experience off the face of the earth.

But the accursed experience is not so easily deleted. The price is always higher than one imagines or could imagine. At the end William Dorrit lapses back pathetically into his memories of the 'good old days' at the Marshalsea:

> Those who are habituated to the – ha – Marshalsea, are pleased to call me its Father. I am accustomed to be complimented by strangers as the – ha – Father of the Marshalsea. Certainly, if years of residency may establish a claim to so – ha – honourable – a title, I may accept the – hum – conferred distinction. My child, ladies and gentlemen. My daughter. Born here!

What we should not forget about this is not just that Dorrit is reminiscing, but that the simple word 'here' has lost its meaning for it no longer carries its simple contextual force. Dorrit's dislocated existence testifies to the destructive power of the alienating urban world, which offers no resting place for the spirit, and shreds memories, associations, identity into so many futile scraps of paper.

Even in *Little Dorrit* hope beckons, but with *Great Expectations* (1860–1) both hope and expectation are tinged with irony from the very start. In the backward glance of the novel, in the pressure that future knowledge exerts back on innocent, uncomplicated beginnings there can be no compulsive narrative drive on the earlier model but only doubt, uncertainty and anxiety. If the world of *Great Expectations* always seems menacing, this is not simply because it begins with a violent nocturnal encounter in a graveyard but because Pip, the hero, seems always a passive victim of circumstance, his life always invaded by obscure forces that he does not understand and over which he has no control. Pip's whole existence is determined by two chance meetings: one with the convict, Magwitch, which produces his great expectations, when Magwitch returns incognito from Australia, determined to make Pip into a gentleman; the other when he first goes to Miss Havisham's and is teased and tormented by Estella, thus laying the foundation for a perverse, masochistic love that will haunt his whole life. It is as if in these vivid moments, so vivid as to be almost suspended from every-day chronology, Pip's life is fixed and frozen as irrevocably as Miss Havisham's when after the calling off of her marriage at the last minute she ordered all the clocks to be stopped. In this novel Dickens comes uncannily close to the tradition of the novel in France, from Stendhal and Flaubert to Proust, in which the world appears as a lure, a false promise, a snare for the unwary, where the one great mistake in life seems to be to surrender to wistful dreams of what will be, precisely to believe in 'great expectations'. Yet Dickens writes in a way that is never cynical, never disillusioned, never simply pessimistic. He avoids the temptation of trying to make his novel into some kind of a tragedy and always maintains a clear, unwavering, poignant, yet unrhetorical tone. Here Dickens never preaches or lectures at the reader, never offers a summing up, and his writing is the more compelling just because there is no verdict. From a certain perspective it seems that Pip would have been happier if he had stayed at the forge with Joe Gargery and had never met Magwitch and Estella, who seemingly bring him so much unhappiness. If it had not been for the contempt of Estella and Miss Havisham Pip would never have wished to be a gentleman, and if he had never assisted Magwitch he would never have been given the means. Yet his role as gentleman is always false and it cuts him off from Joe and from Biddy and the familiar world of the village, which offered him an emotional security and whose loss caused him so much pain and guilt. There is another side, however – for the later Dickens is insistent that we can have no happiness in life unless we can live as much and more for others as we live for ourselves – Pip gains great satisfaction from the help he is able to give his friend Herbert, just as Magwitch has found happiness in helping him. Although Pip's relationships with his benefactor and with Estella are often confused and distressing, so that tension, hostility and fear are as prominent as love, he nevertheless becomes a more complex person himself in accepting that human emotions are often made twisted and perverse by upbringing and circumstance. The lives of Magwitch, Estella and Estella's mother have been as tragically and as irrevocably marked as the deeply scarred wrists of Estella's mother – indeed the wounding and burning of so many characters in the novel from Pip's sister to Miss Havisham suggests a vision of the world in which no one can really hope to be whole and complete. If Pip never finds happiness as such, he is brought to an acceptance of both Magwitch and Estella that would earlier have been beyond him. The novel is dominated by repetition and by an insistent return to earlier scenes – to Miss Havisham's house, to the desolate yet familiar word of the marshes, to the blacksmith's forge – in a way that seems to parallel Magwitch's experiences of escape and release. Pip can never leave the world of his childhood and yet never return to it, just as Magwitch can never leave England, though it is impossible for him to return. In *Great Expectations* everything in life seems to be finally cancelled out, like a giant blackboard in which every word is crudely scored through. In theory this is a vision of life as inexplicably and inexorably threatening, of a sense of futility as omnipresent as Dickensian fog, and yet Dickens suggests that we nevertheless can salvage something, through the concern and sensitivity that we show to others. As when Pip, at the end, takes the desperately injured Magwitch's hand and finally sees him in a transfigured light:

> For now, my repugnance to him had all melted away, and in the hunted wounded shackled creature who held my hand in his, I only saw a man who had meant to be my benefactor, and who had felt affectionately, gratefully, and generously, towards me with great constancy through a series of years. I only saw him a much better man than I had been to Joe.

'Constancy' – the word in relation to the violent, erratic and unpredictable life of such a man as Magwitch is unexpected and is concerting, yet it is utterly right and it reminds us that human beings can maintain something of value even in the face of an unstable and menacing world.

Our Mutual Friend (1864–5), the last novel that Dickens completed, is at once a profoundly unsatisfactory and a profoundly fascinating work. The tortuous plot mechanics surrounding John Harmon's escape from drowning and the various wills left by his father, the way in which Noddy Boffin is transformed from genial philanthropist to hard-hearted skinflint and back again, the fact that Dickens often hardly bothers to establish his characters' motivations, the rather lacklustre social satire centring on the upstart Veneerings and their circle: all this leads one to question Dickens's judgement – which is doubly perplexing in a novelist who was so often uncannily and unerringly right in his overall sense of how a narrative should develop. It is easy to understand Henry James's complaint that Dickens 'has added nothing to our understanding of human character',[5] and with this novel especially to feel that Dickens is doing nothing more than shifting a number of pieces around the board with scant regard for the overall credibility of his narrative, and that he had allowed himself be so blinded by the imaginary security of plot as to offer the reader nothing more than a mass of elaborated fragments. The narrative dynamism and social vision of his earlier work seems lacking.

A natural response to such criticism and complaints would be to argue that they are misconceived because they effectively presume that *Our Mutual Friend* is to be regarded as a naturalistic representation of the world, whereas in this novel especially the allegorical bent that was always strongly present in Dickens's fiction becomes so predominant that it seems more a fable about the possibility of goodness in the world than anything else. In other words, it is rather like another late work, Mark Twain's *The Man Who Corrupted Hadleyburg*, only with the significant difference that whereas Twain gives up on human nature, Dickens still wants to go on believing in it despite strong presumptions to the contrary. Thus Noddy Boffin's pretence at being a ruthless and manipulative miser is both a way of testing the integrity of the other characters and, perversely and paradoxically, of insisting on the importance of human freedom and freewill. That is, Noddy Boffin does not *have* to be corrupted by his accession to power and wealth even though we may more or less take it for granted that this is inevitable; equally neither does Bella Wilfer nor anyone else have to respond to Boffin's new manner in the way that Boffin seems to expect. On the contrary this is the very moment when they have to ask themselves who they are and what they want to be and to stand up for what they believe to be right. In fact one of the major preoccupations of the novel is the fact that many of the characters – such as Rogue Riderhood, Gaffer Hexam, the schoolmaster, Bradley Headstone and Eugene Wrayburn – are obsessive, driven individuals, who seem to lack any capacity to draw back from their involvements and question and criticise their own behaviour. Simply to name these characters is also to point to the way in which the allegorical imperative in the novel is articulated through the recurrent figure of death by drowning, which Dickens uses to suggest the possibility of spiritual renewal and rebirth. Gaffer Hexam drowns himself because he is not prepared to accept any alteration in his relation to his children – for him to give up his power over them is to give up life itself. Yet John Harmon saves himself from a watery death to begin a new life as John Rokesmith, in which he learns that love, independence and self-respect are of far greater importance than money, power or position. Rogue Riderhood and Bradley Headstone, the driven characters, will not learn from their experience. Rogue Riderhood, instead of being grateful for the gift of life and resolving to begin all over again, is, on the contrary, reconfirmed in his arrogant, vindictive behaviour. Bradley Headstone refuses to see that his 'love' for Lizzie is nothing more than his hatred for Eugene Rayburn, and though Eugene may have provoked him beyond endurance, the fact remains that somewhere along the line he has totally lost his humanity and self-respect. In the final analysis he hates and despises others because he hates and despises himself. His deliberate transformation of himself into Riderhood to commit the assault on Wrayburn and their common death by drowning points the symbolic meaning – for Headstone, from being a symbol of all that was noblest and best and a worthy model for the aspirations of others, has turned himself into all that is contemptible and degraded. If he had had more faith in himself and a more balanced perspective on life, the posturings of Eugene Wrayburn could never have hurt him. Eugene himself moves in the opposite direction. Initially an empty character, in every sense of the word, he seems to have not only no occupation but no reason for existing. Like a parasite he attaches himself to others and seeks to reconfirm his sense of identity through the power he can exercise over them. He makes Lizzie Hexham grateful and dependent on him as a patron. He enjoys reasserting his own (weak) sense of superiority by bringing out the underdog in Bradley Headstone. Only by actually facing the prospect of death and by realising the depth of the love that Lizzie bears for him can he finally brought to behave in a natural, unself-regarding and unmanipulative way. What Dickens makes us see is that Eugene is a deeply repressed character because out of arrogance and false pride he has denied his own capacity of love.

Yet the kind of affirmations that Dickens seeks to make seem contradicted on a more fundamental level by the overall pessimism, not to say cynicism, that pervades the book. It is in this specific sense that Stephen Gill's suggestion that *Our Mutual Friend* 'seems the product of not one but many visions of life'[6] is justified. In Dickens's earlier fiction the character who seeks to control, dominate and assert his power over others is the exception and is invariably identified with the villain. But virtually all the relationships in *Our Mutual Friend* have this character. We are always conscious of the existence of power, of dominance and subjection, in the dealings of

the characters with one another. I have already discussed the determination of Eugene Wrayburn to dominate Lizzie Hexham and
Bradley Headstone but we see the same pattern endlessly repeated.
There is Jenny Wren, the crippled doll's dressmaker who nevertheless wields despotic power over her pathetic and despicable drunken
father. There is the power that Riderhood obtains over Bradley Headstone through his knowledge of Headstone's responsibility for the
near death of Eugene Wrayburn. There is the tyrannical authority
that Gaffer Hexham imposes on his children. There is the hypocritical manipulation by Fledbury of those who suppose him to be their
closest friend through the agency of Riah, the reviled but honest Jew.
There is the preposterous yet nevertheless sinister dream of absolute
power, which Silas Wegg believes he is in a position to wield over
Boffin, through his discovery of a will that would leave his employer
penniless. Even the relationship of John Harmon, alias Rokesmith, as
secretary to Boffin seems a relationship of this kind. It seems that
there is hardly a person in the novel who does not seek revenge of
some kind or who wishes to do others an injury. From this malignant
vision of life as one made up of destructive power relations even the
genial Boffin is not exempt. Even before he assumes his identity as a
heartless, unfeeling capitalist we cannot but feel that his authority
over others, even if exerted in a good cause, is nevertheless potentially dangerous. For it seems that money gives Boffin the power to
do virtually anything he likes – so that the sinister, if imaginary, later
Boffin, who says to John Rokesmith of his love for his protégée, Bella
Wilfer, 'we all three know it's Money she makes a stand for – money,
money, money – and that you and your affections and hearts are a
Lie, sir!'

Despite his good intentions in taking both Bella and the child of
Mrs Higden from their families, Boffin causes considerable distress
and confusion and we cannot but wonder whether the purse of
Fortunatus is necessarily the blessing that it is supposed to be. So
Dickens gets caught in a tangle of his own making. Instead of believing, as he asks us to, that money can be used in good ways as well as
bad, we are more likely to conclude that it is as potentially as corrupting for the donor as it is for the recipient. This makes Dickens's
reassertion of the 'good' Boffin something of a nonsense. The parallels between Dickens and Dostoevsky have often been asserted and
nowhere are they more in evidence than in *Our Mutual Friend*: the
novel is a veritable encyclopaedia of the insulted and the injured,
ranging from the malignant Riderhood and the quasi-comic Wegg to

the incurable *ressentiment* – as Nietzsche would call it – of Bradley
Headstone. In theory the underdog mentality is not endorsed in the
novel and Dickens quite unequivocally asks us to condemn all three.
And yet these are the most vivid characters in the novel, and while
we may not necessarily sympathise with them in any straightforward way, we cannot help recognising that life as it is viewed from
the lower depths and through the spectacles of resentment and inner
emptiness is a very different thing for those who enjoy a position in
society or who have something constructive to live for. The venge-
fulness of Silas Wegg is both excessive and ridiculous, yet Dickens
has the power to make us empathise with his anger against the good,
smug and sanctimonious Boffin and even to relish the prospect of
the reversal that he has in store for him:

'Was it to be borne that he should come, like a thief in the dark,
digging among stuff that was far more ours than his (seeing that
we could deprive him of every grain of it, if he didn't buy us at our
own figure), and carrying off treasure from its bowels? no, it was
not to be borne. And for that, too, his nose shall be put to the
grindstone.'
    'How do you propose to do it, Mr Wegg?'
    'To put his nose to the grindstone? I propose,' returned that
estimable man, 'to insult him openly. And, if looking into this eye
of mine, he dares to offer a word in answer, to retort upon him
before he can take his breath, 'Add another word to that, you
dusty old dog, and you're a beggar.'
    'Suppose he says nothing, Mr Wegg.'
    'Then,' replied Mr Wegg, 'we shall have to come to an under-
standing with him with very little trouble, and I'll break him and
drive him, Mr Venus. I'll put him in harness, and I'll bear him up
tight, and I'll break him and drive him. The harder the old Dust is
driven, sir, the higher he'll pay. And I mean to be paid high,
Mr Venus, I promise you.'
    'You speak quite revengefully, Mr Wegg.'
    'Revengefully, sir? Is it for him that I have declined and falled,
night after night? Is it for his pleasure that I've waited at home of
an evening, like a set of skittles, to be set up and knocked over, by
whatever balls – or books – he chose to bring against me? Why,
I'm a hundred times the man he is, sir; five hundred times!'

Here, albeit in a grotesque form, we catch Dickens's growing aware-

ness that deference in Victorian society is crumbling, that even humble individuals from the lowest ranks of society are beginning to
chafe at the position they find themselves in and assert their rights.
And of course Dickens does not approve. He much prefers a man
like Stephen Blackpool, in *Hard Times*, who doffs his cap and speaks
respectfully to his social superiors. Part of Bradley Headstone's crime
is not just that he attempts murder but that he presumes to be the
antagonist of a man of far higher status than himself. Eugene
Wrayburn, as it were, could never conceive of a *duel* with such a man
and could never imagine for a minute that Headstone could be his
rival. Yet Dickens also cannot help showing a world that, aside from
the fantasy of a Boffin, lacks any redeeming values; where human
relationships are corrupted by power; where the would-be benign,
paternalist, Victorian order is threatened by smouldering discontent
and open opposition. If anything the world seems even more menacing than before.

In the fiction of the Brontë sisters, Charlotte and Emily, there is also
a powerful sense of the world as hostile and threatening, but in their
case the danger is formulated in radically subjective terms. The
individual confronts a world that seems to deny her very right to
exist. In their fiction there is always some other who seeks to overwhelm her and envelop her, to suppress and subdue her, to manipulate her and appropriate her. Charlotte Brontë, in two of the very
greatest English novels, *Jane Eyre* (1847) and *Villette* (1853), established completely new parameters for the writing of fiction by beginning not with a preformed identity that could be paraded before the
reader, but rather by demonstrating that the very struggle to assert
and form that identity was to be the subject of her novel. Jane Eyre's
life is a perpetual journey in search of a place where she can belong,
from the hated house at Gateshead where she is cruelly mistreated
and abused to the more supportive yet demoralising world of Lowood
School, from Thornfield Hall where she is acknowledged as a person
yet cruelly tormented, to Moor House where she finds security but
where her right to individuality and independence is subtly denied.
Perhaps significantly her final happiness with Rochester is no longer
identified with any particular place, for Thornfield Hall is burnt to
the ground. Perhaps, at bottom, Jane's desire to find such a homely
place was a vestige of her unhappy childhood, which she is finally

able to leave behind. For now happiness will not be so much something she will 'find' as something she can create herself.

The narrative of *Jane Eyre* is driven by repetition and return. She returns to Gateshead to confront Mrs Reed again. She returns twice to Thornfield Hall. She has to struggle to gain any recognition for herself. Always Jane is the outcast and intruder, a person who seems to exist only on sufferance. At the outset of the novel, on a gloomy day, marked by mist, cloud and ceaseless rain, we encounter Jane hiding behind a curtain, pretending to be an unperson, but even this self-effacement is not enough, since John discovers her, hits her and accuses her of being a worthless dependent who has no rights whatsoever. When she is transported to Lowood School she finds herself in the same predicament. Instead of being allowed to blend into the woodwork she is introduced by the severe and sanctimonious Mr Brockleshurst, in a passage that invokes one of the Brontë sisters' favourite poems, Cowper's 'The Castaway', thus:

> it becomes my duty to warn you that this girl, who might be one of God's own lambs, is a little castaway – not a member of the true flock, but evidently an interloper and an alien. You must be on your guard against her; you must shun her example – of necessity, avoid her company, exclude her from your sports, and shut her out from your converse.

In Mr Brocklehurst's Calvinistic vision of things Jane, once stigmatised as a liar, represents a moral contagion that must be perpetually shunned. Indeed Charlotte Brontë recognises that for the novelist to record in such detail all the events of her 'insignificant existence' represents some sort of imposition on the reader, who may wish to avoid any association with such a lowly person; who presumably anticipates a heroine who if not rich and well-born, will at the very least be beautiful, graceful and not what Jane herself seems to offer: 'Portrait of a governess, disconnected poor and plain'. What makes Jane Eyre so unladylike at bottom is her rebellious, independent spirit. Far from being grateful for the benefits she receives, as is fitting in the Victorian lowly, Jane Eyre is perpetually discontented and chafes against the restrictions of her situation. Even on arriving at Thornfield Hall, where she has in Adèle a vivacious and lively girl to teach and in Mrs Fairfax a genial and kindly companion, she still feels she wants more, significantly to be part of some grander narrative than that which she seems irrevocably assigned:

I climbed the three staircases, raised the trapdoor of the attic, and having reached the leads, looked out afar over sequestered field and hill, and along dim skyline – that then I longed for a power of vision which might overpass that limit; which might reach the busy world, towns, regions full of life I had heard of but never seen; that then I desired more of practical experience than I possessed; more of intercourse with my kind, of acquaintance with variety of character, than was here within my reach. I valued what was good in Mrs Fairfax, and what was good in Adèle; but I believed in the existence of other and more vivid kinds of goodness, and what I believed in I wished to behold.

Who blames me? Many, no doubt; and I shall be called discontented. I could not help it; the restlessness was in my nature; it agitated me to pain sometimes. Then my sole relief was to walk along the corridor of the third story, backwards and forwards, safe in the silence and solitude of the spot, and allow my mind's eye to dwell on whatever bright visions rose before it – and, certainly, they were many and glowing; to let my heart be heaved by the exultant movement, which, while it swelled in trouble, expanded with life; and, best of all, to open my inward ear to a tale that was never ended – a tale my imagination created, and narrated continuously; quickened with all of incident, life, fire, feeling, that I desired and had not in my existence.

It is in vain to say human beings ought to be satisfied with tranquillity: they must have action; and they will make it if they cannot find it. Millions are condemned to a stiller doom than mine, and millions are in silent revolt against their lot. Nobody knows how many rebellions beside political rebellions ferment in the masses of life which people earth. Women are supposed to be very calm generally: but women feel just as men feel; they need exercise for their faculties, and a field of their efforts as much as their brothers do; they suffer from too rigid a restraint, too absolute a stagnation, precisely as men would suffer.

Here speaks a humble governess and yet a Promethean heroine who rejects all the limits that are imposed on her. It is certainly symbolically significant that while she can, from Thornfield Hall, look out over an immense prospect, she is nevertheless constricted and confined, just as her as yet unknown double, the mad Bertha Mason, is constricted and confined. Indeed the sense of confinement is further intensified by Grace Poole, who has been employed to look after

Rochester's wife, but whose apparently complaisant acceptance of a lonely existence on the third floor greatly puzzles Jane. Moreover this place of confinement repeats one of Jane's earliest punishments, when she is locked by Mrs Reed in the sinister red-room upstairs. As the whole tone of the passage makes clear, there was no greater crime for woman than to be discontented and disaffected, and therefore Charlotte Brontë in neither extenuating nor apologising for it strickes a radical note. There are millions who feel thwarted and frustrated, yet such a powerful and universal feeling can neither be spoken of nor named. Jane Eyre violates the deepest of Victorian taboos. For although she is entitled to be miserable and unhappy it is not seemly for this to be grounded in such cosmic discontent. So it is in more than one sense that Jane Eyre is a Romantic heroine.

When Jane Eyre encounters Rochester for the first time she really begins to believe that she can be a person. Rochester is genuinely concerned about her and with what she thinks and feels. From the very beginning he does not simply regard her as a menial in his employ but as an individual, whose responses are genuinely of interest to him. He focuses his attention on her in a quite extraordinary way, and in response to this the submerged and submissive Jane Eyre begins to blossom. Rochester has 'such a wealth of the power of communicating happiness', his smile is 'the real sunshine of feeling'. Admittedly there are times when she finds Rochester's frank enquiries somewhat awkward to handle and she finds it difficult to decipher his candid but enigmatic utterances. Rochester's intimacy is at once flattering and disturbing:

> 'You are afraid of me, because I talk like a sphinx.'
> 'Your language is enigmatical, sir: but though I am bewildered, I am certainly not afraid.'
> 'You *are* afraid – your self-love dreads a blunder.'
> 'In that sense I feel apprehensive – I have no wish to talk nonsense.'
> 'If you did, it would be in a very grave, quiet manner, I should mistake it for sense. Do you never laugh, Miss Eyre? Don't trouble yourself to answer – I see you laugh rarely; but you can laugh very merrily; believe me, you are not naturally austere, any more than I am naturally vicious. . . . I see at intervals the glance of a curious sort of bird through the close-set bars of a cage – a vivid, restless, resolute captive is there; were it but free, it would soar cloud-high.

Jane *is* anxious because although Rochester treats her with a flattering intimacy, he also has an uncanny ability to read her thoughts and emotions, whereas, as he himself points out, he has a complex past and has experienced things of which she can do nothing. So the relationship, though startlingly direct and free from the barriers that would normally separate aristocrat from employee, is nevertheless unequal. At bottom Jane knows that the spontaneity and freedom of Rochester is a class prerogative from which she is debarred. She must always be cautious and careful even when he urges her not to be – perhaps especially when he urges her not to be. Yet she is a free spirit, as Rochester divines, and she genuinely longs to reach a point at which she can be as spontaneous and as open with him as he, apparently, is with her. Yet, of course, her wariness is thoroughly justified. Rochester artfully plays on her emotions by encouraging her to believe that he is in love with Blanche Ingham so as to make her jealous; he poses as a gypsy fortune-teller in order to elicit further revelations from her; he asks her direct questions that she cannot easily brush aside; yet he himself is by no means as straightforward and open as he pretends. He conceals the existence of his mad wife on the third floor in the face of extraordinary pressures to reveal it. He asks Jane to marry him even though he knows that he cannot either legally or honourably do so. Rochester claims to be a reformed rake, which in some doubtful sense he is, but his reformation still has a very long way to go. Moreover we must not overlook the cruelty of Rochester's teasing of Jane Eyre in the scene in the garden where he deliberately causes her to shed tears at the thought that she must leave Thornfield forever, before telling her that he wishes to marry her. So although he sincerely loves Jane there is more than a element of sadism in his overtures towards her. Jane is quite defenceless before his emotional virtuosity and even before she learns that their marriage is impossible she begins to fear again. Marriage with Rochester could not be the consummation that she dreams of because their relationship would be so unequal. Even as she tries to assert her power over him she fears for the future:

> In other people's presence I was, as formerly, deferential and quiet; any other line of conduct being uncalled for: it was only in the evening conferences I thus thwarted him and afflicted him. . . . Yet after all my task was not an easy one; often I would rather have pleased than teased him. My future husband was becoming to me my whole world; and more than the world; almost my hope

of heaven. He stood between me and every thought of religion, as an eclipse intervenes between man and the broad sun. I could not, in those days, see God for his creature: of whom I had made an idol.

Despite all her scruples and all her anxieties Jane is totally infatuated with a man she does not even know. The unexpected discovery that Rochester is, after all, married, to some obscure threatening object: 'it grovelled, seemingly, on all fours; it snatched and growled like some strange wild animal: but it was covered with clothing, and a quantity of dark, grizzled hair, wild as a mane, hid its head and face', is therefore devastating on a multiplicity of levels. Obviously the marriage she has dreamed of is fatally barred, but perhaps even more significantly Jane realises that Rochester has not been as open as she had believed: 'the attribute of stainless truth was gone from his idea', and in addition she now fears that Rochester has already reduced one wife to a caged beast, her hope that she has nothing to fear from him seems utterly unfounded. She has trusted Rochester and been cruelly betrayed even if she is capable of instantaneously forgiving him for his deception.

Up until the moment of her marriage Jane has struggled tirelessly against a menacing world and in the process has achieved both greater self-confidence and a securer sense of her own identity. She has even dared to believe in the possibility of personal fulfilment. Momentarily the grim Bunyanesque picture of the world as an interminable, weary pilgrimage across a hostile landscape seems falsified: 'I wondered why moralists call the world a dreary wilderness; for me it blossomed like a rose.' Yet now just at the very moment when happiness is within her grasp her whole world is brutally shattered. Before she had not dared to hope. Now that she finally has summoned up the courage to assay it she finds that all hope is gone: 'Jane Eyre, who had been an ardent expectant woman – almost a bride – was a cold, solitary girl again: her life was pale; her prospects were desolate. . . . I looked on my cherished wishes, yesterday so blooming and glowing; they lay stark, chill, livid – corpses that never could revive.' Rochester suggests that they can live together abroad. If they love each other that is all that matters. Jane is greatly tempted – one of many temptations that she has to face. For at bottom she is not as repressed and moralistic as she seems and the prospect of living with Rochester is almost as irresistible as marriage itself, especially since she now realises how much he needs her. Yet she knows it is impossible, for in thus submitting herself to Rochester she would lose all dignity and independence and place herself, much as she wants to, totally at his mercy.

Now Jane truly faces the dark night of the soul. Once more an outcast, bereft either of shelter or bread to eat she wanders aimlessly and without hope. She speaks of 'the friendly numbness of death'. Unexpectedly, Providence once more smiles on her and she finds herself again ensconced within a cosy and welcoming environment. Yet she has no further reason to live and now her spirit totally gives way:

> I knew I was in a small room and in a narrow bed. To that bed I seemed to have grown; I lay on it motionless as a stone; and to have torn me from it would have been almost to kill me, I took no note of the lapse of time – of the change from morning to noon, from noon to evening. I observed when anyone entered or left the apartment: I could even tell who they were; I could understand what was said when the speaker stood near me; but I could not answer; to open my lips or move my limbs was impossible.

Now it seems that all her struggles have been in vain. Not only has she lost Rochester but in the same moment she has lost all sense of herself as a powerful, vital, independent person. But gradually the life in her comes ebbing back. She makes friends with Mary and Diana and discovers that she is related to them. At the invitation of St John Rivers she becomes mistress of a village school. She learns that she is now a woman of means, having inherited money from her uncle in Madeira. She tries to make Moor House into a thoroughly comfortable and welcoming home but she is surprised to find that Rivers is displeased, only observing: 'I trust when the first flush of vivacity is over, you will look a little higher than domestic endearments and household joys.'

Rivers means to go to India as a missionary and has decided that Jane has all the qualities requisite in a wife who should accompany him. Now begins an extraordinary series of temptation scenes in which Rivers insists, demands and pleads with Jane to come with him. Jane knows that he is in love with Rosamund Oliver but has rejected her as unsuitable for his purpose. She knows that he views her in purely instrumental terms. Once again she has to stand up to him and oppose him as she has done so many times before. Yet Rivers knows that the idea does have its appeal for Jane. Now that she has given up Rochester and the prospect of personal happiness she is drawn to the idea of dedicating herself to some worthy purpose, if not to Rivers himself. For she is conscious of the way in which he manipulates her and endeavours to make her submit her will to him:

> I found him very patient, very forbearing, and yet an exacting master: he expected me to do a great deal; and when I fulfilled his expectations, he, in his own way, fully testified his approbation. By degrees, he acquired a certain influence over me that took away my liberty of mind: his praise and notice were more restraining than his indifference. I could no longer talk or laugh freely when he was by, because a tiresomely importunate instinct reminded me that vivacity (at least in me) was distasteful to him. I was so fully aware that only serious moods and occupations were acceptable, that in his presence every effort to sustain or follow any other became vain: I fell under a freezing spell. When he said 'go', I went, 'come', I came, 'do this', I did it. But I did not love my servitude: I wished, many a time, he had continued to neglect me.

The difference from Rochester who has been genuinely interested in her and positively valued her liveliness and spirit is very marked. Jane has some intuitive perception that something is wrong with Rochester and returns to find Thornfield Hall burnt to the ground. Rochester has lost a hand and been blinded. This mutilation of Rochester functions on a multiplicity of levels. First, and most obviously, it functions as some kind of retributive punishment for his past actions. Equally significantly, it removes the psychological barriers between them, since Jane no longer feels threatened or overpowered by him: they can be equals. But there is more to it than that. Jane has a deep fear of pleasure and happiness. She distrusts their promise because of the prospect of betrayal and she therefore wants to combine love with personal sacrifice. But until now her person has not seemed worth sacrificing. Now she can give herself to Rochester in the knowledge that he will truly value and respect her as an independent person. Moreover Rochester has himself had the experience of being alone and outcast, which has been Jane's experience all along: 'I was desolate and abandoned – my life dark, lonely, hopeless.' In some sense it is disturbing that Jane Eyre can only be complete when Rochester is maimed, and it is this perverse conclusion that gives the book its uncanny power. It is only now that she realises: 'he, in truth, loved me far too well and too tenderly to constitute himself my tyrant'.

By comparison with *Jane Eyre, Villette* (1853) is a work pitched in a much quieter key. The melodramatic events at Thornfield Hall are replaced by much more humdrum events that take place in the Belgian town of Villette. Although a ghostly nun makes several mysterious appearances, these, as Todorov would say, belong to the realm of the uncanny, and are given a fairly prosaic explanation, when it is revealed that M. de Hamal has used this disguise in order to pay court to the lovely Ginevra Fanshawe. In fact the deliberately unprepossessing narrative is precisely the book's greatest strength, for what Charlotte Brontë seeks to show is that the quiet tenderness that develops between Lucy Snowe and M. Paul Emanuel, the moody and often acerbic teacher, as her obsession with the more glamorous Dr John progressively fades, is something far more precious than any grand passion. Yet, despite this, the world of *Villette* is undoubtedly affected by menace. From the outset, Lucy, like Jane Eyre, finds that her sense of identity is easily threatened. Lucy always seems to be on the point of drowning and at every point when she rises again to the surface it seems that she does so only to be inundated by a still greater wave. It therefore seems that, when she has finally found the possibility of happiness with M. Paul, there is a certain deadly inevitability about the fact that his death at sea is announced on the final page of the novel. This fatalism is probably truer to Charlotte Brontë's own sense of the world than was the conclusion to *Jane Eyre*, since she believed that some people were fated never to find happiness. In *Villette* hope is a deadly lure. Lucy struggles against the temptations that it offers and finds both that she cannot live without hope and that hoping places her under an intolerable psychological burden. If, as she recounts 'A new creed became mine – a belief in happiness', and if she speaks of 'the rising of Hope's star over Love's troubled waters', we are always conscious of the danger that such expectation brings with it. At bottom Lucy feels unworthy of happiness and therefore always expects to find it snatched from her grasp.

From the very moment of her arrival in Belgium and her departure for Villette a sense of menace settles around her: the sky is grey; the landscape is flat; the 'slimy canals' are like 'half-torpid green snakes'; the train moves slowly and is subject to lengthy, unpredictable stoppages. As always, Lucy's hope that her spur of the moment decision to travel to Villette will turn out for the best is beset by feelings of disquiet:

These feelings, however, were kept well in check by the secret but ceaseless consciousness of anxiety lying in wait on enjoyment, like a tiger crouched in a jungle. The breathing of that beast of prey was in my ear always; his fierce heart panted close against mine; he never stirred in his lair but I felt him: I knew he waited only for sun-down to bound ravenous from his ambush.

Lucy goes through the world like a person with her eyes cast down, who fears to look up and boldly confront the world because she cannot perceive this as anything other than reckless and futile bravado. At the station she misses her trunk but after an unknown English gentleman (subsequently identified as Dr John) has escorted her through the streets, she rushes along in a frenzy of anxiety at the sight of two mysterious bearded strangers, 'all my pulses throbbing in inevitable agitation'. Arriving at Madame Beck's school, she asks to see Madame Beck and spends fifteen apprehensive minutes, waiting in the 'cold, glittering salon'. To her relief M. Paul recommends that Madame Beck engage her and 'by God's blessing I was spared the necessity of passing forth again into the lonesome, dreary, hostile street'. Lucy is engaged as a maid but is soon given a position as a teacher. She struggles to learn the French language and to wield authority over her pupils. For a while things seem to improve, but it is not long before she is to be cast down once more.

Lucy's emotional life becomes complex because she has already fallen in love with Dr John, in fact her former acquaintance Graham Bretton. However, Lucy cannot admit this to herself, indeed she positively denies it: 'Suitor or admirer my very thoughts had not conceived.' Strictly speaking, of course, the statement is true, since although Lucy is absolutely besotted with Dr John, he is neither suitor nor admirer and Lucy hardly dare hope that this would be the case. However, she discloses her emotions by the violence of her reaction when she finds Madame Beck going through her things, which is hardly an unexpected occurrence since she awoke on her very first night in Villette to discover a similar search in progress:

> Loverless and inexpectant of love, I was as safe as spies in my heart-poverty, as the beggar from thieves in his destitution of purse. I turned, then, and fled; descending the stairs with progress as swift and soundless as that of a spider, which at the same instant ran down the bannister.
> How I laughed when I reached the schoolroom. I knew now that

she had certainly seen Dr John in the garden; I knew what her thoughts were. The spectacle of a suspicious nature so far misled by its own inventions, tickled me much. Yet as the laugh died, a kind of wrath smote me, and then bitterness followed: it was the rock struck, and Meribah's waters gushed out. I never had felt so strange and contradictory an inward tumult as I felt for an hour that evening: soreness and laughter, and fire, and grief, shared my heart between them. I cried hot tears; not because madame mistrusted me – I cared not twopence for her mistrust – but for other reasons. Complicated, disquieting thoughts broke up the whole repose of my nature. However, the turmoil subsided: next day I was again Lucy Snowe.

For a moment Lucy exults in the belief that Madame Beck has found nothing. She rejoices in her own personal insignificance that makes her no more noticeable than a spider. But then she feels nevertheless that her very soul has been raked over by Madame Beck, since her suspicion that Lucy is in love with Dr John is, after all, correct. Yet what makes this doubly mortifying, brings floods of hot tears is her realisation that there is, in the end, nothing to the accusation, since her love is not reciprocated and Dr John has not the foggiest inkling of it. This moment of exposure is followed by another. At the Fête a girl drops out of the vaudeville that is to be performed and M. Paul asks Lucy to take over the part at short notice. The play centres on the rivalry between two lovers for the hand of 'a fair coquette', played by Ginevra Fanshawe – one is 'a good, gallant but unpolished man', resembling Dr John; the other, 'a butterfly, talker and traitor', is to be played by Lucy. Symbolically Lucy practises her part in a dingy garret – rather like Cinderella – before finally emerging into the theatrical limelight. Although she is playing the part of a man, she insists on retaining her skirt, a gesture of independence no doubt, but more probably a desire to remain feminine and attractive to a man, since she knows that Dr John will be watching. Lucy transforms the part from cynical fop to ardent lover – 'thus flavoured I played it with relish'.

The rivalry involved in the spectacle is complex. By playing her part to the hilt Lucy seeks to demonstrate to Dr John that where Ginevra is concerned he can never hope to win her heart since he will always be outmanoeuvred by a more sophisticated rival, yet at the same time her endeavour to shine on stage places her in a situation of rivalry with Ginevra for his attentions. But her tremendous effort is in vain and Cinderella does not get to try on the glass slipper. The doctor is scarcely aware of Lucy's existence and is rather conscious of himself as the rejected suitor in yet another triangle, in which M. de Hamal constitutes the third term. Lucy, so acutely conscious of her own inferiority, is astonished at the depths of his discomforture: 'an inexpressible sense of wonder occupied me as I looked at this man, and reflected that *he* could be slighted'. The fête occurs at the end of the summer term, and when the long vacation begins Lucy is plunged into a deep depression:

> My heart almost died within me; miserable longings strained its chords. How long were the September days! How silent, how lifeless! How vast and void seemed the desolate premises. . . . Alas! When I had full leisure to look on life as life must be looked on by such as me, I found it but a hopeless desert: tawny sands, with no green field, no palm-tree, no well in view. The hopes which are dear to youth, which bear it up and lead it on, I knew not and dared not know. If they knocked at my heart sometimes, an inhospitable bar to admission must be inwardly drawn. When they turned away thus rejected, tears sad enough flowed; but it could not be helped: I dared not give such guests lodging. So mortally did I fear the sin and weakness of presumption.

On stage she had violently, almost involuntarily revealed her emotions. Now she feels crushed when she ponders their actual insignificance. Ginevra Fanshawe is beautiful and comes from a well-connected family. Lucy is only a teacher, nothing more – how absurd that she should imagine, even for a moment, that she could be her rival. Now Lucy is utterly desolate. She feels she has nothing to live for; she cannot sleep. Finally in desperation, although a Protestant she goes to confession – simply to communicate with someone, to pour out all the thoughts and feelings that she had tried so hard to suppress. But undoubtedly she feels guilty. By playing her part on stage with such vivacity she had deliberately turned the knife in Dr John's wound and at the same time had made a flagrant display of her most intimate feelings. In terms of Charlotte Brontë's Protestant faith, Lucy has sinned and in going to a Catholic confessional she sins again. Emotionally exhausted and in despair she collapses in the street.

Lucy awakens to find herself in the Bretton household where she is attentively watched over by Dr John. But this proves to be a false dawn since he never thinks of Lucy in any romantic way and continues to be infatuated with Ginevra Fanshawe. Under such circumstances Lucy finds her stay in paradise intolerable, and quite out of character she expostulates: 'you are but a slave, I declare where Miss Fanshawe is concerned, you merit no respect; nor have you mine'. This 'culpable vehemence' makes it inevitable that she will have to leave. What makes Dr John so intolerable is that although he is invariably friendly, considerate and cheerful, he is nevertheless unable to pick up on nuances of feeling and attitude: 'Expect refinements of perception, miracles of intuition, and realise disappointment.'

Moreover the reason for this is his complacency and narcissism – his behaviour, even when impeccable, is always self-regarding. Lucy suffers further torments when she accompanies him to a concert at which Ginevra is present, and when she finally returns to Madame Beck's she is reminded of her former desolation and swallows tears 'as if they had been wine'. More significantly M. Paul, unlike anyone else, is sensitive to her grief and though in a way Lucy resents this, she nevertheless feels a sense of relief in crying openly before him. This is one of the very few occasions in the book when she is actually able to let go without any inhibitions. What finally provokes her disillusionment with Dr John is a visit to the theatre to see Vashti, the great tragic actress. For Vashti displays great strength:

> Before calamity she is a tigress; she rends her woes, shivers them into convulsed abhorrence. Pain, for her, has no result in good; tears water no harvest of wisdom: on sickness, on death itself, she looks with a eye of a rebel. Wicked, perhaps, she is, but also she is strong; and her strength has conquered Beauty, has overcome Grace, and has bound both at her side, captives peerlessly fair, and docile as fair.

Vashti represents a spirit of feminine strength and defiance, strength *as* defiance, which is denied the Victorian woman but with which Lucy can passionately identify. In Dr John's incomprehension and insensitively before her dramatic display – 'her agony did not pain him, her wild moan – worse than a shriek – did not much move him' – Lucy sees a mirror of her own condition – but now she sees not *her* weakness but *his*. At this moment her liberation begins.

If the theme of *Jane Eyre* is romantic love realised, that of *Villette* is romantic love transcended. The paradox of the novel is that Dr John, though always kindly and considerate, always seems to her a dominating, overpowering figure, whereas M. Paul, 'whose absolutism verged on tyranny', who is choleric, emotionally touchy, invariably difficult, sometimes ridiculous, nevertheless proves a genuinely open and responsive person towards Lucy. He is like this because he loves her. Lucy is not in awe of him because she can see his vulnerability just as he can see hers. She realises just how much he cares about her when he cannot help revealing his disappointment that she has not brought him any flowers on his fête:

> 'It is well!' dropped at length from the lips of M. Paul; and having uttered this phrase, the shadow of some great paroxysm – the swell of wrath, scorn, resolve – passed over his brow, rippled his lips, and lined his cheeks. Gulping down all further comment he launched into his customary 'discours.'
>
> I can't at all remember what this 'discours' was; I did not listen to it: the gulping down process, the abrupt dismissal of his mortification, or vexation, had given me a sensation which half-counteracted the ludicrous effect of the reiterated 'Est'ce la tout.'

We now realise how often M. Paul has manifested his concern with Lucy and her reactions and in how many different ways, ranging from his embarrassment that he should find her looking at a painting of a nude woman and his sense of shock that she should wear a red dress to his ill-disguised jealousy at her receipt of a letter. M. Paul seems severe, chauvinistic and intolerant, yet in practice this is often modified. He allows her to wear a skirt in the play. He makes no complaint when Lucy shatters his glasses. He is anxious that she should adopt the Catholic faith, yet respects her determination to remain a Protestant. He believes that women are inferior to men yet always takes it for granted that Lucy is a person of considerable intelligence and ability. At bottom he has a real respect for her in a way that Dr John, affable as he is, does not. In the eyes of M. Paul and in the eyes of herself Lucy becomes conscious of herself as a valuable person and he shows his respect for her by leaving her a school so that she can continue in her chosen career. Through the tenderness of M. Paul Lucy discovers that the world need not be threatening. For even Dr John's kindness was oppressive: it did not presume equality.

Charlotte Brontë dedicated the second edition of *Jane Eyre* to Thackeray, a possibly surprising gesture, which she justified in the following terms:

> Why have I alluded to this man? Reader, because I think I see in him an intellect profounder and more unique than this contemporaries have yet recognised; because I regard him as the first social regenerator of the day, as the very master of that working corps who would restore to rectitude the warped order of things.

Charlotte Brontë's response to Thackeray was so enthusiastic because she recognised in the author of *Vanity Fair*, whose serialisation began in 1847, the very year in which her own great novel was published, a kindred spirit. Thackeray was not only a mordant commentator on the ostentatious preoccupation with appearances, hypocrisy and materialism that characterised fashionable society, he was also, in *Vanity Fair* at least, a powerful advocate of the rights of women and he clearly recognised that it was above all women who were the primary victims of contemporary social attitudes. That Thackeray's sympathies were clearly on the side of women is demonstrated by the fact that this novel 'without a hero' has no male character with whom it is possible to sympathise, with the single and problematic exception of Dobbin, although it has two contrasted heroines in Amelia and Becky Sharp. In his *Pilgrim's Progress* Bunyan saw 'Vanity Fair' as being above all a place where things were bought and sold and where the values of the market prevailed:

> a fair wherein there should be sold all sorts of vanity, and that it should last all the year long. Therefore at this Fair are all such merchandise sold, as houses, lands, trades, places, honours, preferments, titles, countries, kingdoms, lusts, pleasures, and delights of all sorts, as whores, bawds, wives, husbands, children, masters, servants, lives, blood, bodies, souls, silver, gold, pearls, precious stones and what not.

Although Thackeray in his analysis of the fashionable world of Vanity Fair lays greater emphasis of its spiritual emptiness and falsity, he by no means loses sight of this original emphasis on the sale of goods or that, specifically, wives are mentioned among them. Thackeray sees that in this materialistic world it is women who become commodities and that they are valued precisely as they are 'worth'. We are asked to share Becky Sharp's initial indignation at her socially disadvantaged position and it strikes, at the outset, a note that is to persist throughout the novel:

> the happiness – the superior advantages of the young women round about her, gave Rebecca inexpressible pangs of envy. 'What airs that girl gives herself, because she is an Earl's grand-daughter,' she said of one. 'How they cringe and bow to that Creole, because of her hundred thousand pounds! I am a thousand times cleverer and more charming than that creature, for all her wealth. I am as well bred as the Earl's grand-daughter, for all her fine pedigree; and yet everyone passes me by here.'

Becky is an independent resourceful person, who refuses to accept the valuation that society imposes upon her and who in consequence always has a socially equivocal status even when she is presented before the King. This presentation is, of course, arranged by Lord Steyne, whose mistress Becky has become, so it may be seen in some sense as the culmination of her socially ambiguous status rather than any actual achievement in itself. Indeed, Thackeray pointedly allows us to draw this conclusion by observing:

> And as dubious goods or letters are passed through an oven at quarantine, sprinkled with aromatic vinegar, and then pronounced clean, many a lady, whose reputation would be doubtful otherwise and liable to give infection, passes through the wholesome ordeal of the Royal presence and issues from it free of taint.

Yet what we must recognise is that the issue is not the morality of Becky Sharp *per se* but the way in which Victorian Society, with a capital s, draws its moral distinctions. It is not that social status or prestige are solely for the virtuous, but rather that there are rituals centring on the institution of the monarchy which have a quasi-religious purifying function and can serve to give the impression that this actually is the case. Moreover, *vis-à-vis* any queries about the morality of Becky Sharp, we would have to raise similar questions about Lord Steyne, yet clearly there could never be any question of Lord Steyne being regarded as unsuitable. So questions about social acceptability, although patrolled and enforced by the female sex, nevertheless most significantly involve taboos that circumscribe the conduct of women.

In thinking about the inequality of the sexes it is rather too easy to focus on particular rights that women were denied – that is, property rights, the right to vote, questions pertaining to divorce and the custody of children, the right to education in schools and universities and to practise middle-class professions (though, of course, the right to work in factories was freely granted). What does need to be stressed therefore is the extent to which middle-class women were confined within the home. Thackeray's quasi-autobiographical novel *Pendennis* (1848–50) offers a classic illustration of this in the disparity between the upbringing of Pendennis himself and his mother's young ward, Laura. Pendennis has a private tutor, who indulges most of his whims, including his affair with a young actress, Emily Fotheringay. He goes to university where he enjoys a considerable income that allows him to give expensive dinners, consume champagne and cigars in abundance and gamble with cards and dice. Even when in disgrace and in financially reduced circumstances he enjoys the freedom of a bachelor's existence while studying for the law in chambers in Lincoln's Inn. While all this is going on Laura simply stays at home – waiting for a husband, Pendennis himself: if he is Pen she is certainly a modern Penelope! As Thackeray well knew there was a whole world outside the home, of drinking clubs, gentlemen's clubs, smoking-rooms, theatres and so forth, which were primarily a gentleman's preserve. In *Vanity Fair* Thackeray presented an extensive gallery of male characters, which includes Lord Steyne, Jos Sedley, Osborne, father and son to Sir Pitt Crawley and his sons, Pitt and Rawdon Crawley, yet it can scarcely be denied – and Thackeray himself would not wish to deny it – that though these characters are skilfully delineated and contrasted, they are, virtually without exception, boorish, mean-spirited, narcissistic and selfish, and it is the women who have to bear the brunt of their boorishness. Of Lady Crawley, Thackeray writes:

> whenever her husband was rude to her she was apathetic; whenever he struck her she cried. She had not character enough to take to drinking, and moaned about, slipshod and in curl-papers all day. O Vanity Fair – Vanity Fair! This might have been, but for you, a cheery lass . . . but a title and a coach and four are toys more precious than happiness in Vanity Fair.

Other wives who suffer from their husband's insensitive, self-centred behaviour are Lady Steyne, Lady Gaunt and Lady Jane

Crawley. Rawdon Crawley is totally lacking in any sense of personal responsibility and after contracting massive debts without blinking an eyelid leaves it up to Becky Sharp to provide for him and sort out all his problems. George Osborne treats Amelia Sedley badly from the very moment he marries her. After his death her father insists on separating the male heir from the mother; the boy is spoiled as Amelia struggles on with little money and diminished social status – proof positive of the difference that it makes to be a man, no matter how diminutive. So Thackeray, as a privileged being at the heart of a male world, is nevertheless conscious of the invisible sufferings of women, who must go through unsung agonies within the privacy of their own home:

> O you poor women. O you poor secret martyrs and victims, whose life is a torture, who are stretched on racks in your bedrooms, and who lay your heads down on the block daily at your drawing-room table; every man who watches your pains, or peers into those dark places where the torture is administered to you must pity you – and – thank God he has a beard.

Significantly, it is in the nature of this description to implicitly couple women's difficulties with such other feminine 'problems' as child-birth and menstruation, which are also hidden from public view. Many male Victorians believed that it was woman's duty to suffer in silence. Thackeray, to his credit, did not.

One of the most striking images in *Vanity Fair* occurs towards the end of the novel when young Georgy Osborne visits the gaming tables at Baden-Baden and is disconcerted by what he sees:

> Women were playing; they were masked, some of them; this license was allowed in these wild times of carnival.
>
> A woman with light hair, in a low dress by no means so fresh as it had been, and with a black mask on, through the eyelets of which her eyes twinkled strangely, was seated at one of the roulette-tables with a card and a pin and a couple of florins before her.

This woman is subsequently identified as Becky Sharp and is described by Thackeray as 'no better than a vagabond upon this earth', and this phase of the novel clearly exemplifies her fall and social disgrace. Yet from another point of view Becky has never been anything else. Becky is one of the many victims of Thackeray's

Vanity Fair and what makes it menacing is not just that it is mercenary and false but that it is heartless and indifferent. The pathos of
Becky's predicament at Baden-Baden goes beyond simply being down
on her luck in her mask and nondescript yet immodest clothing; she
has become an unperson, someone who has lost all her dignity and
about whom no one cares.

Yet the image is simply one that dramatises the cruelty of Vanity
Fair in general. If you have no money, if you have no position, if you
undergo any change of status for the worse, you might just as well
cease to be, for all anyone else cares. Becky reaches these lower
depths but they are also inhabited in their diverse ways by Rawdon
Crawley, by old Mr Sedley and by Amelia. The great irony, of
course, as Thackeray makes clear, is that those who are disgraced are
no more disgraceful than many of those who occupy the highest
positions in the land. What makes disgrace painful is that those who
formerly were anxious to know you are now equally anxious to
avoid you. Where once you were recognised, now you are invisible.
For Thackeray what characterises the fashionable world of Vanity
Fair is the fact that it has no memory. Everything is transitory.
Everything is soon forgotten. As the world is in a constant and
unpredictable process of change, as fortunes rise and fall, as contacts
and associations are made and broken off, it seems that everyone in
fashionable society lives only for the immediate moment. Anything
written down or recorded can have the form of irony:

> Perhaps in Vanity Fair there are no better satires than letters. Take
> a bundle of your dear friend's of ten years back – your dear friend
> who you hate now. Look at a file of your sister's how you clung to
> each other till you quarrelled about the twenty-pound legacy. Get
> down the round-hand scrawls of your son who has half broken
> your heart with selfish undutifulness since; or a parcel of your
> own, breathing endless ardour and love eternal, which were sent
> back by your mistress when she married the Nabob – your mis-
> tress for whom you now care no more than for Queen Elizabeth.
> Vows, loves, promises, confidences, gratitude, how queerly they
> read after a while! there ought to be a law in Vanity Fair ordering
> the destruction of every written document (except receipted trades-
> men's bills) after a certain brief and proper interval. Those quacks
> and misanthropes who advertise indelible Japan ink should be
> made to perish along with their wicked discoveries. The best ink
> for Vanity Fair use would be one that faded utterly in a couple of

days, and left the paper clean and blank, so that you might write on it to somebody else.

Thackeray's reference to a 'proper interval' carries the connotation of deaths and funerals, and we may also note that in the case of the old Sir Pitt Crawley and Osborne Senior Thackeray emphasises how quickly they are forgotten, how little regretted. George Osborne *is* remembered but Thackeray characteristically suggests that it might have been better for all concerned if he had been more quickly forgotten, instead of becoming the subject of a sentimental and un-truthful reverie. *Vanity Fair* is linked with Dickens's *Dombey and Son*, published almost simultaneously in 1847–8, in its stress on the im-personality and instability of the modern world – an emphasis that owed much to the challenge of Chartism even though this is not directly reflected in either book. In retrospect it may be thought that this instability was overstressed. Certainly many modern historians have thought so and certainly within a few years novelists such as Trollope, George Eliot and Margaret Oliphant were to lay much greater emphasis on the principles of order and stability in English society, though they significantly shifted their focus away from the capital to provincial settings where a traditional order of things might be gently shaken but not fundamentally stirred by the onrush of the modern. Of the early Victorian novelists, Thackeray, if not the greatest, was certainly the most disconcerting, if only because he offered so few consolations. Dickens world is always threatening, yet even for a Dombey there is the comfort of home and family, if only he would grasp it. Thackeray's marriages are typically un-happy and unsatisfactory. Whereas Dickens in his novels musters an army of carers, from the Cheerybles to Solomon Gills, to minister to those in trouble or need, the lesson that Thackeray enforces is that those in trouble are likely to find their hardship exploited – as Old Sedley and Amelia are dealt with by Osborne senior. Thackeray, like Stendhal and Proust, is a novelist of disillusion and part of the reason for his decline is that Victorian society found such a tone, when insisted on, demoralising and encouraged Thackeray to mend his ways. Even in 1848 much of the mordant force of Thackeray's social criticism may have been deflected by the thought that *Vanity Fair* is, after all, a historical novel, set in the England of Waterloo. Some contemporary readers, infused with the spirit of Macaulay, may well have been prompted to reflect with some satisfaction on the vast improvements in social tone, morality and manners that had occurred since that time. At the very least, surely, Becky Sharp could never have been presented at court!

In any discussion of Thackeray's antithetical and carefully balanced presentation of his two 'heroines', Amelia and Becky, it is easy to insist on some kind of false polarisation, either to accept the notion that Amelia is passive but good, Becky active, energetic but definitely bad; or, in some putative reversal of this scheme to suggest that Thackeray finds Amelia dull as ditchwater but is obliged to offer up such a heroine to his readers, and that his real sympathies are with the anti-heroine, whose refusal of both humbug and sentiment is, in a Victorian novel, positively refreshing. Such partisanship is understandable since Thackeray himself positively encouraged it, but we must also recognise that Thackeray wanted to dramatise the injustice and insecurity of the fashionable world precisely by showing that you could be damned just as well if you were virtuous as if you were not, that really virtue had nothing to do with it. Thackeray structures the novel in such a way as to show that as the result of quite arbitrary events the fortunes of one are on the ascendant as those of the other are on the wane. What he suggests is that survival skills, which Becky possesses in abundance, are really what is required:

> while Becky Sharp was on her own wing in the country, hopping on all sorts of things, and amid a multiplicity of traps, and pecking up her food quite harmless and successful, Amelia lay snug in her home of Russell Square; if she went into the world, it was under the guidance of the elders; nor did it seem that any evil could befall her or that opulent cheery comfortable home in which she was affectionately sheltered.

Becky encounters disaster, as often, more often, than Amelia, but the difference is that she has learned to be independent. When disaster occurs she is neither disconcerted nor surprised and is full of stratagems for dealing with it. Becky always seems able to bounce back. But Thackeray never loses sight of the arbitrariness of the justice that is dispensed by the proud and pretentious world. Becky is tossed to one side by Jos Sedley when Amelia herself is still considered quite a catch. Yet after the death of George Osborne we find Becky clambering out of her own parlous situation with Rawdon Crawley to social eminence as Lord Stein's mistress, while Amelia finds that she can scarcely make ends meet. The final restoration of

Amelia's fortunes coincides with Becky's nadir as the masked woman at the gaming table. So in a way poetic justice is done. But Thackeray does *not* believe in poetic justice and is actually at pains to show that he does not. He is in no doubt that Vanity Fair is a secular world, that it is 'a very vain, wicked, foolish place', and he is not prepared to foster the pretence that his readers themselves are any more virtuous. Rather he suggests that they are likely to read more virtuously than they actually behave. So the humbug of Vanity Fair – of course – includes the humbug about adultery, sexual impropriety and the general disposition to pretend that sexuality does not really exist. Thackeray the novelist 'professes to wear neither gown nor bands, but only the very same long-eared livery in which his congregation is arrayed', and by denying the workings of some benign providence he can only see at work some kind of parodic antithesis of justice: 'The hidden and awful wisdom which apportions the destinies of mankind is pleased so to humiliate and cast down the tender, the good, and wise, and to set up the selfish, the foolish, or the wicked.' It is precisely the arbitrariness and unpredictability of Vanity Fair that makes it appear so menacing. Good conduct can never guarantee security and men as contemptible as the elder Sir Pitt Crawley and Lord Stein have the money, power and rank to shrug off any comment or criticism that is surreptitiously murmured against them. Therefore for us to analyse *Vanity Fair* in terms of character is rather to miss the point.

In general terms the lives of those fortunate members of the upper and middle classes were remarkably secure, but because the ranks of writers were swollen by those, such as Dickens and Thackeray, who were acutely conscious of their own loss of status, the instability of social existence was a major theme of early Victorian fiction. But there again although bankruptcy or imprisonment for debt may actually have affected comparatively few, it may nevertheless have haunted the lives and imaginations of those who never actually experienced it. For all classes what characterised the Victorian society was the sense that they were walking a tightrope without a safety net. Whether it was a sense of loyalty or mutual obligation within the family, or simply the determination to make the granting of subsistence dependent on the shame and discipline of the workhouse, there was always the feeling that once you started falling you would probably go on doing so. The Tullivers in *The Mill on the Floss* feel no special obligation to help old Mr Tulliver when his attempts to defend his water rights in the courts place him in financial difficulty, and Sir Pitt Crawley sees no pressing reason why he should help his brother Rawdon, though he could very easily do so. Although high social status may enable the individual to contract large debts, those who buy the paper are certainly not great respecters of persons. In Thackeray's world the misery of social rejection and humiliation is omnipresent. Even if you despise those who dispense favour it is nevertheless acutely painful to find it withdrawn. So many of the characters in *Vanity Fair* die the death of a thousand cuts and find themselves flinching before the lash of social ostracism. There is George Osborne, who is shamed and humiliated when on his visit to the office of Higgs and Higgs, he is treated with overt indifference and contempt. Yet his father, unpleasant and ruthless as he is, also suffers at the thought that his social pretensions will be nullified by a favourite son who insists on marrying a bankrupt's daughter. Rawdon Crawley, for his rashness in marrying Rebecca, is disowned and cut in the street by his aunt, who at one time was proposing to settle her fortune upon him. Since she, to rescue her own fortunes, turns more and more to Lord Steine, so Rawdon finds himself reduced to being nothing more than a gofer, 'her upper servant and maitre d'hotel'. Finally, after having been unable to get Becky to release him from his imprisonment for debt, Rawdon returns home to find her yielding to the amorous advances of Lord Steine. Yet Becky in turn is to be humiliated by being repeatedly snubbed, rebuffed and ostracised. Amelia is humiliated by her husband and Rebecca as they repeatedly dance together while she sits ignored in a corner. Her father-in-law will not aid her son unless he can make her feel worthless and rejected as well. Lord Steine actually uses Becky to humiliate the women around him. He enjoys showing his power and making them suffer. The elderly Sir Pitt Crawley also relishes the discomforture he can cause by placing the control of his household in the hands of his mistress and housekeeper, Miss Horrocks. Old Sedley suffers the shame of bankruptcy and social rejection. Dobbin, despite his kindliness, self-sacrifice and helpfulness, is despised by everybody, including Amelia, whom he loves. *Vanity Fair* is a world without dignity or respect, a world where there is status but no honour.

In *Vanity Fair*'s successor *Pendennis* Thackeray seems to have decided to present a critique of worldliness that would be both more subtle and more oblique. Instead of focusing on the opportunism, ruthlessness and insincerity of upper-class society he would present a more genial portrait, which would nevertheless show how the individual can almost insensibly be corrupted by exposure to its values. Pendennis would be presented as a naïve, rather spoilt but nevertheless sincere person, who would, in the course of events, be gradually transformed into a worldly-wise, cynical pragmatist, who somewhere along the line loses his redeeming spontaneity and personal authenticity. The main episodes in Pendennis's initiation into the world – his early affair with the actress Emily Fotheringay, his irresponsible and extravagant lifestyle as an Oxford undergraduate, his bachelor existence in chambers at Lincoln's Inn, his involvement in the world of fashionable journalism and his brief and wholly unsuitable affair with the humble Fanny Bolton – are brilliantly realised. As befits a quasi-autobiographical novel, the world of *Pendennis* seems to be more substantial and to have more colour and shading than *Vanity Fair*, and it is adorned by a vivid gallery of supporting characters: Major Pendennis, the hero's benevolent uncle; the perennially tipsy Captain Costigan; old Mr Bows who takes a proprietorial interest in the fortunes of Fanny; Fanny herself and her eventual husband, Mr Huxter; the swaggering Henry Foker and his London flatmate, George Warrington. Perhaps Thackeray's most interesting creation is his shifting and unstable depiction of that apparently stable figure, Major Pendennis. The Major is vain and always wears a wig – hence his derogatory nickname of 'Wigsby'. Although snobbish and worldly-wise, he is nevertheless – and not just by his own lights – eminently good-natured to the point of being positively self-sacrificing and full of good sense. He is quite surprisingly tolerant. Yet Thackeray suggests that the Major's credo, expressed in his advice to Pendennis:

'Remember, it's as easy to marry a rich woman as a poor woman; and a devilish deal pleasanter to sit down to a good dinner than to a scrag of mutton in lodgings. Make up your mind to that. A woman with a good jointure is a doosid deal easier a profession than the law, let me tell you. Look out: *I* shall be on the watch for you: and I shall die content, my boy, if I can see you with a good ladylike wife, and a good carriage, and a good pair of horses, living in society and seeing your friends, like a gentleman.' It was thus this affectionate uncle spoke, and expounded to Pen his simple philosophy

is nevertheless deeply corrupting. The Major rescues Arthur from the wiles of Emily Fotheringay, the first great love of his life, and is also instrumental in ensuring that he extricates himself from his involvement with Fanny Bolton with the minimum of inconvenience; yet Thackeray suggests that such a rescue is not as straightforward as it seems, for from this point on Pendennis conducts his affairs with an eye to the main chance. But the Fanny Bolton episode also seems a failure of nerve on Thackeray's part. Pendennis's involvement with this young girl – appearing as it does as a repetition of his earlier affair with the actress, yet as one from which Pendennis can emerge with much less credit, since he has encouraged Fanny, who genuinely loves him – strikes at the very heart of Victorian values. If he takes Fanny as his mistress, his claim to genuineness and spontaneity is imperilled. If he marries her, his action can only appear as further folly. Thackeray's description of the moment when his mother, together with Laura, his childhood sweetheart and eventual bride, arrive at Pendennis's chambers, to find him attended in his serious illness by Fanny is one of the most brilliant and surprising scenes in Victorian fiction, and yet Thackeray dare not develop this involvement further. Instead he used it to suggest how worldly Pendennis has become. He now renews his early romantic attachment to Blanche Amory in a more prosaic spirit, no longer avowing the depths of his love for her but rather drawing attention to the advantageous consequences for both sides. Blanche's rejection of Arthur:

> you are spoiled by the world . . . you do not love your poor Blanche as she would be loved, or you would not offer thus lightly to love her or leave her. No, Arthur, you love me not – a man of the world, you have given me plighted troth, and are ready to redeem it; but that entire affection, that love whole and abiding, where – where is that vision of my youth?

should be a pivotal moment, but Arthur is saved from the painful consequences of such an assessment both by the fact that Blanche herself is insincere, since she has – or believes she has – Henry Foker waiting in the wings, but also because Arthur can simply fall back on Laura, who has loved him all along. The argument of the novel demands that Pendennis should pay the price of his insincerity, opportunism and vacillation by losing both, but it nevertheless gets its long-signalled happy ending. As a result *Pendennis* is fatally compromised and a novel that could have stood worthily alongside *Vanity Fair* just misses greatness by a margin that is really as good as a mile. As a result it is impossible not to see some connection between a rather too genial and self-indulgent hero and a rather too genial and self-indulgent author.

Thackeray atoned for the fact that he had made the writing of *Pendennis* rather too easy by making the writing of *Henry Esmond* (1852) extremely difficult; for not only was *Esmond* a historical novel that involved Thackeray in considerable reading, investigation and research, but he made the task harder by presenting the book in the form of memoirs, written in a period style. For Thackeray *Henry Esmond* was very definitely a return to form, in which he sharpened through a historical setting his sense of the threat that the great world could present to the integrity and psychological wholeness of the individual. Indeed, in *Henry Esmond* the whole idea of what it is to be an individual is radically problematised, since the hero goes through numerous changes of allegiance and is subjected to quite varying forms of indoctrination. His early upbringing by Huguenot foster-parents is succeeded by a Catholic education at the hands of a Jesuit priest, Father Holt. He is then taken into the household of the Castlewoods, who are Church of England, and brought up in the expectation that he will become a minister in the church. Having shown his loyalty to the crown by taking his part as an army officer in Marlborough's campaigns in the Low Countries, he finally becomes involved in an unsuccessful plot to restore the Old Pretender. Thus, Scott's premiss of a more or less unattached individual torn by a conflict of loyalties, wavering between alternate possibilities is replaced by a situation where a specific allegiance and definite compliance is called for and where the individual has to work tortuously through in his own mind a stance that will enable him to cope with the conflicting obligations he is placed under. *Henry Esmond* is in many ways an act of homage to Scott in its espousal of the Jacobite theme and in its overt advocacy, announced at the outset, of a history from below:

> The Muse of History hath encumbered herself with ceremony as well as her Sister of the Theatre. She too wears the mask and the cothurnus, and speaks to measure. She too, in our age buries herself with the affairs only of kings; waiting on them obsequiously and stately, as if she were but a mistress of court ceremonies, and had nothing to do with the registering of the affairs of the common people.

Yet it can also be seen as offering a sardonic parody of the assumptions on which the Waverley novels are based. For Scott really does believe in great and noble causes, in outstanding world-historical individuals and in passionate conflicts of principle, even if he may often deplore the consequences and rejoice in the arrival of a more tolerant and temperate age. Thackeray, on the other hand, fundamentally mistrusts the whole idea of 'greatness' and of a great world in which the whole destiny of peoples is to be played out and sees it as nothing more than a servile and deluded ideological construction to which 'history' has perversely dedicated itself. For Thackeray Marlborough was not the great general and patriotic Englishman of history and legend but a ruthless egoist and opportunist who was prepared to sell out his own troops for bribes from the opposing side and to sacrifice wantonly the lives of thousands of troops, simply to restore his general image and credibility. Indeed, as Thackeray sees it, given that Henry Esmond displays both idealism and a fierce sense of personal loyalty towards those with whom he is personally associated, who is there among them who actually deserves it? In the case of Lord Castlewood, for example, Esmond makes considerable efforts to effect a reconciliation between him and his wife. He is himself wounded in the affray that sees Lord Castlewood killed by Lord Mohun. On Castlewood's deathbed he learns that he himself is the true heir to the title, since he is the child of an earlier unacknowledged marriage, and that it has partly been this knowledge that has been responsible for Lord Castlewood's eccentric, guilt-ridden behaviour. Yet he is cruelly reproached by Lady Castlewood for his behaviour and virtually made the scapegoat for her husband's death. Esmond's disenchantment with Marlborough and his military campaigns runs hand in hand with his disillusionment with Lady Castlewood's beautiful daughter Beatrix, with whom he is in love though his own social position effectively debars him from such a match, a cruel irony when he himself is the legitimate heir, who honourably refuses to press his claim. Beatrix's determination to make the best possible match, her shameless dedication to social climbing, make her the character in the novel who corresponds most closely to Major Pendennis, though her exposition of the doctrine is even more unsavoury. As she says to her mother:

> Worldliness! Oh, my pretty lady! do you think that I am a child in a nursery, and to be frightened by Bogey? Worldliness, to be sure; and pray madam, where is the harm of wishing to be comfortable?

When you are gone, you dearest old woman, or when I am tired of
you and have run away from you, where shall I go.

Beatrix – a bit like the Buchanans in *The Great Gatsby* – goes around
smashing things up, most notably an attempt to secure the Stuart
succession on Queen Anne's deathbed, which is destroyed through
amorous dalliance between the Pretender and Beatrix when he should
have been closeted with the Queen. In this narcissistic and opportunistic world Esmond himself becomes something of a guilt-ridden
careerist, only involving himself in the Jacobite cause for his own
advancement:

> horrible doubts and torments racked Esmond's soul: 'twas a scheme
> of personal ambition, a daring stroke for a selfish end – he knew it.
> What cared he in his heart, who was king? Were not his very
> sympathies and secret convictions on the other side – on the side
> of People, Parliament, freedom? And here was he, engaged for a
> Prince that had scarce heard the word liberty, that priests and
> women, tyrants by nature, both made a tool of.

But at least Esmond still has a conscience. He finally rejects the
ambitions and pretensions of the great world, choosing instead exile
in Virginia and marriage to Lady Castlewood, a match perfectly
legitimate in itself but one intensely shocking to the Victorian reader
because she is older than he and has taken the place of his mother all
through the novel. Thackeray especially wanted to administer such
a shock because he had flinched away from it in Pendennis, but it
was also for him a way of demonstrating that individuals must for
their own spiritual health, ignore the fraudulent claims and 'moral'
imperatives that the great world imposes. It is precisely through the
idea of a suitable match that the whole discourse of worldliness is
articulated and given substance. The individual is reduced to a
social commodity, a mere pawn in an interminable social game of
advancement. Henry Esmond loves Lady Castleford – and has perhaps loved her from his first childish encounter with her – and she
represents an unwavering integrity in a world that is constantly
shifting and changing:

> Esmond took horses to Castlewood. He had not seen its ancient
> grey towers and well-remembered woods for nearly fourteen years,
> and since he rode thence with my Lord, to whom his mistress with

her young children by her side waved adieu. What ages seemed to have passed since then, what years of action and passion, of care, love, hope, disaster!

The children were grown up now, and had stories of their own. As for Esmond, he felt to be a hundred years old; his dear mistress only seemed unchanged; she looked and welcomed him as of old.

Thackeray was one of many Victorian novelists who struck a note of nostalgia and regret, indeed this novel more than any other may have made that fashionable. Yet in a novel of contemporary society, in the year following the Great Exhibition – the very apogee of Victorian self-congratulation – it would have struck a very discordant note.

But with *Henry Esmond* the heart went out of Thackeray's fiction. *The Newcomes* (1853–5) is a feeble *Pendennis* clone with the hero now artist rather than man of letters and with Colonel Newcome standing in for Major Pendennis. The principle theme of *The Newcomes*, the failure of Clive Newcome to marry (at least within the confines of an inordinately lengthy novel) his beautiful cousin Ethel, owing to the insistence of her family that she make a glittering match, is, as presented, too slight and too superficial to make a strong claim on the reader's attention. Thackeray conveys the impression of a tired and jaded writer who can scarcely maintain his own interest in affairs let alone anyone else's, and some late machinations by Ethel's wicked banker brother, Barnes Newcome, only serve to make the hollowness of the book even more obvious. Many estimable novels contain their *longeurs* but *The Newcomes* seems to consist of very little else. At least *Pendennis* had a vivid gallery of unorthodox and disreputable characters, whereas the all-pervasive gentility of *The Newcomes* makes it seem like nothing less than a return to the traditions of the Silver Fork School, which Thackeray had supposedly supplanted. The only thing to be said is that, in its obsession with the idea of the perfect gentleman and its consequent general vacuity *The Virginians* (1857–9) is even worse. When Thackeray writes of his hero Harry Warrington: 'His title of Fortunate Youth was pretty generally recognised. Being young, wealthy, good-looking and fortunate, the fashionable world took him by the hand and made him welcome. Harry was liked because he was likeable; because he was rich, handsome, jovial, well-born and brave', we feel not merely that Thackeray's fascination with his own lost *jeunesse dorée* has got out of hand, but that his characters have become all too reminiscent of Mrs Jarley's waxworks: 'All the gentlemen were very pigeonbreasted and very blue about the beards; and all the ladies were miraculous figures; and all the ladies and all the gentlemen were looking intensely nowhere, and staring with extraordinary earnestness at nothing.'

The Newcomes at least continues Thackeray's stress on the demeaning nature of arranged marriages, but Ethel's statement: 'We are sold ... we are as much sold as Turkish women' courts for little in a novel that pivots on the relationship between Newcome father and son and is written from a fundamentally patriarchal point of view. Moreover Colonel Newcome's offer of his entire fortune in order to facilitate the marriage of Ethel and Clive makes a mockery of Thackeray's claim that he is criticising the very foundations of marriage in polite society. The extraordinary rapidity of Thackeray's decline as a novelist can never be adequately explained because so many factors contributed to it. Arguably Thackeray never mastered the basic skills of novel-writing in the first place, and his inability even to get his narrative under way, let alone construct a satisfactory plot, became the more chronic as time went on. Yet the deterioration in his fiction must surely be correlated with the altered mood of the 1850s. The middle classes felt secure. The world no longer seemed as menacing as it once had. Those who in the 1840s had spoken with a shrill or urgent voice seemed to have overplayed their hand. There was no longer a place for biting satire or vigorous social criticism. Poise, balance, self-confidence, *savoir-faire* – these were the qualities that were now called for. Thackeray, who was personally involved in the changes that made *Punch* in the 1850s a very much less radical paper even though he was no longer actually on the staff, was very much a part of all this. The later Thackeray revered integrity and courage, yet the courage and integrity that had once enabled him to challenge and provoke the reader of *Vanity Fair* had now deserted him.

4

Keeping the Faith: Newman, F. D. Maurice, Tennyson and Trollope

This chapter will be concerned with the role of the Anglican church in the cultural world of Victorian England and with the variety of ways in which individuals within it sought to sustain their faith and to maintain what it represented against a variety of forces that were threatening to undermine it. It perhaps needs to be emphasised that this attempt at preservation was, for a long time, comparatively successful. It is often the case that discussions of the place of religion in Victorian society have a way of homing in on the battle between science and religion, the crises of conscience to which this gave rise, the struggle to maintain faith against the manifold and circumambient pressures of doubt. Certainly the trials of the spirit endured by such distinguished figures of the Victorian era as George Eliot, Tennyson, Arnold, Carlyle, Newman, Ruskin and Leslie Stephen are in their very different ways among its most significant and poignant episodes. These are experiences too powerful and too representative to be evaded. Nevertheless to place these events so vividly in the foreground is to misrepresent, subtly yet profoundly, the wider context, to underestimate the persistence of traditional religious beliefs even in the face of admittedly discouraging, even demoralising circumstances; to assume a pattern of social change more rapid and more radical than actually was the case. As Frank Turner has pointed out:

> Paradoxically a religion that is not oppressive, intrusive, or demanding of substantial time and attention or that remains more or less compartmentalised from other social and intellectual concerns . . . does not generate personal crisis and inner conflict. There exists no fervent faith to be lost or to be rejected or to assert its presence in some other problematic manner. . . . Rather it is expan-

sive intensified religion, in this case fostered theologically first by Methodism and the evangelical revival and later by the Oxford Movement, that establishes a faith to be lost.[1]

The pertinence of such an analysis is confirmed by many of the names cited above. Carlyle's background was Scottish Calvinism, George Eliot, Ruskin and Leslie Stephen were shaped by the Evangelical movement. Moreover virtually all the figures mentioned above were intellectuals who subjected their belief to the most strenuous interrogation – the possible exception, Tennyson, was also the one to whom questions of doctrine mattered least. Newman went over to Rome because he had come to the, reluctant, conclusion that the positions adopted by the Church of England were not intellectually sustainable. Yet Newman made demands of the Church of England that it could not possibly acknowledge or respond to, simply because it was too diverse and unwieldy an institution readily to work out a position on anything. Its strength simply lay in the fact that it had for so long represented some kind of loose consensus that could only survive so long as it was not put to any serious test, in that it had acquired a cultural significance that did not necessarily rest on specific points of doctrine, even if the existence of the Thirty-Nine Articles implied that it did. There can be little doubt that it was a massive force for inertia in Victorian culture, despite some spasmodic efforts to address the problems of the day, but, in some sense, to expect more of it would be like asking a shire horse to jump fences and sprint for the finish. Moreover – and this is certainly pertinent – there were many who valued the Church of England precisely because it *was* a force for inertia, because in a changing world it seemed that it might be one thing that could hold Britain's disunited kingdom together, even though it was patently obvious that its established existence was a major source of friction. So just as André Bazin proposed a liberation from the frenetic artifice of montage through the expansiveness of the pan, so it can be helpful to place this dramatic sequence of close-ups within a pattern of establishing shots that can offer a more general view of the terrain. Specifically, to consider the Church of England as a social and cultural institution is to recognise that 'keeping the faith' is as much a cultural dilemma as an individual one.

The paradox and the dilemma of the Anglican church is grounded in the fact that it both is and is not a national church. On the one hand it is an established church whose income from tithes is politically guaranteed and whose leading clerics are ensconced as the result of political appointments and sit in the House of Lords. It is the only church body that possesses the authority to validate births, marriages and deaths. Right up to 1871 it controlled admissions to Oxford and Cambridge through the sanction of the Thirty-Nine Articles – though Cambridge required only a declaration of membership of the Church, not an actual act of subscription. Yet on the other hand the Church of England is *not* the national church of Scotland; it is *not* the church of the 75 per cent of all Welshmen who attend a religious service in 1851; it is emphatically *not* the church of the four and a half million Catholics who make up the vast majority of the Irish people; even in the northern manufacturing areas of England it is outgunned by the vigorously expanding dissenting churches. The persistence of the Church of England as an established church is one of the strongest reasons why England has seen itself as privileged within the United Kingdom and why the lesser regions within the law continue to feel deep resentments against an 'England' that so intermittently and so reluctantly acknowledges them. Yet despite this there are many in the Victorian arena, from Newman and F. D. Maurice to Thomas Arnold and Gladstone, who nevertheless conceive of the Church of England as a great unifying and vivifying force in the life of the nation. As a cultural presence and political force the Anglican church is massively there, yet for all its strenuous and often effective attempts to keep up, whether reflected in the attempts to eliminate absenteeism, the greater dedication of its ministers, or the effort put into the building of new churches and schools, it is always as if its effort has come several decades too late. It always seems too narrowly based. As Owen Chadwick has pointed out: 'The notion of the rural parish still largely conditioned the thinking of the Church of England.'[2] Rural England was its spiritual home.

Although perhaps everyone really knew that many Church of England pastors had not been very conscientious, that many had been worldly and that some had not been very devout, the Church is nevertheless the persistent subject of idealisation and nostalgia. The very fact that it has failed to move with the times means that it comes to stand for a kind of direct and innocent relationship between God and man before more complex doctrinal disputes set in; for a vision of social harmony and Christian comradeship that is now being eclipsed by political activism and class conflict; for an idyll in which beauty in ritual, architecture and nature are lyrically combined. This is the Victorian era's truest pastoral. It asks us to picture the church festively decorated with holly, flowers or fruit at the appropriate season, the parson standing at the wicket-gate on Sunday in his white surplice, rooks cawing in immemorial elms over the old ivy-clad rectory, the sense of a world where everything has its due season and where everything is reassuringly in place. To fill out the tapestry we must imagine a vicar like the one celebrated by Winthrop Mackworth Praed – though Praed more or less inevitably suggests that his type is now departed –

> And he was kind, and loved to sit
> In the low hut or garnish'd cottage,
> And praise the farmer's homely wit,
> And share the widow's homelier pottage:
> At his approach complaint grew mild;
> And when his hand unbarr'd the shutter
> The clammy lips of fever smiled
> The welcome which they could not utter.

Here religion is tranquil, orderly, untroubled. Characteristically John Keble, whose *The Christian Year* (1827) did so much to define Anglican spirituality and to redefine it in terms of a Wordsworthian receptiveness to the beauty of nature, drew a contrast in his poem for the second Sunday after Easter between the violence of Old Testament religion at the time of Moses and the unruffled quiet of the present. The star of faith may be ultimately the same, but

> To him it glared afar,
> A token of wild war,
> The banner of his Lord's victorious wrath:
> But close to us it gleams,
> Its soothing lustre streams
> Around our home's green walls, and on our churchway path.

The star may be nearer because of Jesus Christ's mission to mankind but it is difficult not to feel also that in rural England the divine is closer at hand, as Wordsworth and Coleridge certainly believed. In another poem in the collection, for St Matthew the Apostle, Keble is brought to wonder whether religion can hope to thrive in the drabness of an urban setting:

Say, when in pity ye have gazed
On the wreathed smoke afar,
That o'er some town, like mist upraised,
Hung hiding sun and star,
Then as ye turned your weary eye
To the green earth and open sky,
Were ye not fain to doubt how Faith could dwell
Amid that dreary glare in the world's citadel?

This doubt is, of course, immediately put to rest:

But Love's a flower that will not die
For lack of leafy screen,
And Christian Hope can cheer the eye
That ne'er saw vernal green.

Yet the suspicion inevitably lingers that the northern industrial towns may well be stony ground for the seeds of the gospel and by its very imagery Keble's poem seems to contradict its ostensible celebration of the Christian mission of those 'who carry music in their heart' amid 'this loud stunning tide / Of human care and crime'. It points rather to the harmony that is to be experienced elsewhere. Keble himself held the living at Fairford in the Cotswolds and as a result was largely insulated from the turmoil that surrounded Newman and Pusey, his collaborators in the Oxford Movement. It is as if all the dissonance of the modern world is dissipated in the tranquillity of the country, as if the emotional appeal of Anglicanism is somehow linked with the restorative power of nature. For those who sallied forth to do battle the Church of England in its rural setting becomes a characteristic emblem of enduring values.

In 'He Fell Among Thieves' Sir Henry Newbolt's colonial hero, before his final battle in the mountains of northern India, remembers

the little grey church across the park,
The mounds that hid the loved and honour'd dead;
The Norman arch, the chancel softly dark,
The brasses black and red.

The cultural myth persisted even into the twentieth century, when in the turmoil and confusion of the First World War Rupert Brooke remembered the idyllic calm of 'The Old Vicarage, Granchester'. He was confident that there at least there was 'peace and holy quiet' and that in this place there were those who loved the Good and worshipped Truth. If only it had all been so simple. Nevertheless the actual relevance of the Anglican experience is often perceived as bound up with the physical body of the church and the actual milieu in which it is situated. In *Margaret Percival* by Elizabeth Sewell (1847) Margaret becomes disillusioned with the Church of England partly because the clergy with whom she comes into contact lack dedication, but still more because of the hideousness of her local parish church, which is a 'glaring brick excrescence', 'an awkward ill-arranged conventicle, dirty and neglected, crowded with pews, and dark with galleries'. Significantly even the local chapel of the Plymouth Brethren is a more acceptable place of worship. So it is therefore hardly surprising that when Elizabeth travels abroad and visits the beautiful church of St Ouen in Rouen she should be completely overwhelmed:

> the graceful pillars of the nave, their moulded piers unbroken by capitals, rose up into the vaulted roof; whilst beyond them were mingled arches and columns, altars and chapels, some dark and scarcely to be distinguished, others touched by the light of the dying day, as its mellow rays shone mistily through the deep yet gorgeous colours of the windows. . . . Margaret stood motionless: she thought of nothing, observed nothing – her whole soul was absorbed in a feeling of intense awe.

She is therefore strongly attracted to the religious experience that this Roman church offers and is tempted to leave the Church of England, both for this reason and because she is told that the English church has no validity because it is in a state of schism with Rome. Eventually, and after much internal struggle, she decides to remain faithful to Anglicanism partly because she is persuaded by the High Church arguments of her uncle, Mr Sutherland, that such a course of action would be disloyal and perhaps equally importantly because, at her uncle's church in Alton, she is presented with a more aesthetically appealing side of the Anglican faith:

> Piety had guarded the consecrated ground from profanation, and flowers grew upon the graves, and the cypress and the yew spread their branches over them luxuriant and uninjured. Without a thought of neglect or forgetfulness to jar upon it, the mind could

revert from death to life; and the carefully-tended, peaceful churchyard seemed but a fitting foreground for the beauty which lay
around it. Yet it was not a beauty of any striking kind. The deep
clear stream glided swiftly and noiselessly onward, reflecting the
purity of the summer sky and the fleecy clouds which floated over
its surface; but its winding course was bordered only by broad
green meadows, studded with trees, and backed by a soft, misty
range of low hills. A few thatched cottages, and gardens bright
with flowers, lay to the right; and on the left, a little higher than
the churchyard, stood the vicarage. It was in the spirit which
hallowed it, rather than each separate detail, that the churchyard
at Alton was lovely; but Margaret did not care to enquire into the
sources of her pleasure. It was sufficient that she was calmed and
refreshed by the bountiful gifts of God.

In such a setting, where church and countryside are so lyrically
interfused, the spiritual authenticity of the English church, for so
long a troubling question in Margaret's mind, can no longer be put
in question.

The Church of England was a potent symbol but it was also a
political and economic institution. It was at Westminster that it first
became apparent that, after a serene and relatively untroubled passage, it might now be heading for more turbulent waters. The repeal
of the Test Acts and the passing of Catholic emancipation was greeted
in Oxford in particular with an uncharacteristic mixture of panic and
alarm. The assumption that nothing would ever be done to undermine the privileges of the Church of England was beginning to look
distinctly shaky. It was becoming clear that a likely consequence of
the government's attempt to pacify Catholic opinion in Ireland would
be disestablishment of the Protestant church there and a concurrent
abolition of the compulsory church rate. But under Dissenting pressure it would then seem logical to carry out comparable measures at
home. There might be more to reform than just Reform Bills. The
result would be simultaneously a secular state and an Anglican
church that enjoyed no special status or any of the privileges that
went with it. A further cause of anxiety was that there was a section
of opinion within the English church that agreed that practices,
traditions and emoluments were in need of reform; that was pre-

pared to acknowledge the justice of the Dissenters' claim that they should be admitted to Oxford and Cambridge. From 1830 onwards the existence of a Whig administration under Earl Grey committed to reform, combined with an Irish Catholic and Dissenting interest that could be expected to call for far-reaching changes, left High Church Anglicans feeling dangerously isolated and apprehensive. The writing, as it seemed, was on the wall. Oxford in particular was an obvious target. It was widely regarded as inefficient, intellectually backward and corrupt. Moreover as a traditional centre of High Church and therefore Tory opinion it was just the sort of institution that the Whigs were anxious both to discredit and, contrariwise, to bring into line with 'enlightened' opinion. Yet to a beleaguered Oxford things all looked very different. There, surrounded by architectural memorials of Archbishop Laud and by an acute awareness that it had been at Oxford that Charles I raised his standard, it seemed as if the battle for rightful authority and true religion would have to be fought out all over again. This harking back to the mood of the seventeenth century was the more potent because many of the leading intellectual figures of Oxford, such as John Keble, Edward Pusey and John Henry Newman, who were to become the triumvirate that headed the Oxford Movement, believed that during the eighteenth century religion had become simultaneously too rationalistic and too worldly. What was called for was not an endless interrogation of the tenets of the Christian faith but rather a willingness to assent to them and a determination to make that gesture of assent the foundation of a pious, godly and wholly spiritual life in which fasting and other disciplines of the spirit might well be found effectual. At Oxford there was thus a determination to stand out against the latest forms of infidelity. The particular form that this took, in the first instance, in the meetings where the Oxford Movement first took shape, was an insistence on the doctrine of apostolic succession. By this they meant that the legitimacy of the Church of England was ultimately grounded in the authority of its bishops, which had been handed on in a tradition of authorisation that ultimately went back to the apostles themselves. In this way they emphasised that existence and validity as a church was not necessarily dependent on its connection with the state, and a further corollary was that the state had no right to interfere in matters of the church. This position, though itself one of long standing and though it was undoubtedly sincerely held, was also tactically adroit. If the Church of England really were to face the prospect of disestablishment, then it would already be prepared to face that prospect and in that event it could still hope to come out of the crisis in all other respects essentially untampered with; the alternative was to face endless political tinkerings before the final disestablishment eventually took place. Yet, contrariwise, a firm stand taken now could pre-empt extensive political interference and leave the church in the magnificent position of being simultaneously established and yet effectively independent. Moreover an insistence on the principle of apostolic succession ruled out any possibility of a deal with the Dissenters. The Dissenters were implacably opposed to bishops so could never acquiesce in any such principle, yet if the Church of England was, by virtue of its bishops, the only accredited trustee of the Christian faith, then by that very token there could be no question of abjuring that sacred trust through parleys or negotiations with bodies essentially illegitimate. The status of the Church of England could not be the subject of political discussion. Keble to his credit recognised the inherent contradiction in such a position when the church was already politically established and he refused to join the others in any protest against the separation of church and state. It was precisely the connection between the two that was sinful and therefore he saw no grounds for opposing disestablishment. For Keble the best way to preserve the church was a spiritual body lay in being prepared to go down that road, whereas for the others – Newman, Hurrell Froude, William Palmer, and for Nicholas Rose, editor of the High Church establishment *British Magazine*, who was not actually at the meeting – it was this established position that had to be defended.

Yet even within the small group that started the Oxford Movement – to which we must add Pusey who became its most conspicuous public figure but who only became associated with it through his signed contribution of Tract 18 on the subject of fasting – there were significant differences of emphasis. Palmer and Rose were the most cautious. Palmer was worried at the pugnacious tone of the early tracts and wanted a more elaborate vetting system, since he believed, as it turned out with good reason, that Newman, by publishing anonymously and without consultation, was always in danger of creating an explosive situation in which his collaborators might suddenly find themselves implicated in positions that they had neither sanctioned nor agreed with. For a while Rose was less inclined to be censorious and to begin with disassociated himself from Palmer by indicating that he was not similarly inclined to find the early tracts too strong. But this very formulation suggested that what Rose habitually looked for was moderation. Keble and Pusey were less inclined to pose the issue in precisely these terms, but for them the Oxford Movement was primarily defensive and exemplary. On the one hand the Church of England was to be infused with greater dedication and spiritual piety and to be purged of the laxity that threatened its credibility as a religious body; on the other the traditional prayer book and High Church liturgical practices must be maintained in the face of Broad Church and dissenting pressure. Both Keble and Pusey wanted to keep the Church of England very much as it was and their thinking was always implicitly in terms of an *English* tradition, as represented by Hooker, the Thirty-Nine Articles and such figures as Andrews and Laud. Hurrell Froude was much more radical in his aims. He saw the tracts as necessarily provocative and destabilising. He wanted to make 'a row in the world'.[3] For Froude the Reformation had been a ghastly mistake, which, by attempting to correct errors within the church has been led to the still more serious error of schism, by which the authority of the universal church was imperilled. Although not uncritical of Rome, Froude was prepared to think of Tractarianism as Romeward in tendency in a way that Keble and Pusey certainly never were. Froude believed in real presence in the Eucharist and could not accept that the taking of bread and wine was merely symbolic; he was sympathetic to the idea of devotion to the Virgin Mary; perhaps most significant of all he believed in rituals of penance and even seems to have practised self-flagellation. Perhaps for this very reason he deplored the present laxity of the Roman church. Newman was more judicious. He also deplored the schism of the Reformation and looked back with nostalgia to the early church when dispute within had been readily settled: 'In the Primitive Church there was no difficulty, and no mistaking; then all Christians everywhere spoke one and the same doctrine everywhere, and if any novelty arose, it was at once denounced and stifled.'[4] But in his conception of it the Church of England had a special place as the ideal 'via media' between Rome and Dissent. While the Dissenters slighted tradition and mistakenly tried to make the Bible the sole court of appeal – an undecidable undertaking that in consequence necessarily opened the door to scepticism and infidelity – the Roman church in its dedication to tradition had allowed the faith of the early Fathers to be corrupted. As Newman put it: 'Rome retains the principle of true Catholicism perverted; popular Protestantism is wanting in the principle.'[5]

Thus the Church of England had the unique opportunity of being at once critical and traditional. Unlike other Protestants it could manifest a genuine concern for tradition; unlike Rome it could submit the tradition itself to judicious and critical scrutiny in a way that was impossible for the Roman church itself, which must necessarily presume its own rectitude: 'A Romanist then cannot really argue in defence of the Roman doctrines; he has too firm a confidence in their truth, if he is sincere in his profession, to enable him critically to adjust the due weight to be given to this or that evidence.'[6] Only the Church of England is capable of speaking from the position of truth. For Newman the Tracts were not simply an attempt to defend the Anglican church as it was, they represented a far-reaching and ongoing process of intellectual enquiry in which it would eventually be placed on firm and unshakeable foundations. For Newman the Thirty-Nine Articles in themselves were not enough; they were a provisional starting point: 'the particular forms under which we teach the details of faith, the basis on and out of which the superstructure of theology may be most conveniently raised'.[7] For Newman Tractarianism was always a process of intellectual enquiry, never simply the reiteration of familiar and possibly neglected truths.

Nevertheless in attending to these theological arguments we should not therefore overlook the obvious fact that the Tractarians were arch-reactionaries in their social and political views. Newman regarded any whisper of trouble or dissent out of Ireland as unwarrantable turbulence. For him the figure of Daniel O'Connell, leader of the movement for Catholic emancipation, was an anathema. Hurrell Froude deplored the emancipation of slaves in the West Indies. Newman unashamedly advocated a church that would be an instrument of repression and social control. Of the church he wrote:

> It is a standing army, insuring the obedience of the people to the Laws, by the weapons of persuasion; by services secretly administered to individuals one by one in the most trying seasons of life, when the spirit is most depressed, the heart most open, and gratitude most ready to take root there. And as is evident its growing importance at this era of our history, when Democracy is let loose upon us. Either the Church is to be the providential instrument of re-adjusting Society, or none at all is vouchsafed to us. The Church

alone is able to do, what it has often done before, – to wrestle with lawless minds, and bring them under.[8]

All too often the Oxford Movement is represented as the individualistic pursuit of sanctity and doctrinal purity for its own sake, which was what, in Newman's case, it ultimately became, but for a long time its ambitions were far greater. Then Newman wanted a church that would be a *power* in the world, a power whose authority would be unquestioned and unshakeable, a rock amid stormy seas.

Newman's study of the early church, *The Arians of the Fourth Century* – completed in 1832, before the publication of the Tracts began in 1833, and published the following year – is itself very much a tract for the times. Newman perceived this early dispute over the Trinity as an exemplary instance of how the church, in seeming to take an erroneous course, would nevertheless, under God's providential guidance, be restored to the true path. He believed that this whole critical episode in the history of the church could be read as an allegory on a multiplicity of levels, from which many lessons for the present could be found. The Arian heresy had been to subvert the doctrine of the Trinity by arguing that the Son was secondary and inferior to God the Father, who alone was a First Cause. As Newman saw it the development of this heresy was characterised by the use of a syllogistical form of reasoning and by a disposition to interpret scriptural texts in a figurative way, which in itself inevitably opened the door to heresy. Newman believed that the early church did not openly divulge all its teachings but preserved a *disciplina arcani*, whereby certain teachings were only disclosed to the initiates when they were believed to be ready to receive them. Not everything in Christian doctrine was written down precisely because of the risk for misinterpretation. This argument was subsequently to be the basis of Isaac Williams's Tract 80 on 'Reserve in Communicating Religious Knowledge'. For Newman the very development of the Arian heresy was proof positive of the dangers of a Protestant insistence on using the Bible as the sole key to religious truth without any regard for Christian tradition. Arianism was simply the result of such interpretative licence:

Now first, it may be asked, how was any secrecy practicable, seeing that the scriptures were open to everyone who chose to consult them. It may startle those who are best acquainted with the popular writings of this day, yet, I believe, the most accurate consideration of the subject will lead us to acquiesce in the statement, as a general truth, that the doctrines in question have never been learned merely from Scripture. Surely, surely, the sacred volume was never intended, and is not adapted to *teach* us our creed; however certain it is that we can *prove* our creed from it, when it has once been taught us, and in spite of individual produceable exceptions to the general rule. From the very first, that rule has been, as a matter of fact, for the Church to teach the truth, and then appeal to Scripture in vindication of its own teaching. And from the first, it has been the error of heretics to neglect the information provided from them, and to attempt of themselves a work to which *they* are unable, the eliciting a systematic doctrine from the scattered notices of the truth which Scripture maintains.[9]

It is tradition that is the guardian of authentic interpretation, and had tradition been respected over the doctrine of the Trinity the Arian heresy could never have arisen, whereas the printed texts necessarily generate instability and public controversy,

> oral discourse can maintain a certain discipline and reserve in which the relationship between pupil and teacher is never forgotten.
> Here, again, is strikingly instanced the unfitness of books, compared with private communication, for the purposes of religious instruction; levelling the distinctions of mind and temper by the formality of the written character, and conveying each kind of knowledge the less perfectly, in proportion as it is of a moral nature, and requires to be treated with delicacy and discrimination.[10]

But the whole episode is instructive for other, yet weightier reasons. Arianism developed after Constantine had made Christianity the official religion of the Roman Empire and thus an established church, and though this was in itself beneficial the unfortunate consequence was that Constantine, partly because of his ignorance of theology and partly because of certain fortuitous circumstances, gave substantial support to the Arian cause. Yet Athanasius, whose creed is still in use, though for a long time persecuted and reviled, was ultimately vindicated. For Newman this demonstrated the damage that could result when politicians meddled in church affairs, and indicated that similar damage could be caused by an unholy alliance between Whigs, Irish Catholics and Dissenters. Yet the ultimate failure of Arianism suggested that truth – and the High Church party – would necessarily prevail: for 'Then as now, there was the prospect, and partly the presence in the Church, of a Heretical Power enthralling it, exerting a varied influence and a usurped claim in the appointment of her functionaries, and interfering with the management of her internal affairs.'[11] The unholy alliance of sectarianism and political calculation could be repulsed if only those within the church would stand firm against the danger.

In Oxford in 1836 that danger took the somewhat improbable form of the appointment of the ponderous and intellectually complacent Renn Dickson Hampden as Regius Professor of Divinity. Hampden was already *persona non grata* with the Tractarians as in 1834 he had argued, unsuccessfully, for the admission of Dissenters to the university. Indeed his professorship was almost certainly a reward from the Whig administration for his efforts on that occasion. Hampden was appointed despite the fact that Archbishop Howley had submitted a list to Lord Melbourne that was headed by Pusey and on which Newman and Keble came fourth and fifth. This appointment was a serious setback to the Tractarians and they immediately set about trying to reverse the decision. The subject of their attack was Hampden's Bampton lectures, which he had delivered as far back as 1832 to a very small audience and which almost certainly none of the Tractarians had either attended or read – or they would have objected to them before. Hampden's lectures were on 'The Scholastic Philosophy considered in its Relation to Christian Theology' and in them he attempted to draw a distinction between the facts contained in the Bible and the complex theological interpretation of medieval scholastic philosophy. Hampden claimed that the Christian religion – especially through its doctrine of substance and causation – had been corrupted by attempts to reinterpret it in the light of Aristotelian philosophy. This led both to the intricate and false systematising of Thomas Aquinas and to the Calvinist denial of free will. So Hampden in thus impartially criticising Roman Catholicism and Dissent must have felt that he was on fairly safe ground. Yet it was both an ignorant and arrogant performance since Hampden did not really possess the knowledge of medieval philosophy he claimed – if he had, he could not have presented it in such a unitary and reductive fashion. Moreover his critique went very far beyond this since he deplored the controversies of the early church and denied that even some of the earliest Christian literature outside of the Bible itself could be appealed to. Yet what is at first sight surprising in Newman's outraged response to Hampden is that the two men seem to have so much in common. Both object to a rationalising spirit in religion and see Aristolelianism as a corrupting force. Newman at this time was critical of Rome as 'this technical religion', which 'destroys the delicacy and reverence of the Christian mind'.[12] They both distrust interpretation and rely on an appeal to incontrovertible facts: Hampden claims 'The only ancient, only catholic, truth is the Scriptural fact',[13] and Newman, though possessed of an infinitely more subtle and scrupulous mind, similarly argues: 'History is a record of facts; and "facts", according to the proverb, "are stubborn things".'[14]

Both men want genuine piety and faith and see speculative interpretation as the door through which infidelity enters. Why, then, does Newman regard Hampden as a Socian – that is, one who denies the Trinity and divinity of Christ – indeed see him as being pretty much indistinguishable from an out and out heretic? Obviously personal rivalry and ambition are involved, but Newman does have a point. For Hampden's opposition to the intrusion of dogma into religion, and his protest against the domination of logic, has the effect of suggesting that absolutely everything but the Bible itself is distorted and false, including all subsequent and latter-day interpretations of scripture. So Hampden, despite his undoubtedly sincere protestations of piety, nevertheless presented theology as impossible and left the very idea of Christianity in ruins. It must either be self-evident or impossible. Newman agreed with Hampden about the incompatibility of rationalism and religion but he saw Hampden's lectures as themselves vitiated by a rationalising spirit. Indeed, Hampden seemed to prove Newman's point that the Bible alone was insufficient if not read in the light of Christian tradition – whose history Hampden, in true Protestant spirit, regarded as little more than a relentless tale of corruption and error.

Nevertheless Newman's case against Hampden was overstated and the extracts he selected to make his case undoubtedly misrepresented it. But for the Tractarians Hampden was the thin end of the wedge at Tory and High Church Oxford. His appointment would symbolise the triumph of the weak and wishy-washy liberalism they so heartily detested. Hampden's appointment was therefore opposed, and although it could not be prevented, a motion of censure was passed against him and many tutors forbade their students to attend his lectures. Yet the Tractarians overplayed their hand for few knew enough to follow the theological issues involved and it began to seem as if Hampden had been the victim of personalised and malicious attacks. Effectively the whole episode rebounded on Newman just two years later in 1838 when he published the diaries of Hurrell Froude, who had died in 1836 of tuberculosis after a prolonged illness. Froude's frankly expressed opposition to Protestantism and his obsessive drive to punish every manifestation of sinfulness in himself made these *Remains* the obvious target for an attack on the Tractarians and the book was made the subject of a hostile sermon preached by Dr Godfrey Faussett before the university on the theme of 'The Revival of Popery'.

Newman responded in pugnacious style and in itself this criticism might not have mattered much, but what made his position more problematic was that his bishop. Bishop Bagot, in the course of some generally favourable comments on *Tracts for the Times*, nevertheless objected to certain passages within them. This was awkward for Newman as he had always insisted on the duty of compliance before episcopal authority and for the first time he became acutely aware that it would not be as easy as it had been to keep the Tractarian bandwagon rolling if they were thus hemmed in by admonitions and restraints. Worse still, a scheme was proposed to honour the Reformation bishops Cranmer, Ridley and Latimer in Oxford, which was intended as a symbolic demonstration that what they represented was still respected within the Anglican church, despite the animadversions of Froude. Newman, Keble and Pusey were asked to contribute and declined. Suddenly the leaders of the Oxford Movement found themselves deeply isolated and regarded by some at least as traitors within the gates.

At this point Newman took the extraordinary step of writing a tract – it was to be the last in the series – that argued that there was nothing in the Thirty-Nine Articles that necessarily precluded a number of Catholic beliefs and practices; in particular there was nothing against either purgatory or the Roman mass. Where another man might have bided his time, Newman deliberately threw petrol on the flames. Yet there was a definite logic in his action. As the Oxford Movement went on it developed a certain internal momentum of its own, in which those who were most involved pressed on to more and more advanced positions and almost without being conscious of it opened up a large gap between themselves and members of the Church of England at large – even High Churchmen. Almost imperceptibly they moved from a determination to safeguard the Thirty-Nine Articles from a dissenting and liberal assault to a position where they themselves began to see the Articles as unsatisfactory because of their *ad hoc* and imprecise nature, dictated as they were by the need to find a formula that was acceptable to everyone. Newman began to worry less about schism within the church as represented by Professor Hampden and much more about the schismatical status of the Church of England itself. Symptomatic of this new frame of mind was Hurrell Froude's Roman breviary, which he kept with him at all times and incessantly studied. Froude had opened Newman's eyes to wider religious perspectives and from this standpoint the Church of England began to seem restrictive and narrow. Moreover Newman's position within the Anglican church had been predicated on the idea that the saving remnant of the Tractarians would infuse the church with a new and stronger sense of the tradition of the early Fathers and that their presumption to speak for the church in its hour of danger would be progressively vindicated as more and more came round to their point of view. But Newman now recognised that this had not happened and would not happen. The *via media* was a road that only a few had taken. The real had not tended towards the idea. Yet Newman could not deny the momentum of his own inner convictions. He would press on regardless.

Now began the slow but inexorable progression whereby Newman left the Church of England and became a Roman Catholic. In 1843 he resigned from St Mary's in Oxford and from its associated parish of Littlemore outside the town. He withdrew his criticisms of Catholicism and in October 1845 joined the Roman church. Yet from another point of view this transfer was less inevitable that it subsequently seemed or was made to seem. For Newman was deeply attached to the Anglican church and to his fellow spirits in the Oxford Movement and one suspects that had he been allowed to keep the chapel at Littlemore he might have been as happy to spend his years of obscurity there as at the Oratory in Birmingham. For Newman, despite the dramatic role that he played on the stage of the world, was always a deeply private person. His whole identity was bound up with the development of the Oxford Movement and with Oxford itself and his decision to join the Roman church brought with it a terrible sense of loss. As he wrote in his novel *Loss and Gain*, published in 1848, some sixteen years before the *Apologia*:

He had passed through Bagley Wood, and the spires and towers of the University came on his view, hallowed by how many tender associations, lost to him for two whole years, suddenly recovered – recovered to be lost for ever! There lay old Oxford before him, with its hills as gentle and its meadows as green as ever. At the first view of that beloved place he stood still with folded arms, unable to proceed. Each college, each church – he counted them by their pinnacles and turrets. The silver Isis, the grey willows, the far-stretching plains, the dark groves, the distant range of Shotover, the pleasant village where he had lived with Carlton and Sheffield – wood, water, stone, all so calm, so bright, they might have been his, but his they were not. Whatever he was to gain by becoming a Catholic, this he had lost; whatever he was to gain higher and better, at least this and such as this he never could have again.

This moment of suspension in which Newman's hero Charles Reding finds it impossible to go on seems to stand symbolically for that long and fraught period in Newman's life, between 1839 and 1845, before he made the irrevocable decision. Paradoxically although Newman distrusted reason, it was reason that led him to Rome and the intellectual security of its dogma and thereby to override all his deepest feelings. In the *Apologia* he claimed that such a dedication to dogma was central to his whole intellectual position: 'First was the principle of dogma: my battle was with liberalism; by liberalism I mean the anti-dogmatic principle and its developments. This was the first point on which I was certain.'[15] But this was not really the case even though Newman may subsequently have persuaded himself that it was. Newman wanted a sure and firm foundation for his faith, but he had to explore all the possibilities in his own mind and test them before he could finally commit himself. Newman in theory believed in submission and in an unquestioning and reverent acceptance of the Christian faith, yet it was something that he found difficult to practise himself. Newman had a critical, enquiring and perennially questing mind. He actually enjoyed difficulties. In *Loss and Gain* he drew a truer portrait of himself when he wrote:

Some persons fidget at intellectual difficulties, and, successfully or not, are ever trying to solve them. Charles was of a different cast of temper; a new idea was not lost on him, but it did not distress him, if it was obscure, or conflicted with his habitual view of things. He let it work its way and find its place, and shape itself within him, by the slow spontaneous action of the mind. Yet perplexity is not itself a pleasant state; and he would have hastened its removal, had he been able.

Newman did not believe that Rome was the true repository of tradition; he believed that a true sense of that tradition could emerge from a reverent, scrupulous and dispassionate enquiry. Somewhat naïvely, for all his intellectual sophistication, he believed if only this could be established, a truly authentic and universal church could be created even in the face of an age of liberalism. For one sublime moment all this seemed possible; then the dream collapsed and he had to grasp at Rome, which was at least a powerful and living actuality. Yet the agony for so sincere and scrupulous a man was that he must necessarily incur the charge of bad faith. If he had been heading in the direction of Catholicism all along, then he was both a hypocrite and a cruel Pied Piper to so lead astray his youthful band of followers. If he left the Anglican church of whose *via media* he was the most eloquent exponent, then he was lacking in fidelity to his own church and lacking in intellectual consistency. If he was not these, then he was either vacillating, opportunistic, perhaps even cowardly not to stay and fight his corner within the Church of England. So he had to explain, even if that explanation could never quite do justice to the complex pressures to which he was subjected as it remorsely rested on the level of doctrine. To preserve the faith Newman wanted to see a strong, undivided and universal church, yet his faith led him to a position of profound isolation; distrusting private judgement he was nevertheless compelled to rely upon it; beginning with a far-reaching enquiry into the history of the whole Christian tradition, he ended up by writing the history of his own developing and changing opinions.

Newman, Keble and Pusey were anxious about the tendency in the 1830s for religious issues to become reduced to questions of political expediency. The kind of stance in church affairs that they deplored can be well represented by Thomas Arnold, better known for his pioneering role as headmaster of Rugby, but an eloquent spokesman of religious as well as educational affairs. On the one hand Arnold's attitude to the central importance of the Church of England is both realistic and pragmatic. Arnold is conscious that the stand-pat traditionalism of the Anglican church means that it has become unable to fulfil a meaningful role in contemporary society and that it is in urgent need of reform. Arnold was deeply concerned at what he called 'a monstrous state of society without parallel in the history of the world – with a population poor, miserable, degraded in body and mind, as much as if they were slaves, and yet called freemen',[16] and he was conscious of the fact that because of complacency in the Church of England it had left the lives of people in the industrial north completely untouched. He pointed out that the cause of the extreme unpopularity there both of bishops and of established clergy in general was undoubtedly due to its failure to reach out to this new constituency:

> Whence the hatred with which the whole order of the clergy is sometimes pursued? Is it not because the people have never been made to feel the full amount of good which an Established Church may and ought to effect, and therefore are the more ready to complain of its endowments? Is it not because in our large manufacturing towns the Church has allowed thousands and tens of thousands of its members to grow up in misery and in ignorance; and that a step-mother's neglect is naturally requited by something of a step-mother's unpopularity.[17]

For Arnold it was vital that the church should be reformed both financially and morally so that it could address itself to the urgent issues of the day. He called for flexibility and pragmatism in the relationship of Anglicanism with other denominations. He was honest and forthright enough to call the 'exclusive establishment of a Protestant Church in Ireland', which could therefore levy tithes on Roman Catholics as 'a direct injustice, and therefore a direct sin'.[18] In the interest of Church unity he was prepared to advocate the common use of the local parish church by a variety of denominations. Arnold deplored sectarianism and he saw the United States as the classic instance of the confusion that would ensue if sectarianism was allowed to run riot. He wrote:

> I groan over the divisions of the church, of all the evils I think the greatest – of Christ's Church I mean – that men should call themselves Roman Catholics, Church of England men, Baptists, Quakers, all sorts of appellations, forgetting that only glorious name of CHRISTIAN, which is common to all, and a true bond of union.[19]

What was needed was a comradely and Christian spirit by which all those who owed allegiance to Christ's name would be prepared to sink their differences for the sake of harmony and the greater good instead of petulant and irritable determination on the part of each particular group to insist on precisely those questions of Christian doctrine on which they differ from others:

> It seems to have been the boast hitherto of the several sects of Christians, to invent formulae both of worship and of creeds, which should serve as a test of any latent error; that is, in other words, which should force a man to differ from them, however gladly he would have remained in their communion. May God give us, for the time to come, a wiser and better spirit; and may we think that the true problem to be solved in the composition of all articles and creed and prayers for public use, is no other than this; how to frame them so as to provoke the least possible disagreement, without sacrificing in our own practical worship, the expression of such feelings as are essential for our own edification.[20]

Arnold's whole attitude is clearly and somewhat paradoxically illustrated in his attitude to the Hampden affair at Oxford. In his *Edinburgh Review* article 'The Oxford Malignants and Dr Hampden' Arnold refused to get involved in the actual theological issues deemed to be at stake and focused entirely on personalities. As far as he was concerned Dr Hampden was a good man and a good Christian, the 'right stuff', and the Tractarians were unnecessarily and wilfully persecuting him for their own narrow sectarian ends. In a way Arnold was right but his whole approach to the issue was far too simplistic and crudely dismissive; worse still, in his call for unity and harmony he succeeded in being as abusive and as obnoxious as any. Of course much was at stake and Arnold was evidently alarmed that the Church of England would lose all credibility by the bitterness of its internecine struggles. Yet Arnold himself did much to make them worse. Arnold saw the church as a powerful force for goodness and unity and he believed that the state needed the moral underpinning that only the church could give. They must so interpenetrate one another as to become inseparable and indistinguishable: 'religious society is only civil society fully enlightened: the State in its highest perfection becomes the Church'.[21]

The church, says Arnold, was intended to be 'a society for the purpose of making men like Christ – earth like Heaven – the kingdom of the world the kingdom of Christ'.[22] Yet the problem with this noble vision is that in the process Arnold is never quite clear whether he is really aiming at universal Christian brotherhood or a state firmly grounded on the unity that he believes only the Christian religion can supply. Like many other Broad Church exponents of the unity of church and state, Gladstone for example, Arnold saw Anglicanism as the solution to a problem, of which in reality it was the cause. Arnold did not realise – as Newman did in the case of Ireland – that religion was often a particular articulation of sectional and class differences and that such excluded and underprivileged groups would certainly not want to surrender precisely that which held them together in deference to some factitious principle of unity. Yet even though we can scarcely share Arnold's perspective, we should at least recognise how complex the issue of a national church could seem to all those who addressed themselves to it at this time.

This hostility to sectarianism and concern for Christian unity finds an even more eloquent articulation in the work of Frederick Dennison Maurice, who in retrospect seems unmistakably the most creative intellectual presence within the Church of England even though at the time he appeared more as a maverick than as a representative spokesman. Yet in the final analysis differences of style, tone and address count for more than an ostensible common purpose. For whereas Arnold is pragmatic, Maurice is mystical; where Arnold seeks to negotiate, Maurice engages in a many-sided spiritual dialogue; where Arnold directly concerns himself with contemporary problems, Maurice, like Newman, looks back over the whole historical development of Christianity in search of inspiration and enlightenment; where Arnold is the decisive man of action, Maurice is unashamedly impractical and otherworldly, a visionary who can never quite manage to get on the same intellectual wavelength as anyone else, even when they seem to be speaking the same language.

While Arnold could casually assume that the churchless masses in the north of England were nevertheless *de facto* members of the Church of England, Maurice could never unthinkingly slip into such uncritical Establishment thinking precisely because he was that most unusual thing, a convert to the Church of England. Maurice was brought up in the Unitarian church, the son of a Unitarian minister, and while he was to repudiate Dissenting positions because he had experienced these at first hand, he was well aware of the issues involved, whereas High Church Anglicans simply regarded Dissent as an unspeakable abomination that did not even bear thinking about – let alone arguing with. Maurice well understood that part of the appeal of the more uncompromising sects was their claim to be at once more godly and more intransigent than the rest, and he recognised that their fanatical pursuit of purity was both misconceived and impossible: 'Every experiment to make bodies holy by cutting off the supposed holy portions from the rest, has proved the more unsuccessful and abortive, the more consistently and perseveringly it has been pursued.'[23]

Maurice was equally suspicious of the absolutism of those involved in the Oxford Movement, even though he shared their belief in the importance of the apostolic succession and their desire for an undivided universal church. He simply felt that their intransigence and their relentless drive against what they perceived as deviance was wholly incompatible with the spirit of Christian fellowship that he personally advocated. He saw them as symptomatic of 'the destructive spirit of the age, at times endeavouring to pull down other men's truth because it is not the same position as their own'.[24] For Maurice if there were to be unity amongst Christians, it would have to be a substantial and palpable unity, grounded in the most common and fundamental traditions of the church, and it would have to be brought about in a spirit of sincerity, dialogue and goodwill. He felt that Newman's attempt to represent the Church of England as a *via media* was nothing more than a complicated fiction based on the drawing of highly arbitrary distinctions in which the complexity of history was not so much confronted as suppressed:

> After all those splendid assurances, that the Church really exists, and that it is endowed with such mighty powers, how grievous it is to find that the most strange uncertainty about the terms under which she exists; whether only as a splendid dream, whereof the record is preserved in the writing of the Fathers, and which may some day be realised; or as a potentiality, which was made a fact during the Middle Ages by the supremacy of the Pope; or, lastly as an invisible equatorial line between Romanism and Protestantism; a line of which some dim traces may, from time to time, be discovered, with the help of powerful glasses, in our English history, but which has gradually been lost in the dark ground upon one side of it.[25]

For Maurice this attempt to erect an Anglican half-way house was itself at a crossroads between pedantic antiquarianism and downright fantasy. Maurice simply did not believe that unity could be hypothesised and dogmatised about. It would have to be worked for. Maurice's own way was that of debate, discussion and dialogue. In *The Kingdom of Christ* – in its origin a series of letters addressed to Quakers – Maurice sets up a complex and many-sided conversation with Unitarians, Quakers, Lutherans, Calvinists and Catholics, and endeavours to answer any objections that they might be expected to raise to the positions that he puts forward. So Maurice practises what he preaches, which is that the answer to the superficiality of the present day is not the childlike spirit of submissiveness advocated by the Tractarians but rather a 'spirit of earnest and deep reflection'.[26]

If Maurice wanted to see a vital connection between church and state this was because he saw modern society as fragmented, deeply divided and characterised by a spirit of selfishness. Maurice saw this spirit of modern society as epitomised in Benthamite Utilitarianism and in his early novel, *Eustace Conway*, he described how his youthful hero, after joining a Benthamite discussion group, clearly the London Debating Society founded by John Stuart Mill, 'forced himself, though with much inward loathing, to swallow down whole pails-ful of metaphysical water-gruel'.[27] It is only subsequently that, in discussions with an Anglican clergyman, Mr Wilmot, that he encounters a more constructive answer to the problem of a self-centred and alienating individualism: 'the Bible expounds this miracle also. It proclaims the law which connected each man with his Creator, and likewise that (dependent upon this primary one) by which he is connected with his fellows.'[28] This was the conviction to which Maurice held onto tenaciously in all his thinking. All questions about man's relationship to God were bound up with his relationship with others in society; and vice versa. Maurice's argument about the role of the church and society is not just that state needs the church's support, it is rather that the church's order always precedes and is more deeply rooted than any order of the state. In *The Kingdom of Christ* Maurice argues that Constantine simply took over an ecclesiastical order that the church had already made: 'But the most vigorous of all the persecutions failed of its object; the new kingdom could not be put down; under Constantine, the eagle did homage to it.'[29] Moreover Maurice is also prepared to argue that the work of constructing the different national societies that arose in the Middle Ages was also the work of the church: 'The ecclesiastical society was the main instrument in creating within each of these tribes a distinct national organisation.'[30]

While the state and civil society in Maurice's conception of them are always brittle and superficial, it is only a spirit of Christian fellowship and brotherhood that can foster a more organic and more fundamental sense of unity. Thus he enunciates it not as a desirable goal but as an inevitable state of affairs that a nation must be spiritual in its very essence: 'I solemnly deny that a Nation is a secular thing.'[31] The church is a vital centre that resists all tendencies to anarchy and disorder:

> The Universal Church, constituted in its Universal Head, exists to protest against a world which supposes itself to be a collection of incoherent fragments without a centre, which, where it reduces its practice to a maxim, treats every man as his own centre. The Church exists to tell the world of its true Centre, of the law of mutual sacrifice by which its parts are bound together. The Church exists to maintain the order of the nation and the order of the family, which this selfish practice and selfish maxim are continually threatening.[32]

Without this, the state becomes a 'mere civil body' that 'will of necessity resort to force again for the putting down of opinion',[33] and which therefore damages the church by 'using vulgar visible arms, for the accomplishment of an invisible spiritual end'.[34] However, in his enraptured presentation of the religiously knit-together society, Maurice, like Arnold, manages to lose sight of the simple fact that many of the most critical sources of division in Victorian society are precisely religious. The church as a centre of national life does not exist; or if it does, it does so only to be a source of cultural oppression to a variety of so-called minorities. It is one thing for Maurice to see Christian unity as something towards which the world is irresistibly working, quite another to imply, wittingly or no, that the Church of England is that unity, and that the millennial prospect towards which he elsewhere reverently gestures is actually already in place.

Since Maurice is a believer in church unity above all else, his characteristic emphasis is to devalue the significance and interpretation of the Bible, which has been a perpetual source of conflict and division, and rather lay emphasis on the traditions and ritual that Christians have in common – or at any rate should have in common. For Maurice the kingdom of Christ is a universal community that men and women enter through the ceremony of baptism. Its essential faith is spelled out in the creed and its common ritual is the ceremony of the eucharist, which Maurice argues was inaugurated by Christ precisely as a means of uniting the faithful. Thus he indicts the Quakers, who refuse to acknowledge it, as follows:

> The sin which I do charge them with is this: that when Christ had, of His loving mercy to mankind, provided them with a simple and wonderful testimony against these narrow notions and dividing tendencies; when He had embodied in a living feast the complete idea of His kingdom, which we, looking at things partially from different sides, through the prejudices and false colourings of particular times and places, are continually reducing under some name, notion or formula of ours; when He has made this feast effectual for imparting to men a faith far above the level of their ordinary theories and speculations; when He had given it as a bond to all peoples and languages and generations – they chose to fancy that His ordinances signified nothing, that they had a much better storehouse for His truths in their own fine thoughts and apprehensions.[35]

Thus to insist on exclusive truths and particular doctrines is itself a denial of Christ's universal message. The kingdom will only be truly realised when men are prepared to sink their differences and to acknowledge their community with one another. So Maurice conjures up a transcendental vision of an all-embracing Christian fellowship in which human beings will be brought together in a spirit of reverence and mutual goodwill, in which conflict and division will finally be brought to an end. Thus Christ's gospel of peace on earth is for Maurice the most significant part of his message. Yet Maurice's playing down of the importance of the Bible and his insistence on the importance of the apostolic succession and on the role of bishops in guiding men to a right understanding of the Bible is distinctly reminiscent of Newman. Maurice even goes so far as to argue that it is Christ who matters as the instigator of this universal brotherhood, as the founder of the church, and that in this light the Bible itself is by no means indispensable: 'The Kingdom exists he is not afraid of losing it or of losing his place in it, even if God thought fit to take away the book altogether.'[36]

What makes Maurice's sense of this kingdom quite complex, however, is that he sees it as the product of a complex process of dialectical development in which God has actually permitted, indeed initiated, division – only to set in motion a process by which the diverse sects will once again be reintegrated. Unlike Newman, who looked back to the time of the early Christian fathers and hoped to recapture the clarity and simplicity of their faith, Maurice is a progressive. His Kingdom is unmistakably located in the future, indeed his sense of it is often distinctly apocalyptic. The struggle between Protestantism and Roman Catholicism will not have been in vain, for it will usher in a new age of unity, which Maurice actually sees as imminent:

> From that time it has been evident to thinking persons, that there are two principles struggling in Christendom for supremacy: the one, that is embodied in Protestantism, resisting the claim of the spiritual power to any extra-national domination, and always tending to set at naught spiritual authority altogether; the other, that which is embodied in Romanism, resisting the attempts of particular states to divide their own subjects from the rest of Christendom, continually striving to uphold the Church as a sepa-rate power, and to set at naught the existence of each particular nation. These principles have fought together in Europe for centu-ries. If it be really the purpose of God in our age to reconcile them, and to cast out the element in each which is contrary to His will, and which has been introduced to it by the perverseness of men, shall we whine about the loss we have sustained by not being born at a time when the Church was making its first struggling efforts to assert its own unity? Shall we not rejoice and gives thanks, that we are born in these latter days of the world, when all things are hastening to their culmination, and when the unity of the Church shall be demonstrated to be the ground upon which all unity in nations and in the heart of man is resting.[37]

So Maurice courageously and optimistically refuses any nostalgia for the fourth century when the church managed to summon up its energies to condemn Arianism, and looks for a still more impressive assertion of such a spirit in his own day. Indeed, given the bitterness of strife not only between Anglicanism, Catholicism and Dissent at the time – leaving aside all question of their complex internal contro-versies – Maurice's desire to bring such dissent to an end seems as quixotic as it is noble. Does Maurice *really* believe that the sound and fury that surrounds him is simply a prelude to perpetual peace? Although Maurice's willingness to address a variety of religious issues in detail without ever descending to pettiness and without ever losing sight of his greater goal is intellectually impressive, there is always an air of unreality about his reflections, earnest though they undoubtedly are. It is therefore difficult at such moments not to recall Carlyle's description of Maurice's 'way of thought' as 'mainly moonshine and *Spitzfindigkeit*' and his attempt to endow the Church of England with significance as a 'vehement earnestness in twisting such a rope of sand'.[38] Maurice's attempt to make Christianity more coherent, more immediate and more relevant in practice always seemed to be inexplicably out of phase with the world to which it was ostensibly addressed.

This comes out with particular clarity in Maurice's involvement with the Christian Socialist movement, which began when he came in contact with J. M. Ludlow, an idealistic young barrister who had experienced at first hand the French Revolution of 1848. Ludlow was a man who genuinely sympathised with the people and was anxious to bring about a radical improvement in their condition. Maurice also wanted to help the working class and bring about a less divided society, but he was at bottom quite out of sympathy with the idea of radical social change or with anything that savoured of rocking the boat. When the Amalgamated Society of Engineers were locked out over their refusal to work overtime he advised them to give into the employers and thereby win public sympathy. He disliked confrontation, which he associated with radical politics. He likewise distrusted radical thought, which, from his characteristically conservative point of view, was unduly abstract and destructive of social coherence. Maurice disliked all intellectual systems and he reinterpreted liberty, equality and fraternity in Christian terms, whereby all men would be free and equal before God as members of a universal Christian fellowship. Maurice believed it would be possible to institute God's kingdom here and now, not 'in some distant Utopia, but here on your own soil', but leave the existing ranks and social classes as they were:

> We would have you just what you are – tailors, shoemakers, bakers and printers; only we would have you in these positions be men feeling and sympathising with each other. . . . We will help you in fighting against the greatest enemy you have, your own self-will and selfishness.[39]

So that what Maurice offers is primarily an uplifting social message that will head off any social revolution, and where Ludlow endeavours to reinterpret socialism in Christian terms, Maurice's objective is to replace it with Christianity. From the lofty perspective of Maurice's Kingdom of Christ, the ballot box and greater economic equality are largely irrelevant. Maurice perceived 'combination' as one of the great principles of the age, but he could not support combination when it took the form of trade unionism, since this was combining *against* others (the employers) not with them. At bottom Maurice was more interested in lecturing the workers than in actually listening to what they had to say. He therefore quickly found Christian Socialism something of an embarrassment and found a more congenial role as Principal of the Workingman's College. Maurice's idealism did finally take a practical and positive form but it was always deeply disabled by his unwillingness to think about the causes of social conflict, instead of simply deploring it and disassociating himself from it. The intellectual flexibility he displayed over theological issues in *The Kingdom of Christ* was never reflected in his thinking on social issues.

Maurice was a lifelong friend and intimate of the poet laureate, Alfred Tennyson, a friendship that began in their undergraduate days at Cambridge in the 1820s and only ended with Maurice's death in 1872. Maurice dedicated his *Theological Essays* of 1853 to Tennyson. Tennyson celebrated his friend in his well-known poem 'To the Rev. F. D. Maurice' and asked him to be godfather to his son, Hallam. The connection between them goes beyond their familiarity and mutual respect, for it is evident that they shared certain intellectual convictions that were in turn shaped by their youthful days at Cambridge. Tennyson, Maurice, John Sterling, Arthur Hallam, who Tennyson passionately worshipped, along with James Spedding, Richard Moncton Milnes and John Kemble, the Saxon historian, were all members of the Apostles, a society dedicated to the discussion of serious philosophical questions, in which Platonic idealism and Platonic friendship were inextricably intertwined. The Apostles was a mutual admiration society in the best sense. At a time when Cambridge was largely a playground for the idle rich, the Apostles were unusual in that, while certainly capable of high spirits and good humour, they approached life in a spirit of intellectual seriousness and high moral earnestness and saw their own ability and commitment as itself offering some foretaste of a better world. They had high hopes both for themselves and each other – the group were convinced of Tennyson's future greatness as a poet long before he had written anything that altogether warranted it, while the early deaths of Arthur Hallam and John Sterling (aged twenty-two and thirty-eight respectively) led not to obscurity but to their becoming the most celebrated and memorialised figures of the age. Hallam, of course, was the subject of *In Memoriam*, while John Sterling, within a few years of his death, had been made the subject of biographies by Julius Hare, his old tutor, and Carlyle who, while their estimates widely differed, were nevertheless united in revering the man. To try to understand why Hallam and Sterling should have been so rapidly elevated to Victorian sainthood will take us a long way towards understanding the intellectual milieu of the Apostles and, in turn, the perplexities and anxieties of *In Memoriam*.

At Cambridge both Maurice and John Sterling, the two figures most actively involved in constituting the Apostles as an effective group, were pupils of Julius Hare. From 1822 to 1832 Hare was a Fellow of Trinity and college lecturer in classics. What marked out Hare as unusual at this time was his strong interest and affinity with German culture. He had learned German at an early age while living with his parents in Weimar; he collaborated in translating Niebuhr's *History of Rome* and in the course of his studies and researches amassed a collection of some 3000 German volumes. Hare has been justifiably characterised as a Coleridgean and it has been suggested that his most significant role was to transmit to such figures as Maurice something of Coleridge's concern to preserve the organic unity of society and his belief in the necessary interconnection of church and state.

However, what such an account passes over is that what Hare believes in above all is *progress* – to be understood as the spiritual development of man that is moving ultimately in the direction of perfectability. Hare's view is one formed under the influence of German idealism and German Romanticism – with perhaps Schelling and Hegel as the most significant figures – and perhaps what most significantly defines it, as against the contemporary gospel of technological and material progress and as contrasted with the Enlightenment faith in a secularising, critical reason, is that it is Christianity that has above all been a progressive force in human history. As Hare argues in *Guesses at Truth* (2nd series) the perfectability of man is a comparatively modern belief, yet it is only Christianity that can give it meaning:

Only through Christianity has a nation ever risen again: and it is solely on the operation of Christianity that we can ground anything like a reasonable hope of the perfectability of mankind; a hope that which has often be wrought in individuals, may in the fulness of time be wrought by the same power in the race.[40]

We have already seen how such a similarly optimistic view is worked out in Maurice's sense of an unfolding Kingdom of Christ, but what also needs to be emphasised here is the importance of individuals: for such exemplary lives, in Hare's perception of it, serve to validate the wager that there is, indeed, a progressive and perpetually developing movement in human history, which while it is never unchecked or uniform, nevertheless transcends the rise and decline of particular cultures. This belief in a universe in which man, despite many setbacks, is ever becoming nobler and ever drawing closer to God is, I believe, quite central to an understanding of what the Apostles were all about. In their criticism of modern commercial society and their concern with the exemplary significance of individuals there was much that could align them with Carlyle's indictment of capitalism in *Chartism* and *Past and Present* and with his celebration of greatness in *Heroes and Hero Worship*, but where they differed from him was that they were more concerned with looking forward to the future than with looking back nostalgically to the past; they had a greater belief in the existence of a divine plan and they put much more faith in organised religion and in the Anglican church in particular. The difference in tone is brought out well in John Sterling's objection to Carlyle's claim that the operation of genius in great men is always unconscious:

Depart then, ye profane! who fancy that life and light are not only organised and methodized in our structure according to a plan which we may partly decipher, but that they enable us to apprehend and meditate on the limits which divide this conscious being of ours from the ocean of divine existence surrounding it and sustaining it. Yet is it not rather certain that, only by such meditation, and the actions which it both prompts and purifies, can our humanity be preserved at once integral and progressive, neither closing itself against the radiance of the objective universe, nor letting itself lazily dissolve and be lost in those currents, from which, not by chance nor vainly, was it distinguished and impersonated into man.[41]

Carlyle, of course, despite his convoluted and inflated rhetoric, nevertheless prided himself on being, Scot that he was, hard-headed, practical and realistic. He admired men of action above all and Sterling, at least, tried to become one, both by serving as a country parson and by aiding General Torrijos to get to Spain at the time of the Spanish insurrection of 1830. But Sterling, like his fellow Apostles, was not a very practical man and this is rather absurdly demonstrated by the way in which both Hare and Carlyle try to celebrate the ten months he spent as a parson as a kind of heroic engagement with reality. Perhaps what characterised this Cambridge milieu of Maurice, Sterling, Hare, Hallam and Tennyson was a too intense idealism and faith in human potential, which therefore could all too easily be discouraged when it encountered early reversals or disappointments. At all events, I would want to argue that *In Memoriam* should be seen as the trial and testing of such a progressive faith rather than as the somewhat generalised mid-Victorian contest between science and religion that critics have so often put on display.

At the very outset of *In Memoriam* Tennyson invokes in the past tense his belief in a progressive human development:

> I held it truth, with him who sings
> To one clear harp in divers tones,
> That men may rise on stepping-stones
> Of their dead selves to higher things

but this optimistic faith is shattered by the news of Arthur Hallam's death. The paradox of *In Memoriam* is that the ostensible task the poet addresses – that of remembering and celebrating Hallam – is one that the poet actually finds quite beyond him. To write in the elegiac manner would call for powers of detachment and lucidity that Tennyson in his moment of loss simply does not possess. To invoke Arthur, even to name him, would be deny the very sense of loss that the poet finds so spiritually numbing and so utterly overpowering. Indeed Tennyson's grief actually goes beyond this. He now recognises more clearly than ever before how deeply his own identity has become bound up with Hallam's, through his adulation of Hallam as 'one half divine', through his attempt to model himself upon him and follow in his footsteps, through his utter dependence on Hallam's bestowal of recognition and approval. In the first instance, therefore, Tennyson is primarily conscious of his own helplessness and powerlessness:

> My will is bondsman to the dark;
> I sit within a helmless bark.

So before Tennyson can grieve for Hallam he must first grieve for himself, and Tennyson can only be praised for the extraordinary honesty with which he is prepared to expose this even though, in consequence, the poem has struck some critics as narcissistic, which indeed it is.

Yet we must also recognise that what is involved in this transaction is a cancellation of Arthur Hallam as an actual living person. We should note that while the use of initials in the title of the poem may be regarded merely as conventional decorum, this has also led to the naming of the poem as *In Memoriam*, which itself is highly paradoxical since the person ostensibly to be remembered actually disappears. Would we dream of describing a poem as 'In Loving Memory Of'? In a way our usage is highly disrespectful yet it does serve as a pointer to some puzzling features of the poem. Again, Arthur is indeed named within the poem, but only three times, which seems remarkably little in relation to its overall length. In so saying I am by no means trying to imply that Tennyson does not care about Hallam, rather that, because he cares so much, the poem cannot, as it were take, the form of a capture of Hallam, a grasping of him as the object of reverence and memory, but must instead take the form of a frank confession of Tennyson's inability to do so. What produces a cognitive dissonance in Tennyson's mind is that the Hallam he remembers, or desperately tries to remember, was above all an intensely vivid physical presence, yet he can now only think of him as a disembodied spirit or shade. The shadow of death has fallen between them. But Tennyson cannot accept this. The movement of the poem cannot be seen as a coming to terms with this inescapable fact but must rather be seen as a desperate struggle against it. The figure of the return of Hallam's ashes from Vienna, where he died, can stand as a sign that Hallam, like Christ, will indeed come back from the dead, and to think this is not at all surprising:

> And I perceived no touch of change,
> No hint of death in all his frame,

But found him all in all the same,
I should not feel it to be strange.

Of course in a way this is, as Tennyson recognises, an impossible dream, yet the poet's frantic insistence on the vacancy of the world without him and his refusal to come to terms with the fact of Hallam's death also creates the possibility that at some future date the world can be replenished with a sense of Arthur's *presence*:

Thy voice is on the rolling air;
I hear thee where the waters run;
Thou standest in the rising sun,
And in the setting thou art fair.

The uncrossable bar that stands between Tennyson and Hallam is one that will nevertheless be traversed not through any act of suicide in which Tennyson would

Leap the grades of life and light,
And flash at once, my friend, to thee

but rather through a multiform act of *recalling* in which Tennyson, through endeavouring faithfully to remember, will actually be able to restore the cancelled presence to him. Thus what is involved in the unfolding of the poem is a subtle process of role reversal. At the outset Hallam is an all-powerful, all-encompassing, semi-divine figure in whose loss Tennyson became acutely conscious of his own insignificance and inadequacy. It suddenly seems that the sense of fraternal equality that he experienced was nothing more than an illusion. So Tennyson has lost Hallam in a double sense: not only is he physically absent but his death also destroys his own fragile identity, which had been validated through his friendship with Hallam. But Tennyson now assumes the role of shaman and witch-doctor, who will through the incantatory rhetoric of the poem transform Arthur from a numinous and threatening absence into a vivid restorative presence – as indeed happens in the vision of section 95. But since this is the work of the poet himself he now feels infused with a feeling of power that will finally make it possible for him to celebrate Hallam in a way that was impossible before. What this also means is that Tennyson is able to overcome his irrational sense that somehow or other Arthur has betrayed and abandoned him at the very moment when he most needed him: behind the intensity of Tennyson's grief is also impotence, frustration and anger.

Certainly the unexpected and inexplicable death of Hallam at the very moment when Tennyson was expecting to become his brother-in-law following Hallam's engagement to his sister was an utterly demoralising event in Tennyson's life and one that he simply refused to come to terms with. The suggestion that such losses are everyday and commonplace, incorporated by Tennyson into the argument of the poem at its very beginning, was one that he ostensibly accepted by insisting nevertheless on the intensity of all such experiences. In this way Tennyson writes, like Whitman, as the poet of democracy, in his determination to celebrate all such experiences of grief no matter how simple or humble the setting in which they are to be found. Later Tennyson transposed his own experience of desperate isolation into the popular folk-tale of *Enoch Arden* in which through a shipwreck Enoch Arden and his wife Annie are tragically separated and where Annie the wife, who seemed to grieve too desperately and too long, is paradoxically if ironically justified since her faith that her husband was still alive turns out after all to have been correct. This poem was a kind of vindication of Tennyson himself by demonstrating that there is nothing perverse about a prolonged period of mourning. It is precisely the willingness, even the eagerness, on the part of Tennyson to make the death of Hallam into the exemplary instance of a grief that is universally felt that accounts for its great popularity in the Victorian age – the poem becomes a kind of frame into which any likeness can be inserted, or like the poem in a birthday card that can be addressed to any recipient. Yet, at the same time, it seems very surprising not just that the poem should acquire such a polyvalency but that Tennyson himself should have wanted it. For Tennyson ultimately did *not* believe that his grief was commonplace. On the contrary he believed that it was exceptional and he objected strongly to the moral complacency that would run together the vacant chaff of pious memorialising with the authentic grain of a shameless and desperate grief that is so caught up in its own deeply personal sense of loss that it is indifferent to all conventions and proprieties. For this reason also, Tennyson, like Shelley in *Adonais*, the poem that it most closely recalls, is prepared to admit that he is above all concerned with his own feelings and emotions even if the exposure of them is doubly embarrassing, as both excessive and inappropriate. By so insisting on the physicality of his sense of loss, on his desperate desire to feel once more the touch of Hallam's body, and by so dwelling on the sheer sensuousness of their moments together, Tennyson risks the accusation of paganism.

> We talked: the stream beneath us ran,
> The wine-flask lying couched in moss,
>
> Or cooled within the glooming wave;
> And last, returning from afar,
> Before the crimson-circled star
> Had fallen into her father's grave,
>
> And brushing ankle-deep in flowers,
> We heard behind the woodbine veil
> The milk that bubbled in the pail,
> And buzzings of the honied hours.

Yet he is prepared to take that risk because he believes that without invoking the sheer magic and plenitude of this tangible and seemingly inexhaustible presence, the sheer terror of absence can never be explained. And to speak of vacancy is immoral also.

The great paradox of *In Memoriam* is how it manages to be at once an intensely private expression of grief and at the same time such a universally revered and respected literary monument. It is haunted by this doubleness and we might even perceive the poem itself as precisely a veil that at once conceals and discloses; or to put it another way, it is a multistoreyed mansion of grief in which the many small poems that together make one great work figure as the endless opening and closing of doors in which bemusement, reticence and revelation are intriguingly combined. As Alan Sinfield has pointed out: 'Repeatedly Tennyson seems to say both more and less than is appropriate, and if we allow ourselves to hear these dissonances customary notions of masculinity are confused and violated.'[42]

The apparent repetitiousness of the poem seems to render its content innocuous, yet the reader is also presented with the problem of piecing together the fragments of personal experience that lie behind and actually prompt this exemplary utterance. For after all, even in a culture where mourning was conspicuously displayed, especially when it was that of a widow for her husband, Tennyson's mourning *was* exceptional, not just because Tennyson as a man assumes, as the poem itself recognises, a feminine role, but because he continued to wear black, as it were, for seventeen years. In this Tennyson and Queen Victoria have much in common for her grief was also seen as excessive and reading *In Memoriam* served to validate the truth of her experience. Nevertheless grief and mourning are rather different things. What is surprising about *In Memoriam* is that Tennyson is able to maintain this spontaneity of expression which we would associate with grief over an infinitely protracted period of time. But we must also wonder why the writing of *In Memoriam* should have been so infinitely protracted and so endlessly elaborated. From a commonsensical point of view it might seem that the time for Tennyson to write, complete and publish the poem was in the immediate aftermath of Arthur's death. In that way the poem might have seemed more immediate and spontaneous and also would have been much more likely to have achieved its object of drawing attention to the tragically early death of such a promising young man. To publish such a work seventeen years later is definitely odd.

The death of Hallam was a terrible blow to Tennyson's whole sense of identity. It was as if at that moment the clock stopped and Tennyson would forever after feel suspended and paralysed, incapable of picking up the threads of ordinary life:

> Break, thou deep vase of chilling tears
> That grief hath shaken into frost!

Precisely because of the depth of his grief and its essentially private nature Tennyson felt cut off from the rest of the world. He vowed to make it his task, his duty, his burden to celebrate Arthur's spiritual greatness; to take time out from life until this act of piety had been accomplished. Yet Tennyson felt unworthy of the task. While Arthur lived, Tennyson was content to love and reverence him, to remain perpetually in his shadow. He willingly surrendered his own career, even his own identity to Arthur simply because he loved to bask in the sun of greatness. Tennyson had made himself totally dependent on Hallam's approval; it was as if he only existed at all in so far as Hallam was prepared to acknowledge him as a person, but so long as Arthur was there to love him he did not even ask for this. He was happy in the role of lover, acolyte and companion. Hallam's death was therefore all the more traumatic because it seemed to remove every reason for Tennyson's existence. Simply, he was nothing without Hallam. He was incomplete. So the attempt to write a poem was fraught with contradiction. On the one hand Tennyson genuinely felt that the task of celebrating Hallam was beyond him. He could never hope to express in words either Arthur's extraordinary personal magnetism or what Arthur had meant to him personally. Thus Tennyson was caught in an extraordinary series of double binds. To complete a poem about Arthur would be to say that he had finally got Arthur out of his system, whereas his very reason for writing the poem was to celebrate him and to proclaim an eternal love. Moreover to finish it would be to suggest that Tennyson as a poet felt that his poetry was wholly adequate to its theme, whereas Tennyson felt that this would always lie beyond the possibilities of language, and so the gesture of finishing the poem would involve both pride and insincerity. The task of writing the poem thus went on interminably and with it came Tennyson's private recognition that the project was necessarily interminable. The passage of time made the very idea of *In Memoriam* more and more quixotic. It would have been one thing to have celebrated Arthur in the twilight of Romanticism, with its extraordinary emphasis on individual genius; it was quite another to try to do so in an age of scientific objectivity and in the aftermath of Chartism where the claim of the individual seemed far more problematic:

> A third is wroth: 'Is this the hour
> For private sorrow's barren song,
> When more and more the people throng
> The chairs and thrones of civil power?
>
> 'A time to sicken and to swoon,
> When Science reaches forth her arms
> To feel from world to world, and charms
> Her secret from the latest moon?'
>
> Behold, ye speak an idle thing:
> Ye never knew the sacred dust:
> I do but sing because I must
> And pipe but as the linnets sing

Here Tennyson is honest in acknowledging the sense of compulsion under which he writes, but somewhat misleading in implying that his obsessional dedication to his theme makes him as spontaneous as the linnet. On the contrary, Tennyson is proud to be an anachronism and to go against the spirit of the age. He rejoices in the perversity of his grief, because in this very inconsolability he proves himself the hero. Thus Tennyson's poem of 1833, 'St Simeon Stylites' is both curiously autobiographical and prophetic. In this poetic monologue Simeon admits that the fanatical determination that has led him to live in solitary isolation on top of a pillar for thirty years is a sign at once of his determination to achieve sainthood, and, at the same time, of his own deep uncertainty as to whether he could ever be worthy of it. In the same way Tennyson's pertinacity in going on writing *In Memoriam* long after the moment for writing it had past is an attempt to achieve greatness through sheer pertinacity. In its very iterativeness, in its very interminableness the poem will achieve the sublime. Like St Simeon, Tennyson feels that his project simply *has* to succeed through sheer will power:

> What am I?
> The silly people take me for a saint,
> And bring me offerings of fruit and flowers:
> And I in truth (thou wilt bear witness here)
> Have all in all endured as much, and more
> Than many just and holy men, whose names
> Are register'd and calendar'd for saints.

Yet he doubts whether he will be numbered among the elect all the same. His task is complicated by further feelings of guilt. While Arthur Hallam was alive Tennyson lived vicariously through him; now, through writing the poem, Hallam must live vicariously through him. But in consequence instead of celebrating his friend and mentor he seems to be broaching a dangerous rivalry in which Tennyson, far from writing in all humility, seems dangerously set on becoming the master. So to complete the poem will be at once as gesture of liberation and an act of impiety.

As Tennyson piously procrastinates, ostensibly for fear of striking the wrong note, he at the same time acquires greater confidence in his own role, since what he lacks in Hellenic grace he makes up for in Hebraic determination:

> Nor mine the sweetness or the skill,
> But mine the love that will not tire.

So Tennyson, in going on writing, increasingly becomes the unacknowledged hero of his own poem. Yet in this very reluctance to complete his elegy and finally surrender it both to Arthur and to the general public Tennyson makes his own task more difficult. For as time goes on his project of celebrating Hallam appears more and more paradoxical, not simply because, it seems, the age of heroes is past but because Lyellian geology opens up such incredible vistas of time as to virtually cancel any ready assumption that memorialisation is actually possible:

> What hope is here to modern rhyme
> To him, who turns a musing eye
> On songs, and deeds, and lives, that lie,
> Foreshortened in the tract of time.

Moreover in the long and complex process of writing and rewriting the poem Tennyson has come to recognise that the genre of elegy necessarily predicates a stability in the significance of the person who is to be celebrated, and a certain poise and coherence in the poet who eulogises – and he also realises that whatever virtues *In Memoriam* may possess these are not among them. For Tennyson's understanding of what Hallam signifies for him is continually subject to reinterpretation, while the Tennyson who at the age of twenty-four was totally devastated by Arthur's death was by no means the same person as the poet who published *In Memoriam* seventeen years later. So in a way what *In Memoriam* comes to be about is simultaneously the necessity and impossibility of trying to write such a poem since it is bound to move towards a closure that the poet himself can never be at ease with. Yet the poem does possess a certain emotional trajectory, of which critics from Bradley onward have tried to offer some sort of account. One way of putting it would be to say that Tennyson begins with a sense of nullity and desolation in which he feels totally bereft of his friend's presence, but in his constant reflection upon everything that he has meant to him it is as if the presence of Arthur becomes restored to his mind. But this in turn only makes more poignant Tennyson's recognition that the loss is permanent and unalterable:

> I hear it now, and o'er and o'er.
> Eternal greetings to the dead;
> And 'Ave, Ave, Ave,' said,
> 'Adieu, adieu' for evermore.

In this discursive switch from Latin to French the hails becomes strangely conflated – even identified – with farewells, which at this moment is precisely Tennyson's mood. Subsequently Tennyson tries to console himself with the thought that this recognition can be almost indefinitely postponed through the actual writing of the poem:

> The high Muse answered: 'Wherefore grieve
> Thy brethren with a fruitless tear?
> Abide a little longer here,
> And thou shalt take a nobler leave.'

In a way it might seem paradoxical that Tennyson should write this almost immediately after intimating his own poetic inadequacy to his task: 'But I shall pass; my work will fail', but the real significance of this is that Tennyson now recognises that his poem will always be essentially private. No one else could ever hope to understand what Hallam had meant to him, nor in all honesty could he either hope to convey this in language and pierce the veil that necessarily divides him from his readers – all he can do is continue with the poem as a kind of private contract between Arthur and himself. Of course, *In Memoriam* unexpectedly *does* contain an increasingly confident public dimension as Tennyson, who now, as the result of certain mystical experiences, believes that he has been imbued and infused with Arthur Hallam's spirit, and therefore is in a position to deliver oracularly such a message of hope as Hallam himself would have believed in, a vision of progress and social harmony:

> Ring out a slowly dying cause,
> And ancient forms of party strife;
> Ring in the nobler modes of life,
> With sweeter manners, purer laws.
>
> Ring out the want, the care, the sin,
> The faithless coldness of the times;
> Ring out, ring out my mournful rhymes,
> But ring the fuller minstrel in.
>
> Ring out false pride in place and blood,
> The civic slander and the spite;
> Ring in the love of truth and right,
> Ring in the common love of good.

But Tennyson's whole formulation is deeply problematic. For the ringing in of Hallam's optimistic message is to be at the expense of

Tennyson's own 'mournful rhymes' so that Tennyson, in desperately trying to be the voice of Hallam, is at the same time trying to drown out the truth and authenticity of what he actually feels. Indeed Tennyson subsequently confessed that the poem was more optimistic than he actually felt, a devious confession that in aspiring to act as a medium for Hallam's convictions he had actually betrayed his own. But of course the contradiction here is inescapable: the whole of *In Memoriam* is an attempt on the part of Tennyson to close the gap between himself and Hallam, coupled with the deeper recognition that this can never actually take place.

The significant component of Romantic optimism from which Tennyson felt debarred was Wordsworthian pantheism. In part this was due to the commitment Tennyson felt to a Platonic idealism that was grounded both in the discussions of the Cambridge Apostles and in his admiration for Shelley. Tennyson simply could not accept that spirit could ever be placed on the same level as matter, and for this reason he believed that man, far from finding his place in nature, was absolutely separate and discontinuous from it. In this, for all his interest in evolutionary and cosmological theory, Tennyson's standpoint was utterly opposed to that of T. H. Huxley. Whereas Wordsworth could find tranquillity in thinking of Lucy rolled around with rocks and stones and trees, Tennyson could never see the material universe as anything other than a veil dividing the soul from the purity and ideality of the pure forms, of which Arthur and Hallam was certainly one. Since Tennyson had experienced the painfulness of separation division, a picture of the world that was completely permeated by and unified by the indwelling presence of God was one that had strong attractions for him, yet he found it impossible to accept such a postulated unity precisely because it would involve a sacrifice of the particular, of absolutely everything that one unique human being, Arthur Hallam, had meant to him:

> That each, who seems a separate soul,
> Should move his rounds, and fusing all
> The skirts of self again, should fall
> Remerging in the general Soul,
>
> Is faith as vague as all unsweet:
> Eternal form shall still divide
> The eternal soul from all beside;
> And I shall know him when we meet

The very way that Tennyson's sense of the absence and presence of Arthur constantly varies in response to his changing experiences and moods makes it impossible for Tennyson to absolutise their feelings and project them onto the universe as Wordsworth had done. At the beginning of *In Memoriam* Tennyson is only conscious of a terrible, demoralising blankness:

> He is not here; but far away
> The noise of life begins again,
> And ghastly through the drizzling rain
> On the bald street breaks the blank day.

Towards the end of the poem he feels the reverse as he becomes overwhelmingly conscious of Arthur's presence, both in the multiplicity of recollections that swim before his consciousness:

> I climb the hill: from end to end
> Of all the landscape underneath,
> I find no place that does not breathe
> Some gracious memory of my friend

and, more profoundly, in a feeling that the whole sense of the physical world is irradiated by an intuition that he is *there*:

> Thy voice is on the rolling air;
> I hear thee where the waters run;
> Thou standest in the rising sun,
> And in the setting thou art fair.

Although it is possible to read these lines in a Wordsworthian way, the difference is that Tennyson is more acutely aware of the psychological dimension, more conscious of the fragility and transitoriness even of such powerful and apparently uncancellable moments of consciousness. Both Wordsworth and Tennyson are committed to the visionary, but whereas for Wordsworth poetic vision offers access to a perennial and unchangeable state of affairs, for Tennyson it offers only glimpses of the eternal that go against the grain of our ordinary everyday experience. For Tennyson life necessarily involves the experience of contradiction and unity is really no longer possible since even Christianity can no longer offer a completely coherent account of experience. The visionary is a way of filling in the gaps, yet its power and poignancy depends on the very fact that our everyday sense of the world *is* incomplete. *In Memoriam* for Tennyson, like *Paradise Lost*, was a way of negotiating the gap between the Christian faith and the complexities of a world that often seemed to belie and contradict it.

Consequently I believe that one of the most common ways in which Tennyson is misread is through the apparently plausible suggestion that Tennyson's religious faith was severely shaken by his exposure to the perception of Nature as a harsh and brutal struggle for existence, a view effectively Darwinian but to which Tennyson was exposed through his reading of such precursors as Charles Lyell and Robert Chambers, author of the popular *Vestiges of Creation*. The effective source for many of these views is the chapter on 'The *Princess* and Evolution' in John Killham's *Tennyson and The Princess*, and while I would not question that Tennyson was familiar with these works or that Tennyson took his suggestion of a possible 'crowning race' that might succeed man from Chambers, I do believe that the issues are significantly misrepresented by presenting all this as a religiously demoralising proto-Darwinism. I would suggest that a clearer picture of the kind of views prevalent in the circles in which Tennyson moved and of the questions he specifically addressed in *In Memoriam* can be obtained by also taking into account such a work as the two-part *Guesses at Truth*, which Julius Hare co-wrote with his brother Augustus Hare, the two volumes of which appeared in 1827 and 1848. The issue to which Julius Hare in particular returns over and over again, in the true spirit of Hegel and Fichte and German idealism in general, is affirming the possibility of progress and equally of affirming that such a view of human progress, far from being secular, is validated and underwritten by our belief in the goodness of God. Such a conception of Christian progress became an integral part of Broad Church Anglicanism in the 1840s and 1850s – in *Barchester Towers* (1857), for example, Mr Arabin, who typifies the more forward-looking tendencies in the Church, responds to Eleanor's suggestion that 'the world grows more worldly every day' by saying: 'If we believe in Scripture, we can hardly think that mankind in general will now be allowed to be retrograde.'

Such a position defines itself in opposition simultaneously to the conservative insistence on original sin as an ineluctable limit on the one hand, and on the other to the radical and rationalistic emphasis on revolutionary change. What Julius Hare insists on is the immense slowness and gradualness of such processes of change. The Christian optimist can take the long view quite as well as a Lyell or Darwin:

> From what we have said, we may perceive that the progress of mankind is not in a straight line, uniform and unbroken. On the contrary it is subject to manifold vicissitudes, interruptions, and delays; ever advancing on the whole indeed, but often receding in one quarter, while it pushes forward in another; and sometimes retreating altogether for a while, that it may start afresh with greater and more irresistible force. . . . It is like the progress of the year, in which after the blossoms of spring have dropped off, a long interval elapses before the autumnal fruits come forward conspicuously in their stead: and these too anon decay; and the foliage and herbage of one year mixes up with the mould for the enriching of another.[43]

What is particularly notable here is the attempt on the part of Julius Hare to reconcile an overall sense of progress with an insistence on the stability of the structure of cyclical recurrence that lies behind it since it recalls Stephen J. Gould's suggestive presentation of Lyell's geology as an attempt to reconcile an overall theory of evolution with uniformitarianism – time's arrow with time's cycle. At times Hare and Lyell seem to speak a common language in their concern to deny the meaningfulness of violent, catastrophic change, as when Lyell writes:

> When we are unable to explain the monuments of past changes, it is always more probable that the difficulty arises from our ignorance of all the existing agents, or that all their possible effects in an indefinite lapse of time, than that some cause was formerly in operation which has ceased to act; and if in any part of the globe the energy of a cause appears to have decreased, it is always probable, that the diminution of intensity in its action is merely local, and that its force is unimpaired, when the whole globe is considered.[44]

Lyell regarded Cuvier's catastrophism as unscientific since it seemed to deny that the action of natural forces was always regular and uniform, yet the actual presentation of radical or violent change as *unreal* in his theory did have obvious political implications in the age of the First Reform Bill, the debate around which precisely coincided with his *The Principles of Geology* (1830–3). If changes in Nature always took place immensely slowly, then the pace of reform should not be forced – man should learn from Nature, which was the conclusion drawn by Julius Hare. Hare contrasted the ways of Nature: 'who can produce nothing great, except by slow and tedious processes of growth and assimilation. How tardily and snail-like she crawls to her task. She never does anything *per saltum*',[45] with the attempts following the French Revolution hastily to draw up new and abstract constitutions, which he likens to the creation of Frankenstein's monster. Although Hare believes that we should profit from the example of Nature, he nevertheless insists on the absolute discontinuity between man and Nature, which is attributable to man's possession of spiritual powers, and suggests his potential is therefore virtually unlimited:

> while each individual animal in a manner fulfils the whole purpose of its existence, nothing of the sort can be predicated of any man that ever lived, but only of the race. All the organs and faculties with which the animal is endowed, are called into action: all the tendencies discoverable in its nature are realised. Whereas every man has a number of dormant powers, a number of latent tendencies, the purpose of which can never be accomplished, except in the historical development of the race. . . . Moreover there is a universal law, of which we have a twofold assurance, – both from observation of all the works of nature, and from the wisdom of their author, that no tendency has been implanted in any created thing, but sooner or later shall receive its accomplishment, that God's purposes cannot be baffled, and that his word can never return to him empty. Hence it follows that those tendencies in man's nature, which cannot be fulfilled immediately and contemporaneously, will be fulfilled gradually and successively in the course which mankind are to run.[46]

Such a view makes explicit the connections between Neoplatonism and Hegel's philosophy and history, and suggests how, in the intellectual circles of Hare, Sterling, Hallam and Tennyson, a Platonic distrust of the world of physical appearances could be linked with a vision of human spiritual development.

In such a vision Nature's profusion and indifference, alluded to by Tennyson in *In Memoriam*, can simply be invoked in order to stress man's much greater potential for development. Hare writes:

Among the numberless marvels, at which nobody marvels, few are more marvellous than the recklessness with which priceless gifts, intellectual and moral, are squandered and thrown away. Often have I gazed with wonder at the prodigality displayed by Nature in the cistus, which unfolds hundreds and thousands of its white starry blossoms morning after morning, to shine in the light of the sun for an hour or two, and then fall to the ground. But who, among the sons and daughters of men, gifted with thoughts 'which wander through eternity', and with powers which have the god-like privilege of working good and giving happiness, who does not daily let thousands of these thoughts drop to the ground and rot? Who does not continually leave his powers to draggle in the mould of their own leaves? The imagination can hardly conceive the heights of greatness or glory to which mankind would be raised, if all their thoughts and energies were to be animated with a living purpose, or even those of a single people, or even the educated among a single people. But as in a forest of oaks, among the millions of acorns that fall every autumn, there may perhaps be one in a million that will grow up into a tree, somewhat in like manner fares it with the thoughts of man.[47]

In the spirit of that great exponent of original genius, Edward Young, Julius Hare draws attention to the imaginative potential that we all possess within us and his necessary conclusion is that man should cherish and tender those sparks of creativity rather than squander this potential as Nature does. So the example of Nature is invoked only to be hypothetically surpassed. My purpose in citing these reflections of Julius Hare is not to suggest that they are the canonical text that *In Memoriam* glosses, but rather to question the cliché of a Tennyson simultaneously shattered by the death of Hallam and by the findings of the new sciences by suggesting that Tennyson was in contact with a tradition of Christian progressive thought that could not only take such findings in its stride but was perfectly capable of being harmonised with them. If there *was* a contradiction between God and Nature:

> Are God and Nature then at strife,
> That Nature lends such evil dreams?
> So careful of the type she seems,
> So careless of the single life

– and that contradiction might itself be altogether in the realm of appearances – it can be dealt with by the wager that there is a planned and progressive scenario for man that is being steadily implemented despite man's evident difficulty in believing that this is actually so. Here again, *In Memoriam* is like *Paradise Lost* in insisting that things are not really as bad as they may seem; that there is an

> Eternal process moving on,
> From state to state the spirit walks,
> And these are but the shattered stalks,
> Or ruined chrysalis of one.

Tennyson did believe that Hallam was a truly exceptional, godlike human being, created like Michaelangelo's Adam:

> For what wert thou? Some novel power
> Sprang up forever at a touch

and the very mysteriousness of his extraordinary, yet transitory power did make him seem precisely the herald of a better world. But Tennyson's problem was not so much that he could not believe in such a better world, but rather that even the possibility of this could never reconcile him to the loss of a unique, irreplaceable human presence.

In the 1850s there was a marked shift away from a concern with theological and doctrinal issues, which under the influence of Newman and the Tractarian Movement had seemingly dominated English cultural life in the 1830s and 1840s. An important reason for this was the impact of Chartism, as it seemed that this movement had drawn its strength from the large industrial cities and much of its energies from the dissenting churches that had become so firmly established there. This suggested that the Anglican church had allowed itself to be distracted into a confrontation with Rome when the real battles to be fought were more pragmatic and closer at hand. This diagnosis was confirmed by the religious census of 1851 which showed that church attendances on 30 March of that year numbered

5,292,551 for the Church of England, 4,536,264 for the various dissenting bodies (Methodist, Presbyterian, Congregationalist, Baptist), while there were 383,630 Catholics in church, nearly 50 per cent of them in London or Liverpool, the majority of them Irish immigrants. It became clear that the overwhelming task for the Church of England was, as Thomas Arnold had long since suggested, to bring the gospel to the working classes in the industrial cities and to build churches there. But the reaction against Tractarianism also took a more spiritual form. Many now began to feel that niceties of religious doctrine or theological interpretation mattered far less than the personal virtuousness and godliness of the individual and that religion needed to be brought down from its ivory tower in order to address itself to the problems of common life. In *Oakfield* (1853) William Arnold, Matthew Arnold's younger brother, describes how his hero gives up the idea of a career in the church in favour of service in India:

> For some time he inclined to the Tractarian influence then so prevalent in Oxford, and thought for a while that he had found the help he needed; when lo! again, in a hour of startling conviction, he found that the forms which he had been so busily lulling his conscience had as little of the Divine in them as the forms of common worldly society. The re-action followed, and he hated the church which he thought had deceived him. The idea of taking orders became intolerable, and the question of what he should do came before him . . . by obtaining an Indian appointment a maintenance would be secured to him, while he, under utterly new circumstances, might begin life anew, try once more to realise his theory of bringing religion into daily life; without the necessity of denying it at every turn in obedience to some fashion or dogma of society; and then, as to his work in life, was not every European in India engaged in the grand work of civilising Asia.

Oakfield finds that in practice the imperial mission is considerably less exalted than he had expected and he becomes disillusioned, but the turn to practical activity is itself characteristic. We find a similar turn in Browning's *Men and Women* where Gigadibs, after a lengthy exposure to Bishop Bloughram's convoluted and tortuous exposition of his religious position, responds as follows:

He did not sit five minutes. Just a week
Sufficed his sudden healthy vehemence.
Something had struck him in the 'Outward-bound'
Another way than Bloughram's purpose was:
And having bought, not cabin-furniture
But settler's-implements (enough for three)
And started for Australia – there, I hope,
By this time he has tested his first plough
And studied his last chapter of St John.

Thus, one of the most conspicuous consequences of this pragmatic turn is the way in which the truths of Christianity become bound up with the development of the British Empire and England's sense of world-mission. An early, though equivocal instance of this is George Borrow's *The Bible in Spain* (1843), where Borrow, at the very moment when the church is in turmoil and Newman is vacillating between Canterbury and Rome, takes great delight in cocking a snoot at the Pope by setting up shop to sell Bibles for the SPKC at the very heart of Madrid and in one of the great bastions of Catholic power and authority. Since this concession has been obtained through British influence it points to the way in which British commercial success can pave the way for missionary endeavours. Certainly the turn towards pragmatism could not be more clearly exemplified than by John Speke, who in his *Discovery of the Source of the Nile* (1863) informs the African ruler, Rumanika, that the true superiority of the Bible over the Koran does not simply consist in the fact that Christians have two holy books whereas Moslems only have one:

> but the real merit lies in the fact that we have got the better *book*, as may be inferred from the obvious fact that we are more prosperous, and their superiors in all things, as I would prove to him if he would allow me to take one of his sons home to learn that *book*; for then he would find his tribe, after a while, better off than the Arabs are.[48]

Has the Protestant ethic ever been more baldly stated? Yet Speke was by no means alone in estimating the worth of English religion in terms of the triumphal expansion of English commercial and political power.

Nevertheless the new activism had more intellectual substance than this. Above all it drew sustenance from the writings of Carlyle, who, no churchman himself and indeed a persistent critic of the Anglican church, nevertheless provided it with the most powerful arguments against Tractarianism. Carlyle celebrated the religious and celebrated the hero yet he brought them into a complex symbiosis in which each was redefined in terms of the other. Cromwell, above all, epitomised this. Cromwell was intensely pious and deeply conscious of the presence of God in his own life, yet he was also a pragmatist and a man of action who moved instinctively in the direction he felt was right, despite the intricacy of the religious and political disputes whose Gordian knots he so sharply severed. Accordingly to Carlyle it is by Great Men that religion itself is established, yet he is at pains to emphasise that *real* religion is not grounded in intellectual arguments but rather:

> the thing a man does practically believe (and this is often enough *without* asserting it even to himself, much less to others); the thing a man does practically lay to heart, and know for certain, concerning his vital relations to this mysterious Universe, and his duty and destiny there, that is in all cases the primary thing for him, and creatively determines all the rest.[49]

With Carlyle the emphasis decisively shifts away from the book, doctrine or creed as a measure of validity in religion to the life itself, to the exemplary individual whose history is the only witness or evidence we need. Under Carlyle's influence Richard Moncton Milnes, Lord Houghton, in his *Palm Leaves* (1844), a collection of poems inspired by a visit to the Middle East, could even argue that Christians, unlike Mohammedans were *not* people of the book for they were not so much governed by commandments like those laid down in the Koran as moved by the astonishing example of goodness that was to be found in the life of Jesus:

> Mohammed's truth lay in a holy Book,
> Christ's in a sacred Life.
>
> So, while the world rolls on from change to change,
> And realms of thought expand,
> The Letter stands without expanse or range,
> Stiff as a dead man's hand;

While, as the life-blood fills the growing form,
The Spirit Christ has shed
Flows through the ripening ages fresh and warm,
More felt than heard or read.

In this way Christ continues to be a living example and his influence escapes the dead hand of interpretative controversy. The
power of the exemplary is also found in Thomas Hughes's novel
about Rugby School, *Tom Brown's Schooldays*, for role models abound.
Thomas Arnold, the Headmaster, demonstrates to the boys the
importance of living the Christian life and of behaving towards
others with Christian kindness and charity. Little Arthur, the weakly
boy whose father has been a clergyman ministering to the poor, is
himself inspired by his father's noble example and he could well
become an object of derision among the other boys, were it not for
his courage in saying his prayers in front of the others and for
the security of Tom Brown's protection. Under the influence of
Arnold and Arthur, Tom Brown himself becomes a better and more
Christian person. His muscular strength is devoted to a noble cause.
So although Hughes *did* emphasise the importance of reading and
reflecting on the Bible, his main emphasis falls on personal example
and on hero-worship as the way towards spirituality: as he writes at
the end of the novel: 'Such stages have to be gone through, I believe,
by all young and brave souls, who must win their way through hero-
worship, to the worship of Him who is the King and Lord of heroes.'
Yet even the triumph of piety over paganism at Rugby School pales
before the extraordinary altruism of Charlotte Yonge's saintly hero,
the exemplary Guy de Morville, of *The Heir of Redclyffe* (1853). Guy is
a sensitive young man, hereditarily prone to fits of melancholy and
anger, who is viewed rather suspiciously by his sanctimonious and
self-righteous cousin Philip. But as Amy observes at an early stage in
the novel: 'If people are to be judged by their deeds, no one is as
good as Guy.' As a child Guy shows an extraordinary kindness to
animals. As a young man he goes out of his way to save his uncle,
Sebastian Dixon, from debts he has largely incurred supporting his
sister and her husband, even though in paying off his uncle's gambling debts he incurs the unjust suspicion, which he will not refute,
that these are debts he has incurred himself. Subsequently Guy saves
some fishermen from drowning and then just manages to rescue
Amy, his beloved, when she is on the point of falling down a preci-
pice when they are walking in the Swiss Alps. Finally Guy nurses the

insufferable Philip when he is seriously ill with a fever, catches the fever himself and dies. Altruism, it seems, could go no further and its merit is the greater because all along Guy has had to struggle against hereditary flaws in his character!

This concern to present character and good deeds as the essence of Christian virtue did arouse a certain uneasiness in some minds. To celebrate action and virtuousness pure and simple might seem to slight the truth of Christian revelation and to promise a return to pre-Reformation times when good works were exalted at the expense of faith. In *The Experience of Life* by Elizabeth Sewell, Mr Rivers the Anglican clergyman is concerned by the fact that the Dissenting cause seems to be gaining ground, and he is exacerbated, rather than mollified by Lady Emily's suggestion that their creed is validated by their own personal goodness. Lady Emily argues: 'But if John Simpkins is an angel of goodness his opinion of what is truth will have considerable weight', to which Mr Rivers replies:

> If you smile now at the notion of turning first Independent, then Baptist, and then Quaker, because the teachers of these sects happen to be good men, so you might, if a heathen, have despised the notion of giving up your former guides for Christian teachers. You might have said, 'Socrates and Plato were excellent persons; why am I not to be contented with their instructions but to follow instead the apostles of Christ.'

Elizabeth Sewell writes from a High Church point of view and what is at stake here is that the Broad Church preoccupation with good works and moral example can weaken the authority of the church and open the door to Dissent. A similar concern about justification by works is displayed in Charles Reade's popular novel of medieval life, *The Cloister and the Hearth* (1861). The life of his hero, Gerard, is split between sacred and secular worlds. The early part of the novel is devoted to a series of boisterous adventures as Gerard, separated from his intended by the intervention of the church, wanders across Europe towards Rome, where he achieves great success as an artist and copyist. Yet he subsequently becomes a monk and a hermit revered for his holiness and with his dying breath insists to his fellow monks: 'we are justified not by our own wisdom, or piety, or the works we have done in holiness of heart, but by faith'. On the one hand *The Cloister and the Hearth* insists that a multiplicity of decadent Roman doctrines must be brought before the bar of common sense, yet on the other it argues that if religion *is* to be given a more worldly orientation, it must not lose sight of the Reformation insistence on faith. Although *The Cloister and the Hearth* is not a work of theology and it would be absurd to treat it as such, Reade does seem to be suggesting that Protestants, in reacting against formal theology are in danger of throwing out the baby along with the bathwater.

Nevertheless there is an increasing feeling that religion is above all a personal matter and that controversy is idle if it becomes a distraction from the obligation to lead a religious life. Thus Kingsley deliberately sets *Hypatia* in the Egypt of the fifth century when Christianity is not only struggling against other creeds but is internally divided by doctrinal disputes and personal rivalries. While Newman in his study of the period was led to insist on the importance of tradition and the authority of the church, Kingsley, on the contrary, sees this only as the discordant setting against which each individual – from Philammon, the young monk, to Hypatia, the high priestess of Greek philosophy, to Raphael Ben Ezra, the sceptical Jew – must decide how best to lead his or her life. As his subtitle 'New Foes with an Old Face' clearly indicates, Kingsley clearly intends his novel to have a contemporary significance: he warns against fanaticism and opportunism alike, and in Hypatia in particular he represents the seductive charms of the Roman Catholic church. But the overriding message of the book is that only personal morality matters, for of the disputing sects within the church he writes: 'Orthodox or unorthodox, they knew not God, for they knew neither righteousness, nor love, nor peace.' In the final analysis they compare most unfavourably with Raphael, the old Jew, now converted to Christianity, whose ambitions are simpler and who asks for nothing more than 'To do a little good before I die', even if this is in atonement for what has gone before.

Beyond the pages of Kingsley's novel both the emotional turmoil induced by doctrinal conflict and the desire to live an exemplary Christian life are vividly illustrated by the experience of Christina Rossetti. In 1848, when Christina was only seventeen, she became engaged to James Collinson, a young painter who had become a member of the Pre-Raphaelite Brotherhood. Rossetti's biographers have been rather disappointed by Collinson, who was a short, dumpy man, but there can be little doubt that their relationship was intense and that they were both passionately devoted to each other. In her poetry Rossetti suggests that it was Collinson who was the more serious to begin with. His eagerness to obtain Christina's hand in marriage was such that he abandoned his plans to join the Catholic church. With such very earnest and devout young people their ability to see eye to eye in matters of faith was clearly very important. For Christina her love of God and her love for Collinson were inextricably woven together – as she subsequently wrote in the sonnet sequence 'Monna Innominata':

> Trust me, I have not earned your dear rebuke,
> I love, as you would have me, God the most . . .
>
> Yet while I love my God the most, I deem
> That I can never love you overmuch;
> I love Him more, so let me love you too;
> Yea, as I apprehend it, love is such
> I cannot love you if I love not Him.
> I cannot love Him if I love not you.

It was precisely this passionate blending of sacred and profane love – or rather a love that seemed altogether sacred and dedicated to God – that made Collinson's decision to join the Catholic church such a shattering blow for Christina. It seemed to destroy absolutely everything in her life that mattered. Christina broke off the engagement. Collinson went to Jesuit community at Stonyhurst as a lay-brother. Christina seems to have regretted breaking off the engagement, but she really had no choice since by going over to Rome at such a critical juncture in both their lives Collinson was indicating unmistakably that they could not continue together. On the one hand Christina accepted Collinson's right to follow the dictates of his conscience and in a perverse way even respected him for his sense of vocation:

> Thinking of you, and all that was, and all
> That might have been and now can never be,
> I feel your honoured excellence, and see
> Myself unworthy of the happier call

yet at the same time she undoubtedly felt a strong sense of personal betrayal at the step he had taken, even though this word was one she was always careful never to use in the very many poems that allude to their break-up. What made the gulf that had opened between them seem especially paradoxical was the fact that the Pre-Raphaelite Brotherhood was precisely the kind of movement where such barriers were being erased. Moreover, though both Christina's parents were of Italian descent, Christina's mother had been born in England and was an Anglican, while her father was a Catholic. So Collinson's Catholicism as such need not necessarily have been a stumbling block. But clearly both Collinson and Christina could be very intransigent where religion was concerned and at the time the decision to go over to Rome was generally perceived as a duplicitous and perfidious abandonment of the Anglican tradition, since in High Church eyes there was no necessity for taking so radical a step. Christina clearly felt that Collinson had sprung the decision on her in order to make the double break without giving her the opportunity to discuss it with him. Certainly she was deeply disillusioned and in the poem 'Memory' she speaks of 'Breaking mine idol':

> I broke it at a blow, I laid it cold,
> Crushed in my deep heart where it used to live
> My heart dies inch by inch; the time grows old,
> Grows old in which I grieve

yet the poem immediately continues with an affirmation of loyalty to her lover's memory:

> I have a room whereinto no one enters
> Save I myself alone:
> There sits a blessed memory on a throne,
> There my life centres.

Christina Rossetti has to destroy her memory of Collinson the betrayer in order to preserve her memory of him as he once was.

In Rossetti's poetry there is a complex rhetoric of remembering and forgetting that becomes closely bound up with her own identification with the reviled, suffering, persecuted figure of Christ, who also specifically asked his disciples to remember him. In 'Remember' the poet insistently demands of her love that he remember her, yet it also leaves open the possibility of forgetting:

> Better by far you should forget and smile
> Than that you should remember and be sad.

Christina herself could not and would not forget: remembering was her own personal form of Calvary.

Although Christina Rossetti is habitually linked with the Tractarian movement, her religious sense is profoundly Protestant: her intensely private sense of self, her wish for a personal, unmediated relationship with God, her distrust of the snares and vanities of the world. If she is a puritan it is because the very strength of her desire for pleasure, of her longing for voluptuousness becomes perilously destabilising and fraught with danger. For Christina the very idea of happiness came to be a treacherous lure just because it could collapse so suddenly into disappointment and despair. One paradoxical result of the breaking-off of her engagement was that she could now recognise how deeply passionate and physical had been her love for Collinson and this made her feel guilty and ashamed:

> Now all the cherished secrets of my heart,
> Now all my hidden hopes, are turned to sin.
> Part of my life is dead, part sick, and part
> Is all on fire within.

The perilous nature of sensual pleasure was a persistent and powerful theme in Rossetti's poetry. In an early poem 'The Dead City' she describes how, on rambling through the mysterious mazes of a wood, she comes across a dead city. A magnificent banquet has been prepared and there are gold and silver vessels filled with rich and exotic fruits, but the revellers have all been turned to stone. The poem concludes with the narrator kneeling to pray. The luscious, tempting fruits reappear in 'Goblin Market', Rossetti's most vivid and compelling poem, which inescapably depicts the uncontrollable nature of sexual passion. Laura insists on peeping at the goblin men, even though she knows she should not, and after following them and tasting their fruits 'until her lips were sore' she can think of nothing else. In a characteristic image that Rossetti was to repeat in many other poems her desire is seen as a mirage;

> She dreamed of melons, as a traveller sees
> False waves in desert drouth
> With shade of leaf-crowned trees,
> And burns the thirstier in the sandful breeze.

Lizzie saves her sister by going after the goblin men and suffers a kind of martyrdom by submitting herself to their insults and physical abuse:

> Barking, mewing, hissing, mocking,
> Tore her gown and soiled her stocking,
> Twitched her hair out by the roots,
> Stamped upon her tender feet,
> Held her hands and squeezed their fruits
> Against her mouth to make her eat.

Only when Laura kisses and licks the juices from Lizzie's face can she be cured of her erotic passion, since she discovers that what she had once desperately desired is now bitter-tasting and repellent. The goblin men seem to offer instant pleasure, their cooing voices sound 'kind and full of loves', but the reality is coarse, undignified, violent. The deeper and darker threat is an abandonment of the essential, private self – which was perhaps the real reason why Christina Rossetti never married.

In Christina Rossetti's poetry the gulf between her former self and her later self is as absolute as the division between BC and AD. In her earlier life she dreamed and hoped, she longed for fulfilment and plenitude. Now she must learn to live with absence, vacancy, and with a hope deferred – that always seems just out of reach –

> For I am bound with fleshly bands,
> Joy, beauty, lie beyond my scope;
> I strain my heart, I stretch my hands,
> And catch at hope.

She is shut out from the enchanted garden that has once been hers and now she must dream of some higher fulfilment in heaven. The complex mixture of hope and despair, of mistrust and inner confidence is epitomised by the simple-seeming but deeply resonant lines of 'Yet a Little While':

> I dreamed and did not seek: to-day I seek
> Who can no longer dream;
> But now am all behindhand, waxen weak,
> And dazed amid so many things that gleam
> Yet are not what they seem.
>
> I dreamed and did not work: to-day I work,
> Kept wide awake by care
> And loss, and perils dimly guessed to lurk;
> I work and reap not, while my life goes bare
> And void in wintry air.

I hope indeed; but hope itself is fear
Viewed on the sunny side;
I hope and disregard the world that's here,
The prizes drawn, the sweet things that betide;
I hope, and I abide.

Who but Christina Rossetti could have uttered the extraordinary paradox at the opening of the third stanza, but it is spoken calmly by one who has looked at things from both sides and who has learnt to come to terms with everything in her existence. Through her poetry and her Christian faith Christina Rossetti survived, and in reading poetry that can seem to be filled with a spirit of utter desolation, we must not miss the great underlying strength that enabled her to write about it and face it. In the poetry of Christina Rossetti we see how religious controversies and religious uncertainty had the perhaps surprising effect of making the traditional security and consolation of religion seem even more appealing. In a confusing and turbulent world it was possible to attain peace and security through an intensely personal and private faith; in the covert perhaps of 'Spring Quiet':

Full of sweet scents
And whispering air
Which sayeth softly;
'We spread no snare;

'Here dwell in safety,
Here dwell alone,
With a clear stream
And a mossy stone.

'Here the sun shineth
Most shadily;
Here is heard an echo
Of the far sea,
Though far off it be.

This emphasis on a more personal religion is also to be found among the contributions to the notorious collection of progressive Anglican opinion, *Essays and Reviews*, of 1861. In what was perhaps the most heavyweight contribution to that work, Benjamin Jowett's

'On the Interpretation of Scripture', Jowett, though emphasising a highly critical approach to the reading of the Bible quite foreign to Kingsley's own disposition and temperament nevertheless endorses an approach to the Christian religion that is very much in accordance with the spirit of *Hypatia*:

> Criticism is not only negative; if it creates some difficulties, it does away others. It may put us at variance with a party or sections of Christians in our own neighbourhood. But on the other hand, it enables us to look at all men as they are in the sight of God, not as they appear to the human eye, separated from each other by lines of religious demarcation, it divides us from the parts to unite us to the whole. That is a great help to religious communion. It does away with the supposed opposition of reason and faith. It throws us back on the conviction that religion is a personal thing, in which certainty is to be slowly won and not assumed as the result of evidence or testimony. It places us, in some respects (though it be deemed a paradox to say so) more nearly in the position of the first Christians to whom the New Testament was not yet given, in whom the Gospel was a living word, not yet embodied in forms or supported by ancient institutions.[50]

Hopefully intellectual turmoil and the dissipation of older certainties may lead, not to disillusionment and despair, but to the creation of a vital and living faith within the heart of every individual. Despite all appearances the world is not grown grey and the Christian faith has just the same chance to prosper and flourish in the modern age as it ever did in ancient times.

Anthony Trollope is often seen as the affectionate satirist of a worldly Church of England, epitomised by his description of Archdeacon Grantley reading Rabelais in a study lined with theological tracts and tomes. Ostensibly Trollope is a worldly figure, little concerned with the minutiae of theological controversy, content to present his readers with a gallery of ecclesiastical types, who are perceived in essentially secular terms. Yet the Church of England means a great deal to Trollope. For all its faults it remains a rocky island of stability, lashed by the waves of change, a more or less constant reference point in a world subject to instability and change. For this very reason Trollope felt that the controversies within the church, whether instigated by *Tracts for the Times* or by *Essays and Reviews*, gave deep cause for concern. For faith, though ostensibly strong, was actually a very fragile thing. Once the effective power of religion in society was weakened and the influence of the Church of England diminished, there could be no expectation that such a state of affairs could be readily rectified. In an early novel, *The Bertrams*, published in 1859, immediately after *Barchester Towers* and *Doctor Thorne*, Trollope describes the dramatic impression made by two Greek Orthodox Christians on his hero, George Bertram, when he visits the Tabernacle of the Holy Sepulchre in Jerusalem and places his hand on the marble tomb:

> But he did put his hand on the slab of the tomb; and as he did so, two young Greeks, brothers by blood – Greeks by their creed, though of what actual nation Bertram was quite unable to say – pressed their lips vehemently to the marble. They were dirty, shorn about the heads, dangerous looking, and skin-clothed, as we have described; men very low in the scale of humanity when compared with their fellow-pilgrims; but nevertheless, they were to him, at that moment, objects of envy. They believed: so much at any rate was clear to him. By whatever code of morals they might be able to govern their lives, whether by any, or as, alas! might be too likely, by none, at least they possessed a faith. Christ, to them, was an actual living truth, though they knew how to worship him no better than by kissing a stone, which had in fact no closer reference to the Saviour than any other stone they might have kissed in their own country. They believed; and as they reverently pressed their foreheads, hips and hands to the tops and sides and edges of the sepulchre, their faith became ecstatic.

Bertram's respect for these individuals is the more striking precisely because he is strongly tempted, like many other English visitors to the Holy Land, to reject such a display as nothing more than empty and ignorant fanaticism. Yet, despite all his inclinations, he cannot help being impressed. At this moment he decides to become a clergyman, but the ambition is short-lived for almost immediately afterwards he falls desperately in love with a well-bred young lady, Caroline Waddington, who makes it abundantly clear that she could never envisage marriage with a man who adopted such a lowly profession. But George's crisis of faith is real enough. His desire to believe with a similar fervour actually reflects his general uncertainty and inability to do so. His lack of conviction is all too representative of the times. To his clergyman friend, Arthur Wilkinson, Bertram not only confesses his own lack of faith but provocatively insists that the very possibility of it no longer exists:

> Your flocks do not believe, do not pray, do not listen to you. They are not in earnest. In earnest! Heavens! If a man could believe all this, could be in earnest about it, how could he possibly care for other things? But no; you pride yourselves on faith; but you have no faith. There is no such thing left. In these days men do not know what faith is.

The pugnacious, combative tone is not Trollope's own – indeed to him, as to many Victorians, such a fervent espousal of controversy was a positive anathema, yet he was equally concerned at the loss of faith, at the fact that the foundations of the Church of England were being undermined from within, a process started by Newman. Discussing the emancipated, liberal clergyman, 'the Clergyman Who subscribes for Colenso' in his *Clergymen of the Church of England* (1866), Trollope commented:

> he has cut the rope which bound his barque to the old shore, and . . . is going out to sea in quest of a better land. Shall we go with him, or shall we stay where we are?
>   If one could stay, if one could only have a choice in the matter, if one could really believe that the old shore is best, who would leave it? Who would not wish to be secure if he knew where security lay? But this new teacher, who has come amongst us with his ill-defined doctrines and his subrisive smile – he and they who have taught him, – have made it impossible for us to stay. With hands outstretched towards the old places, with sorrowing hearts, – with hearts which still love the old teachings which the mind will no longer accept, we, too, cut our ropes, and go out in our little boats, and search for a land that will be new to us, though how far new, – new in how many things, we do not know. Who would not stay behind if it were possible to him?[51]

So Trollope strikes a very characteristic note. The old comfortable dwelling place must be abandoned, there is absolutely nothing that can be done about it and yet the desire to stay on is so intense as virtually to outweigh the apparent necessity for departure.

This theme was already articulated in *The Warden* (1855), which

was Trollope's first novel with an English setting and the inauguration of the Barsetshire novels. Trollope's motive in writing the novel
was clearly to put in question the early Victorian concern with social
reform and to suggest that the time had come to call a halt. The
moment was propitious. Calls for reform had seemed both urgent
and credible against a general background of Chartism and social
unrest, but with the repeal of the Corn Laws and the defeat of the
Chartists in 1848 it now seemed possible to take a more relaxed view
of things, to suggest that both criticism and agitation have been
overdone. It is significant that in the novel Trollope parodies the
most strident voices of the preceding decade – *The Times* newspaper,
Dickens and Carlyle – and deliberately presents as his test case a
situation that the reformers seriously misconstrue. Septimus Harding
is precentor of Barchester Cathedral but he also holds the office of
warden to an almshouse established by John Hiram in 1434 in order
to support twelve elderly wool-carders. Now a dozen deserving
cases are lodged, fed and clothed there and in addition to a payment
of one shilling and fourpence a day receive an extra twopence from
the pocket of Septimus Harding himself. As warden, Harding receives £800 a year – a comfortable sinecure – but he does seriously
concern himself with the welfare of the old men. But it is alleged by
John Bold, a local radical and agitator, that there is no warrant for
such a substantial payment to the warden and that these funds
should go by right to the inhabitants of Hiram's Hospital. Bold is
eventually persuaded to withdraw the legal proceedings he has
instituted by Eleonor Harding, the warden's daughter, with whom
he is in love. But it is too late. Harding, a kindly, virtuous and well-
meaning old man, has been ridiculed and disgraced by adverse
comment in the press and feels that he can no longer hold up his
head if he remains in the post, despite the strong urging of Archdeacon Grantly that it is his duty to do so. Harding withdraws to
lodgings in the town, and the hospital, once a picturesque and well-
cared for place, goes to rack and ruin:

> The Warden's garden is a wretched wilderness, the drive and
> paths are covered with weeds, the flowerbeds are bare, and the
> unshorn lawn is now a mass of long damp grass and unwhole-
> some moss. The beauty of the place is gone: its attractions have
> withered. Alas! a very few years since it was the prettiest spot in
> Barchester, and now it is a disgrace to the city.

The Warden is a skilfully written and carefully characterised novel that can be enjoyed simply for its human interest, but it is impossible not to read it also as an allegory of the condition of the Church of England. A stable, traditional and well-ordered way of life that could have survived more or less indefinitely has been wilfully destroyed by a futile, self-dramatising will to controversy. As Trollope sees it, the preoccupations with righting 'wrongs' produces more wrong than right, and furthermore, by destabilising a well-established and morally secure order of things, incalculable harm is done.

The Warden's successor, *Barchester Towers*, is a reprise of the same themes in a comic mode. Its comic focus is on the oily personality of Mr Slope who presses his unwanted favours both on Harding's daughter, who is now a widow, and the voluptuous Signora Neroni, and who changes sides over the allocation of the office of warden when he realises that to support Harding may aid his access to the £1200 a year that Eleonor Bold possesses. Trollope's mocking exposure of the ineffectualness of Bishop Proudie, who can barely muster the courage to stand up to his domineering wife, and his renewed emphasis on the worldliness of Archdeacon Grantley may encourage the reader to think that Trollope's main interest is in exposing human foibles and in stressing that even in the ecclesiastical world the ambitions and follies of men and women are as evident as anywhere else.

There is some truth in this. The three centres of contention in the book – the struggle for Eleonor Bold's hand between Slope, Bertie Stanhope and Mr Arabin, the controversy as to whether Mr Harding or Mr Quiverfull will be warden, the battle to keep Mr Slope out of the deanery – are placed on a similar footing, and are all shown not to be simple questions of right or wrong but matters that involve considerable negotiation and intrigue among a very wide range of 'interested' parties. There is considerable irony in the way in which things turn out so unexpectedly: the shameless Signora Negroni nevertheless helps to bring about the marriage of Eleonor and Mr Arabin, which might otherwise have been prevented by pride, prejudice and nervous hesitation. Quiverful and Arabin become warden and dean respectively just when it had seemed certain that these offices would go to Harding and Slope. Yet this transposition is not adventitious, for Trollope believes it to be morally right. At bottom Trollope is *not* even-handed because we are asked to rejoice that Arabin, the pious, diffident and righteous High Churchman wins a overwhelming victory over the manipulative, self-advertising Low Churchman Slope by marrying Eleonor Bold and obtaining the deanship as well. Once again the forces of innovation are discomforted and the church's traditional ways vindicated. For all the book's wit and humour Trollope ends it on a serious note, leaving the reader with the image of old Mr Harding as the pious unworldly pillar of the Church of England who, in being left uncomplainingly empty-handed, demonstrates that we should not be fooled by the crusading rhetoric of *The Jupiter* when it speaks of 'easy couches to worn-out clerical voluptuaries'. Harding seeks no such easy couch. He is a truly virtuous man:

> He is still Precentor of Barchester, and still pastor of the little church of St Cuthbert's. In spite of what he has so often said himself, he is not even yet an old man. He does such duties as fall to his lot well and conscientiously, and is thankful that he has never been tempted to assume others for which he might be less fitted.

The author now leaves him in the hands of his readers; not as a hero, not as a man to be admired and talked of, not as a man who should be toasted at public dinners and spoken of with conventional absurdity as a perfect divine, but as a good man without guile, believing humbly in the religion that he has striven to teach, and guided by the precepts that he has striven to learn.

In *The Warden* and *Barchester Towers* Trollope had mounted a strong case for the defence of the Church of England against the charge that it was spiritually moribund, out of touch with the times and overloaded with corrupt sinecures and offices. If the church was not in tune with the modern age, so much the better for the church if this meant the kind of piety and dedication represented by Septimus Harding. If there were sinecures, this did not necessarily mean that such offices did not fulfil a worthwhile social function or that the beneficiaries were necessarily pampered or lacking in a sense of religious vocation. Perhaps there were worldly clerics like Archdeacon Grantly, but at least this meant there were men in the church with a strong sense of realism. Trollope had no objection to worldliness and his typical response to any such possible reproach was to demand of his readers whether they were not worldly also. If men like Archdeacon Grantly strive to ensure that such a man as Dr Arabin is installed as Dean of Barchester rather than a vulgar

Low Churchman like Slope, then the church, despite superficial appearances, is still in good hands. But in *Framley Parsonage* Trollope performed a more or less complete volte-face. In this novel it is suggested that the carryings on of such a worldly and social climbing parson as Mark Robarts do offer grounds for anxiety about the spiritual integrity and moral standing of the Church of England, and that the kind of attack mounted by *The Times* on the extraordinary disparities of income that may exist, for example, between a parson and a cleric who performs the same duties in his absence may well be justified. It is for this reason that Trollope introduces the character of Mr Crawley, who was to be the central character of the culminating *Last Chronicle of Barset*. Crawley's plight is particularly unjust since he is conscientious and genuinely devout clergyman, yet his income of £130 a year is less than a tenth of what Mark Robarts receives, when his prebendary stall at Barchester is included. Mr Crawley lives in poverty in the dreary village of Hogglestock, desperately trying to support an ailing wife and four children. Roberts lives in a grand house with footman, groom and sundry domestics and spends several days a week hunting with the local aristocracy. In this novel *The Jupiter*'s attack on church corruption in such individuals as Robarts, who has achieved a prebendary stall – normally a way of rewarding much more senior clergyman – before the age of thirty through underhand political dealings, appears not so much as preposterous and unwarranted rhetoric as the plain and unvarnished truth. By slanting *Framley Parsonage* in the opposite direction Trollope may have had an eye for the main chance, for he may have realised that such an attack on the church would arouse more attention and interest. Certainly *Framley Parsonage* was his greatest success to date. It was the novel above all that established him as one of the major Victorian novelists and ensured both a wide readership and, for a while at least, that his books were read with a good deal of critical respect. Yet Trollope was not necessarily insincere: his very desire to believe in the Church of England and think well of it went hand in hand with a deep anxiety about its welfare and its moral influence in society. It is this anxiety that is reflected in *Framley Parsonage*.

Perhaps what is crucial about *Framley Parsonage* is that Trollope allows many of the aspects of contemporary English society that gave him cause for disquiet to seep back into a fictional world that had been deliberately created to exclude them. The whole point of *Barchester Towers* was to present a struggle or series of struggles in miniature, a fight with snowballs in which a good time would be had by all but in which no one would be seriously hurt. But in *Framley Parsonage* Trollope was not only forced to concede that corruption in the church was a more serious matter than he had previously been prepared to acknowledge, but also that it could well be regarded as part of general laxity about moral questions that pervaded the whole of mid-Victorian society. Admittedly, this concern is articulated along party political lines and is, in Trollope's expression of it, distinctly melodramatic, but the buckling of rural Barchester before powerful pressures from the centre does nevertheless have a certain poignancy:

> there Mrs Robarts received her letter. Fanny, when she read it, hardly at first realised to herself the idea that her husband, the clergyman at Framley, the family clerical friend of Lady Lufton's establishment, was going to stay with the Duke of Omnium. It was so thoroughly understood at Framley Court that the duke and all belongings to him were noxious and damnable. He was a Whig, he was a bachelor, he was a gambler, he was immoral in every way, he was a man of no Church principle, a corruptor of youth, a sworn foe of young wives, a swallower up of small men's patrimonies.

This information is the more disconcerting because Mark's letter arrives from Chaldecotes, the home of Mr Sowerby, a financially hard-pressed MP who is something of an artist in avoiding payment of his debts and in getting others to assume responsibility for them. Mark is already on foreign ground and Gatherum Castle, where he is headed next, might as well be on another planet. We are told that the idea that the Duke and his associates are wicked is the view of Lady Lufton, but this is also the general perspective of the novel. For what is alarming about the situations that Mark gets into is not just that he becomes tainted by associating with such men as Sowerby or even that he gets into serious financial difficulties, but rather that he loses all moral perspective on his actions. For Trollope makes it clear that a man like Sowerby will manipulate his bills and unload as much of his debt onto others as he possibly can. The question is rather why Mark Robarts should be getting involved in such matters when his association with the Whig clique is causing concern at home? The only possible answer to this must be that he gets into such difficulties only because he has become a social climber. Moreover he is not the only person in the novel to be affected in this way:

Archdeacon Grantly is ensconced in London trying to get himself made Bishop of Westminster through political influence, while his daughter manages to nail the incredibly affluent Lord Dumbello. In effect Mark had taken as his credo the tolerant and broad-minded kind of Christianity that, in *Barchester Towers* at any rate, Trollope had suggested was greatly to be preferred to the hypocritical moralism of Mr Slope:

> It had been his intention, in reviewing what he considered to be the necessary proprieties of clerical life, in laying out his own mode of living, to assume no peculiar sacerdotal strictness; he would not be known as a denouncer of dancing or of card-tables, of theatres or of novel reading; he would take the world around him as he found it, endeavouring by the precept and practise to lend a hand to the gradual amelioration which Christianity is producing; but he would attempt no sudden or majestic reforms. Cakes and ale would still be popular, and ginger be hot in the mouth, let him preach ever so – let him be never so solemn a hermit; but a bright face, a true trusting heart, a strong arm, and a humble mind, might do much in teaching those around him that men may be gay and yet not profligate, that women may be devout and yet not dead to the world.

This is by no means a doctrine of worldliness but rather the kind of energetic, practical Christianity of which most Victorians approved – which makes it all the more alarming when he goes so badly wrong. The problem is that he does not only take the world as he finds it but leaves it that way: the precept and practice on his own part are lacking. The fact that at Chaldecotes he almost arrives late for a service at which he is officiating and that he rewrites his sermon to preclude any laughter from his cynical cronies shows just how rapidly he loses his independence and integrity. By consciously involving himself in Sowerby's purposes and lending his support to such dubious affairs, his conduct becomes far more reprehensible than that of Lydgate, in *Middlemarch*, who is in no way a party to Bulstrode's schemes. Robarts's dereliction of duty evoked a powerful response from Trollope's readers because it touched on their anxiety that the Church of England lacked real moral fibre, that it was not strong enough to battle with the problems of the age. Having initially disagreed with this view, Trollope now gave it his reluctant assent.

In *Framley Parsonage* Trollope had made Josiah Crawley, the poor curate of Hogglestock, the voice of conscience of the Church of England, and his sincere and outspoken reproach to Mark Robarts – 'You become a hunting parson, and ride with a happy mind among blasphemers and mocking devils – you, whose aspirations were so high' – is one that scarcely any other Trollopian clergyman could have plausibly made. In *The Last Chronicle of Barset* Crawley himself moves to centre stage and the story of how he comes to be accused, falsely, of misappropriating a cheque and the agonies and humiliations that he suffers provide the central interest of the book. Certainly there is little else, since the narrative is interlarded with no less than four of those interminably protracted courtship rituals that Trollope had brought to a fine art in his novels immediately preceding *The Last Chronicle*: *The Belton Estate* (1866) and *The Claverings* (serialised in 1866–7). Of *The Belton Estate* Henry James acidly remarked:

In the tale before us we slumber on gently to the end. There is no heroine but Miss Clara Amedroz, and no heroes but her two suitors. The lady loves amiss, but discovers it in time, and invests her affections more safely. Such, in strictness, is the substance of the tale; but it is filled out as Mr Trollope knows how to fill out the primitive meagreness of his dramatic skeletons.[52]

Some critics have seen the predicament of Mr Crawley as constituting Trollope's finest hour as a novelist, as for once he written about real troubles and sufferings, rather than about slights, suspicions and scandals. Here, at least, there is real substance. But the rights and wrongs of Trollope of a novelist are more problematic than this. In a perceptive review of *Framley Parsonage*, J. A. wrote in *Sharpe's London Magazine* (July 1861): 'The only conscience in the book is, "What will the world say?", the only morality, "such conduct does not become such a position."'[53]

On the face of it Mr Crawley's conduct in *The Last Chronicle* serves as a complete refutation of this charge, since Crawley does not really concern himself with public opinion, refuses to take obvious steps such as obtaining a lawyer, which would help to protect his reputation, and generally acts in a thoroughly unworldly, not to say perverse manner. Crawley is finally vindicated when Mrs Arabin is able to confirm that it was she who gave him the cheque, which had not therefore been carelessly misappropriated as public opinion had supposed. Nevertheless there is much truth in J. A.'s charge. Throughout the Barchester novels, whether in the case of Septimus Harding, Josiah Crawley, the Greshams in *Doctor Thorne*, or Mark Robarts, Trollope lays great emphasis on the agonies of embarrassment and public disgrace. Moreover Trollope's women characters are no different. Both Lucy Robarts and Grace Crawley are so desperately anxious that no one will think badly of them that they would rather give up the man they love than face such a fate worse than death. Trollope does try to show the action of individual conscience at work in a way that is independent of public opinion, namely by having Harding resign even when others are pressing him to stay and when Robarts deliberately chooses to face the humiliation of having the bailiffs come in. But perversely this only confirms J. A.'s point as Trollope does believe that going against public opinion is the highest form of courage. He also believes that anyone who does so is more than a little of a Don Quixote. The real betrayal, both of Mr Crawley and of Trollope's own deepest instincts, lies in the fact that having drawn the character of a poor, conscientious, hardworking, intensely virtuous Church of England clergyman, Trollope cannot avoid suggesting that such a man *must* be eccentric, not to say slightly mad. Trollope is more authoritative on the agonies of the worldly.

Nevertheless, there remains a sense in which Trollope is interested in virtuous conduct – precisely because there is no longer any power in society that requires it. Virtue in being 'eccentric' may therefore also be noble – especially where well-born characters are involved. For if virtue could not realistically be expected of Church of England parsons, neither could it be presumed that the legal system would deliver justice: there is only the individual conscience to appeal to where social institutions fail. In *Orley Farm* (1862) Lady Mason forges a codicil to her late husband's will in order to ensure that the property of Orley Farm is passed on to her own son Lucius. Many years later, thanks to the intervention of Mr Dockwrath, an attorney who takes up the matter in a spirit of revenge when he is given notice to quit his tenancy, the whole murky episode is in danger of being brought to light. But Lady Mason, in Trollope's eyes, goes a long way towards redeeming herself both because she takes the difficult step of confessing her crime to her elderly lover, Sir Peregrine Orme, and because, though she is acquitted in court of all criminal intent, thanks to the skill of her attorney, Mr Chaffenbrass, she nevertheless gives up the property. In *The Eustace Diamonds* (1873) Trollope strikes a more cynical note. Lizzie Eustace first takes possession of some valuable diamonds and refuses to give them up despite the fact that she has no legal right to them. Then she pretends that they were stolen from her at Carlisle, though they were not in the black box that was opened by thieves, since she had kept them under her pillow. Lizzie lies to the police and again subsequently when the diamonds are in reality stolen from her house in Hertford Street, London. Although it is poetic justice that she should nevertheless lose the jewels that she has struggled so desperately to keep, she is acquitted of the perjury that she has undoubtedly committed. What concerns Trollope is not just that Lizzie should be dishonest – and, to return to that point made by J. A., it is the more serious because of her high social position – but that society has neither the will nor the power to do anything about it.

The sense of a topsy-turvy world, where there are no stable reference points or recognised moral standards, already adumbrated in *Framley Parsonage*, reaches its climax in *The Way We Live Now* (1876), where Augustus Melmotte, the expatriate financier, presides over a world of financial dealing and double dealing, a world where there is no sense of honour and decency, even among lovers and friends. That Melmotte should be unscrupulous does not really concern Trollope. He is just the sort of person that might have been expected to behave in this fashion. He has no real doubts about what he has done:

> There was much that he was ashamed of, – many a little act which recurred to him vividly in this solitary hour as a thing to be repented of with inner sackcloth and ashes. But ever once, not for a moment, did it occur to him that he should repent of the fraud in which his whole life had been passed. No idea ever crossed his mind of what might have been the result had he lived the life of an honest man. Though he has inquiring into himself as closely as he could, he never ever told himself that he had been dishonest.

What does concern Trollope is the general moral laxity displayed by various members of the British aristocracy, who should know better, ranging from Lady Carbury and her son Felix to Paul Montague, Lord Niddersdale, Miles Grendall and the Longstaffes. Alas, Trollope's hero, Roger Carbury, the good, old-fashioned Suffolk country gentleman, seems not so much old-fashioned as positively antediluvian. Trollope does introduce a pious old bishop of the Church of England into the novel, but he no longer seems to think that such a person matters a great deal in the real world. In the twenty years separating *The Warden* from *The Way We Live Now* the Church of England had been radically marginalised. Then Trollope had deplored the fact that it was the subject of so much public concern, yet now even he is not really convinced that it matters or could matter.

Trollope's concern about the future of Christian values was shared by Tennyson. For Tennyson the publication of *In Memoriam* in 1850 had brought not simply instantaneous success but also instant respectability through his appointment as Poet Laureate. Moreover as he followed Wordsworth in this office and was also a spokesman for orthodox Christianity and the Church of England, there was a definite sense in which the Poet Laureate could be construed as some kind of *ex-officio* bishop. In many ways Tennyson welcomed this role and with the later *Idylls of the King*, which was issued in sections from 1859 to 1874, he wrote another great national poem, based on the Arthurian legends, in which Arthur is shown to be simultaneously concerned with the defence of the realm and the defence of the Christian faith against the forces of irreligion and paganism. But in *Maud* Tennyson quite deliberately published a poem that not only was not a manifesto of orthodoxy but was bound to give considerable offence. The speaker's morbid and rancorous response to his displacement as Maud's intended by an insipid but enormously wealthy young lord might itself have appeared in poor taste, but Tennyson compounded the offence having him launch a comprehensive attack on the decadence of British society and by concluding the poem with an unequivocal celebration of war: 'The blood-red blossom of war with a heart of fire.'

The equivocal nature of this enterprise has always made the poem very difficult to interpret. Clearly Tennyson's appointment as Poet Laureate unleashed a torrent of bitterness in his mind as he recalled the many slights and rebuffs he has suffered, especially his rejection by the affluent Rosa Baring and the incredible delays that held up his marriage to Emily Sellwood until after the publication of *In Memoriam* as Tennyson's finances were not deemed sound enough to permit it.

In *Maud* Tennyson gives free rein to the anger and bitterness of that former self, secure in his conviction of the narrative's overall deniability. In a way this is impressive. Tennyson assaults the brutality and hypocrisy of Victorian capitalism with an explicitness that is worthy of Blake. His exposure of a character who is at once authentic and unadmirable recalls Dostoevky's underground man. Furthermore for Tennyson to have voiced such criticism in the 1840s might have been just acceptable, but in the 1850s such thoughts were distinctly untimely and out-of-season. It was as if Tennyson was deliberately trying to irritate middle-class society with shrill reminders of all that it was trying to forget. Above all, why was such a pathetically inadequate character, a man so obviously eaten up with self-pity, envy and resentment, trying to proclaim 'the glory of manhood' and 'the wrongs and shames' that stemmed from an inglorious love of peace? How ludicrous to make the experience of being jilted in love the basis for a political manifesto! What is more, *Maud*'s narrator freely acknowledges himself to be weak – indeed almost glories in exposing to the world an existence that has been totally shattered by Maud's infidelity:

> Maud could be gracious too, no doubt
> To a lord, a captain, a padded shape,
> A bought commission, a waxen face,
> A rabbit mouth that is ever agape –
> Bought? what is it he cannot buy?
> And therefore splenetic, personal base,
> A wounded thing with a rancorous cry,
> At war with myself and a wretched race,
> Sick, sick to the heart of life, am I.

By comparison with the expression of grief in *In Memoriam*, the narrator's emotional display is indecorous in the extreme.

The narrator sees his personal misfortune as merely symptomatic of the parlous state of modern England, in which dignity, honesty, compassion and a sense of personal responsibility have been replaced by cynicism, opportunism and the cash-nexus. But there is also a sense of cosmic disillusionment. 'The drift of the maker is dark' and instruments of modern astronomy are:

Innumerable, pitiless, passionate eyes,
Cold fires, yet with a power to burn and brand
His nothingness into man.

Certainly the narrator's pessimism seems to verge on nihilism and
his invocation of God at the end of the poem:

Yet God's just wrath shall be wreaked on a giant liar

$\cdot \quad \cdot \quad \cdot \quad \cdot \quad \cdot \quad \cdot \quad \cdot \quad \cdot \quad \cdot \quad \cdot$

I embrace the purpose of God, and the doom assigned.

seems to represent little more than a mood of fatalism and a mega-
lomaniac desire for purification and vengeance. Since there can be
little doubt that Tennyson does share the narrator's Carlylean analysis of the state of England, are we to take it that in *Maud* Tennyson
came close to abandoning the desperately hard-won faith of *In
Memoriam*? On the face of it this seems unlikely – and yet why
should Tennyson have been so fond of reading from the poem and
so sensitive to criticism of it if there was not a strong element of self-
revelation in it? Again it is difficult not to think that Tennyson
himself is implicated in the bellicose conclusion to the poem; it
would seem that the protagonist is freed from his own personal
neurosis by his involvement with England's cause in the Crimean
War. He awakens to a better and presumably more healthy mind. He
finds a sense of purpose in fighting for a good cause rather than
simply complaining about his misfortunes. He feels a sense of solidarity with the British people – 'I am one with my kind.' At this
point we are confronted with the paradox that if the narrator's state
of mind in some way corresponds with Tennyson, then Tennyson
was able to overcome his sense of personal alienation by writing
'The Charge of the Light Brigade', when what actually seems much
more likely is that it is actually Tennyson's assumption of that official bardic role that actually *produces* his alienation. At all events
both versions cannot be correct.

In this critical predicament I do not think we can overlook the fact
that it was precisely *Maud*'s intentional blood-thirstiness that gave
most offence, and I think we can reasonably assume, that in a poem
written to give offence, Tennyson foresaw this. By adding the half-
crazed voice of *Maud*'s narrator to the chorus of patriotic solidarity
over the Crimean War Tennyson brought a skeleton to the feast and

gave the whole proceedings an unnecessarily gruesome character. *Maud's* narrator is a prophet of destruction, not the dispenser of consolation, and I would suggest that in writing it Tennyson mocked both the bardic role and his own 'ignoble' assumption of it. Tennyson seems to be saying to the British public: 'Yes, I will celebrate Britain's cause if you want me to, but I think you may well find that you've summoned the wrong man – someone who's distinctly inclined to speak out of turn.' Only by reserving his right to anarchic and untimely utterance could Tennyson convince himself that he remained a free man. It is impossible to resist the feeling that Tennyson, in saying 'I embrace the purpose of God, and the doom assigned', is ironically alluding to his own assumption of the Laureateship!

Tennyson's *The Idylls of the King* is often seen as a rather limp attempt to translate Malory's complex and many-sided work into a somewhat schematic celebration of the Victorian gentlemanly ideal, as projected back into the distant past. Just as Trollope regrets the passing of Roger Carbury in *The Way We Live Now*, so Tennyson regrets the passing of Arthur. Indeed it is not hard to think of Arthur as a rather fine but slightly distant headmaster, who has in the past found that it has worked quite well not to enquire too deeply into what the boys get up to but who now detects a definite decline in the school spirit. Some boys have been regularly cutting chapel and afternoon rugger practice. There are rumours of bullying and of playing cards for money. Some of the fellows have been spotted in the town with girls and there have even been strong suggestions that the headmaster's wife is sweet on the headboy. Arthur, more in hope that expectation, continues to cry 'Play up, play up, play the game' and has even had to give the boys a serious talking to, but no one seems to be listening. Such a parodic view of *The Idylls of the King* does have a certain validity – indeed it *would* be surprising if Tennyson did not reinterpret the Arthurian legends in terms of the values and attitudes of his own day. Moreover to talk of a public-school ethos or of team spirit is actually to get very close to the issues that Tennyson is concerned with in the poem. But I would argue that the fundamental questions raised by the poem are religious. Like many in the Church of England at this time, Tennyson is not particularly concerned with whether certain specific doctrines or beliefs are true. What he is concerned with is the loss of confidence which that uncertainty causes, the tendency for people to go off in different directions and to work out their own *ad hoc* beliefs, with the way in which a perceived loss of meaning in the world can generate a sense of purposelessness and futility in the lives of individuals, a lack both of integrity and trust. Herbert F. Tucker's suggestion that 'What Tennyson regrets is the self's passing away'[54] does have a certain validity here. Further, if Tennyson is concerned with such questions, then the very idea of uttering some inspirational summons to a life of virtue becomes deeply problematic. There is much in *The Idylls of the King* both to suggest that the disintegration of the Round Table was the product of complex cultural forces beyond the control of any single individual, and also – perhaps more perversely – that the collapse of Camelot occurred not so much because Arthur's knights ceased to be noble, brave and good but because they began to spend too much time worrying whether they were or not!

From the very outset Tennyson was very much more interested in the paradoxical, indeed on the face of it more or less unaccountable, fact that such a pre-eminent body of men as King Arthur and his knights should have progressively lost both the moral stature and the cohesion that had once made them unchallengeable. Since Tennyson actually began the sequence of poems by writing 'The Passing of Arthur', the books that followed it but ostensibly preceded it were always under pressure to signal ahead the collapse that was to come. So in Tennyson's version of Arthur there is never any one moment when the court at Camelot can be tranquil and shining. It takes almost no time at all for the birds of ill omen to gather over Camelot so that *The Idylls of the King* is never idyllic: it is a poem with a beginning and a long drawn-out end but almost no middle. Tennyson cannot simply celebrate the deeds of Arthur's knights as Malory can. It is as if Malory himself belongs to a naïve age that cannot even begin to understand history as process; so, Tennyson, coming after, cannot simply take one thing at a time, but must see to it that every moment is saturated with implications of futurity. The contradictions in Tennyson's poem are particularly evident in *Balin and Balan*, the last of the idylls to be written but placed fifth in the overall sequence. Clearly Tennyson wanted to simulate a point of balance in the poem that he felt it lacked, which would serve as a point of transition between the comparative innocence of 'Geraint and Enid' and the moral corruption of 'Merlin and Vivien', yet in supplying this lack Tennyson also shows that there actually could never ever be such a point in the poem. Balin and Balan clearly foreshadow later pretenders and challengers to Arthur's pre-eminence in *The Idylls* but because they are easily defeated by Arthur they are forced to recognise that the reputation

of Camelot is fully justified and are themselves honoured to be
inaugurated as knights of the Round Table. Balin is desperately
anxious to carry on his standard the crown of Guinevere herself, yet
he becomes anxious that he is unworthy of the distinction that has
been accorded him:

> Too high this mount of Camelot for me;
> These high-set courtesies are not for me.
> Shall I not rather prove of the worse for these?
> Fierier and stormier from restraining, break
> Into some madness even before the Queen.

These doubts are banished when Balin, in the garden, overhears
Guinevere reproach Lancelot for neglecting her, and disturbed by
these intimations of an illicit passion dashes away 'mad for strange
adventure'. In the hall of Pellam Sir Garlon asks Balin why he wears
this insignia, to which Balin proudly replies:

> The queen we worship, Lancelot, I, and all,
> As fairest, best and purest, granted me
> To bear it!

But he is rapidly deflated by Sir Garlon's cynical and worldly-wise
response, which confirms his own worst suspicions:

> Fairest I grant her: I have seen; but best,
> Best, purest? *thou* from Arthur's hall, and yet
> So simple! hast thou eyes, or if, are these
> So far besotted that they fail to see
> This fair wife-worship cloaks a secret shame?
> Truly, ye men of Arthur be but babes.

Sir Balin represents simultaneously the moment when the aura of
Camelot can wield an irresistible power over others – much as
Byzantium did over the states of the Eastern empire – and yet also
the moment when the shining glamour of Camelot begins to be
tarnished. Yet in a way it is an illusion, made possible only by Balin's
naïvety. But if he was taken in by Arthur's court, this has a further
disturbing implication that Tennyson cannot altogether dispel,
namely that Camelot's grandeur may always have rested on some

kind of deception. For Malory, of course, the love between Lancelot and Guinevere did not pose the same moral problem that it did for Tennyson, since it so clearly exemplified a pure yet transgressive passion sanctioned by the traditions of courtly love. For Tennyson the question is whether Camelot was a flawed diamond, or whether it was an apple, rotten at the core.

As far as Tennyson is concerned if there ever was one single reason for the loss of morale at Arthur's court then that reason was undoubtedly the infidelity of Guinevere with Lancelot. It led Geraint to leave the court for the Welsh Marches and prompted Sir Balin's departure also. Guinevere's infidelity is dangerous because it undermines Arthur's authority and threatens a reversal of sex roles in which the real power at Camelot is effectively wielded by a woman. The attempt to seize and capture male power is most obviously epitomised by Vivien, who only attempts to obtain Merlin's magic charms after she has unsuccessfully set her cap at Arthur. For Tennyson, as for most Victorians, the ideal woman is Enid, the loyal and always submissive bride, who obediently puts on her most faded dress when her husband commands her to and who makes preservation of his life and general well-being her primary duty.

It is through the power and malign influence, when uncontrolled, of feminine sexuality that the mutual loyalty and male bonding among the knights of the Round Table is progressively undermined. A curious aspect of the collusion that surrounds the relationship between Lancelot and Guinevere is that it very largely depends on Lancelot's own authority as the most eminent of all the knights of the Round Table, as the incomparable star of the jousting-field. It is really in deference to him rather than to Arthur that a discreet silence is maintained as it is Lancelot who is the real glory of Camelot, Lancelot who inspires others to feats of emulation, Lancelot who makes Camelot worthy to be celebrated in verse. As Lancelot himself points out:

> But now my loyal worship is allowed
> Of all men: many a bard, without offence
> Has linked our names together in his lay,
> Lancelot, the flower of bravery, Guinevere,
> The pearl of beauty: and our knights at feast
> Have pledged us in this union, while the King
> Would listen smiling.

In trying to recentre the Arthurian narrative onto Arthur himself Tennyson finds the materials more recalcitrant that might have been anticipated; for the praise of Arthur must function, in a very real sense, at the expense of Camelot itself. If Lancelot is noble, then all can be noble; but if Arthur in his virtuousness is the true pattern of nobility, then it is bound to seem as if the Round Table has actually turned out to be something of a disappointment.

To say this is also to recognise how very important the whole idea for fidelity was for Tennyson, and I would argue that the ultimate reason for this is religious. For Tennyson the knights of the Round Table lived, like the Victorians, in a time of difficulty and danger where the whole existence of the Christian faith was under threat. What matters about such religious faith is that it is, above all, something shared. It is a focus of community, of common values, it can serve as a powerful bond between individuals, inspiring them to feats of courage, nobility and of genuine piety, which they would never be capable of on their own. What Tennyson is really saying, if we transpose *The Idylls of the King* back into the key of the Victorian age, is that the real spirit of religion is not to be found in quibbles over the Thirty-Nine Articles or in debates about the relationship between the findings of geology and the chronology of the Bible. Tennyson was certainly concerned about this. In *Maud* he had written:

> But the churchmen fain would kill their church
> And the churches have killed their Christ.

Since such debates are inherently divisive it makes more sense to be true to the Church of England, particularly since the authentic Christian life, is, as at Arthur's court, a matter of deeds and action not words. In 'The Last Tournament' there is a crucial moment when Isolt insists that Tristram must swear fidelity to her:

> Swear to me thou wilt love me even when old,
> Gray-haired, and past desire, and in despair.

But Tristram refuses. He regrets having swore the original oath to Arthur in the first place since he was not able to keep it and thus feels dishonoured. The very idea of an oath has become contaminated as it no longer implies an act of commitment freely, even joyfully given, but rather an undertaking so relentlessly restrictive and binding that no one should have to enter into it, or indeed even been asked to do so. Arthur's demands on the knights of the Round Table are unrealistic – they go against the whole grain of human nature:

> a doubtful lord
> To bind them with inviolable vows,
> Which flesh and blood perforce would violate:
> For feel this arm of mine – the tide within
> Red with free chase and heather-scented air,
> Pulsing full man; can Arthur make me pure
> As any maiden child? Lock up my tongue
> From uttering freely what I freely hear?
> Bind me to one? The wide world laughs as it.

Sir Tristram's refusal to enter into any kind of commitment can certainly be seen as foreshadowing the many versions of modern infidelity and his victory over Lancelot at the last tournament is the occasion when it finally becomes clear that the great historical moment of Arthur and the knights of the Round Table is finally over. The vivifying and unifying spirit of Camelot has finally departed. Yet Sir Tristram's claim that the knightly oath goes against the grain of human nature cannot be dismissed out of hand. It is Arthur himself who warns his knights of the dangers of the quest for the Holy Grail:

> O my knights,
> Your places being vacant at my side,
> This chance of noble deeds will come and go
> Unchallenged, while ye follow wandering fires
> Lost in the quagmire.

The implication of this is that the perfect sainthood that is called for if a person is to be vouchsafed a vision of the Grail is beyond the range of ordinary human possibility and therefore it is perhaps even impious to seek it. There are many ways of living a virtuous and Christian life that do not call for a person to be a saint. Indeed it can be argued that it is not the love of Lancelot and Guinevere that destroys the fellowship of the Round Table but rather the pursuit of the Grail, which sends each knight on a purely individual spiritual quest and which must leave the majority, as Arthur foresaw, feeling spiritually unworthy and demoralised. But there is a very important difference between the realism of Arthur and the realism of Tristram. For Arthur realism means setting oneself high, but nevertheless possible goals, where the constant striving to become better never lapses into hopelessness or cynicism; Tristram wants to avoid disappointment by refusing to make a commitment of any kind. For Tennyson keeping the faith means remaining true to one's original commitment even as you recognise that you cannot be true to it as you would ideally like. The alternative is anarchy and despair.

5

Victorian Intellectuals and their Dilemmas: Mill, Huxley, George Eliot and Matthew Arnold

The emergence of the intellectual is a characteristically nineteenth-century phenomenon and the term implies not merely a person of intelligence and independent mind but one who uses that intelligence *against* rather than *for* the *status quo*. The reality, inevitably, is rather more complex but in this chapter I shall discuss four representative and significant Victorian combatants – John Stuart Mill, Thomas Henry Huxley, George Eliot and Matthew Arnold – and consider to what extent their thinking and mode of argumentation can be regarded as oppositional. Certainly if we reflect on the nature of Victorian institutions for any length of time we must be impressed by the strength and relative homogeneity of the cultural establishment. For instance, periodical articles in such journals as the *Edinburgh Review* were quite clearly written with a view to influencing government policy, and even articles and speeches that were critical of the government or of particular social institutions were nevertheless framed and argued in such a way as to make it absolutely clear that no thoroughgoing transformation of society was envisaged. With the eclipse of the 'philosophical radicals' in the 1830s and the recognition that 1832 was not to a prelude to yet further reform, and with the defeat of Chartism in 1848, it was crystal clear that any changes that might be made to the structure of society would be from the top down rather than through pressure from below, even though there might always be a glimmer of a pre-emptive motive. From this it followed that there was little to be gained simply by challenging or attacking the Victorian establishment; what mattered was to be *influential* – to be taken seriously by those in the higher echelons of society – and this implied a much more focused and nuanced mode of presentation, a clear recognition that all such con-troverted questions could really only be adjudicated by a social élite. Neither Mill, Huxley, Eliot nor Arnold was finally a Christian in the conventional sense of the word and their views did represent a challenge to the Anglican establishment centred on the universities of Oxford and Cambridge; yet, I would want to argue, though these thinkers *did* want to unsettle the cultural orthodoxy, they were as deeply concerned about deference and social stability as those they sought to oppose. In other words, just as Brecht saw in Galileo's recantation a refusal to use scientific knowledge as a progressive social force, so, correspondingly, the Victorian intellectuals were reluctant to allow radical ideas or critical thinking to be deployed in ways that could be socially subversive.

Nevertheless we do see the development of spheres of intellectual activity that takes place outside, and even in conscious opposition to, the English universities. The clearest instance of this is Utilitari-anism as an intellectual movement. Thus James Mill, Bentham's great supporter and populariser, was successively a minister, a jour-nalist and a high official in the service of the East India Company. He did not go to either Oxford or Cambridge and educated his son himself rather than send him there which would, of course, have involved acquiescence in the Thirty-Nine Articles of the Church of England. As a secular philosophy Utilitarianism was perceived as a threat to the Anglican universities and therefore in these centres of privilege and sometimes culture there was a conscious effort to oppose it. Utilitarianism was not seen to have penetrated these au-gust citadels until 1874, when Henry Sidgwick published his *Meth-ods of Ethics* – by which time, of course, Oxford and Cambridge were no longer specifically Anglican institutions, having been effectively disestablished in 1871. As far as the sciences are concerned the question is more complex. Certainly at Cambridge where William Whewell, Master Trinity, was a leading light – simultaneously scien-tist, moralist, theologian and philosopher of science – there was a conscious effort to show that religion was perfectly compatible with the development of science. In his *History of the Inductive Sciences* (1873) Whewell went so far as to argue that the Roman Catholic church had treated Galileo very reasonably and had only moved against him when absolutely forced to do so. Whewell's views on science will be discussed presently.

Here it is sufficient to say that it is exceedingly improbable that

Darwin could have developed his views on evolution within such an institutional setting not simply because of its subversive message but also because Darwin's empirical mode of enquiry was not in accordance with Whewell's understanding of scientific method. Yet, by the same token, it seems highly probable that James Clerk Maxwell was only able to develop his pioneering theory of electromagnetic fields as the result of his dependence on the 'intuitionist' philosophy of Hamilton and Whewell. Nevertheless the fact remains that Oxford and Cambridge were closed communities in more ways than one, and as a result some of the most powerful minds of the Victorian era, whether university educated or not, were only able to achieve what they did by educating themselves. Huxley, of course, was the archetypal self-made man, yet George Eliot's own programme of self-education was even more remarkable. In addition to being a great novelist and translator of Feuerbach, she was also extremely well informed about a variety of scientific fields. For a woman of the time, of course, a university education would have been an impossibility and the educational milieu of the time would certainly have discouraged the interests she actually pursued. But in pondering the relationship between intellectuals and the university Arnold is the most complex case. Arnold was the only one of these strenuous figures actually to attend Oxford or Cambridge and he certainly thought of himself as an Oxford man and remembered his time there with great affection. Arnold always thought of Oxford at its best, especially as represented by Newman, as representing a force for good in the world, yet even he, perhaps especially he, was conscious of the provinciality of English universities. In his essay 'The Literary Influence of Academies' Arnold referred to Renan's astonishment that 'a recent article . . . should have brought forward as the last word of German exegesis a work like this, composed by a doctor of the University of Cambridge, and universally condemned by the German critics', and ruefully commented:

you see what he means to imply: an extravagance of this sort could never have come from Germany, where there is a great force of critical opinion controlling a learned man's vagaries and keeping him straight: it comes from the native home of intellectual eccentricity of all kinds, – from England, from a doctor of the University of Cambridge; – and I daresay he would not expect much better from a doctor of the University of Oxford. (III, 243)

Yet Oxford's honour is more or less saved since Arnold immediately goes on to cite Newman as an exemplary instance of precisely the catholicity, the breadth of learning and outlook, the urbanity of style that he values. But, of course, Arnold also knows that Newman was driven out of Oxford.

If any one man epitomised the high Victorian intellectual establishment that man was William Whewell, who from relatively humble origins, as the son of a Lancashire carpenter, made his way to become Professor of Moral Philosophy at Cambridge in 1838, and Master of Trinity from 1841 until his death. Whewell was a huge, overbearing, irascible and physically intimidating man, whose personality was reflected in a series of equally intimidating, if not always intellectually formidable volumes. He wrote a three-part *History of the Inductive Sciences* (1837) and the equally massive *Philosophy of the Inductive Sciences* (1840). He also published a two-volume work on ethics and a treatise on *The Plurality of Worlds* (1853). Whewell was an expert on the subject of tides and a syllabus reformer, who introduced a revised Mathematics Tripos and a new Moral Sciences Tripos. Whewell gave the impression of being a polymath, but he was at heart a censorious busybody, who made it his self-appointed task to police a variety of fields of knowledge to ensure that what went on there was in accordance with sound learning, scholarship and the Thirty-Nine Articles of the Church of England. Whewell's overall intellectual and religious standpoint is best approached through his Bridgewater treaties of 1833, *Astronomy and General Physics considered with reference to Natural Theology*. Here Whewell argued that a whole variety of regularities and structured symmetries in the relationship between living organisms and their terrestrial environment offered decisive proof of the existence of a benevolent creator. Thus the fact that the length of the year and the recurrence of the seasons is precisely as it is is absolutely crucial to the existence of all life on earth: 'now, if any change of this kind were to take place, the working of the botanical world would be thrown into utter disorder, the functions of the plants would be entirely deranged, and the whole vegetable kingdom involved in instant decay and rapid extinction'.[1] Whewell's method was effectively to begin with Pope's dictum 'Whatever is, is right' and then illustrate it with a variety of circumstantial evidence. Thus the alternation of periods of activity and sleep in man and other animals is tied in with the alternation of day and night. Our own ability to walk conveniently and the general stability of objects around us depends on the fact that the gravity of the earth is so much and no more. Our ability to hear sounds and therefore to communicate depends on the fact that our ears are precisely attuned to the sound waves that carry them. Whewell's whole argument was that the earth had been especially constructed with man in mind and it was therefore inconceivable, on purely logical grounds, that there could be intelligent life anywhere else in the universe. But Whewell went beyond the purely physical evidence to claim that if God made the atmosphere and the means that made communication possible, he must also have created the mental capacities that are realised in language and speech. Moreover if all the evidence demonstrated what care God had gone to in order to ensure that the world was fitted to man, it necessarily followed that he must be as equally concerned with man's moral development as with his physical well-being. In this way, and in accordance with the overall objective of the Bridgewater treatise, science does not undermine religion but confirms it.

This theological perspective shaped Whewell's understanding of the nature of scientific enquiry, and it actually enabled him to produce a better understanding of what is actually involved in scientific research than those, like John Stuart Mill, who approached the question from a more secular point of view; though Whewell, in this, was undoubtedly aided by the fact that he had a much more thorough grounding in the history of science and therefore knew more about the actual circumstances of scientific discovery. At Cambridge it was Whewell's intention to oppose Lockianism, which he correctly perceived as offering an understanding of scientific enquiry that could dispense with any religious assumptions. For Whewell the fact that God had made man and had made the world in such a way that he could live in harmony with it also meant that it was possible for man to arrive at basic insights about the nature of this God-given reality. What was crucial to his 'intuitive' theory of science was that it was not necessary for man to proceed laboriously to build up his understanding of the world, working up from the most rudimentary fundamentals, from simple building blocks to a more complex understanding. Whewell did believe that science was progressive, but he also insisted that man had the ability to break through to an understanding of the nature of things, through what he called 'happy guesses'. Whewell denied that it was possible to reach such an understanding merely through the accumulation of facts. What was required was rather a hypothesis that could give order and meaning to a variety of facts that might otherwise seem disparate and unconnected. In this way Whewell's philosophy of science has been seen as prefiguring Popper's analysis of scientific enquiry in terms of 'conjectures and refutations'. Whewell writes:

> Yet still, we may do something in tracing the process by which such discoveries are made; and this is our business to do. We may observe that these, and the like discoveries, are not improperly described as happy *Guesses*; and that Guesses, in these and other instances, imply various suppositions made, of which some one turns out to be the right one. We may, in such cases, conceive the discoverer as inventing and trying many conjectures, till he finds one which answers the purpose of combining the scattered facts into a single rule.[2]

Whewell's favourite instance of this process at work was Kepler's attempt to calculate the orbit of the planet Mars. Kepler only came to the conclusion that the path of the planet was an ellipse after trying nineteen other hypotheses, yet this one proved to be correct. What was alarming about this version of science to some was precisely that Whewell made it seem something of a hit-or-miss affair, and not the rigorously grounded and inexorable process that it surely ought to be. For Whewell there was no royal road to knowledge. What guaranteed knowledge was not so much the steps that lead to it as the existence of God – who, as Einstein subsequently suggested, would not play with dice. Chance could not play a significant role in the universe and it was this that made science possible. Contrariwise, from this point of view it was Darwin's very emphasis on random variation that made his theory of evolution improbable, *purely on scientific grounds*.

As a moral philosopher Whewell is distinctly unimpressive. Since he sees himself as defending some kind of Christian moral consensus he more or less takes it for granted that his views are 'sound' and has no hesitation in appealing either to legal traditions or to some presumed unanimity of respected opinion. Nevertheless he does make certain strategic emphases that are of interest, if only because they indicate that combatting the heresy of Utilitarianism was a cause dear to his heart. Yet, somewhat unexpectedly, we find that Whewell is not one of those believers in Original Sin, who hold that immorality and wickedness have been fairly constant through the ages. Like John Stuart Mill, Whewell believes that there has been progress in morals. Even more paradoxically he argues this case on

Lockian grounds: 'As the intellectual culture of the nation proceeds, abstract words are used with more precision; and in consequence, the conceptions, designated by such words, grow clearer in men's minds.'[3]

As his title, *The Elements of Morality including Polity*, suggests Whewell was very much concerned with the political and legal dimension of morality. He laid great emphasis on the importance of submission to political authority and was even prepared to suggest that anyone who was disposed to resist the state was in some way unnatural: 'Disloyalty to the Sovereign, Disobedience to Authority, Sedition, Treason, Rebellion, are, in themselves looked upon with feelings of Dislike and Indignation. If a person does not participate in these feelings, he is not likely to possess Benevolent Affections at all.'[4] Unlike the Utilitarians, whose arguments were premissed on the assumption of a self-regarding individual, who would naturally seek pleasure and avoid pain, Whewell emphasised the collectivity over the individual:

> the Supreme Law of Human Action must be a Law which belongs to man as man; a thing in which all men sympathise, and which binds together man and man by the tie of their common humanity. It excludes all that operates merely to separate men; for example, all Desires that tend to a centre in the Individual, without any regard to the common sympathy of mankind.[5]

Although Whewell did use two of the key terms of Utilitarians, 'Happiness' and 'Desire', he was at pains to use them in a very different sense. He would have no truck with bodily desires at all: sexual desire was roundly condemned as fornication. For Whewell these terms could only be given meaning not through hedonism but through a traditional theory of moral obligation:

> Since Happiness is necessarily the Supreme Object of our Desires and Duty the Supreme Rule of our actions, there can be no harmony in our being, except our Happiness coincide with our Duty. That which we contemplate as the Ultimate and Universal Object of Desire, must be identical with that which we contemplate as the Ultimate and Supreme Guide of our Intentions. As moral beings, our Happiness must be found in our Moral Progress, and in the consequences of our Moral Progress: we must be happy by being virtuous.[6]

With so much heavy capitalisation the case seemed proved. Whewell objected to the Utilitarian principle of the greatest happiness of the greatest number on the grounds that it was impossible to predict or evaluate the consequences of any action on such a basis:

> How are we to measure Happiness, and thus to proceed to ascertain, by what acts it may be increased? If we can do this, then, indeed, we may extract Rules and Results, from the Maxim that we are to increase our own and others' Happiness: but without this step, we can draw no consequences from the Maxim. If we take the Conception in its just aspect, how little does it help us in such questions as occur to us! I wish to know whether I may seek sensual pleasure; whether I may tell a flattering lie.
>
> I ask, Will it increase or diminish the Sum of Human Happiness to do so? This mode of putting the question cannot help me. How can I know whether these acts will increase or diminish the Sum of Human Happiness?[7]

Whewell had a point – but he was not likely to submit his own equation of happiness with virtue to the same kind of scrutiny. In morals as in science, Whewell believed that all must follow the same straight and narrow road and he was impatient with any attempt to leave what he saw as the main highway or to strike out on some essentially deviant and subversive path.

John Stuart Mill was not only one of the most influential thinkers of the high Victorian period, he was also the most persistent advocate of a secular point of view – a complex undertaking in an age when religious thinking continued to be powerful. Mill's own education had been such as to make religion the very last item on the intellectual agenda rather than, as was more common, the very first, and he was determined to struggle against all those who believed the truths of religion could be taken for granted. On the other hand Utilitarianism could not hope to achieve significant influence if it did not also become respectable, so Mill was prepared to make significant modifications to it in order to achieve this objective. As Mill saw it, the main stumbling blocks in the way of developing a field of scientific, rational, secular enquiry was what he called 'intuitionism', both as represented by the ideas of Whewell and, equally importantly, by the philosophy of Sir William Hamilton. Hamilton's reputation was made by a series of articles that appeared in the *Edinburgh Review* between 1829 and 1836, and his authority was such that Mill felt obliged to publish his critique of Hamilton's philosophy some thirty years later in 1865. Hamilton is now virtually unread and his enormous standing may therefore seem something of a puzzle. But Hamilton was a man who was formidably knowledgeable about the history of philosophy at a time when such expertise was extremely rare, and he was probably the only British philosopher (excluding, of course, Coleridge, whose claims to such a designation are somewhat problematic) who was well acquainted with such figures from the German philosophical tradition as Kant, Fichte and Schelling. Hamilton was often linked with Kant because of his insistence that things in themselves were ultimately unknowable and because he could be seen as stressing, in the manner of Kant, the power of the mind to organise experience, but the overall thrust of his philosophy was really quite different. Hamilton took a phenomenalist – or what was often described as a relativist – approach to our knowledge, whereby without denying that the external world was the cause of our sensations, he nevertheless insisted that these sensations were all that we could really know. He wrote:

> Our whole knowledge of mind and matter is relatively conditioned. Of things absolutely or in themselves, be they external, be they internal, we know nothing, or know them only as incognisable; and become aware of their incomprehensible existence only as this is indirectly and accidentally revealed to us through certain qualities related to our faculties of knowledge. . . . All that we know is, therefore, phenomenal – phenomenal of the unknown. The philosopher, speculating the worlds of matter and mind, is thus, in a certain sort, only an ignorant admirer.[8]

Hamilton's way of arguing left ample space for theological argument. For if there was much in the universe that lay beyond our ken, then a certain amount of humility was called for, and it could be argued that someone must be capable of such absolute (rather than man's relative) knowledge – and that person must be God. Hamilton also claimed that we could only know the world through processes of difference and comparison, but since the absolute, that is, God, could not be known in this way, he must lie beyond ordinary human cognition. Therefore there could be no question, as it were, of questioning God's existence. Hamilton was also disposed to use the word 'belief' to refer to man's relative mode of perception, which, Mill felt, tended to promote religious ways of thinking and arguing. Actually Mill himself, by defining matter as a 'Permanent Possibility of Sensation', conceded quite a lot to Hamilton's philosophical position, but at the same time he was anxious to insist that human knowledge and scientific activity did have real validity. He therefore saw Hamilton's work as presenting a challenge to the empiricist research programme.

The problem with the empiricist research programme, as adumbrated by Mill, however, was that it was daunting in the extreme. Following Locke, Mill suggested that our knowledge was derived by assembling comparing and contrasting innumerable atomic facts. There could be no short cuts or imaginative solutions. Human knowledge might be seen either as a giant castle of facts that had been carefully built up, brick by brick, or fact by fact. Alternatively it might be viewed as a gigantic necklace of facts, strung together on the chain of theory. For a theory to be true it would have to be a final, absolute knowledge that would be true for all facts or all conceivable facts, so that it could never be contraverted. For one who claims to be an empiricist Mill's view of scientific truth seems strangely theological and reminiscent of Sir Thomas Browne on predestination – 'a definitive blast of his will already fulfilled'. With Mill there seem to be no stages on the route to truth; no process of trial, error, of corroboration or disconfirmation. If truth is not complete, total and final it is virtually non-existent. At bottom it is the discovery of the computer as much as quantum physics that unravelled the empiricist dream, for we can now see that even if we had a supercomputer into which we could feed all known facts, we would still have to programme it, we would still have to tell it what to look for. Yet for the true empiricist such a prejudgement of the facts is heresy. It is characteristic of Mill that he is very anxious to downgrade the value of a hypothesis, precisely because it must necessarily be narrow, partial, tendentious. Hypotheses, Mill concedes, may have a certain limited value in suggesting possible experiments that may shed light on the real properties of the given phenomenon, but he adds:

> But to this end it is by no means necessary that the hypothesis be mistaken for scientific truth. On the contrary, that illusion is in this

respect, as in every other, an impediment to the progress of real knowledge, by leading inquirers to restrict themselves arbitrarily to the particular hypothesis which is most accredited at the time, instead of looking out for every class of phenomena between the laws of which and those of the given phenomena any analogy exists, and trying all such experiments as may tend to the discovery of ulterior analogies pointing in the same direction.[9]

On the face of it Mill's discussion here is fairly incomprehensible – why if one analogy is restrictive will this not apply to the others also, and why does he assume that they will point *in the same direction*? Presumably what Mill has in mind is Whewell's well-worn instance of Kepler and the orbit of Mars, and what he is suggesting is that Kepler's earlier conceptions may well have got in the way of the final analogy of an ellipse. But by discouraging analogy and frowning on trial and error, Mill only served to devalue the kind of untheological, empirical enquiry that he was allegedly trying to promote. Certainly Darwin's work could only seem a tower of fanciful speculation rather than a well-built fortress of knowledge from a Millian point of view.

If Mill's struggle against any alliance between science and theology was unremitting but not altogether successful, his intervention in the field of ethics was a great deal more conciliatory. His development of the principles of Utilitarianism, which he inherited from Bentham and his father, was designed to resist any implication that Utilitarianism was crude, immoral or impractical. Mill's most significant departure from classical Utilitarianism was to admit the distinction between higher and lower pleasures that Bentham had always denied. As we know from the vital role that the poetry of Wordsworth fulfilled in helping Mill out of his own spiritual crisis, which the Utilitarian creed had largely induced, Mill had strong personal reasons for resisting Bentham's refusal to distinguish between the pleasures of pushpin and poetry; but in making this crucial concession he blunted the challenge that Utilitarianism presented to traditional ethics. For Utilitarianism, in the tradition of Hobbes, presented itself as an analysis of human behaviour as it actually was rather than as it theoretically ought to be. Instead of endlessly recommending virtue, the moralist had to begin with the recognition that human beings sought pleasure and tried to avoid pain. You had to think of happiness itself as constituting a positive good. Moreover for Bentham pleasure was by no means an empty word. Not the least of his criticisms of Christianity was that it was a religion that both promoted hypocrisy and, in its habitual asceticism, positively proscribed pleasure. In particular Bentham was not afraid to describe sexual pleasure as the 'highest enjoyment' that life could offer. Yet of three crucial words in the Utilitarian lexicon – desire, pleasure and happiness – Mill undoubtedly found pleasure the most embarrassing. Instead of challenging Christian antagonists in their habitual talk of 'animal pleasures', which invariably led to diatribes against the sin of fornication, Mill in his famous formulation 'It is better to be a human being satisfied than a pig satisfied; better to be Socrates dissatisfied than a fool satisfied', effectively conceded the argument and made his peace with Victorian prudery.

Moreover such a denial of the body has far-reaching social implications, for it can lead to the conclusion that the physical hardship and material deprivation that the majority of people in Victorian society suffered from is not something that can be placed on the ethical agenda. Mill to his credit *did* want to place this on the agenda but by acquiescing in the point of view of his opponents he sacrificed an important dimension of his argument. Furthermore the recognition that pleasures cannot readily be equated has a corollary that they cannot easily be hierarchised. Once we start ranking them in this way we are not merely refusing to acknowledge their extraordinary range, complexity and diversity (which is after all part of the point of disagreeing with Bentham), but are also refusing to acknowledge the fact that pleasure is a highly subjective matter. Mill himself writes at one point: 'The ingredients of happiness are very various, and each of them is desirable in itself, and not merely when considered as swelling an aggregate' (33–4). But he does not allow this to modify his overall argument.

We must also recognise, however, that Mill was not simply concerned to make Utilitarian principles more palatable but to extend and transform them through a complex dialectic of development. Like Whewell, Mill believed that there had been and would continue to be progress in morals. In effect Mill was prepared to believe, following Hobbes, that in the earliest stages of society men had pursued their own narrow self-interest to the exclusion of everything else, but he wanted to demonstrate that such self-interest could nevertheless be transformed into the acknowledgement of a collective interest and even into altruistic behaviour, that from such primordial beginnings even relatively sophisticated values such as virtue and justice could result, and be themselves actively desired.

Moreover such a view of progressive moral development also underpins Mill's theory of government, for Mill not only defined 'Conduciveness to Progress' as constituting the 'whole excellence of government' (190) but also saw representative government as a powerful instrument of moral improvement:

> In all states of human improvement ever yet attained, the nature and degree of authority ever yet attained, the nature and degree of authority exercised over individuals, the distribution of power, and the conditions of command and obedience, are the most powerful of the influences, except their religious belief, which makes them what they are, and enables them to become what they can be. (197)

Part of the paradox of Mill's argument, therefore, is that despite a moral strenuousness that insists each individual shall calculate his or her actions so as to promote the greatest happiness, it nevertheless seems that virtue is no longer solely a matter for individuals – mankind will become more moral and more virtuous largely as the result of the irreversible process of world history and through the conscious creation of governments.

What is radical in Utilitarianism is precisely the fact that since, in Bentham, it is bound up with a legislative and administrative perspective, it is perhaps the first ethical system to address directly questions of government policy, to begin with the consequences for society as a whole rather than with the motives of an individual. When Mill is discussing questions of justice he seems to assume that the greatest happiness principle is some kind of super-standard that can adjudicate a variety of ethical principles – and in a way he is right. The Utilitarian perspective, by speaking frankly in terms of consequences for the majority, does actually make is possible to discriminate between a variety of courses of action in ways that would otherwise be impossible, and although we may not always be conscious of it has implicitly figured in a whole range of twentieth-century controversies. For instance, although happiness as such may not have a great deal to do with it, the saturation bombing of Dresden and the dropping of atomic bombs on Hiroshima and Nagasaki were justified at the time on the grounds that these actions would actually save lives by bringing the war to an end more speedily. In a wholly different context, it can be argued that the benefit to contemporary society derived from cheaper aerosols does not justify long-term damage to the ozone layer, or that a few should not benefit from the destruction of vast areas of the Brazilian rain-forest when the consequences for many others are so serious. Again, the greatest happiness principle can be used to adjudicate questions of spending on the National Health Service or in the field of education. In *Utilitarianism* itself, one of Mill's most telling arguments was to point to 'the present wretched education, and wretched social arrangements', and to insist 'utility includes not solely the pursuit of happiness, but the prevention or mitigation of unhappiness' (12).

In saying this, however, I am not suggesting that the greatest happiness principle is unchallengeable, only that it has introduced an important perspective that we cannot ignore. Equally it is clear that there remain powerful moral imperatives that cannot necessarily be suppressed or swallowed up in such a calculus: we may argue that the environment must be preserved and that the mass destruction of cities is morally wrong. Yet even here we would have to recognise there would be quantitative implications to a moral judgement – it is above all *massive* destruction that provokes moral indignation. At the time few objected to ordinary run-of-the-mill bombing. Moreover while we might still want to object to the burning of the Brazilian rain-forest, if this had taken place on a considerably reduced scale it might not have had the same effect on the ozone layer. Mill seems to have individualised the greatest happiness principle when it would have had far more radical implications if he had been more determined to politicise it.

The work on which Mill's reputation finally rests, however, is *On Liberty* (1859). This essay is elegantly and carefully argued, yet is written with so much eloquence and conviction that it commands admiration and suspends dissent. It seems merely carping to complain that Mill is really saying nothing very new, that his attempt to distinguish public and private spheres is unsustainable, or that his position is essentially élitist. What surely matters is that Mill saw the need to argue forcefully and uncompromisingly for this one single principle when, both then and now, there have been all too many who, while paying lip-service to liberty in principle, have nevertheless been only to ready to sacrifice it in the face of other, more pressing considerations. Nevertheless *On Liberty* is a puzzling and problematic work because it is hard to understand what circumstances can have inspired the writing of it or given it its tone of mingled pessimism, urgency and qualified optimism. In the case of some of the classic works of political theory, by Hobbes, Locke and

Rousseau, it is not hard to connect them with a specific social and political context or to grasp the issues they tried to address. But with *On Liberty* the case is rather different. The problem that Mill addressed – the potential threat to freedom of discussion posed by a democratic society – was a largely hypothetical one. Only the United States could be regarded as a concrete instance of such a society, though Mill clearly viewed post-1832 England as an incipient democracy and saw it as sharing many of the same characteristics. Nevertheless we must wonder why Mill seemed more concerned at a possible threat to freedom of opinion with the realisation of a democratic society, when in much of the world that prospect was very far distant and the threat posed to such freedom by censorship in a variety of autocratic countries from France to Austria and Russia was very real. Is not this rather like worrying about the dangers of over-eating in some future world of plenty when the present actuality is one of starvation and malnutrition? The obvious answer to this, of course, is to reply that in the century or more since *On Liberty* was written Mill's fears about freedom of expression have proved to be well founded; we should therefore rather commend him for his insight than complain about his disposition to prophesy. But Mill's worry about such a future mass society was especially odd because he was in favour of democracy. It is one thing to deplore the prospect and oppose any extension of the franchise like Carlyle, and something quite else, when like Mill, you worry deeply about a development that you ostensibly welcome. Mill's misgivings about democracy can be traced back to the 1830s when he was associated with the *Westminster Review* and the Philosophical Radicals – a small group of reformers of a generally Benthamite persuasion. The Radicals and perhaps especially Mill's father, James Mill, had believed that in the struggles of reason against entrenched prejudice and tradition the people would be on the side of reason and would both follow and defer to their intellectual betters. But their hope of mobilising public opinion to shake the establishment was destroyed on two fronts. When Grey insisted that 1832 was not a halfway house but a final solution he isolated the small group of radicals from the majority opinion in Parliament. At the same time Chartism began to develop as a lower-class political movement, under its own independent leadership. Thus a guided democracy under the leadership of the best minds no longer seemed a possibility and the example of the United States suggested on the contrary that the bad currency would drive out the good. It can thus be argued that *On Liberty* is

Mill's attempt to come to terms with this and to lower his expectations: if the intellectuals cannot be philosopher kings, they have, at
the very least, the right to be heard. But we can measure Mill's
pessimism by the fact that he did not believe that even this could
be taken for granted. In *Utilitarianism* Mill referred favourably to a
state of affairs in which there would be more social and intellectual
unanimity:

> In an improving state of the human mind, the influences are
> constantly on the increase, which tend to generate in each indi-
> vidual a feeling of unity with all the rest; which, if perfect, would
> make him never think of, or desire, any beneficial condition for
> himself, in the benefits of which they are not included.   (30)

Yet in *On Liberty* he suggested more sombrely: 'the tendency of all
the changes taking place in the world is to strengthen society, and
diminish the power of the individual, this encroachment is not one
of the evils which tend spontaneously to disappear, but on the
contrary, to grow more and more formidable' (77).

Of course, there is no necessary contradiction. Mill feared the
possible relapse of Western societies into a stationary state in which
the existing arrangement would be so habitual as to become unquestionable: a more egalitarian and fraternal society might therefore
also be one that was lacking both in dynamism and the capacity for
self-criticism. But there again such a worry seems relatively recondite and Mill's real target seems to be something much more immediate – his sense that intolerance is natural to mankind, that collective mediocrity is the oppressive reality, and that 'public opinion
now rules the world' (123). It is the press above all that is responsible
for this deadly uniformity, but in *Representative Government* Mill sees
the existence of a free press as an essential safeguard of democratic
freedoms. The press may well be both at once, and we need not
stigmatise Mill for these differential emphases. What is disconcerting, however, in view of the care with which he generally formulates
his arguments, is that he sees no necessity for developing a more
connected analysis of its overall impact, especially if the press is as
important as Mill says it is. Again, the United States is Mill's exemplary instance of democracy in action and he leans heavily on de
Tocqueville's classic analysis of the tyranny of public opinion in
Democracy in America – yet this had appeared twenty years prior to
the writing of *On Liberty* and there were good reasons why Mill

might have reconsidered de Tocqueville's verdict. The United States was now deeply divided between north and south and was scarcely a good example of social unanimity, even if each section imposed a powerful consensus within it. Moreover the role of slavery within American culture raised important questions about the relationship between thought and action, about individual freedom and about the right of governments to constrain individuals that Mill could usefully have addressed. Yet he did not choose to do so. The paradox of *On Liberty* is that the moral indignation that informs it is clearly provoked by contemporary circumstances yet its argument stresses universal considerations and seems to focus more on past and future than on the immediate present.

While I am not disposed to deny that Mill was concerned by the possible threat to freedom of conscience posed by a future mass society or that the argument is primarily focused on the relationship between the individual and the state, I nevertheless feel that there is much that such an analysis omits. In my view, *On Liberty* contains a sometimes discreetly veiled, yet always powerful sub-text, which is an attack on established religion in general, and on the Anglican church in particular. As I have already suggested, Mill felt it was his mission to promote both Utilitarianism as a philosophy, and, as' a concomitant goal, the development of a secular society, yet he had not had very much success. Whewell and Hamilton seemed to have seen off any possible challenge of science to religion, and the controversies surrounding the Oxford Movement had made it seem that any threat to Anglicanism was a threat to England itself. If even Newman, who after all only tried to push a well-established and powerfully connected High Church ethos a little further in the direction of a *rapprochement* with Rome, was to be regarded as an enemy within, what hope was there for those who sought to resist the role of religion altogether? In *Utilitarianism*, which was published in *Fraser's Magazine* two years after *On Liberty*, Mill himself tried to validate his secular creed by writing: 'In the golden rule of Jesus of Nazareth, we read the complete spirit of the ethics of utility. To do as you would be done by, and to love your neighbour as yourself, constitutes the ideal perfection of utilitarian morality' (16).

Mill was always torn between the desire to be reasonable and conciliatory, to win converts by speaking the language of his opponents, and the somewhat vacillating desire to stand up to and challenge the cultural establishment. *On Liberty*, his boldest work, and in this respect undoubtedly written under the influence of Harriet

Taylor, was just such a challenge. For if, as Mill argued, England was indeed in the grip of a deadly consensus, it was scarcely enough to argue theoretically for the right to a heterodox point of view, what was called for was a challenge to that orthodoxy itself. I would claim that this is just what *On Liberty* is, even if its subversive implications are consciously muffled. What Mill sought to do was to start out with a value – liberty – to which no one could seriously object, but to develop and extend its implications in such a way that they would nevertheless prove unacceptable to the supporters of the cultural establishment. The ideological thrust of Mill's emphasis on the single principle of liberty was that though this was a principle to which everyone was prepared to pay lip-service, in practice it was one to which no spokesman for organised religion, whether Anglican, Methodist or Catholic, could genuinely subscribe.

Equally it is clear that Mill was deeply concerned at the unfair deal given to atheists and non-believers under the existing dispensation. It is significant that the most contemporary references in the text cite several cases in 1857 where such persons were unfairly treated by the law. Thomas Pooley was sentenced to twenty-one months imprisonment simply for writing some blasphemous words on a gate. George Holyoake and Edward Truelove were excluded from jury service because they did not profess any religious belief. The Baron de Gleichen was refused justice against a man who had robbed him for similar reasons. So Mill's argument against the state – 'All attempts by the state to bias the conclusions of its citizens on disputed subjects are evil' (162) – is not just an argument against the state, since Mill's secular state would have no opinions, but an argument against the power and authority of the state being used to support specific religious doctrines. Moreover Mill does not believe that religions can do without such coercive measures. It is true that Mill seems to support the idea of a religious education that is independent of the state but only because he believes it is relatively less harmful. Mill throws down the gauntlet of liberty to religions of whatever description precisely because he is confident that they will not be able to pick it up. Mill does not believe that the religiously minded will be prepared to subject their beliefs to an indefinite process of intellectual scrutiny and critical enquiry; but even if they are he is confident that such an interrogation will be fatal. Mill is confident that neither Anglicans, Catholics nor Methodists will feel able to subscribe to his ideal of diversity, derived from Wihelm von Humboldt, since such diversity would strike at the existence of all institutional structures and mean that every church could only have a membership of one. Liberty, as Mill conceives it, is too large for religion to swallow – even the greediest and most ambitious of theological pythons must perish in the attempt.

In his overall picture of man and history Mill was very much the child of the Enlightenment. He believed that the overall movement of history was progressive and that progress had manifested itself in the increased predominance of reason in human affairs. Everywhere reason was triumphing over superstition, prejudice and custom. Reason prospered under conditions of liberty, and, contrariwise, a society where reason flourished, as in the France of the *philosophes*, was also one that would be favourable to the development of personal and political liberty. In general, therefore, Mill was an optimist, though that optimism was tempered to some degree by his reading of de Tocqueville. But in view of the fact that an important part of Mill's argument for freedom of thought and discussion in *On Liberty* was connected with the prosecution of Thomas Pooley for writing some anti-Christian sentiments on a gate and with the penalties suffered by George Holyoake, Edward Truelove and Baron de Gleichen for refusing to swear on the Bible as to the truthfulness of their evidence, and in view of the fact that religion was the traditional enemy of reason as Mill understood it, Christianity nevertheless is handled with extraordinary leniency in his discussion. Mill suggests that in the past the arm of the law has been misguidedly employed 'to root out the best men and the noblest doctrines' (85), yet despite this the endeavour failed:

> Socrates was put to death, but the Socratic philosophy rose like the sun in heaven, and spread its illumination over the whole intellectual firmament. Christians were cast to the lions, but the Christian church grew up a stately and spreading tree, overtopping the older and less vigorous growths, and stifling them by its shade. (93)

This linking of Socrates and Jesus may seem obvious enough but in the overall context of Mill's argument it has some rather curious implications and repercussions. For one thing, whatever influence we may feel that Socrates has had in Western culture it is certainly very slight by comparison with Christianity. Moreover Mill's whole way of arguing is such as to suggest that ideas or beliefs that prevail do so in the long run because they are true; indeed Mill's very definition of progress involves the multiplication of such accepted truths: 'As mankind improves, the number of doctrines which are no longer disputed or doubted will be constantly on the increase: and the well-being of mankind may almost be measured by the number and gravity of the truths which have reached the point of being uncontested' (103). This is, of course, reason's eye view of history and it is to be sharply contrasted with the tendency he deplores: 'the fatal tendency of mankind to leave off thinking about a thing when it is no longer doubtful, is the cause of half their errors' (103).

But what exactly is Mill saying? Presumably doctrines that are no longer disputed or doubted and taken to be true will, by Mill's own definition, not be doubted, but if this is so, is not this a fatal error? Mill would no doubt want to differentiate between doctrines that have been subjected to the most stringent tests that reason is capable of and those that simply persist on the say so of the eminent and because they have never been critically examined at all. The distinction is between ideas that have been brought before the bar of human reason and those that have not. But where does Mill stand with regard to Christianity? In fact he wants to have it both ways. He wants to criticise Christianity and defend the right of atheists and freethinkers to attack it, but at the same time he wants to imply that the suppression of Christianity was an early instance of the suppression of truth. But if Mill, though respecting Jesus as a moral thinker, is nevertheless suspicious of Christianity and its claims, then it is really rather strange of him to cite its historical triumph as something admirable. If Mill is a rationalist he should assess the truth of doctrines on their own merits and not evaluate them by their comparative success or failure. This kind of historicism also makes a nonsense of Mill's argument about freedom of discussion as Mill himself recognises when he emphasises that truths have not always prevailed over persecution. The convenient citation of Jesus and Socrates and of Marcus Aurelius begins to seem distinctly awkward and double-edged since these examples actually seem to show that persecution does not hinder the spread of ideas and may actually help to disseminate them. They also serve to highlight the fact that Mill finds it handy to assume that a truthful idea is a successful one, without considering the social processes that operate upon them. Moreover if Mill believes that the mass of mankind are naturally intolerant, we must wonder quite what is the purpose of his essay. Is he self-consciously and fruitlessly arguing a case that he actually knows will never be accepted?

The strange consequences for Mill's argument that ensue from his reliance on a particular kind of historical determinism are also evident in his discussion of the question of individuality in modern cultures. For Mill, following de Tocqueville, the very idea of the individual is under threat. On this analysis in democratic societies, such as the United States, no one wishes to contract the solid majority, nor would it even occur to them to do so:

> Thus the mind itself is bowed to the yoke: even in what people do for pleasure, conformity is the first thing thought of; they like in crowds; they exercise choice only among things commonly done: peculiarity: peculiarity of taste, eccentricity of conduct, are affirmed equally with crimes: until by dint of not following their own nature they have no nature to follow: their human capacities are withered and starved: they become incapable of any strong wishes or native pleasures, and are generally without either opinions or feelings of home growth, or properly their own.   (119)

It is this analysis that gives a distinct poignancy to Mill's epigraph to *On Liberty* from Wilhelm von Humboldt: 'the absolute and essential importance of human development in its richest diversity', since von Humboldt advocates and believes in it, whereas Mill advocates it but does not really believe in it. Diversity will *not* characterise future societies, which will indeed have grown incapable of it; the only question is whether a handful of exceptional individuals, geniuses in fact, can keep the flame alive. But even here there is a problem since while genius may still possess the capacity to think differently it may no longer possess the self-confidence to set itself up in opposition: 'the amount of eccentricity in a society has generally been proportional to the amount of genius, mental vigour, moral courage it contained. That so few now dare to be eccentric marks the chief danger of the time' (125). In the ancient world and in the Middle Ages 'the individual was a power in himself'; today 'individuals are lost in the crowd' (123).

But if Mill is right, then his demand for freedom of discussion is in vain because while the social, political and legal remit will be there, the impulse that once produced controversy, the force of will that once instigated it – as Luther once nailed his theses to the door at Wittenberg – will be lacking. We should also note that Mill's determination to polarise the idea of controversy around the notions of reviled and uncomprehended genius show a distinct lack of faith in the idea of freedom of discussion that he himself advocates. For the genius is a beacon of truth in a world of darkness, so there is actually no real perception that divergences of opinion can be productive or that truth may not necessarily be the property of one side in the argument, even though Mill in other places in the text puts this forward as one of the fundamental reasons why freedom of discussion is crucial. But, of course, much of our misapprehension of Mill stems from the banal assumption that he is issuing some kind of clarion call, whereas he was doing little more that repeat the commonplaces of his day. Victorians believed there *was* freedom of discussion, even though the working classes were largely excluded from it. In an age ruled and dominated by élites, Mill sought to defend such élites from a presumed and hypothetical threat to their power – which is hardly a very radical position. With hindsight we can see the parallels between Mill's position and the law of copyright introduced by Sergeant Talfoord. Ideas are to be viewed as the private property of individuals and this property must be defended at all costs, because what is at stake is simultaneously capitalism and individualism. There is an unwillingness to recognise that ideas (that is, ideologies) may be connected to specific social groups, and a comparable unwillingness to consider the fact that ideas may have far-reaching social consequences or that they may be politically destabilising – which is why, for one thing, Mill is puzzled that Marcus Aurelius should have been bothered by Christianity. Mill criticises Christianity as a 'doctrine of passive obedience', yet in reality he has no sympathy whatsoever with doctrines that question or challenge state power. Mill defends a freedom of discussion that will be uncontroversial, without consequences, impotent. He looks back nostalgically to the open and fearless characters of the past, yet in the present he would almost certainly find them irrational, absurdly dogmatic, obsessively concerned to provoke conflict and social disruption. Mill admired frank and fearless characters precisely because he himself hesitated to challenge Victorian orthodoxy even when it was his moral duty to do so. Deep down he knew that *power* was the real issue, yet he advocated freedom of discussion in terms that notably failed to address it. In the final analysis Mill fails to say what he needs to say but defends to the very death his own right to say it – presuming he had!

The whole of Victorian intellectual life was significantly modified and reconstructed through the lengthy and protracted debates that took place first over Lyell's geological speculations that the Earth must be older than had previously been assumed by many millions of years, and secondly over Darwin's hypothesis that species had developed over a corresponding period due to the effects of 'natural selection'. What needs to be stressed above all about such debates was the way they engaged the interest and curiosity not only of the educated middle-class public but also the way in which such issues also came to the forefront in the development of colleges and educational programmes designed for working men. Yet what equally needs to be emphasised is that in practice such disputes could not be easily adjudicated or resolved. This was not simply because of the intellectual complexity of the issues, though that was considerable, or even because of the lack of obvious ways by which their validity could be confirmed or denied; but because the world of science was still essentially one of learned amateurs, where the problem was not so much that of shaking the received wisdom, as so many accounts of Darwinism might lead one to believe, but rather the difficulty of reaching a clear and undisputed consensus. Indeed this very problem can shed some light on the whole strange 'conflict' that took place between science and religion. As Owen Chadwick has emphasised, many clergymen were well disposed towards new scientific thinking and James Moore has described how the notion of a developing warfare between them was largely promoted in the United States by such works as John Draper's *History of the Conflict between Religion and Science* and Andrew Dickson White's *The Warfare of Science*.[10] In fact science and religion frequently had a mutually supportive relationship. Many notable scientists, including of course Darwin himself, were clergymen, and from the seventeenth century onwards there was a persistent tendency to see the universe as stable and rule governed, subject to laws that were simultaneously the laws of God and the laws of science. In particular there was resistance to the idea that God found it necessary or desired to intervene repeatedly in the universe that he had created. Science and religion, of a Protestant kind, could agree in finding the belief in miracles neither sound religion nor plausible science. The same general arguments could be applied to the notion that each species was specially created, a position repeatedly criticised by Darwin in the *Origin of Species*. It could seem more consistent with the grandeur of God that he created the universe through a small number of fundamental principles than that he should have been constantly engaged in tinkering with the whole system. It seemed more theological to think of God as a mathematician than to conceive of him as some kind of insatiable inventor who could never stop fiddling with his universe or leave well alone. So there was much in Darwin's argument that was altogether consistent with the general direction in which the Victorian church was moving. I would want to argue that the relationship between science and religion needs to be seen much more in terms of a struggle for position and influence by such scientific intellectuals as Huxley. Huxley wanted to be accepted as part of the cultural establishment and knew that he could only achieve this if he first played the part of the turbulent priest. But the challenge to religion was also strategically useful because the scientific controversy was being so endlessly prolonged that there seemed little prospect of resolving it. Yet if 'science' could not speak authoritatively – and here we must note Huxley's desire to preach 'Lay Sermons' and construct a 'Church of Science' – then it could not hope to wield the influence in Victorian society that Huxley believed it should. We may also note that Darwin came from an affluent family and was therefore not obliged to support himself in any way, whereas Huxley needed to obtain an income from his scientific work and scientific writings. He therefore thought of himself as a professional in a way that Darwin did not. Huxley's conflicts and controversies with churchmen and other scientists were designed to promote science as some new and more powerful form of truth and this claim could be made the more effectively in the public arena than it could in a purely scientific context, where victories were not only less easily won, but it often seemed doubtful if they could ever be won at all.

If there is one thing about Darwin's *theory* that we are most often prone to forget it is that in his own day it was most often regarded as a hypothesis, even by those who were sympathetically disposed towards it. Thus John Stuart Mill, who was at the time the leading philosopher of science, described Darwin's 'remarkable speculation' on the origin of species as an 'inimpeachable example of a legitimate hypothesis' but he immediately went on to emphasise that he could not be expected to be governed by the rules of induction and proof, since 'Mr Darwin has never pretended that his doctrine was proved.' Darwin's real achievement was to make what at first seemed an extraordinary and improbable conjecture 'admissible and discussable', but nevertheless as conjecture not fact.[11] The real advantages of Darwin's hypothesis were not scientific at all. Darwin offered a series of extremely bold and original conjectures about the origins and development of life on Earth that had the power to appeal to the popular imagination, yet this was at the same time an argument developed in a careful and copiously illustrated way, using arguments from the breeding of pigeons and other domesticated plants and creatures, which seemed the more plausible because of their very homeliness and familiarity. Moreover what gave Darwin's argument added conviction was the fact that it fitted in so well with other ideas of the time. If Darwin agreed with Lyell, that made both men seem that much more convincing, and when Darwin saw eye to eye with Malthus and the classical economists on life as a struggle for existence he reinforced population theory and classical economics as much as those disciplines lent weight to his interpretation of biology. Although the consequences of Darwin's arguments were far reaching and might for some be difficult to accept, the arguments themselves fitted into the intellectual context of their day like a red leather chair into the lounge of a London club. They blended into the background.

Nevertheless there were real obstacles to the acceptance of Darwin's style of argument. The most important and most obvious of these was that Darwin placed the activities of the plant breeder and the pigeon fancier at the centre of his picture of the transmission of species and baldly denied that there was any real difference between a variation and a species. In many ways this was Darwin's boldest argumentative move because he knew that by simply asserting this and by implying that the distinction between them was essentially a metaphysical one he had, as it were, already got the door open and from there on it was simply a matter of maintaining a firm and continuous pressure. Yet while it might seem obvious to a modern biologist that all species must once have been variations as Darwin claimed, to Darwin's contemporaries it seemed as if Darwin was trying to shrug aside the massive weight of evidence against him: on the one hand the fact that no evidence of such variations or intermediate species could be found in the geological record; on the other that there was equally abundant evidence of the extraordinary persistence and stability of the known species and the well-known fact that the vast majority of all hybrids were sterile. Against this Darwin claimed that the geological record was incomplete and that further evidence might yet be found but his strongest argument appeared to be the appeal to the enormous span of historical time, which Lyell's researches had opened up. Although the production of wholly new species might seem implausible in the short term, given such a colossal time frame it was surely reasonable to conclude that just as rock formations might be worn down by the erosion of centuries, so too must the cumulative effect of many small variations eventually add up to something far more significant. Yet in reality this assumption was one of the weakest points in Darwin's whole argument. In the first place it meant that Darwin's hypothesis, by his own admission, was virtually unverifiable because of the aeons that must elapse before all the evidence itself was in. Moreover because Darwin insisted on the complexity of the processes at work and the multiplicity of factors involved:

> Throw up a handful of feathers, and all must fall to the ground according to definite laws; but how simple is this problem compared to the action and reaction of the innumerable plants and animals which have determined, in the course of centuries, the proportional numbers and kinds of trees now growing on the old Indian ruins.[12]

it was therefore obvious that there could be no real possibility of making predictions, which was one of the most obvious ways in which a scientific theory could be validated. Indeed Darwin's style of writing – indeed its most characteristic and eloquent moments – invites the reader to wonder rather than to calculate, to marvel at the countless miracles that Nature ceaselessly generates, albeit by a process of natural selection. A further problem with the small variations was to understand how a species could drive out an 'inferior' predecessor if its competitive advantage was so slight. It was easy enough to believe that in the struggle for existence the strong would prevail over the weak, but much harder to see how the very marginally more strong should prevail over the only very marginally less strong. Again, as Darwin's critics hastened to point out, the new variation, being a minority, would much more likely be overwhelmed or genetically swamped by the more numerous if slightly less advantageous variation. The most powerful and subtle critique of Darwin's hypothesis, and the one that most disconcerted Darwin himself, was that advanced by Fleeming Jenkin. As Jenkin recognised, although Darwin was ostensibly opposed to teleological thinking and had down his utmost to eliminate it from his argument for natural selection, Darwin nevertheless did think teleologically in assuming that variation would accumulate and reinforce a certain tendency in nature; his belief that small variations would eventually have a cumulative effect posited not only directionality but actually a capacity for this that far surpassed the obviously motivated efforts of the domestic breeder. Jenkin writes:

Experience with domestic animals and cultivated plants shows that great variability exists. Darwin calls special attention to the difference between the various fancy pigeons, which, he says, are descended from one stock; between various breeds of cattle and horses, and some other domestic animals. He states that these differences are greater than those which induce some naturalists to class many specimens as distinct species. These differences are infinitely small as compared with the range required by this theory, but he assumes that by accumulation of successive differences any degree of variation may be produced; he says little in proof of the possibility of such an accumulation, seeming rather to take for granted that if Sir John Sebright could with pigeons produce in six years a certain head and beak of say half the bulk possessed by the original stock, then in twelve years this bulk could be reduced to a quarter, in twenty-four to an eighth, and so farther. Darwin probably never believed or intended to teach so extravagant a proposition, yet by substituting a few myriad of years for that poor period of six years, we obtain a proposition fundamental to his theory. That theory rests on the assumption that natural selection can do slowly what man's selection does quickly; it is by showing how much man can do, that Darwin hopes to prove how much can be done without him. But if man's selection cannot double, treble, quadruple, centuple, any special divergence from a parent stock, why should we imagine that natural selection should have that power? When we have granted that the 'struggle for life' might produce the pouter or the fantail, or any divergence man can produce, we need not feel one whit the more disposed to grant that it can produce divergences beyond man's power. The difference between six years and six myriads, binding by a confused sense of immensity, leads men to say hastily that if six or sixty years can make a pouter out of a common pigeon, six myriads may change the pigeon to something like a thrush; but this seems no more accurate than to conclude that because we observe that a cannon-ball will traverse a mile in a minute, therefore in an hour it will be sixty miles off, and in the course of ages that it will reach the fixed stars.[13]

Of course, Jenkin's imagery has its rhetorical force just as Darwin's does. Darwin implies that given world enough and time enough the apparent fixity of species is only an illusion; Jenkin that there are inherent laws operating in the natural world that prevent any single tendency getting out of control. The idea of a quantum leap is unnatural. Yet the irony of this aspect of Darwin's argument is that it is implicitly theological, for though he progressively lost his own Christian faith, he significantly invokes the powers of God in the celebrated passage in which he compares the eye with a telescope and subsequently argues:

> In living bodies, variation will cause the alterations, generation will multiply them almost infinitely, and natural selection will pick out with unerring skill each improvement. Let this process go on for millions and millions of years; and during each year on millions of individuals of many kinds; and may we not believe that a living optical instrument might thus be formed as superior to one of glass, as the works of the creator are to those of man?[14]

Once again this was a bold argumentative move on Darwin's part, since the complexity of the eye was precisely adduced by Darwin's critics as a compelling reason why natural selection could not possibly achieve all that it was supposed to. But Darwin implied that anything human selection could do, natural selection could do *better*, both because it had more time at its disposal but also because it could be seen as fulfilling the divine purpose. As Darwin originally saw it, the quantum leaps of nature could scarcely be doubted since they demonstrated the power and the grandeur of God.

If it was somewhat troubling to be regularly reminded that the *Origin of Species* was a speculative hypothesis, this nevertheless had its advantages in that it was therefore that much more difficult to disprove. Indeed Darwin clearly adopted the position that while he would listen to what his critics had to say, he would only regard their comments as marginal to his argument. He never for one moment thought that it could be falsified. Again, since Darwin recognised that so many different factors were in operation, of which natural selection was only one, it was hard to pin him down to any categorical assertion or to evade the charge of wilfully perverting and simplifying his argument. Moreover despite the morally evaluative language that Darwin employed his argument involved circularity and more than a whiff of Pope's 'whatever is, is right': those species that survived did so because they were the more able to do so.

Yet if this is a platitude it is also one that verges on untruth, for with this emphasis Darwin seems to lose sight of his own emphasis elsewhere that 'fitness' is not an absolute but has to be understood in relation to a particular ecological environment and in terms of finding a specific ecological niche. He suggests quite happily that most British species are innately superior to those to be found in New Zealand – an argument with a distinctly colonialist ring. Darwin speaks moralistically of natural selection 'rejecting that which is bad, preserving and adding up all that is good',[15] yet it is hard to see how this language applies to the flightless insects of Madeira, which are selected because those with wings would be blown away, or to his fantasy of a bear catching flies in the river that might eventually turn into a whale. This latter speculation represents the kind of argument that Darwinians habitually ridicule in Lamarck, but it is actually important for Darwin's case as a way of trying to explain how creatures can eventually be modified by their environment. But if Darwin thus seems to be claiming that 'anything goes', it is that much harder to view the *Origin of Species* as a network of undeviating and inexorable laws.

What becomes increasingly evident in retrospect is that the controversy over the *Origin of Species* was not one in which impeccable scientific reasoning confronted emotional and woolly appeals to the sanctity of Holy Writ, but one in which the scientific proponents of evolution were as prone to use rhetoric and special pleading as their opponents. In this connection the intellectual position of T. H. Huxley, 'Darwin's Bulldog', is especially curious. Despite the fact that Huxley made himself a massive reputation as the belligerent advocate of the new scientific thinking and though he did as much as anyone to suggest that the scientific knowledge would drive forward as inexorably as waves upon the shore despite the puny and ineffectual attempts of latter-day Canutes to stop it, it is nevertheless remarkable that Huxley did *not* accept natural selection as the mechanism by which species had evolved. In the context of scientific controversy the idea of evolution itself was not new. It had been propounded by Erasmus Darwin, Goethe, Lamarck and Chambers, while as Huxley himself pointed out, the theory of natural selection based on the idea of the survival of the fittest had already been suggested by Wells in 1813 and again in greater detail by Matthew in 1831. Yet just as Alfred Russell Wallace, co-propounder of the hypothesis with

Darwin, had doubts about natural selection, so too did Huxley. In his first comments on the *Origin* in 1859 he suggested that the only proper attitude to take towards it was 'active doubt', and in his 1860 review he stated quite categorically that:

> It is our clear conviction that, as the evidence stands, it is not absolutely proven that a group of animals, having all the characters exhibited by species in Nature, has ever been originated by selection, whether artificial or natural. Groups having the morphological character of species – distinct and permanent races in fact – have been so produced over and over again; but there is not positive evidence, at present, that any group of animals has by variation and selective breeding given rise to another group which was, even in the least degree, infertile with the first.[16]

In fact Huxley, the 'supporter' of Darwin, shared most of the reservations about the principle of natural selection of Darwin's opponents. Huxley was not convinced that the variations produced by selective breeding could necessarily be produced in Nature, and like some of Darwin's adversaries he was wary of the implication that Nature could 'select' in broadly comparable fashion. He felt that the infertility of many natural species with one another was not consistent with evidence of species changes under the circumstances of domestication. Consequently this did appear to create difficulties for Darwin's argument. In 'Man's Place in Nature' he wrote:

> But for all this, our acceptance of the Darwinian hypothesis must be provisional so long as one link in the chain of evidence is wanting: and as long as all the animals and plants certainly produced by selective breeding from a common stock are fertile and their progeny are fertile with one another, that link will be wanting. For, so long, selective breeding will not be proved to be competent to do all that is required of it to produce natural species.[17]

In addition to this Huxley was doubtful about Darwin's argument that new species were brought about by the accumulation of small variations. Although Huxley never actually said so, his reservations on this point may well have stemmed from his recognition of the teleological implications of such a position, since he was always very severe on teleological arguments and indeed believed – or purported to believe – that Darwinism provided the strongest possible arguments against them:

> For the teleologist an organism exists because it was made for the conditions in which it is found; for the Darwinian an organism exists because, out of many of its kind, it is the only one which has been able to persist in the conditions in which it is found.[18]

Darwinism could be used to refute Paley's analogy between man and an accidentally discovered watch, which were held to offer similar evidence of deliberate contrivance and design. So Huxley was disposed to steer clear of Darwin's accumulation of variations to suggest that 'Nature does make jumps now and then, and a recognition of the fact is of no small importance in disposing of many minor objections to the doctrine of transmutation.'[19]

Huxley simply threw this out in passing and subsequently was disposed to repeat it, but in so doing he never seems to have acknowledged that such a shift in emphasis was theoretically so highly significant that not merely did it mark out a divergence from Darwin but could even be regarded as an alternative theory. Huxley was alluding to the well-documented existence of 'sports' in domesticated breeding but he never addressed either Darwin's own reasons for rejecting radical jumps and discontinuities or those of Fleeming Jenkin. Huxley's argument was maintained on the easiest of terms, as part of a Victorian mode of pontificating that he, above all, was to make his own, despite the insistence on scientific rigour that was also so much a part of his style. We should also add that though, in public, Darwin was the esteemed and august master whose praises he never ceased to sing, Huxley privately felt that Darwin's rambling and high-level style of argument fell far short of total scientific demonstration – indeed in the early days he virtually said as much when he referred to the *Origin* as 'a mass of facts crushed and pounded into shape, rather than held together by the ordinary medium of an obvious logical bond; due attention will, without doubt, discover this bond, but it is often hard to find'.[20] Huxley's constant reference to the difficulty of the *Origin of Species*, while perhaps designed to favour his own role as an interpreter, does seem to reflect his own genuine feeling that Darwin's argument was neither completely clear nor readily disentangleable from the 'evidence' with which it was intertwined.

So the puzzle we are left with is why Huxley, who seems to have had almost as many reservations about the *Origin of Species* as its opponents, should nevertheless have become the book's most prominent advocate and defender? Was Huxley insincere? Did he suppress his own doubts and reservations in the interests of science in general and his own career? Certainly Huxley was acutely conscious of the difficulties of making a living out of science in mid-Victorian England. He wrote:

> My opportunity for seeing the scientific world in England forces upon me every day a stronger and stronger conviction. It is that there is no chance of living by science. . . . There are not more than four or five offices in London which a Zoologist or Comparative Anatomist can hold and live by. Owen, who has a European reputation, second only to Cuvier, gets as Hunterian Professor 300 a year! which is less than the salary of many a bank clerk.[21]

Without being cynical it is nevertheless easy to imagine that Huxley saw that he could only hope to establish himself through the patronage of a senior and well-respected scientific figure such as Darwin, and he must have believed that his own work on the comparative morphology of species would both be supportive of Darwinism and in turn be enhanced and confirmed by it. We may also note that Huxley was clearly envious of Owen's prestige. Huxley's demonstration of affinities between the skull of the ape and that of man, which Owen had denied, was both the moment that made his own reputation and destroyed Owen's but also marked one of the most significant triumphs of Darwinian theory since it was one of the few instances where an appeal to the evidence was clear-cut and decisive. So for all his reservations Huxley undoubtedly saw Darwinism as an expanding research programme that it would be advantageous to be associated with. In any event, Huxley perceived the arguments over natural selection and evolution in his own very characteristic way. As far as he was concerned the question was whether all species had been specially and separately created or whether they had been produced by 'transmutation', as he was always disposed to formulate it. The former view was inconsistent with the scientific evidence; the latter had at first been urged by figures such as Lamarck and Chambers whose arguments were too eccentric to be taken entertained by the scientific community. But with Darwin, a reputable scientist who staked out the province of his argument with extreme caution, the case for transmutation had to be taken seriously. What Huxley welcomed in Darwin was the emphasis on the normal occurrence of fortuitous variations from a basic type. Moreover as a student of morphology and a comparative anatomist, Huxley was not really interested in the precise historical working out of some evolutionary narrative.

Huxley himself prefers to argue through the demonstration of structural resemblances, vividly brought home through the use of illustration, as in the ascending order of skeletons from gibbon, orang-utan and chimpanzee through the gorilla to man, or a pile of primate skulls arranged in rank order. In his contribution to *The Life and Letters of Charles Darwin* Huxley wrote of his attitude prior to the publication of the *Origin*:

> I took my stand upon two grounds: firstly, that up to that time the evidence in favour of transmutation was wholly insufficient; and secondly, that no suggestion respecting the causes of the transmutation assumed, which had been made, was in any way adequate to explain the phenomena.[22]

While the first statement does bring out why Darwin's work was genuinely important for Huxley, the second is somewhat disingenuous as it is actually doubtful whether Huxley really thought that natural selection was adequate either. Huxley simply felt that what Darwin had written was good enough to be going on with and that what really mattered was to raise the status of science and the scientist and to promote the importance of scientific thinking. While scientists themselves needed to be sceptical, it was simultaneously necessary that their views should be deferred to by the general public. Part of the reason why Huxley was never much concerned to defend the principle of natural selection, apart from the fact that it was difficult for him to do so because he did not believe in it, was his realisation that this would have the effect of putting science on the defensive and of taking the debate into complex areas where the issues could not be definitely resolved and where a popular audience could not follow. Rather Huxley's way – and this goes a long way to explain the 'conflict between science and religion', such as it was – was to take the battle to his opponents. Huxley would question the merit of using the Old Testament as a source of scientific knowledge, point to problems in the arguments for special creation and then suggest that science was a more reliable guide. For Huxley the scientific world-view with its scepticism and demand for evidence and proofs was infallible, even if particular scientific theories were not. Yet Huxley's arguments fell far short of the claims he made for such a scientific world view. In his 1860 article on the *Origin of Species* in response to the cogent argument that 'there is no real analogy between selection which takes place under domestication by human influence and any operation which can be effected by Nature, for man interferes intelligently',[23] the best Huxley can manage is to appeal to the miraculous: 'Mix salt and sand, and it shall puzzle the wisest of men, with his mere natural appliances, to separate all the grains of salt from all the grains of sand; but a shower of rain will effect the same object in ten minutes.'[24] Both Huxley and Darwin implicitly reply on the argument that Nature, like God, works in a mysterious and purposive way and are as happy as Paley simply to invoke a sense of wonder that this should be so. What needs to be stressed is that what made their arguments credible to the contemporary public was just this and not any supposed hardheaded reasonableness of science – though of course the belief that science *was* hard-headed and reasonable undoubtedly helped.

Whereas John Stuart Mill's thinking develops out of and in response to English philosophical and cultural traditions, George Eliot's attitude to England and English culture was much more ambivalent and complex. The writing of the French woman novelist Georges Sand and the findings of German biblical scholarship loomed large in her own personal intellectual universe and she could not but be aware of the provinciality and narrowness of many of her contemporaries. Yet at the same time provinciality had very positive connotations for George Eliot. She was deeply attached to the people and landscape of Warwickshire, where she was brought up, and she valued and respected the complex ties that bound people to their fellow human beings and their customary environment. Unlike Mill, George Eliot received a narrow and censorious religious upbringing from which she was emancipated through her association with the free-thinking industrialist, Charles Bray. Through her translations of David Strauss's *Life of Jesus* (1846) and Ludwig Feuerbach's *The Essence of Christianity* she became the medium through which unorthodox new ideas on the subject of Christianity reached Britain. Strauss went through the New Testament in scrupulous and exhaustive detail, pointing out all the many implausibilities, contradictions and inconsistencies both in the various biblical narratives and in their relationship to one another. After he had finished it would never again be possible to believe that the Gospels were literally true or even that they contained much truth at all. Feuerbach, a disciple of Hegel, suggested that man had become alienated by projecting all his finest qualities onto the idea of God; he could regain his dignity and self-respect only by acknowledging that what he had hitherto regarded as divine was actually *human*. Instead of reverencing God, we must reverence man. Feuerbach's influence on George Eliot's 'religion of humanity' has often been commented upon but the influence of Strauss was almost equally significant. For Strauss always insisted that he was not a rationalist and his intention was not so much to debunk the biblical stories but to understand what motivated them. This was the goal of his mythological analysis. As Strauss saw it, the composers of the books of the New Testament were haunted by the Old and by the obligation to confirm Jesus as the true Messiah. Far from being original narratives they were compelled to repeat and confirm what had been said of old. So Jesus's birth to a virgin, Mary, was dictated by the need to fulfil a prophecy that the Messiah would be born in just such a way. The miracle of the loaves and fishes demonstrated that Jesus could miraculously provide sustenance for his followers, just as Moses had caused manna to rain down in the desert. Jesus's transfiguration on a mountaintop repeated the experience of Moses and thus confirmed his right to leadership of the Jewish people. The subtle implication of Strauss's text was that if we later generations find the transcendental demands and prodigious events of the New Testament a burden, we have the consolation of knowing that they were just as much a burden for Jesus and his early followers. For whatever the true circumstances of Jesus's life may have been, the fact remains that Jesus could not simply lead a spontaneous existence as an inspired moral teacher; he was obliged to work his way through an arduous programme of prophetic fulfilment, or at least chroniclers, in later days, had to do that for him. The conclusion that George Eliot drew from this is that is unreasonable for us to form superhuman expectations of people or to demand heroes and heroines that are wholly admirable and without stain. We need to develop an infinitely greater respect for ordinary, everyday human qualities, to reverence the courage and fortitude that men and women can show, even in the humblest circumstances, simply in struggling against the vicissitudes and discouragements that life has to offer, whether lack of money, sickness or simply the hostility and suspicion of other people. Amos Barton, the protagonist of the first story in *Scenes of Clerical Life* (1857), is just such a man. He is a badly paid curate who arrives in a small conservative parish and endeavours to improve the religious life of the community, which has become somewhat lax because of the worldliness of his predecessor. Their complacency is such that when he speaks to Mrs Patten about her sins she is quite indignant, protesting later:

Now, Mr Hackett, I have never been a sinner. From the fust beginning since I went into service, I al'ys did my duty by my employers. I was a good wife as any in the county – never aggravated my husband. The cheese-factor used to say that my cheese was al'ys to be depended on.

However, although George Eliot is interested in the impact of a new preacher on the small community of Shepperton, she is equally interested in his own inner life, in precisely that which escapes the prying, inquisitive and inveterately gossipy collective consciousness. There is always a tension between George Eliot's realism, which lovingly details the buildings, bric-à-brac and customs of a bygone age – for in some sense George Eliot's fiction is inveterately backward-looking and nostalgic – and her desire to disclose the deeper feelings of her characters, which will never be in the public eye. But Amos is far from being a model parson. Though undoubtedly sincere, his preaching is awkward, lacks eloquence and is not finely tuned towards the prejudices and sensibilities of her hearers. Amos is always in debt and because of the perpetual pressure on his finances his mind is as much focused on worldly as on heavenly things. Moreover he is insensitive to the way in which he is perceived by others and fails to realise that the prolonged stay of the beautiful Countess Czerlaski in his household has given rise to speculation that there is some romantic attachment between them. His reputation is only redeemed when the Countess eventually leaves and his wife, exhausted by stress and overwork, finally dies after a long illness. For George Eliot both Amos and his wife – 'gentle, uncomplaining Millie' – truly noble characters, who despite all their faults and the limited sphere in which they move are nevertheless worthy of our deepest admiration. At first glance the second of these sketches, 'Mr Gilfil's Love-Story', is the slightest, since it is 'only a love story', and lacks both the subtly sketched social canvas of 'Amos Barton' and the complex argumentation of 'Janet's Repentence', yet it is a masterly work nevertheless and one, which like others, points forward to her later concerns. Caterina, the young Italian girl, who has been brought up in an aristocratic English household, is in many ways a privileged person, yet she feels acutely her own position of dependence and subservience. She is very much under the control of others, and the splendid Gothic of Cheverel Manor, where she resides under the benign patronage of Sir Christopher Cheverel, is little more than a gilded cage for a singing bird. Indeed George Eliot's stress on the Gothic character of the building is filled with allusive irony. Caterina has fallen desperately in love with Captain Wybrow, Sir Christopher's nephew and heir, who has been flirting with her. Although she really knows her love is hopeless, she is made even more unhappy and resentful when Wybrow brings home the well-connected Miss Assher as his wife to be. The helpless observer of these proceedings is the young clergyman, Mr Gilfil, who has long loved Caterina yet knows that his love is not returned. Caterina is plunged into a state of emotional trauma when rushing out with a knife, intending to kill her unfaithful lover, she is shocked to find him already dead from a premature heart attack. Through the loving care of Mr Gilfil she is gradually restored to health, but dies only a year after her marriage to him. Ostensibly the point of the story is to show that even a complacent old bachelor like Mr Gilfil, the old parson, may once have loved deeply and truly, but what it also stresses is the isolation of individuals, so that Caterina can scarcely communicate the depth and complexity of her feelings to anyone. However, of the three stories it is 'Janet's Repentence' that articulates the concerns of the collection most clearly and suggests why George Eliot was attracted to the idea of writing about 'clerical life'. Some critics such as David Lodge have suggested that in this story Eliot 'finally made peace with the religion of her childhood and youth',[25] but I believe that such a characterisation of the story profoundly misses the point. Of course, George Eliot had powerful memories of the struggles over Evangelicalism and she still respected those clergymen who had gone forth to preach the word to lax congregations, well knowing that they would be received with suspicion and even downright hostility, but as the result of her reading of Strauss and Feuerbach her former perspective on all this had been radically transformed. Particularly crucial was the radical distinction that Feuerbach made between faith and love:

Faith is the opposite of Love. Love recognises virtue even in sin, truth in error. It is only since the power of faith has been supplanted by the power of the natural unity of mankind, the power of reason, of humanity, that truth has been seen even in polytheism, in idolatry generally . . . love is reconcilable with reason alone, not with faith; for as reason, so also love is free, universal, in its nature; whereas faith is narrow-hearted, limited.[26]

So George Eliot recognises that the attempt of Mr Tryan to bring a new and more radical gospel, based on justification by faith, is always potentially divisive, and is as likely to set one Christian against another as to promote a moral transformation of the community. Admittedly there is a narrow and bigoted group, led by the solicitor, Mr Dempster, Janet's husband, who see this as an opportunity to assert their authority over the community by presenting Tryan as a pious fraud, and George Eliot is scarcely anxious to defend such a person, who in any event also behaves like a terrible and unreasonable tyrant to his wife. What she does seek to suggest is that there are various people in the community, such as Mr Jerome, who is actually a dissenter, and Janet herself, who can look past these labels and see Tryan as a good and virtuous man who is, at bottom, simply trying to help others along life's way. This is the story's fundamental humanist message. Tryan's crusade may not have been altogether successful and the energies he poured into it may simply have accelerated his own death, but its one great success is that through his own honesty about his past life he was able to give Janet the courage to stand up for herself in the depth of despair and adversity and give her a reason to go on living. As George Eliot sees it, what really matters is not faith or doctrine, but that rare miracle: direct and open communication with another human being – and the love and compassion that must necessarily go with it.

Adam Bede (1859), George Eliot's first full-length novel, is a miracle of realism; her depiction of the small village of Hayslope between the years 1799 and 1801 is so life-like and so exquisitely detailed that a gasp of wonder and admiration seems the only appropriate response. Although the narrative has a powerful moral interest, the vividness of the representation so rivets the attention that it seems more like a landscape painting than a novel. Even George Eliot, great artist that she was, was never again able to reproduce the remarkable effects she achieves here. Yet, for all its perfection, *Adam Bede* is strangely flawed and even those critics who have most admired the book have been forced to concede its faults. Does the novel's very virtuosity lead us to become hypercritical – peering at the canvas in search of faulty brushstrokes and errors of perspective, or does this nagging sense of dissatisfaction point to some kind of problem with the project of realism itself? But before we can answer this we first need to decide just what the components of George Eliot's realism are. Certainly an important part of it is the suppression, though not the elimination, of cultural change. We cannot fail to note that like *Waverley* the novel harks back to a time that is precisely sixty years since, or that its untroubled surface contrasts greatly with the sense of cultural dissonance we get from *The Origin of Species* or Mill's *On Liberty*. George Eliot likes to suspend time; to draw a magic circle around a particular time and place and to transform it into a kind of shimmering dream of unchangeableness, which not even our knowledge of change can destroy. In this, Mrs Gaskell's *Cranford* was certainly her model, yet George Eliot manages to avoid an excess of nostalgia because she knows that at any moment and in any place there is always strife, discord and unhappiness. In *Adam Bede* we are made aware that England is at war with France, that there is a tension between Methodism and the Church of England, and that Dinah Morris, as a woman preacher, is a phenomenon uniquely of this moment, since there were women preachers neither earlier nor since. An equally striking aspect of the book is the complex sense George Eliot gives us of the topography of the village and its surrounding landscape from the moment at the opening of the novel, when we learn that Dinah is to preach out in the open, on the green, which lies on the edge of the village beyond the Donnithorne Arms and the parish church, in a setting of rich woods and pastureland, but with a 'bleak treeless region' of 'barren hills' in the distance. So many events in the novel are subtly bound up with a particular ambience, so that we are conscious not merely of a movement in the narrative, but of many emotional modulations and changes of key. Hetty's belated introduction follows a loving description of Hall Farm and its dairy, but the moment where she is brought to smother her illegitimate baby occurs in 'a wild brake, where there had once been gravel pits, leaving mounds and hollows studded with brushwood and small trees'.

This environment is bleak, but it is also deliberately banal and commonplace. George Eliot contrasts the deceptive idyll in the garden, where Hetty is picking redcurrants and when Adam mistakenly believes that Hetty is falling in love with him when in reality she is infatuated with the young squire, Arthur Donnithorne, with the stark hillside at Snowfield where Adam and Dinah agree to marry. What also contributes to the novel's sense of realism is George Eliot's ear for everyday speech. Dinah's address to the people shows not merely that such a Methodist sermon has a dialectical movement from reassurance to warning and intimations of damnation and back again to a message of comfort and the promise of divine love, but that it is itself eloquent and artfully calculated to move its unsophisticated audience. Mrs Poyser's expostulations and tirades are especially memorable. She is so skilfully drawn and her speech so vivid that she often comes near to dominating the whole book – especially when she courageously 'has her say out' to the old squire. But perhaps what is most striking in *Adam Bede* is the way in which George Eliot shows her many characters relating to one another, in ways that always seem right and appropriate. We think of the loyalty that the misogynistic old schoolmaster, Bartle, shows towards Adam; or of Mrs Poyser's attempts to talk Dinah out of preaching; or of the conversations Mr Irvine has with Arthur Donnithorne and Adam Bede. Indeed it may well be part of George Eliot's nostalgia that such frank and open communication between individuals – even, as between Arthur and Adam, across class barriers – is still shown to be possible. Admittedly Hetty does not, in the garden, tell Adam everything that is in her heart, and Arthur misses a crucial opportunity to confess to the vicar, but these omissions are notable because they are unusual. Elsewhere in George Eliot's novels the opportunities for spontaneity and confession are very much less.

If there is a flaw in *Adam Bede* it is associated with the character of Hetty Sorrel and her overall role in the narrative, because it seems that either she dominates it too much, or else that George Eliot seems to grudge her the prominence that she has come to assume and fails to grant her both the centrality and the tragic stature that seem rightfully hers. In any event it is clear that Hetty's murder of her illegitimate child irrevocably shatters the stable and relatively harmonious world of Hayslope. Indeed from a certain perspective, we are asked to see this as the real disaster. George Eliot suggests that the thoughtless passion of Arthur Donnithorne for Hetty and Hetty's own vanity and day-dreaming, though seemingly harmless, are nevertheless fraught with serious consequences that go far beyond themselves. It is not just that Hetty's own life is ruined or that Arthur can no longer hope to be the well-loved and respected squire, presiding over a happy and harmonious community. Adam's dream of marriage is destroyed. The Poysers are deeply shamed by what has happened and feel that they can never hold their heads up again. The stain and misery touches everyone. From an artistic point of view the drama surrounding Hetty takes the novel dangerously far into melodrama – there is the violence of the fight between Arthur and Adam, where George Eliot allows the reader to believe for a moment that Arthur may be dead, the arrival of Arthur with a paper announcing that the death penalty for Hetty is to be reprieved, the sordid nature of the baby's death. Doubtless all this is perfectly plausible, but the shift from lyrical realism to dirty realism is abrupt. On the other hand the transition has great emotional power for that very reason. Moreover it dramatises for us the fact that, beneath the tranquil surface, there are real class tensions: the threat posed by the appeal of Methodism to the lower classes; Mrs Poyser's anger at the old squire's plans to displace them from the farm; the blazing up of a deep resentment in Adam against Arthur, whom he has hitherto always respected. Perhaps Hayslope was never quite what it seemed.

Nevertheless, it seems a more weighty criticism of the novel that George Eliot appears to take Hetty almost too lightly and to take rather a patronising attitude towards her. Of course, Hetty's disappearance from the last section of the novel after being sentenced to transportation, to which Henry James strongly objected, can be defended on the grounds that it is Adam Bede who is the central character and that it is only right that Dinah Morris, who has been absent from Hetty's section of the narrative, should now assume centre stage. To have made Hetty the tragic victim of Arthur Donnithorne would have made the novel still more melodramatic and one-sided. George Eliot wanted to establish a sense of proportion between *all* the characters and to make the reader feel that Hetty's misfortune was the kind of thing that could happen to any attractive young girl with dreams of a life above her station. Hetty's fate must be a warning to others:

> Poor, wandering Hetty, with the rounded childish face, and the hard unloving despairing soul looking out of it – with the narrow heart and narrow thoughts, no room in them for any sorrows but her own, and tasting that sorrow with the more intense bitterness! My heart bleeds for her as I see her toiling along on her weary feet, or seated in a cart, with her eyes fixed vacantly on the road before her, never thinking or caring whither it tends, till hunger comes and makes her desire that a village may be near.

What will be the end? – the end of her objectless wandering,
apart from all love, caring for human beings only through pride,
clinging to life only as the hunted wounded brute clings to it.

God preserve you and me from being the beginnings of such
misery.

George Eliot's description of Hetty's terrible isolation is so powerful
that we cannot help sympathise with her – and for that very reason
we feel quite indignant that George Eliot can be so severe and
censorious. How could a young girl facing ostracism be concerned
with anyone but herself? Surely she deserves something more from
the novelist than to become an example for self-satisfied moral superiority. At this point George Eliot asks us to see Hetty only as a
sinner, and had not Feuerbach in *The Essence of Christianity* written:

> Now, by what means does man deliver himself from this state of
> disunion between himself and the perfect being, from the painful
> consciousness of sin, from the distressing sense of his own noth-
> ingness? How does he blunt the fatal sting of sin? Only by this;
> that he is conscious of *love* as the highest, the absolute power and
> truth. . . . No man is sufficient for the law which moral perfection
> sets before us; but, for that reason, neither is the law sufficient for
> man, for the heart. The law condemns; the heart has compassion
> even on the sinner.[27]

Why has George Eliot come close to losing sight of the insight that
she was so conscious of in writing *Scenes of Clerical Life*? Perhaps, at
such a moment as this, she is too severe but we must also recognise
how impossible it was for George Eliot – and surely for any writer –
to achieve or desire to achieve so perfect a realism that the scales
would never be tilted in any direction. George Eliot became a novelist because she wanted to describe truthfully the moral dilemmas of
ordinary life, but she could never do this without also being anxious
to communicate her own point of view. So while we may wish that
George Eliot had loved Hetty just a little more, so that she would
have judged her less harshly, we must also recognise that the act of
judgement itself was inescapable.

The Mill on the Floss (1860) is a novel that is also haunted by the
dream of a suspension of time, but now George Eliot is reluctantly
forced to admit that that dream can never be realised. The world of
Dorlcote Mill in the novel itself is exposed to all the pressures –
economic and psychological – of the modern world, yet the Mill, as

it *was*, nevertheless remains a powerful symbol of a place of peace, security and tranquillity, of an unchangeable rural way of life that can never be touched by either commerce or industrialism. The Tullivers lose Dorlcote Mill and in regaining it lose it once more. At the end of the novel the Mill, after being badly damaged in the floods, is rebuilt – a fact that gives added poignancy to the start of the novel where the lyrical opening description of Dorlcote Mill in its original majesty and stability is revealed to be only a dream. So the novel actually begins with a moment of loss, which is to be repeated again and again. In the opening lines of the novel we learn of the vigorous commercial life of the river: 'On this mighty tide the black ships – laden with the fresh-scented fir-planks, with rounded sacks of oil-bearing seed, or with the dark glitter of coal – are borne along to the town of St Ogg's', yet the Mill itself seems completely enclosed and shut off from all this. The 'trimly-kept', comfortable dwellings are encircled with elm trees and chestnuts, the stream is bordered by a withy plantation. The muddy mill pool is a place where the horses pulling the waggons heavily loaded with grain can rest and drink. The sound of the millstream, itself seems to suspend all sense of the outside world: 'The rush of the water and the booming of the mill bring a dreamy deafness which seems to heighten the peacefulness of the scene. They are like a great curtain of sound, shutting one out from the world beyond.'

This description is all the more significant because it dramatises the suspension of consciousness that underpins that sense of security. We recognise that in consequence old Mr Tulliver is so strong in his sense of possession and in the fullness of his traditional rights that he never imagines that his position at the Mill can be shaken or that he could ever lose a legal battle over water-rights. The law belongs to another world, the modern world, the world of Philip Wakem and his father, to which Tulliver himself could never belong. Tulliver inhabits a biblical world, where matters must be settled directly on a personal level and where personal reputation and the desire for vengeance on one's enemies are overwhelming moral imperatives. Tom Tulliver, the son, is able to regain the Mill, which has been lost to the Wakems, by a entrepreneurialism that is very much in keeping with the spirit of the times, but this is not enough for old Tulliver who must administer a personal thrashing to his employer in order to make the act of restitution complete. This is his own personal way of denying the force of modernity – a denial that the novel cannot altogether endorse or decisively repudiate.

In *Adam Bede* Hetty became the unsuitable and unwanted heroine of the novel – stealing the limelight by sheer fecklessness from more repressed and worthier individuals, and, for George Eliot, there is a similar guilt attached to the way in which Maggie Tulliver comes to dominate *The Mill on the Floss*. For Maggie is emotional, impulsive, disobedient, reckless and irresponsible, and therefore it may also seem that her pre-eminence is 'undeserved'. Of course, to say this is quite absurd, but we have to recognise that even George Eliot, the leading novelist of her time and herself a woman bold enough – reckless enough – to live with a man who was not and could not be her husband, nevertheless felt that there was something slightly improper in Maggie's usurpation of the narrative – why should we concern ourselves with teenage turmoil, when there are important matters at stake – like recovering the ownership of Dorlcote Mill? At the beginning of Book 5, which is significantly the moment when Maggie's star comes into the ascendant, George Eliot writes:

> While Maggie's life-struggles had lain almost entirely within her own soul, one shadowy army fighting another, and the slain shadows forever rising again, Tom was engaged in dustier noisier warfare, grappling with more substantial obstacles, and gaining more definite conquests. So, it has been since the days of Hecuba, and of Hector, tamer of horses: inside the gates, the women with streaming hair and uplifted hands offering prayers, watching the world's combat from afar, filling their long, empty days with memories and fears: outside, the men in fierce struggle with things divine and human, quenching memory in the stronger light of purpose, losing the sense of dread and even of wounds in the hurrying ardour of action.

It is precisely because George Eliot writes as a woman that she knows that there is more to life than this glamorous, precipitous recital of events. If the Victorian novel becomes increasingly centred on the unspoken drama of the inner life, this shift is very much the work of women novelists such as George Eliot herself and her great predecessor, Charlotte Brontë. Yet the difficulty of accomplishing this recentring must not be underestimated: it involves not merely revaluing what women do – and do not do – but also accepting the possibility of a narrative centre that is anchored in the unfolding consciousness of a woman. To begin with Maggie cannot be such a centre and knows it. She is introduced listening to old Mr Tulliver's great plans for Tom's education, plans that frankly have their origin in her father's recognition that Tom is Maggie's intellectual inferior, yet her intervention takes the form of a plea on her brother's behalf. She too must wring her hands, as the 'real' action, the loss and recovery of the Mill, takes place elsewhere and quite beyond her control. The difference between the part of the narrative that concerns Maggie and the part that concerns her father, brother and the Mill is that where the mill is concerned we are never in any doubt as to where the right lies, whereas with Maggie we are always plunged into uncertainty and ambiguity. It is never quite clear just what she intended or where the line should be drawn. Admittedly there is a consistent pattern in Maggie's actions which is one of disobedience and transgression – she runs away to the gypsies, she has secret meetings with Philip Wakem, the son of her father's deadly enemy, at Red Deeps, finally she is led into a river journey with Stephen Guest from which she returns unharmed but which is understood by public opinion to be morally compromising. Yet the implied repetition is actually deeply misleading because the circumstances in each case are very different and, as a young woman at least, Maggie never actually feels that she is doing anything wrong. The first meeting in the woods at Red Deeps is at Philip's instigation and Maggie sees no real harm in meeting a boy with whom she has been friendly and whom she pities because of his deformity, even though there is hostility between their parents. Are we to regard this phase in her life as an earlier temptation that prefigures her subsequent disgrace? In a way, yes, since by continuing these clandestine meetings she encourages Philip to believe that she reciprocates his love for her and even comes to believe this herself. Consequently the situation becomes morally confused in a way that Victorian readers could scarcely approve. Moreover Philip himself figures as a kind of tempter figure who in answer to Maggie's (and George Eliot's!) doctrine of resignation: 'Our life is determined for us – and it makes the mind very free when we give up wishing and only think of bearing what is laid upon us and doing what is given us to do', replies:

> But I can't give up wishing. . . . It seems to me we can never give up longing and wishing while we are thoroughly alive. There are certain things we feel to be beautiful and good, and we *must* hunger after them. How can we ever be satisfied without them until our feelings are deadened.

But on the other hand we feel that Maggie shows a praiseworthy spirit of independence and moral courage in meeting Philip, and that her discussions with him contribute significantly to her moral development. For George Eliot there can be no moral development without the ability to make mistakes and a set of ethical rules serves both to cramp individual spontaneity and seriously to underestimate the complexity of the circumstances that we have to contend with. Moreover Philip does have a point; desire is legitimate since without it there would be nothing to drive us toward higher goals. For George Eliot, writing as she saw it in the twilight of faith, the judgement of the individual is even more important when the church can no longer serve as an authentic and unimpeachable guide. Yet the complexity, the seriousness, the earnestness of this task is destroyed if we assume that conduct has hard and fast rules. The mission of the novel is precisely to show just how complex life is and to call in question 'the men of maxims':

> All people of broad, strong sense have an instinctive repugnance to the men of maxims; because such people early discern that the mysterious complexity of our life is not to be embraced by maxims, and that to lace ourselves up in formulas of that sort is to repress all the divine promptings that spring from growing insight and sympathy. And the man of maxims is the popular representation of the minds that are guided in their moral judgement solely by general rules, thinking that these will lead them to justice by a ready-made patent method, without the trouble of exerting patience, discrimination, impartiality, without any care to assure themselves whether they have the insight that comes from a hardly-earned estimate of temptation, or from a life vivid and intense enough to have created a wide fellow-feeling with all that is human.

This is one of the most eloquent and praiseworthy passages in George Eliot's fiction and we must rejoice that with *The Mill on the Floss* she made up her mind to present the moral dilemmas of her heroine in all their complexity instead of judging her as severely as she had Hetty Sorrell. Nevertheless there is a price to be paid for all this: if she is to be indulgent to Maggie, then she had to place most of the blame for what takes place onto the tempter figures of Philip Wakem and Stephen Guest. Thus Philip tempts Maggie by suggesting that she is artificially suppressing her brilliant and imaginative nature, by suggesting that their meetings will serve to overcome the family feud and by pretending that their encounters will not be clandestine if he comes upon her by chance. Philip can perhaps be partially excused for this because he is deformed and lacks love – but he *is* responsible nevertheless in a way that Maggie is not.

Of course this may well be part of George Eliot's argument – though she never expressly says so – because the social code that governs the relationship between men and women is unfairly tilted towards the male sex, since men have a far greater freedom to act in such situations and are granted far more indulgence even when it is clear that they have acted with impropriety, whereas a woman has very little freedom of action and will always be deemed to have acted improperly no matter what the actual circumstances may be. *The Mill on the Floss* reverses this set of expectations and suggests that it is rather the man who should be blamed. For if Maggie is led to shed bitter tears after Tom has condemned them for meeting surreptitiously and is now acutely conscious of the misery that had perturbed the clearness and simplicity of her life, George Eliot's own attitude to this is rather ambiguous. For on the one hand if anyone has disturbed this clarity it is Philip, who must be held responsible – yet, on the other, George Eliot knows that 'a lasting stand on serene heights above worldly temptations and conflict' is very difficult if not impossible, so that, apart from anything else, a virtue that could not contemplate the possibility of difficulty would be a very poor virtue indeed. George Eliot both wants to strike at the Pharisees, like Tom, who set themselves up as shallow, tinpot tribunals, yet she also wants to believe that blame can be apportioned all the same. What George Eliot really wants to say is that perhaps – in the very *last* analysis – Maggie should not have acted quite as she did, but we have to arrive at a more complex analysis of her error that is not simply based on some crude knee-jerk reaction.

Such considerations apply even more forcefully to the climactic episode in the novel when Maggie is brought to a situation that is explicitly described as a temptation, in which she is led to take a protracted journey down the river with Stephen Guest. What makes the biblical implications thicken even more irresistibly is that Maggie is once more cast in the role of the betrayer. Before it had been her brother and her father, now it is Lucy, her friend to whom Stephen is engaged, and Philip, who still has some hope of a relationship between them. From a certain point of view the situation and the moral responsibility could not be more clear-cut and yet the narrative implication of that journey down the river is powerfully allegorical. Maggie represents the modern sensibility, the contemporary conscience that, borne on the stream of history, is floating further and further away from 'home' and the simple moral certainties associated with it. She is embarking on a journey into the unknown in the course of which she will have to encounter unforeseen problems and will have to decide unaided what to do about them. Of course, this is more ideological freight than the episode itself will really bear and George Eliot knows this, but still she does want us to feel the difficulty of Maggie's situation: which is that whatever she decides to do will necessarily be wrong, and the bravest, most courageous and most authentic decision wrongest of all. Since Stephen loves Maggie and is prepared to marry her he is no conventional seducer and their elopement, though a cruel blow to Lucy, would nevertheless be something to which society would eventually grant its retrospective sanction; whereas Maggie's actual decision to return home after being absent for a day necessarily leads not just to the assumption that she is a fallen woman but the very reverse of what is actually the case – that she has no sense of moral responsibility. For George Eliot the social ostracism both of Maggie and of Dr Kenn, the vicar who initially tries to take her part, points to the loss of a genuine sense of community. Dr Kenn speaks of the danger of losing heart when he observes 'the want of fellowship and sense of mutual responsibility among my own flock. At present everything seems tending towards the relaxation of ties'. Maggie and Kenn becomes the types of the modern intellectual, who, far from being admired for their courage and moral righteousness, will only find themselves the victims of idle and malicious gossip. So the predicament of Amos Barton is repeated. Men and women judge by appearances, yet the truth itself is often difficult to know. Yet if it is George Eliot's intention to call in question the conventional morality, why does she end the novel with a return to origins, in which Maggie is reunited in death with her estranged brother – a conclusion which seems to negate the whole movement of the novel? The answer to this may lie in George Eliot's whole ambivalent attitude towards the Christian moral code and the kind of complacent moral certainty represented by Tom, whose intolerable status is intensified by the fact that he represents an unshakeable patriarchal authority that constantly undermines Maggie's struggle towards independence and self-realisation. We have to recognise that though George Eliot values independence and self-realisation, she values renunciation and self-abnegation more. But, crucially, renunciation is only possible for those who have something to renounce. So Maggie, having achieved a sense of her own independence, both from Tom and from the other men in her life, can now return to Dorlcote Mill to rescue Tom. Now, at last, and for a moment *he* is dependent on *her* and all the barriers are down. After for a long time navigating the muddy waters of experience, her death is intended as a gesture of renunciation in which clearness and simplicity are finally recovered. Yet, George Eliot really knows that this clearness and simplicity is a dream – just like the memories of Dorlcote Mill.

At the same time, however, the strength of that longing for clearness and simplicity cannot be underestimated. In *Silas Marner* (1861) the longing to suppress the modern and return to the certainty and stability of the past is even more strongly in evidence. Silas Marner, the weaver who has lost his religion and is cut off from all sense of community and social ties, and who only lives for his work and the gold coins that it brings him, is the very type of the modern alienated worker. Yet George Eliot, by setting her fable back in the time of the Napoleonic Wars is able to suggest that he can overcome his alienation eventually by a return to the untarnished world of the countryside. Admittedly such a cure cannot easily be effected since Marner has lost his faith in human nature after being unjustly accused of theft, and the country people themselves, though good natured at heart, are nevertheless suspicious and superstitiously afraid of such an outsider. The apparently familiarity of *Silas Marner* is derived from its evocation of Dickens's *A Christmas Carol*; a hard-hearted miser is recalled to the importance of love and human ties by the unexpected arrival at his cottage of a baby girl, whom he brings up as his own daughter. Yet, for George Eliot, obviously the implications are rather different. Marner, who has become disillusioned with religion as the result of his persecution at the hands of an evangelical sect, discovers through the love of Eppie the religion of humanity. It is not just that he loves her and that she loves him, but that through her presence he becomes reintegrated into the community, so that many other people in the village are able to express their concern and sense of fellowship with him. For George Eliot this idea of a caring community is itself religious. She believes that if religion – which is, in her view, after all only humanity's awareness of its own spiritual worth – is deeply woven into the fabric of everyday life, then it will be truer and more authentic than some externally imposed standard, which is why she does not now necessarily disapprove of the more worldly type of parson:

> Already Mr Macey and a few other privileged villagers, who were allowed to be spectators on these great occasions, were seated on benches placed for them near the door; and great was the admira-

tion and satisfaction in that quarter when the couples had formed themselves for the dance, and the Squire led off with Mrs Crackenthorp, joining hands with the Rector and Mrs Osgood. That was as it should be – that was what everybody had been used to – and the charter of Raveloe seemed to be renewed by the ceremony. It was not thought of as unbecoming levity for the old and middle-aged people to dance a little before sitting down to cards, but rather as part of their social duties. For what were these if not to be merry at appropriate times, interchanging visits and poultry with due frequency, paying each other old-established compliments in sound traditional phrases, passing well-tried personal jokes, urging your guests to eat and drink too much out of hospitality, and eating and drinking too much in your neighbour's house to show that you liked your cheer? And the parson naturally set an example in these social duties. For it would not have been possible for the Raveloe mind, without a peculiar revelation, to know that a clergyman should be a pale-faced memento of solemnities, instead of a reasonably faulty man whose exclusive authority to read prayers and preach, to christen, marry, and bury you, necessarily co-existed with the right to sell you the ground to be buried in and to take tithe in kind; on which last point, of course, there was a little grumbling, but not to the extent of irreligion – not of deeper significance than grumbling at the rain, which was by no means accompanied by a spirit of impious defiance, but with a desire that the prayer for fine weather might be read forthwith.

There was no reason, then, why the Rector's dancing should not be part of the fitness of things quite as much as the Squire's.

The dance is a secular, yet sacred ceremony in which the community, at Christmas time especially, establishes its sense of mutual goodwill and solidarity of old and young, high and low, male and female.

From this sense of fellowship Silas Marner is excluded – but it is at this very moment that he discovers Eppie. The importance of belonging – not just for Silas Marner but for everyone else as well – is underlined at the end of the novel with Eppie's marriage to Aaron; for now Silas has a loving family and is at the centre of affairs, while old Mr Macey, so long a figure of importance in Raveloe, is consigned to the sidelines and is too ill to be at the wedding feast as he is racked with rheumatism – but they all make a point of pausing to speak and shake hands with him as they pass. Silas Marner himself has returned to his home town only to find it a soulless industrial city in which all the old landmarks have been swept away. But the novel has made possible a journey back into the past. The rents, tears and dislocations of the modern manufacturing world can all be reworked and rewoven in the timeless world of Raveloe.

A particular puzzle in *Silas Marner* is the sense that George Eliot strongly conveys of the workings of providence. Dunsey is punished for his unscrupulousness and irresponsibility by drowning almost immediately after stealing Silas Marner's money. Godfrey is punished for his lack of concern both for his unacknowledged wife and daughter by losing Eppie to Silas Marner, and by facing the humiliation of hearing Eppie express both her love for Silas and her dislike for him. Silas Marner finds in Eppie a miraculous replacement for the gold that he has lost. Clearly the fable points an obvious moral lesson, but how can George Eliot as person who is no longer a believer in God justify a story with such a providential design? The question of divine providence and specifically of the human need to believe in such action of providence was, of course, addressed by Feuerbach in *The Essence of Christianity*. Feuerbach writes:

Providence is the privilege of man. It expresses the value of man, in distinction from other natural beings and things; it exempts him from the connection of the universe. Providence is the conviction of man of the infinite value of his existence; it is the idealism of religion. . . . Faith in Providence is faith in one's own worth, the faith of man in himself; hence the beneficient consequences of this faith, but hence also false humility, religious arrogance, which, it is true, does not rely on itself, but only because it commits the care of itself to the blessed God. God concerns himself about me; he has in view my happiness, my salvation; he wills that I shall be blest; but that is my will also: thus my interest's is God's interest, my own will is God's will, my own aim is God's aim, – God's love for me nothing other than my own self-love deified. Thus when I believe in Providence, in what I do believe but in the reality and significance of my own being?[28]

For Feuerbach providence means God's care for man, which in the post-Christian era must be reinterpreted as man's concern for himself, for his own spiritual importance. Such an analysis is certainly relevant to *Silas Marner*. The consequence for Silas of belonging to the evangelical church is that, when lots are cast to discover whether he is guilty of the crime of which he is accused and he is found guilty, his life is thrown into a terrible obscurity. He cannot understand how this could have happened to him. It goes against everything that he has thought and believed. What George Eliot stresses in Silas Marner is that though it may have been chance that sent Eppie to Silas, it is Silas *himself* who confers meaning on the event, both by deciding to bring the child up – a most unexpected thing for him to do – and by seeing the event as an act of providence. It was not that God has sent Eppie to Silas; it is that Silas himself has decided to make Eppie the agent of his own spiritual regeneration into the religion of humanity. The real significance of the event is that since we can never know or foresee what will happen to us, we must make the most out of such opportunities as present themselves to us. As Dolly Winthrop says:

> it's like the night and the morning, and the sleeping and the waking, and the rain and the harvest – one goes and other comes, and we know nothing how nor where. We may strive and scrat and fend, but it's little we can do after all – the big things come and go wi' no striving o' our'n – they do that they do; and I think you're in the right on it to keep the little un Master Marner, seeing as it's been sent to you, though there's folks as think different.

There is no absolute justice in the world. At the end Silas believes he can finally clear himself of the old accusations, but finds that the enterprise is hopeless. We have to make our life out of the materials we possess.

In *Romola* (1862–3) George Eliot's fiction took a radical new turn. Instead of looking back to the recent English past, she made the decision to set her novel in the Renaissance and, more specifically, to set it in the Florence of Savonarola, the formidable critic of abuses within the Roman church, in the years from 1492 to 1498. What made her approach to the historical novel distinctive was she did not see the dilemmas of that time as being locked into some historical time capsule, but, on the contrary, regarded them as essentially analogous to the situation of intellectuals who had to live in the aftermath of faith. For it was in the Renaissance that pagan values, as articulated in the Greek classical texts, emerged as an alternative value-system to Christianity; while it was at this very same moment that the Catholic church itself came under attack from within, at the hands of Savonarola, whose assault on ecclesiastical corruption prefigured the later and more damaging indictments of Luther and Calvin. Moreover in this novel George Eliot transformed the marginality of her heroine, Romola, into a positive moral advantage, since Romola, exposed to the siren voices of Machiavellian opportunism and religious fanaticism, succeeds in passing between Scylla and Charybdis unscathed, even if, like Ulysses, she is compelled to experience acute psychological distress. *Romola* is the forerunner of a whole tradition in modern fiction where the hero or heroine, despite strong inducements to do so, refuses commitment, in the belief that they can best maintain their integrity by standing aloof from enterprises that are morally flawed. Such an attitude also involves, in the tradition of Scott, an interest in the lost causes of history, since there is the strong possibility that those parties that may have been less effective and less successful may nevertheless less have had right on their side. The paradox of *Romola* is that while it is heavily weighted, indeed overloaded with historical detail, over which George Eliot expended great pains, it is very much an allegory of the contemporary Victorian situation, and thus risks being radically unhistorical, as many contemporary critics observed. Specifically Tito's determination to sell off the remarkable classical library of Romola's father for his own personal benefit raises questions that pertain to the rights of women to own property, which were not to be addressed in Victorian England until the Married Women's Property Act of 1870. Moreover Romola's desire to separate herself from Tito on the grounds that she should not be obliged to share her life with a selfish and morally corrupt individual, though severely criticised by Savonarola, nevertheless does represent a kind of plea for divorce that is more in tune with the Victorian situation (and with George Eliot's decision to live with a man who could not under any circumstances obtain a divorce) than it is with the fifteenth century. Again, although Tito clearly represents a Machiavellian approach to politics, he is also offered as a critique of Utilitarian ethics and of the idea that life can in any way be meaningfully perceived as involving the pursuit of pleasure. For George Eliot such issues actually had a greater moral significance now that it was very difficult for any intelligent person to believe in revealed Christianity and the Bible. In the post-Christian era there were now no obvious sanctions against unscrupulous or immoral behaviour, which made the task of combatting it all the more urgent.

It is symptomatic of the extraordinary value that the Victorians put on moral strenuousness that the most damaging criticism George Eliot's feels she can make of the kind of self-regarding Utilitarianism represented by Tito is not just that it is selfish or even morally wrong, but that it always involves taking the easiest way out. Mill, of course, would have been swift to respond that it is precisely the Utilitarian who does *not* take the easy way out; on the contrary to weigh carefully, in every situation, precisely which course of action will most contribute to the happiness of the greatest number is both difficult and daunting. Yet even if George Eliot were to concede this point, she would nevertheless be disposed to argue that Utilitarian ethics is unduly abstract and mathematical in its calculations. She would insist that every individual is born into a very specific situation with ties both to family and community, and it is always these that must take precedence over any theoretical notion of universal humanity. Thus, with Romola, her first duty must be to her father and her family, after these she owes an obligation to Florence, the city where she has lived and been brought up. It is precisely George Eliot's fear that the force of modernity will dissolve all such traditional ties and obligations so that the individual becomes an alienated, self-interested person, who in thinking of no one but himself actually deprives himself of the very real satisfaction that comes from acknowledging a relationship to others and from striving to help them. Tito represents precisely this baleful modernity. Arriving in Florence with some precious objects, whose value he should put to use in searching for and rescuing his father, Tito chooses to betray this obligation on the ground that this wealth can benefit him more:

> Certainly the gems and therefore the florins were, in a sense, Baldassare's; in the narrow sense by which the right of possession is determined in ordinary affairs: but in that large and more radically natural view by which the world belongs to youth and strength, they were rather his who could extract the most pleasure out of them.

For George Eliot, Tito's unthinking instinctive hedonism is such that he cannot even begin to be a moral individual. Since he has never put the interests of another person before his own he has no inner authenticity on which to build. Both personal identity and personal morality must be created out of the decisions that we make in daily life, and to have acted greatly, even once, creates within us the possibility that we can do so again. But Tito's desire to avoid giving pain – also seen as an Utilitarian priority – has never extended to the point of actually doing positive good. His decision always to take the easy way leads him into a moral miasma of his own devising as he is tortured by fear, guilt, and the dread of being detected in all his subterfuges and lies. Tito does not have the bottle to be a true Machiavellian:

> his dread generated no active malignity and he could still have been glad not to give pain to any mortal. He had simply chosen to make life easy for himself – to carry his human lot, if possible, in such way that it should pinch him nowhere; and the choice had, at various times, landed him in unexpected positions. The question now was, not whether he should divide the common pressure of destiny with his fellow-men; it was whether all the resources of lying would save him from being crushed by the consequences of that habitual choice.

Tito's vocation is to be a manipulator, a man who uses others to achieve the goals that he seeks. He is ruthless in relation to those who love him or have come to depend on him: to Baldassarre his father, to Bardo and Romola, and to Tessa, the simple peasant girl whom he seduces. To many readers Tito may seem too much the exemplification of an alien world-view to carry much conviction, and the novel undoubtedly suffers from George Eliot's remorseless determination to expose his moral emptiness and total worthlessness. In consequence he seems more a cardboard cut-out than a man. But George Eliot feels bound to campaign against him because the temptations that he represents are doubly dangerous in a world that is losing its belief in hell and even in the power of evil.

That Romola should reject Tito, explicitly described as 'the Great Tempter' is inevitable but her response to Savonorola, whose dedicated follower she becomes, is more complex. Effectively, through Romola, George Eliot expresses her own attitude towards historical Christianity and risks becoming unhistorical as a result. What matters to Romola are 'the grand energies of Savonorola's nature' rather than any specific 'dogmas and prophecies' to which he may be committed. Savonarola's desire to cleanse church and state of corruption is praiseworthy and can be seen, if this is not anti-climactic, as prefiguring such things as Strauss's life of Jesus and the 1832 Reform Bill, yet at one and the same time Savonarola is a fanatical and often opportunistic man who will use superstition, prejudice and political circumstances to achieve his ends. Savonarola's spirituality and personal dedication can scarcely be faulted. He is just the man that the times call for. Yet he cannot but be of these times and in becoming politically effective always runs the risk of becoming just another politician. On the other hand, Savonarola's devotion to his own city and his insistence to Romola on the importance of duty:

> You are seeking your own will, my daughter. You are seeking some other good other than the law you are bound to obey. But how will you find good? It is not a thing of choice: it is a river that flows from the foot of the Invisible Throne, and flows by the path of obedience. I say again, man cannot choose his duties. You may choose to forsake your duties, and choose not to have the sorrow they bring. But you will go forth; and what will you find, my daughter? sorrow without duty – bitter herbs, and no bread with them

makes him a forerunner of the religion of humanity. Romola, by putting her own desires first, risks following in the footsteps of Tito, even though she is in all respect his moral superior.

It is at this crucial point in the narrative that George Eliot becomes entwined in a complex moral confusion of her own, already broached in *The Mill on the Floss*: the problem of how freedom and personal fulfilment are to be estimated within the context of an overwhelming emphasis on the importance of renunciation, duty and the obligation that every individual owes to others. Romola does indeed return to her husband and to assist the plague victims of Florence, yet George Eliot cannot accept that Romola owes any duty to her husband, so the pattern of flight is repeated at the end:

> The bonds of all strong affection were snapped. In her marriage, the highest bond of all, she had ceased to see the mystic union which is its own guarantee of indissolubleness, had ceased even to see the obligation of a voluntary pledge: had she not proved that the things to which she had pledged herself were impossible? The impulse to set herself free had risen again with overmastering force; yet the freedom could only be an exchange of calamity. There is no compensation for the woman who feels that the chief relation of her life has been no more than a mistake. She has lost her crown. The deepest secret of human blessedness has half-whispered itself to her, and then forever passed her by.

Despite these admonitory words George Eliot knows that marriage to such a man as Tito is not the deepest secret of human blessedness or anything like it; so Romola finally repudiates both Tito and Savonarola, the two men who have thus far dominated her life, and once more leaves Florence in search of liberation. Yet George Eliot cannot altogether disguise the emptiness of this gesture by making her into a mysterious saint-like figure who saves a community of Jews from the worst evils of the plague. The problem with this conclusion is not that it is too idealised, but that, for the novelist at least, it is too easy. George Eliot will not allow herself to say outright that Romola is justified in leaving Tito, so in this respect Romola seems less positive than she might; but equally her abandonment of Florence and Savonarola has negative implications, since she also seems to be leaving behind all the difficult moral choices that would face her if she stayed. It is no good writing a novel of the Renaissance unless you are convinced that life also had an urgency then. *Romola* asks all the searching and difficult questions but uses the genre to avoid giving any seriously thought-out answers.

With *Felix Holt* (1866) George Eliot returned to her preoccupation with the recent English past and the problem of change and continuity in English life. The novel has two interwoven and symbolically related strands. One strand deals with the unsuccessful attempt of Harold Transome, who has returned from the Middle East with a large fortune, to win the parliamentary seat of Treby Magna as a Radical candidate in the election of 1832. Felix Holt, a forthright and uncompromising young watchmaker, who supports the Radical cause, successfully manages to prevent a disorderly mob committing more serious violence, but for his pains is taken to be their ringleader and sentenced to four years in prison for manslaughter. Interwoven with this political narrative is a complicated story of entailment and inheritance, from which it emerges that Esther, apparently the daughter of Rufus Lyon, a dissenting preacher, is, in reality, the true heir to Harold Transome's estate at Transome Court. Esther loves Felix but when Harold Transome makes overtures towards her she is almost led to adopt his point of view: that Felix is no longer a suitable person for someone of her social pretensions. However, Esther is convinced of Felix's moral superiority, whose altruism is in marked contrast to Harold's way 'of virtually measuring everything by the contribution it made to his own pleasure'.

She gives up her claim to the estate and marries Felix when he is pardoned and released from prison. The strength of *Felix Holt* lies in its strong democratic thrust. The novel deliberately dallies with the possibility that Esther will marry Harold – a consummation that George Eliot knows that most of her readers regard not simply as desirable but inevitable – only to frustrate it at the end. In her brilliant portrait of Rufus Lyon, the dissenting minister – surely one of the most memorable characters she ever created – George Eliot presents us with a man who is solemn, serious , indefatigably loquacious, saturated in biblical lore, yet strongly democratic in his sympathies and quite unexpectedly open minded. Although he often appears in a comic light, as when he uses the gratitude of Philip Dubarry over the return of some valuable as a pretext for staging a public confrontation between Dissent and the Church of England, he remains a complex, many-sided human being who retains our respect. George Eliot makes us feel through Rufus and Felix Holt that there is an integrity and commitment in Dissenting culture, which those who have been raised in the aristocracy and the Church of England do not possess and could never emulate. George Eliot at her best, however, is a novelist who stresses the complexity and difficulty of life and the often painful consequences of the decisions we make. In *Romola* she certainly had achieved this but in *Felix Holt* we cannot seriously take Esther's decision not to marry Harold as a gesture of renunciation – since she loves Felix and knows that life with him will bring her personal happiness in a way that Transome Court could not. It is only painful by the standards of the shallowest reader of fashionable novels. The novel is also weakened, as many readers from Henry James onward have pointed out, by the fact that Felix Holt is not radical in any meaningful sense at all, and the novel's melodramatic preoccupation with the dangers of mob violence shows a distrust of ordinary people that is seriously at odds with the general spirit of George Eliot's work. George Eliot never seems to have grasped that the whole point of extending the franchise, both in 1832 and 1867, was precisely to defend the existing political structures by broadening their social base. Moreover this social base would have been extended still further by granting votes to women, which George Eliot could scarcely have regarded as a step that would be fraught with possibilities of social disorder and violence. With *Romola* it was easy to imagine that the difficulties that George Eliot had in framing a suitable course of action for her heroine were bound up with powerful social restrictions on the freedom of action of women. But in *Felix Holt* we see that this is not a complete explanation since Felix is also unable to find a course of action through which he can express his personality and convictions. He is not a convincing embodiment of the importance of public order, and we are conscious of a certain hollowness in a 'free' character who seems to spend most of his time trying to prevent other people – Esther, his mother or the mob – from doing things. George Eliot sees Felix as a pure and unstained potentiality that can only become muddied and obscured in the field of action.

Through her decision to give her fiction the calmness and lucidity of retrospection George Eliot had made it difficult for herself to articulate the difficulties that she experienced as an intellectual and a woman in her own time. Indeed, her very impulse to write fiction sprang from a desire to affirm that there were indeed principles of stability and continuity in the world even if it was no longer possible to believe in the workings of divine providence. In *Romola* she had come closest to expressing a many-sided discontent – with the dependent position of women, with the structures of power from which women are excluded, with the difficulty for a woman of finding a sphere of action in which she could adequately define herself – yet the credibility of the Renaissance milieu, ostensibly so apt an analogy for the modern, was always in danger of being shattered, like a venerable old bottle that is suddenly filled with new and effervescent wine. *Felix Holt* ostensibly addressed itself to the problem of change but leant too far the other way – Felix Holt wanted to make an omelette without even thinking of cracking eggs. Yet in *Middlemarch* (1871–2) George Eliot finally and triumphantly brought these divergent concerns together, showing the complex interaction between intellectuals and idealists, who believe that they have a mission in life they must fulfil, and an ordinary community that looks for nothing better than to carry on in the time-honoured ways. Moreover after the passing of the Second Reform Bill in 1867 it became easier to see 1832 as a moment that represented not a radical transformation of the social order so much as a steady and stabilising transition. Recognising, no doubt, that her anxieties over the Second Reform Bill had been exaggerated, it now became possible to take a cooler view of 1832. Although no Hegelian, George Eliot had been instructed by those in his shadow, and *Middlemarch* became an essay in dialectic, in the complex interaction between the ideal and the real.

At first sight nothing could strike a more disconcerting note than the prelude to *Middlemarch*, in which George Eliot invokes the spirit of St Theresa – for what could be more embarrassing for a Victorian audience than such a heavily signalled allusion to a Catholic saint famous for her mystical, distinctly erotic visions. Surely this could not be an appropriate aspiration for the Victorian girl. The modern reader is likely to be equally puzzled. Sainthood can hardly be an appropriate subject for the realistic novelist, and if Dorothea is disposed to ponder Theresa's example, then we can only regard this as one of her many mistakes. Yet George Eliot has a serious point about the limited field of action that was open to an intelligent woman in the nineteenth century. If Theresa 'found her epos in the reform of a religious order', her successors are faced with the prospect of 'a life of mistakes, the offspring of a certain spiritual grandeur ill-matched with the meanness of opportunity' whose struggles seemed 'mere inconsistency and formlessness'.

For George Eliot, as we have already seen in *Romola*, the problem of vocation was particularly acute if you were a woman, and clearly it is with the restrictions on women that she is most concerned. Yet, arguably, the problem is more far-reaching since Victorian intellectuals were unable to find a role within the church, which in earlier generations would have been the obvious place in which to pursue a career and the opportunity of wielding power and influence. We may note Arnold's occupation as Inspector of Schools, John Stuart Mill's employment in the Civil Service, Leslie Stephen's position as a magazine editor, Shaw's employment as music and drama critic, George Eliot's own position as translator and novelist as representative instances of the ways in which intellectuals found employment. The obvious response to this is to argue that we should not too readily endorse some imaginary demand on the part of Victorian intellectuals for higher social status, nor should we acquiesce in the presumption that the church in former times would have offered the kind of situation in which they would have thrived. Yet such figures as Carlyle, Eliot and Arnold were acutely conscious of their own social marginality. They had no obvious constituency to which they could appeal – neither the aristocracy, the commercial industrial middle class, nor the working class – so they had to predicate a kind of enlightened constituency of people like themselves who would be prepared to think critically and address issues in a way that was not based purely and simply on self-interest. A major theme of *Middlemarch* is therefore to show just how complex and daunting is the task of the intellectual in the modern world. If you set yourself high goals and if you have some hopes of bringing about a better world, then your first task must be to focus your activity and decide in what way and by what means you will promote improvements or add something to the total of human achievement. But this in itself by no means simple. The life of Casaubon demonstrates just how easy it is for a person to embark on some ambitious project and then lose his way; to reach a point where it becomes virtually impossible to admit that the whole endeavour is in vain. It is easy to criticise Casaubon but this is hardly the point. His spectre haunts the novel and the consciousness of George Eliot precisely because it represents in the most tangible and nightmarish form the dangerous and menacing isolation of the intellectual life. As a writer George Eliot is preoccupied with the possibility of making mistakes. Such mistakes are never a trivial matter but always involve a tremendous price. For once you have gone down the wrong path it is impossible to go back. In life it is possible to go astray by taking the easy way, as with Fred Vincy or Lydgate, yet it is also possible to be mistaken in choosing a hard and rocky road, as Dorothea knowingly does in marrying Casaubon. There are times where George Eliot seems to see life as involving some kind of inadvertent but irrevocable Faustian contract, as when apropos of Ladislaw's involvement with Rosamund she writes: 'it seemed to him as if he were beholding in a magic panorama a future where he himself was sliding into that pleasureless yielding to the small solicitations of circumstance, which is a commoner history of perdition than any single momentous bargain'. Ladislaw, like the other characters in the novel, is struggling to find his path in life. He starts out as a painter, then becomes a newspaper editor and through his desire to be near Dorothea becomes entangled in a compromising situation with Rosamund that risks the loss of whatever slender chances of happiness he has.

Dorothea believes that marrying Casaubon will give her life both intellectual companionship and a sense of direction and purpose, in which expectation she is sadly disappointed. Yet Lydgate, who attaches no real importance to such considerations, marries a girl who comes close to destroying his whole life precisely because she has no interest in his work and researches and refuses to communicate with him on any level. For George Eliot the intellectual will necessarily be a lonely person since it is difficult to explain to others the extraordinary frustrations that must beset his or her mission. She writes of Lydgate:

there are episodes in most men's lives in which the highest qualities can only cast a deterring shadow over the objects that fill their inward vision: Lydgate's tender-heartedness was present just then only as a dread lest he should offend against it, not as an emotion that swayed him tenderness. For he was very miserable. Only those who know the supremacy of the intellectual life – the life which has a seed of ennobling thought and purpose within it – can understand the grief of one who falls from that serene activity into the absorbing soul-wasting struggle with worldly annoyances.

This is the dilemma of the modern intellectual. In a world without God a self-appointed task or mission can give meaning and a sense of direction to life, yet the possibility of external validation and confirmation that existed for St Theresa is denied. In consequence the individual may find his original clear purpose fraying, his path through life petering out in the wilderness. Without God and without a mission he is truly a lost soul – or, at best, as Gillian Beer puts it a 'mitigated failure'.[29]

George Eliot, like John Stuart Mill, was powerfully attracted to the ideal of a relationship between men and women that would involve not simply financial convenience, sexual attraction or the desire for a family but would above all be a marriage of minds, a true intellectual partnership. Such was the relationship that George Eliot formed with G. H. Lewes and such was the relationship between John Stuart Mill with Harriet Taylor. It was appropriate and even gratifying that such an association should exist outside marriage – Mill only married Harriet Taylor, whom he had known for many years, after the death of her husband – since it served to demonstrate just how scandalous and incomprehensible to the ignorant majority such a spiritual connection could be. Although George Eliot hypothesised marriage itself as an intellectual affinity – such as Dorothea Brooke sought with Casaubon – she was acutely conscious both that such an ideal was deeply subversive of conventional ideas about marriage, and, equally, that such ideas could well stand in the way of a more equal, comradely and developed understanding. Certainly in *Daniel Deronda* (1876) Gwendolen Harleth is not just apprehensive about Grandcourt but about marriage in general – since she 'never saw a married woman who had her own way' and 'she had not observed husbands to be companions'.

Thus, George Eliot's demand for equality and companionship in marriage, though to our eyes perhaps unexceptional, is a large time-bomb, quietly and menacingly ticking away. For George Eliot herself doubts whether it can be truly realised in more than a very small number of cases, yet even the arousal of such an expectation can only have the effect of focusing attention on the unequal power relations within marriage and of dramatising the hollowness of a connection where there is no true meeting of minds. Marriage, instead of being represented as the cosy, warm and morally sustaining milieu of the family, becomes the deepest and most intense form of loneliness in which men and women, chained to one another, not only cannot communicate but dare not let slip any revelation of their true feelings to the menacing other who threatens the deepest sources of their being. In *Middlemarch* George Eliot brutally rips back the lace curtain that shrouds the intimacies of man and wife to expose not love but a damaging and interminable struggle for power. But what she also shows is that this struggle is not what it seems – the woman is the stronger. Casaubon imagines that in marrying Dorothea he will acquire a gentle, docile and reverential helpmate, who will minister to his every whim and regard his pretensions to scholarship with uncritical adoration. So he makes a mistake just as Dorothea and everyone else makes a mistake, which, of course implies not so much that mistakes have been made as that the marital enterprise is characterised by mistakenness. Marital violence, psychological or actual, is thus the explosive eruption of frustration, anger and disappointment that the other is not as we dreamed, which is intensified by surprise that this should not be so. It was not what they had expected – nor could it have been. Yet most surprising of all is the strength of the women. Rosamund masters Lydgate. Dorothea humiliates Casaubon by seeing through his pretensions. Mrs Bulstrode retains her dignity, courage and self-possession even when her husband shatters the whole fabric of their existence by telling her of his sins of commission and omission. Mary Garth is sufficiently sure of herself to insist that if she is to marry Fred Vincy it will only be on her terms. The men are weak because they imagine that everything will go their way, while the women become stronger because they know they will have to struggle. But this sense of marriage as a struggle for existence, in which absolutely no holds are barred, also serves to problematise George Eliot's notional ideal of spiritual partnership. We may say that Dorothea's marriage with Casaubon fails because he is not prepared to make his enquiry a joint enterprise and is not even prepared to entertain the relatively submissive and secondary role that Dorothea is prepared to assign to herself. He is proud and inflexible because deep down he is conscious of his own inadequacy. Yet we also know that there could never be a novel in which Dorothea found spiritual partnership with a man, even if George Eliot found it herself. For, at bottom, there would always be the dominance of the man, who, as it were, 'allows' the woman to be equal with him when what she seeks is no such concession or condescension but a right that she herself claims and asserts. Here, one cannot help thinking of Lewes himself in his role as a perceptive critic of George Eliot's work, for what he praises is her painstaking realism – so that she, in implicit rebellion embarks, with *Romola*, on novels of a much more intellectual character that focus on a woman's demands. We are bound to read *Middlemarch* not just as painstaking realism, but also as myth in which a young and vital woman slays the old and ineffectual masculine priest, who has maintained his unjustified dominance by purporting to be the guardian of sacred and impenetrable mysteries. With the death of God comes the death of the omniscient, omnipotent father.

For Feuerbach another corollary of the death of God was the development of a humanist morality in which instead of allowing our actions to be dictated by the presumed commands of a divine being, we are placed in a position in which we only can assume the burden of responsibility for the morality of our actions. In one sense this is existentialism *avant le lettre*, but from another point of view such a designation is wrong since for Feuerbach moral action does not necessarily involve alienation and *angst* but rather predicates a need to confirm the worth of our actions by the summoning of a human other who will, as God did formerly, by confirming the dictates of our own best self. The relationship with the other makes possible a genuine dialectic since the other can truly respond to our doubts and questioning in a way that God himself never could. The existence of such a significant and *concerned* other restores the possibility of meaning and of righteousness. Feuerbach writes:

Doubtless the essence of man is *one*, but this essence is infinite; its real existence is therefore an infinite, reciprocally compensating variety, which reveals the riches of this essence. Unity in essence is multiplicity in existence. Between me and another human being – and this other is the representative of the species, even though he is only one, for he supplies to me the want of many others, has for me a universal significance, is the deputy of mankind, in whose name he speaks to me an isolated individual, so that, when united only with one, I have a participated, a human life; – between me and another human being there is an essential qualitative distinction. The other is my *thou*, – the relation being reciprocal, – my *alter ego*, man objective to me, the revelation of my own nature, the eye seeing itself. In another I first have the consciousness of humanity; through him I first learn, I first feel, that I am a man: in my love for him it is first clear to me that he belongs to me and I to him, that we two cannot be without each other, that only community constitutes humanity. But morally, also, there is a qualitative, critical distinction between the *I* and *thou*. My fellow-man is my objective conscience; he makes my feelings a reproach to me; even when he does not expressly mention them, he is my personified feeling of shame. The consciousness of the moral law, of right, of propriety, of truth itself, is indissolubly united with my consciousness of another than myself.[30]

In Feuerbach's phenomenological and idealised description the other is a perfect mirror who sends back to the individual a vivified and clarified sense of his own spiritual integrity. Nevertheless George Eliot, in translating this analysis, cannot but have been conscious of its presumed masculinity, the idea of a female other, let alone a female subject scarcely enters. But George Eliot was gripped by the idea of such a significant other who could help and guide others along life's way by offering them moral support just when their situation seemed darkest and most obscure. In theory anyone could fulfil such a role, but George Eliot undoubtedly believed that it could only be truly fulfilled by a woman. In theory Will Ladislaw is capable of being such a significant other. He offers comfort and admiration to Dorothea and Rosamund in the difficulties of their marriage and he has sympathy for Lydgate in his struggles to improve medical care in the district, since this corresponds with his own mission to raise the standard of political debate. A significant moment that dramatises the issues at stake occurs when Dorothea is remonstrating with her uncle because his political ambitions are not matched by his own actions:

you mean to enter Parliament as a member who cares for the improvement of the people, and one of the first things to be made better is the state of the land and the labourers. Think of Kit Downes, uncle, who lives with his wife and seven children in a house with one sitting-room and one bed-room hardly larger than this table! – and those poor Dagleys in their tumble-down farmhouse, where they live in the back kitchen and leave the other rooms to the rats.

Dorothea's generosity of spirit not only shows up Mr Brooke, who until now has scarcely given the matter a second thought, but also Will Ladislaw, whose admiration is tinged with a certain resentment:

> Dorothea had gathered emotion as she went on, and had forgotten everything except the relief of pouring forth her feelings unchecked: an experience once habitual with her, but hardly ever present since her marriage, which had been a perpetual struggle of energy with fear. For the moment, Will's admiration was accompanied with a chilling sense of remoteness. A man is seldom ashamed of feeling that he cannot love a woman so well as when he sees a certain greatness in her; nature having intended greatness for men.

This may only be a passing moment but it nevertheless is one that lingers in the mind, especially since it ominously connects the frustration of Dorothea's spontaneity and authenticity at the hands of Casaubon with the man who will be her second husband. But be that as it may, George Eliot believes that since a woman's mind and heart are not hedged around with such petty restrictions, only a woman is really capable of playing the part of Feuerbach's other. Early in the novel Dorothea confirms Will in his decision to become financially independent of Casaubon and to take up a career in journalism. She offers encouragement and financial assistance to Lydgate when his work at the hospital is running into difficulties. But most significant of all is her intervention at the crucial moment in Lydgate's existence, when, though altogether innocent, he is judged by public opinion to have been complicit with Bulstrode in the death of Raffles. In helping Lydgate Dorothea shows particular courage since she not only has to stand out against the immense force of public opinion but has to make a kind of moral wager on Lydgate's integrity when the actual circumstances are doubtful. She also has the difficult task of convincing Rosamund that the slurs on her husband's character are unjustified when it would be all too easy for Rosamund to disown him completely. But Dorothea does not simply rescue Lydgate; she gives back to him the most precious thing that he has lost – a sense of his own personal worth:

Lydgate turned, remembering where he was, and saw Dorothea's face looking up at him with a sweet trustful gravity. The presence of a noble nature, generous in its wishes, ardent in its charity, changes the lights for us: we begin to see things again in their larger, quieter masses, and to believe that we too can be seen and judged in the wholeness of our character. That influence was beginning to act on Lydgate, who had for many days been seeing all life as one who is dragged and struggling amid the throng. He sat down again, and felt that he was recovering his own self in the consciousness that he was with one who believed in it.

Dorothea's respect is both energising and revivifying. Lydgate, who has felt himself simply to be what others believed him to be, the guilty appendage and accomplice of Bulstrode, now regains not only his self-respect but the faith that he can carve out his own, independent, autonomous sphere of action. The illumination that formerly came in a blinding flash of light on the road to Damascus can now be felt simply in the confident and respectful gaze of the other.

In *Middlemarch* we have a strong sense of characters stumbling and losing their way, yet often regaining the right path: we are always conscious of their potential freedom of action and thus their ability to undo to some degree what they may have already done. Yet with Gwendolen Harleth, the heroine of *Daniel Deronda* (1876), we are conscious of an inexorable, inevitable movement in which character itself becomes a principle of fatality. It scarcely seems possible to think of Gwendolen struggling against her fate since she herself is that fate. All the options, all the excuses, all the alibis that George Eliot permitted Dorothea over her fateful decision to marry Casaubon are denied Gwendolen. George Eliot makes her fully and totally responsible for her actions. She can never claim, as Dorothea might, that she did not know what sort of a man she was marrying since she marries him after meeting the mistress whom she has so shabbily treated, and she marries him in full knowledge of his sadistic, overmastering will. But she believes that she can conquer him. The disturbing image that focuses the meaning of the novel is that of Gwendolen recklessly gambling at the casino. On the one hand it signifies courage, power and independence that might, in Victorian eyes, seem disconcerting in a woman, yet it also conveys a sense of emptiness, frustration, inner despair. Like Charlotte Brontë, George Eliot wishes to cancel any sense her readers might have that a woman's lot is either a comfortable or a cosy one. She wants to show that a woman's life also involves risk, daring and danger. On her wedding day Gwendolen feels 'a sort of exulting defiance as she felt herself standing at the game of life with many eyes upon her, daring everything to win much – or if to lose, still with *eclat* and a sense of importance'.

Gwendolen has for long enjoyed the exhilarating sense of power that comes from the knowledge that a wealthy and powerful man stands wholly at the mercy of her whim, yet such power of frustration is ultimately empty. It implicitly predicates an eventual 'concession' through which her existence will be doubly valorised, since she obtains the great match of which other women can only dream, yet seemingly without wanting it or valuing it. Although Gwendolen is not really free anyway, since the reduced circumstances of her family virtually requires that the opportunity be snatched at while there is still time, paradoxically it is her own will to power that compels the marriage rather than any financial pressure:

> The word of all work Love will no more express the myriad modes of mutual attraction, than the word Thought can inform you what is passing through your neighbour's mind. It would be hard to tell on which side – Gwendolen's or Grandcourt's – the influence was more mixed. At that moment his strongest wish was to be completely master of this creature – this piquant combination of maidenliness and mischief: that she knew things which had made her start away from him, spurred him to triumph over that repugnance; and he was believing that he should triumph, and she – ah, piteous equality in the need to dominate – she was overcome like the thirsty one who is drawn towards the seeming water in the desert, overcome by the suffused sense that here, in this man's homage to her lay the rescue from helpless subjection to an oppressive lot.

Here is George Eliot's rather more disenchanted tableau of 'Modern Love' – a struggle for dominance that necessarily must lead to emptiness, in which every party is the 'victor'.

In the dark night of despair Gwendolen desperately clutches at Daniel Deronda as the significant other, who can give her a sense of perspective on her predicament and who can stabilise and reinforce her own best self. Deronda in some mysterious way becomes 'a part of her conscience', 'the strongest of all monitors'. Through his ideal, imaginary gaze she can purge herself of all the impurities of her existence:

> she had learned to see all her acts through the impression they would make on Deronda. . . . He seemed to her a terrible-browed angel from whom she could not think of concealing any deed so as to win an ignorant regard from him: it belonged to the nature of their relation that she should be truthful, for his power over her had begun in the raising of a self-discontent which could be satisfied only by genuine change.

However, the whole notion of the significant other in *Daniel Deronda* begins to acquire sinister connotations of which George Eliot herself may not have been aware. For whereas in *Middlemarch* Dorothea's faith in Lydgate is genuinely vivifying, the fact that Deronda, after hearing Gwendolen's confession that she wished for her husband's death, refuses either to exonerate or forgive her, saying only 'you may become worthier than you have ever yet been', places her in a state of perpetual probation and makes her even more helplessly dependent on him: 'she could not spontaneously think of an end to that reliance, which had become to her imagination like the firmness of the earth, the only condition of her walking'.

Far from strengthening her, her involvement with Deronda seems only to have sapped the independence of a once strong woman – and of this George Eliot seems to approve. Matters are of course complicated by the fact that the always implicit erotic attachment between the two has now turned into a kind of love on Gwendolen's side, so Deronda can scarcely encourage further confessions without bad faith:

> his strong feeling for this stricken creature could not hinder rushing images of future difficulty. He continued to meet her appealing eyes as he spoke, but it was with the painful consciousness that to her ear his words might carry a promise which one day would seem unfulfilled: he was making an indefinite promise to an indefinite hope.

So his determination to maintain an almost clinical detachment can be justified on compassionate grounds. Yet in so mingling his life with hers, he has always been on treacherous ground, and in her desire to criticise Gwendolen's narcissism George Eliot makes it rather too easy for him to walk away. Although Daniel Deronda could not be a more idealised representation of the power of the significant other in a secular world, we cannot help feeling that such power is dangerous.

Many critics, most notably F. R. Leavis, have objected to the Jewish counterplot to the story of Gwendolen Harleth on the grounds that it is artistically inferior. There is an artistic imbalance in the novel in the sense that with Gwendolen Harleth George Eliot treated a subject she knew well – the spiritual dilemmas of the Victorian woman – whereas, though well intentioned, she knew very much less about the sufferings of European Jewry, so that the chapters dealing with Mirah and Mordecai are very much the stuff of romance. Yet we must not dismiss this section of the book too readily since it was here that George Eliot finally addressed a question that she had interminably postponed and which lay closest to her own predicament as a non-believer and an intellectual: how is it possible to live in a world without God? It must be admitted in some sense the novel cannot and does not address this since the Jewish people *do* believe in God, so that George Eliot, by making Daniel Deronda allegorical of her own situation, creates a multiplicity of misconstructions and misrecognitions. As I have already pointed out, for George Eliot what the modern intellectual and the modern world had lost was a sense of community, and the drive to reconstruct a world where a concern for others survived lay behind all her earlier fiction. As a project what *Daniel Deronda* promised was both to restore the Jews, the lost and excluded nation, to the community of European nations and to offer a model of harmony for the alienated intellectual. Deronda, by acknowledging his identity as a Jew is not merely restored to a living community, but finds his identity enhanced through a sense of commitment and social mission: 'It was as if he had found an added soul in finding his ancestry – his judgement no longer wandering in the mazes of impartial sympathy, but, choosing, with the noble partiality which is man's best strength, the closer fellowship that makes sympathy practical.' Among the Jews Deronda finds a role, whereas before he has been confused and aimless – which is why if he is the significant other for Gwendolen, *he* is also her double. In the model of Jewish history and in its concern with the handing on of tradition, which must at the same time be creatively revitalised, George Eliot saw a way out of the impasse of the intellectual whose life seems dominated by rejection and refusal of the past in the name of reason. The intellectual, as master of knowledge, is also concerned with the transmission of culture and of values. She or he cannot begin just with a blank page: there must be a dialectical relationship with the past. So just as Deronda needs Mordecai, so Mordecai needs Deronda. Each completes the other. Mordecai says to Daniel: 'you will be my life: it will be planted afresh; it will grow', and Daniel reflects:

> Nay, it was conceivable that as Mordecai needed and believed that he had found an active replenishment of himself, so Deronda might receive from Mordecai's mind the complete ideal shape of that personal duty and citizenship which lay in his own thought like sculptured fragments certifying some beauty yearned after but not traceable by divination.

The metaphor is revealing as it implies the hypothetical reconstruction of a Greek and pagan ideal of beauty, yet this will also in some sense be a religion. For George Eliot religion has come to imply an aesthetical, moral and social condition where the beliefs themselves really do not much matter – which is why she showed a sneaking and rather unexpected sympathy with the Anglican church. George Eliot saw in the Jewish faith a way of bringing back passion, community and conviction to a world that lost it. She mingled Jewish wishes and hopes with her own in order to give them a local habitation and a name, but the result, necessarily, was a piously embarked upon, well-intentioned muddle. It is the desperation of Gwendolen, her anxiety, 'world-nausea' and 'spiritual dread' that is truer to George Eliot's own situation.

Like Mill and George Eliot, Matthew Arnold saw himself as an embattled intellectual struggling against the ignorance, complacency, facile optimism and lack of seriousness that he discerned in Victorian public life, and he made it his mission in life to discredit these attitudes. Indeed this question of the tone of public life was of far greater importance to him than it was to Mill and Eliot, for although Arnold did want his own views to be heeded and respected, he did not think this could come about until public debates were conducted in a more calm, disinterested and critical spirit. Arnold's emphasis on the function of criticism, the critical spirit and on the importance of rational discussion seemingly links him with Mill and Eliot, yet the thrust of such terms in his own argument is very different. For Mill and Eliot criticism implied above all secularisation – a spirit of scientific and critical enquiry, as represented by geology, Darwinism and German biblical criticism that would challenge theological dogma. Arnold was opposed to dogma but he was also opposed to the kind of rationalism that Mill and Eliot represented; faced with a confrontation between dogma and reason, Arnold's response was to look for some alternative, which he found both in imaginative literature and in the idea that the Bible itself must be understood as a kind of poetry. Arnold did make very significant concessions to modern science and to biblical criticism. There is a strange concurrence between Mill and Arnold that what can be salvaged from historical Christianity is the idea of Jesus as an outstanding moral teacher, yet Arnold could not accept the idea of morals without religion – much of *Literature and Dogma* is concerned to articulate his view that religious morality, or righteousness does represent an infinitely superior kind of spirituality. For Arnold criticism as he understood it was not to be identified with any fixed intellectual standpoint or determination to adopt some preconceived standpoint; it meant rather a free and disinterested spirit of enquiry, a willingness to sift, interrogate and scrutinise, but which would end, nevertheless, not in scepticism but in a rigorous and clearly worked out position.

In considering Arnold's thinking on the relationship between criticism and modernity it is impossible to overlook the extraordinary influence that Newman exerted upon him. Arnold himself was never a member of the Oxford Movement and was scarcely even a fellow-traveller. His own tendency in religious questions was not to move towards dogma in matters of religion but rather to react strongly against it. Yet Arnold was strongly impressed by what Newman represented – which was the determination to work out a clear and consistent intellectual position, coupled with the conviction that nothing less than this could possibly do. The alternative to this was muddle, carelessness, a spirit of *laissez-faire* in which no point of view could be regarded as better than any other and where inconsistency was more virtue than vice. Newman's code word for this was 'Liberalism'. In an extended discussion of the topic in his *Apologia* he argued that the influence of theological Liberals in the Oxford of his day had produced an unjustifiable 'licence of opinion': 'In their day they did little more than take credit to themselves for enlightened views, largeness of mind, liberality of sentiment, without drawing the line between what was just and what was admissible in speculation, and without seeing the tendency of their own principles.'[31]

In his own way Arnold also objected to such Liberalism, though he did not use the term – it is reflected in his criticism of those English people who will defend and justify anomalies on the grounds that anomalies are a good thing, and in his stern criticism in *Culture and Anarchy* of 'doing as one likes', which leads to 'action with insufficient light, action pursued because we like to be doing something and doing it as we please, and do not like the trouble of thinking and the severe constraint of any kind of rule' (v, 116). Arnold agrees with Newman that Liberalism leads to anarchy, is indeed incipiently anarchic in itself. Arnold would have understood Newman's criticisms of Evangelicalism:

it had no intellectual basis; no internal idea, no principle of unity, no theology. 'Its adherents,' I said, 'are already separating from each other; they will melt away like a snowdrift. It has no straightforward view on any one point, on which it professes to teach, and to hide its poverty, it has dressed itself out in a maze of words. We have no dread of it at all; we only fear what it may lead to. It does not stand on entrenched ground, or make any pretence to a position; it does but occupy the space between contending powers, Catholic Truth and Rationalism.'[32]

Arnold could not accept Newman's presentation of these alternatives as an absolute either/or. He too attempted to articulate an alternative space and realised that he would have to develop his position with the same earnestness and dedication that Newman had brought to his own intellectual quest. In his critical essays Arnold sought to correct and reform England by comparing it, unpatriotically and unfavourably, with France and Germany, yet in his own mind the home-grown example of Newman may actually have been of most significance. Certainly his essay on 'The Literary Influence of Academies' goes out of its way to praise Newman for his 'balance of mind', his 'intellectual delicacy' and 'urbanity of style' – all qualities that English culture in general lacks (III, 250). It is also of particular significance that this first collection of essays appeared in 1865, immediately after the controversy between Kingsley and Newman and Newman's subsequent publication of the *Apologia* in self-vindication. When Arnold refers to the *brutalité des journaux anglais*

(III, 250) he certainly must have had in mind the indecorous violence of Kingsley's personal attack on Newman, even though he nowhere mentions Kingsley by name. If the intellectual tendencies that Newman represents are to be combatted, this requires decorum on the part of those who oppose him and a comparable intellectual rigour. Arnold recognises that the violence is precisely a substitute for care and scrupulousness in argument, so that the first step is to create a climate of opinion in which such vicious polemicising is impossible. The struggle for culture must simultaneously be a struggle against barbarism.

Arnold's first major critical intervention, the essay 'On Translating Homer' of 1861, is remarkable precisely for the dexterity with which it manages both to delineate Arnold's own critical position, and, at the same time, to strike out at so many tendencies in English culture to which Arnold was opposed. The essay itself exemplifies so many of the qualities that Arnold advocated; it is calm, learned, both flexible and judicious in argument – above all it is authoritative. Most Victorian writers aspired to authoritativeness. With Carlyle and Ruskin this could take the form of a strident assertiveness, of a sort that Arnold deplored. The alternative mode was that established by the *Edinburgh Review* – a kind of Olympian pontificating, in which the author suggested that he and he alone was knowledgeable enough to have grasped the nature of the problem – and hence was the only person in any sort of position to offer either prescriptions or solutions. Like the Edinburgh Reviewers Arnold is concerned to establish his own credentials, so that it is by no means accidental that he begins by observing that it has often been suggested to him that he translate Homer, and in general his way is to suggest that he has thought more purposefully and more deeply about the matter than anyone else and therefore to imply that his 'advice' can hardly be ignored. Where he differs from the writers for the *Edinburgh Review* is that his analysis depends upon the qualities of his own close reading of Homer and his translators: effectively Arnold challenges Homer's translators and his readers to challenge his readings – *if they can*. He aims to be authoritative yet concedes the possibility of a response. For Arnold the example of Homer was a potent one since it raised the possibility – already triumphantly exemplified in Goethe – as to whether it was possible to be a classic in an age where everything mitigated against it. Here Arnold was at once able to make amends for his breach with Clough by suggesting that Clough pre-eminently possessed the Homeric qualities of 'out-of-doors freshness, life, naturalness, buoyant rapidity' (I, 216), while at the same time parenthetically implying the decadence of Tennyson, the dominating figure of the day. The whole point about Tennyson, as Arnold sees it, is that he is not and never can be the poet of the grand style – as Arnold himself aspires to be: Tennyson is neither plain, simple nor direct and he is certainly not rapid. Homer is therefore a very convenient stick to beat Tennyson with, even though this may not be the ostensible object of the exercise. To speak of Homer and to focus on the problem of translating Homer is also to foreground what is worst in English poetry and criticism – its whimsicality, arbitrariness and excess.

Arnold's essay is not just another view of Homer nor does it concede that one view is just as good as another. Arnold insists that only the scholarly and the discriminating can have a view about translating Homer in the first place. This is not a matter for the common reader and Arnold, in addressing common readers, wants above all to make them aware of their own limitations as well as of the limitations of translators. Yet for all the dangers of dogmatism the essay is a remarkable triumph. In his eighth paragraph Arnold baldly states that the translator of Homer

> should above all be penetrated by a sense of four qualities of his author: – that he is eminently rapid; that he is eminently plain and direct, both in the evolution of his thought and in the expression of it, that is, both in his syntax and in his words; that he is eminently plain and direct in the substance of his thought, that is, in his matter and ideas; and finally that he is eminently noble. (I, 102)

He immediately concedes that this specification may seem too general as to be virtually valueless, yet he then goes on to show in abundant detail how such apparently simple requirements cannot be met by most Homeric translators and to show that there is very much more to saying this than meets the eye. Arnold thus shows himself at once a virtuoso of practical criticism and a cogent theorist of translation. When he has finished it is hard to dismiss this as just another point of view and while, in general, in literary criticism we tend not to be very well disposed towards attempts to lay down the law, Arnold has achieved his own objective, since the criteria that he lays down have been very widely accepted since. Yet in so saying we can also recognise in Arnold and in his age a metaphysical demand for certainty that is alien to us – we would not necessarily agree that the existence of standards depends on the existence of arguments and claims that cannot be controverted. In thinking this Arnold is much more like Mill than he would be disposed to admit.

In Arnold's criticism the idea of the modern looms large, it seems the pivotal concept around which all his thinking revolves, yet in many ways this is strange since, especially as a young man, Arnold gave every indication of being an arch-conservative, an aspirant poet who defined his identity through an intransigent opposition to the modern. If anyone in Victorian England heeded Carlyle's admonition 'Close thy Byron; open thy Goethe', that person was certainly Arnold – and Arnold pursued the implications of that choice with a quite extraordinary severity. In part this was because in rejecting the Romantics Arnold was also reacting against Carlyle as well. Arnold disliked Carlyle's overblown rhetoric and stylistic vehemence; he above all seemed to typify the lack of balance and indifference to reasoned argument that, for Arnold, was all too prevalent in English life. His reading of Keats – suddenly fashionable thanks to the edition of his poetry published by Moncton Milnes – convinced him that the great vice of English poetry, for which Shakespeare must be held ultimately responsible, is the victory of style over content. Keats's determination to 'load every rift with ore' leads in 'Isabella' to a situation in which the narrative is effectively destroyed by the linguistic excess. 'Isabella' is 'a perfect treasure-house of graceful and felicitous words and images', it contains a greater number of 'happy single expressions' than the complete works of Sophocles, yet the action is so feebly conceived that the effect produced by it is 'absolutely null' (I, 10). For Arnold the lesson of this was that it was absolutely imperative to subordinate style to content and this Neo-classical distinction was one that would remain central to his thinking. Yet the Arnold who repudiated Shakespeare and the Romantics on Neo-classical grounds, insisting on 'the all-importance of the choice of subject; the necessity of accurate construction; and the subordinate character of expression' (I, 12), was also the man who was summarily to dismiss Dryden and Pope as 'classics of our prose' (IX, 189). Arnold had contrived to dismiss the greater part of English literature, yet his verdict on the classics of Roman literature was equally sweeping. Virgil wants cheerfulness, Horace wants seriousness, Lucretius is 'overstrained, gloom-weighted, morbid' (I, 34). In their very different and diverse ways Arnold finds none of them 'adequate'. The phrase itself suggests a schoolmasterly censoriousness, and when Arnold states categorically 'If human life were complete without faith, without enthusiasm, without energy, Horace, like Menander, would be the perfect interpreter of human life: but it is not; to the best, to the most living sense of humanity, it is not; and because it is not, Horace is inadequate' (I, 36) we are conscious of Arnold pontificating from a university lectern, which, to all intents and purposes, might just as well be a pulpit. Horace, we feel, has been slumming it when he should have been getting on with his studies. Literary texts are found wanting in terms of a public-school ethos that seems to preclude the existence of diversity in literature as well as morals. Of course many readers of Arnold may feel that he is entitled to express his point of view and that even if it too readily aspires to authoritative and canonical utterance at least we do know where he stands. Equally it can be argued that Arnold's interventions are above all strategic and closely related to his own developing career as a poet. Whatever the merits of his own poetic precursors and contemporaries, it is imperative that he find his own path, that – as T. S. Eliot was to do later – he should look for inspiration and example beyond the English tradition. Arnold's criticism of Roman literature must be seen rather as an assertion of the supremacy of Greek literature within the classical tradition, where the balance is all too readily tilted towards Latin – a salutary insistence on 'the absolute, the enduring interest of Greek literature, and, above all, of Greek poetry' (I, 37).

Arnold's cultural conservatism, however, actually goes much further than this. Although he takes his cultural bearings from the 'classicism' of Goethe and Schiller, he stresses in a way that they do not the need for absolute fidelity to the models provided by Greek literature and warns quite categorically against the dangers of a modern subject. For Arnold the claims of the classical subject, whether Empedocles or Merope, were strong since this was one of the most important ways in which the poet could evade the transitoriness of the age: 'A great human action of a thousand years ago' will involve the passions even of a contemporary spectator more deeply than 'a smaller human action of today' (I, 4). In his Preface to the first edition of his poems Arnold seems to make very few concessions to the modern. He admits that 'the present age makes great claims upon us' (I, 13), yet he implies that the only way the poet can maintain his sanity is to block out this clamour and concentrate single-mindedly, even obsessively, on the still relevant – never more relevant – model of classical Greece. He finds his only solid footing 'among the ancients' (I, 14). Even the claim that we must emulate rather than merely imitate the great classical authors such as Aeschylus and Sophocles is not really conceded by Arnold since he really does not believe that imitation would be unworthy. Reading and rereading the great classics of antiquity can actually save us: 'They can help to cure us of what is, it seems to me, the great vice of our intellect, manifesting itself in our incredible vagaries in literature, in art, in religion, in morals: namely, that it is *fantastic*, and wants *sanity*' (I, 17).

For Arnold, as for Goethe and Schiller, the artist had somehow to maintain his poise and serenity in a world that was confused and discordant. Arnold is one of the very first critics explicitly to insist that the task of the artist is emphatically not to imitate the chaos and disorder of the modern world – which is why the idea of imitating the classics is no longer to be seen, as it was by Edward Young, as inferiority confessed. In his letters to Clough he suggested that the contemporary world was insufficiently nourishing for the artist and saw analogies with the decline of the Roman Empire – which was why the example of Marcus Aurelius held such a fascination for him. He exploded:

> My dearest Clough these are damned times – everything is against one – the height to which knowledge is come, the spread of luxury, our physical enervation, the absence of great *natures*, the unavoidable contact with millions of small ones, newspapers, cities, light profligate friends, moral desperadoes like Carlyle, our own selves and the sickening consciousness of our difficulties.[33]

As so often with Arnold, the incipient hysteria seems strangely mingled with a certain superior smugness and yet, despite this, we can sympathise with his dilemma. For it increasingly becomes Arnold's conviction that the artist can no longer simply create, no longer unselfconsciously express the consciousness of his age. Now he needs to be a critic before he is an artist, both because it is essential for him to 'begin with an idea of the world in order not to be prevailed over by the world's multitudinousness',[34] and because in a period of social and intellectual confusion it is more necessary than ever that the reading public should be educated, that standards should be maintained. If the age's pretensions are false then they will need to be combatted by an art that does not accede to them and by a criticism that resists them. So Arnold could not draw back from the recognition that of the two tasks, criticism was the more urgent.

Arnold's sense that the modern age was an age of criticism was not peculiar to himself, it was a perception that he shared with Mill, George Eliot and many others. Yet his understanding of what the idea of criticism implied was actually very different. For Mill the modern age was characterised by the dominance of a rational, scientific spirit that necessarily set itself at odds both with tradition and with established forms of religion. Up to a point Arnold also accepted this. He knew that religion would have to be rethought in the light of modern demands and that in the face of a comprehensive interrogation of religious truth claims many concessions would have to be made. His most explicit acknowledgement of the corrosive power of the modern spirit occurs, appropriately enough, in his essay on Heinrich Heine, where he writes:

Modern times find themselves with an immense system of institutions, established facts, accredited dogmas, customs, rules, which have come to them from times not modern. In this system their life has to be carried forward; yet they have a sense that this system is not of their own creation, that it by no means corresponds exactly with the wants of their actual life, that, for them, it is customary, not rational. The awakening of this sense is the awakening of the modern spirit. The modern spirit is now awake almost everywhere; the sense of want of correspondence between the forms of modern Europe and its spirit, between the new wine of the eighteenth and nineteenth centuries, and the old bottles of the eleventh and twelfth centuries, almost everyone perceives. (III, 109)

Moreover Arnold, though conceding that Heine himself is 'not an adequate interpreter of the modern world' but 'only a brilliant soldier in the war of liberation of humanity', nevertheless pointedly cites him as a *locus classicus* – if the phrase is not too perverse – of the modern (III, 107). Here Arnold seems clearly to indicate that he is on the side of the modern and against the unthinking traditionalism, chauvinism and philistinism of English culture. In his own attack upon it he sees Heine as a useful ally, yet already in this crucial qualification that Heine is not an adequate interpreter of the modern world we can detect Arnold's search for an alternative perspective. This alternative is that it is neither possible nor desirable to imagine that you are on the side of the modern or of progressive ideas in general, as Mill and George Eliot, for example, might have thought

they were. Although Arnold continues to acknowledge the significance of criticism in discrediting outworn ideas and systems of
belief, he is more concerned to stress the preservative role of criticism. Its task is not so much to destroy and dissolve as to promote an
awareness of the 'best that has been known and thought in the
world' – with the clear implication that it is not necessarily the
moderns who have the best ideas.

Arnold, though conscious of modernity as a problem, could not
believe in any unilinear, unproblematic notion of progress, and he
was at his shrewdest and most perceptive in his determined resistance to what the Victorians took to be the most self-evident of
doctrines. Arnold recognised that what many took to be a fact was
actually little more than a complacent state of mind, and it was
symptomatic of his intellectual adroitness that he could begin,
almost ironically, by first apparently conceding Macaulay's claim
that the literature in English now surpasses the literature that existed
in all languages three hundred years ago, and then adding, very
coolly:

> only, remembering Spinoza's maxim that the two great banes
> of humanity are self-conceit and the laziness coming from self-
> conceit, I think it may do us good, instead of resting in our
> pre-eminence with perfect security, to look a little more closely
> why this is so, and whether it is so without any limitations.
> (III, 232)

We hear little about why this is so – much more about the provinciality of English culture – of which, we may take it, Macaulay is
symptomatic. Yet if Arnold could not accept assumptions about
cultural progress, he nevertheless had to find his own interpretation
of the problem of the modern. His response, in his Oxford lecture
'On the Modern Element in Literature', was to deploy the organic
analogy – to suggest that all cultures have their stages of growth,
maturation and decay, and to argue that the modern is that particular phase in the development of culture where it has become more
advanced, more complex, but also subject to incipient processes of
decay. Undoubtedly Gibbon's *Decline and Fall of the Roman Empire*
had an important influence on his thinking, and his essay on Marcus
Aurelius he drew significant parallels between past and present:

> Christianity was a new spirit in the Roman world, destined to act
> in that world as a dissolvent; and it was inevitable that Christian-

ity in the Roman world, like democracy in the modern world, like every new spirit with a significant mission assigned to it, should at its first appearance occasion an instinctive shrinking repugnance in the world which it was to dissolve. (III, 144)

For Arnold the modern represents an advanced stage of culture in which

there is greater prosperity, where war no longer significantly impinges on the lives of the majority of people, where it is possible to pursue more sophisticated and refined pursuits, and where, most significantly of all: the intellectual maturity of man himself; the tendency to observe facts with a critical spirit; to search for their law, not to wander among them at random; to judge them by the rules of reason, not by the impulse of prejudice or caprice. (I, 24)

Yet there are also periods where this critical discrimination is most needed, since what characterises the modern is a certain cognitive dissonance, engendered by the existence of a plurality of ideas and creeds, all of which are struggling for predominance: 'an immense, moving confused spectacle, which, while it perpetually excites our comprehension, perpetually baffles our comprehension' (I, 20). Therefore what modern periods really need – and here Arnold would have agreed with Comte – is a principle of order and stability, yet what can provide this is not uncritical acceptance of tradition, as Burke would have it, but the critical intelligence itself made socially central, elevated, institutionalised as in the Académie française. Arnold agreed that the modern age was characterised by a plurality of opinions, but he could not accept that such a pluralism, at once endemic and undecidable, was a desirable state of affairs.

The great irony of Arnold's career is that *Culture and Anarchy* (1869), the work by which he is best known and which has been most influential, is also that which least exemplifies his own definition of what constitutes good criticism. For Arnold good criticism should be lucid and discriminating, it should subtle and flexible in argument, it should above all seek to persuade. Yet for Arnold in *Culture and Anarchy* the matter is too urgent, the hour too late for such intellectual niceties, he seems like a man bent, like Milton, on abandoning all fugitive and cloistered virtue for the dust and heat of public battle. Arnold is convinced that if he is to guard the last citadel of truth from encircling, ladder-scaling barbarian hordes he has no alternative but to empty buckets of pitch over the wall, to smite his adversaries hip and thigh. Arnold seeks to defend and promulgate Hellenic values in a manner that is distinctly Hebraic in tone and smacks more than a little of the uncompromising, fire-breathing chapel rhetoric that he so greatly deplores. In 'On the Literary Influence of Academies' Arnold had deprecated the narrow and provincial spirit of English culture:

> it does not persuade, it makes war; it has not urbanity, the tone of the city, of the centre, the tone, which always aims at a spiritual and intellectual effect, and not excluding the use of banter, never disjoins banter itself from politeness, from felicity. But the more provincial tone is more violent and seems rather an effect upon the blood and senses than upon the spirit and intellect; it loves hard hitting rather than persuading.   (III, 249)

Yet here Arnold himself seems to have succumbed to this English predilection for 'vigorous' controversy – perhaps because only in this way could he overcome the mood of powerlessness expressed in 'Dover Beach'. In his defence Arnold would almost certainly claim that while he might deplore English provinciality and wish that it did not exist, he nevertheless had to acknowledge that it did and act accordingly. Arnold had found that his attempts to adopt an Olympian tone were distinctly ineffective – it was this that prompted the *Daily Telegraph* to style him 'an elegant Jeremiah'. In the controversies over *Culture and Anarchy* there must have been moments when Arnold must have called to mind Heine's lines in 'Atta Troll'

> Doch mit schlechtgeleckten Töpeln
> Täglich mich herumzubalgen
> In der teurer Heimat, dessen
> Ward ich endlich überdrüssig.

[But in the end I grew tired of scuffling daily in my beloved homeland with ill-mannered louts]

The double bind Arnold found himself in was that to be effectual he needed to become something of a stump orator, yet in so doing he risked putting in jeopardy the ideals of culture, of sweetness and light that he espoused. Indeed much of the pent-up frustration released in *Culture and Anarchy* stems from Arnold's own baffled awareness that to defend an ideal of culture in a society that does not recognise it is a virtually impossible task. Culture, as Arnold sees it, involves some kind of recognition of a higher authority that his English critics simply refuse to concede. In the essay on academies he suggested that

> deference to a standard higher than one's own habitual standard in intellectual matters, a like respectful recognition of a superior ideal, is caused, in the intellectual sphere, by sensitiveness of intelligence. Those whose intelligence is quickest, openest, most sensitive, are readiest with this deference; those whose intelligence is less delicate and sensitive are less disposed to it. Well, now we are on the road to see why the French have their Academy and we have nothing of the kind.   (III, 237)

But, of course, seeing it does not really help. Arnold's arguments about culture presume an authority, predicate a deference, postulate a consensus that does not exist, so that he is both in and out of the battle, both insisting on culture's importance to those like Frederick Harrison who perceive the man of culture as 'one of the poorest mortals alive' (v, 87), and yet also thinking of culture as some kind of irresistibly historical force, a drive towards perfection, that will both transform and transcend a world that denies it. In this Arnold sees the operation of culture as something very like historical development of Christianity, a force born into a pagan world and despised within it, but a force that will nevertheless ultimately and inevitably transform that pagan world into something else. Yet, like Marx, Arnold both knows that his cause will eventually triumph, yet worries that it may not.

Modern discussions of *Culture and Anarchy* have tended to focus, almost obsessively, on Arnold's conception of culture, yet it could certainly be argued, contrariwise, that all this talk of culture is very much by the by, and that Arnold's real purpose in *Culture and Anarchy* is to defend both the idea of an established church and the High Church Anglican establishment. Certainly Arnold himself did much to encourage such a view, especially in his Preface, and so in considering the complexity of texts we have to recognise that in addition to a complexity in the development of an argument, there may also be a complexity that stems from an attempt, within a text, to transmit two different messages simultaneously. Certainly, although Arnold's whole analysis of contemporary 'anarchy' embraces such things as the disorders in Hyde Park and a man's right to marry his deceased wife's sister, there can be little doubt that the thing that troubled Arnold the most was the proposal to disestablish the Irish church. Arnold recognised that the existence of an established church whose views were not shared by the majority of the population led to a great deal of unfairness, yet the destructive conjunction of Fenianism on the one hand and English Nonconformism on the other made him cling to the idea of a central institution. Ever since the collapse of Chartism the power of the coalition between the English aristocracy and the middle class had been unchallenged. Now at last this hegemony was being threatened, and Arnold, like many others, was perturbed by such polyglot and polymorphous insurrections. The whole idea of a guiding and ruling centre had suddenly become problematic. The dangerous prospect was that of a society fragmented into a variety of special interest groups, each with their own specific axe to grind, where all that would matter would be power and numbers, epitomised by Hepworth Dixon's description of the Mormons: 'The great facts remain. Young and his people are at Utah; a church of 200,00 souls; and army of 20,000 rifles' (v, 148).

In the Preface to *Culture and Anarchy* Arnold seems to delight in presenting himself as a conservative of the old school, praising the edifying qualities of Bishop Wilson's *Maxims*, so profusely cited in the text itself, and observing:

> To me and to the members of the Society for Promoting Christian knowledge his name and writings are still, no doubt, familiar. But the world is fast going away from old-fashioned people of his sort, and I learnt with consternation lately from a brilliant and distinguished votary of the natural sciences, that he had never so much as heard of Bishop Wilson, and that he imagined me to have invented him.   (v, 231)

The talismanic importance attached to Bishop Wilson strongly suggests that those, like Arnold and Wilson, who know Latin and Greek are probably better Christians than those Nonconformists who do not, and that right reason and the will of God are to be identified with the Anglican church. Certainly the case for church establishments is strongly argued in the Preface: there are the customary laudatory references to Hooker; there is the claim that 'the fruitful men of English Puritanism and nonconformity are men who were trained within the pale of the Establishment, – Milton, Baxter, Wesley' (v, 237–8); the suggestion that 'the Nonconformist is not in contact with the main current of National life, like a member of an Establishment' (v, 238).

Arnold looks forward to the disappearance of Nonconformity just as he looks forward to the disappearance of the Welsh language. Divergence and plurality are an anathema to him, even though he also says that those who live in the modern era have to learn to live with diversity. Yet, at the same time, behind this parade and appearance of orthodoxy lurk more heretical messages. There is the insinuation that since neither the aristocracy or the middle classes have the credentials to govern, the future lies with an objective and impartial intelligentsia. There is the suggestion that there is no point actually in talking about preserving national unity or consensus and tradition, since they no longer exist, if they ever did, and will have to be constructed from scratch through a Prussian system of national education. There is the troubling implication that Christianity has actually had its day, that the positive phase of its historical mission is largely over and that its negative effects and consequences are now in danger of outweighing its actual and very real achievements. One side of Arnold actually recognises, under protest, that it is not altogether preposterous to think Bishop Wilson imaginary or to think of consigning Christianity to the past.

In the whole argument of *Culture and Anarchy* Arnold's emphasis on the value of 'Sweetness and Light', a formulation that he believes epitomises the spirit of Greek culture, is clearly of crucial importance. Yet considering the overall length of his text it is surprising how little space Arnold devotes to elucidating and elaborating what he means by this and how little detailed discussion there is either to Greek culture itself or of its major intellectual figures and philosophical ideas. Arnold does indeed mention Socrates as an exemplary figure, yet he seems scarcely to consider the awkwardness Socrates might present for his own argument. Socrates was, after all, a sceptic and he made it his task to interrogate and discomfort those who, like Arnold, were confident of their own possession of the truth. Arnold seeks to enhance and strengthen the power of the state, yet Socrates was executed precisely because of the challenge that he presented to the authority of the Athenian state. One wonder how Arnold would have responded to a request from Socrates to explain what he means by 'Sweetness and Light' and why he believes that this is to be identified with right reason and the will of God. In defence of Arnold it can reasonably be claimed that he had already developed his own understanding of Greece in earlier essays and that at the time there was a fairly general consensus about the values that Greek culture stood for. Yet there does remain a certain irony in the fact that Nietzsche should have written *The Birth of Tragedy* in 1870–1, almost immediately after the publication of *Culture and Anarchy*. The point is not that Nietzsche was right about the Greeks and that Arnold was wrong, but that Arnold's way of thinking seems to exclude both the possibility that there actually can be divergent interpretations of the significance of Greek culture and the likelihood that there may be diverse and contradictory tendencies within Greek culture itself. We may of course concede that Arnold is at liberty to invoke some kind of Greek ideal without necessarily committing himself to the view that most or even much of ancient Greek society corresponded to it. Nevertheless there is a significant hiatus in the argument here. Arnold, in speaking of sweetness and light, of balance, of harmonious development, of openness and flexibility of mind, is above all invoking an interpretation of Greek culture associated with such figures as Goethe and Schiller, Herder, von Humboldt and Hegel. It is here that we find a great stress on the idea of *Bildung*, on aesthetic education, on the idea that there has been a progressive movement in history, on the role of the state in promoting human development. These thinkers were certainly inspired by the example of Greek culture, but the ideas themselves are not specifically Greek, and the Greeks, who had no notion of progress in history, might well have found some of them puzzling. Had Arnold spelled out this German intellectual background more fully his position would have been both clearer and more accessible, but the possibility cannot be discounted that had he done so the secularising implications of this position would have been made more obvious and that he would therefore have found it more difficult to give sense to his claim that 'The aim and end of both Hebraism and Hellenism is . . . one and the same' (v, 164).

Arnold's consistent position is that Hellenism must correct Hebraism, and he does not want to argue too openly that Hellenism should replace it, even though he seems to envisage that, in the long run, this is what will happen. A particular puzzle is the relation of religion to science, which is one of the many hidden sub-texts of *Culture and Anarchy*. Arnold sees the origins of the development of science in Greek culture, in the desire to see the object as it really is, and sees that goal as having been revived in the Renaissance.

But does Arnold believe that Hebraism must be corrected by this side of Hellenism, that its myths and misrepresentations must recede before the light of science? Perhaps he does, even if he does not openly say so; but if he does, where does this leave 'right reason and the will of God'? If Arnold ridicules Robert Buchanan for thinking that it is the will of God that he 'would *swarm* the earth with beings' (v, 214), how does he know that his own sense of the will of God is more just? How is it that Arnold, who claims to be an intelligent and sophisticated man with a flexible mind, fails to recognise, as have many much more simple minds, that it is no easy matter to interpret what the will of God is? Still, Arnold does have an argument, which centres on the idea of Sin. Arnold believes that the avoidance of sin may well have been a worthy and even necessary development in the early stages of human history, but now, like the American Transcendentalist, he believes that this goal has become too limiting; it actually stands in the way of a fuller conception of a human development, of an odyssey towards perfection. The Greek ideal was premature:

The indispensable basis of conduct and self-control, the platform upon which alone the perfection aimed at by Greece can come into bloom, was not to be reached by our race so easily; centuries of probation and discipline were needed to bring us to it. Therefore the bright promise of Hellenism faded and Hebraism ruled the world. (v, 169)

But now the case is different. Hebraism was right in the infancy of the human race; now as humanity reaches towards a fuller and more harmonious conception of spiritual development, it is the example of Greece that can lead it there.

Such a ringing affirmation of the value of the example of Greek culture is undoubtedly present in *Culture and Anarchy*, but Arnold's utterances are always more strategic and more equivocal than they might seem, so it is not always easy to know how to take them. Although Arnold was himself suspicious of rhetoric – coming down particularly heavily, for example, on Macaulay, whose exhilarating periods he found unsatisfactory, despite their undoubted interest for the intellectual novice – he was a considerable rhetorician himself. Much of the impact of *Culture and Anarchy* stems from its predilection for the device of zeugma, the fate that it can speak of beauty and perfection in one and the same breath as the largest truss manufacturer in Europe and Mr Murphy's advice to Protestant husbands: 'Take care of your wives!' (v, 121, 131). Indeed it is impossible not to suspect Arnold of a deliberate and complex irony in speaking of beauty and perfection, knowing full well that even the use of such words will send his bourgeois adversaries into absolute paroxysms of indignation. Certainly, *Culture and Anarchy* is at its best when fighting philistinism; at its weakest when suggesting what the alternative might be. Arnold ostensibly writes in defence of flexibility and openness of mind, yet even as the reader is gladly concurring with Arnold on the inestimable value of these qualities, he is brought up short when Arnold glosses 'the want of flexibility of our race' as follows:

> I mean, it being admitted that the conformity of the individual reason of the fanatical Protestant or the popular rioter with right reason is our true object, and not the mere restraining them, by the strong arm of the state, from Papist-baiting, or railing-breaking, – admitting this, we English have so little flexibility that we cannot perceive that the State's restraining them from these indulgences may yet fix clearly in their minds that, to the collective nation, these indulgences appear irrational and unallowable, may make them pause and reflect, and may contribute to bringing, with time, their individual reason into harmony with right reason. (v, 160)

Arnold is clearly entitled to argue for a stronger role for the state, and his own role in promoting the idea of state education was both far-sighted and honourable, yet here it becomes all too clear that his talk of flexibility and openness means little more than that his opponents should come round to his point of view, which is of course to be identified with right reason. Arnold clearly had plenty of justification for criticising the often confused and irrational *mêlée* of Victorian controversy, yet it often seems that he is more interested in silencing it than in improving the overall quality of debate.

What makes the apparent clarity of Arnold's endorsement of Greek culture and of sweetness and light all the more confusing is that, only four years later, with the publication of *Literature and Dogma* in 1873, Arnold's emphasis has shifted again. Reading *Culture and Anarchy* in isolation it would certainly be possible to conclude that there was in Victorian England an ongoing aesthetic tradition, rippling out from its centre at Oxford University, which embraced such diverse, yet linked phenomena as the concern in the Oxford

Movement with 'the beauty of holiness', the stress on the vital importance of art by such Oxford men as Ruskin, Morris, Swinburne and Burne-Jones, the aesthetic, hedonistic creed of Walter Pater, Arnold's own emphasis on beauty, harmoniousness, perfection. But in *Literature and Dogma*, published, ironically, in the very same year as Pater's *Studies in the Renaissance*, Arnold's position seems light years away. The assault on Nonconformity, of course, continues, with Arnold insisting:

> Our mechanical and materialising theology with its insane license of affirmation about God, its insane license of affirmation about a future state, is really the result of the poverty and inanition of our minds. . . .
> [T]o understand that the language of the Bible is fluid, passing, and literary, not rigid, fixed, and scientific, is the first step towards a right understanding of the Bible. But to take this very first step, some experience of how men have thought and expressed themselves, and some flexibility of spirit, are necessary; and this is culture.   (VI, 152)

Here Arnold seeks to make good the implicit promise of *Culture and Anarchy* that the Christian heritage must be exposed to the possibility of an intellectual critique. Yet Arnold's own sense of the balance between Hebrew and Hellene has nevertheless shifted again, even if he seems to be only repeating what he has already said before:

> Every educated man loves Greece, owes gratitude to Greece. Greece was the lifter-up of the banner of righteousness. Now the world cannot do without art and science. And the lifter up of the banner of art and science was naturally much occupied with them, and conduct was a homely matter. Not enough heed, therefore was given by him to conduct. But conduct, plain matter as it is, is six-eighths of life, while art and science are only two eighths. And this brilliant Greece perished for lack of attention to *conduct*; for want of conduct, steadiness and character.   (VI, 388)

But in *Culture and Anarchy* Arnold had suggested that Greece offered a higher moral vision, for which the world was not yet ready, whereas now he imputes to Greece a serious defect that even the passing centuries cannot redeem. Moreover, with Pater hovering in the wings, we may note that Arnold deliberately sets his face against any form

of the hedonist creed. He goes out of his way to criticise the Bohe-
mian lifestyle, 'the ideal, free, pleasurable, life of Paris':

> Plausible and attractive as it may be, the constitution of things
> turns out to be somehow or other against it. And why? Because
> the free development of our senses all round, of our *apparent* self,
> has to undergo a profound modification from the law of our
> higher *real* self, the law of righteousness.   (VI, 391–2)

The Hebrews were right after all. But if so we are bound to wonder
that Arnold can change his perspective so rapidly and so radically,
while nevertheless speaking with great confidence of the constitution of things and of right reason. Arnold calls for flexibility and
openness of mind, he calls for criticism, yet at bottom no one is more
dogmatic and lacking in self-criticism than he.

Nevertheless Arnold in his criticism is confident in a way that he
rarely is in his poetry. In the poetry what is especially surprising is
that the concept of the modern, which proved – to use one of his
favourite words – so *energising* as far as his criticism was concerned,
seemed to have quite the reverse effect on his verse. Arnold found
the task of the modern poet daunting, the example of the classical
past at once intimidating and humbling. The great poets of ancient
Greece, like Rustum in Arnold's 'Sohrab and Rustum', are mighty
warriors beside whom the modern lyricist seems as slender and
delicate as a girl. As Rustum suggests, and Arnold fears, this later
generation can never hope to win true renown in its own right, but
must try to steal it by feigning a challenge to open combat that they
could never actually hope to win. *Hamlet* is, in all respect, a key text
for Arnold, with its sense that the time is out of joint, its sense of a
hero who feels inadequate to the demands laid on him and who feels
unable to cross the Rubicon which leads from contemplation into
action. It was therefore not surprising that Arnold should have tried
to rewrite *Hamlet* as *Merope* – though *Merope* is more obviously a
repetition and recasting of the Oedipus story. *Merope* also suggests
that the *Daily Telegraph*'s charge that he was indifferent to politics
was not entirely justified. Admittedly Arnold had grave misgivings
about politics in general and was made yet more apprehensive by
the prospect of mass democracy, even if he was hardly unique in
this, but his very anxiety mean that such questions actually did
surface in his writing. 'Balder Dead', for example, both suggests the
impossibility of obtaining concerted action for even the worthiest of

causes – it also hints obliquely at the possible irrelevance of Christianity, since we must assume, by analogy, that even if there were the possibility that Christ could return to Earth it is by no means certain that everybody would want it. *Merope* agonises over the validity of political action in a way that no Greek tragedy ever actually does. For Arnold it is by no means obvious that the killing of Polyphontes, King of Messenia, can be justified, even if he is both a murderer and a usurper, since the issue is not simply one of vengeance or abstract justice, but one that involves questions of loyalty and political obligation, so that if the action is to be legitimised the people themselves will have a part to play. Although in his criticism Arnold was never in much doubt that all important issues should be decided by wise and judicious persons like himself, in *Merope* this automatic assumption of righteousness is problematised by the Chorus;

> But who can say, without a fear:
> *That best, who ought to rule, am I;*
> I the one righteous, they the many bad?

The political conflict in Messenia stems from the fact that Cresphontes, the murdered king, ruled by virtue of the fact that he was leader of a band of Dorians who conquered and made subjects of the Messenian people, but Cresphontes established his position by treating the Messenians favourably and constructing alliances with them. Polyphontes justifies his action on the grounds that Cresphontes was betraying his own kin, whereas Merope argues that her husband's goal of social unity is more important. She asks rhetorically:

> Whether is better, to abide alone,
> A wolfish band, in a dispeopled realm,
> Or conquerors with conquer'd to unite
> Into one puissant folk, as he designed?

For Arnold the problem, as always, as in *Culture and Anarchy*, is how it is possible to transcend factionalism and anarchy, if everyone is committed to local and factional causes. So Merope insists to her son Aeptus, after he has murdered Polyphontes, that his action can only be justified if he commits himself single-mindedly to justice and truth, and if his own actions have an exemplary significance for his people:

But thou, my son, study to make prevail
One colour in thy life, the hue of truth;
That justice, that sage order, not alone
Natural vengeance, may maintain thine act,
And make it stand indeed the will of Heaven.
Thy father's passion was this people's ease,
This people's anarchy, thy foe's pretence.
As the chiefs rule, my son, the people are.
Unhappy people, where the chiefs themselves
Are like the mob, vicious and ignorant.

We should also note that the killing of Polyphontes by Aeptus is a public, not a private act, in which he calls on the people to save both themselves and him from the power of the Dorian overlords, thus giving his act a democratic legitimation. Yet at bottom the real burden of the play seems Merope's – a strong sense that all action is doubtful and morally compromised.

The contradictions between Arnold's criticism and his poetry are nowhere more evident than in his dramatic poem *Empedocles on Etna*: the poem was first published in Arnold's collection of 1852, yet already by 1853 Arnold had decided to suppress it on the grounds that no enjoyment can be derived from the representation of situations

> in which suffering finds no vent in action; in which a continuous state of mental distress in prolonged, unrelieved by incident, hope or resistance; in which there is everything to be endured, nothing to be done. In such situations there is inevitably something morbid, in the description of them something monotonous. (I, 2–3)

Arnold's rapid change of mind was puzzling – particularly since the faults he imputes to *Empedocles* could be quite plausibly imputed to such a canonical work of Greek classicism as Sophocles' *Oedipus the King*. Of course, in Victorian times the charge of pessimism was a very serious one, more serious that we can readily imagine, so Arnold may have been reluctant to be thus characterised and so stigmatised this early in his career. The whole episode seems all too reminiscent of Shostakovich's willingness to accept a similar indictment of his Fourth Symphony. With hindsight it would indeed be too easy to dismiss *Empedocles* as 'uncharacteristic' – surely the critic who defined the Greeks in terms of sweetness and light could not have chosen to represent the balanced and rational spirit of Greek culture through a man who chooses to hurl himself into a volcano! Yet the Greek context is actually quite misleading since *Empedocles* was undoubtedly Arnold's attempt to rewrite Byron's *Manfred* for a later generation. From this point of view too Arnold's admission that the work was morbid seems odd, since Arnold had leant over backwards to disassociate Empedocles from the cosmic dissatisfaction of the Romantics and from the insatiability of Romantic aspiration, through his advocacy of 'moderate desire':

> I say: Fear not! Life still
> Leaves human effort scope.
> But, since life teems with ill
> Nurse no extravagant hope;
> Because thou must not dream, thou need'st not then despair!

Yet precisely because Empedocles's credo seems so sensible and balanced, because it seems determined to avoid absolutism and the tragedy that stems from it, his decision to kill himself seems puzzling. What Arnold wants to insist upon here is that the alienation of the philosopher/artist is not purely self-generated but stems rather from his contradictory relationship to society – how can he reconcile his duty to the world with his obligation to his deeper self? He becomes a victim not of desire but of contradiction:

> Take thy bough, set me free from my solitude;
> I have been enough alone!
>
> Where shall thy votary fly then? back to men? –
> But they will gladly welcome him once more,
> And help him unbend his too tense thought,
> And rid him of the presence of himself,
> And keep their friendly chatter at his ear,
> And haunt him, till the absence from himself,
> That other torment grows unbearable;
> And he will fly to solitude again,
> And he will find the air too keen for him,
> And so change back; and many thousand times
> Be miserably bandied to and fro
> Like a sea-wave, betwixt the world and thee,

Thou young, implacable God! and only death
Can cut his oscillations short, and so
Bring him to poise.

Yet, of course, we are bound to note that the harmoniousness that
Arnold elsewhere advocates is here presented as an impossibility for
the thinking man. Indeed harmoniousness would be a kind of betrayal. Empedocles is thus a troubling hero, whom Arnold feels
obliged to disown.

The Scholar-Gypsy is also a troubling hero, but in a completely
different way. In reading the poem we have to acknowledge that
Arnold's unequivocal endorsement of Glanville's lad, who abandons his studies to join a company of vagabond gypsies in order to
discover the secrets of their arcane lore, is in many ways surprising.
Arnold distrusted the Romantic quest for the absolute, with which
the Scholar-Gypsy is clearly allied. Even in Glanville's brief text the
disturbing failure of the Scholar, now Gypsy, to return is
foregrounded. We are bound to wonder: has he, without realising it,
lost his way or has he rather consciously abandoned his scholarly
mission for a carefree life of pleasure? Has he been duped and
deceived? Of course it can be plausibly argued that Arnold is not
much concerned with such matters, that 'The Scholar-Gypsy' is nothing if not an escapist poem, in which Arnold, now an Inspector of
Schools, rather whimsically celebrates a sense of freedom and irresponsibility that he knows is now denied him. In some sense the
poem can be seen as a valediction to his own former carefree self and
to the innocence of the life he once led at Oxford, when he did not
feel the cares of the world or the difficulties of supporting a wife and
family pressing upon him. Indeed Arnold even permitted himself to
follow Keats in luxuriating in the splendours of poetic language,
which his critical self knew to be a serious vice. Nevertheless the
poem does raise serious questions about the modern predicament.
Arnold sees the Scholar-Gypsy as an exemplary figure who represents everything that the modern age lacks: optimism, energy, decisiveness, clarity of purpose. In reading the poem we cannot fail to
recognise affinities with other critics of the nineteenth century,
whether it is Nietzsche's attack on 'paralysis of the will' or
Kierkegaard's statement that 'Purity of heart is to will one thing.'
Yet, once again, it is *Hamlet* that stands in the background – the
Scholar-Gypsy is not troubled by excessive introspection, by doubt
or hesitation; he is able to act on impulse in the clear conviction that

his goal is worthy and that his decision is for the best. In the nineteenth century such commitment is impossible, because the individual faces such strong pressures from without, such devastating conflicts within, that he is invariably deflected from the path that he should follow. Yet Arnold's own case is subtly different – though doubtful and hesitant in his poetry, in his criticism he strove for a clearness and clarity of purpose that he did not always entirely feel.

6

The Necessity of Art: Browning, Ruskin and the Pre-Raphaelites

In Victorian culture an unexpected but significant development is the way in which painting, sculpture and architecture assume a greater cultural importance. Never before had the visual arts been the subject of such widespread debate and discussion. Of course it does not therefore follow that such interest was either discriminating or informed, but the very fact that art became a matter of public concern at all was itself an important step forward. To say this is not to gloss over the negative side. As Ruskin repeatedly emphasised, Turner, the greatest of all English painters, turned his back on the world in the face of so much ignorance and incomprehension. The Pre-Raphaelite painters, though much talked about, nevertheless encountered much hostility and more significantly faced an ongoing lack of patronage that would have discouraged more dedicated spirits. Dante Gabriel Rosetti notoriously refused to continue to exhibit his paintings in public. Thomas Woolner, the sculptor, emigrated to Australia. Moreover the charge of philistinism so often levelled at the British public was not unmerited. We have only to compare the interest and enthusiasm for art displayed by such figures in French cultural life as Diderot, Baudelaire and Zola with the indifference, even hostility, shown to the visual arts displayed by such representative Victorian figures as Carlyle, Thackeray and Mill to perceive the difference. Dickens, despite his friendship with illustrators and artists, launched a savage attack on Millais. Arnold, who spoke a great deal about philistinism, seems to have had little interest in art himself. Nevertheless if we compare the situation with France, where such figures as Flaubert and Mallarmé self-consciously turned their backs on the complacent middle-class audience, what is striking about the situation here is the way in which poets, artist and critics, though extremely anxious to retain both high artistic standards and their own personal integrity, were anxious that art should play a significant role in society. The movement from isolation to cultural engagement is repeated. Browning, after writing such notoriously obscure and intransigent works as *Paracelsus* and *Sordello*, then produced the more accessible collection of *Men and Women* – but in reaching an audience Browning did not necessarily cease to be difficult. Ruskin, after championing the visionary art of Turner, which, he admits is inaccessible to the majority of people, turns in *The Stones of Venice* to the ideal of a society that will be permeated by art. Morris, after producing rare and costly artefacts for the rich, becomes a convert to socialism and to a more democratic conception of art. Yet in every case compromise was not so much ruled out as never even considered.

In Victorian culture the applied arts become extremely significant. Such activities as book illustration, the production of decorated china, of ornamental tiles, of fabrics and materials, the design of furniture and other everyday objects begin to make a considerable impact on the everyday world. From a certain point of view the world had never before seen so much art. Moreover with the tremendous expansion of population and the growth of large cities and industrial towns there was a great demand for buildings, whether industrial, ecclesiastical, municipal or private, which had to be answered, and in consequence the questions of what architectural style or styles they were to be built in had sooner or later to come onto the agenda. Yet, at the same time, all this activity arguably made the struggle for *art* more difficult rather than less. For was it not precisely all this mass-produced, mechanically produced work that led to Ruskin's powerful diatribe in 'The Nature of Gothic'?

And now reader, look round this English room of yours, about which you have been proud so often, because the work of it was so good and strong, and the ornaments of it so finished. Examine again all those accurate mouldings, and perfect polishings, and unerring adjustments of the seasoned wood and the tempered steel. Many a time you have exulted over them, and thought how great England was, because her slightest work was done so thoroughly. Alas! if read rightly, these perfectnesses are signs of a slavery in our England a thousand times more bitter and more degrading than that of the scourged African or helot Greek. Men may be beaten, chained, tormented, yoked like cattle, slaughtered like summer flies, and yet remain in one sense, and the best sense,

free. But to smother their souls with them, to blight and hew into
rotting pollards the suckling branches of their human intelligence
to make the flesh and skin which, after the worm's work on it, is
to see God, into leathern thongs to yoke machinery with, – this is
to be slave-masters indeed.   (x, 193)

What makes Ruskin's attack so thoroughly disorientating is that his
imagery stresses that the human beings are more completely the
objects of the power and violence of the industrial process than the
artefacts he asks his readers to survey. He compels them to recognise
not simply that mass production has human cost that is *not* out on
display, but equally to recognise that the finish, accuracy and perfection they admire is inhuman in every sense of that word. Yet at the
same time this judgement, this reading is not made in the name of
high art and high culture, but, on the contrary, simultaneously leads
to a dissolution and liquidation of the concept of art as traditionally
understood: Ruskin recognises that since the concept of perfection
leads to unfreedom it is better that the workman should be free even
if this means that less is to be expected of him. Thus it is not simply
a question of remaining the intransigent but neglected artist or of
giving way to the demands of the market, as the contrast between
Millais and Ford Madox Brown might suggest, but rather a complex
confrontation and mutual interrogation between the values of art
and the presumptions of mass culture in which the idea of art is not
compromised so much as forged and toughened in the fire. What is
significant about all the writers, artists and critics discussed in this
chapter – Browning, Ruskin, the Rossettis, Swinburne, Morris, Pater
– is not that they were compelled to adjust their perception of art to
the exigencies of the real world but rather what an extraordinarily
exalted conception of art they had and how persistently and untiringly
they advocated it. Symptomatic of this intransigence is a letter written by Browning to, of all people, Ruskin – who was wont to urge a
realism on others that he disdained for himself – in the aftermath of
Browning's publication of *Men and Women* in 1855. *Men and Women*
is often seen as marking a more pragmatic turn in Browning's work
where he abandons the earlier visionary and difficult poetry of
'Paracelsus' and 'Sordello' for a more approachable and intimate
style of verse that deals with the emotions of ordinary people; just as
Ibsen's master-builder abandons his project of building great churches
to construct homes for ordinary people. Yet at this juncture Browning not only insists on his right to be difficult, but refuses to accept

that any problems the reader may encounter are to be laid at his door. He refuses to make any concessions whatsoever:

> For the deepnesses you think you discern, – may they be more than mere blacknesses! For the hopes you entertain of what may come of subsequent readings, – all success to them! For your bewilderment more especially noted – how shall I help *that*? We don't read poetry the same way, by the same law; it is too clear. I cannot begin writing poetry till my imaginary reader has conceded licences to me which you demur at altogether. I *know* that I don't make out my conception by my language; all poetry being a putting the infinite within the finite. You would have me paint it all plain out, which can't be; but by various artifices I try to make shifts with touches and bits of outlines which *succeed* if they bear the conception from me to you. You ought, I think to keep pace with the thought tripping from ledge to ledge of my 'glaciers', as you call them; not stand poking your alpenstock into the holes, and demonstrating that no foot could have stood there; – suppose it sprang over there?[1]

But Browning not only rejects any straightforward model of literary communication and throws the whole onus of understanding back on the reader; he goes on, somewhat exasperatedly, to argue that no generalised or popular understanding of poetry is actually possible: 'Do you think poetry was ever generally understood – or can be? . . . Do you believe people understand *Hamlet*?'[2] In the year of publication of his most popular work Browning tells Ruskin – and the general public – to go to hell!

While, in the most general terms, the development of a conception of art that is perceived as being involved in a struggle with society clearly reflects the tension between Romantic ideals and the values of middle-class society, it nevertheless has a specific history. Browning's own reference point was undoubtedly Shelley, and Shelley as man, poet, political radical and author of *A Defence of Poetry* is one of the major shapers and formulators of Victorian ideas about the arts. Admittedly there is something paradoxical in this since Shelley always speaks of *poetry*, and believes that poetry constituted in language has an expressive purity denied to the other arts: 'For language is arbitrarily produced by the imagination, and has relation to thoughts alone; but all other materials, instruments, and conditions of art, have relations among each other, which limit

and interpose between conception and expression' (279–80). Here
Shelley is in agreement with the Renaissance men of letters. Yet at
the same time Shelley's erasure of the boundaries between poetry,
prophecy and philosophy and his conception of the poet as a visionary and a seer offered the possibility of a more flexible interpretation
that could encompass the other arts as well. The fundamental contradiction of *A Defence of Poetry*, which Shelley both masks and
acknowledges, is that Shelley maintains that poets are absolutely
central to the constitution of human culture and yet in the modern
age they are effectively marginal – which is why poetry has to be
defended. While Shelley seems to acknowledge that the nineteenth
century presents an entirely new set of circumstances in which the
development of science and technology have led to human alienation – 'man, having enslaved the elements, remains himself a slave'
(293) – and where poets are challenged 'to resign the civic crown to
reasoners and mechanists' (291), he does not therefore conclude that
the contemporary function of poetry has to be rethought and rather
reasserts and elaborates what he conceives to have been its traditional function. Although Shelley believes that 'Poets are the
hierophants of an unapprehended inspiration; the mirrors of the
gigantic shadows which futurity casts on the present' (297), *A Defence of Poetry* is largely a nostalgic, lingering backward look at the
heroic cultures of the past when things were better; yet in more
recent times, *King Lear*, 'the most perfect specimen of the dramatic
art existing in the world', was produced in 'narrow conditions' (284).
Even Shakespeare had to struggle against the limitations of his age.
Many of the puzzles in Shelley's argument derive from his attempt
to work two different models of development simultaneously: on
the one hand a falling away from the ideal of the poet as prophet and
legislator (originally broached by the eighteenth-century writer John
Brown), on the other the advance of the human spirit towards freedom and equality as it struggles against religion, tyranny and superstition, the faith of the Enlightenment. Shelley *does* believe in the
greatness of modern poetry – the problem is that this greatness is not
recognised and the poet is denied the cultural centrality that rightfully should be his.

The young Browning openly acknowledged himself to be an acolyte
of Shelley and endeavoured to follow in his footsteps, yet he found

that task fraught with difficulty. One way of analyzing this would be to say that Browning could neither rise to Shelley's self-confidence – if confidence it was – about his own visionary powers nor resolve the problem that this posed as to how the poet could hope to reach, let alone sway, an audience. Certainly Browning did find Shelley's conception of the poet's role daunting, since Shelley demanded that the poet be both a genius and an exemplary human being. But it was not so much that Browning tried to follow in Shelley's footsteps and then gave up as that he found the problem of following Shelley involved great difficulties of interpretation – and it is to that task of interpretation that much of Browning's subsequent poetry is addressed. In particular Shelley's life and his prescriptions for poetry in *A Defence* are often at odds. Shelley in life was the proponent of many causes, from socialism to atheism, from sexual equality to vegetarianism, yet Shelley is critical of poetry with a narrowly didactic aim or with a specific axe to grind. He criticises Euripides, with whom we might expect him to sympathise, for being too moralistic and his praise is reserved for Homer, Aeschylus and Sophocles. For Shelley the task of poetry is to 'enlarge the circumference of the imagination' (283), and therefore he should not simply use his writing to articulate contemporary notions of morality. Here Shelley seems to advocate poetry that is either amoral or indifferent to the explicit articulation of moral values, yet in the same passage he argues that poetry *does* act morally, through the power of love that leads us to identify with others:

> The great secret of morals is love; or a going out of our own nature, and an identification of ourselves with the beautiful which exists in thought, action or person, not our own. A man to be greatly good, must imagine intensely and comprehensively; he must put himself in the place of another and of many others; the pains and pleasures of his species must become his own.　(282–3)

Shelley claims that dramatic poetry is the highest form of poetry, yet his own verse is regarded as essentially lyrical, epitomising John Stuart Mill's conception of poetry as something overheard: 'A poet is a nightingale, who sits in darkness and sings to cheer its own solitude with sweet sounds; his auditors are as men entranced by the melody of an unseen musician, who feel that they are moved and softened, yet know not whence or why' (282). Shelley is characteristically perceived by his critics, Browning included, as the subjective poet *par excellence*, yet his own precept stresses poetry's universality and higher objectivity, so that the poet speaks not just for himself but for others.

Pauline, published anonymously when Browning was twenty-one, spells out both the necessity and the impossibility of the poet's vocation after Shelley. The strangeness of the work resides in the fact that it is a poetic utterance without speaker or audience. *Pauline* not only has no identifiable author: it issues from a poet figure who is never named and is addressed towards an interlocutor, who, though named, is nevertheless mysterious and vague. Through this device of addressing Pauline, Browning circumvents the whole problem of communicating with the public and such complex indirections, including the personal code through which Shelley is addressed as 'sun-treader', make it hardly surprising that John Stuart Mill should have viewed the poem as confessional. At all events it is certainly a discourse that asks to be overheard. The opening reference to 'wild dreams of beauty and of good' already strikes a dissonant note. Browning seems to suggest that such exalted goals may be impure – unworthy even – if they are incapable of realisation, yet in another part of the poem he goes on to stress the nobility of the poet's vocation and aims. The deeper cause of the poet's sense of dissatisfaction and failure is never clearly articulated. Has he failed in his vocation or has his vocation failed him? Browning became a passionate devotee of Shelley and all that he represented, but as he himself recognises, his sense of Shelley was private and personal to himself. It was not Shelley the radical bard of freedom and democracy, the opponent of political tyranny, that captivated him so much as Shelley the visionary and seer, the exponent of an esoteric doctrine that could only be grasped by the favoured few. Shelley's genius has been neglected and scorned, so that Browning feels a peculiar affinity with him that verges on total identification:

> But thou art still for me who have adored
> Tho' single, panting but to hear thy name
> Which I believed a spell to me alone,
> Scarce deeming thou wast a star to other men.

Browning was captivated by the thought of Shelley's poetry as simultaneously shrouded mystery and lucid vision – or as Shelley puts it: 'whether it spreads its own figured curtain, or withdraws life's dark veil from before the scene of things' (295) – and he speaks of the rapture with which he launched himself on the task of decipherment:

> such first
> Caught me and set me, slave of a sweet task,
> To disentangle, gather sense from song:
> Since, song-inwoven, lurked there words which seemed
> A key to a new world, the muttering
> Of angels, something yet unguessed by man.

Yet it is one thing to fall in love with the idea of an angelic discourse, another actually to transcribe it. Browning's narrator suggests that in some way the project goes awry through a loss of faith in Shelley's political programme in which 'Men were to be as gods and earth as heaven', but the problem goes deeper since he is brought to the point of self-distrust. Effectively the poet requires an extraordinary faith in his own powers and at the same time some kind of external validation, through the people, of his mission. Browning, or Browning's poet, feels that he can only validate his sense of mission through the conviction that it is divinely inspired, yet Shelley's atheism seems to preclude the one possibility that can offer him reassurance, except perhaps the love of a woman, Pauline. The poet believes that he is defined above all by a insatiable, enquiring and searching spirit that can never be at rest. He speaks of

> a principle of restlessness
> Which would be all, have, see, know, taste, feel, all
> This is myself

and sees such an endless pursuit as an ineluctable destiny:

> Souls alter not, and mine must still advance
> .   .   .   .
> It has strange impulse, tendency, desire,
> Which nowise can I account for nor explain,
> But cannot stifle, being bound to trust
> All feelings equally, to hear all sides.

Thus on the one hand Browning is torn towards an Shelleyan 'immorality' that insists the soul must follow its own desires and dispositions regardless, and a confused and equally unaccountable feeling of guilt that his desires are both impossible and improper, perhaps, in the tradition of Faust, actually impious. *Pauline* never resolves these contradictions in the poet's role, while much of the poem has the feeling of a recantation and seems to express a longing for the 'normal'. It concludes with a reaffirmation of the poetic mission: 'I shall be priest and prophet as of old', and an attempt to reconcile that with the idea of God. In open disagreement with Shelley, Browning affirms:

> Sun-treader, I believe in God and truth
> And love

yet nevertheless asks for the atheist poet's blessing: 'Love me and wish me well.' Both God and Shelley will guide the poet's future.

In *Paracelsus* (1835) Browning attempts to explore more fully the moral dilemmas of the questing hero and poetic visionary that he in many ways aspired to be, taking as his starting point the man deemed at once a pioneer of medicine and modern scientific enquiry and a quack, imposter and charlatan. But Browning always felt deeply sympathetic to those whom the world estimates as charlatans, from Chatterton to Paracelsus, precisely because Browning regards the world's estimate as being of very little value. *Paracelsus*, despite its many twists, turns and qualifications, declares itself as an apology for the romantic artist as much in its conviction that genius must remain true to itself as in its distrust of popular opinion. At the outset of his attempts to penetrate the secrets of the universe, Paracelsus is not mistrustful of his undertaking, like the poet of *Pauline*, but, on the contrary, completely confident, because he believes that it is inspired by God. Paracelsus has the Renaissance confidence that God, far from believing that man's knowledge must be limited, is actually anxious to open his creation to the inspection of the human understanding. Thus, although *Paracelsus* has many similarities with the Faust myth, both in its concern with intellectual enquiry and its suggestion that this pursuit may lead to a disastrous severing of human ties, it is nevertheless distinguished from it because it is by no means taken for granted that such a quest is either impious or forbidden. Certainly, Paracelsus, in the beginning, has no such doubts and Browning, throughout the poem, suggests that such a conviction, so long as one can possess it, is both healthy and beneficial. Paracelsus speaks of his unwillingness to abandon 'God's great commission' of his

> ready answer to the will of God
> Who summons me to be his organ;

while Festus, his friend, refers his determination to 'gain one prize':

> the secret of the world,
> Of man, and man's true purpose, path and fate.

While Festus believes that Paracelsus's ambitions court danger in so far as they lead him into solitariness and into 'strange and untried paths', Paracelsus expresses the romantic faith that visionary truth is only to be found within:

> There is an inmost centre in us all
> Where truth abides in fulness. . . .
> . . . and to KNOW
> Rather consists in opening out a way
> Wherein the imprisoned splendour may escape.

In any event Paracelsus believes that his craving to know must be divinely inspired since God could not have implanted this impulse within him if that impulse itself were unworthy. Yet at the same time Paracelsus's drive to understand is not a desire for knowledge pure and simple but potentially a noble attempt to dignify and enhance man's sense of his own worth:

> Know, not for knowing's sake
> But to become a star to men for ever.

Yet the Renaissance concern with honour and fame was always potentially corrupting – as it was to be in Paracelsus's own case – and he goes on to speak of gain, praise and wonder. But for the moment Paracelsus's trajectory is upward.

In the second part, at Constantinople, Paracelsus is presented as having made significant intellectual advances towards his goal, without, at the same time, having reached it. This places him in an equivocal position. On the one hand he is glad at the progress he has made, but the fact that he lacks any unified idea or theory makes him wonder what it all really amounts to. It is not really possible for Paracelsus to take a dispassionate view of his achievement because he is conscious of the price he has paid in the loss of all personal relationships and because he now lacks the confidence and the sense of a divine mission that originally inspired him:

> Give me but one hour of my first energy,
> Of that invincible faith, but only one!
> That I may cover with an eagle-glance
> The truths I have, and spy some certain way
> To mould them, and completing them, possess!
> Yet God is good: I started sure of that,
> And why dispute it now?

The corner that Paracelsus has got himself into is that he started out convinced of God's goodness, but, as it were, provisionally, since it required the success of his enterprise to finally underwrite it. Now Paracelsus must either doubt God's goodness or admit that he has somehow misconstrued God's intentions. No wonder Paracelsus subsequently is angered by confident references to God's will, as if

> Man had but merely to uplift his eye,
> And see the will in question charactered
> On the heaven's vault.

In Constantinople Paracelsus finds a poet, Aprile, who treats him as a prophet and visionary but who stresses the importance of love and sympathetic understanding over the claims of knowledge, the need to address the human as much as the natural world:

> Marts, theatres, and wharfs – all filled with men,
> Men everywhere! And this performed in turn,
> When those who looked on, pined to hear the hopes
> And fears and hates and loves which moved the crowd,
> I would throw down the pencil as the chisel,
> And I would speak; no thought which ever stirred
> A human breast should be untold.

Aprile seeks to restore Paracelsus to humanity and asks him to take on board another set of values; as Paracelsus says 'Are we not halves of a dissevered world', but the moment for reuniting them has not yet come.

In Part III Paracelsus returns to Switzerland and as a result of his performing many miraculous cures is made a professor at Basle, where he ridicules the wisdom of the ancients and burns the works of Galen and Aristotle. For a moment he is vouchsafed fame, fortune and uncritical adulation but the tide rapidly turns, as Paracelsus foresaw it would, and soon he is hounded out of his position, reviled as an imposter and a charlatan. But this only teaches Paracelsus the futility of trying to take his specific mode of understanding to the multitude, since they can only latch on to spectacular cures or obvious truths and cannot grasp either the real scope of his knowledge or its actual limitations. In defeat Paracelsus becomes mocking, humorous and, apparently, light-hearted. He is more disposed to be philosophical and more ready to come to terms with his situation, yet without altogether giving up on the tasks he once set himself:

> I am a wanderer: I remember well
> One journey, how I feared the track was missed,
> So long the city I desired to reach
> Lay hid; when suddenly its spires afar
> Flashed through the circling clouds; you may conceive
> My transport. Soon the vapours closed again,
> But I had seen the city, and one such glance
> No darkness could obscure: nor shall the present –
> A few dull hours, a passing shame or two,
> Destroy the vivid memories of the past.
> I will fight the battle out; a little spent
> Perhaps, but still an able competent.

As Paracelsus now sees it, the quest for knowledge is not so much a matter of winning as of worthily taking part.

Sordello, published in 1840 only to be meet with indifference, incomprehension and disdain, was begun before *Paracelsus* yet was only completed a long time afterwards. Browning was distracted from it by his attempts to write for the stage but clearly for a time he either lost interest in the work or lost his way in the writing of it. He was finally able to complete it after a visit to Italy in 1838 that revived his interest in the poem and gave him some new perspectives upon it. Many readers have found *Sordello* baffling and frustrating and while this is in part due to Browning's elliptical and elusive style, it must also be attributable to the fact that their expectation that they will read a poem about 'Sordello', the poet as hero, is very largely frustrated. It is, of course, part of Browning's war with his potential audience – to whom, as ever, he refuses to make concessions – that he constantly teases them with the promise that they will, indeed, after many digressions, 'Hear Sordello's story told', only to launch into yet another convoluted account of the struggle between Guelf and Ghibelline in which Sordello seems only a very marginal and parenthetical figure. Yet there is a serious intention behind all this as Browning wants to dramatise the gulf that exists between life as we actually experience it and as it more definitively appears under the eye of history. For a patriotic nineteenth-century historian like Sismondi, it is wrong to perceive the struggles in northern Italy in the thirteen century either simply as a battle for supremacy between the Emperor and the Pope, or else as a largely opportunistic struggle between a multiplicity of cities and local warlords who constantly make new alliances and change sides to promote their own advantage. What is really at stake is Italian independence and freedom from centuries of foreign invasion and domination on a variety of pretexts, and it is therefore the Guelfs, siding with the Pope, who have history on their side. Or, to put it another way, the Pope sides with the free cities precisely because he knows that they are opposed to the German Emperor. Yet this could not be perceived with the same clarity at the time. Similarly very little is known about the historical Sordello and he is remembered largely because Dante praises him for the part he played in developing the Italian language. Thus Sordello figures as Dante's precursor, yet Sordello himself can have no idea of what his part in history is to be.

Sordello continues Browning's exploration of the problem of the artist's identity and vocation, with the examples of both Shelley and Dante in mind, but the real precedent for the poem is Shakespeare's *Hamlet*, with its contrast between Fortinbras, the man of action, and Hamlet, the reflective individual, who recoils from the possibilities of action because he can never bring them into alignment with the inner workings of his mind. As Browning sees it, the artist's problem is how to reflect the world and at the same time remain true to himself, how to be at once universal and particular – which is in some sense the same generic question raised by Hegelian philosophy. Yet to make this connection is also to recognise that, in the final analysis, Browning is on the side of the universal against the particular; for if the artist immerses himself too deeply in the particular and becomes too totally enmeshed in specific causes, he risks triviality and one-sidedness. Indeed Browning felt that even Shelley, the very epitome of the transcendent powers of mind, had nevertheless succumbed to this. According to Browning, the youthful poet actually possessed 'a low practical dexterity' that was his undoing:

the early fervour and power to *see*, was accompanied by a preco-
cious fertility to contrive: he endeavoured to realise as he went on
idealising; every wrong had simultaneously its remedy, and out of
the strength of his hatred for the former, he took the strength of his
confidence in the latter – till suddenly he stood pledged to the
defence of a set of miserable little expedients, just as if they represented great principles, and to an attack upon various great principles, really so, without leaving himself time to examine whether,
because they were antagonistical to the remedy he had suggested,
they must therefore be identical or even essentially connected
with the wrong he sought to cure, – playing with blind passion
into the hands of his enemies, and dashing at whatever red cloak
was held forth to him, as the cause of the last fireball he had last
been stung with – mistaking Churchdom for Christianity, and for
marriage, 'the sale of love' and the law of sexual oppression. [3]

Only later, says Browning, was Shelley 'raised above the contemplation of spots and the attempt at effacing them, to the great Abstract
Light'. [4] Thus the artist is presented with a pattern of development.
To begin with he possesses an inner illumination and power that is
untramelled and unconfined because it has not become attached to
some specific object. So Browning writes of Sordello:

> Men no more
> Compete with him than tree and flower before.
> Himself, inactive, yet is greater far
> Than such as act, each stooping to his star,
> Acquiring thence his function; he has gained
> The same result with meaner mortals trained
> To strength or beauty, moulded to express
> Each the idea that rules him; since no less
> He comprehends that function, but can still
> Embrace the others, take of might his fill
> With Richard as of grace with Palma, mix
> Their qualities, or for a moment fix
> On one, abiding free meantime.

– the oblique reference to Shakespeare is symptomatic. Although
Shakespeare is taken by Browning as well as others to typify the
objective artist, Shelley the subjective one, he nevertheless believes
that what makes the artist is a refusal of the specific role, the es-

pousal of a particular star that is ultimately narrowing, and for the artist actually disabling. In his early success in the contest of troubadours, Sordello, inspired by the love of Palma, is able to compose a poem that is completely unified and untroubled by this problem of vocation. But subsequently in this struggle with language he loses his rapport with his audience while at the same time his concentration on his poetic craft leads him to forget his higher spiritual mission; as he subsequently laments after abandoning Mantua:

> Why fled I Mantua, then? – complained
> So much my Will was fettered, yet remained
> Content within a tether half the range
> I could assign it? able to exchange
> My ignorance (I felt) for knowledge, and
> Idle because I could thus understand –
> Could e'en have penetrated to its core
> Our mortal mystery, yet – fool – forbore,
> Preferring elaborating in the dark
> My casual stuff, by any wretched spark
> Borne of my predecessors, though one stroke
> Of mine had brought the flame forth? Mantua's yoke,
> My minstrel's trade, was to behold mankind, –
> My own concern was just to bring my mind
> Behold, just extricate for my acquist,
> Each object suffered stifle in the mist
> Which hazard, custom, blindness interpose
> Betwixt things and myself.

In beholding mankind the artist loses touch with his own inner vision, and subjective and objective are once more wrenched apart. Nevertheless at this point the standpoint of the poem is still very similar to that of *Paracelsus*: the artist must not be lured by siren voices of popularity or fame and must not be led to lose sight of his deeper purpose by the senseless and uncomprehending murmurs of the crowd. The rejection of public opinion is clear even if the alternative way forward is not.

In the ensuing years Browning was led to interrogate this doctrine of artistic purity both because he became somewhat less confident about his own artistic mission – though the massive failure of *Sordello* itself did not deflect him from his goal of being among the English poets – and because the rise of social discontent and of Chartism in the late 1830s forced him to think about the artist's social responsibilities. The pauper girl who pulls him by the sleeve as he sits on a ruined palace step in Venice:

> You sad dishevelled ghost
> That pluck at me and point

might have come up to him at any place and any time, but in 1838 this serves as a reminder to the Orphic poet of the pressing claims of the real world and of the sufferings of the working class. Browning now recognises that there has been more than an element of narcissistic self-regard in his discussion of Sordello's sufferings – a fact that he wryly acknowledges when he writes in Book v:

> I circumvent
> A few, my masque contented, and to these
> Offer unveil the last of mysteries –
> Man's inmost life shall have yet freer play:
> Once more I cast external things away,
> And nature's composite, so decompose
> That. . . . Why, he writes *Sordello*.

But of course this throwaway remark is ironic in more than one sense as Browning did not have any single intention in writing *Sordello*, and while he did want to stress the importance of subjectivity and the inner life, he was also anxious to counterbalance this with the claims of the world and of political action. Against Sordello the poet he counterposes Taurello Salinguerra, the chief lieutenant of Ecelin of the House of Romano, who in turn is the leading supporter of the Emperor, Frederick Barbarossa, who is a man who really understands the political world and who is shrewd and calculating in his actions. By presenting Taurello's perspective on the current Italian political scene, Browning exposes the naïvety of Sordello's dream of siding with the people, throwing his own influence behind the Guelphs and thus ridding Italy of foreign domination; partly because Sordello, as the poet he is, cannot really expect significantly to affect things, but more importantly because Taurello recognises that as there are so many separate factors that enter the equation and so many values that remain unknown, there is no way of foreseeing what the outcome will be. It is only for a poet like Sordello that the world of action is endowed with an imaginary clarity. In the course of their conversation Taurello reveals to Sordello that he is his son and offers him insignia that would make him the leader of the Ghibelline faction in Italy. But Sordello refuses it and, with this gesture, disappears from history. Sordello preserves his integrity as a poet, but in consequence loses his chance of making his mark on the world stage. Instead of becoming a central figure in a crucial phase of Italian history and with a real opportunity of contributing to the advancement of the cause of Italian freedom, Sordello abandons himself to the fate of becoming little more than a footnote to Dante. Was this the wrong decision? Perhaps, but what is really in Browning's mind is that political action and poetry are incommensurable worlds, so that the question can never be satisfactorily answered.

Sordello was itself a disastrous failure and it was to be a very long time before Browning was able to establish himself as a prominent poet of the Victorian age. He was not to publish *Men and Women*, the collection that made his reputation, for a further fifteen years, when he was forty-three – two years older than Tennyson when he became Poet Laureate – yet the reputation itself was still longer in arriving, since the first reviews of that volume were predominantly critical, not to say disparaging. These wilderness years must have been very demoralising for Browning, despite the happiness he found in his relationship with Elizabeth Barrett, whom he married in opposition to her father's wishes in 1846. Although Browning was still convinced that the poet must be, like Shelley, an endlessly questing spirit and although he still believed that poetry should address itself to life's most difficult questions with determination and intellectual rigour, he nevertheless came to believe that his path had been mistaken. He now believed that in concentrating so exclusively on the long poem and in making each work so narcissistically concerned with the poet's mission he had not merely condemned himself to an indefinitely protracted spiritual isolation – a fate that at first he had willingly, gladly embraced – but that in the process he had lost sight of what poetry really was. In explicit and mocking criticism of his earlier ways in 'Transcendentalism', subtitled 'A Poem in Twelve books' though in fact only fifty-one lines in length, he wrote:

> Stop playing, poet! may a brother speak?
> 'Tis you speak, that's your error. Song's our art:
> Whereas you please to speak these naked thoughts
> Instead of draping them in sights and sounds.
> – True thoughts, good thoughts, thoughts fit to treasure up!

But why such long prolusion and display,
Such turning and adjustment of the harp,
And taking it upon your breast at length,
Only to speak dry words across its strings?
Stark-naked thought is in request enough –
Speak prose and holloa it till Europe hears!
The six-foot Swiss tube, braced about with bark,
Which helps the hunter's voice from Alp to Alp –
Exchange our harp for that, – who hinders you?

Browning now recognised in the prolixity of his earlier works an attempt to amplify his message that resulted in crudity rather than complexity. He decided to make his poetry more evocative, allusive and compressed, but at the same time to make it directly address the reader, whose hypothetical and actual patience he had formerly been happy to abuse. Instead of a head-on confrontation with the absolute that was allegedly its own *raison d'être*, he would dramatise his ideas by presenting them through the mouth of a variety of vividly realised speakers, who would themselves summon up a specific historical context, right down to its very sights and sounds. As he wrote to Isa Blagden after his departure from Florence: 'Do be minute – tell me trifles – no trifles to me.'

As Browning reformulated the opposition between the finite and the infinite in his mind it became an opposition between the transcendental and a perennially varying, perennially unrolling contingency of the present, so that all ages are equally close to the infinite, yet equally far away. He came to believe, like Ranke, that all historical periods are equal in the eyes of God, yet, unlike Ranke, the believer in objectivity, he endowed this conviction with more relativist implications. This made Browning sceptical of any possibility of certainty, whether scientific or otherwise, and led to a questioning and interrogative poetry that does not seek finality, but rather asks for some kind of accommodation with intellectual uncertainty. Instead of asking his readers' indulgence, Browning presented them with individuals who could challenge them with a skilfully argued and compellingly presented point of view. In terms of John Stuart Mill's distinction between poetry and eloquence, Browning had abandoned unpremeditated lyrical effusion for the glittering public art of rhetoric. As Mill had defined it:

Poetry and eloquence are both alike the expression or utterance of felling. But if we may be excused the antithesis, we should say that eloquence is *heard*, poetry, is *over*heard. Eloquence supposes an audience; the peculiarity of poetry appears to us to lie in the poet's utter unconsciousness of a listener. Poetry is feeling, confessing itself to itself in moments of solitude, and embodying itself in symbols, which are the nearest possible representations of the feeling in the exact shape it exists in the poet's mind. Eloquence is feeling pouring itself, out to other minds, courting their sympathy, or endeavouring to influence their belief, or move them to passion or action.[5]

Browning's poetic interlocutors insidiously draw the reader into their own intellectual and imaginative world and endeavour either to persuade him or to recognise, at the very least, that they have some justification for holding the beliefs that they do. Mill's suggestion that poetry should be composed for its own sake without any instrumental purpose recalls Kant's perception of aesthetics in the *Critique of Judgement*, yet although Browning was still unwilling to compromise his own convictions by writing *for* an audience, he was perfectly prepared to direct his poetry *at* an audience in a way that would provoke, challenge and unsettle them. Indeed Browning, as such Pre-Raphaelite poets as Dante Gabriel Rossetti and Swinburne were to recognise, can be seen as being, in many ways, the first British avant-garde poet, both because to begin with he had a 'underground' reputation and because he saw his relationship with the reader as essentially an antagonistic one. For all his parade of bluff good humour, Browning never expected to be read in the same spirit as Dickens or Tennyson and would not have wished for such a relationship even if he could have had one. Through his personae Browning sidles up to the reader, presenting them with a face so embarrassingly close that all the pores are visible, yet Browning himself is always at a distance, conducting his negotiations with the reader by proxy.

In the writing of his historical poems and dramas Browning had become fascinated with the way in which human beings could perceive the world from totally different points of view, both because they might belong to a totally alien culture or historical context, but also because, even sharing that same context, they might have been conditioned, or so shaped themselves, to look at events in a completely different way. Thus Sordello's understanding of thirteenth-century Italian politics is quite different from that of Taurello Salinguerra, even though in Browning's scenario they are father and son. More significantly, perhaps, Strafford and Pym are close personal friends and have political convictions in common, yet Strafford is to become wholly identified with the royalist cause, while Pym epitomises the spirit of parliamentary resistance to kingly power. Browning recognised that experience actually has no centre – even though the citizens of great empires (Roman or British) inevitably believe that it does. What lies on the periphery of my experience may be at the centre of yours – and vice versa. It was precisely this puzzle that Browning attempted to explore in 'An Epistle Containing the Strange Medical Experience of Karshish, the Arab Physician' and 'Cleon', which respectively depict the Arab and Greek responses to the emergence of a Christian world. It would be easy to imagine, as so often with Browning, that his intention is to make some oblique affirmation of the Christian faith – especially when the 'epistle' deals with the miracle of the raising of Lazarus as miracles were still a contentious issue – but Browning's concerns are a good deal more complex than this. What Browning is trying to show is that religious belief, and indeed any kind of belief, requires a particular kind of cultural support that will make that belief credible. If this is lacking, then it may well be dismissed as 'madness'. Karshish, though interested and sympathetically involved in the 'case' of Lazarus, cannot help but regard Jesus as a fellow-practitioner and Lazarus cannot denote, for him, what it signifies for the committed Christian. Similarly Cleon rejects the testimony of Paul, not because he knows anything about it, but because it has arisen on the cultural periphery and therefore cannot, by definition, be significant. In considering Browning's attitude towards Christianity we need to recognise that what made Christianity something completely new in world history was the fact that it was not a settled, stable set of beliefs but a dynamic, unsettling, endlessly striving religion. Christianity, for Browning, is like art: it expresses man's aspiration towards the infinite. It is always pressing against limits and boundaries and therefore the 'case' of Lazarus is symbolically important here because Lazarus is a living instance of a man who has erased the boundary between this world and the next. Karshish is presented relatively sympathetically because his imagination can rise to the extraordinary challenge that Lazarus represents, despite the rather pedantic background of his medical training, while Cleon, who boasts of being able to unite all the arts, is a man both complacent and limited, who can give no meaning to art because the dimension of struggle and aspiration is lacking. His powers are significant since, in 'One

Word More', Browning regrets that he cannot thus express himself in more than one art and then goes on to cite examples of such left-handed expression – the sonnets of Raphael, Dante's picture of an angel, which may have conveyed a particular sincerity and genuineness of feeling, just because of their lack of technical ability. Thus Browning always distrusts artistic counsels of perfection.

In Victorian England the critique of art that aims primarily at artistic perfection is by no means confined to Browning – Rio, Ruskin and the Pre-Raphaelites had all stressed the virtues of directness and sincerity and had deplored empty accomplishment, which they associated, in particular, with the later Raphael and his successors. What makes Browning unusual is that this emphasis does not involve a rejection of the Renaissance for its lack of genuine faith, but, on the contrary, goes hand in hand with a warm regard for Renaissance art, as typifying the striving and aspiring qualities he most valued and a complementary tendency to view some medieval art as mechanical and empty. Thus in 'Pictor Ignotus' Browning's unknown artist claims that he too possessed the capacity to create great art

> to scan
> The license and the limit, space and bound
> Allowed to Truth made visible in Man

but he became anxious at the implications of his transgression: 'The world seemed not the world it was before!', and he decides to stick to familiar routine and what he knows best, churning out endless series of Saints and Madonnas that never surprise or trouble any one. For Browning there is only one sin – the lack of courage or nerve to follow through the dream, desire or design that you have conceived in your mind, once you have conceived it. The Duke and the Lady create a statue and a bust, so that in effigy the Duke will always ride across the square and look up at the lady whom he loves, who in turn will always look down at him in marble from a window. Yet Browning believes their love scarcely warrants such commemoration if they in living flesh can be no more than stone and if they were too reticent to actualise their illicit passion in the first place. Similarly the lady in 'The Glove', who flamboyantly and recklessly throws her glove into the lion's den, expecting her admirer, De Lorge, to retrieve it, is not as irresponsible as she may seem. For life is full of moments when we must face tests, make irrevocable decisions, and cross visible and invisible barriers, and there must necessarily be moments when experience becomes critical – dangerous even. In his acute and influential essay, 'The Poetry of Barbarism', George Santayana criticised Browning for what he perceived as the mindless advocacy of an instinctive activism:

> His notion is simply that the game of life, the exhilaration of action is inexhaustible. You may set up your tenpins again after you have bowled them over, and you may keep up the sport for ever. The point is to bring them down as often as possible with a master-stroke and a big bang. They will tend to invigorate in you that self-confidence which in this system passes for faith.[6]

Santayana's depiction of Browning in terms that suggest a large, ungainly and somewhat bumptious youth engaged in rather boisterous play comes cruelly close to the mark in homing in on that self-confident side of Browning that always seems to lurk behind the scepticism – so that to some critics like Santayana the parade of scepticism is little more than a façade. Admittedly in 'The Statue and the Bust' Browning goes out of the way to present his call to action in a form that is unmistakeably immoral. He does not even allow his readers the indulgence of beaming favourably on a young and romantic lover who rescues his bride from a loveless and ill-fated marriage with a powerful Duke, but by making the Duke a marriage breaker presents them with a much more problematic case. He then turns the screw even further by turning to his audience and asking:

> You of the virtue (we issue join)
> How strive you? De te, fabula!

Browning is not, like Milton, insisting that a fugitive and cloistered virtue could not be virtue, but rather arguing that inactivity and indecision make the very possibility of moral behaviour impossible. Browning's position is not as crude as Santayana makes it look because he believes that to be moral agents we must be able to choose, and further that we must necessarily implement the consequences of those decisions and be prepared to live with them. But it has to be recognised that Browning's view does have the secular implication that if we are to be punished at all for what we do, we will punish ourselves for what we do or do not do, just as the Duke and the Lady are punished for failing to make the commitment to one another that they feel in their hearts. For Browning action is at once moral education and a form of self-knowledge. It is part of a dialectical process of growth and development, in the course of which by being 'something' it becomes possible to transcend that and become something better. Although Browning recognises the existence of good and evil, he denies that they can be separated – as he writes in 'Old Pictures in Florence':

> When a soul has seen
> By the means of Evil that Good is best,
>   And through earth and its noise, what is heaven's serene, –
> When its faith in the same has stood the test.

Browning does not believe that a person could be truly good who was wholly content with himself and with his own saintliness. He places in a madhouse Johannes Agricola, who believes that God has singled him out for glory above other men and who is convinced

> I have God's warrant, could I blend
> All hideous sins, as in a cup,
> To drink the mingled venoms up,
> Secure my nature will convert
> The draught to blossoming gladness fast.

For Browning such effortless and instantaneous goodness would make a mockery of all men's struggles and aspirations. In 'Old Pictures in Florence' Browning claims that the perfect ideality of classical sculpture seemed so wholly beyond the attainment of ordinary men and women, so finished, final and complete, that it simply mocked them without giving them any goal to aim at. Moreover classical art seems beyond time and circumstance, whereas the art of the Renaissance is fully conscious of its own temporality. The Renaissance artists knew their works might not last and they had to live with the fact that they would not have time to complete their most cherished projects, as Giotto as was not able to finish the Campanile in Florence. They accept that the human situation is necessarily flawed, and Browning, in his own antiquarian endeavours to revive and restore their work to the public consciousness, becomes a secret sharer in their hopes and visions. For perfection can teach us nothing, whereas in the incomplete and unfinished is a reminder that the struggle is never actually over. Indeed it was probably just as well that Browning never became a painter, for he could never have allowed a picture to leave his studio without feeling he had succumbed to a fatal complacency.

What made life seem always ominous for Browning was its incompleteness. Experience, as he saw it, was a mass of fragments without any obvious centre that could make it cohere; while individuals might endeavour to give meaning to their lives through some particular project or quest, it was almost inevitable that they would in some way be thwarted or frustrated in their attempts to reach it. In certain moods Browning could be philosophical about this failure: what mattered was not the achievement itself but the effort that had gone into it. Moreover he had argued in *Sordello* that no one can ever hope to see their dreams realised; they must recognise that they are part of an ongoing endeavour on the part of the whole of humanity and that therefore it will be left to the generations that come after finally to realise what their precursors could only dream. Yet this involved some kind of wager on the future coming up trumps that might itself only be an appealing fiction. Browning was haunted by the nightmare that life was inescapably fragmentary and incomplete. Browning claimed to believe in God – indeed in his own way almost certainly did so – yet this belief seems to have offered him no assurance that the world was ultimately meaningful. For if man was haunted by a lack of meaning derived from his own experience, then it would be no consolation to know that there was some higher transcendental point of view from which this perception might be dismissed as a merely local and partial illusion. For Browning this sense of life as always potentially without focus or meaning was epitomised by the bleak and arid area around Rome, known as the Campagna, which became the starting point for several poems in *Men and Women*. Browning exorcised its spell most easily in 'Love Among the Ruins', the opening poem of the collection where the lovers, secure in their love, can perceive it as cancelling the relentless temporality that has brought innumerable emperors low and destroyed endless dreams of magnificence and power. On a site where great spectacles and battles once took place, there is now only a tranquil prospect of ruins and grazing sheep. The vacancy that now exists can be filled by love.

However, 'Childe Roland to the Dark Tower came', which also seems to invoke the barrenness and inhospitality of the campagna in its references to 'that ominous tract', 'such starved ignoble nature' and 'penury, inertness, grimace' is more sinister. Browning sets this poem in an imaginary medieval world where a knight, embarked on some great quest, after a seemingly perpetual journey through a hostile landscape, finally reaches the 'Dark Tower' that has been the traditional goal of knightly endeavour and blows his horn as a sign that he is ready to do battle. Yet with the hindsight that only intermittently brings wisdom it is impossible not to read this poem in the light of Ruskin's remarks on the subject of 'Pathetic Fallacy' made only a year later in 1856. For the knight continually attributes human qualities to the natural world; it is 'petty', it is 'spiteful', it is 'desperate' and 'grim'. What is alarming about 'Childe Roland' is not so much this sense of menace as our unfolding recognition that the knight has projected this sense of menace onto the landscape in order to validate his quest and give meaning to the world. Without this transcendental mission the world would still be bleak, inhuman and hostile but it would not seemingly offer confirmation of the validity of his quest, which seeks to cancel through sheer energy and determination the lack of meaning that the world presents. So in this poem action is by no means the solution; indeed Browning, by failing to report on the upshot of the knight's mission, thereby suggests that the mission itself scarcely matters. It seems significant that in the chivalric world invoked by Browning there is no sense of a divine world order that these powers of evil seek to undermine. The knight struggles on in a universe where all illumination is denied.

A similar obscurity threatens the lovers in 'Two in the Campagna', though the tone of the poem is deceptively lighter and the campagna is evoked in such a lyrical way that it seems shrug off the associations that might otherwise be summoned up:

> The champaign with its endless fleece
> Of feathery grasses everywhere!
> Silence and passion, joy and peace,
> An everlasting wash of air –
> Rome's ghost since her decease.

Yet the imagery of the spider threads, suggestive at once of the poet's own elusive train of thought and of the insubstantial nature of the filaments that constitute our own personal experience, acquires, like the beetles blindly groping in the honey meal, overtones that are no less menacing than Roland's iconography of palsied oaks and great black birds. The poem concedes that even where the desire for love, happiness and fulfilment is intense, it may nevertheless be elusive: love, far from being some powerful dyke that can hold out against the destructive waters of time, may be as subject to its depredations as everything else. In this crucial instance Browning is unable to hold onto his habitual consolation that human striving is self-validating. He seems to concede that to recognise that if the lovers can never find themselves on the same spiritual wavelength despite all their efforts to do so and if they suddenly find their relationship invaded by emptiness, then such a recognition must be deeply demoralising – not because of the failure of the relationship in itself but because the implication is that human emotions are neither as strong nor as stable as we would like them to be.

The depth and complexity of *Men and Women* as a collection stems from the diversity of moods and feelings that it represents. In contrast with 'Two in the Campagna', 'Fra Lippo Lippi' depicts an attitude to life that is happy, easy going and contented, though since Browning is Browning it does not follow that the poem is as straightforward as the character it presents. 'Fra Lippo Lippi' has a particular importance in the collection since it is the first full portrait of a historical individual and it is also the poem in which the distinctive character of *Men and Women*, as a series of meditations on art, life and personal identity, becomes apparent. While some critics of Browning would stress his own distance from such poetic personae and yet take Lippi's gospel of realism for Browning's own, my own position would be very much the reverse, since I would want to stress the strength of Browning's identification with the painter-priest and yet warn against taking the poem as the unequivocal expression of his philosophy of art. To understand fully 'Fra Lippo Lippi' we need to remember that the young Browning had thought of poetry as a priestly vocation and had believed, following Shelley, that to be a good poet it was also necessary to be a good man. Moreover Browning went on believing this despite the doubts about his own personal worthiness expressed in *Pauline*, and as late as 1852, only three years before the publication of *Men and Women* was still defending Shelley as 'a moral man', because he was 'true, simple-hearted and brave', and as a 'man of religious mind' even in the face of a public opinion that generally regarded Shelley as both an atheist and an immoralist.[7] But Browning had found this exalted conception of the poet a burden and not the least blessing of his marriage to Elizabeth Barrett was that it freed him from the isolation and psychological pressure that the role seemed to entail. Browning felt that with his clandestine marriage and elopement to Italy, he too had climbed over the wall. In his newfound relationship he was able to luxuriate not only in the joy of loving and of being loved in return, but in a sense of freedom bordering on irresponsibility that he had never before enjoyed as he had struggled ineffectually to make his way in the world of the London theatre. Since his wife was a poet too, and since she had a strong sense of the power of poetry to calm all his nagging doubts, Browning no longer felt called upon to justify either himself or his chosen career. For the first time he could be himself without anxiety or guilt – and it is this side of Browning that goes into the writing of 'Fra Lippo Lippi'.

Indeed, in writing the brief, immensely diversified poems of *Men and Women* Browning felt himself to be a Lippo Lippi – a man freed from the burden of an arduous spiritual programme, albeit self-imposed, who is now free to look around him and rejoice in the plenitude and diversity of existence, in the sheer beauty and physicality of the world – as Lippo Lippi says:

> If you get simple beauty and nought else,
> You get about the best thing God invents.

'Fra Lippo Lippi' is a radical statement because in it Browning adumbrates what was to become the core of the aesthetic of 'Art for Art's Sake' – the belief that art has nothing to do with morality, or if it does then only because it embodies its own higher moral and artistic imperatives, which have absolutely nothing whatever to do with the petty, conservative moralism of the bourgeoisie. Browning suggests that the devoted servants of the church can never see the world truly because they are blinkered by doctrine and the power of tradition. It takes an anarchic and libertine spirit like Lippo Lippi to see it as it really is. Moreover Lippo Lippi's sense of the physical is actually truly religious and reverent as it involves a profound respect for the world that God has made and a delight that comes naturally to unlearned people:

> You be the judge!
> You speak no Latin more than I, belike –
> However, you're my man, you've seen the world
> – The beauty and the wonder and the power,
> The shape of things, their colours, lights and shades,
> Changes, surprises, – and God made it all!

With a typical Browningesque transvaluation of values, Lippo Lippi's hedonism begins to look like a higher form of spirituality.

Nevertheless it would be mistaken to rest in a one-sided view of 'Fra Lippo Lippi' that sees no more in the poem than what the libertine monk and artist has to say for himself: the poem needs to be grasped dialectically. As Browning sees it, the medieval church goes astray in laying too much emphasis on the soul and spiritual values, for in so doing it cuts itself off from the ordinary worshippers it should be addressing and becomes involved in promulgating a creed that seems to have no purchase on everyday existence. Hence the realism of Lippo Lippi and Masaccio comes as a valuable corrective, both because it enables the church to address the lives of ordinary people and because it restores the soul to the body and resituates the claims of the spirit within a context that can acknowledge the actual weaknesses and temptations of the world. A religion that loses sight of this, as in the Prior's remonstrance to the painter:

> Your business is not to catch men with show,
> With homage to the perishable clay,
> But lift them over it, ignore it all,
> Make them forget there's such a thing as flesh

is a religion that, in its wilful blindness, makes goodness seem unnaturally simple, since all the difficulty of existence is left out. Lippo Lippi's characteristic cheek is displayed in the painting he contemplates where he will dare to include himself in the exalted company of God, Jesus and the Virgin Mary, Saint John, Saint Ambrose and Job; yet Browning suggests that such an effort of the imagination is necessary since Christianity is nothing if it cannot address its promise of salvation to sinners as well as the virtuous. Yet while all this must be recognised in any assessment of the poem, we must also see that Fra Lippo Lippi is in danger of forgetting what is most valuable in human nature – its constant tendency to strive beyond its own limitations. Lippo Lippi is too easily satisfied, too readily contented, ultimately too complacent, so that though Browning envies the tranquillity, truthfulness and assurance of his art, and though he would gladly identify with the model he represents, he knows that to be Lippo Lippi would be to suppress the ceaseless questioning of his own unquiet spirit. The nomad can only linger at the oasis for so long.

Just as 'Two in the Campagna' seems antiphonal to 'Love among the Ruins', so 'Andrea del Sarto' seems to answer and counterbalance 'Fra Lippo Lippi'. The freedom and irresponsibility of Lippo

Lippi is denied to Andrea who is presented 'fettered fast' by the chains of circumstance, careworn and lacking the drive and ambition to be the truly great painter, which he once had the potential to be. The enigma as to why, with all his extraordinary gifts, Andrea remains only 'the faultless painter' is one that the poem sets out to explore. It may have been simply that because his art came so easily to him he never felt impelled to strive to do something better, so that he never conveys the sense of aspiration and power that we encounter in Leonardo or Michelangelo. It may be that in sacrificing a promising career at the court of the King of France in response to the demands of his wife Lucrezia, Andrea knowingly abandoned the golden world of fame and ambition for a grey domesticity

> A common greyness silvers everything, –
> All in a twilight.

It may be that Lucrezia dragged him down with her shallow self-centredness and materialistic values, but it may also be that Andrea himself once decided that a more limited, humdrum environment would suit him best. Andrea is tempted to blame his wife, yet he also recognises that 'incentives come from the soul's self'. Andrea is a tragic figure because he seems to have sacrificed much for personal happiness, yet it still eludes him since his wife is unfaithful. Undoubtedly this poem expresses Browning's own guilt and anxiety about abandoning, or seeming to abandon, his vocation as an artist by marrying Elizabeth Barrett and thus apparently prioritising her future over his own – since she was already famous, he was virtually unknown. By putting personal happiness first he has placed his identity as a poet in jeopardy, yet that happiness is itself a fragile thing which may offer no compensation for what he has given up. Indeed Browning's premonition was at least partly justified as Elizabeth died in 1861, only six years after the publication of *Men and Women*. Yet recognition as a major figure in Victorian poetry was to be still slow in coming – J. Fotheringham in his *Studies in the Poetry of Browning* (1898) suggests that it only begins to grow after 1870.[8] Because Andrea seems heroic in his self-knowledge and acceptance of limitation, he is not complacent about it. For so gifted an artist he is strangely apologetic and humble. So Browning suggests that there may be salvation in hanging on to his conviction that art must be a struggle *against* limitations, even when the struggle itself seems too great.

Of all Browning's dramatic monologues, 'Bishop Bloughram's Apology' is the most celebrated and it is difficult to know which to admire more, the adroitness of the arguments that Bloughram puts forward in defence of his own position, or the many deft touches by which Browning sketches the portrait of a thoroughly worldly and self-satisfied churchman. The real puzzle presented by the poem is to decide whether the poem is as straightforward as it appears to be and to determine what Browning's motive was for writing it in the first place. In some sense the reader is freed from the obligation of responding to Bloughram's actual intellectual arguments, both because his interlocutor does not – his departure for Australia with settler's tools and a copy of the Bible is comment enough – and because though the arguments themselves are often persuasive in theory, the reader is always conscious that Bloughram is a man who has no real convictions and simply adopts a particular point of view to suit his own comfort and convenience:

> What suits the most my idiosyncrasy,
> Brings out the best of me and bears me fruit
> In power, peace, pleasantness and length of days.
> I find that positive belief does this
> For me, and unbelief, no whit of this.

Nevertheless although the poem can be readily interpreted – as it was by Browning's Victorian contemporaries – as a satire on Catholic hypocrisy, its actual motivation is more devious because much of what Bloughram has to say is not specifically associated with Catholic theology, and Browning, had he wished, could just as easily have presented Bloughram as a bishop in the Church of England. This would have been more apt in many ways, since the Catholic church insists on the literal truth of its own doctrines, while it was in the Church of England that there was a disposition to argue for Christianity in more instrumental terms, stressing the advantages both for the individual and society that accrue as the result of holding such beliefs. The actual awkwardness of the poem is that it seems to undermine some perfectly good and widely held arguments for Christianity by attributing them to such a venial man. Bloughram's claim that since absolute certainty in belief is impossible it makes sense to adhere to the values and traditions in which you have been brought up, has much in common with the conservatism of Burke and Coleridge. Indeed, in the mid-nineteenth century it was commonplace to view religion as a kind of glue that could stabilise society and the life of each individual man and woman. Bloughram's insistence that faith and doubt are interconnected and inseparable strikes the same note as Tennyson's *In Memoriam*. Moreover if Bloughram seems irreverent when he suggests that beliefs are a kind of baggage that we carry through the world, Carlyle had already made a similar suggestion through the clothing metaphor of *Sartor Resartus*, whose force is both to suggest that beliefs are historically contingent and that, in all cases, *something* is better than nothing – precisely the position of Bloughram. Browning seems to admit that there is a danger that the opinions he presents may be devalued by their proponent by the strange and rather unexpected way in which he emerges, speaking in an unaccustomed *propria persona* to warn: 'He said true things, but called them by wrong names.' But one nevertheless suspects that Browning was more than a little suspicious of those who had managed to cut down the bulky impedimenta of traditional religion so that it would fit more readily and easily into the confined spaces of the present day. For Browning's readers Bloughram's principal fault would have been his lack of genuine piety, but Browning's own criticism is more that Bloughram's religion involves neither tension nor effort. This is particularly apparent in Bloughram's discussion of Shakespeare:

> 'But try,' you urge, 'the trying shall suffice;
> 'Try to be Shakespeare, leave the rest to fate!'
> Spare my self-knowledge – there's no fooling me!
> If I prefer to remain my poor self,
> I say so not in self-dispraise but praise.
> If I'm a Shakespeare, let the well alone;
> Why should I try to be what now I am?
> If I'm no Shakespeare, as too probable, –
> His power and consciousness and self-delight
> And all we want in common, shall I find –
> Trying for ever?

Here was the really dangerous thrust of Bloughram's Mephistophelean gospel which Browning felt all too acutely, since he placed in the bishop's mouth all those doubts he felt about his own career as a poet. Over the two decades since the publication of *Pauline* Browning had striven to be another Shelley but had altogether failed to achieve the recognition he had sought. Now ingratiating voices insinuated that he should now give up the vain struggle that had so far only served to bring him unhappiness. All he had to do to obtain happiness and make his peace with the world was to recognise that he was not and never would be a Shelley or a Shakespeare. Admittedly, for Browning to reconcile himself to the idea that he could only ever hope to be some sort of literary hanger-on, like Gigadibs, was utterly out of the question, but what the poem dramatises is his fear that having spurned the opportunism of a Bloughram he might end up without either the gifts of the world or the spirit.

Where Bloughram becomes a particularly subtle devil's advocate is in his contemptuous demolition of Gigadibs's belief in sincerity and the integrity of the personality. Bloughram knows that Gigadibs despises him for his hypocrisy but he in turn despises Gidgadibs's simplistic assumption that he can be 'whole and sole yourself', his credo 'Best be yourself, imperial, plain and true.' Browning himself had come to distrust this unitary view of the self and the writing of *Men and Women* was eloquent testimony to his conversion. For Browning this romantic ideal of the self implied an impossible dream of total self-transparency and a self that was never beset by doubt or subject to internal conflict or division. Yet Browning also recognised that his understanding of the poet's mission predicated precisely such a harmonious self, for only in this way could the poet formulate his goals and then steadfastly set about the task of realising them. In his *A Defence of Poetry* Shelley had written: 'the frequent recurrence of the poetical power, it is obvious to suppose, may produce in the mind a habit of order and harmony correlative with its own nature and with its effects upon other minds'. Shelley admitted that in the intervals of inspiration the poet would become as other men and subject to similar pressures, but Shelley's whole conception of poetry implied that the poet must be able to transcend ordinary human weaknesses. Bloughram turns the tables on the poetic idealist, whether Browning or Shelley, by suggesting that it is the visionary who is the hypocrite because of the gap between his aspirations and reality, whereas Bloughram is not only a realist, but intellectually honest as well. As he says to Gigadibs:

> How one acts
> Is, both of us agree, our chief concern:
> And how you'll act is what I fain would see
> If, like the candid person you appear,

You dare to make the most of your life's scheme
As I of mine, live up to its full law
Since there's no higher law that counterchecks.

The challenge that Browning the sceptic throws down to Browning
the visionary dreamer is that he shall give force and substance to the
idea of personal integrity – a challenge that Browning was to take up
in his great work, *The Ring and the Book*.

The Ring and the Book is a long and complex poem that presents the
events in a seventeenth-century Roman murder trial from a number
of different points of view. Yet Browning's intention was not so
much to demonstrate the relativity of human perception as to insist
on the importance of *judgement* even where the events and circumstances may be such as to make judgement so difficult as to verge on
the impossible. In *The Ring and the Book* Browning's intention is both
to show the general inscrutability of human behaviour as it presents
itself to the public gaze, and yet, at the same time, to suggest that a
careful sifting of the evidence will make truth possible. But there is
a paradoxical twist to his argument, which is that this truth may only
be discovered in the overall articulation of the poem, which, by the
power of art, may achieve a clarity that might never be achieved
under ordinary circumstances. The ring – the poem – has a brilliance
and definiteness of form that the book – a jumble of disparate documents – lacks. Moreover the whole question of judgement is made
the more intricate because in the writing of *The Ring and the Book*
Browning is acutely conscious that he is describing no ordinary
murder trial, but one that took place under a very particular set of
circumstances. The fascination of the trial for Browning, quite apart
from the intrinsic interests of the case, lies in the fact that it represents a conjunction of the ancient and the modern. On the one hand
the verdict, handed down by the court and confirmed by the Pope,
implied the modern judgement that a woman who is terrorised and
oppressed by her husband has every right to leave him and resist
any attempt on his part to get her back or impose his will upon her;
yet on the other the trial in 1698 represented perhaps the last moment, before the onset of eighteenth-century rationalism and anti-
clericalism, when such a matter could have been adjudicated in the
belief that the verdict represented absolute justice, rather than the
merely relative opinion of a particular social group. For we like to
believe that justice is absolute, but in practice we recognise that the
most that can be expected is that the jury will deliver a verdict that

reflects the beliefs and prejudices of the age. In the trial that is the subject of *The Ring and the Book* this did not happen – Count Guido expected that his patriarchal rights over his spouse would be upheld, in accordance with tradition and a wide spectrum of public opinion. Yet they were not – and the Pope upheld the verdict. This result was at once innovative and conservative, the product of a distinctive and unusual set of circumstances.

For Browning the fascination of this murder by Count Guido of his wife Pompilia was that it did not take place immediately after her clandestine departure from his home in the company of a handsome young priest, but only subsequently, after her release from a convent into the house of her 'parents'. While the general contours of the story were familiar it nevertheless had a number of puzzling features. While certain facts were contested – had Pompilia and the priest exchanged love letters? was Guido drugged? – they were by no means crucial to the interpretation of the events, many of which – Guido's confrontation with his wife and Caponsacchi after he had caught up with them at Castelnuovo, outside Rome; Guido's responsibility for the murder of his wife and her 'parents' – were not in dispute.

What was interesting was that the 'same' story could be told in quite different ways and with such an entirely different moral emphasis that the ostensible unity of the narrative could be totally fractured. What was so subtle in Browning's treatment of the story was not so much that he presented the events from different points of view, innovative as that was, as that he recognised that the characters and the circumstances in which they were placed could not be viewed purely and simply as they 'were', but only in terms of stereotypes and the complex webs of attitude and belief that such stereotypes represent. For Browning it was of the essence that the trial had engaged the popular imagination of the Roman people and that all over the city people were taking sides, as this demonstrated that they had already preconstructed it as narrative in their minds. The most obvious response was to read the case as a grotesque Boccaccian comedy of the deceived and cuckolded husband. On this view Count Guido Francescini is duped by the crafty old wife Violante not just into a misalliance with lowly commoners, but into accepting as his wife the illegitimate child of a common prostitute. The young bride naturally finds marriage to an unattractive and tyrannical old husband irksome and seizes on the opportunity of elopement with a handsome priest, who is inevitably not the innocent he appears. This same comedy can be made more serious by reflection from either a male aristocratic, or 'feminine', priestly point of view. As the supporters of Count Guido see it, he has been shamefully mistreated, first by the old couple who deceived him and then held him up to ridicule, then by his wife and the priest, and finally, adding insult to injury, by the courts. His revenge is a wholly justified assertion of his rights as a husband. For those who sympathise with Pompilia, she has suffered much and unjustly at the hands of her husband and was fully justified in accepting the assistance of Guiseppi Caponsacchi in running away, whatever his motives in the affair may have been. Yet all of these versions represent a kind of pre-cognition of the story, so that it is already possible to take sides without really reflecting on the testimony that is given in court. Yet the court proceedings offer further scope for mystification and confusion as the advocates on either side pile on the similes, metaphors and typological analogies in terms of which they wish the case to be viewed. De Archangelis, for the defence, compares Guido's tribulations in Rome with the suffering of Samson amongst the Philistines and likens him to Virginius, who killed his own daughter rather than see her become the slave of Appius Claudius. Bottinius, for the prosecution, asks the court to see Violante, Pietro and Pompilia as the Holy Family, Guido as the cruel destroyer Herod. He favourably compares Pompilia with Judith, who slew Holofernes to defend her honour; with Dido, who fled from Tyre with hidden treasure to Carthage; and with Hesione, who was offered as a sacrifice to Apollo and Poseidon. This barrage of types, stereotypes and precedents may serve to impress or persuade, yet the overall effect is of obfuscation. For Browning the real question is – can we see Guido or Pompilia plain?

Certainly the decision of Pompilia to leave her husband with the aid of Guiseppi Caponsacchi does possess a miraculous clarity and decisiveness. It would be all too easy to underestimate the courage that was called for to take this step, especially when all the appearances were against her. Browning is convinced that both Pompilia and Caponsacchi acted with perfect rectitude, and what validates that is the speed and spontaneity with which they acted. Had they lingered or prevaricated, or had they allowed themselves to be overwhelmed by the possibilities for misconstruction that their behaviour invited, they would have become either paralysed or compromised. The clarity of their purpose is, for Browning, a refutation of Bloughram's insinuation that the pretension to 'be yourself, imperial, plain and true' must always be fatally flawed. Bloughram is right to the extent that if the individual becomes mesmerised by the interpretative possibilities that his or her action open up, then it will become a matter of calculating what people are likely to conclude and action will be transformed into pantomime and theatre. So the assessment of character must be guided by a contrary logic in which we must assume that a strong presumption of innocence must be attached to those who are prepared to risk seeming guilty. As the priest points out, had he wished to pursue an affair with Pompilia it would have made more sense for him to remain with her at Artezzo than to embark on a course that must necessarily seem incriminating. Similarly the Pope finds the letters that are supposed to have passed between Pompilia and Caponsacchi are not merely proved false but are a decisive pointer to the depths of depravity underlying Guido's actions, since their contents are so blatantly discrepant with everything else that we know about them:

> Why then,
> Craft to the rescue, craft should supplement
> Cruelty and show hell a masterpiece!
> Hence this consummate lie, this love-intrigue,
> Unmanly simulation of a sin,
> With place and time and circumstance to suit –
> These letters false beyond all forgery –
> Not just handwriting and mere authorship,
> But false to body and soul they figure forth –
> As though the man had cut out shape and shape
> From fancies of that other Aretine,
> To paste below – incorporate the filth
> With cherub faces on a missal-page.

Whereas Bottinius, for the prosecution, feels that Pompilia and Caponsacchi claim a virtue that is so excessive as to be unbelievable, and therefore makes numerous concessions – that Pompilia may have been able to read, despite her denials; that the priest may have had some romantic feelings towards her; that she may have taken some money from her husband to pay for the jury – the Pope is prepared to believe that Pompilia is 'perfect in whiteness'. Indeed her wager that her actions will appear innocent and justified require to validate them a comparable wager from the Pope to follow his own intuition. Yet appearances must still remain against her; just as the earlier tribunal, while not supporting Guido, nevertheless pre-

sumed by its decisions that some measure of guilt attached both to
her and her rescuer. Indeed for Browning the very idea and possibility of human goodness necessarily flies in the face of public opinion,
which can never entertain it as a realistic possibility.

After the Pope's deeply serious meditations on good and evil, life
and death, and the fragility of justice, it is something of a shock to be
plunged back into the narcissistic, endlessly self-justifying mentality
of Guido as he once more renews his protestations on the threshold
of the gallows:

> innocent am I
> As Innocent my Pope and murderer,
> Innocent as a babe, as Mary's own,
> As Mary's self.

Guido's language is scandalous. Even Dominus Hyancinthus de
Archangelis and Doctor Johannes-Baptista Bottinius would never
have allowed their fondness for similitude to stretch as far as this,
and even before Guido has launched himself into yet one more
defence Browning has ensured that we are utterly alienated from
him. We begin to recognise how, from book to book, our perception
of Guido has been radically altered. To begin with it seemed that it
was possible to take sides in the trial and that the issue was doubtful.
Guido's case seemed quite persuasive. He seemed like an ill-used,
long-suffering nobleman, who, after enduring endless abuse and
quite scandalous assaults on his honour, had been finally driven to
a retribution that seemed the more justified because it had been so
long delayed. But step by step Guido's self-righteous anger is exposed as the cruel vanity it is. Through the testimony of Pompilia
and the priest we realise that Guido's behaviour has been cruel,
calculating and inhuman, that he has never for one moment thought
of Pompilia as a person, or seen her as anything other than a chattel
and a bargaining tool to be used and misused as he sees fit. So we are
hardly likely to sympathise when Guido demonstrates in the most
unequivocal manner that he is utterly indifferent to any point of
view but his own, that he is contemptuous of everyone, and that he
feels neither shame nor remorse. Yet even at this point there is
nothing of the two-dimensional in Browning's approach to the story
and he contrives to bring forward arguments that are more than a
little unsettling. For if Browning, as the rescuer of Elizabeth Barrett,
well understood patriarchal tyranny and inevitably sympathised

with wife and priest, there was another side to Browning, the frustrated and neglected poet, which could understand very well the ignominy and desperation that Guido had suffered. Of course, Guido exposes himself in such an utterly shameless way that we can scarcely harbour any illusions about him. He admits that his 'moral' code is a brutally utilitarian one – 'Get pleasure, 'scape pain' – and he also concedes that his speech is calculated solely to persuade and does not profess to articulate any real self:

> You understand me and forgive, sweet Sirs?
> I blame you, tear my hair and tell my woe –
> All's but a flourish, figure of rhetoric!
> One must try each expedient to save life.

But if the sudden switch from the transcendental position of the Pope to the uncompromisingly worldly position of Guido comes as a violent shock, we cannot, at the same time, altogether deny Guido's worldly logic. As a matter of fact Guido *was* extremely unlucky and if things *had* worked out even only slightly differently he would either have escaped the law or escaped punishment. Further, while only Guido would be shameless enough to invoke his wife's miraculous survival of his brutal scheme as just another instance of his bad luck, he is clearly right in claiming that her death-bed narration necessarily carried much more conviction than her original testimony in court. So we are not just concerned with evidence but with typology and symbolic action. Most ingeniously of all, Browning has Guido turn the argument about the inscrutability of human motivation, which he has used to plead the case of Pompilia and Caponsacchi, to his own advantage. If Pompilia was indeed innocent, how could he, a mere mortal, be expected to have known:

> All those eyes of all husbands in all plays,
> At stare like one expanded peacock-tail,
> Are laughed at for pretending to be keen
> While horn-blind: but the moment I step forth –
> Oh, I must needs o' the sudden prove a lynx
> And look the heart, that stone-wall, through and through!
> Such an eye, God's may be, – not yours nor mine.

What Guido is suggesting is that the transcendental position of God or the Pope involves assumptions about the clarity and certainty of experience that are denied in normal experience, and that he should be judged by less exalted and more conventional criteria. Since husbands have traditionally been supported in their claims to absolute sovereignty over their wives, he is entitled to the same right – and why should he be denied it by the whim of a Pope, with intimations of immortality on his mind.

It is easy to underestimate the force of this argument, just because Guido, in putting it, seems at the same time to condemn himself utterly. It is Browning's way to make life difficult for his readers even if they may not be disposed to take up the challenge he presents them with. What Browning suggests is that condemnation of Guido is the only right and proper verdict – but that no ordinary court of law could possibly be justified in handing such a verdict down, because it could never possess either the certainty or the unimpeachable moral authority that would justify it.

In the Victorian age the visual arts acquired a curiously important position not so much because they were valued for their own sake as because they were regarded as a significant index of the health and vitality of the national culture. At an early date Victorian art critics began to worry that artistic tradition, which seemed to have reached some kind of culmination with the work of Joshua Reynolds, might have already entered into a period of senescence and decline even as Sir Joshua himself was directing his students in the emulation of Raphael and Michelangelo. In an article in *Blackwood's* for July 1836, 'The British School of Painting', Archibald Alison deplored the fact that though England could boast of an unrivalled tradition in poetry from Shakespeare and Milton to the Romantics, she seemed to possess no painters who could be mentioned in the same breath as Raphael, Michelangelo and Claude Lorrain. He believed that in all the major fields of painting, whether historical, landscape, portraiture or Dutch genre, the English artists were inferior. Alison believed that English artists were shirking direct confrontation with the great masters and would not be spurred to greater heights until there were galleries in England that had works of the very highest class on display. But what lies behind this demand is Alison's sense that while England's greatness on the stage of nations is an unquestionable, indubitable fact, that greatness nevertheless needs to be announced and bodied forth in commanding works of art, as has been the case with the great civilisations of the past. Alison's fear is that the moment for such a burst of creativity may have already past:

> We are in that state of national existence when excellence in the fine arts might naturally be expected, in which Athens raised the matchless portico of the Parthenon, and Rome the stately dome of the Pantheon, and modern Italy gave birth to Raphael and Domenichino. Unless something is done now, and that too, speedily, we shall arrive at the stage of the corruption of taste before we have passed through its excellence; like the Russians, we shall be rotten before we are ripe. The vast growth of opulence, the taste for gorgeous display and rich decoration, the passion for theatric spectacles, the turn of our literature and manners, all mark too clearly the approach of the corrupted era of national feeling.[9]

What makes Alison's anxiety about the possibility of giving British culture 'a refined and classic direction'[10] is not just that England does not have the artists, but that the very notion of the classic is itself imperilled and becoming impossible to achieve precisely because there is no adequate public consciousness of what classic art is. What is on trial is not just English art but the national spirit itself. It is ironic that John Ruskin, who tried more determinedly than anyone to refute Alison's disparagement of the English landscape painters and his claim that they had produced nothing that could stand comparison with the work of Claude, Salvator Rosa and Poussin, should nevertheless have shared this sense of national crisis and should, at the opening of *The Stones of Venice* (1951–3) have struck a similar note of warning even in the very aftermath of the Great Exhibition:

> Since first the dominion of men was asserted over the ocean, three thrones, of mark beyond all others, have been set upon the sands: the thrones of Tyre, Venice and England. Of the First of these great powers only the memory remains; of the Second, the ruin; the Third, which inherits their greatness, if it forgets their example, may be led through prouder eminence to less pitied destruction. (x, 193)

Both Alison and Ruskin were concerned about the future of English art, but while the former wanted to educate public opinion through the diffusion of the best examples from the past, the latter believed that great art could only come from the faithful study of nature and through an emancipation of English art from the corrupt traditions of the past of which Claudian landscape painting was the supreme instance. While it is often felt, quite rightly, that the emergence of Ruskin as a critic of culture rather than as a critic of art pure and simple is associated with *The Stones of Venice* it is worth stressing that there are intimations of such a cultural perspective even in the early volumes of *Modern Painters*. Ruskin, under the tutelage of Shelley and Wordsworth, believed strongly in the virtues of originality and the vices of imitation, and this made him resist the idea that excellence in art could only be attained *á la* Reynolds by following the strongest masters of the past. He was doubly suspicious of Claude, because he felt that, as an expatriate Frenchman who spent his entire adult life in Rome, Claude has become an inauthentic artist and had completely lost touch with his native culture and tradition. It therefore follows that Ruskin also disagreed with Alison over his insistence on 'the vast, incalculable advantage of foreign study'.[11] Against this Ruskin stressed, in Wordsworthian fashion, that what was crucial for the development of greatness in a painter was the influence of his native surroundings and therefore any period of residence in Italy to study the antique, far from broadening horizons and enlarging the capabilities, could only lead to falsity and artistic decline:

> Expression, character, types of countenance, costume, colour, and accessories are with all great painters whatsoever those of their native land, and that frankly and entirely, without the slightest attempt at modification; and I assert fearlessly that it is impossible that it should ever be otherwise, and that no man ever painted or ever will paint well anything but what he has early and long seen, early and long felt, and early and long loved. How far it is possible for the mind of one generation to be healthily modified and taught by the work of another, I presume not to determine; but it depends upon whether the energy of the mind which receives the instruction be sufficient, while it takes out of what it feeds upon that which is universal and common to all nature, to resist warping from national or temporary peculiarities. Nino Pisano got nothing but good, the modern French nothing but evil, from the study of the antique; but Nino Pisano had a God and character. All artists who have attempted to assume, or in their weakness have been

affected by, the national peculiarities of other times and countries, have instantly, whatever their original power, fallen to the third-rank, or fallen altogether, and have invariably lost their birthright and blessing, lose their power over the human heart, lost all capability of teaching or benefitting others.   (III, 229–30)

With these terms of analysis Ruskin has effectively demolished the whole notion of the antique as an object of cultural reverence and study. It is one thing for an Italian painter to learn from *his own* cultural tradition but something quite other for a Frenchman to come from the outside and *copy*: 'Titian being the most remarkable instance of the influence of the native air on a strong mind, and Claude, of that of the classical poison on a weak one' (III, 233).

By contrast it is possible for Turner to be a strong painter in a way that Claude is not because everything in his painting testifies to the fact that the scenery of his native Yorkshire has been deeply implanted in his soul: 'There is in them little seeking after effect, but a strong love of place, little exhibition of the artist's own powers or peculiarities, but intense appreciation of the smallest local minutiae' (III, 233). In Ruskin's perception of it, classical landscape is a hybrid, fabricated invention that calls for admiration of the artist's skill, while in an authentic artist such as Turner there is no display as the artist totally loses himself in and subordinates himself to the truthful rendering of that which he dearly loves.

For Ruskin the essential problem with the powerful traditions of art history of his day was that they left no space for the modern artist, so in describing his work as *Modern Painters*, in dedicating it to the English landscape painters and in claiming that it was dedicated to 'the advancement of the cause of real art in England' (III, 6) he deliberately threw down a challenge to the whole idea of a classical tradition. For if Raphael and Michelangelo were 'mortal gods' as Vasari had suggested and if their art really represented a 'perfection', an unsurpassable high point from which declension was the only conceivable outcome, then Vasari's notion of a progressive history of art, so optimistic in its day, could only cast a baleful shadow over the efforts of those whose fate it was to come after. This was the model that Ruskin perpetually tried to revise and recast, yet the general presentation of art in terms of bold but naïve beginnings leading to a mature and balanced consummation, which in turn would produce exaggeration, one-sidedness and decadence was one that he always accepted. In *The Stones of Venice* Ruskin rejected

Vasari's prioritising of the Renaissance – indeed to call it Renaissance at all was a misconception – for the artistic achievement of St Mark's in Venice belongs to the twelfth and thirteenth centuries and Ruskin therefore set the decline of Venice as far back as 1418. If the peak was here, then the Renaissance itself was belated. The Renaissance in architecture itself was also inauthentic as it rested on a revival of dead classical models and involved a final betrayal of the vital traditions of Gothic. This narrative also involved a reversal of the relationship between architecture and painting since it was architecture that was the crucial index of cultural development.

Yet Ruskin could also work the progressive model the other way, pointing to progressive possibilities *beyond* the Renaissance in the modern era. Landscape painting was important precisely because it represented one area where the great artists of the preceding centuries really could be surpassed. In his *Lectures on Architecture and Painting* delivered at Edinburgh in 1853 Ruskin claimed that there were advances in landscape painting in Italian art from Giotto and Orcagna to Raphael, Leonardo and Perugino and again with Corregio and Titian. Yet the further step forward which should have been taken to free landscape painting from conventionalism was made by Claude and Salvator Rosa in a way that was fundamentally superficial and unserious so that it became

> like a scene in a theatre, viciously and falsely painted throughout, and presenting a deceptive appearance of truth to Nature; understood, as far as it went, in a moment, but conveying no accurate knowledge of anything, and, in all its operations on the mind, unhealthy, hopeless, and profitless.   (XII, 117)

What we must particularly note here is that Ruskin is not primarily concerned to labour the decadence of Claude and Salvator Rosa, much as he deplores their artistic methods, but rather to insist on the missed opportunity. The fourth step in this progressive movement from Giotto onwards still remains, and thus the way lies open for Turner to reach the apogee of landscape painting: 'none before Turner had lifted the veil from the face of Nature; the majesty of the hills and forests had received no interpretation, and the clouds passed unrecorded from the face of the heaven which they adorned, and of the earth to which they ministered' (XII, 129). It has been left to Turner to shake off his classical predecessors, like a pack of baffled and bemused foxhounds who have lost the scent, for his art stands on its own in its ability to render nature truthfully, indeed to be nothing less than a 'transcript of the whole system of nature', which necessarily makes Turner 'the most perfect landscape painter the world has ever seen' (III, 616).

The confidence that underpinned the early volumes of *Modern Painters* was based on Ruskin's faith in Christianity as a progressive system of revelation in which, as ignorance and idolatry were extinguished and the scope of human knowledge extended, man would be gradually brought closer to God. As he wrote in his 1847 review of Lord Lindsay's *The History of Christian Art*:

> The vision of the cloister must depart with its superstitious peace – the quick apprehensive symbolism of early Faith must yield to the abstract teaching of disciplined Reason. Whatever else we may deem of the Progress of Nations, one character of that progress is determined and discernible. As in the encroaching of the land upon the sea, the strength of sandy bastions is raised out of the sifted ruin of ancient inland hills – for every tongue of level land that stretches into the deep, the fall of Alps has been heard among the clouds, and as the fields of industry enlarge, the intercourse with Heaven is shortened.   (XII, 247)

Indeed the evidence is that Ruskin at this time genuinely believed that modern man was being offered cosmic revelations that had never hitherto been disclosed and he was perfectly sincere in his original claim – which *Blackwood's* found so blasphemous that it was deleted from subsequent editions – that Turner was 'sent as a prophet of God to reveal to men the mysteries of His universe, standing, like the great angel of the Apocalypse, clothed with a cloud, and with a rainbow upon his head, and with the sun and stars given into his hand' (III, 254).

While Ruskin was subsequently to feel the conflict between science and religion so acutely that this lead temporarily to a loss of faith, the evidence is that in the 1840s he believed that science and painting could together serve to disclose the divine will as immanent in Nature. The truth and importance of painting will be enhanced if its accuracy can be confirmed by directly referring to the evidence of the natural world, while at the same time the sciences of botany and geology can be used to discredit the empty and mendacious 'idealism' of the Grand Style. Up until now art criticism had been essentially circular. The Old Masters could never be themselves criticised or their practice questioned since all the concepts and values of discourse about art were derived precisely from the practice of the Old Masters. On this basis it was impossible, for example, to say, as Ruskin wanted to, that Turner was a better painter than Claude since Claude was inevitably the standard by which Turner was to be judged. Against this Ruskin stressed that whereas Claude simply deployed a repertoire of improbable clichés, Turner offered real knowledge. Indeed there can be no doubt that Ruskin found in Turner a unique power to disclose the world as it truly was. In a letter to his father from Venice in 1845 he was struck by the fact that Turner's *The Sun of Venice Going to Sea* could not simply be regarded as colourful or picturesque since it possessed such an astonishing accuracy:

> I *was* a little taken aback when yesterday, at six in the morning, with the early sunlight just flushing its folds, out came a fishing boat with its *painted* sail full to the wind, the most gorgeous orange and red, in everything, form, colour & feeling, the very counter-part of the Sol di Venezia – it is impossible that any *model* could be more rigidly exact than the painting, even to the height of the sail above the deck.[12]

Consequently Ruskin was simply not prepared to remain within the parameters of the old art criticism and he was impatient with those who were: 'Ask the connoisseur, who has scampered over all Europe, the shape of the leaf of an elm, and the chances are ninety to one that he cannot tell you' (III, 146).

The advantage of an art criticism that summons all paintings before the bar of truth and looks initially only for a clear downright statement of the facts is not simply that such an approach will decisively validate Turner and the English landscape artists: it also offers the only route whereby criticism can be at once authoritative and objective. The drawback is that Ruskin, in his enthusiasm for science and nature, is often in danger of losing sight of painting altogether; as his eye zooms in on minute particulars whose accuracy can be verified he often loses sight of the composition as a whole and completely suppresses all consideration of style, subject or period. In particular Ruskin's knowledge of botany and geology led to a veritable obsession both with the painting of rocks – to which he devoted the whole of Book 4 of *Modern Painters* – and with the accurate painting of foliage in the foreground, which often became a touchstone for his treatment of painting in general. Ruskin praises Turner for being 'as much of a geologist as he is a painter' (III, 429), and insists that it is a particular merit of his *The Upper Fall of the Tees* that 'With this drawing before him, a geologist could give a lecture upon the whole system of aqueous erosion' (III, 488).

Undoubtedly this approach leads to a strange warping of Ruskin's perception not merely of individual paintings but of the whole history of painting, since he often seems only interested in pictures in so far as they offer grist to his own particular mill. Thus Mantegna figures primarily in *Modern Painters* as an accurate painter of stones, while Masaccio's *Tribute Money* is of interest for its relatively accurate painting of mountains. Similarly the accurate painting of rocks is a significant feature of three well-known Pre-Raphaelite paintings – the portrait of Ruskin himself by Millais, John Brett's *The Stone-Breaker* and his *Val d'Aosta* – and Ruskin could happily expatiate on their geological accuracy, yet it is as if he lacks the terms to discuss what differentiates them as distinct from what they might apparently have in common. Thus while Millais was undoubtedly prompted by personal pique in his disparaging reference to *Val d'Aosta* as 'a wretched little work' when Ruskin was praising it 'sky-high' while showing little interest in Millais's own work, his suggestion that Ruskin's eye was 'only fit to judge the portraits of insects'[13] had more than a grain of truth in it. Yet the Pre-Raphaelites had undoubtedly been persuaded by Ruskin's criticism to labour very intensively at the foreground painting of foliage, which virtually takes the form of a collective signature in such well-known works of the school as Millais's *Ophelia* and *The Huguenot*, Holman Hunt's *Valentine Rescuing Sylvia from Proteus* and *The Hireling Shepherd*, Arthur Hughes's *April Love* and *The Long Engagement*. When Ruskin later stressed that they had followed his advice to 'go to nature in all singleness of heart' (III, 624), he might have added that he had also advised: 'Then let the details of the foreground be studied, especially those plants which appear peculiar to the place' (III, 627).

At its most pedantic Ruskin's criticism could lead to the creation of fetishised zones within the picture which consequently assumed the whole burden of mimesis. Yet Ruskin was by no means consistent in this. Indeed at the very end of his essay *Pre-Raphaelitism* he complained that the Pre-Raphaelites were in danger of being *too* careful and too preoccupied with attention to detail. It is very characteristic of Ruskin's criticism that he always wants to have it both ways; he will insist on literal accuracy and yet at the same time call for poetry and imagination, which must always be there to infuse and subtly transcend a representation that is scrupulously accurate in itself. It is characteristic of Ruskin that in his observations on the painting of architecture should state:

> The difference between the drawing of the architect and artist ought never to be, as it now commonly is, the difference between lifeless formality and witless licence; it ought to be between giving the mere lines and measures of a building and giving these lines and measures with the impression and soul of it besides. (III, 222–3)

Yet Ruskin's theory of art seems to offer very little space for creativity and imagination even though Ruskin himself eagerly responds when he is confronted with the evidence of them. What Ruskin was never prepared to admit was that the question of truth in painting could be interpreted in different ways and that there was no single, infallible yardstick that could be applied. Ruskin revelled in the brilliancy of Turner's rendering of light and rejoiced in his dazzling colour, yet he could combine this with a Lockian insistence that colour was a mere secondary and unimportant characteristic of objects. Similarly Ruskin could never fully bring himself to acknowledge that in Turner's later work the effect of light is to dissolve and dissipate the solidity of objects, thus putting in question Ruskin's assumptions of painterly realism and his belief that paintings must convey as much information as possible. The claim that Turner is a more truthful painter than Canaletto cannot be validated, as Ruskin liked to pretend, simply by an appeal to the Venetian facts. At bottom Ruskin knew that this was so and as his admiration for such Venetian painters as Tintoretto and Bellini increased, so he also came to realise how unsoundly based was his antithesis between the ancients and the moderns. In the successive volumes of *Modern Painters* Ruskin conducted his education and re-education in public as perhaps no other critic has ever done, yet in the final analysis the whole project is flawed simply because Ruskin was reluctant to abandon the iconoclastic fervour of the Reformation preacher, who seeks the destruction of all false and idolatrous images. As he wrote in the first volume of *Modern Painters*:

> if there be neither purpose nor fidelity in what is done, if it be an envious or powerless imitation of other men's labours, if it be a

display of mere manual dexterity or curious manufacture, or if in any other mode it show itself as having its origin in vanity, – Cast it out.   (III, 174)

Such violent antitheses were of the very essence for Ruskin and it was precisely this that enabled him to infuse the role of the art critic with such passionate urgency. To prevent bad art driving out the good the critic must be relentless and unappeasable in his struggle to drive out the bad.

A particularly curious aspect of Ruskin's art criticism at this time in the light of his later emphasis on the social mission of the visual arts was that it was almost completely untouched by the new public role assigned to painting through the open competitions that were held for paintings to be installed in the rebuilt Houses of Parliament, following the great fire of 1833. Indeed it is important to emphasise that while artists such as Holman Hunt, Rossetti and Whistler might be disposed to regard the Victorian public as Philistine, the fact remains that the visual arts became significant for a far wider audience than hitherto, as attendances at the Royal Academy exhibitions and the interest aroused by such pictures as Frith's *Derby Day* demonstrate. What was noteworthy about the exhibition of cartoons for the Palace of Westminster that was held in 1843 was that it became a great public event of interest to all sections of the population. Lady Eastlake, wife of the President of the Royal Academy, wrote in her diary:

The daily throng is immense; the public takes great interest, and the strongest proof is thus given of the love of the lower orders for *pictures*, when they represent an event. I abridged the catalogue to a penny size for the million, but many of the most miserably dressed people prefer the sixpenny ones, with the quotations, and it is a very gratifying sight to witness the attention and earnestness with which they follow the subject with books in their hands.[14]

What was particularly important about the competition was the tremendous boost it gave both to the genre of historical painting, which had never been able to find either patrons or an audience in England despite the fact that it was regarded as the summit of artistic achievement, and to England's newfound interest in her own earlier history. By a significant yet pathetic irony of fate, Benjamin Haydon, who had for years been clamouring in vain for recognition for the grand style, was finally led to take his own life at the very moment when his call was at last being answered – leaving on his easel a picture that could not have been more apropos, King Alfred and the first English jury. If the 1840s became a significant turning point in the history of British art, this was because there was a shift away from the portrait and the landscape towards moralising genre pieces, drawn from literature, history or with an obvious contemporary message, pictures that not only told a story but used the narrative mode to draw exemplary lessons. Victorian painting was characteristically didactic, yet Ruskin, the didactic critic par excellence, made virtually no contribution to this decisive trend apart from his enigmatic insistence on the important of ideas in painting, which was subsequently to inspire such artists as William Morris and Edward Burne-Jones. It was above all in the short-lived Pre-Raphaelite journal, *The Germ*, that the new doctrine was formulated. John L. Tupper insisted that the artist should only choose morally worthy and exemplary subjects, which 'address and excite the activity of man's rational and benevolent powers' and he began his extensive list with acts of justice, mercy and good government.[15] Tupper was opposed to base and unworthy subjects in art and he had a particular dislike of still-life paintings since he believed they only addressed man's physical appetites, not his spiritual powers. Similarly Frederic Stephens saw the visual arts as a force that could serve to enhance England's purity and spiritual grandeur:

> the Arts have always been most important moral guides. Their flourishing has always been coincident with the most wholesome period of a nation's growth. . . . If we have entered upon a new age, a new cycle of man, of which there are many signs, let us have it unstained by this vice of sensuality of mind.[16]

One of the unspecified targets of this style of criticism was the highly erotic nude painting of William Etty who, as Holman Hunt recorded in his memoirs, was a major influence on young art students of the 1840s. The new styles of painting would not simply aim at representation of the physical world, since this on its own was always potentially decadent, but would strive to embody and create higher spiritual values just like such naïve precursors of Raphael as Fra Angelico and Benozzo Gozzoli. The critic who went furthest of all in this direction was John Orchard, who in his 'A Dialogue on Art' (*The Germ*, May 1850) presented his views through a dialogue between

Kalon and Christian, thus demonstrating his conviction that Christian moral values must predominate over mere beauty: 'A picture, poem, or statue, unless it speak some purpose, is mere paint, paper, or stone. A work of art must have a purpose, or it is not a work of fine art'.[17]

Perhaps because Victorian art could be sentimental or sanctimonious, and often both at once – as in its endless fascination with the theme of the fallen woman – there has been a tendency to gloss over, neglect or deliberately misrecognise not simply the didacticism of Victorian art but also the degree to which Victorian painting was heavily *textualised*, to the point at which not simply elaborate titles but even comprehensive programme notes became crucial for their elucidation. A note of impatience with such an approach to painting was sounded early by the celebrated French critic Hyppolyte Taine in his *Notes sur l'Angleterre* (1872):

Never has so much effort been expended in trying to address the mind by way of the senses, illustrate an idea or a truth, or in collecting a greater mass of psychological observations into a surface twelve inches square. What patient and penetrating criticisms! What clever contrivance, and what aptitude in rendering moral values into physical terms. And what admirable vignettes these artists might have drawn to illustrate an edition of Sterne, Goldsmith, Crabbe, Thackeray or Eliot! . . . *But what a pity it is that these artists, instead of writing took to painting!*[18]

The implication is that there is something slightly unnatural, not to say perverse, about the endeavour, and it cannot be denied that in many cases pictorial and plastic values were neglected – as Taine himself went on to deplore: 'I do not believe that pictures so very disagreeable to look at have ever been painted. Impossible to imagine cruder effects, colour more brutal or exaggerated, more violent and gaudy discords, harder or falser juxtapositions of tones.'[19] Yet already in this indictment one begins to wonder whether Taine is quite as advanced and sophisticated as he claims, for these were the charges routinely advanced against some of the most innovative works of the Pre-Raphaelite school. The problem today is more that since the art of our own day has characteristically undervalued subject matter and insisted that what the artist chooses to paint is *per se* unimportant, we are ill prepared to approach paintings that are

pinned to specific quotations and texts and were intended to stimu-
late a particular train of reflection. In the case of Holman Hunt or
Rossetti the symbolic intention can scarcely be missed and Rossetti's
Beata Beatrix deliberately draws attention to its own allusiveness by
the way in which the text is actually incorporated into the structure
of the image itself. Yet such textualisation is a pervasive feature of
Victorian painting. Even Ruskin's beloved Turner was prone to link
his paintings with quotations and sometimes with anonymous poetic fragments composed by himself. The full title of Holman Hunt's
Rienzi is 'Rienzi vowing to obtain justice for the death of his young
brother, slain in a skirmish between the Colonna and Orsini factions', while the catalogue supplied a quotation from Bulwer Lytton's
Rienzi: Last of the Tribunes. The version of Ford Madox Brown's *Work*
in the Birmingham Art Gallery has an elaborate frame into which are
inset the following biblical quotations:

> Neither did we eat any man's bread for nought; but wrought with
> labour and travail night and day.

> Seest thou a man diligent in his business? He shall stand before
> Kings.

In this way the painting's concern to dramatise the dignity of work
is further emphasised. In the same way Alfred Rankley's *Old School-
fellows* was supplied with a motto from Proverbs: 'A friend loveth at
all times and a brother is born for adversity'. The Victorian artist
often perceived himself as painting sermons in paint; he hoped to
spur the spectator either to admire and emulate the moral grandeur
that his brush depicted, or else to steer well clear of the primrose
path leading to the everlasting bonfire. The Victorian painter was
more concerned with influencing conduct than with representing
reality pure and simple. As Holman Hunt subsequently wrote of the
Pre-Raphaelite Brotherhood: 'It will be seen that we were never
realists. I think art would have ceased to have the slightest interest
for any of us had the object been only to make a representation,
elaborate or unelaborate, of a fact in nature'.[20] Hence the awkwardness of the alliance between the Pre-Raphaelites and Ruskin, since
the critic saw in the artists, and the artists saw in the critic, just what
they wanted to see and no more.

Since the young Ruskin as a critic was infatuated with Turner it
was inevitable that he would see in historical painting and the grand

style just an aggravated pretext for falsity and insincerity in painting. Indeed when he openly addressed the issue for the first time in
the third volume of *Modern Painters* he reluctantly conceded the
painter's right to choose a high and noble subject, but only 'if the
choice be sincere' (v, 49) – a significant qualification since Ruskin did
not really believe that such a project in the modern age could be
other than flawed. Ruskin did not believe that historical painting
could be true because he felt that it was exceedingly unlikely that it
could be historically accurate; but the real reason for such a persistent problematising of the genre was more that it served to under-
score the higher truth claims of his beloved landscape painting.
Ruskin's early career as a critic of art was caught up in a strange
contradiction of which he was subsequently to become conscious:
that on the one hand he sought to be influential and a critic and to
proselytise on behalf of the genius of Turner (and to a lesser extent
on behalf of the Pre-Raphaelites), yet on the other hand Ruskin was
an ultra-élitist who did not believe that the majority of people were
capable of appreciating great art and who further believed that the
tiny coterie who *did* claim to appreciate it simply did not know what
they were talking about. Ruskin held that the art critic needed to be
well versed in botany and geology, he needed to be artist enough
himself to appreciate the actual problems and difficulties that painters encountered, and he also needed to have the eloquence in words
that would do justice to eloquence in paint. Only Ruskin himself
possessed these qualities. Indeed who but Ruskin would have challenged some of the great European painters to rival on canvas his
skill and accuracy in word-painting, and he implicitly suggested
that he alone was the equal of Turner in possessing the power to
capture the spirit of Venice:

> But let us take with Turner, the last and greatest step of all. Thank
> heaven, we are in sunshine again, – and what sunshine! Not the
> lurid, gloomy, plague-like oppression of Canaletti, but white, flash-
> ing fulness of dazzling light, which the waves drink and the
> clouds breathe, bounding and burning in intensity of joy. That sky
> – it is a very visible infinity, – liquid, measureless, unfathomable,
> panting and melting through the chasms in the long fields of
> snow-white, flaked, slow-moving vapour, that guide the eye along
> their multitudinous waves down to the islanded rest of the
> Euganean hills. Do we dream, or does the white forked sail drift
> nearer, and nearer yet, diminishing the blue sea between us with

the fulness of its wings? It pauses now; but the quivering of its bright reflection troubles the shadows of the sea, those azure, fathomless depths of crystal mystery, on which the swiftness of the poised gondola floats double, its black beak lifted like the crest of a dark ocean bird, its scarlet draperies flashed back from the kindling surface, and its bent oar breaking the radiant water into a dust of gold dreamlike and dim, but glorious, the unnumbered palaces lift their shafts out of the hollow sea, – pale ranks of motionless flame, – their mighty towers sent up to heaven like tongues of more eager fire, – their grey domes looming vast and dark, like eclipsed worlds, – their sculptured arabesques and purple marble fading farther and fainter, league beyond league, lost in the light of distance. Detail after detail, thought beyond thought, you find and feel them through the radiant mystery, inexhaustible as indistinct, beautiful, but never all revealed; secret in fulness, confused in symmetry, as nature herself is to the bewildered and foiled glance, giving out of that indistinctness, and through that confusion, the perpetual newness of the infinite, and the beautiful.

Yes, Mr Turner, we are in Venice now.   (III, 257)

Ostensibly Ruskin is praising the truthfulness of Turner's painting, but in reality he is seeking to enter into the world of Turner's imaginative vision and to create a prose style that would so triumphantly rise to the awesome challenge set by Turner's art that writer and painter would merge in their sublime endeavour to write a commentary on the infinite. Did the Latin critic who coined the phrase *ut pictura poesis* ever envisage anything like this? Yet inevitably if Turner's painting offered such a visionary experience, it was one available to few others beside Ruskin himself. As he wrote in *Modern Painters:*

But the highest art, being based on sensations of particular minds, sensations occurring to *them* only at particular times, and to a plurality of mankind perhaps never, and being expressive of thoughts which could only rise out of a mass of the most extended knowledge, and of dispositions modified in a thousand ways by peculiarity of intellect – can only be met and understood by persons having some sort of sympathy with the high and solitary minds which produced it – sympathy only to be felt by minds in some degree high and solitary themselves. He alone can appreciate the art, who could comprehend the conversation of the painter, and share in his emotion, in moments of his most fiery passion and most original thought.   (III, 135–6)

Like Tolstoy and God, Ruskin and Turner were like two bears in one den; but such exalted and pristine communication must necessarily be rare. Hence Ruskin felt that with an artist like Turner 'the true meaning and end of his art' must necessarily 'be sealed to thousands or misunderstood by them' (III, 136). Ruskin never seriously modified his sense that painting was an art open only to the most knowledgeable and dedicated of initiates, and if anything both the hostile criticism he received over *Modern Painters* and the acrimonious controversy over the Pre-Raphaelites only served to convince him that he was struggling against an almost invincible ignorance. In his commentaries on painting he felt that he was appealing to criteria that were too esoteric to be grasped by the general public, yet at the same time, by challenging concepts of ideal beauty and artistic tradition, he was setting himself at odds with those connoisseurs who set themselves up as arbiters of taste. Ruskin had hoped to reach out to a new and more responsive audience, but after the Pre-Raphaelite wars that earnest expectation was dimmed. If Ruskin in his *Lectures on Architecture and Painting* stressed somewhat melodramatically the alienation of the later and more radical Turner, saying of him: 'He retired into himself; he could look no longer for help, or counsel, or sympathy from anyone; and the spirit of defiance in which he was forced to labour led him sometimes into violences from which the slightest expression of sympathy would have saved him' (XII, 379), this was because Ruskin felt that, in his capacity as Turner's advocate, he had experienced vicariously but in full measure the rejection suffered by his idol.

The turn to architecture, then, which was so decisive a moment both in Ruskin's own intellectual development and in the history of the Victorian response to the arts, was undoubtedly motivated by Ruskin's disillusionment with the whole notion of fine art. Indeed although his hostility to the Renaissance was grounded in a multiplicity of arguments ranging from the preoccupation with technique in Renaissance painting to the rigid application of classical models in Renaissance architecture to what he termed the Renaissance pride in knowledge, there can be little doubt that he also traced back to the Renaissance the élitist traditions of connoisseurship that he had confronted in his defence of Turner. Ruskin believed that before the fourteenth century the arts had been more open, less specialised and more democratic, but that from that time onward a deadly rivalry for status and precedence was instituted which shattered the harmonious interplay between the arts of architecture, painting and sculpture that had previously existed. The painters of the Renaissance were not the heroes that Vasari presented but dangerous and destructive egoists:

> The merely decorative chequerings on the walls yielded gradually to more elaborate paintings of figure-subject; first small and quaint, and then enlarging into enormous pictures filled by figures generally colossal. As these paintings became of greater merit and importance, the architecture with which they were associated was less studied; and at last a style was introduced in which the framework of the building was little more interesting than that of a Manchester factory, but the whole space of the walls was covered with the most precious fresco paintings . . . in proportion as the architect felt himself thrust aside or forgotten in one edifice, he endeavoured to make himself principal in another; and in relation for the painter's entire usurpation of certain fields of design, succeeded in excluding him totally from those in which his own influence was predominant.   (XI, 29–31)

Thus in considering Ruskin's relationship with architecture we have to recognise that though he continued to revere his favourite painters, he had nevertheless come to distrust the elevation of painting that characterised post-Renaissance art as simultaneously élitist, arrogant and a significant moment both in the development of the division of labour and of the alienation and disunity that developed along with it. Ruskin no longer perceives painting purely and simply as some kind of irresistible surge towards truth driven by artistic genius, but rather as the epitome of a deeply troubling and ambivalent moment in Western culture where privileges reserved for the few are bought at the price of tyranny and oppression for the many. What is extraordinary about Ruskin's analysis is that he starts out from an essentially aesthetic perspective, yet his sense of what is most deeply valuable in art leads him to a viewpoint that puts that very aestheticism in question. He had now come to realise that what mattered was what touched the lives of the vast majority of men and women and therefore that his great crusade conducted against Claude and Poussin in *Modern Painters* had been almost entirely pointless. What really mattered was architecture:

Claude and Poussin were weak men, and have had no serious influence on the general mind. There is little harm in their works being purchased at high prices: their real influence is very slight, and they may be left without grave indignation to their poor mission of furnishing drawing-rooms and assisting stranded conversation. Not so the Renaissance architecture. Raised at once into all the magnificence of which it was capable by Michael Angelo, then taken up by men of real intellect and imagination, such as Scamozzi, Sansovino, Inigo Jones, and Wren, it is impossible to estimate the extent of its influence on the European mind; and that the more, because few persons are concerned with painting, and of those few the larger number regard it with scant attention; but all men are concerned with architecture, and have at some time of their lives serious business with it.   (IX, 46)

Yet even this passage dramatically understates the radical shift in Ruskin's perception of the arts. For his reference to serious business would doubtless have to the ordinary middle-class reader intimations of buying a house or employing an architect, which is certainly what the passage implies, whereas what has really changed for Ruskin is that he is no longer concerned with the aesthetic of consumption but with the ethics of production. Whether or not French landscape paintings are used to adorn genteel interiors is for him a relatively trivial issue. What does matter, and this is what 'architecture' stands for in Ruskin's mind, is a world where work is meaningful and enjoyable. As he wrote in *The Seven Lamps of Architecture*:

I believe the right question to ask, respecting ornament is simply this: Was it done with enjoyment – was the carver happy while he was about it? . . . For we are not sent into the world to do anything into which we cannot put our hearts . . . there is dreaming enough, and earthiness enough, and sensuality enough, without our turning the few glowing moments of it into mechanism.   (VIII, 218)

However, the question of the relationship between aesthetic values and actual life was for Ruskin a more complex one than this quotation alone would suggest. Ruskin's reflections on this topic are inspired by the city of Venice and the significance it has for the nineteenth-century world, but that is deeply problematic since Venice, though still *there* as a spectral, luminous presence, is also in some sense almost beyond the interrogation of the present. So *The*

Stones of Venice is not just a description of Venice as an unique architectural ensemble but a decipherment of what that really represents, in which Venice's composite, simultaneous present will be broken down into a diachronic narrative from its early settlement to its peak under the Doge, Andrea Dandolo, and its subsequent decline. Ruskin has to insist that Venice is more than it appears to be, for what saves Venice from Ruskin's Protestant point of view is the fact that in St Mark's especially there can be discerned an authentic Christian piety that has survived the decadence of medieval Catholicism, the pride of the Renaissance, the indifference of the present. Venice is a *northern* city and that means that the principles of decoration and colour, so dear to Ruskin's heart, can be rescued from all imputation of popery and irreligion. Here the Gothic is a universal language; here at least, in the stones of Venice the true voice of Christianity can be heard. St Mark's is a Bible in stone, and articulates a spiritual message through every apse, dome, pillar and portico. Ruskin believes that through a return to origins, through a spiritual traversal of the outer islands of Murano and especially Torcello, where men 'in flight and distress' built a church as a 'shelter for their earnest and sorrowful worship' (x, 13), it is possible to grasp the real significance of Venice and to perceive that its existence was once firmly grounded in piety and deep sincerity even if those qualities have long since been lost. To many nineteenth-century visitors it seemed that Venice could never be anything more than a melancholy relic of the past. Ruskin, on the other hand, believes that Venice, alien as she can often seem, nevertheless *does* have something to teach the industrialised world if only it will make the effort to listen to her. One of the most powerful rhetorical devices in the whole of *The Stones of Venice* – so powerful indeed that it must have provided Proust with the starting point for *A la recherche du temps perdu* – is the contrast that Ruskin makes, at the end of Volume I and the beginning of Volume II, of the two ways by which it is possible to approach Venice. The modern traveller, arriving from Mestre, is greeted by this:

> Now we can see nothing but what seems a low and monotonous dockyard wall, with flat arches to let the tide through it; – this is the railroad bridge, conspicuous above all things. But at the end of these dismal arches there rises, out of the wide water, a straggling line of low and confused brick buildings, which, but for the many towers which are mingled among them, might be the suburbs of

an English manufacturing town. Four or five domes, pale, and apparently at a greater distance, rise over the centre of the line; but the object which first catches the eye is a sullen cloud of black smoke brooding over the northern half of it, and which issues from the belfry of a church.

It is Venice.   (ix, 415)

In this description Venice is virtually dematerialised into a few shadowy domes; what really remains in the mind's eye is the wall, the railway bridge, the cloud of smoke, which obscure Venice almost to the point of replacing it. But how different were things in the old days when the traveller first approached Venice by sea:

when first upon the traveller's sight opened the long ranges of columned palaces, – each with its black boat moored at the portal, – each with its image cast down, beneath its feet, upon that green pavement which every breeze broke into new fantasies of rich tessellation; when first, at the extremity of the bright vista, the shadowy Rialto threw its colossal curve slowly forth from behind the palace of the Camerlenghi; that strange curve, so delicate, so adamantine, strong as a mountain cavern, graceful as a bow just bent; when first, before its moonlike circumference was all risen, the gondolier's cry, 'Ah! Stali,' struck sharp upon the ear, and the prow turned aside under the mighty cornices that half met over the narrow canal, where the splash of water followed close and loud, ringing along the marble by the boat's side; and when at last that boat darted forth upon the breadth of the silver sea, across which the front of the Ducal palace, flushed with its sanguine veins, looks to the snowy dome of Our Lady of Salvation, it was no marvel that the mind should be deeply entranced by the visionary charm of a scene so beautiful and so strange, as to forget the darker truths of its history and its being.   (x, 6)

To see Venice imaginatively in this way and to come at it from this direction is to pass through the looking-glass into an enchanted world and to be freed from the drab literalism of modernity. For the true Venice, which lies almost hidden under a thick layer of dull brown varnish, represents a city where faith and beauty were united, a city that was itself a work of art, but also represented an ideal harmony of man and nature, an almost impossible combination of order, stability and perfect balance – epitomised by the tides that have made Venice possible and could not vary a fraction more or less without destroying her. Ruskin's dream is that the extraordinary qualities of Venetian Gothic will not remain imprisoned and pent-up within the confines of Venice herself but will reach far beyond the grim barricades of Mestre to become a universal architectural style. Venice instead of succumbing to the power of the modern can herself conquer through the force of her beauty. The whole world can be Venetian.

In his writing about Venice we see the first gleams of Ruskin's humanism, which was to lead him away from God and the exaltation of nature above the works of man. For the buildings of Venice are human productions and the freedom that Ruskin delights in ascribing to the individual sculptor and carver he could never concede to the art of painter, where the expression of individuality was typically seen as a prideful dereliction from nature and the truth. *The Stones of Venice* was both Ruskin's wisest and most influential book because in it he temporarily turned his back on his censorious insistence on literalism in painting to celebrate creativity and the imagination. A good griffin does not necessarily *resemble* anything. Art is the product of happy and harmonious being, of minds that have been released from servitude, servility and fear.

As the result of thinking about the significance of Venice, and also about early Italian art, which he had been largely unfamiliar with when he produced the first two volumes of *Modern Painters*, Ruskin had effectively abandoned his assumptions about progress in art, in which art's powerful cognitive ambitions necessarily linked it with developments in science. Now Ruskin recognised that in a narrow obsession with the measurable and the quantifiable, contemporary culture had lost touch with much that was of still greater value. Art had actually been devalued and cut off from ordinary life by the arrogant and flashy art of the Renaissance, which was simply designed to impress wealthy patrons. Ruskin was now convinced that for art to become something more it would also have to be something less. As he put it in *The Two Paths* (1858):

We may abandon the hope – or if you like the words better – we may disdain the temptation, of the pomp and grace of Italy in her youth. For there can be no more the throne of marble – for us no more the vault of gold – but for us there is the loftier and lovelier privilege of bringing the power and charm of art within the reach of the humble and the poor; and as the magnificence of past ages failed by its narrowness and its pride, ours may prevail and continue, by its universality and its lowliness.   (xvi, 342)

Art must become more democratic, more approachable, more sincere; it will be valued not for its technical sophistication but because it is able to touch the lives of ordinary people. In fact it must be able to fulfil very much the same role that it had in the early Middle Ages when artists, themselves pious but relatively uneducated men, were able to communicate both more directly and more profoundly:

> whatever can be measured and handled, dissected and demonstrated, – in a word, whatever is of the body only, – the schools of knowledge do resolutely and courageously possess themselves of, and portray. But whatever is immeasurable, intangible, indivisible, and of the spirit, that the schools of knowledge do as certainly lose, and blot out of their sight. . . . Giotto gives it us: Orcagna gives it us; Angelico, Memmi, Pisano, – it matters not who, – all simple unlearned men, in their measure and manner, – give it us; and the learned men that followed them give it us not, and we, in our supreme learning, own ourselves at this day farther from it than ever.   (xi, 61–2)

Ruskin still reverences Turner but he is now less inclined to write in terms of a triumphant ascent towards truthful representation, and in the last volume of *Modern Painters* he sees Turner more as a despairing prophet at odds with his time. In his early response to the Pre-Raphaelite movement Ruskin was primarily interested in the work of Millais and Hunt for its truthful depiction of nature, and he deeply distrusted the Catholicising and medievalising tendencies of Rossetti. But now he found himself very much on the same wavelength as Rossetti since he had come to feel that spirituality, beauty and sincerity were actually more important than technical accuracy or what he would otherwise call 'truthfulness'. In the late 1850s, after the publication of *The Stones of Venice*, Ruskin became quite friendly with Rossetti and praised his work, a step that subtly contributed to the redefinition of Pre-Raphaelitism. For Rossetti, from being seen as a minor follower was increasingly viewed – and with some justification – as both the key figure of the movement and its prime instigator. In fact a belated desire to rebut this claim seems to have been one of the principal reasons why Holman Hunt was driven to write *The Pre-Raphaelite Brotherhood*. In *Pre-Raphaelitism* Ruskin had still very much conceived his role to be that of an advocate for *modern* painting and he had expressed the hope that they would not succumb to the dangers of medievalism:

> If they adhere to their principles and paint Nature as it is around them, with the help of modern science – with the earnestness of the men of the thirteenth and fourteenth centuries, they will, as I said, found a new and noble school in England. If their sympathies with the early artists lead them into medievalism or Romanism they will of course come to nothing.   (XII, 358)

At this time, in the aftermath of Newman's conversion to Rome, Ruskin still saw himself as the zealous defender of Protestant truth against Roman corruption and falsity. The history of landscape painting in particular was one of continuous progress culminating in Turner. Now, only two years later, in completing *The Stones of Venice* Ruskin saw things very differently. The medieval period, which he had once spoken of patronisingly, now seemed exemplary – a period where artistic freedom and artistic achievement went hand in hand. Work itself was creative. Now it was science and the false pride of science that was the enemy. He could no longer speak confidently of the 'modern'.

With hindsight it is clear that the extraordinary antipathy that the early exhibitions of Pre-Raphaelite painting aroused was to be of crucial significance for the whole history of the arts in Britain in the nineteenth century. The years 1850 and 1851 might well have been auspicious for modern British painting, since the stimulus to painting offered by the project to decorate the new House of Commons was followed by the Great Exhibition, which offered a forum for the applied arts, and both represented a unique opportunity to bring art before audiences who had never before been offered such easy access to them. It was not art that was the problem so much as religion, and the Pre-Raphaelite painters incurred the odium of being regarded, like Newman, as traitors to the national church. A cloud of suspicion would hang over them for a very long time to come. Self-confident as England appeared to be in those years, there were nevertheless certain topics – Chartism, Catholicism, Ireland – that aroused considerable unease and anxiety even though the threat they presented might already have passed. So Pre-Raphaelitism was perceived as being not so much a new approach to representation as the Trojan horse of Rome. This paranoia had massive consequences. Ruskin decided that there was little point in any further struggles on behalf of what was in any event a minority art and turned his attention to architecture. Millais adopted a more commercial style that was to damage irretrievably his reputation as a painter. Rossetti, in some ways the most exposed, because, to the vulgar mind, most evidently Catholic, took the opposite course and gave up exhibiting in public altogether.

For the remainder of his life Rossetti was to be the most private of artists, inhabiting a private world of Dantesque visions and Arthurian mythology, painting over and over again beautiful women, primarily Elizabeth Siddall and Jane Morris, who had become for him an all-encompassing obsession. Unlike Holman Hunt and Millais, who went out into the fields to paint directly from nature as Ruskin had taught, Rossetti was fundamentally uninterested in depicting the external world directly as it appeared to the eye. On an expedition to Sevenoaks with Holman Hunt he typically complained that the leaves were the wrong colour, because it was autumn they were red and yellow whereas he wanted to paint them green. Like one of his early idols, Blake, Rossetti seems to have felt that depicting the world as it really was could only serve to weaken the power of the imagination. Rossetti's father was an Italian political exile and Rossetti spoke Italian fluently, worshipped Dante and inspired others with his great love for the naïve style and glowing colours of the Pre-Raphaelite painters, yet he never once visited Italy, though he had both the time and the money to do so. So we must conclude that Rossetti would probably have agreed with Des Esseintes, the hero of Huysman's novel *A Rebours* – 'Travel, indeed, struck him as being a waste of time, since he believed that the imagination could provide a more-than-adequate substitute for the vulgar reality of actual experience.'

Although Rossetti was responsive to the demand for truthfulness in art, he always saw this in terms of truth to the imagination rather than in some presumed correspondence with the external world. Part of the appeal of the early Italian painters to him lay in their essentially flat, formalised images and sharply defined patches of colour in which there was no obligation to acknowledge either the rules of perspective or the effects of light. Rossetti himself strove for a clarity of vision that would, as in his *Beata Beatrix* or *Dantis Amor*, transcend the ordinary sublunary world with its humdrum shadows and background detail. Rossetti's painting dedicates itself to the art of the close-up – to the presentation of an image that is refined precisely to eliminate all such extraneous detail. There are flowers in the foreground of *The Bower Meadow*, yet no one would imagine that this was an attempt to go humbly to nature in the spirit of Ruskin. On the contrary, though green fields are shown, the painting's unusual composition and highly patterned structure proclaim it a work of deliberate artifice and complex personal symbolism. Rossetti likewise is uninterested in the use of colour to promote greater realism. One of his very earliest paintings, *Ecce Ancilla Domini*, though it depicted the Annunciation, was also quite self-consciously a study in white. This restricted palette was to be very characteristic of Rossetti's art: *Dantis Amor* was a study in blue and gold; *The Bower Meadow* was confined almost exclusively to green and puce; *Veronica Veronese* of the same year (1872) was, as Rossetti described it, 'a study of varied greens'.

In this it might be said that Rossetti anticipated Whistler – though Whistler obviously followed him – yet Rossetti was the more radical since Whistler still tried in his own way to depict the external world. Rossetti's symbolist use of colour is most strikingly evident in his late repainting of an early work, Dante's *Dream at the Time of the Death of Beatrice*, in which the earlier reds, blues, greens and purples give way to a more unified colour field, in which red angels and poppies gleam against an overwhelmingly sombre background and where even the doves are red. Rossetti's construction of a private world in paint is often seen as a later development and critics such as Christopher Wood have spoken of a change in style that follows the death of Elizabeth Siddal in 1862.[21] While there is indeed such a change in style, it is nevertheless important to note that Rossetti's espousal of such an interiorised art comes very early in his career, in his story 'Hand and Soul', which was published in *The Germ*, the short-lived Pre-Raphaelite journal, in 1849, in the same year that he exhibited his first important picture, *The Childhood of Mary Virgin*, and at the very moment when the Pre-Raphaelite movement first came to the attention of the public. In this narrative the Italian painter, Chiara, becomes disillusioned with his role as a public painter when two rival factions in Pisa become engaged in a brutal affray directly in front of his allegorical fresco of Peace, so that blood actually streams down the walls on which it is painted. This convinces him that it is a complete waste of time to address his work to an audience that, at bottom, cares neither for art nor morality. Subsequently Chiara is confronted with the image of a beautiful woman, dressed in green and grey, who tells him that she is the image of his own soul and that he must paint her to attain self-knowledge: 'Do this; so shall thy soul stand before thee always, and perplex thee no more.' But for this dedication to inner truth there is a price to be paid. Centuries later the narrator comes upon this painting of Chiara's in Florence where he hears it discussed by an uncomprehending group of spectators. An Englishman describes it as '*Very* odd' and a Frenchman suggests that since he cannot understand it, it cannot possibly mean anything. This story is prophetic both of Rossetti's own career and of symbolist and modernist art in general; for the likelihood is that the deeply personal significances that have been encoded into the work of art will remain indecipherable to the general public. Yet Rossetti believes the artist *must* take this step regardless of the consequences.

Rossetti's life and art are full of paradoxes, most of which relate to his complexly divided attitude towards women. In many respects Rossetti appears as an advanced and progressive figure, a man engaged in a heroic struggle against the taboos and prejudices of the age. He wrote frankly and explicitly about prostitution when this was a subject that few writers could even acknowledge let alone discuss. By celebrating physical love in some of the sonnets in *The House of Life* he became, at the hands of the Scottish poet and critic Robert Buchanan, a subject of scandal and concern and founder of the so-called 'Fleshly School of Poetry'. Rossetti not only wanted to make profane love into a sacred love, like Dante's love for Beatrice, he also wanted to erase the boundaries between platonic and erotic love, to create a sense of personal identity that could express and acknowledge both. At a time when it would have been easy for him to confine Elizabeth Siddall, a girl of lower-class origins, to the role of companion and model, Rossetti encouraged her in her aspirations to be a painter and poet. Yet at the same time Rossetti was very much a child of his time and he was never really able to shake off either the influence of an upbringing that was very nearly as repressive as Ruskin's or free himself from the prejudices that he consciously resisted but which nevertheless brought him great personal unhappiness. Thus Rossetti's relationship with Elizabeth Siddall became a torment for both of them, partly because their relationship as lovers and as artist and model was so overwhelming and all absorbing as to become positively oppressive. Since Rossetti placed Elizabeth on a

pedestal and transformed her through his art into a figure of transcendent purity, this in itself created a barrier between them, so that
Rossetti was compelled from time to time to escape into casual, easy-
going sexual relationships with other women simply because he
found them less demanding. Ostensibly the relationship was an
equal one – yet Elizabeth was Rossetti's creation, her light always a
reflected one and there was no space for her to acquire an identity of
her own, no matter how hard she tried, other than that which he
graciously conferred on her. There was no malice in Rossetti but a
good deal of thoughtlessness behind his general parade of attentive-
ness and concern. Yet Rossetti was also wracked by guilt over his
manifold transgressions, which also made him all the more determined to recommit himself to an ideal of pure and utterly spiritual
love. 'Jenny' is a Browningesque dramatic monologue in which the
narrator muses over the nature of love in the early hours of the
morning, by the bedside of a prostitute who is sleeping. He wishes to
celebrate her for her youthful innocence and beauty and to link her
with that archetypal Pre-Raphaelite symbol of purity, the lily, and
yet he cannot accept that this could be other than a compelling
illusion since a woman who possesses not merely carnal knowledge
but an awareness of the intricacies of male desire can never be pure.
There could never ever be such a thing as a technician of the sacred.
Jenny is an impossible chiasmus: 'so pure, so fall'n'. The narrator
realises that he can never 'love' Jenny, no matter how much he might
be tempted to do so, because she can never be the transcendent other
that he seeks. His attempts to idealise her fly in the face of 'reality' –
but what Rossetti cannot acknowledge is that the barrier is not in
reality as such, so much as in his own tormented mind.

Rossetti's anxieties about feminine sexuality are most clearly reflected in his early Browningesque dramatic monologue 'A Last
Confession' of 1848. The narrator describes how he cared for a young
and innocent Italian girl who was abandoned by her parents in time
of famine. The poem is concerned with the moment when the girl
crosses the borderline from childhood into womanhood and with
the narrator's realisation that his feelings towards her are no longer
those of a father or brother, but of a lover. This is prefigured by the
narrator's gift to his adopted daughter of a glass Cupid, which,
when she 'kissed me and kissed me' is shattered and cuts her hand.
Symbolically this is loss of innocence and virginal purity, an initiation into the pains of love – in which the narrator will join her. As the
narrator's passion for the girl becomes more and more intense, so he

becomes conscious of a growing indifference on her part, as she
becomes self-consciously aware of the effect of her beauty upon
others:

> as all men's eyes
> Turned on her beauty, and she seemed to tread
> Beyond my heart to the world made for her.

Her fall away from fidelity and purity into a threatening feminine
fickleness is symbolically represented by her rejection of the old and
dignified Madonna in the Duomo at Monza before which they had
worshipped together in favour of a tawdry modern image, 'tinselled
and gewgawed' –

> The old Madonna? Aye indeed,
> She had my old thoughts, – this one has my new.

When on a visit to the village fair the narrator identifies her as the
'brown-shouldered harlot' whom he sees through a tavern window
being kissed by another man, he stabs her to death in a fit of jealousy
with the horn and pearl handled dagger that he had once bought for
her as a present. What the poem asserts is that the moment of
puberty, when a woman at once discovers her own sexuality and her
power over men, is a dangerous one, for at this moment she can
assert her independence and refuse to represent the qualities of
purity, innocence and fidelity with which she should rightly be
identified. Although it is ostensibly very different, Rossetti's contro-
versial painting of 1850, *Ecce Ancilla Domini*, reveals similar preoccupations. When it was first shown it was identified as a Tractarian
proto-Catholic work by its Latin title and emphasis on the figure of
the Virgin. Yet the painting is not solely a vehicle for religious
meanings but is also concerned with the transition from girl to
woman. At the front of the picture the cloth embroidered with a lily
on which Mary was working in Rossetti's earlier *The Childhood of
Mary Virgin* stands completed – a sign that this phase of her life is
over. The Annunciation by an angel that she is to be the mother of
Christ, usually a joyous if serious occasion, is with her laden with
fear and anxiety. Mary, dressed wholly in white, draws her knees up
on the bed in a protective gesture and seems mesmerised by the lily
stalk that the angel thrusts towards her. The lily acquires strangely
phallic connotations and it is as if Mary flinches away from the

prospect of an initiation into motherhood and womanhood. The doubled lily, on the cloth and in the hand of the angel, seems to express the psychological need to assert the idea of purity the more strongly just because, when childhood is over, it is the more profoundly threatened.

In his life and in his art Rossetti's deepest dream and desire was to unite spiritual with physical love – a dream that he perhaps only attained in his later paintings of Jane Morris as a love goddess, since such works as *Mariana*, *Proserpine* and *Astarte Syriaca* contrive to be at once sensual and unearthly – though, of course, this also removes them from the Christian ambience of many of Rossetti's other works so that they seem distinctly pagan. More typically Rossetti's attempts to unite the physical with the spiritual are haunted by a sense of the impossibility of such a consummation. In a rangefinder camera the subject is brought into focus when two separate images coincide, but with Rossetti this moment is endlessly and frustratingly postponed: the fractured identities are held apart by some powerful yet invisible barrier. Part of the reason for Rossetti's interest in Poe was his fascination with the theme of the double, that emerges most strikingly in his painting *How They Met Themselves*. Two young lovers encounter their other selves in the wood – the youth holds a sword and seems tortured with guilt; the girl swoons and holds out her hands. Clearly they are 'fallen' as the result of a sexual initiation and the problem the picture poses lies in its symbolic asymmetry: it is possible to cross from the left to the right of the picture, but it seems that once that transition has been made there can never be any going back. Although Rossetti wishes to assert and indeed does assert the purity of sexual love, he is nevertheless tortured with anxiety about its shamefulness and impurity. Rossetti is never sure whether love is redemptive or corrupting, whether it is to be associated with life or death. In 'The Kiss', for example, one of the earliest poems in *The House of Life*, Rossetti's celebration of this moment of desire is perversely introduced with this rhetorical question:

> What smouldering sense in death's sick delay
> Or seizure of malign vicissitude
> Can rob this body of honour, or denude
> This soul of wedding-raiment worn to-day?

For although this question seems to be raised only to be dismissed, the language seems already to pre-empt and disqualify the ecstatic

conclusion – 'Fire within fire, desire in deity.' It is as if all representations of the body lie in the shadow of its eventual dissolution, so
that the profane love can never escape its destiny no matter how
much it may strive to overcome it. All Rossetti's images of profanity
and transcendence are haunted by profane doubles: Dante and
Beatrice by Paolo and Francesca, the Virgin Mary by Mary Magdalene,
the lilies of the field by lilies that fester. Indeed the lily in particular
is a curiously bivalent symbol. In 'Love-Lily', one of the final songs
in *The House of Life*, the lily is taken to symbolise not virginal purity
but the intense mingling of sexual and spiritual love:

> Brows, hands, and lips, heart, mind, and voice,
> Kisses and words of Love-Lily, –
> Oh! bid me with your joy rejoice
> Till riotous longing rest in me!
> 'Ah! let not hope be still distraught,
> 'But find in her its gracious goal,
> Whose speech Truth knows not from her thought
> Nor Love her body from her soul.

In one of the most explicitly erotic poems of the collection, 'Nuptial
Sleep', in which breasts and genitals are compared to flowers growing from either side of a single stem, the imagery certainly invokes
the example of the lily, though no flower is actually specified. In
'Barren Spring' it is the corruptibility of the lily that is foregrounded.
The poet insists that he is dead to the promise of spring and that it
can elicit from him 'no answering smile':

> Behold, this crocus is a withering flame;
> This snowdrop, snow; this apple-blossom's part
> To breed the fruit that breeds the serpent's art.
> Nay, for these Spring-flowers, turn thy face from them,
> Nor gaze till on the year's last lily-stem
> The white cup shrivels round the golden heart.

Here the golden warmth of love is enclosed in the shrivelling whiteness of death, which it is ultimately unable to evade. Such paradoxes
about the nature of love underpin one of Rossetti's most personal
and complex works in poetry and art, 'The Blessed Damozel', which
clearly invokes his relationship with Elizabeth Siddal. The Blessed
Damozel, leaning out from the gold bar of heaven, carrying lilies in

her hand and with stars in her hair seems an image of transcendental purity, yet by leaning out the Damozel seems to resist the denial of the physical that the idea of Heaven seems to represent. As the souls mounting to God pass her like 'thin flames', she herself is tangible, physical, erotic:

> And still she bowed herself and stooped
> Out of the circling charm;
> Until her bosom must have made
> The bar she leaned on warm,
> And the lilies lay as if asleep
> Along her bended arm.

The Damozel speaks of her dream of being reunited with her lover, but the question is whether the physical and spiritual consummation of earthy love can be renewed in heaven:

> Alas! we two, we two, thou say'st!
> Yea, one wast thou with me
> That once of old. But shall God lift
> To endless unity
> The soul whose likeless with thy soul
> Was but its love for thee?

For although the Damozel's lover may have loved her for her purity, this does not mean that he may have attained a similar purity himself. The Damozel speaks of asking the Virgin Mary to intercede for him, but the poem ends with her weeping, face in hands, against the golden barrier. In the painting the youth who loves her is separated from the promise of happiness she represents by a bar within the picture itself, but behind the Damozel there are endlessly repeated images of lovers kissing, which suggests that she, though in heaven, is also excluded from felicity. Thus the painting is haunted by a multiplicity of absences. Fulfilment is always somewhere else, perhaps neither in earth *nor* heaven.

The young Swinburne was the most ardent of Rossetti's disciples and it is certainly possible that in some sense Swinburne himself was the master, since his early verse prefigures in poetic language what was to be the animating spirit of Rossetti's later painting: the idea of woman as a cruel, voluptuous enigmatic goddess. Yet the mood of Swinburne's writing, though ostensibly faithful, seems always to transcribe into a slightly different and perhaps deliberately more discordant key. Whereas Rossetti often seemed personally haunted by the obsessional character of his loves, Swinburne positively celebrates obsessive, captive and compulsively driven love as the only authentic form of erotic experience – as perhaps might be expected from a man who found the greatest stimulation in bitings and beatings. Whereas Rossetti strives for a union between spiritual and physical love, Swinburne emphasises their tendency to pull destructively apart. Whereas Rossetti turned aside from the world, as if unconcerned with public reactions to his work, Swinburne was a propagandist and an eager and able controversialist. Whereas Rossetti had a genuine reverence for the traditions of Christianity, so that even his use of sacred figures to speak of profane love involves a kind of piety, Swinburne was anxious to present carnal love as a pagan, perhaps even satanic, religion with its own dark and mysterious sacrifices – a creed that puts all conventional morality in question, since it seeks to expose Christianity's mild gospel to be hopelessly naïve, and to problematise the Utilitarian distinction between pleasure and pain by showing how inextricably they are linked. The young Swinburne is very much an immoral philosopher with a doctrine to expound, a stance that is in some ways at odds with the doctrine of *l'art pour l'art* with which he is also associated.

Swinburne was one of the earliest figures in England openly to proclaim the doctrine of art for art's sake, though, as I have suggested, it was clearly implicit in the trajectory of Rossetti's artistic career. In his later criticism, for example in his essay on Hugo's *Année Terrible* of 1872, Swinburne took a very balanced and judicious view of the whole question, stressing on the one hand that 'No work of art has any worth or life in it that is not done on the absolute terms of art. . . . The rule of art is not the rule of morals',[22] and on the other 'refusing to admit that art of the highest kind may not ally itself with religious passion, with the ethics or the politics of a nation or an age'.[23] At this point in time Swinburne has come to distinguish between the crassly simplistic 'moral' demands of some contemporary critics and the actual perspectives of the texts themselves. Indeed, in one of Swinburne's many anticipations of T. S. Eliot, he suggested that a genuine system of belief was more likely to produce good art than scepticism or uncertainty – as he wrote in his essay on Arnold: 'Nothing is to be made by an artist out of scepticism, half-hearted or double-hearted doubts or creeds; nothing out of mere dejection and misty mental weather'.[24] However, despite the undoubted sophistication and penetration of the later Swinburne's thoughts on this topic in the 1860s, in the dawn of his poetic career he was much more concerned to stress the radical and unsettling implications of the doctrine, to imply that if anything art had a duty to be amoral. In his early essay on Baudelaire's *Les fleurs du mal* he warns against both the demand that poetry shall be morally uplifting and edifying and against the call for poetry to fulfil a social role. Swinburne's contemporary readers may therefore have been somewhat disconcerted to encounter the following bald announcement: 'the sharp and cruel enjoyments of pain, the acrid relish of suffering felt or inflicted, the sides on which nature looks unnatural, go to make up the stuff and substance of this poetry. Very good material they make, too.'[25]

In a significant anticipation of the problems his own poetry was to face, Swinburne noted that 'paganism' had become an issue in the discussion of Baudelaire's poetry. He objected strongly to the demand for a conventional didacticism: 'If any reader could extract from any poem a positive spiritual medicine – if he could swallow a sonnet like a moral prescription – then clearly the poet supplying these drugs would be a bad artist; indeed, no real artist, but a huckster and vendor of miscellaneous wares',[26] though he was both honest enough and perceptive enough to recognise that Baudelaire was a moralist of a more subtle kind. Swinburne could not have been more temperamentally at variance with Arnold, yet they shared a reverence for Greek culture and a hostility to the philistinism of the present age. Swinburne saw the ignorance, narrowness and imperceptiveness of the reading public and of some prominent critics (such as Alfred Austen and Robert Buchanan) as the major problem. In reading the great Elizabethan and Jacobean dramatists Swinburne was conscious – and frankly envious – that they could write for a public that was more intelligent, more discriminating and more broad-minded. In the later Victorian period, by contrast, the more open and explicit treatment of love and sexuality became strangely bound up with gender stereotyping. Buchanan and Austen were particularly anxious to charge Rossetti and Swinburne with effeminacy, a charge that was particularly odd since they equally clearly felt that their subject matter was not suitable for ladies. Thus Robert Buchanan in his notorious attack on Rossetti, 'The Fleshly School of Poetry', found in his verse as in his painting: 'the same thinness and transparency of design, the same combination of the simple and the grotesque, the same morbid deviation from unhealthy forms of life, the same sense of weary, wasting, yet exquisite sensuality; nothing virile, nothing tender, nothing completely sane.'[27] The complex binary set, in which health, sanity, masculinity, decency and plenitude are ranged against morbidity, insanity, effeminacy, sensuality and insubstantiality, may not be wholly original with Buchanan but it was certainly to show a remarkable persistence in intellectual discussions of the period, both culminating and reaching its intellectual nadir, in so far as that is possible, with Max Nordau's *Degeneration*. For Alfred Austen the crucial question to be asked of Swinburne's poetry is:

> Has Mr Swinburne . . . turned his back on the haunts of feminine muses, struck out a masculine strain, and wrung from strenuous chords nervous and extolling hymns worthy of men and gods? . . . what have men – men brave, muscular, bold, upright, chivalrous – I will not say chaste, for that is scarcely a masculine quality ('I will find you twenty lascivious turtles ere one chaste man,' says no less in authority than Shakespeare), but at any rate clean – men with 'pride in their port, defiance in their eye', men daring, enduring, short of speech, and terrible in action – what have these to do with Mr Swinburne's Venuses and Chastelards, his Anactorias and Faustines, his Dolores, his Sapphos, or his Hermaphroditus? . . . I do not say that they are not fair, much less illegitimate, subjects for the poet's pen; but are they masculine? That is the question?[28]

Interestingly enough Swinburne was not prepared to accept this accusation but instead repolarised the argument, by suggesting that literature is emasculated when it is subjected to moral censorship, when it cannot deal 'with the full life of man and the whole nature of things'. He looks forward to the day when

> it will once more be remembered that the office of adult art is neither puerile nor feminine, but virile; that its purity is not that of the cloister or the harem; that all things are good in its sight, out of which good work may be produced. Then the press will be as impotent as the pulpit to dictate the laws and remove the landmarks of art; and those will be laughed at who demand from one thing the qualities of another – who seek for sermons in sonnets and morality in music. Then all accepted work will be noble and chaste in the wider masculine sense, not truncated and curtailed, but outspoken and full grown.[29]

In the medieval chivalric romances adultery and sexual desire enter the narrative primarily as a lure that distracts the knight from his goal of spiritual purity and from the pursuit of the Holy Grail, just as Circe imperils Odysseus' journey homeward. The struggle against carnality makes the ideal of the spotless knight more vivid and more compelling. In Swinburne's 'Laus Veneris' the reverse is the case. For Swinburne the interest of the story of the knight's obsession with Venus lies in the fact that for him the whole idea of being pure and without sin has become utterly impossible. The knight is a Faust figure who will sacrifice his very soul for passion – not willingly but simply because he can do nothing else: he is the quintessence of the erotic captive, believing in Christ perhaps, but nevertheless helplessly entangled in the toils of Venus. As Swinburne himself noted in his defence of the poem: 'Once accept or admit the least admixture of pagan worship, or of modern thought, and the whole story collapses into froth and smoke.'[30] The characteristically Swinburnian move in the poem, which makes it so typical of the aesthetic tendency, is that belief is itself aestheticised and simply used as a compositional element. Swinburne himself is the advocate of love as a pagan creed, but this implies neither guilt, repentance nor shame. So there is no one who can be such a total slave to love as the knight who experiences all this as well as the complex pleasures and pains of love, and who despite this finds it totally impossible to escape love's bondage. Indeed, for him pleasure and damnation have become inseparable:

> And I forgot fear and all weary things,
> All ended prayers and perished thanksgivings,
> Feeling her face with all her eager hair
> Cleave to me, clinging as a fire that clings
>
> To the body and to the raiment, burning them
> As after death I know that such-like flame
> Shall cleave to me for ever; yea, what care,
> Albeit I burn then, having felt the same.

Instead of showing how desperately difficult it is to be a worthy servant of Christ, Swinburne shows how yet more desperately difficult and intense are the sufferings of those who involuntarily serve Venus. They alone have totally surrendered themselves. They have no will of their own.

As the poet of sexual love Swinburne may seem at once perfervid and excessively mannered, but in the chaste and decorous context of Victorian love poetry his ecstatic celebration of masochistic delights must have been as sensational as an attempt to deliver a kissogram in the middle of divine service. Swinburne created a poetic language of whirling, swirling figures, which seek themselves erotically to intertwine, to blend, melt and intermingle symbolic contraries. Swinburne's women, in true Pre-Raphaelite tradition, are cold and pale, yet such words as 'cool' and 'pallor' typically generate a love that is fiery and passionate, that is characterised by such words as 'flame', 'burn', 'blush', 'blood', that revels in such oxymoronic linkages as 'fruitful and virginal', 'splendid and sterile', 'barren delights' or 'crown and caress thee and chain'.

The young Swinburne is also a brilliant and shameless parodist who does not merely present Dolores, 'Our Lady of Pain', as an antitype to the Virgin Mary but insists that only through her irresistible nexus of pleasure and suffering can man be redeemed from the vapidities of Christianity. What Dolores represents, Swinburne insists is *real*

> Thine, thine the one grace we implore us,
> Who would live and not languish or feign,
> O sleepless and deadly Dolores,
> Our Lady of Pain.

At times Swinburne's eroticism may seem all to reminiscent of Count Dracula, but what does give his early poetry real bite is his disconcerting willingness to explore not merely the world in which God is dead, but a world in which Christian ethics are an irrelevance, where man is compelled to confront sexuality and mortality as the only certainties that experience can offer. What is equally disorientating is that Swinburne's sense of the world derives from the very same Greek culture that Arnold, contemporaneously, was taking as synonymous with 'sweetness and light'. For Swinburne, as for Pater – but, let us not forget, writing in 1866, long before the publication of *The Renaissance* in 1873 – what matters above all is that experience be vivid.

Swinburne's defence of virility in art seems ironic in the light of his decision to write a poetic drama based on Greek mythology, *Atalanta in Calydon*, for what is interesting about it is that the fable represents a defence of the feminine principle in the face of a culture that would deny it (likewise, of course, *The Oresteia* and *The Bacchae*). The goddess Artemis punishes Oeneus, king of Calydon, who has sacrificed to all the gods but her, by sending a monstrous wild boar, which no man can slay, to menace his kingdom. Meleager falls in love with the beautiful huntress, Atalanta, who is beloved of the gods, a maiden so pure and chaste that she can return no man's love. Through Artemis's intercession Meleager is able to kill the boar, but Toxeus and Philippus are indignant when he presents the spoils to Atalanta, and Meleager is compelled to kill them to defend her honour. These are the brothers of his mother, Altheaea, and in retribution she casts on the fire the brand that represents his span of life, so condemning him to death. Clearly what fascinated Swinburne in this legend was this image of absolute female power – the goddess Artemis, who terrorises the kingdom; Atalanta who elicits from Meleager a tribute that initiates the tragedy; Altheaea who has absolute power of life and death over her own son. But what also interested him was the sense of the ephemerality of human life. Meleager lives only to kill the boar and present it to Atalanta – in this single gesture love and death are united. *Atalanta in Calydon* represents the triumph of an extraordinary aestheticism in which Swinburne was able to write a poetic drama almost as if no interval of time had elapsed since the drama of Euripides, as if he were not writing in a Victorian world of railway trains and industrial mass production. Swinburne's power to simulate the poetry of Greek tragedy is positively uncanny, so uncanny in fact that it makes nonsense of Arnold's claim that the great literature of the past is not subject to the transitoriness of the present. Swinburne's massive suppression of the present, his weirdly compelling historical masquerade, cannot but foreground the artifice of his project. Admittedly the nineteenth century becomes highly visible in the Choruses of *Atalanta*, in which the gods are forcefully attacked for perverse, irrational and repressive treatment of man, but even this only represents an intensification of the kind of criticism of the gods that can be found in Euripides. In *Atalanta* the representational function of art virtually disappears and Swinburne comes close to achieving the Keatsian dream of melting into his own legend, of stepping without resistance into the frieze that encircles the Grecian urn.

Swinburne's progressive movement away from a conception of art identified with neutrality or indifference to moral values towards a sense of art that could communicate, like Baudelaire, a more subtle morality is interestingly exemplified by his Mary Queen of Scots trilogy, *Chastelard*, *Bothwell* and *Mary Stuart*. *Bothwell*, though now an almost totally forgotten work, is actually very impressive, one of the finest attempts at drama by any Romantic or Post-Romantic poet. *Chastelard* (1865) is a highly characteristic rendition of Swinburne's early gospel of pagan love, in which Mary Queen of Scots inevitably figures as the irresistibly alluring, yet cruel queen, who lures men on to their death, like some Venus flytrap. Darnley says 'her love is like a briar that rasps the flesh', and Chastelard speaks of

> her mouth,
> A flower's lip with a snake's lip, stinging sweet
> And sweet to sting with: face that one would see
> And then fall blind and die with sight of it
> Held fast between the eyelids.

Chastelard's obsession with the Queen is very much in the spirit of the Wagnerian Liebestod. He conceals himself in her bedroom, knowing full well that the penalty for his discovery there is death:

> Prithee, love, come fast,
> That I may die soon; yea, some kisses through,
> I shall die joyfully enough, so God
> Keep me alive till then.

Chastelard is arrested and condemned to death, but though Mary subsequently pardons him, Chastelard subsequently tears the pardon up. Mary is seen as the vacillating and dangerous, if sometimes tender woman; Chastelard as her inevitable victim. With *Bothwell*, written nine years later in 1874, it would have been easy for Swinburne to have presented Darnley, and indeed Bothwell too, as moths flitting desperately round her brilliant flame, inevitably lured to their own destruction, but Swinburne did not yield to this temptation. He does not develop the play purely in terms of personal relationships, important as they are, but shows how complexly they are bound up with the whole political and religious life of Scotland. History returns. The action is not confined to Mary, Bothwell and Darnley but convincingly brings in a wide range of characters, virtually all of whom are quite sympathetically presented, even John Knox, whom the younger Swinburne would almost certainly have presented as a ridiculous, sanctimonious humbug. Through the figure of Darnley, Swinburne presents a probing and sophisticated critique of the view of woman with which he himself was once closely identified. Darnley is at once unstable, anxious and unreliable in his perceptions of others. He is all too ready to believe the worst of Mary and to perceive her as a typically manipulative, untrustworthy woman. Darnley's desire to assert himself as a man, combined with his insecurity and paranoia, has the effect of making Mary's own position completely untenable. Since he is all too readily manipulated by others he becomes a focus for various plots and intrigues directed against her, while his anxieties about her sexual infidelity – typified by the execution of both Chastelard and Rizzio – serves to damage further her reputation. Swinburne makes us see that Mary is virtually compelled to turn to Bothwell at such a juncture, since he is strong, courageous, determined, ready to stand on his own two feet and completely and utterly loyal – the complete reverse of Darnley. Swinburne so involves the reader in the complexity of her predicament that we begin to see that, in the context of the *realpolitik* of the time, Darnley's death is more or less inevitable and even to assent to the idea that it might be justified. But at this moment Swinburne turns the tables, by bringing out the full horror of the machinations surrounding Darnley's murder, in which Mary simultaneously tries to save him and dupe him. Now all the characters seem like victims. The great irony is that while Darnley has been wrong about Mary all along, her involvement in his death seems to prove him right. On one level it seems that she is the cruel queen after all, yet on another the whole action of the play has been to show how serious and how superficial a misjudgement this is. *Bothwell* is an extraordinary work, the real vindication of Swinburne's claim that no complex work of art can conspicuously thrust its moral judgements into the foreground.

Paradoxically it is William Morris rather than either Rossetti or Swinburne who represents the most extreme repudiation of the claims of contemporary reality. Although Morris in his later life became famous as a socialist and a political activist, he had earlier shown little interest in politics. His many-sided involvement in radical causes really began in 1876, when he was forty-two, with his involvement in a campaign of protest against Disraeli's support of the reactionary regime in Turkey and eventually led to his joining the socialist Democratic Federation in 1883. In such earlier poetry as *The Life and Death of Jason* and *The Earthly Paradise* Morris made it abundantly clear that he wanted nothing to do with the ugliness and spiritual poverty of the Victorian present; he wanted either to abolish it or to escape from it. Swinburne suppressed the contemporary completely in *Atalanta in Calydon*. Morris introduced it only as a point of departure for an imaginative journey, which would *not* be taken by train and through which the world would become magically rinsed clean of pollution:

> Forget six counties overhung with smoke,
> Forget the snorting steam and piston stroke,
> Forget the spreading of the hideous town;
> Think rather of the pack-horse on the down,
> And dream of London, small, and white, and clean,
> The clear Thames bordered on its gardens green.

With such an introduction it would be easy to accuse Morris of using art as a form of escapism, and certainly many contemporary readers grasped eagerly at the opportunity to suspend, if only for a few hours, their consciousness of contemporary actuality. The reviewer for the *Pall Mall Budget*, who may have been Sidney Colvin, commented:

> Every reader almost was glad to retire from the stress and cares of his ugly workaday English life and to be entertained, for no matter how long with that succession of gracious pictures and pleasant incidents of a remote romantic world – remote –, but conceived and set forth with the inexhaustible detail of a loving eyewitness.[31]

Indeed, we suspect that the leisurely and protracted character of the poems in *The Earthly Paradise* may have been precisely what was appreciated, for an illusion sustained is greatly to be preferred to one whose ephemerality is manifest. Morris would certainly have been quite unabashed by any attempt to make all this into a criticism. Although Morris may never have been a platonist as such, he certainly believed that it was no part of the purpose of art to copy an imperfect and degraded world. Its mission was, on the contrary, to present a world more beautiful, more noble and more radiant; not to hold up the mirror to nature but to envision the world in a manner radically transformed. The artist had to think of the possibility of an earthy paradise even if he was nevertheless acutely aware of the formidable obstacles that might prevent its possible realisation. Since Morris believed that all art involves some element of idealisation, he felt that the demand for realism would always be made in bad faith.

In *News from Nowhere*, in response to Clara's questions: 'Are we not good enough to paint ourselves? How is it that we find the dreadful times of the past so interesting to us – in pictures and poetry?', old Hammond replies:

> It is true that in the nineteenth century, when there was so little art and so much talk about it, there was a theory that art and imaginative literature ought to deal with contemporary life; but they never did so; for, if there was any pretence of it, the author always took care (as Clara hinted just now) to disguise, or exaggerate, or idealise, and in some way or another make it strange.

Morris's retelling of Greek and Nordic myths in *The Earthly Paradise* is carefully inserted into an elaborate textual frame. The Northern wanderers who arrive in Greece after having searched the world in vain for the Earthly Paradise take part with their hosts in a round of story-telling in which the search for some paradisal world is itself an obsessive theme. So although in a way Morris's theme is the frustration of human desire and the vanity of the quest for perfect love and for an ideal world, it is revalorised by the sense that it is this very drive that has characterised all men in all ages. So to tell stories of the past, even as men did in the most historically remote times, involves not so much escapism and nostalgia as a powerful sense of human community, and we trace in the old narratives a complex yet compulsive pattern in which we find our own wishes and desires so vividly interwoven. These repetitions thus articulate the deepest of all truths.

In many respects the perception of the world that Morris articulates in *The Earthly Paradise* is remarkably similar to Swinburne. Morris clearly chose his setting both to bring out the parallels between two apparently diverse mythological traditions and to celebrate values that can be seen as essentially pagan. Under Christianity joy in the pleasures of this world, delight in the sheer clarity and vividness of sensory experience are suppressed through an insistence on the priority of the next. The idea of God expresses a demand for transcendental meaning that the terrestrial world necessarily lacks. It is only when the other-worldly perspective is lacking that humankind's intense desire for paradise here and now can be given full and authentic expression. In pagan mythology the gods rather become the name for some obscure and perverse principle in human existence that seems constantly to hold man back from the perfect fulfilment of sexual love and from a world that might otherwise be free from fear, anxiety and pain. When John in 'The Land East of the Sun' protests:

> O idle Maker if the world,
> Art thou content to see me hurled
> To nought, from longing and from tears,
> When thou through all these weary years
> With love my helpless soul has bound,
> And fed me in that narrow round
> With no delight thy fair world know?

we realise that what interests Morris in Greek and Nordic religion is that it bears within it an explosive moral charge. It is always possible within such a framework for man to express his anger and indignation when happiness seemingly slips through his fingers, whereas with Christianity he is offered no prospect of earthly happiness and God's decisions must always be perceived as just. In the tales of *The Earthly Paradise* and in *The Life and Death of Jason*, which became so long that it was published separately, Morris returns again and again to the desire for an untroubled, blissful world and the strange and by no means inevitable shadow that always seems to stand between man and the realisation of his desperate dreams. *The Life and Death of Jason* epitomises this. Jason is the archetypal questing figure who goes in search of the Golden Fleece, yet in Morris he is a far from triumphal figure: though he does return with the trophy, the prospect of an earthly paradise eludes him just as surely as the Nordic wanderers. Where Morris most notably departs from his mythological sources is in his idealised presentation of Medea, who effectively becomes the dominating presence of the poem. As Henry James pointed out in his review:

> From the moment that Medea comes into the poem, Jason falls into the second place, and keeps it to the end. She is the all-wise and all-brave helper and counsellor at Colchis, and the guardian angel of the returning journey. She saves her companions from Circean enchantments, and she withholds them from the embraces of the Sirens. She effects the death of Pelias, and assures the successful return of the Argonauts. And finally – as a last claim upon her interest – she is slighted and abandoned by the man of her love. Without question, then, she is the central figure of the

poem, – a powerful and enchanting figure, a creature of barbarous arts, and of exquisite human passions.[32]

The question for Morris becomes: why it should be that Jason and Medea cannot find happiness together? The fable is transformed into a tale of foreboding, of inexorable postponement and delay, in which Jason returns, having triumphed over innumerable obstacles, only rashly to throw away Medea's love by deserting her for the beautiful Glause, daughter of Creon. The crew of Jason's ship are often happy, never knowing

> that they
> Must wander yet for many an evil day
> Or ever the dread Gods should let them come
> Back to the white walls of their long-left home.

Jason and Medea are also happy, yet for Morris this possibility of happiness is always intertwined with pain, with shadow that always interposes its troubling presence between:

> So out into the fresh night silently
> The lovers passed, the loveliest of the land;
> But as they went, neither did hand touch hand,
> Or face seek face; for gladsome as they were,
> Trembling with joy to be at last so near
> The wished-for day, some God yet seemed to be
> 'Twixt the hard past and their felicity.

After Jason's return, Creon, who is anxious that his own daughter shall marry so great a hero, insinuates that Medea is not to be trusted and Jason is immediately transformed into a man tormented by insecurity and anxiety – a recurring figure in Morris's poetry:

> Jason, left alone and pondering,
> Felt in his heart that still increasing dread,
> And he was moved by that great elder's face,
> For love was dying in the ten year's pace.

Jason, like many characters in *The Earthly Paradise*, seems strangely passive for so active a hero. Although, like Othello, he is a man who

> Like the base Indian threw a pearl away
> Richer than all his tribe

he is also like Othello something of an innocent who cannot really be held responsible for what he does. For in the magical world of Morris's tales the perfect happiness that his characters momentarily enjoy is so dreamlike that awakening seems inevitable. Yet what differentiates Morris's treatment of the idea of erotic bliss both from his mythological sources, and from the German *Märchen*, which were certainly a significant influence, is that Morris invariably suppresses the implication that any entanglement with gods or magical powers must necessarily be fraught with danger and inevitable disillusionment. When in 'The Land East of the Sun' John is transported by his swanmaid to some faraway kingdom where he even forgets the existence of grief, such a forgetting is for Morris far more natural and understandable than its antithesis: a forgetting of the possibility and actual existence of real happiness on the return to the everyday world. Morris regards this visionary world as the more real and he implies that the human failure to achieve such happiness begins with an inability to believe that it actually is possible. In 'Ogier the Dane' Ogier dies to awaken in the land of Avalon where

> everything was bright and soft and fair
> And yet they wearied not for any change,
> Nor unto them did constancy seem strange,
> Love knew they, but its pain they never had,
> But with each other's joy were they made glad.

Often Morris seems to recall Spenser on the mutability of things, but what Morris really seems to be saying is that human beings are so accustomed to the idea of impermanence that they can never possess the inner tranquillity that perfect happiness would require, even when all the other ingredients are there. Morris concludes 'The Watching of the Falcon' by saying

> a land it is
> Where men may dwell in rest and bliss
> If they so will – Who yet will not,
> Because their hasty hearts are hot
> With foolish hate, and longing vain
> The sire and dam of grief and pain.

This perversity of spirit is most clearly exemplified in the most naturalistic of the tales, 'The Lovers of Gudrun', in which Gudrun is loved by four men, yet Kiartan, the only one she does not marry, is the one she really loves. Kiartan sails away from Iceland to Denmark, where he becomes involved with Ingioborg and fails to return when expected. This delay proves fatal since Gudrun then makes the equally fateful decision to marry Kiartan's friend, Bodli. All three are then tortured by the falseness of the situation they have got themselves into. This unhappiness is entirely of their own making and once this dark shadow has fallen over their lives there is nothing whatsoever they can do to lift it. Here more than anywhere else – and the story clearly alludes to the triangle of Morris, Rossetti and Jane Burden – Morris seems to accept the idea of personal responsibility, but even here he stresses how seemingly insignificant are the contingencies through which disaster may come.

There is a distinct appropriateness both in the fact that Walter Pater should have reviewed *The Earthly Paradise* in the *Westminster Review* of October 1868, and that that review should conclude with the paragraphs that were to become vastly more celebrated as the conclusion to *The Renaissance* (1873), which became the definitive articulation of Pater's aesthetic creed, for Pater clearly responded positively to the invocation of a hedonistic, pagan world in the poetry of Swinburne and Morris. Indeed, though Pater's views struck many as dangerous and daringly modern, they are very much in the tradition of the poets, critics and artists whom I have already discussed. Although Pater's view of art was radically opposed to that of Ruskin at many points, his sense of the painter as visionary owed much to Ruskin's own eloquent defence of Turner. It was almost certainly in response to the poetry of Browning that Pater came to value the Renaissance more positively than either Ruskin or the Pre-Raphaelites and to interpret it in terms of a tension between the infinite and the finite. Rossetti seems equally important through his own personal dedication to beauty and his quiet determination to turn his back on the task of representing the external world in favour of an art that would be idealistic and symbolic. Nevertheless there is a significant difference of tone. Although, in response to criticism, Pater was compelled to withdraw the conclusion to *The Renaissance* for a while, what is noticeable is that while Rossetti, Swinburne and Morris are, in their different ways, tortured souls, who are always as conscious of pain, guilt and suffering as they are of pleasure, Pater's exposition of his credo, though ecstatic, is nevertheless serene and unruffled. Pater's harmonious and lyrical insistence 'To burn always with this hard gem-like flame, to maintain this ecstasy, is success in life' seems to be not just decades but light years away from the angst-ridden moral earnestness of Carlyle, who had made the gospel of work into an overwhelming Victorian imperative. Yet Pater was indifferent to social issues. It was Morris who, in *News from Nowhere* (1891), conjured up a world of pleasure and beauty, which would also be a socialist Utopia:

> my heart swelled with joy as I thought of all the beautiful grey villages, from the river to the plain and the plain to the uplands, which I could picture to myself so well, all people now with this happy and lovely folk, who had cast away riches and attained to wealth.

7

Breaking the Silence: Collins, Meredith and Hardy

The Victorian novel was a rich and complex genre, which opened up not one but many windows onto the dizzying panorama of Victorian culture, but it remained constricted and inhibited by a diversity of restrictions and tacit prohibitions. Most obviously there was the demand for something protracted and elaborately plotted. Clearly there were demands for decency and decorum in the representation of relationships between men and women. But over and beyond that there was the question of stereotyping, especially where women characters were concerned, which may well have been the most powerful imperative of all, since both in fact and fiction the protocols of respectable behaviour bore down most heavily on women. In addition there was the implicit expectation of a happy ending, which could be avoided, at best, by a not unhappy ending. Among the later Victorian novelists Collins, Meredith and Hardy stand out as independent-minded, courageous writers who were always prepared to offer the reading public something rather different from what they were accustomed to expect. New and unexpected chords are heard – breaking in upon a cultural silence.

If there is any one writer who is responsible for unsettling the comfortable mood of mid-Victorian England and for inaugurating a shift towards a literature that is less sentimental, more critical and more able to portray the sexes on a basis of equality, that writer is Wilkie Collins. Collins was distinctly unorthodox in his attitudes, as his maintenance of two completely separate households suggests, and though he was by no means an outspoken social critic, he was little inclined either to indulge in or to humour the most insufferable forms of Victorian humbug. Indeed his own attitude to complacencies of Victorian fiction is amusingly suggested in *Armadale*, where the bent doctor who runs the sanitarium in which Allan Armadale is to die says to a company of visitors that he restricts the fiction that can be read there:

> 'Only such novels as I have selected and perused myself, in the first instance' said the doctor. 'Nothing painful, ma'am! There may be plenty that is painful in real life – but for that very reason we don't want it in books. The English novelist who enters my house (no foreign novelist will be admitted) must understand his art as the healthy-minded English reader understands it in our time. . . . All we want of him is – occasionally to make us laugh; and invariably to make us comfortable.'

Collins's own fiction shocks on more than one level. He was not just a writer of thrillers or mystery stories, but created an entirely new fictional world, filled with danger, uncertainty and a definite feeling of moral discomfort, so that his novels might well be described as 'Satan Among the Sofa Cushions' – to quote *The Moonstone*. He reinvented the Gothic in a form that made it both contemporary and credible, whether it centred on the development of private mental asylums and sanitoriums or on the presence in England of clandestine societies of Italian revolutionaries or disguised Indian priests engaged on an errand of restitution. In Collins we become acutely aware of the way in which improved railway services, a more widespread use of newspapers and the postal service had affected the middle-class perception of time. Collins's world is one in which everything has been speeded up. Thus the correspondence between Maria Oldenshaw and her protégée in crime, Lydia Gwilt, the ruthless governess who is at the centre of the machinations of *Armadale*, is ostensibly a return to an eighteenth-century tradition, but the interchange often of very brief communications rather suggests the urgency of the proceedings, in which time, and the ability to steal a march on one's adversaries, is of the essence. Collins is fond of describing places that are slightly disreputable or seedy, new housing developments on the fringes of London, or dingy accommodation addresses and boarding houses, but he does not shrink from more brutal descriptions or from the kind of outspoken comment

that was now beginning to seem slightly *passé*. In *No Name* he introduces the old ecclesiastical palace of Lambeth and then shifts the
focus to the nearby Vauxhall Walk:

> The network of dismal streets stretching over the surrounding
> neighbourhood contains a population for the most part of the
> poorer order. In the thoroughfares where shops abound, the sor-
> did struggle with poverty shows itself unreservedly on the filthy
> pavement; gathers its force through the week; and, strengthening
> to a tumult on Saturday night, sees the Sunday morning dawn in
> murky gaslight. Miserable women, whose faces never smile, haunt
> the butchers' shops in such London localities as these, with relics
> of the mens' wages saved from the public-house, clutched fast in
> their hands, with eyes that devour the meat they dare not buy,
> with eager fingers that touch it covetously, as the fingers of their
> richer sisters touch a precious stone. In this district, as in other
> districts remote from the wealthy quarters of the metropolis, the
> hideous London vagabond – with the filth of the street outmatched
> in his speech, with the mud of the street outdirtied in his clothes –
> lounges, lowering and brutal, at the street-corner and gin-shop
> door; the public disgrace of his country, the unheeded warnings of
> social troubles that are yet to come. Here, the loud self-assertion
> of Modern Progress – which has reformed so much in manners,
> and altered so little in men – meets the flat contradiction that
> scatters pretensions to the winds. Here, while the national
> prosperity feasts, like another Belshazzer on the spectacle of its
> own magnificence, is the Writing on the Wall, which warns the
> monarch, Money, that his glory is weighed in the balance, and
> found wanting.

Whereas twenty years earlier, in the fiction of, say, Bulwer-Lytton,
such an excursion into the back-streets would have been an exercise
in the picturesque, Collins's description is both more brutal and
more vivid and it is linked with a clear warning of impending social
unrest. In describing the back-streets of English cities Collins clearly
knew what he was talking about. The Skeldergate area of York
introduced in *No Name* is described by the historian Frances Finnegan
in *Poverty and Prostitution*, a study of Victorian prostitutes in York, as

> the most unsavoury and least frequented of all notorious districts
> in the city, with prostitutes living rather than working in the area

and being housed mainly in unhealthy yards off the main street. Any men returning with such women to their squalid lodgings, which can hardly be described as brothels, or even houses of ill fame, must have been almost as destitute as were the whores themselves.[1]

If Collins is critical of self-regarding, middle-class affluence, he is equally sceptical of law and justice. When, in *The Woman in White*, Walter Hartright, the drawing-master, goes to see the lawyer, Mr Kyrle, to see what can be done about the swindle effected by Count Fosco and Sir Percival Glyde, by which the death of Anne Catherick has been passed off as that of Lady Glyde, he learns that there is no redress – there is absolutely no way in which the truth could be legally established. Although Collins is an expert in plot mechanics and a master of suspense, he deprives his readers of the comfortable expectation that his novel will end with a convenient restoration of the status quo ante, that there is a kindly providence at work in the world that will set everything to rights. Collins's characters know that they will have to fight, scheme and struggle for absolutely everything they can get, whether they are unscrupulous adventuresses like Lydia Gwilt or righteous individuals like Hartright. They live in a universe that is not predictable, where chance, coincidence and uncertainty rule. So although, in one sense, their fate is in their own hands, they still face the possibility that everything they have striven for may be snatched from their hands. Lydia Gwilt and Magdalene Vanstone are determined, strong-minded women who have set their sights on a prosperous match by unscrupulous means. Ostensibly Victorian readers should rejoice at the downfall of their nefarious schemes, yet Collins has so artfully involved them in the predicament of his heroines – for that is what they are or become – that they are bound to experience much of their bafflement, rage and frustration. For what Collins suggests is that the world of settlements and wills through which property is arranged and distributed is highly arbitrary, whimsical and unfair, and it is on such circumstances that the likes of Sir Percival Glyde and Count Fosco rely. If there is immorality, Collins suggests, the law is more likely to give it aid and support than resist it. As Court Fosco points out:

John Bull does abhor the crimes of John Chinaman. He is the quickest old gentleman at finding out faults that are his neighbours', and the slowest old gentleman at finding out the faults that are his own, who exists on the face of creation. Is he so very much better in his way than the people he condemns in their way? English Society, Miss Halcombe, is as often the accomplice as it is the enemy of crime.

It is a singular feature of Collins's fictional world that there are seldom any stable family structures. The solid, reliable father is conspicuous by his absence. In *The Woman in White* Marian Halcombe and Laura Fairlie are half-sisters who are brought up by an uncle who takes no interest in them. Ann Catherick, the woman in white, knows nothing of her father and even the villain, Sir Percival Glyde, loses his parents in early youth. In *No Name* Magdalene and Nora Vanstone are not only orphaned by the death of their parents but also learn that they are illegitimate as well. In *Armadale* neither Armadale nor Midwinter, his double, ever knew their father. Miss Gwilt is an orphan. Even the setting for *The Moonstone* – a highly respectable English country house – still represents a household without men. Although these circumstances are often necessary to enforce Collins's characteristic mysteries of identity, they are nevertheless significant in that they permit, and even compel his women characters in particular to be more articulate, more independent and more persistent in defending their own interests than might otherwise be the case. While all too many other Victorian heroines are surrounded by a retinue of attendants, imprisoned within the Victorian household, Collins's characters are obliged to fend for themselves, to stand on their own two feet. They are also not afraid of strong emotion. Lydia Gwilt loves Midwinter passionately and possessively and resents the depths of his intimacy with Armadale. She writes ironically in her diary:

> If so ladylike a person as I am could feel a tigerish tingling all over her to the very tips of her fingers, I should suspect myself of being in that condition at the present moment. But with *my* manners and accomplishments the thing is, of course, out of the question. We all know that a lady has no passions.

In *No Name* Collins contrasts the depth of the passion that Magdalen feels for Frank with the shallowness of emotion that he feels for her, and stresses that this powerful love, though frustrated, is nevertheless crucial in strengthening her character:

the passionate strength of Magdalen's love clung desperately to the sinking wreck of her own delusion – clung, until she tore herself from it by main force of will. The woman never lived yet who could cast a true love out of her heart, because the object of that love was unworthy of her. All she can do is to struggle against it in secret – to sink in the contest, if she is weak; to win her way through it, if she is strong, by a process of self-laceration, which is of all mortal remedies applied to a woman's nature, the most dangerous and the most desperate; of all moral changes that is surest to mark her for life. Magdalen's strong nature has sustained her through the struggle; and the issue of it had left her – what she was now.

Victorian critics purported to be shocked by the immorality of Collins's story, but what really disturbed them was Collins's suggestion that a woman could feel like this. Even to suggest such a depth of emotional involvement is to imply something rather improper – for the basis of such a love as this must implicitly be sexual. Equally her reluctance to go through with the marriage to Noel Vanstone must stem from the same cause. Indeed Collins's main concession to Victorian propriety lay in acknowledging that, with such feelings, Magdalen Vanstone could not really be a proper person.

Wilkie Collins habitually depicts forceful, self-reliant women and even suggests, as with Count Fosco's admiration for Marian Halcombe, that men may be attracted to them for this very reason. However, the Victorian novelist who went furthest in reversing sex-role stereotyping was George Meredith, who not only wrote about strong and independent women but frequently contrasted them with men who were hesitant, insecure and vacillating. Many critics have taken this aspect of Meredith's novels to be autobiographical. Certainly Meredith recognised that women found decisiveness attractive even if he felt that there might be a price to be paid for this:

Wouldst thou, O man, amorously inclining! attract to thee superior women, be positive. Be stupidly positive, rather than dubious at all. Face fearful questions with a vizor of brass. Array thyself in dogmas. Show thy decisive judgement on the side of established power, or thy enthusiasm in the rebel ranks, if it must be so; but be firm. Waver not. If woman could tolerate wavering and weakness, and did not rush to the adoration of decision of mind, we should not behold them turning contemptuously from philosophers in their agony, to find refuge in the arms of smirking orthodoxy. (p. 59)

In *Sandra Belloni* (originally *Emilia in England*, 1864), where this heart-felt advice appears, Emilia, a young Italian girl with a magnificent voice, becomes the protégée of Mr Pole, a wealthy city merchant, and falls passionately in love with his son, Wilfred, a handsome army officer. Characteristically, when they kiss it is he who draws away 'almost bashfully'. Wilfred plans to marry Lady Charlotte Chillingworth since this will be an advantageous match that will also please his father. He is therefore somewhat taken aback when Emilia tells him that she will sacrifice her career in Italy as an opera-singer for the sake of his love:

He had some little notion of the sacrifice; but, as he did not demand any sacrifice of the sort, and as this involved a question perplexing, irritating, absurd, he did not regard it very favour-ably. As mistress of his fancy, her prospective musical triumphs were the crown of gold hanging over her. As wife of his bosom, they were not to be thought of.   (pp. 200–1)

Wilfred desultorily reviews her prospective advantages in his mind without finding any of them irresistible; what is sufficient is that 'he was her prime luminary' (p. 202). Wilfred strings her along without much thought of the consequences until finally she hears him deny to Charlotte that he has ever loved her. Emilia runs away to London, where lonely and deeply distressed by the cruelty of Wilfred's be-trayal, she even contemplates suicide. Wilfred now comes to the conclusion that he may have made a mistake and that he really does love Emilia after all, but she has now made up her mind to go to Italy both to sing and to get involved in revolutionary activity, so she rejects him. In the novel's sequel *Vittoria* (1867) there is further irony as Emilia, now known as 'Vittoria' – her stage name in Italy – marries Count Ammiani and finds that her role in life is equally restricted. Laura comments:

It is the curse of man's education in Italy? He can see that she has wits and courage. He will not consent to make use of them. You know her: she is not one to talk of these things. She who has both heart and judgement – she is merely a little boat tied to a big ship. Such is their marriage. She cannot influence him. She is not allowed to advise him. And she is the one who should lead the way.   (pp. 553–4)

As far as Hardy is concerned, the most significant of Meredith's novels is *Rhoda Fleming* (1865). Indeed Siegfried Sassoon suggested that it gave 'the curious impression of having been written in collaboration with Hardy'. In the context of Meredith's own fiction *Rhoda Fleming* has many unusual features: the rural theme, the strongly melodramatic plot, the emphasis on chance, the tragic conclusion. Certainly the disposition towards melodrama suggests that Meredith may himself have been brought temporarily under the influence of Wilkie Collins. William Fleming is an impoverished Kentish farmer who has long struggled to make a living and, at the same time, as he sees it, done his best to indulge the whims and wishes of his wife and two daughters, Dahlia and Rhoda. Dahlia goes away to London and there falls in love with Edward Blancove, the son of a wealthy banker, who takes her with him on a tour of Europe but cannot make up his mind to marry her for fear of crossing his father. Dahlia tells her family that she is married but her family conclude that she is disgraced – as the old farmer bluntly puts it 'My first girl's gone to harlotry in London' (p. 123). Robert Eccles, his assistant, who loves the other daughter, Rhoda, is determined to confront the Blancove family. He is badly beaten by a brutal thug called Nicodemus Sedgett and then seeks a duel with Edward, which is denied. Edward leaves for the continent again, planning to extricate himself from the situation by arranging Dahlia's marriage to Sedgett, but when he finally receives all the letters he has a change of heart and returns to England intent on marrying her only to learn that she has taken poison. She recovers but now cannot possibly contemplate marriage to the man she once desperately loved. The story is strained by Meredith's rather paradoxical determination to make Edward a morally contradictory figure:

Hero and villain are combined in the person of Edward, who was now here to abase himself before the old man and the family he had injured, and to kneel penitently at the feet of the woman who had just reason to spurn him. He had sold her as a slave is sold; he had seen her plunged into the blackest pit; yet she was miraculously kept pure for him, and if she could give him her pardon, might still be his.   (pp. 482–3)

These lines call to mind both *Tess of the d'Urbervilles* and *The Mayor of Casterbridge* even though *Rhoda Fleming* is scarcely fit to touch the hem of their garment, since Meredith does not do enough to make Edward's vacillations credible or to make us view the situation, even momentarily, through his eyes. But the negative reversed, with the focus on the character of the woman, is certainly in keeping with the character of Hardy's work. Where Meredith can be praised is in his rejection of the fallen woman stereotype, as in his reference to 'all these false sensations, peculiar to men, concerning the soiled purity of woman, the lost innocence, the brand of shame upon her'. Again, it is hard here not to think of the subtitle of *Tess*.

It is, however, *The Ordeal of Richard Feverel* (1859) that constitutes one of the most significant landmarks of later Victorian fiction. It is Meredith more than anyone who dismantles the conventions of the Victorian three-volume novel and who exhibits the narrowness of its fictional conventions and of the social morality that these ultimately rest upon. In so many Victorian novels there are apparently insuperable barriers of class and status that stand in the way of the love of two young people, yet the audience knows that these barriers will, after much heartache, eventually be removed, either through a change in status of the humbler party or through a relenting on the part of the intractable parents. *The Ordeal of Richard Feverel* promises to be just such a novel. Sir Austin Feverel is an enlightened aristocrat who has elaborate plans for his son Richard's future. He cares a great deal for his son, whom he has brought up without a mother, and Richard is devoted to his father. But the father's schemes seem thwarted when Richard falls passionately in love with Lucy, the daughter of a farmer and thus hardly a great match, and arranges to marry her secretly in London. Now it seems that it is only a matter of winning the father round, and since both care a great deal for each other, a happy ending seems already assured and Meredith goes out of his way to hint to the reader that this will be the case. However, Sir Austin makes use of his influence with Richard to bring about his separation from his wife and endeavours to destroy the marriage by placing Mrs Mount, an attractive courtesan, in Richard's way, thus leaving Lucy exposed to the attention of Lord Montfalcon. Lucy goes mad and dies, while Richard, who is seriously wounded in a duel with Lord Montfalcon, is left to contemplate the fatal circumstances that have led to such a denouement. But for Meredith this is not just a tragedy of individuals but a demonstration of the way in which healthy and natural instincts can be perverted by culture. Early in the novel, Adrian tells Richard that he is an animal, a conclusion that he resists, but in Meredith's own view man is part of nature and it is the attempt to separate him from all that is instinctual and spontaneous, as happens with Sir Austin's 'system', that leads to tragedy. Towards the end of the novel, in a chapter entitled 'Nature Speaks', Richard experiences a belated change of heart when he is caught in a thunderstorm in the German forest and experiences a sense of kinship with nature. This feeling is intensified when he finds a tiny leveret that clambers all over him and then begins gently to lick his hand. Suddenly all the tender feelings that he has repressed are reawakened and he hurries home to see his wife and child. But of course it is too late. *The Ordeal of Richard Feverel* was influential not simply because Meredith surprised people by writing a tragic novel, but because he showed the arbitrariness of such a conclusion and suggested that the imperatives of culture do violence to human nature.

In the light of his future career it was certainly significant that Hardy began his attempt to support himself as a novelist with a melodrama, written very much under the aegis of Wilkie Collins, since this was a genre in which the broaching of taboo subjects was not only possible but virtually *de rigueur*.

Take bigamy or the possibility of bigamy as a case in point. Bigamy, or the possibility of bigamy, was effectively launched by Mary Braddon in *Lady Audley's Secret* and *Aurora Floyd* and was taken up by Wilkie Collins in *Armadale*, by George Meredith in *Rhoda Fleming*, by Charles Reade in *Griffith Gaunt* and by Hardy in *Desperate Remedies*. Doubtless, bigamy as a crime has long since lost whatever shock value it had, but obviously what made the offence disturbing was not simply the fact that it involved breaking the law but the strong sexual message that it conveyed. Clearly anyone who was prepared not simply to abandon their wife but to risk a prison sentence into the bargain must have been driven by powerful emotions, and if these emotions were given even partial legitimation – as they certainly were in *Griffith Gaunt* – then many assumptions about marriage and respectability might be put at risk. For the whole point about moral conventions that are presumed to have an inexorable force within a society that is deeply conformist is that even if one single individual transgresses, if he does so without any show of repentance and remorse, then his refusal can have a very powerful impact indeed. We are often inclined to imagine that Victorian morality was strict – but its very strictness necessarily led to double standards and to a kind of *de facto* recognition that 'cheating' within limits was acceptable, provided that it remained properly clandestine and shame-faced. The melodrama of Collins and his successors was always potentially subversive simply because to write it and even to read it involve a certain brazenness in acknowledging the existence of matters that might more appropriately be denied. As much as anything else, the wearing down of a presumed Victorian moral rigidity came about through a gradual extension of the frontiers of what could be discussed. Moreover it should be emphasised that this melodrama was in its own odd way highly proper. Few Victorian novelists, for example, would have dared to describe a character who kept a mistress, even though Dickens and Collins did so, but to write about a bigamist at least had the air of virtue and suggested at the very least that an involvement with two different women must be criminal.

In *Desperate Remedies* (1871) Hardy combined Collins's emphasis on patterns of fatality and chance with Meredith's preoccupation with characters who hesitate or remain indecisive at pivotal moments in their lives. The conjunction was to prove deeply significant for the future development of his work. This already creates a complex response in the mind of the reader: on the one hand the tendency of a character to pause or change his or her mind at the moment of decision seems to dramatise their own independence and freedom of will; yet on the other hand the pressure and arbitrariness of external events seems to force them along a pathway that they never envisaged or intended. We thus have a sense, though not a theological one, that

> There is a divinity that shapes our ends
> Rough-hew them how we will.

In *Desperate Remedies* Cytherea's perplexing existence begins when her father accidentally falls from a building where he is architect in charge. She only obtains her employment with Miss Aldclyffe when Miss Aldclyffe, after dismissing her as unqualified, decides to take her on after all. She becomes involved with Edward Springrove, her future husband, when her brother injures his ankle and is forced to take the train home while Springrove joins her on the boat. Aeneas Manston only answers Miss Aldclyffe's advertisement on the third insertion and even then only after she has had it sent directly to him. Cytherea is caught between two men, Springrove and Manston, while Springrove is caught between Cytherea and Adelaide Hinton. The chance burning down of The Three Tranters when some long smouldering couch-grass ignites, a disaster that apparently brings with it the death of Manston's wife, though obviously melodramatic, initiates a whole series of complex ironies. For Manston should not really have responded to Mrs Aldclyffe's advertisement at all, as it called for a single man, and he would not then have encountered Cytherea. Had not the burning of The Three Tranters placed an opportunity in his way he would never have been tempted to murder his wife. The unkindest cut of all is that having apparently achieved the object of his desire and married Cytherea, his hopes are dashed by reports that his wife is still alive after all. Moreover he cannot seriously instigate enquiries into his wife's whereabouts for fear of arousing suspicions that she may be dead. Although Manston seems a fairly cold-blooded character, with whom it is difficult fully to sympathise, he is the first Hardy character who both tries to struggle against the arbitrariness of existence and yet finds himself defeated by it. Unlike the others he is not indecisive and knows what he wants in life, yet this clarity of purpose is also the cause of his undoing.

In *Under the Greenwood Tree* (1872) and *A Pair of Blue Eyes* (1873) Hardy introduced what was to become a characteristic preoccupation of his work: the conflict between the old and the new. Although this conflict is one that is articulated in many diverse ways in his fiction, it is pertinent to stress at the outset that his presentation of women is very much at the centre of it. It is not just that, as common parlance has it, Hardy is concerned with the 'new woman', but that woman becomes the signifier of the new. This is the case in *Under the Greenwood Tree* where Fancy Day, the newly arrived teacher in Mellstock, becomes a threat to the customary folkways of the community when the vicar decides to replace the traditional instrumental band with the more modern sound of the harmonium, as played by Fancy Day. Fancy is courted by Dick Dewy, the son of a Tranter and a member of the orchestra, despite the fact that he might be deemed to have aspirations above his station. For a moment Fancy dallies with the idea of marrying the vicar, in a typically Meredithian moment of hesitation, but in the end decides in favour of her more ardent but humbler lover. In this way a perfectly harmonious balance is achieved between past and present – for if the vicar is victorious over the harmonium, he is defeated in love. All the various forces are reconciled. In the end the fraying web of tradition is effortlessly rewoven. Fancy's presence in the village proves to be not quite as destabilising as it had once threatened to be. Hardy's presentation of an essentially similar theme in *A Pair of Blue Eyes*, however, could not be more different in either characterisation or style – the consolations of *Under the Greenwood Tree* can here be understood in only the most ironic spirit. Already we are confronted with the characteristic contradiction of Hardy's work that he can write both as the nostalgic traditionalist and in a way that is self-consciously and abrasively modern – and moreover is capable of doing both these things simultaneously. In *A Pair of Blue Eyes* all three principal characters can be seen as distinctively modern types. Elfride, though an unsophisticated country girl and daughter of a clergyman, is nevertheless a forceful, independent person who declines to remain in the prescribed orbit of the conventional young woman, perhaps in part because she has no mother. Elfride plays chess, writes her father's sermons and is the author of a historical novel. Indeed it is the very fact that she has to act as hostess to Stephen Smith, a young man from an architectural partnership in London who has come to make sketches of the village church, that leads to the development of a relationship between them. This relationship is characterised by a certain impropriety because Stephen is not what he seems. The mere fact that he arrives from London seems to give him social position and cachet – yet he is in fact the son of John Smith, a local mason, which from the point of view of Elfride's father makes their relationship distinctly embarrassing as well as unforeseen. As Elfride remarks subsequently: 'To think *you*, the London visitor, the town man, should have been from here, and have known the village so many years before I did. How strange.' Yet much of the irony of the book stems from the fact that the demure Elfride, 'a pair of blue eyes', proves equally disconcerting to the men in her life. Stephen falls passionately in love with her but when he realises that this social position places an insuperable obstacle in the way of their marriage – at least as far as Elfride's father is concerned – he suggests an elopement. Indecision characteristically ensures. Stephen bungles the arrangements by imagining that they have to go through the ceremony at St Launces when the licence he has is actually only valid in London. They travel up there, but then Elfride insists: 'I am so miserable! I must go home again – I must – I must! forgive my wretched vacillation. I don't like it here – nor myself – nor you.' However, she is really testing out Stephen's own determination, and when he indecisively falls in with her apparent wishes she is disappointed in him:

> Rapture is often cooled by contact with its cause, especially if under awkward conditions. And that last experience with Stephen had done anything but make him shine in her eyes. His very kindness in letting her return was his offence. Elfride had her sex's love of sheer force in a man, however ill-directed; and at that critical juncture in London Stephen's only chance of regaining the ascendancy over her that his face and not his parts had acquired for him, would have been by doing what, for one thing, he was too youthful to undertake – that was, dragging her by the wrist to the rails of some altar, and peremptorily marrying her. Decisive action is seen by appreciative minds to be frequently objectless, and sometimes fatal; but decision, however suicidal, has more charm for a woman than the most equivocal Fabian success.

Frustrated in his expectations Stephen leaves for India to pursue his career as an architect in the hope that he will be able to return and claim Elfride, but in his absence she falls in love with his friend and mentor, Harry Knight, a successful reviewer and prominent figure on the London literary scene. Knight is both a stronger and more forceful personality than Stephen, and is able to dominate Elfride and win her respect in a way that Stephen never could. In theory at least he is a sophisticated man of the world, yet in practice he is extremely insecure in his relationships with women and finds the very idea that she should be anything other than an artless *ingénue* at once unthinkable and intolerable. When she refuses his gift of earrings out of a sense of loyalty to Stephen, to whom she is still betrothed, Knight interprets this as bashful innocence:

> He read her refusal so certainly as the bashfulness of a girl in a novel position that, upon the whole, he could tolerate such a beginning. Could Knight have been told that it was a sense of fidelity struggling against new love, whilst no less assuring to his ultimate victory it might have entirely abstracted the wish to secure it.

When Knight discovers that Elfride has had more than one previous admirer and has been actually been kissed before he is virtually unmanned. Having himself been the commanding, authoritative figure, he now feels himself to have been made a laughing stock, deceived by the wiles of an ostensibly virtuous woman: 'Certain it was that Knight's disappointment at finding himself second or third in the field, at Elfride's momentary equivoque, and at her reluctance to be candid, brought him to the verge of cynicism.' However, we also know that it is Elfride's disposition to be candid and that she is only compelled to equivocate because Knight is so absurdly sensitive to any possibility of a slur on his 'knightly' honour. Knight concludes that the relationship must be broken off. But subsequently he encounters Stephen, now returned from India and a successful man, and his interest in Elfride is reawakened. Both men decide separately to travel down to St Launces and ask for Elfride's hand but they are disconcerted once more when they learn that Elfride is dead and encounter Lord Luxellian in mourning over his wife's grave. The irony is that Elfride finally achieves the upwardly mobile marriage envisaged for a person in her station, but only because two intellectually advanced and thoroughly contemporary men have been unable to rise to the challenge that she represents. Hardy indicates that even the slightest shift in the ground-rules governing the relationship between the sexes can be thoroughly unnerving as far as men are concerned. What *do* you do with a woman who does not always act as proprieties dictate?

These changes in the nature of interpersonal relationships are accompanied by still more far-reaching changes in the nature of religious belief. The paradoxical efforts of the Church of England to renew itself under the competitive pressure of Methodism are reflected in the project of 'church restoration' on which Stephen is engaged, in the service of which the old tower, around which Elfride once so recklessly walked, is deliberately demolished in order to make way for what Elfride's father, Mr Swancourt, calls 'a splendid tower – designed by a first-rate London man – in the newest style of Gothic art, and full of Christian feeling'. The tower takes with it Mrs Jethway, the only witness of Elfride's former improprieties: it is as if the destruction of the tower really does represent a powerful wish to abolish the past, which serves as a construction and a limit. Yet these changes in the church are overshadowed by the impact of Darwinism, epitomised by the striking scene in the book, at once melodramatic and symbolic, in which Knight, with Elfride, slips on the cliff edge and is left for several minutes perilously hanging on for his life:

> By one of those familiar conjunctions of things wherewith the inanimate world baits the mind of man when he pauses in moments of suspense, opposite Knight's eyes was an imbedded fossil, standing forth in low relief from the rock. It was a creature with eyes. The eyes, dead and turned to stone, were even now regarding him. It was one of the early crustaceans called Trilobites. Separated by millions of years in their lives, Knight and this underling seemed to have met in their place of death. It was the single instance within reach of his vision of anything, that had ever been alive and had had a body to save, as he himself had now.
>
> The creature represented but a low type of animal existence, for never in their vernal years had the plains indicated by those numberless slaty layers been traversed by an intelligence worthy of the name. Zoophytes, mollusca, shell-fish, were the highest development of those ancient dates. The immense lapses of time each formation represented had known nothing of the dignity of man. They were grand times, but they were mean times too, and mean were their relics. He was to be with the small in his death.

The 'gaze' of the Trilobite is a contemporary equivalent of the *momento mori*, and what it dramatises is life as physical rather than spiritual – an incredibly protracted and more or less shapeless process in which man is diminished in importance into something very like a crustacean since he can no longer regard himself as a privileged being who somehow stands above and outside this process as some special creation of God. For Hardy, like many of the more sensitive minds of his generation, the most damaging consequence of the Darwinian theory of evolution was both to deny any sense of providential design and, still more dispiritingly, to suggest that man, far from being captain of his fate and 'master of his soul' (as W. E. Henley stoically and contemporaneously put it), was no more than flotsam and jetsam tossed about on the waves of chance. This very scene – one of many such Hardyesque 'conjunctions' – is designed to demonstrate just this point, since Elfride, venturing forth with a telescope to see the return of Stephen's ship, *The Puffin*, accidentally encounters Knight on the cliffs. Through the act of rescuing Knight from death she finds herself in his arms with her whole future now irrevocably set on a different course. Hardy is often criticised for his use of coincidence, which is allegedly part of his inability either to avoid melodrama or create a well-constructed story, but Hardy's motives are actually very different. His use of chance, coincidence and conjunction is intended to dissipate any conviction in the reader that his characters live in a world that is providentially governed, rational and predictable. It is designed to show just how powerfully our lives can be shaped by fortuitous events. Moreover Hardy wants to suggest, as he was to do still more powerfully in *Tess*, that we are always prone to exaggerate our own importance and uniqueness, little realising that we may simply be following in the footsteps of many others. Although Hardy *does* suggest that Knight's jealousy is pathological and excessive, there is an uncanny pattern of repetitions in the book – so that, for example, Knight not only follows Stephen in buying ear-rings for Elfride but is even led to discover her lost ear-ring and so recall the moment when she lost it. The lost ear-ring symbolises a loss of innocence and is a kind of jinx that threatens her relationship with both men, yet what it points to on a deeper level is the ultimate insignificance of the individual, who is always capable of being replaced by another. This is ironically demonstrated in the scene in the crypt of the church where Stephen encounters Elfride with Knight, who introduces her to Stephen as his fiancée. At the time the ostensible sense of the scene is that Stephen has been replaced by Knight, yet its setting by the graveside of Lady Luxellan points to a yet unforeseen substitution in which Elfride will take Lady Luxellan's place – even to the point of being mourned in turn – while both Stephen and Knight are supplanted by Lord Luxellan, whom they never envisage as a possible rival. So at the end their sense of their own special identity and special relationship is utterly undermined: 'We have no right to be there. Another stands before us – nearer to her than we!' They have become shadows.

In *Far from the Madding Crowd* (1874) Hardy's sense of the destructive power of chance and passion in human lives is intensified into tragedy, yet is at the same time softened and moderated by the power of tradition. In a desacralised world men and women are compelled to confront yet more nakedly the disturbing power of their own emotions, which threaten to overwhelm them totally – a demonic other for which no reason can be given. Thus all are victims and for Hardy what matters is how they cope with that situation, whether they can find within themselves the resources to survive. Nature appears in an ambiguous light in the novel: on the one hand its customary patterns offer a ritualistic sense of order; yet at the same time it is the inscrutable source of cataclysmic events in which all sense of reason and harmony is overturned. It is significant that the novel is anchored in the personality of Gabriel Oak, who initially appears as a somewhat comic figure as he sets off on his inept attempt to woo Bathsheba Everdene, using

> all the hair-oil he possessed upon his usually dry, sandy, and inextricably curly hair, till he had deepened it to a splendidly novel colour, between that of guano and roman cement, making it stick to his head like mace round a nutmeg, or wet seaweed round a boulder after the ebb.

While Gabriel never quite shakes off the absurdity of his initial characterisation as the novel progresses, we are forced to take him more seriously. In this the early destruction of his whole flock of sheep and thus of his future as an independent farmer is crucial. It seems that his whole life is in ruins just because of the playful nature of a young dog, yet Gabriel has no alternative but to accept this. Although Hardy describes Gabriel on the first page of the novel as a churchgoer and subsequently presents him at prayer after the death of Fanny Robin, there is nevertheless something almost pagan about the quiet stoicism with which Gabriel unquestioningly accepts the cruel blows that life has dealt him. It is this that gives him the strength to survive, to take life as it comes, to look on 'good and ill alike':

> Gabriel was paler now. His eyes were more meditative, and his expression was more sad. He had passed through an ordeal of wretchedness which had given him more than it had taken away. He had sunk from his modest elevation as pastoral king into the very slime-pits of Siddim; but there was left to him a dignified calm he had never before known, and that indifference to fate which, though it often makes a villain of a man, is the basis of his sublimity when it does not. And thus abasement had been exaltation, and the loss gain.

Gabriel never again falls so low as when he is playing his flute for coppers at the Casterbridge hiring fair, yet the fortitude he gains at so early an age stays with him. As Hardy sees it, Gabriel is also sustained by his sense of belonging to a traditional rural community, in which each person has their due position and place, and where, just as Oak himself is looked up to for his skills as a shepherd, so too such a person as the Old Maltster is respected and revered. Hardy suggests that this sense of community with its rituals and traditions is not just a substitute for religion but is itself capable of sustaining a religious view of the world. The great barn where the sheep-shearing takes places resembles a church and rivals the local church in its antiquity – yet it has a continuing purpose and relevance in a way in which the church itself does not. Its very persistence invokes a sense of piety:

> Standing before this abraded pile, the eye regarded its present usage, the mind dwelt on its past history, with a satisfied sense of functional continuity throughout – a feeling almost of gratitude, and quite of pride, at the permanence of the idea which had heaped it up. The fact that four centuries had neither proved it to be founded on a mistake, inspired any hatred of its purpose, nor given rise to any reaction that had battered it down, invested this simple grey effort of old minds with a repose, if not grandeur, which a too curious reflection was apt to disturb in its ecclesiastical and military compeers. For once medievalism and modernism had a common standpoint. The lanceolate windows, the time-eaten arch-stones and chamfers, the orientation of the axis, the misty, chestnut work of the rafters, referred to no exploded fortifying art or worn-out religious creed. The defence and salvation of the body by daily bread is still a study, a religion, and a desire.

Here Hardy provocatively questions the distinction between body and soul – so dear to the Victorians – and suggests that there may be more truth and dignity simply in man's struggle to satisfy the most basic needs. Moreover in reading this description we cannot help noting the parallel between the unpretentious barn, a 'simple grey effort', and Gabriel Oak himself, who for so much of the novel blends into the background while the action focuses on such vivid, prideful figures as Sergeant Troy, Farmer Boldwood and Bathsheba Everdene. Oak, we may recall, loses his right to be called 'Farmer' in the very first pages of the novel.

Of course, Hardy can also satirise this sense of rustic tradition as when Jan Coggan, at the Buck's Head, admits that the advantage of being a member of the Church of England over Methodism is that you do not need to bother your head about points of doctrine, and declares that he will stand by it through thick and thin even if it does mean that he is much less likely to get to heaven:

'Chapel-folk be more hand-in-glove with them above than we,' said Joseph thoughtfully. 'Yes', said Coggan. 'We know very well that if anybody do go to heaven, they will. They've worked hard for it, and they deserve to have it, such as 'tis. I bain't such a fool as to pretend that we who stick to the Church have the same chance as they, because we know we have not. But I hate a feller, who'll change his ancient doctrines for the sake of getting to heaven. I'd as soon turn king's evidence for the few pounds you get.'

Yet behind the humour there is a serious point. Methodism represents the assertive, self-seeking, self-regarding modern spirit, while those who cling to tradition in a seemingly irrational way have recognised their place in a customary way of life and feel neither the need nor the desire to insist on their own will to be different. There is a certain humility involved. Gabriel Oak is, of course, the clearest embodiment of this spirit. He addresses only the task regardless of his own personal importance. Early on he saves the hay-ricks from fire and is the hero of the hour, surrounded by many participants and onlookers, yet later he saves the stacks from rain completely alone until Bathsheba joins him. Oak's acceptance of his own small place in the scheme of the universe comes from experience, yet for Hardy himself it is a lesson intellectually enforced by the Darwinian theory of evolution. It gives Gabriel a kind of grandeur, which even Bathsheba in the midst of her misfortunes comes to recognise as exemplary:

> What a way Oak had, she thought, of enduring things. Boldwood, who seemed so much deeper and higher and stronger in feeling than Gabriel, had not yet learnt, any more than she herself, the simple lesson which Oak showed a mastery of by every turn and look he gave – that among the multitude of interests by which he was surrounded, those which affected his personal well-being were not the most absorbing and important in his eyes. Oak meditatively looked upon the horizon of circumstances without any special regard to his own standpoint in the midst. That was how she would wish to be.

Oak is content to be on the periphery, while Troy or Bathsheba must always be the centre of attention. Oak is content for much of the novel to play second-fiddle to more exalted and glittering personages, to be part of the side-show amongst the rude mechanicals: yet for Hardy, he is always a prince in disguise.

Far from the Madding Crowd is a prolonged meditation on the power of the unpredictable and the unforeseen in human affairs. It is not just that individuals are affected by forces that they are unaware of, but they also find themselves the victims of circumstances that they themselves have instigated. Bathsheba further enmeshes Gabriel in love's snares by rushing after him to tell him that she has no sweetheart, and achieves the same object by sending Boldwood the Valentine, yet these light-hearted, spur-of-the-moment actions are fraught with complex consequences for herself. However, the most catastrophic enmeshing, an entanglement both literal and figurative, occurs when she bumps into Sergeant Troy in the darkness. Bathsheba strikes against 'warm cloth and buttons':

> It was immediately apparent that the military man's spur had become entangled in the gimp which decorated the skirt of her dress. He caught a view of her face.
>
> 'I'll unfasten you in one moment, miss,' he said, with new-born gallantry.
>
> 'O no, – I can do it, thank you,' she hastily replied, and stooped for the performance.
>
> The unfastening was not such a trifling affair. The rowel of the spur had so wound itself among the gimp cords in those few moments that the separation was likely to be a matter of time.
>
> He too stooped, and the lantern standing on the ground betwixt them threw the gleam from its open side among the fir-tree needles and the blades of long damp grass with the effect of a large glow worm. It radiated upwards into their faces, and sent over half the plantation gigantic shadows of both man and woman, each dusky shape becoming distorted and mangled upon the tree-trunks till it wasted to nothing.
>
> He looked hard into her eyes when she raised them for a moment; Bathsheba looked down again, for his gaze was too strong to be received point-blank with her own. But she had obliquely noticed that he was young and slim, and that he wore three chevrons upon his sleeve.
>
> Bathsheba pulled again.
>
> 'You are a prisoner, miss; it is no use blinking the matter,' said the soldier drily, 'I must cut your dress if you are in such a hurry.'

Hardy's undoubted genius as a novelist expresses itself in such scenes as this: at once, vivid and powerfully realised, yet with complex symbolic overtones. The spur and the gimp chords in the dress are the lures of male and female sexuality that lead to their mutual imprisonment in a relationship from which they cannot break free. The gigantic shadows cast by the lantern suggest the way in which this moment will come to dominate the novel, yet Hardy's specific reference to the dissipation of these images 'to nothing' at the same time tends to diminish it. Hardy means to imply that in a very real sense this entanglement is bigger than they are. It is not anything that either Troy or Bathsheba can master: they are powerless in the face of it. It is easy simply to see Troy as a glamorous, cynical womaniser, but it is always part of Hardy's purpose to suggest that he is a victim too; neglectful of Fanny, certainly, but swept off his feet by Bathsheba while always wanting to believe that he is in control. Under the power of love the characters are humbled and become ridiculous – there is Fanny's pathetic letter to Gabriel Oak; Bathsheba's midnight journey on a lame horse; Boldwood's attempt to buy Troy off; and, perhaps most absurd of all, the quirk of fate that compels Troy to play the part of Dick Turpin without speaking when he realises that Bathsheba is to be in the audience. It is here that an ironic reversal of their original meeting occurs which also overturns his former dominance of Boldwood, as he is shocked to hear her talking with a man – 'surely she was not so unprincipled as to flirt in a fair' – and is reduced to voyeur and cuckolded husband as he cuts a peephole in the tent:

> Troy took in the scene completely now. She was leaning back, sipping a cup of tea which she held in her hand, and the owner of the male voice was Boldwood who had apparently brought the cup to her. Bathsheba, being in a negligent mood, leant so idly against the canvas that it was pressed to the shape of her shoulder, and she was in fact, as good as in Troy's arms; and he was obliged to keep his breast carefully backward that she might not feel its warmth through the cloth as he gazed in.

The effect of this scene is to parody and diminish the original meeting in which their physical contact held such an erotic charge that it must necessarily shape their destinies. Now the physical contact only serves to emphasise the colossal gulf that separates them. Troy, like the male characters in *A Pair of Blue Eyes*, has become a ghost, who must deny his own presence both here and in the theatrical performance. This moment also returns us to Troy's original *coup de théâtre*: his dramatic display of the sword exercises. Few commentators have failed to stress the erotic nature of this scene but what also needs to be emphasised about it is the quality of control. Troy's display is masterful and faultless. He never once touches Bathsheba but when he so desires he can cut off a lock of her hair or spear a caterpillar on the point – 'My sword never errs.' Yet Troy is not able to show the same control in his own personal life. Ostensibly Troy and Boldwood are very different. Troy is flamboyant, extrovert, magnetic, gregarious, fluent and fulsome of speech. Boldwood is reclusive, solemn, serious and relatively uncommunicative. He has never been interested in women until he meets Bathsheba. Yet they are at bottom very similar. Both men are deeply self-centred and indifferent or unresponsive to the feelings of others – Hardy says of Boldwood 'he could not read a woman'. Each in his own way seeks to assert control of affairs. Troy imposes his will on Bathsheba after their marriage. Boldwood also seeks to control events and to bind others, whether this involves paying off Troy or getting Bathsheba to commit herself to marrying him in the distant future. The presents labelled 'Bathsheba Boldwood' are a grotesque instance of this, but his willingness to kill Troy, who stands in his way, is a more sinister manifestation of the same compulsion. Neither Troy nor Boldwood has learnt the humility enforced upon Gabriel Oak, who stands at the hiring fair with all the others 'waiting on Chance'. Troy's determination to impose himself on events is manifested in his rapid decision to buy an expensive gravestone for Fanny Robin, whom he neglected in life, and have it immediately erected. By this gesture and the planting of flowers Troy seeks to validate himself and his original love and at the same time to deny Bathsheba. It is a symbolic statement that seeks to cancel the power of time and make him the master of all their existences. This is also what Hardy, somewhat disparagingly, calls 'Troy's Romanticism'. In a passage thick with Darwinian implications, water from a gargoyle erupts onto the grave, ruining all of Troy's handiwork. It is at this moment that Troy's narcissism is destroyed and he is made conscious of his own powerlessness to shape events:

> Troy had felt, in his transient way, hundreds of times, that he could not envy other people their condition, because the possession of that condition would have necessitated a different person-

ality, when he desired no other than his own. He had not minded the peculiarities of his birth, the vicissitudes of his life, the meteor-like uncertainty of all that related to him, because these apper-tained to the hero of his story, without whom there would have been no story at all for him; and it seemed to be only in the nature of things that matters would right themselves at some proper date and wind up well. This very morning the illusion completed its disappearance, and, as it were, all of a sudden, Troy hated himself. The suddenness was probably more apparent than real. A coral reef which just comes short of the ocean's surface is no more to the horizon than if it had never even been begun, and the mere finishing stroke is what often appears to create an event which has long been potentially an accomplished thing.

Thus, although *Far from the Madding Crowd* is itself a powerfully plotted story with vividly drawn characters, it is also a warning against the illusory providential patterns of Victorian fiction. Troy has fancied himself the hero of such a grand narrative and now that dream is over. Yet Hardy characteristically concludes the passage by stressing that it has been a delusion all along. Perhaps all human lives, no matter how effortfully built, are little more than submerged, invisible fragments of coral, without even a God to witness them.

In *Far from the Madding Crowd* Hardy had, in the person of Bathsheba Everdene, once more depicted a forceful, independent woman who was capable of taking over and running her own farm, and yet the novel, in its single-minded obsession with cosmic themes tended to gloss over disparities in social class. Through their emotional in-volvement with Bathsheba, a shepherd a soldier and a gentleman farmer are all placed on the same level. Oak, Bathsheba and Troy experience radical changes in status that imply the effect of chance and circumstance but also put in question the reality of those differ-ences. What is unusual about *The Hand of Ethelberta* (1876), therefore, is that it both mocks and satirises the British class system, but at the same time takes those differences very seriously. On the face of it the aspirations of Ethelberta – ironically endowed with a aristocratic Saxon name – to rise in society may seem laughable when she is, in reality, the daughter of a butler, and it may seem equally grotesque that much of the interest that is aroused by her verse and her attempt to launch herself as a story-teller stems from the fact that she is taken to be a fashionable lady of society who is assuming an unaccus-tomed role. Ethelberta can only succeed if she is not perceived as an adventuress. Like Trollope's *The Way We Live Now*, which was published in the same year, the novel projects fashionable society as a topsy-turvy world so thoroughly invaded by *arrivistes* and the *nouveau riche* as to have no real basis of legitimacy. Hardy delights in the ironic reversal whereby the story climaxes in an attempt to stop the lowly born Ethelberta marrying the affluent but aged Lord Mountclere, not to save Lord Mountclere but to save Ethelberta. As Mrs Doncastle observes: 'The times have taken a strange turn when the angry parent of the comedy, who goes post-haste to prevent the undutiful daughter's rash marriage, is a gentleman from below stairs, and the unworthy lover a peer of the realm.' The collapse of gentility is typified by the episode in which Ethelberta, intrigued by the social pretension of her suitor, Mr Neigh, makes a clandestine visit to check out his country estate at Farnfield. But she finds there no great house: 'where should have been the front door of a mansion was simply a rough rail fence, about four feet high', beyond which are some horses 'in the last state of decrepitude' intended for the knacker's yard – this in fact being Neigh's line of business. Ethelberta feels that this visit deflates Neigh's social pretensions, yet Neigh himself, who has found out about her visit, feels that this determined spirit of enquiry makes her into a laughing-stock. No one is quite what they seem to be, there is much pretence and sham, yet the aristocratic ethos supposedly presumes that one can take ones peers on trust. Ethelberta realises that she must marry well before her lowly origins are found out, since at bottom skills and talent count for nothing, as Christopher, the musician who truly loves her, discovers in another way. As Ethelberta's mother points out: 'Marriage is a thing which, once carried out, fixes you more firmly in a position than any personal brains can do.' On the face of it Ethelberta triumphs both by marrying Lord Mountclere and by establishing herself against all the odds as unchallenged mistress of his household, yet for this she pays a great price, giving up both the love of Christopher and the intimacy of her own family. As Hardy had earlier observed: 'How far any known system of ethics might excuse her on the score of those curious pressure which had been brought to bear on her life, or whether it could excuse her at all, she had no spirit to enquire.'

After *The Hand of Ethelberta*, *The Return of the Native* (1878) can easily be read in a similar light, as a rejection of the worldliness of the great city and as a reassertion of traditional values. Clym Yeobright hates the 'flashy business' of selling jewellery in the glamorous city of Paris and returns to Egdon Heath determined to start a new life as a teacher. He is now so little ambitious that when his eyesight begins to fail he gladly takes up the lowly occupation of a furze-cutter and appears quite contented with his lot. It seems that Clym acts out what Ethelberta only enunciates: 'I am sick of ambition. My only longing now is to fly from society altogether, and go to any hovel on earth where I could be at peace.' Indeed it would be easy to read the novel autobiographically as constituting Hardy's own rejection of the superficial, ephemeral urban world in favour of the enduring values of nature and the rural world. Just to look on Egdon Heath is to listen to a sermon on human vanity, for it seems to suggest that what is unvarying is also what is enduring:

> It was at present a place perfectly in accordance with man's nature – neither ghastly, hateful, nor ugly: neither commonplace, unmeaning, nor tame; but, like man, slighted and enduring; and withal singularly colossal and mysterious in its swarthy monotony. . . . Civilization was its enemy; and ever since the beginning of vegetation its soil had worn the same antique brown dress, the natural and invariable garment of the particular formation. In its venerable one coat lay a vein of satire on human vanity in clothes.

Hardy's tone suggests that he is sympathetic to Carlyle's critique of modern society in *Sartor Resartus* and that he too can see some point in George Fox's suit of leather. The Egdon–Paris opposition is crucially focused on the question of fashion and the desire for self-assertiveness in modern culture that this represents. As a furze-cutter Clym has no desire to see the world simply as the stage for his own existence but is content to blend into the landscape:

> This man from Paris was now so disguised by his leather accoutrements, and by the goggles he was obliged to wear over his eyes, that his closest friend might have passed him by without recognising him. He was a brown spot in the midst of an expanse of olive-green gorse and nothing more.

So it would seem that we find in *The Return of the Native* a reassertion of the humility represented by Gabriel Oak in *Far from the Madding Crowd*. But here Hardy's position is more tortuous and more ambivalent, for he recognises that it is one thing to live out one's life as Wordsworth would say 'under the eye of Heaven', and quite another thing to come back to such a life after sampling something else.

The awareness of coexisting, contrasting possibilities can create as much discord in the mind as any resentment or revolt against the familiar. Hardy had described Sergeant Troy as a Romantic, and here also we find a critique of the Romantic imagination, but Hardy seems much more ready to recognise that there is no easy cure for romantic restlessness. It is all very well urging the virtues of tradition on the modern spirit and preaching humility to those who are bold and rebellious, but Hardy realises that the advice is not always easy to take. Egdon Heath may itself be an unchanging world, yet the world of the novel *is* a changing one. Clym has amazed the locals by his proficiency in learning and by his ability to leave the community for success in the great world. Wildeve too is restless and with the money he inherits plans to travel around the world. Eustacia is deeply discontented with her lot and is desperate to escape her apparent destiny, namely to live out her life by Egdon Health. Like Emma Bovary she is mesmerised by the possibilities that the world seemingly offers and which yet seem cruelly denied to her. Hardy is critical of such 'idealism', yet he knows and understands it because he has experienced it himself and he also realises that it is not really possible to expose the futility of those desires to those who are yet more deeply conscious of their own frustrations. Clym's words to Eustacia:

> Now, don't you suppose, my inexperienced girl, that I cannot rebel, in high Promethean fashion, against the gods and fate as well as you. I have felt more steam and smoke of that sort than you have ever heard of. But the more I see of life the more do I perceive that there is nothing particularly great in its greatest walks, and therefore nothing particularly small in mine of furze cutting

seem both sensible and even wise: all things are equal in the eye of heaven. Yet to the modern sensibility, narrowness, closure and stability are intolerable, and Eustacia would literally rather die than take his advice.

That *The Return of the Native* is to have a Promethean theme is announced in Hardy's opening description of the festivities on the Heath to mark November the 5th. His symbolic intentions are very apparent, for though in human eyes the fires are vivid and dramatic they are diminished almost into insignificance by the surrounding darkness and by the unfathomable vastness of the Heath itself. If, as Hardy says, the lighting of a fire 'indicates a spontaneous, Promethean rebelliousness against a fiat that this recurrent season shall bring foul times, cold darkness, misery and death', the fires themselves are nevertheless transitory and ineffectual statements – transient blazes soon extinguished. Significantly the fire that burns the longest is a bonfire of wood not straw of furze, which has been lit by Eustacia to attract Wildeve. Equally significantly it is a private gesture not a public one, the expression of a rebellious, individualistic self-assertion, since although Eustacia has learnt that Wildeve's marriage could not proceed, it is nevertheless a highly disruptive gesture to seek a secret meeting with the bridegroom on his wedding day. This meeting initiates Hardy's tragic plot, yet it also serves to demonstrate how problematic for Hardy the very idea of tragedy is. In the post-Darwinian world there are no gods to be indignant. Promethean rebellion serves to dramatise and magnify the importance of human existence – a project with which Hardy is in sympathy – yet to invoke it now may seem mere nostalgia. If nature in the struggle for existence is concerned to preserve only the species, and only some of them, and if on a cosmic scale the life of the individual scarcely matters, how is the novelist to think about the problem of human destinies? Are they necessarily ironised by such a biological overview, or is it possible to think of them as both great and insignificant at one and the same time. In *The Return of the Native* Hardy keeps twisting and turning his telescope – one of his favourite motifs by the way – at one moment showing us his characters in dramatic close up and then suddenly reversing the perspective to show them as small, insignificant objects. Hardy aspires to be a tragic novelist in a world in which he believes tragedy is no longer possible.

It is for this reason that Eustacia figures so paradoxically both as a tragic queen and a tragic queen in inverted commas. Eustacia believes that she has been called to a great destiny. She is proud and ambitious but the only way in which her overmastering desire for fulfilment and self-realisation can be actualised is through love: 'To be loved to madness – such was her great desire. Love was to her the one cordial which could drive away the eating loneliness of her days. And she seemed to long for the abstraction called passionate love more than for any particular lover.' In this sense Eustacia is the true romantic, the feminine counterpart to Faust and Don Juan in that it is clear that her desire could never find an adequate object, that her discontent is unquenchable and unappeasable. Superficially Eustacia and Wideve are symmetrical. They both always desire what they do not have and do not value what they possess. They can only love when their passion is infused with a spirit of rivalry. Each seeks to master the other. Eustacia seeks to assert her power over Wildeve and Thomasin simultaneously since in this way she will be acquiring an intensified sense of her own value. Yet when she learns that Thomasin may not wish to marry Wildeve after all, her obsession with him is almost instantaneously stifled:

> Was it really possible that her interest in Wildeve had been so entirely the result of antagonism that the glory and the dream departed from the man with the first sound that he was no longer coveted by her rival. She was, then, secure of him at last. Thomasin no longer required him. What a humiliating victory!

The word 'victory' is significant here just as is her admiration for the 'high gods' of William the Conqueror, Strafford and Napoleon Bonaparte – all personalities as masterful as she seeks to be herself. The difference between Eustacia and Wildeve, however, is that whereas Wildeve is vain, frivolous and easily distracted, Eustacia is intensely serious. When she decides upon an objective she will go to almost any lengths to achieve it as both her determination to win back Wildeve and her plan to marry Clym clearly demonstrate. Hardy observes: 'her plans showed the comprehensive strategy of a general than the small arts called womanish'.

Yet if Eustacia always takes herself seriously, Hardy does not always encourage the reader to do likewise. There is something ridiculous about Eustacia's mortification that she cannot display her beauty to Clym at the performance by the mummers since she is dressed as a Turkish Knight and the 'wild jealousy' she experiences because Thomasin, her deadly rival, is there looking at her best. The mood Hardy creates is positively grotesque as this intense young woman experiences 'a fearful joy' in her situation, while causing a glass of elderflower wine to vanish inside the ribbons of her costume. She is filled with fear, anxiety and shame at the possibility of detection, yet she has gone to such lengths only to see Clym Yeobright's face for the first time. It is as if Eustacia, by her very disposition, can create tragic possibilities out of the most unpromising materials. Eustacia's recklessness is particularly striking because she herself recognises that the great passion she seeks will necessarily be ephemeral, that it will be 'A blaze of love, and extinction.' Ostensibly the choice for Eustacia is between a stable relationship with Yeobright or a romantic involvement with Wildive, made fascinating by the very fact that it is taboo. Certainly, as Hardy repeatedly stresses,

Eustacia is in love with the very idea of love and the fascination that both Wildeve and Clym have for her really has very little to do with them as particular individuals. What drives Eustacia is a restlessness and compulsion to break free from her situation whatever that may be. She is a depressive, melancholy character. She attributes her escapade with the mummers to depression and it is depression that drives her to the accidental and ill-fated encounter with Wildeve at the dance on the green: 'No one shall know my suffering. I'll be bitterly merry, and ironically gay, and I'll laugh in derision.'

At bottom, Eustacia recognises the futility of her own dreams, which only serves to make her situation all the more galling. Clym and Wildeve are equal in that both disappoint her; neither is a worthy object of her desire. She drowns herself not so much because she is unhappy emotionally but because she sees the death of all her aspirations. Wildeve is simply not worth sacrificing herself for: 'He's not *great* enough for me to give myself – he does not suffice for my desire!' Hardy's introductory comment on her words is ironic and deprecating: 'When a woman in such a situation, neither old, deaf, crazed, nor whimsical, takes upon herself to sob and soliloquise aloud there is something grievous the matter.' Hardy admits that his heroine is in a state of extreme unhappiness and yet he mocks her. Eustacia is self-pitying, self-indulgent and narcissistic and Hardy will not allow us to take her sense of 'the cruel obstructiveness of all about her' at face value since she would feel this no matter where she was or what her circumstances were. Eustacia typifies the *malaise* of the modern spirit which rebels against the pettiness of circumstance. Hardy contrariwise insists on the need to reject this romanticism and to come to terms with the pettiness of circumstance, to give up the idea of glamour, which a return to Egdon represents. Yet he also realises that tradition does not offer a complete answer for the modern sensibility which has severed all connection with it. Eustacia and Clym may seem very different, but in their alienation they are one.

The problem of discontinuity between past and present was one that continued to haunt Hardy's fiction even as he consciously sought to evade such discouraging implications. In *The Trumpet-Major* (1880), a self-consciously simple tale of a girl who is loved by two brothers, each of whom tries to defer to the presumed rights of the other, Hardy suppressed the issue by setting his story at the time of the Napoleonic Wars, but in *A Laodician* (1881), written during his convalescence, he used the vacillation of Paula Power between two lovers to reopen the question. Somerset is an architect, a connoisseur of Gothic architecture. Captain de Stancy is an impoverished aristocrat, whose family formerly owned the great house that is now Paula's residence. Paula, the daughter of a wealthy railway engineer and Dissenter, is taken by Somerset to epitomise the modern: 'you represent the march of mind – the steamship, and the railway, and the thoughts that shake mankind.'

The electric telegraph that she eagerly installs at Stancy Castle seems to epitomise the way the wind is blowing, yet the whole question of what is to be regarded as modern is one that becomes deeply troubling and confused. Somerset as a professional man, the son of a successful painter, is in many ways a modern type, yet his love for the architecture of the past means that he often feels at odds with the present age. Contrariwise, although de Stancy is at pains to stress his own pedigree, his own father is quite unsentimental about such matters and Dare, a photographer and his illegitimate son, seems in his unscrupulous narcissism to represent a peculiarly modern form of inauthenticity. Paula herself seems increasingly drawn to the past, as Somerset disconsolately observes, since this becomes associated with the idea of a marriage to de Stancy: 'Veneration for things old, not because of any merit in them, but because of their long continuance had developed in her; and her modern spirit was taking to itself wings and flying away.'

In theory Somerset's own architectural designs for remodelling the castle represent some kind of ideal bridge between old and new that can combine the best to both, but the novel ends ironically with the destruction of the castle by fire and with Paula consenting to marry Somerset, yet saying: 'I wish my castle wasn't burnt; and I wish you were a de Stancy.' By this Hardy implies that everything the family and the castle may have represented is really gone and that modernity has nothing definite to put in its place. For what Paula really does represent is the Laodiceanism, the indecisiveness, the eclecticism of the modern that can vacillate interminably between different alternatives because it lacks the courage of its own convictions. Paula's father never doubted either his Nonconformist principles or the value of his railway tunnels, but the second generation is one that, in every sense, cannot truly believe.

Hardy clearly regretted writing such a conventional novel of manners as *A Laodicean* for in *Two on a Tower* (1882) he deliberately set out to shock and to demonstrate his disdain for conventional social values. The eponymous tower is a place set apart from the everyday world, a place of romantic assignation for Lady Constantine and the glamorous blond astronomer, Swithin St Cleeve. Watching the heavens from this lofty standpoint they are made conscious simultaneously both of the urgency and the insignificance of sublunary things. Just as geological discoveries have made man conscience that his life is merely instant when set against the aeons of time, so an awareness of the innumerable galaxies beyond the solar system totally transforms man's perceptions of space. Swithin points out to Lady Constantine that whereas she can see no more than three thousand stars with the naked eye, with a telescope it is possible to view more than twenty million. But the tower itself offers further evidence of human insignificance. It is built on an ancient barrow that once memorialised hundreds of ancient Britons and while it was itself erected as a memorial that original *raison d'être* has been forgotten:

> Here stood that aspiring piece of masonry, erected as the most conspicuous and ineffaceable reminder of a man that could be thought of; and yet the whole aspect of the memorial betokened forgetfulness. Probably not a dozen people within the district knew the name of the person commemorated, while perhaps not a soul remembered whether the column was hollow or solid, whether with or without a tablet explaining its date or purpose.

In his latterday preface to *Two on a Tower* Hardy particularly stressed his wish 'to set the emotional history of two infinitesimal lives against the stupendous background of the stellar universe', and purported to be surprised that the book should have been regarded as morally improper and as a satire on the Church of England. In so saying, however, Hardy was certainly being disingenuous. *Two on a Tower* presents the love affair of an older woman for a younger man, where the woman is a distinguished member of the aristocracy, the man the offspring of a curate and a farmer's daughter. The affair begins before Lady Constantine learns that her husband is dead. She goes through a clandestine marriage with Swithin but the marriage is invalidated because her husband actually dies at a later date than she had originally believed, and so she subsequently finds herself facing the sad predicament of being an unmarried mother. Since Swithin is now on the other side of the world pursuing his astronomical researches she is forced into a 'respectable' marriage with a bishop. As if this were not shocking enough by the standards of the day, Hardy ironises the denouement still further by earlier introducing Andrew Green, a humble rustic, who remarks:

> But 'tis wearing work to hold out against the custom of the country, and the woman wanting 'ee to stand by her and save her from unborn shame, so, since common usage would have it, I let myself be carried away by opinion, and took her. Though she's never once thanked me for covering her confusion, that's true.

For Hardy, once one has glimpsed the voids and interstellar spaces of the universe, the 'ragged boundary which divides the permissible from the forbidden' must necessarily figure as both trivial and arbitrary. Lady Constantine and Swithin are brought together by the force of genuine passion that can only be diminished in a social context into the adventures of a coral bracelet – 'the little red scandal breeding thing'. The gulf between such feelings and the tenets of respectable society is brought into sharp relief when Lady Constantine, in a state of desperation at the perverse conjunction of circumstances that finds her both pregnant and unmarried at the very moment when Swithin is thousands of miles away, is told by her considerate brother Louis that the bishop is the solution to her problems. As indeed he is. The hopelessly conventional Louis had earlier impressed on his sister that marriage to the bishop would be 'a stepping stone to higher things'. For Hardy's novelistic precursors such a grand match would indeed have been a serious matter, but for Hardy the proposal is at once laughable and grotesque. All such mundane considerations must recede in the face of the urgency of human emotions and the vastness of the universe. The mistake made by Lady Constantine and Swithin was not that they were too daring but that they were far too cautious.

The distinct falling off in the quality of Hardy's fiction after *The Return of the Native* was undoubtedly connected with his disinclination to continue writing in a tragic vein, but with *The Mayor of Casterbridge* (1886) he returned to it, in what was unquestionably his bleakest and most uncompromising work to date. There is much in *The Mayor of Casterbridge* that seems to allude quite self-consciously to the tradition of Greek tragedy and especially to Sophocles' *Oedipus the King*. Henchard is a man who achieves greatness and respectability within the community but who is then humbled by the discovery of events from his distant past. Henchard's selling of his wife in a fit of drunkenness parallels Oedipus' murder of his father at the crossroads, not simply because this event returns both to haunt and destroy them, but because there is a deep ambiguity about their personal accountability for what they did. For while they cannot deny that they are responsible, they were not really aware either of what they were doing or what the consequences of their actions would be. Henchard's status as tragic hero is given further weight by the way in which Hardy allows him to dominate the book to a quite extraordinary degree, an aspect of *The Mayor* that has been remarked on by numerous critics. Ian Gregor sees this 'dominance of Henchard' as defining both the strengths and limitations of the novel and he believes that Hardy's emphasis on 'one man's deeds ... drains life out of the other characters'. [2] Irvine Howe sees Hardy's design as requiring a sharp contrast between 'the looming protagonist' and the other characters in which Henchard must always be 'somewhat larger than life'.[3]

For J. Hillis Miller, Henchard is a man driven by the desire to possess and dominate who is directly responsible for his own fate, which is 'determined not by a "power" external to himself, but by his own character'.[4] If *The Mayor of Casterbridge* is 'a study of man of character', we are to think of that character as the bearer of its own destiny. However, I would want to question the overall thrust of this analysis, which I believe ultimately leads to a serious misreading of the book. Henchard is central certainly, but Hardy's intention is both to present us with that centrality and at the same time to interrogate it and undermine it. In the first place we must remember that if *The Mayor of Casterbridge* is a tragedy, it is also Hardy's most important venture onto the terrain of the historical novel. As he points out in the Preface:

> The incidents narrated arise mainly out of three events, which chanced to range themselves in the order and at or about the intervals of time here given, in the real history of the town of Casterbridge and the neighbouring country. They were the sale of a wife by her husband, the uncertain harvests which immediately preceded the repeal of the Corn Laws, and the visit of a Royal personage to the aforesaid part of England.

Since the Corn Laws were repealed in 1846 and Prince Albert passed through Dorchester in 1849, this would suggest that the main action of the novel can be located in the 1840s. In this Hardy was true to

Scott's own example in *Waverley* of writing about a time that was distant enough to seem historically remote and yet still close enough to be within living memory. What is significant about the historical novel as practised by Scott is that Scott suggests that events are always beyond the control of particular individuals, no matter how eminent or celebrated. Great battles and what Hegel would call world-historical individuals do appear in Scott's novels but always in an oblique and elliptical way. Scott consciously refuses to centre his narrative around them and thereby diminishes them. Their belief that they can shape or control events is always exposed as an illusion, even if they are, like Macbeth, often temporarily deceived. Such a view was certainly congenial to Hardy and while he does allow Henchard seemingly to command *The Mayor of Casterbridge*, the whole action of the novel is designed progressively to marginalise, indeed to empty, his whole existence of any significance. Symptomatically the high point of the book, the visit of the 'Royal Personage' to Casterbridge, is also Henchard's low point. Since he has for so long been Mayor, the 'powerfullest member of the Town Council and quite a principal man in the country round besides', he cannot imagine that he would not play a prominent part in such a great occasion. He is determined to be at the centre:

> The carriages containing the Royal visitor and his suite arrived at the spot in a cloud of dust, a procession was formed, and the whole came on to the Town Hall at a walking pace.
> This spot was the centre of interest. There were a few clear yards in front of the Royal carriage, sanded; and into this space a man stepped before any one could prevent him. It was Henchard. He had unrolled his private flag, and removing his hat he staggered to the side of the slowing vehicle, waving the Union Jack to and fro, while he blandly held out his right to the Illustrious Personage.

As Hardy describes it, this represents the invasion of the sacred by the profane, but as Farfrae hastily drags him out of the way we are also reminded of Henchard's original crime since in proposing to sell his wife he also transgressed against respectability and decency. Yet, at the same time, it is also somewhat misleading to refer to the wife-selling in this way, since this would imply that Henchard is more instrumental than he actually is. Henchard is, of course, an extremely arrogant, over-bearing and self-centred man – as he clearly demonstrates in this opening episode. He takes it for granted that his wife and child are his possessions, who are there for him to dispose of as he thinks fit. This is what it is to be 'a man of character'. But we must not forget that his wife, Susan, has character too. Henchard does not really sell his wife, both because he is too drunk to know what he is doing and because he has no legal power to do so. It is Susan herself who makes the decision. Refusing to allow herself to be publicly shamed in this way – for Henchard, drunk as he is, obviously expects her to plead with him to keep her – she takes him at his word. It is she who leaves him. So even here Henchard's determination to be master and controller of events is deeply undermined.

Indeed the humbling lesson of *The Mayor of Casterbridge* is that it is distinctly dangerous for the individual to assume that life can be stabilised or to take it for granted that they can be the permanent focus even of their little world, let alone of the larger community. Hardy had a long-standing fascination with situations involving substitution and displacement. In *A Pair of Blue Eyes* Knight supplants Stephen in Elfride's affections; but both are displaced by Lord Luxellan. In *Far from the Madding Crowd* these patterns of substitution become more complex and circular: Oak, Bathsheba's first suitor, is briefly replaced by Boldwood until she falls passionately in love with Sergeant Troy. But Troy is himself displaced by Boldwood until with the killing of Troy by Boldwood Bathsheba returns to the patient and ever-enduring Oak. Bathsheba herself supplants Fanny Robin in Troy's affections, but when Fanny dies Troy insists on his love for her so vehemently that it is as if Bathsheba has been supplanted in turn. In *The Mayor of Casterbridge* Farfrae is actually described as 'the supplanter' and his acts of usurpation and appropriation are so extensive as almost to parody the idea that it is Henchard who is possessive. Farfrae not only replaces Henchard in command of the corn trade and marries Lucetta, but also becomes Mayor himself, lives in Henchard's house and finally marries his daughter. In reading *The Mayor of Casterbridge* one takes it for granted to refer to Henchard himself, especially since it is subtitled 'the story of a Man of Character', yet it seems to me that Hardy consciously intended this title to be ironic since there remains a certain ambiguity in the designation, expressive of the pervasive way in which Henchard is haunted by doubles – not just Farfrae but also Newson, the father of 'his' child. It is not only Henchard who finds himself displaced. When Susan Henchard returns to Casterbridge she supplants Lucetta whom Henchard was on the point of marrying. In marrying Farfrae, Lucetta displaces Elizabeth-Jane, who had hoped to marry him herself, which she is eventually able to do after the death of Lucetta following the skimmity ride. The skimmity ride itself, involving the stuffed figures and false faces of Henchard and Lucetta, itself involves some complex substitutions. In this representation Henchard in effigy displaces the man who has in such a multiplicity of ways displaced him; yet Henchard himself is saved from death by the shock of seeing his own image floating in the river:

> In the circular current imparted by the central flow the form was brought forward, till it passed under his eyes; and then he perceived with a sense of horror it was *himself*. Not a man somewhat resembling him, but one in all respects his counterpart, his actual double, was floating as if dead in Ten Hatches hole.

What makes this moment especially demoralising for Henchard is that he had already felt as if every aspect of life through which he has defined himself has been taken away from him; now, contemplating suicide, it is as if that final and most personal gesture has also been taken from him. Of course it can be argued that in some very complicated and oblique sense Henchard brings about his own downfall. In particular, his decision to open prematurely the letter from Susan which informs him that Elizabeth-Jane is not his daughter produces a certain distance between them as the result of which Henchard does not choose to visit her at Lucetta's house. In consequence it is Farfrae, not Henchard, who appears there, a turn of events that eventually leads to the secret marriage of Lucetta and Farfrae. But these twists, turns and reversals are so complex that it would be absurd to try to explain them in terms of human agency.

Of all Hardy's novels *The Woodlanders* is thickest with echoes and allusions, whether to Shakespeare, Shelley or his own earlier novels. It is as if Hardy needs to recapitulate, consolidate and look back before moving forward. Giles Winterbourne, both in his deep affinity with the rhythms of nature and in his loss of social status, through the expiration of the lease on his cottages, recalls Gabriel Oak. Grace Melbury, the educated and upwardly mobile woman, invokes such earlier Hardy heroines as Elfride and Ethelberta. The episode where Grace stays in Giles's humble cottage seems like an ironic transposition of the episode in *Two on a Tower* when Swithin and Lady Constantine inaugurate their marriage in humble surroundings, for here the issue is not marriage but the very impossibility of such a consummation. *The Woodlanders* seems a nostalgic work with its strong invocation of a traditional way on life in which human beings still live in harmony with the rhythms of nature, epitomised by the seasonal nature of the work undertaken by Melbury and Winterbourne, who work together and help one another out. Most of the activity in Melbury's timber business takes place in winter and spring, while Winterbourne's business in the cider and apple trade is concentrated in the autumn. The village of Little Hintock seems a place almost untouched by the contemporary world as its secluded situation, hidden deep in the woodland, might suggest. Budmouth, here, seems infinitely further afield than it ever did in *The Return of the Native*. In Hardy's introductory description of it, it is 'one of those sequestered spots outside the gates of the world where may usually be found more meditation than action, more listlessness than meditation'. Yet here Hardy already strikes a more unsettling note. Although urban readers might envy them their rustic idyll, the inhabitants of Little Hintock are by no means as settled and contented as their situation might suggest. What is particularly striking in *The Woodlanders* is the loss of any real sense of community. The break from this community is, of course, epitomised by Grace Melbury's departure in order to receive a genteel education, since on her return she is unsettled and unable to fit into the old way of life. On her return, as Giles is drawing her attention to the large crop of bittersweets, her mind is elsewhere, thinking of her school, with its broad lawns in the fashionable suburb of a 'fast city'. It is very difficult if not impossible for her to be again what she was. Yet if Grace is unsettled and isolated, so are most of the other characters in the novel. We first encounter Marty South desperately working through the night, making the spars her father is too ill to make himself. Both Fitzpiers and Mrs Charmond, as newcomers and outsiders, feel cut off from contact with others and cannot really settle. Yet this sense of alienation and displacement extends both to such a pillar of the community as Giles, who loses his hoped-for wife, his place in society and his home, and to Suke Damson and Timothy Tangs, who at the end of the novel are preparing to leave for Australia. The world of Little Hintock is slowly dying and behind the reassuring rhythm of the changing seasons lies a more ominous sense of life as a struggle for existence, in which some thrive and others are defeated. So here, just as much as in the city slum, Hardy discerns nature's botched and bungled purposes: 'the leaf was deformed, the curve was crippled, the taper was interrupted; the lichen ate the vigour of the stalk, and the ivy slowly strangled to death the promising sapling'. What makes *The Woodlanders* so very disconcerting is that Hardy does not simply suggest that this world is threatened by outside forces, but that it is already subject to its own internal warping. The loss of a sense of community in Little Hintock is very marked when we compare it with, say, *Under the Greenwood Tree*. It is epitomised by the one great communal gathering in the book, the party Giles Winterbourne gives in the hope of recommending himself to Grace. On such occasions, not just in Hardy, but in George Eliot and Trollope as well, distinctions of class momentarily recede into the background in a revelry without barriers. But here, despite the fact that Grace and her parents throw themselves into helping with the preparations, the occasion does not go well, possessing neither graciousness nor conviviality. Giles is disconcerted to find that Cawtree and the hollow-turner, whom he had envisaged as part of the supporting cast, now embarrassingly dominate the scene with their noisy game of langterloo. Grace has forgotten the old rustic dances and so does not take part. The party, far from melting the ice and breaking down barriers, actually serves to remind all the participants of their own isolation.

Thus, although *The Woodlanders* may seem a more conventional work than *The Return of the Native*, the sense of restlessness and dissatisfaction, which Hardy saw as characteristic of the modern spirit, is here far more pervasive. In that novel the sense of being limited and thwarted by a provincial existence was concentrated in the figure of Eustacia Vye, while Clym Yeobright, who had actually been to Paris, had no desire to return there. In *The Woodlanders* the modern characters are the outsiders Fitzpiers and Mrs Charmond, but since Grace is strongly linked to both through her marriage to Fitzpiers and through her earlier desire to be the friend and companion of Mrs Charmond the influence they exert is considerable. It is Grace's aspiration to move on their level that undermines her father's original plan to bring her and Winterbourne together – itself symptomatic of the narrow, enclosed community that is being invaded and undermined from within – since it was after all Melbury's desire to see his daughter an educated woman that sets the whole train of events in motion. Felice Charmond is presented as a character without any real core of identity. She is moody, capricious and lethargic – taking up Grace and dropping her as her fancy takes her, abruptly leaving the village and returning through boredom or loneliness. At bottom she is really rather a sad person. Fitzpiers is equally whimsical and unstable. He can never settle himself to any definite action or commit himself to one thing rather than another. Thus his promiscuous love life, in which he can be 'possessed by five distinct infatuations at the same time', is echoed in his intellectual dilettantism:

> The real Dr Fitzpiers was a man of too many hobbies to show likelihood of rising to any great eminence in the profession he had chosen, or even to acquire any wide practice in the rural district he had marked out as his field of survey for the present. In the course of a year his mind was accustomed to pass in a grand solar sweep throughout the zodiac of the intellectual heaven. Sometimes it was in the Ram, sometimes in the Bull; one month he would be immersed in alchemy, another in poesy; one month in the Twins of astrology and astronomy; then in the Crab of German literature and metaphysics.

As the Victorians would have said, he lacks bottom. Fitzpiers fancies himself a philosophical idealist and as a man more immersed in the ideal than the real, but really this is another name for the chilly self-centred narcissism that leads him both to neglect Grace and to regard the likes of Grammer Oliver and Joe South as nothing more than materials for his own desultory scientific study. In Fitzpiers the great Romantic figure of Faust is parodied and trivialised, just as his suggestion that human love is nothing more than self-projection renders his citation of Shelley's *The Revolt of Islam* a mockery. Despite the harm that his narcissism brings on others, he can still only feel neglected and unappreciated: 'I am doomed to live with the trades-people in a miserable little hole like Hintock.'

Yet, paradoxically, though he sees himself as the embodiment of the progressive scientific spirit, he is only respected by the villagers by virtue of his aristocratic descent. It is not the 'extrinsic, unfathomed gentleman of limitless potentiality, scientific and social' that is greeted by a deferential touching of hatbrims, but the man who is perceived as one of the last of the old Oakbury Fitzpiers. Thus the confusions of ancient and modern that marked *A Laodicean* are repeated here. There is no reality to Fitzpiers since he proclaims principles that he has no intention of putting into practice. He portentously informs Grace that the cardinal virtues according to Schliermacher are 'Self-control, Perseverance, Wisdom, and Love', yet as the context implies it is Giles Winterbourne, who is very far from being an intellectual, who exemplifies these virtues, not he.

In *The Woodlanders*, more forcefully even than in *Two on a Tower*, Hardy insists on the way in which people's lives are botched and distorted by notions of decorum and propriety and by the perverse arbitrariness of social conventions. Although Hardy was a strong believer in social mobility, in *The Woodlanders* he suggests that the characters are made unhappy by the very uncertainty of their own social position, which causes them to be pulled in contradictory directions. Felice Charmond was an actress who married into the aristocracy. Fitzpiers belongs to a family that once enjoyed high status. Grace is the daughter of a tradesman who aspires higher. Winterbourne, once more or less on a level with Melbury, is dragged down by ill luck. They are all, like Grace, 'in mid-air between two stories of society', which means not only that they do not really know who they are but also that they do not really know what they want. Yet despite this indefiniteness Hardy also shows that the class distinctions are nevertheless clearly marked. Grace cannot be a suitable match for Winterbourne after he has lost his cottages, and Winterbourne himself could never consider marriage with Marty South. Fitzpiers sees himself as drawn by desire into a match that is shamefully beneath him: 'I stooped to mate beneath me; and now I rue it.' In these tangled situations it is those with money and status who enjoy the power. Confronted with the liaison between Mrs Charmond and Fitzpiers, Melbury feels helpless:

> what could he and his simple Grace do to countervail the passions of those two sophisticated beings – versed in the world's way, armed with every apparatus for victory? In such an encounter the homely timber-dealer felt as inferior as a savage with his bows and arrows to the precise weapons of modern warfare.

Mrs Charmond rules over the village with an absolute *driot de seigneur*, taking from others whatever she needs – or does not need. She takes Marty South's hair. She deprives Winterbourne of his cottages, Grace of her husband. Yet Fitzpiers is equally imperious, seducing Suke Damson, and by a cruel irony, using the horse that Winterbourne bought for Grace to facilitate his liaison with Felice. Divorce, as the novel powerfully underlines, is also very much a class matter where the rich enjoy rights that are not extended to other members of society. Grace and Giles are cruelly misled into hoping that it may eventually be possible to marry by the seductive promises of Fred Beaucock. In consequence, through the arbitrary and repressive character of civilisation, Giles is made to feel guilty about his spontaneous and heartfelt kiss: 'The wrong, the social sin, of now taking advantage of the offer of her lips, had a magnitude in the eyes of one whose life had been so primitive, so ruled by household laws as Giles's which can hardly be explained.' The grotesque culmination of such respect for appearances is Giles's insistence on leaving Grace alone in the cottage for propriety's sake, which actually brings on his own death. Even the respectable Grace can see the absurdity of such a sacrifice. At this point the novel seems to cry out for some act of social defiance; but Hardy felt that it would be more damaging to show his characters paying the price. This also explains why he chooses to close the novel not on a quasi-tragic note with Winterbourne's death, but with the ironic twist whereby the mantrap intended to Fitzpiers catches Grace's dress. Grace can only free herself by removing her dress, a symbol of propriety and civilisation, in a gesture that returns her to the husband whom she does not love; when with Winterbourne, whom she loved, it proved impossible for either to disencumber themselves of the mental obstacles to their love. Through affectation and observance of the niceties, men and women can deny their own deepest needs and capacity for happiness.

When Hardy published *Tess of the d'Urbervilles* in 1891 he had been a practising novelist for twenty years and it was with this great novel that he finally broke the Victorian silence surrounding sexuality. Yet this breaking of the silence involves no sudden explosion, no violent clashing of cymbals, but seems almost to be a work of silence itself. For as has often been noted, Hardy's allusion to the rape of Tess by Alec d'Urberville could not be more oblique: it is as if Hardy himself hesitates to embark on the work of desecration to which he is committed. It is significant what he *does* say is that 'an immeasurable social chasm was to divide our heroine's personality thereafter from that previous self of hers who stepped from her mother's door to try her fortune at Trantridge poultry-farm'.

What Hardy means by this is that Tess is now to be regarded as belonging, through no fault of her own, to that great and unquestioned category of Victorian society: 'the fallen woman'. But as Hardy's description suggests, this 'chasm' is very much one determined by consciousness and social attitudes – even in the mind of Tess herself. In *Tess of the d'Urbervilles* the Meredithian novel of hesitation finds its strangest apotheosis, since Tess's grounds for hesitation are infinitely more compelling, given the prejudices of the era, than anything that Meredith or even Hardy himself had formerly envisaged. Tess believes in telling the truth, and in repudiating the prudent counsel of her own mother she unquestionably brings about her own downfall. Hardy shows how the depth of the cultural taboos surrounding sexuality directly contributes to such situations. Angel Clare blames Tess for not telling him before their marriage, yet Hardy shows how difficult – not to say impossible – such a confession is for a woman. When the subject of the widow who marries Jack Dollop is raised in the dairy there is some controversy as to whether she should have told him that she would lose her fifty pounds a year on marrying, when this money had been Jack Dollop's motivation for marriage in the first place. Tess, with her own situation in mind, tries to be emphatic: '"I think she ought – to have told him the true state of things – or else refused him – I don't know," replied Tess, the bread-and-butter choking her', but as this final collapse into uncertainty suggests, it is by no means easy to be categorical since men are unwilling to accept any conceivable compromising of feminine purity even in acknowledging their own 'weakness'. Tess, despite her great love for Angel, does everything that she can to 'save' him from her. When she finally agrees to marry him after his repealed urging she breaks down and cries. She insists that she is not worthy of him. She is reluctant to name the wedding day. When a day is set she tries to postpone it. She writes him a letter confessing her 'crime' but pushes it under the carpet – a gesture that ironically suggests Victorian society's own approach to such matters. When she eventually rediscovers the letter – she tears it up. She is relieved when after their marriage Angel confesses to his own sexual misdeeds, but when she speaks of her own past she finds that confession is not symmetrical, even though she was the innocent party in a way that Angel Clare was not. Yet the very tortuousness of the process whereby Tess's confession is dragged into the open mimics the convolutedness of Hardy's novel, which *must* speak of things that nevertheless cannot be spoken of.

In retrospect it seems surprising that it took so long for Hardy to reach this point. After all his very first novel of 1871, *Desperate Remedies*, was definitely *risqué*, and with *Two on a Tower*, written a decade later in 1881, Hardy quite self-consciously challenged all the Victorian proprieties surrounding marriage. Another decade was to pass, however, before the silence could finally be broken. Had events in England followed developments in Europe, 1880 might have been expected to mark a decisive turn. The year 1880 saw the publication of France of Zola's *Nana*, with its explicit treatment of prostitution, and also marked the first performance of Ibsen's *Pillars of Society* in England. However, *A Doll's House*, the most crucial work, in which Nora, in slamming the door on her husband, finally shatters the Victorian idyll of domesticity, was not staged in England until 1889 – a full decade after its original appearance. Later Victorian England was actually even more censorious than early Victorian England. Thackeray, who contrived in his own way to be fairly outspoken, felt a nostalgia for the eighteenth century that his successors could not share. In 1862, the *Art Journal*, celebrating the sobriety and decorum of modern English art, observed:

> We have now seldom to complain of intentional coarseness: Hogarth's works would, in this day, be intolerable. We are, in like manner, preserved from the *double entendre* in which the French rejoice. Virtue is respected; vice, as in Mr Egg's Tryptych, *Past and Present*, a depiction of prostitution and its costs, has a moral tagged on to it, generally, in short, is found 'the awakened conscience' somewhere, which, in the end, sufficiently well reconcile aesthetic effects to ethical laws.[5]

Over twenty years later, in her 'A Dialogue on Novels' (1885), Vernon Lee, often regarded as an intellectually progressive figure, expresses virtually identical thoughts through her character, Baldwin:

> I ask you again, Mrs Blake – for you know the book – could you conceive a modern girl of eighteen, pure and charming and loving, as Fielding represents his Sophia Western, learning the connection between her lover and a creature like Molly Seagrim, without becoming quite morally ill at the discovery? But in the eighteenth century a nice girl had not the feelings, the ideal of repugnances, of a nice girl of our day. In the face of such things it is absurd to pretend, as some people do, that the feeling of mankind and of womankind are always the same.[6]

The class bias is very evident. Following Macaulay, the Victorians rejoiced at the growth in moral sensibility, through which their own age manifested its superiority over its predecessors, and, like Vernon Lee, many attributed this increase in cultivation to the influence of woman. So Hardy must have been conscious of the irony of the fact that it was precisely women like Tess who became the victims of this new moral dispensation.

Tess of the d'Urbervilles is an impressive novel, without doubt Hardy's greatest novel, not just because of the magnificent challenge it hurls down to Victorian values, or because of the vividness of its characterisation, or through its many-sided evocation of rural English life in the process of change, but also because it contains Hardy's most subtle treatment of the question of modernity. In writing *Tess* Hardy realised that the novel could not just be centred on the time-honoured assumption that it was normal for aristocratic men to have their way with working-class lasses, though he certainly did want to stress both the class and sexist foundation of contemporary morality. Undoubtedly it is deeply disconcerting that Tess both has the pride and courage to challenge Alex d'Urberville and the ability to shame him, yet Hardy also knew that he would not have probed the depths of Victorian sexual repression unless he could show how complexly it could affect even a comparatively enlightened individual – even someone so 'modern' as Angel Clare. Angel is undoubtedly a symbol of the 'modern' – yet we need to retain the parentheses, since Hardy believes that Angel, relatively emancipated as he is, has not only been unable to come to terms with the real implications of modernity, but is actually totally incapable of doing so. If Angel is to be compared either with his father or with his two clergymen brothers, he seems quite remarkably emancipated. Angel has refused to become a minister of the church in defiance of his father's wishes – a destiny that his brothers have accepted without question. He is independent enough to think of a career in farming and even to contemplate the possibility of emigrating. While Angel's brothers, despite their alleged Christian principles, typify the blinkered prejudices and extraordinary narrowness of the sympathies of their class: 'Each brother candidly recognised that there were a few unimportant scores of millions of outsiders in civilised society. Persons who were neither University men nor churchmen; but they were to be tolerated rather than reckoned with and respected.' Angel, however, shows a remarkable openness to the lives of the peasant girls at Talbothays dairy and Hardy is at pains to stress – by contrast with Alex – the depths of his respect for Tess: 'Tess was no significant creature to toy with and dismiss; but a woman living her precious life – a life which to herself who endured it or enjoyed it, possessed as great a dimension as the life of the mightiest to himself.'

Yet, despite all this, when it comes right down to it Hardy shows that Angel Clare is as deeply implicated in Victorian sexual stereotypes as anyone else. Despite his apparent flexibility and openness he is deeply, deeply prejudiced. He makes the usually perfunctory confession of his own sexual peccadilloes – since this is how they are to be regarded under the customary rubric – little dreaming that Tess herself can be regarded as having something also to confess, or that if she did – as she does – that would be something that could also be overlooked. As John Goode points out: 'He is bewildered to find such a sophisticated consciousness in so simple a nature.'[7] The whole situation is absolutely absurd, yet it is also fraught with the most terrible potential for tragedy. Angel, in marrying out of his class, is, deep down, quite unable to accept Tess as a real person; he can only view her as cliché: 'I thought – any man would have thought – that by giving up all ambition to win a wife with social standing, with fortune, with knowledge of the world, I should secure rustic innocence as surely as I should secure pink cheeks.' Yet what gives this unforgivable statement a strange pathos is the fact that Angel's relationship has been both innocent and deeply erotic. On a subconscious level he has found real contentment with Tess, yet when he learns of her 'past' he becomes as tormented as Othello or his precursor, Knight, in *A Pair of Blue Eyes*. However, Hardy does not explain this in terms of jealousy but in terms of convention and social prejudice: 'With all his independence of judgement, the advanced and well-meaning young man of the last five-and-twenty years, was yet the slave to custom and conventionality when surprised back into his early teachings.' Arnold had identified the modern spirit as an enquiring, critical spirit, possessed of a certain maturity and self-confidence that would enable it to cope with both complexity and diversity, and which was therefore tolerant and open-minded. In the light of this exacting standard Angel Clare proves woefully deficient.

It needs to be added, however, that Angel Clare is not just another character whom the reader can stand back from and evaluate dispassionately. In the final analysis Angel Clare is the enlightened reader of Hardy's own day, and just as Hardy knows that Angel cannot accept Tess, so he writes into his novel through Angel the reaction to *Tess* that he is certain the novel will evoke. Tess's manifold doubts and wavering about whether it is right to tell Angel about her past and her determination to do so despite her mother's explicit warnings parallels Hardy's own hesitations about the wisdom of challenging the hypocrisy, inconsistency and evasiveness of Victorian sexual morality. Although Hardy was to treat the idea of the modern more sympathetically in *Jude the Obscure*, here his evaluation of the modern world is much more negative. It is epitomised by the opposition of Talbothays and Flintcomb Ash. Talbothays is a world of peace and beauty, where life is still governed by instinctual rhythms. It is a world where sexual desire naturally finds expression; where individuality still has a very definite place: all the cows have names and Tess is given to milk those who get on best with her. The farm at Flintcomb Ash, on the other hand, is a world of unfeeling exploitation where Tess is given the job of feeding the mechanical threshing-machine, a task that reduces her to a mindless automaton and scarcely gives her time to eat and no opportunity to talk with the other girls. This denial of the individual is paralleled by Angel Clare's attitude towards Tess, who always imagines that in the final analysis he will not be able to deny his spontaneous feelings towards her and will be able to accept her for what she is. But Angel typifies the drive towards abstraction that characterises modernity. He becomes incapable of seeing her as an innocent and loving woman. Unable to accept her as she is, Angel cannot help placing her in the time-honoured category of 'fallen woman' despite the unfairness, perversity and incongruity of doing so. Moreover, despite his rejection of ancient families, it is he more than anyone who insists on viewing her as a 'd' Urberville'. At the point of transition between two worlds Tess becomes for Hardy a complex synthesis of the ancient and the modern. In her strength, her integrity and her self-reliance she belongs to the world of the past, but in her simultaneously ability to resist so much of the contemporary cant about morality and to listen to her own inner voice she is undoubtedly modern. For much of the novel Tess is judged and rather passively acquiesces in the verdicts that are pronounced upon her, but in the end she resists. She writes her devastating letter to Angel – so different from the one she sent to him in Brazil:

> O why have you treated me so monstrously, Angel. I do not deserve it. I have thought it all over carefully and I can never, never forgive you! You know that I did not intend to wrong you – why have you wronged me? You are cruel, cruel indeed. I will try to forget you. It is all injustice I have received at your hands.

She finally takes her revenge on Alex who has also refused to acknowledge her as a person. So the novel works its way towards an intensifying crisis of conflicting judgements – the reader judges Tess, Tess turns the moral tables on Angel, Tess is judged by society and hanged – but Hardy uses that verdict to condemn Victorian society. Justice is rightly placed in inverted commas. The reader's right to come to his own conclusions about the matter is put in question. For those readers must acknowledge their own guilty complicity in the Victorian values that drive the wheels of the plot.

What makes the major novelist so often is the determination to worry away at a relatively small number of themes and through that very obsessiveness produce works that exhibit progressively greater insight and greater intensity. This is certainly the case with Hardy, but in reading Hardy we are conscious not merely of artistic development but of an increasing determination to shock and to disconcert, to violate the taboos of Victorian society with such clarity and determination that there can be no possibility of misunderstanding. Yet Hardy shows such considerable courage in *Tess of the d' Urbervilles* and *Jude the Obscure* that in some perverse and imperceptive way we feel almost bound to speculate why it should have taken so long for Hardy – always a bold writer – to shatter the silence. One way of approaching this question would be to see Hardy as a man using a battering ram to break down the doors of the antique Victorian castle. The first blows are perhaps somewhat tentative and exploratory. The doors seems solid enough to withstand a lengthy siege. More powerful assaults also seem somewhat ineffectual and it appears that the mighty archway is still impassable, though now there is a distinct sensation that the doors are vibrating. Then, suddenly, under the impact of a final, almost despairing thrust, the doors unexpectedly burst open: the appearance of impregnability has gone. Hardy's concern with the way in which the institution of marriage warps and distorts human lives and with the sheer desperation of his characters' attempts to escape from the shackles that they themselves have so willingly embraced is already announced in *Desperate Remedies*. However, although Hardy had so often shown his men and women mismatched and unhappy, it was not until *Jude the Obscure* that he saw fit to argue quite unmistakeably that it was marriage itself that was to blame. A possible reason for this may have been Hardy's changing attitude to the question of divorce. After all, the reformed divorce law of 1857 had been in place long before Hardy started writing. As a result of this legislation a divorce would cost between forty and sixty pounds, which though considerably less than before was nevertheless a considerable sum, so that what the legislation really represented was an extension of this social privilege from the aristocracy to the affluent middle class. Before 1918 there were never more than a thousand divorces a year, but of that number there were some from the lower orders. In *Putting Asunder* Roderick Phillips writes:

> Of a sample of 101 cases of divorce reported in the London *Times* between 1860 and 1919 the occupational groups must commonly represented by husbands were the military, trade (such as shop-keepers), workers (butlers, sailors), professionals, clerks and men of independent means. Working men were represented, but disproportionately infrequently, accounting for only one-sixth of the husbands whose occupation were reported.[8]

Clearly it is relevant that persons who were butlers or sailors would be more easily able to save money than the average working man. Where Hardy may seem inconsistent is that in *The Woodlanders* he suggests that the costs of divorce would have been an insuperable obstacle for the comparatively prosperous Giles Winterbourne, whereas Jude, who is only a stonemason, nevertheless finds the money for his divorce from Arabella. What does seem to be the case is that with the passing of years the idea of divorce had become more familiar, even if getting one was still just as difficult. In consequence Hardy now recognised that the issue was not really divorce as such. There was still a massive social stigma attached to divorce, so the issue was not simply the cost but the fact that millions of people entered into marriage without giving a moment's thought to the unhappiness it might cause them and, once married, did not have either the temerity to stand up to public opinion or the willingness to accept a life sentence of social ostracism.

The paradox of Jude as hero in *Jude the Obscure* is that Hardy see him as being at once belated and too early. For although Jude's ambition to win a degree at Christminster, the transparent synonym for Oxford, is perhaps out of the question for a man of his background, at the same time his very desire to go there, which causes him so much unhappiness, is actually based on the assumption that Oxford is still as idealistic and as devoted to rigorous intellectual inquiry as it had been some sixty years earlier in the 1830s. Tractarianism is actually rather important for *Jude the Obscure* since Sue Bridehead is clearly identified with High Church sympathies and her own tendency to question things is shown as stemming from this. Hardy saw Newman as a man driven by an irresistible impulse to question, enquire and interrogate rather than as the advocate of tradition and conformity to Rome – a view that would seem to be confirmed by the Roman church's general suspicion and distrust of Newman after his conversion, despite the great victory which that seemed to represent for the fortunes of Catholicism in England. But of course Newman's Oxford has gone and the irony of Jude's whole situation is that he is an obscure, unimportant hero, pursuing a dream of Oxford that is insubstantial, deceitful and unreal – and one that will poison his whole life. From the very first, Jude's aspirations are saturated with a deep sense of futility and when Hardy writes of his early days at Christminster;

> From his window he could perceive the spire of the Cathedral, and the ogee dome under which resounded the great bell of the city. The tall tower, tall belfry windows, and tall pinnacles of the college by the bridge he could also get a glimpse of by going to the staircase. These objects he used as stimulants when his faith in the future was dim.

It is already evident that Jude's faith in Christminster is already a kind of substitute for religion, and one that will prove to be equally disappointing. In *Jude the Obscure* we recognise that the modernity of the novel does not derive from some contemptuous disregard for the past, but is a stance progressively forced on Jude after he has made many exhausting attempts to make dry bones live. In *Jude* it becomes clear that though Hardy is still preoccupied with the idea of tragedy, it has come to mean something very different from what it did even in *The Return of the Native* or *The Mayor of Casterbridge*. In Hardy's perception of things there are two serious errors that can be made in life: to be too bold and reckless, and to be too cautious. The reckless, self-willed characters are Troy and Bathsheba in *Far from the Madding Crowd*, Eustacia in *The Return of the Native*, Henchard in *The Mayor of Casterbridge*, but in his later novels Hardy became rather more interested in characters who are hesitant, cautious and ridden with self-doubt. In this respect the writing of *A Laodicean* and *Two on a Tower* was an important turning point. Hardy no longer saw this tendency to be vacillating and indecisive as a sign of weakness; indeed he did not see it as a character trait at all. Indecisive characters were modern characters and what made them that way was an internal contradiction, as they were pulled in one direction by their own deepest impulses and desires, but pulled the other way by the imperatives of culture and 'morality'. People literally do not know what they want. Paradoxically, although their desires are the more powerful because there is less of a disposition to deny them, at the same time since they think more critically they are also more prone to scepticism and disillusionment. So Hardy's version of tragedy is now one that is riddled with question marks and inverted commas. It is not against gods that men struggle but 'only men and senseless circumstances'. Jude is not the Promethean hero struggling melodramatically against the cosmos, but only a humble stonemason who is progressively worn down by 'the grind of stern reality'. Jude's tragic error, flaw or mistake is not to be proud or overweening in the conventional sense though there is a pride there: it is his fateful belief that he can somehow give meaning to a decaying and moribund world. Everything that Jude turns his hand to involves perpetuating a shoring up the past, whether it is aiming to be an academic or a minister of the gospel, or whether, most ludicrously of all, it is relettering the Ten Commandments in the chancel of a local church. In a sense Jude is not really tragic, despite the apparent failure of his life, since his fate, his achievement even, is to recognise his own modernity and therefore to perceive that that very condition will make him dislocated and disconnected from the activities that normally make life seem worthwhile. As a writer who was as deeply preoccupied with tradition as he was with the question of modernity, Hardy perceived that scepticism was not a state of reflection which you could abandon, like Hume, simply by going back to the billiard table but a comprehensive mode of being. For even living simply from day to day calls for a definite commitment. Jude never lacks commitment. He throws himself energetically and wholeheartedly into everything he does, but by that very dedication he comes close to recognising the truth of Nietzsche's aphorism 'Better to have a void for a purpose than to be void of purpose.' Carlyle and his contemporaries had used the gospel of work and self-dedication as a substitute for religion, but Hardy is perhaps the first Victorian writer to sense the hollowness behind so much endeavour and to exhibit it for the reader to see.

What remains striking about *Jude the Obscure* is the way in which Jude, Sue and Phillotson are impelled into some new spiritual universe in which conventional ideas of morality have neither force nor jurisdiction, so they must at once assume the burden of insecurity and social disapproval. Phillotson pays dearly for his willingness to acquiesce in Sue's decision to leave him for Jude because of the spiritual affinity he has observed between them, but the deepest irony of the novel is that Jude and Sue, despite his magnaminity, still cannot find happiness. Sue is, of course, the blazing signifier of the modern, who by her frankness, her directness, her spontaneity and her extraordinary honesty shatters all the protocols that were supposed to govern the lives of women. It is through Sue that Hardy makes manifest his conviction that there really is no such thing as personal identity at all since if we are to be free, then that capacity for freedom will make it impossible for the individual ever to be moored in any one single place. As Sue says:

> I have been thinking that the social moulds civilization fits us with have no more relation to our actual shapes than the conventional shapes of the constellations have to the real star patterns. I am called Mrs Richard Phillotson, living a calm wedded life with my counterpart of that name. But am not really Mrs Richard Phillotson, but a woman tossed about, all alone, with aberrant passions and unaccountable sympathies.

For this reason both Sue and Jude are unable to go through the ceremony of marriage since they feel that to bind themselves in this way will destroy the freedom of the impulse that has brought them together in the first place. As an epigraph to the second book of the novel Hardy uses a phrase of Swinburne's: 'Save his own soul he hath no star', but it is a mark of the complexity of Hardy's thinking about personal identity in this novel that he both believes this – since he believes that individuals must follow their own deepest impulses – and disbelieves what it seems to imply, which is that such a credo can only lead to personal fulfilment and happiness and also that people really can be totally confident of what they want. Sue's return to Phillotson is seen by Jude as a betrayal, a crumbling back into the conformity that she had formerly turned her back on. She is the victim of a repressive culture, which makes freedom such an intolerable burden that she returns to what she believes is her duty with a positive sense of relief. Yet Jude himself finds the uncertainty and insecurity of his relationship with Sue almost intolerable, and it is therefore not only Sue who is open to the charge of insincerity and inconsistency. To invoke the idea of inconsistency, however, is to reinstate the very perception of human identity of which Hardy has mounted such a critique. It is remarkably that Hardy, in advocating an ideal of personal authenticity, simultaneously recognises what an insuperably difficult goal it represents. In part this is because since individuals are shaped and conditioned by the culture in which they find themselves, they are always caught in the binary oppositions that culture constructs, but it is also because the price that such a quest imposes, as Jude suggests, is extraordinarily high. After the horrifying death of the children, Sue, in a state of shock, says:

> My eyes are so swollen that I can scarcely see; and yet a little more than a year ago I called myself happy! We went about loving each other too much – indulging ourselves to utter selfishness with each other! We said – do you remember? – that we would make a virtue of joy. I said it was Nature's intention, Nature's law and *raison d'être* that we should be joyful in what instincts she afforded us – instincts which civilization has taken upon itself to thwart. What dreadful things I said! And now Fate has given us this stab in the back for being such fools to take Nature at her word!

Here, it is impossible not to think of the last line of *Tess*: 'The President of the Immortals had finished his sport with Tess', for here that kind of determinism can no longer gain the same purchase. As Sue, ridden with guilt, tries to take back her former words, all these words are rendered problematic. At bottom they are all uncertain and unstable interpretations for which there is no real warrant, desperate attempts to cover over the void of uncertainty that opens up. It might be that freedom and spontaneity would not necessarily mean clarity and joy, they might also imply, as in this novel, grief and confusion and an uncomfortable recognition of the depths of the division within the self. Sue is never more spontaneous than when she is vacillating or contradicting herself, and it is actually this capacity to be unstable that Jude admires – yet spontaneity is at odds with any notion of personal responsibility. In a world where all the idols have crumbled, the landscape necessarily looks bare and the silence seems deeper than before.

Notes

NOTES TO THE INTRODUCTION

1. David Roberts, *Paternalism in Early Victorian England* (New Brunswick, NJ, 1979) p. 39.
2. Quoted in A. Brundage, *England's Prussian Minister* (Pennsylvania State University Park and London, 1988) pp. 155–6.
3. Clive H. Church, *Revolution and Red Tape* (Oxford, 1981) p. 298.
4. Sir Norman Chester, *The English Administrative System, 1780–1870* (Oxford, 1981) pp. 166–8.
5. E. Mogg, *Paterson's Roads*, 18th edn (London, 1826) pp. 240–1.
6. Quoted in Ford M. Ford, *Ford Madox Brown* (London, 1896) p. 189.
7. Henry Mayhew, *London Labour and the London Poor*, 4 vols (London, 1967) vol. I, p. 2.
8. Ibid.
9. Gertrude Himmelfarb, *The Idea of Poverty* (London, 1984) p. 398.
10. John Hollingshead, *Ragged London in 1861* (London, 1986) p. 85.
11. Ibid., p. 2.
12. Mary Cowling, *The Artist as Anthropologist* (Cambridge, 1989) pp. 236–7, 242–3.
13. Nancy Boyd, *Josephine Butler, Octavia Hill, Florence Nightingale* (London, 1982) pp. 186–7.
14. William Landels, *Woman's Sphere and Work* (London, 1859) pp. 156–7.
15. Ibid., p. 30.
16. Ibid., p. 31.
17. Ibid., p. 61.
18. Quoted in Valerie Sanders, *Reason over Passion* (Brighton, 1986) p. 88.
19. John Stuart Mill, *The Subjection of Women* and Harriet Taylor Mill, *Enfranchisement of Women*, introduction by Kate Soper (London, 1983) p. 147.
20. Ibid.
21. Ibid., p. 83.
22. Ibid., p. 59.
23. Thomas Babington Macaulay, *Critical and Historical Essays*, 2 vols (London, 1966) vol. I, p. 479.
24. Ibid.
25. Eliot Warburton, *The Crescent and the Cross*, 2 vols (London, 1846) vol. I, p. 324.
26. Sir William Sleeman, *A Journey through the Kingdom of Oudh*, 2 vols (London, 1858) vol. II, p. 279.
27. Richard Burton, *Sindh* (London, 1851) p. 2.
28. David Livingstone, *Missionary Travels and Researches in South Africa* (London, 1857) p. 28.
29. William Hughes, *The Treasury of Geography* (London, 1869) p. 156.

30. Ibid., p. 42.
31. Matthew Arnold, *Lectures and Essays in Criticism*, ed. R. H. Super with Sister T. M. Hocter (Ann Arbor, Mich., 1952) p. 245.
32. Frederick Harrison, *National and Social Problems* (London, 1908) p. 332.
33. Walter Bagehot, *Physics and Politics* (London, 1872) p. 204.
34. M. Thorpe (ed.), *Clough: The Critical Heritage* (London, 1972) pp. 192–3.

NOTES TO CHAPTER 2: ENGLAND

All references to works by Thomas Carlyle included in the text in this and the following chapter are to the Ashburton edition in seventeen volumes published in London by Chapman and Hall (1885–8).

1. David Ricardo, *The Principles of Political Economy and Taxation*, introduction by Donald Winch (London, 1973) p. 55.
2. Ibid., p. 175.
3. Ibid., p. 17.
4. Edward Baines, *On the Moral Influence of Free Trade* (London, 1838) pp. 21–2.
5. John R. McCullough, *Principles of Political Economy* (New York, 1965) p. 141.
6. Ibid.
7. Nassau Senior, *Selected Writings on Economics* (New York, 1966) pp. 6–7.
8. Alexis de Tocqueville, *Journey to England and Ireland*, ed. K. P. Mayer, trans. G. Lawrence and K. P. Mayer (London, 1958) p. 107.
9. *Edinburgh Review*, vol. 77, February 1843, p. 215.
10. Ibid., pp. 191–2.
11. Ibid., p. 194.
12. Ibid.
13. Ibid., pp. 197–8.
14. Ibid.
15. Ibid., p. 195.
16. Ibid., pp. 202–3.
17. Ibid., p. 201.
18. Ibid., p. 227.
19. David Hume, *The History of England*, continued by William Cooke Stafford, 4 vols (London, 1868–71) vol. I, p. 2.
20. Ibid.
21. Ibid., p. 8.
22. Ibid., p. 15.
23. Charles Knight, *Old England*, 2 vols (London, 1845) vol. I, p. 55.
24. Henry Hallam, *The Constitutional History of England*, 3 vols (London, 1897) vol. I, p. 1.
25. Ibid., vol. I, p. 2.

26. Ibid.
27. Charles Kingsley, *The Roman and the Teuton* (London, 1864) p. 249.
28. Thomas Arnold, *Introductory Lectures on Modern History* (London, 1860) pp. 23–4.
29. Hume, *History of England*, vol. I, introduction, p. 12.
30. Ibid., introduction, p. 16.
31. Henry Thomas Buckle, *History of Civilization in England*, 2 vols (London, 1936) vol. I, p. 409.
32. Sharon Turner, *History of the Anglo-Saxons*, 3 vols (London, 1823) vol. I, p. 116.
33. Ibid., vol. I, p. 242.
34. Ibid., vol. III, p. 232.
35. Sir Francis Palgrave, *The Rise and Progress of the English Commonwealth* (Cambridge, 1921) p. 574.
36. Ibid., p. 196.
37. Ibid., p. 5.
38. J. M. Lappenberg, *A History of England under the Saxon Kings*, trans. B. Thorpe, 2 vols (London, 1845) vol. II, pp. 256–7.
39. Ibid., vol. II, p. 306.
40. Ibid., vol. I, pp. 134–5.
41. Ibid., vol. II, pp. 83–5.
42. John Mitchell Kemble, *The Saxons in England*, 2 vols (London, 1849) vol. I, pp. 319–20.
43. Ibid., vol. II, p. 240.
44. Ibid., vol. I, pp. 70–1.
45. Ibid., vol. I, p. 326.
46. Ibid., vol. I, pp. v–vi.
47. Thomas Babington Macaulay, *The History of England from the Accession of James II*, 3 vols (London, 1935) vol. II, p. 212.
48. Ibid., vol. II, p. 212.
49. Ibid., vol. I, p. 219.
50. Thomas Babington Macaulay, *Critical and Historical Essays*, 2 vols (London, 1966) vol. I, p. 292.
51. Macaulay, *History of England*, vol. I, p. 228.
52. Nassau Senior, *Journals, Conversations and Essays Relating to Ireland*, 2nd edn, 2 vols (London, 1868) vol. I, p. 22.
53. Palgrave, *Rise and Progress*, p. 60.
54. Macaulay, *History of England*, vol. II, p. 442.
55. Ibid., vol. II, p. 460.
56. Ibid., vol. I, p. 605.
57. Ibid., vol. I, p. 611.
58. Ibid.
59. Thomas Babington Macaulay, *Miscellaneous Writings and Speeches* (London, 1897) p. 658.
60. Quoted in E. D. Steele, *Irish Land and British Politics* (London, 1974) p. 37.
61. Quoted in Dorothy Thompson, *The Chartists* (London, 1984) p. 83.
62. William Cobbett, *A History of the Protestant Reformation in England and Ireland* (Leamington, 1896) p. 93.

63. Quoted in Christopher Hill, *Puritanism and Revolution* (London, 1958) p. 96.
64. Quoted in Raymond Williams, *Cobbett* (Oxford, 1983) p. 17.
65. *Poor Man's Guardian, 1831–1835*, introduction by Patricia Hollis, 2 vols (London, 1969) vol. II, p. 445.
66. *Northern Star*, April 27 1839, p. 7.
67. John D. Rosenberg, *Carlyle and the Burden of History* (Oxford, 1985) p. 11.
68. Conor Cruise O'Brian (ed.), *Edmund Burke: Reflections on the Revolution in France* (London, 1968) pp. 172–3.
69. Ibid., p. 106.

NOTES TO CHAPTER 3: THE MENACING WORLD

1. Raymond Williams, *The Country and the City* (London, 1973) p. 154.
2. Edmund Wilson, *The Wound and the Bow* (London, 1952) pp. 9–13.
3. John Lucas, *The Melancholy Man*, 2nd edn (London, 1980) p. 136.
4. David Trotter, 'Circulation, Interchange, Stoppage', in R. Giddings (ed.), *The Changing World of Charles Dickens* (London, 1983) p. 170.
5. Roger Gard (ed.), *Henry James: The Critical Muse* (London, 1987) p. 53.
6. Charles Dickens, *Our Mutual Friend*, ed. Stephen Gill (London, 1971) p. 12.

NOTES TO CHAPTER 4: KEEPING THE FAITH

1. Frank Turner, 'The Victorian Crisis of Faith and the Faith that was Lost', in R. J. Helmstadter and B. Lightman (eds), *Victorian Faith in Crisis* (London, 1990) pp. 14–15.
2. Owen Chadwick, *The Victorian Church*, 2 vols (London, 1970), part II, p. 214.
3. George Prevost, *The Autobiography of Isaac Williams* (London, 1892) p. 63.
4. John Henry Newman, *The Via Media of the Anglican Church* (London, 1877) vol. I, p. 260.
5. Ibid., p. 41.
6. Ibid., pp. 68–9.
7. Ibid., p. 237.
8. Ibid., vol. II, p. 84.
9. John Henry Newman, *The Arians of the Fourth Century* (London, 1833) pp. 55–6.
10. Ibid., p. 152.
11. Ibid., p. 422.
12. Newman, *Via Media*, vol. I, p. 91.
13. R. D. Hampden, *The Scholastic Philosophy and its Relation to Christian Theology* (London, 1833) p. 149.

14. Newman, *Via Media*, vol. I, p. 38.
15. John Henry Newman, *Apologia Pro Vita Sua*, ed. A. D. Culler (Boston, Mass., 1956) pp. 65–6.
16. Arthur Penrhyn Stanley, *The Life and Correspondence of Thomas Arnold*, 2nd edn, 2 vols (London, 1845) vol. II, p. 178.
17. Thomas Arnold, *Miscellaneous Works* (London, 1845) p. 210.
18. Ibid., p. 445.
19. Stanley, *Life and Correspondence*, vol. I, p. 285.
20. Arnold, *Miscellaneous Works*, p. 285.
21. Ibid., p. 332.
22. Stanley, *Life and Correspondence*, vol. II, p. 15.
23. Quoted in A. R. Vidler, *F. D. Maurice and Company* (London, 1966) p. 79.
24. F. Maurice (ed.), *The Life of Frederick Denison Maurice*, 3rd edn, 2 vols (London, 1884) vol. I, p. 205.
25. F. D. Maurice, *The Kingdom of Christ*, 2 vols (London, 1906) vol. II, p. 311.
26. Maurice, *Life of Maurice*, vol. I, p. 226.
27. F. D. Maurice, *Eustace Conway* (London, 1834) vol. I, p. 159.
28. Ibid., vol. III, p. 114.
29. Maurice, *The Kingdom of Christ*, vol. II, p. 185.
30. Ibid., vol. II, p. 106.
31. Quoted in Vidler, *F. D. Maurice*, p. 164.
32. Quoted in ibid., p. 65.
33. Maurice, *The Kingdom of Christ*, vol. II, p. 243.
34. Ibid., vol. II, p. 244.
35. Ibid., vol. II, p. 54.
36. Ibid., vol. II, p. 151.
37. Ibid., p. 249.
38. Quoted in Charles Richard Sanders, *Coleridge and the Broad Church Movement* (New York, 1972) footnote, p. 158.
39. Quoted in Charles E. Raven, *Christian Socialism, 1848–1854* (London, 1960) p. 90.
40. Julius and Augustus Hare, *Guesses at Truth* (London, 1905) pp. 248–9.
41. John Sterling, *Essays and Tales*, 2 vols (London, 1848) vol. II, pp. 332–3.
42. Alan Sinfield, *Alfred Tennyson* (London, 1986) p. 150.
43. J. and A. Hare, *Guesses at Truth*, p. 273.
44. Charles Lyell, *Principles of Geology*, 11th edn, 2 vols (London, 1872) vol. I, pp. 164–5.
45. Hare, *Guesses at Truth*, p. 64.
46. Ibid., pp. 269–70.
47. Ibid., pp. 358–9.
48. John Hanning Speke, *Journal of the Discovery of the Source of the Nile* (London, 1906) p. 197.
49. Thomas Carlyle, *Works*, vol. VI, p. 2.
50. *Essays and Reviews* (London, 1860) pp. 431–2.
51. A. Trollope, *Clergymen of the Church of England* (London, 1974) pp. 128–9.
52. D. Smalley (ed.), *Trollope: The Critical Heritage* (London, 1969) p. 255.

53. Ibid., p. 131.
54. H. F. Tucker, *Tennyson and the Doom of Romanticism* (Cambridge, Mass., 1988) p. 23.

NOTES TO CHAPTER 5: VICTORIAN INTELLECTUALS AND
THEIR DILEMMAS

All references to works by John Stuart Mill included in the text are to John Stuart Mill, *Utilitarianism, On Liberty and Considerations on Representative Government*, ed. H. B. Acton (London, 1972). All references to prose works by Matthew Arnold are to *The Complete Prose Works of Matthew Arnold*, ed. R. H. Super (Ann Arbor, Mich.: University of Michigan Press, 1960–).

1. William Whewell, *Astronomy and General Physics considered with Reference to Natural Theology* (London, 1832) p. 23.
2. R. E. Butts (ed.), *William Whewell's Theory of Scientific Method* (Pittsburgh, 1968) p. 134.
3. William Whewell, *The Elements of Morality including Polity*, 2 vols (London, 1845) vol. ɪ, p. 307.
4. Ibid., vol. ɪ, pp. 176–7.
5. Ibid., vol. ɪ, p. 135.
6. Ibid., vol. ɪ, p. 359.
7. Ibid., vol. ɪ, p. 362.
8. Quoted in Andrew Seth, *Scottish Philosophy* (London, 1899) p. 156.
9. John Stuart Mill, *A System of Logic* (London, 1965) p. 368.
10. James R. Moore, *The Post-Darwinian Controversies* (Cambridge, 1979) pp. 19–49, and Owen Chadwick, *The Victorian Church* (London, 1970) vol. ɪɪ, pp. 23–33.
11. Mill, *System of Logic*, p. 328, footnote.
12. Charles Darwin, *The Origin of Species*, ed. J. W. Burrow (London, 1968) p. 126.
13. David L. Hull, *Darwin and his Critics* (Cambridge, Mass., 1973) pp. 305–6.
14. Darwin, *Origin*, p. 219.
15. Ibid., p. 133.
16. Thomas Henry Huxley, *Darwiniana* (London, 1893) p. 74.
17. Thomas Henry Huxley, *Man's Place in Nature* (London, 1906) p. 149.
18. Huxley, *Darwiniana*, p. 84.
19. Ibid., p. 77.
20. Ibid., p. 25.
21. Quoted in James G. Paradis, *T. H. Huxley: Man's Place in Nature* (Lincoln, Nebr. and London, 1978) pp. 27–8.
22. Francis Darwin (ed.), *Life and Letters of Charles Darwin*, 3 vols (London, 1887) vol. ɪɪ, p. 188.
23. Huxley, *Darwiniana*, pp. 75–6.
24. Ibid., p. 76.
25. George Eliot, *Scenes of Clerical Life*, ed. D. Lodge (London, 1973) p. 30.

26. Ludwig Feuerbach, *The Essence of Christianity*, trans. George Eliot (New York and London, 1957) p. 257.
27. Ibid., p. 47.
28. Ibid., p. 105.
29. Gillian Beer, *George Eliot* (Brighton, 1986) p. 199.
30. Feuerbach, *Essence*, p. 158.
31. Newman, *Apologia Pro Vita Sua*, ed. A. D. Culler (Boston, Mass., 1956) p. 271.
32. Ibid., p. 111.
33. H. F. Lowry (ed.), *The Letters of Matthew Arnold to Arthur Hugh Clough* (Oxford, 1968) p. 111.
34. Ibid., p. 97.

NOTES TO CHAPTER 6: THE NECESSITY OF ART

All references to works by Shelley included within the text are to David Lee Clark (ed.), *Shelley's Prose* (London, 1988). All references to works by John Ruskin included within the text are to *The Works of John Ruskin*, Library Edition in thirty-nine volumes (London: George Allen, 1903–12).

1. S. Nowell-Smith (ed.), *Browning: Poetry and Prose* (London, 1950) pp. 751–2.
2. Ibid., p. 753.
3. Ibid., p. 683.
4. Ibid., p. 684.
5. Joseph Bristow (ed.), *The Victorian Poet: Poetics and Persona* (London, 1987) p. 37.
6. N. Henfrey (ed.), *Selected Critical Writings of George Santayana*, 2 vols (Cambridge, 1968) vol. I, p. 109.
7. Nowell-Smith, *Browning*, p. 685.
8. W. J. Fotheringham, *Studies in the Poetry of Browning* (London, 1898) p. 3.
9. J. C. Olmsted (ed.), *Victorian Painting: Essays and Reviews*, 2 vols (New York and London, 1980) vol. I, p. 132.
10. Ibid.
11. Ibid., p. 131.
12. H. T. Shapiro (ed.), *Ruskin in Italy* (Oxford, 1972) p. 202.
13. Quoted in Allen Staley, *The Pre-Raphaelite Landscape* (Oxford, 1973) p. 130.
14. Bernard Denvir (ed.), *The Early Nineteenth Century: Art, Design and Society, 1789–1852* (London, 1984) p. 68.
15. J. C. Olmsted (ed.), *Victorian Painting*, vol. II, p. 32.
16. Ibid., p. 45.
17. Ibid., p. 83.
18. Quoted in Richard D. Altick, *Paintings from Books* (Columbus, Ohio, 1985) p. 239.
19. Ibid.

20. William Holman Hunt, *Pre-Raphaelitism and the Pre-Raphaelite Brother-hood*, 2 vols (London, 1905) vol. I, p. 150.
21. Christopher Wood, *The Pre-Raphaelites* (London, 1981) pp. 95–6.
22. Clyde K. Hyder (ed.), *Swinburne as Critic* (London, 1972), p. 147.
23. Ibid.
24. Ibid., p. 79.
25. Ibid., p. 30.
26. Ibid., p. 32.
27. Bristow (ed.), *Victorian Poet*, p. 143.
28. Clyde K. Hyder (ed.), *Swinburne: The Critical Heritage* (London, 1970) p. 96.
29. Clyde K. Hyder (ed.), *Swinburne Replies* (Syracuse, NY, 1966) p. 32.
30. Ibid., p. 26.
31. P. Faulkner (ed.), *William Morris: The Critical Heritage* (London, 1973) p. 102.
32. Ibid., p. 91.

NOTES TO CHAPTER 7: BREAKING THE SILENCE

1. Frances Finnegan, *Poverty and Prostitution* (Cambridge, 1979) p. 43.
2. Ian Gregor, *The Great Web* (London, 1974) pp. 115–16.
3. Irving Howe, *Thomas Hardy* (London, 1985) p. 96.
4. J. Hillis Miller, *Thomas Hardy: Distance and Desire* (Cambridge, Mass., 1970) p. 150.
5. Quoted in Lynda Nead, *Myths of Sexuality* (Oxford, 1988) p. 57.
6. Edwin M. Eigner and George J. Worth (eds), *Victorian Criticism of the Novel* (Cambridge, 1985) p. 237.
7. John Goode, *Thomas Hardy: The Offensive Truth* (Oxford, 1988) p. 115.
8. Roderick Phillips, *Putting Asunder* (Cambridge, 1988) p. 421.

Bibliography

HISTORY: GENERAL AND POLITICAL

Bentley, M., *Politics without Democracy, 1815–1914* (London: 1984).
Best, G. F. A., *Mid-Victorian Britain, 1851–75* (London: 1975).
Blake, R., *Disraeli* (London, 1969).
Briggs, A., *The Age of Improvement* (London, 1961).
Burn, W. L., *The Age of Equipoise* (London, 1964).
Coleman, B., *Conservatism and the Conservative Party in Nineteenth-Century Britain* (London, 1988).
Edsall, N. C., *Richard Cobden: Independent Radical* (Cambridge, Mass., 1986).
Evans, E. J., *The Forging of the Modern State, 1783–1870* (London, 1983).
Gash, N., *Aristocracy and People, Britain 1815–1865* (London, 1985).
Hanham, H. J., *Elections and Party Management in the Time of Disraeli and Gladstone* (London, 1960).
Harrison, J. F. C., *The Early Victorians, 1832–1851* (London, 1971).
Matthew, H. C. G., *Gladstone, 1809–1874* (Oxford, 1986).
Read, D., *Peel and the Victorians* (Oxford, 1987).

THE SOCIAL AND CULTURAL CONTEXT

Crouzet, M., *The Victorian Economy* (London, 1982).
Dyos, H. J., and Wolff, M. (eds), *The Victorian City*, 2 vols (London, 1973).
Epstein, J., *The Lion of Freedom: Feargus O' Connor and the Chartist Movement, 1832–1842* (London, 1982).
Epstein, J., and Thompson, D. (eds), *The Chartist Experience: Studies in Working-class Radicalism and Culture, 1830–1860* (London, 1982).
Gates, B. T., *Victorian Suicide* (Princeton, NJ, 1988).
Girouard, M., *The Return to Camelot: Chivalry and the English Gentleman* (New Haven, Conn. and London, 1981).
Goubert, J.-P., *The Conquest of Water*, trans. A. Wilson (Oxford, 1989).
Hobsbawm, E. J., and Ranger, T. (eds), *The Invention of Tradition* (Cambridge, 1984).
Horn, P., *Labouring Life in the Victorian Countryside* (Dublin, 1977).
Houghton, W. E., *The Victorian Frame of Mind, 1830–1870* (New Haven, Conn., 1957).
Jones, G. S., *Outcast London* (London, 1971).
Jones, G. S., *Languages of Class* (Cambridge, 1983).
Marcus, S., *The Other Victorians: A Study of Sexuality and Pornography in Mid-Nineteenth Century England* (New York, 1966).

Nead, L., *Myths of Sexuality: Representations of Women in Victorian Britain* (London, 1988).
Roberts, D., *Paternalism in Early Victorian England* (New Brunswick, NJ, 1979).
Savile, J., *1848* (London, 1987).
Taylor, B., *Eve and the New Jerusalem* (London, 1983).
Thomas, W., *The Philosophical Radicals* (Oxford, 1979).
Thompson, F. M. L., *The English Landed Classes in the Nineteenth Century* (London, 1963).
Trench, R., *Arabian Travellers: The European Discovery of Arabia* (London, 1986).
Vicinus, M. (ed.), *A Widening Sphere: Changing Roles of Victorian Women* (Bloomington, Ind., 1977).
Williams, R., *The Country and the City* (London, 1973).
Wright, D. G., *Popular Radicalism: The Working-Class Experience 1780–1880* (London, 1988).

RELIGION

Bradley, I., *The Call to Seriousness: The Evangelical Impact on the Victorians* (London, 1976).
Chadwick, O., *The Victorian Church*, 2 vols (London, 1971–2).
Chadwick, O., *Newman* (Oxford, 1983).
Clark, G. K., *Churchmen and the Condition of England, 1832–1885* (London, 1973).
Cunningham, V., *Everywhere Spoken Against: Dissent in the Victorian Novel* (Oxford, 1975).
Inglis, K. S., *Churches and the Working Classes in Victorian England* (London, 1963).
Jay, E., *Faith and Doubt in Victorian Britain* (London, 1986).
Martin, B. W., *John Keble* (London, 1976).
Norman, E., *The Victorian Christian Socialists* (Cambridge, 1987).
Prickett, S., *Romanticism and Religion: The Tradition of Coleridge and Wordsworth in the Victorian Church* (Cambridge, 1976).
Reardon, B. M. G., *Religious Thought in the Victorian Age* (London, 1980).
Rowell, G., *Hell and the Victorians: A Study of the Nineteenth-Century Theological Controversies Concerning Eternal Punishment and the Future Life* (Oxford, 1974).
Sellers, I., *Nineteenth-Century Nonconformity* (London, 1977).
Vance, N., *The Sinews of the Spirit: The Ideal of Christian Manliness in Victorian Literature and Religious Thought* (Cambridge, 1985).
Vidler, A. R., *F. D. Maurice and Company: Nineteenth-Century Studies* (London, 1966).
Willey, B., *More Nineteenth-Century Studies* (London, 1956).

PHILOSOPHY AND SCIENCE

Beer, G., *Darwin's Plots* (London, 1983).
Burrow, J. W., *Evolution and Society: A Study in Victorian Social Theory* (Cambridge, 1966).
Butts, R. E. (ed.), *William Whewell's Theory of Scientific Method* (Pittsburgh, 1968).
Chapple, J. A. V., *Science and Literature in the Nineteenth Century* (London, 1986).
Cosslett, T. (ed.), *Science and Religion in the Nineteenth Century* (Cambridge, 1984).
Cowling, M., *Mill and Liberalism* (Cambridge, 1963).
Gillespie, C. C., *Genesis and Geology: The Impact of Scientific Discoveries upon Religious Beliefs in the Decades before Darwin* (London, 1959).
Girouard, M., *Alfred Waterhouse and the Natural History Museum* (London, 1981).
Goldman, M., *The Demon in the Aether: A Study of James Clerk Maxwell* (Edinburgh, 1983).
Halevy, E., *The Growth of Philosophical Radicalism* (London, 1949).
Knight, D., *The Age of Science: The Scientific World-view in the Nineteenth Century* (Oxford, 1986).
Kuhn, T. S., *The Essential Tension* (Chicago, 1977).
Moore, J., *The Post-Darwinian Controversies: A Study of the Protestant Struggle to Come to Terms with Darwin in Great Britain and America, 1870–1900* (London, 1979).
Paradis, J. G., *T. H. Huxley: Man's Place in Nature* (Lincoln, Nebr. and London, 1978).
Plamenatz, J., *The English Utilitarians* (Oxford, 1958).
Quinton, A., *Utilitarian Ethics* (London, 1989).
Rees, J. C., *John Stuart Mill's 'On Liberty'* (Oxford, 1985).
Russett, C. E., *Sexual Science: The Victorian Construction of Womanhood* (Harvard, 1989).
Ryan, A., *The Philosophy of John Stuart Mill* (London, 1970).
Skorupsky, J., *John Stuart Mill* (London, 1990).
Wright, T., *The Religion of Humanity: The Impact of Comtean Positivism on Victorian Britain* (Cambridge, 1986).
Young, R. M., *Darwin's Metaphor: Nature's Place in Victorian Culture* (Cambridge, 1985).

HISTORY AND ECONOMICS

Bann, S., *The Clothing of Clio* (Cambridge, 1984).
Blaug, M., *Ricardian Economics: A Historical Study* (London, 1958).
Burrow, J., *A Liberal Descent* (Cambridge, 1981).
Clive, J., *Thomas Babington Macaulay: The Shaping of a Historian* (New York, 1973).

Crosby, C., *The End of History: Victorians and 'The Woman Question'* (New York and London, 1991).

Culler, A. D., *The Victorian Mirror of History* (New Haven, Conn., 1985).

Dale, P. A., *The Victorian Critic and the Idea of History: Carlyle, Arnold, Pater* (Cambridge, Mass., 1977).

Deane, P., *The Evolution of Economic Ideas* (Cambridge, 1978).

Fetter, F. W., *Development of British Monetary Orthodoxy, 1797–1875* (London, 1965).

Hamburger, J., *Macaulay and the Whig Tradition* (Chicago, 1976).

Jann, R., *The Art and Science of Victorian History* (Columbus, Ohio, 1985).

McClelland, C. E., *The German Historians and England* (Cambridge, 1971).

Meek, R. L., *Economics and Ideology* (London, 1967).

O'Brien, D. P., *The Classical Economists* (Oxford, 1975).

Peardon, T. P., *The Transition in English Historical Writing* (New York, 1966).

Rosenberg, J. D., *Carlyle and the Burden of History* (Oxford, 1985).

Shaw, C., and Chase, M. (eds), *The Imagined Past: History and Nostalgia* (Manchester, 1989).

Williams, R., *Cobbett* (Oxford, 1983).

Winch, D., *Malthus* (Oxford, 1987).

THE ARTS

Altick, R. D., *Paintings from Books* (Columbus, Ohio, 1985).

Anthony, P. D., *John Ruskin's Labour* (Cambridge, 1983).

Bermingham, A., *Landscape and Ideology: The English Rustic Tradition, 1740–1860* (London, 1987).

Bell, Q., *A New and Noble School: The Pre-Raphaelites* (London, 1982).

Fuller, P., *Theoria: Art, and the Absence of Grace* (London, 1988).

Girouard, M., *The Victorian Country House* (London, 1979).

Gloag, J., *Victorian Comfort: A Social History of Design from 1830–1900* (London, 1961).

Hilton, T., *The Pre-Raphaelites* (London, 1970).

Holman Hunt, W., *Pre-Raphaelitism and the Pre-Raphaelite Brotherhood*, 2 vols (London, 1905).

Hunt, J. D., *The Pre-Raphaelite Imagination: 1848–1900* (London, 1968).

Iser, W., *Walter Pater: The Aesthetic Moment*, trans. D. H. Wilson (Cambridge, 1987).

Landow, G., *William Holman Hunt and Typological Symbolism* (New Haven, 1979).

Maas, J., *Victorian Painters* (London, 1978).

Pevsner, N. (ed.), *Seven Victorian Architects* (London, 1977).

Pointon, M. (ed.), *The Pre-Raphaelites Revisited* (Manchester, 1990).

Read, B., *Victorian Sculpture* (New Haven, Conn., 1982).

Reynolds, G., *Victorian Painting* (London, 1966).

Robertson, D., *Sir Charles Eastlake and the Victorian Art World* (Princeton, NJ, 1978).

Staley, J., *The Pre-Raphaelite Landscape* (Oxford, 1973).
Strong, R., *'And When Did You Last See Your Father?': The Victorian Painter and British History* (London, 1978).
Thomson, P., *The Work of William Morris* (London, 1967).
Wood, C., *The Pre-Raphaelites* (London, 1981).

LITERATURE: GENERAL WORKS

Armstrong, I., *Language and Living Form in Nineteenth-Century Poetry* (London, 1982).
Ashton, R., *The German Idea: Four English Writers and the Reception of German Thought, 1800–1860* (Cambridge, 1980).
Brantlinger, P., *Rule of Darkness: British Literature and Imperialism, 1830–1914* (Ithaca, NY, 1988).
Bristow, J. (ed.), *The Victorian Poet: Poetics and Persona* (London, 1987).
Buckley, J. H., *The Victorian Temper: A Study in Literary Culture* (London, 1952).
Chandler, A., *A Dream of Order: The Medieval Ideal in Nineteenth-Century English Literature* (London, 1971).
David, D., *Intellectual Women and Victorian Patriarchy: Harriet Martineau, Elizabeth Barrett Browning and George Eliot* (Ithaca, NY, 1987).
Foster, S., *Victorian Women's Fiction: Marriage, Freedom, and the Individual* (London, 1985).
Gallagher, C., *The Industrial Reformation of English Fiction: Social Discourse and Narrative Form, 1832–1867* (Chicago, 1985).
Garrett, P. K., *The Victorian Multiplot Novel: Studies in Dialogic Form* (New Haven, Conn., 1980).
Gilbert, S., and Gubar, S., *The Madwoman in the Attic: The Woman Writer and The Nineteenth-Century Literary Imagination* (New Haven, Conn., 1979).
Gilmour, R., *The Novel in the Victorian Age: A Modern Introduction* (London, 1986).
Gross, J., *The Rise and Fall of the Man of Letters* (London, 1969).
Hawthorn, J. (ed.), *The Nineteenth-Century British Novel* (London, 1986).
Holloway, J., *The Victorian Sage* (London, 1953).
Hughes, W., *The Maniac in the Cellar: Sensation Novels of the 1860s* (Princeton, NJ, 1980).
Jenkyns, R., *The Victorians and Ancient Greece* (Oxford, 1980).
Johnson, E. D. H., *The Alien Vision of Victorian Poetry* (Princeton, NJ, 1952).
Kestner, J., *Protest and Reform: The British Social Narrative by Women, 1827–1867* (London: 1985).
Kettle, A., *The Nineteenth-Century Novel: Critical Essays and Documents* (London, 1981).
Kucich, J., *Repression in Victorian Fiction: Charlotte Brontë, George Eliot, and Charles Dickens* (Berkeley, Calif., 1987).
Landow, G., *Victorian Types, Victorian Shadows: Biblical Typology in Victorian Literature, Art, and Thought* (Boston, Mass., 1980).

Lerner, L. D. (ed.), *The Victorians* (London, 1979).
Levine, G., *The Realistic Imagination* (Chicago, 1981).
Lucas, J., *The Literature of Change: Studies in the Nineteenth-Century Provincial Novel* (Hassocks, 1977).
Lucas, J. (ed.), *Literature and Politics in the Nineteenth-Century* (London, 1971).
Miller, J. H., *The Disappearance of God: Five Nineteenth-Century Writers* (Cambridge, Mass., 1975).
Prickett, S., *Victorian Fantasy* (Hassocks, 1979).
Qualls, B., *The Secular Pilgrims of Victorian Fiction: The Novel as Book of Life* (Cambridge, 1982).
Richards, B., *English Poetry of the Victorian Period, 1830–1890* (London, 1988).
Rowell, G., *The Victorian Theatre, 1792–1914* (Cambridge, 1978).
Sanders, A., *The Victorian Historical Novel, 1840–1880* (London, 1978).
Stein, R. L., *Victoria's Year: English Literature and Culture, 1837–1838* (Oxford, 1987).
Stone, D. D., *The Romantic Impulse in Victorian Fiction* (Cambridge, Mass., 1980).
Turner, F. M., *The Greek Heritage in Victorian Britain* (New Haven, Conn., 1981).
Vicinus, M., *The Industrial Muse: A Study of Nineteenth-Century British Working-Class Literature* (New York, 1974).
Wheeler, M., *English Fiction of the Victorian Period* (London, 1985).
Williams, A. S., *The Rich Man and the Diseased Poor in Early Victorian Literature* (London, 1986).
Woolf, R. L., *Gains and Losses: Novels of Faith and Doubt in Victorian England* (New York, 1977).

POETRY: STUDIES OF INDIVIDUAL AUTHORS

Matthew Arnold

Buckler, W. E., *On the Poetry of Matthew Arnold: Essays in Critical Reconstruction* (New York, 1982).
Collini, S., *Arnold* (Oxford, 1989).
Culler, A. D., *Imaginative Reason: The Poetry of Matthew Arnold* (London, 1966).
Honan, P., *Matthew Arnold: A Life* (London, 1981).
Riede, D. G., *Matthew Arnold and the Betrayal of Language* (Richmond, Va., 1987).

Elizabeth Barrett Browning

Leighton, Angela, *Elizabeth Barrett Browning* (Brighton, 1986).

Robert Browning

Armstrong, I. (ed.), *Robert Browning: Writers and their Background* (London, 1974).
Dew, P. (ed.), *Robert Browning: A Collection of Critical Essays* (London, 1966).
Hassett, C. W., *The Elusive Self in the Poetry of Robert Browning* (Athens, Ohio, 1982).
Korg, J., *Browning and Italy* (Athens, Ohio, 1983).
Langbaum, R., *The Poetry of Experience* (New York, 1957).

Arthur Clough

Biswas, R. K., *Arthur Hugh Clough* (Oxford, 1972).
Houghton, W. E., *The Poetry of Clough* (New Haven, 1963).

Christina Rossetti

Harrison, A. H., *Christina Rossetti in Context* (Brighton, 1988).

Algernon Swinburne

Conolly, T. E., *Swinburne's Theory of Poetry* (London, 1964).
Louis, M. K., *Swinburne and his Gods: The Roots of and Growth of an Agnostic Poetry* (Montreal, 1990).
McGann, J. J., *Swinburne: An Experiment in Criticism* (Chicago, 1972).

Alfred Tennyson

Goslee, D., *Tennyson's Characters: 'Strange Faces, Other Minds'* (Iowa City, 1989).
Kilham, J. (ed.), *Critical Essays on the Poetry of Tennyson* (London, 1960).
Ricks, C., *Tennyson* (London, 1972).
Sinfield, A., *Alfred Tennyson* (Oxford, 1985).
Sinfield, A., *The Language of Tennyson's 'In Memoriam'* (Oxford, 1971).
Tucker, H. B., *Tennyson and the Doom of Romanticism* (Cambridge, Mass., 1988).

FICTION: STUDIES OF INDIVIDUAL AUTHORS

Emily and Charlotte Brontë

Eagleton, T., *Myths of Power* (London, 1975).
Maynard, J., *Charlotte Brontë and Sexuality* (Cambridge, 1984).
Peters, M., *Unquiet Soul: A Biography of Charlotte Brontë* (London, 1975).

Charles Dickens

Carey, J., *The Violent Effigy* (London, 1973).
Chittick, K., *Dickens and the 1830s* (Cambridge, 1990).
Collins, P., *Dickens and Crime* (London, 1962).
Garis, R., *The Dickens Theatre* (Oxford, 1965).
Hollington, M., *Dickens and the Grotesque* (London, 1984).
House, H., *The Dickens World* (Oxford, 1960).
Lucas, J., *The Melancholy Man* (Brighton, 1980).
Morris, P., *Dickens's Class Consciousness: A Marginal View* (London, 1991).
Schlicke, P., *Dickens and Popular Entertainment* (London, 1985).
Schwarzbach, F. S., *Dickens and the City* (London, 1979).

George Eliot

Barrett, D., *Vocation and Desire: George Eliot's Heroines* (London, 1989).
Beer, G., *George Eliot* (Brighton, 1986).
Hardy, B., *The Novels of George Eliot* (London, 1959).
Harvey, W. J., *The Art of George Eliot* (London, 1961).
Newton, K. M. (ed.), *George Eliot: A Critical Reader* (London, 1991).
Paris, B. J., *Experiments in Life: George Eliot's Quest for Values* (Detroit, Mich., 1965).
Paxton, N. L., *George Eliot and Herbert Spencer: Evolution and the Reconstruction of Gender* (Princeton, NJ, 1991).
Shuttleworth, S., *George Eliot and Nineteenth-Century Science* (Cambridge, 1984).
Smith, A. (ed.), *George Eliot: Centenary Essays and an Unpublished Fragment* (London, 1980).
Uglow, J., *George Eliot* (London, 1987).

Elizabeth Gaskell

Craik, W. A., *Elizabeth Gaskell and the English Provincial Novel* (London, 1975).
Lansbury, C., *Elizabeth Gaskell: The Novel of Social Crisis* (London, 1975).
Stoneman, P., *Elizabeth Gaskell* (Brighton, 1987).

Thomas Hardy

Boumelha, P., *Thomas Hardy and Women: Sexual Ideology and Narrative* (Hassocks, 1982).
Goode, J., *Thomas Hardy: The Offensive Truth* (Oxford, 1988).
Gregor, I., *The Great Web* (London, 1974).
Howe, I., *Thomas Hardy* (London, 1968).
Hillis Miller, J., *Thomas Hardy: Distance and Desire* (London, 1970).
Widdowson, P., *Thomas Hardy and History* (London, 1989).
Williams, Merryn, *Thomas Hardy and Rural England* (London, 1972).

William Thackeray

Carey, J., *Thackeray: Prodigal Genius* (London, 1977).
McMaster, R. D., *Thackeray's Cultural Frame of Reference: Allusion in 'The Newcomes'* (Toronto, 1991).
Peters, C., *Thackeray's Universe: Shifting Worlds of Imagination and Reality* (London: 1987).
Stevenson, L., *The Showman of Vanity Fair* (New York, 1947).
Sutherland, J., *Thackeray at Work* (London, 1974).

Anthony Trollope

Halperin, J. (ed.), *Trollope Centenary Essays* (London, 1982).
Kincaid, J. R., *The Novels of Anthony Trollope* (Oxford, 1977).
Letwin, S. R., *The Gentleman in Trollope: Individuality and Moral Conduct* (London, 1982).
McMaster, R. D., *Trollope and the Law* (London, 1986).

Index